BIG ROAD ATLAS
BRITAIN
AND NORTHERN IRELAND

Collins

Published by Collins
An imprint of HarperCollins Publishers
Westerhill Road, Bishopbriggs, Glasgow G64 2QT

www.harpercollins.co.uk

Copyright © HarperCollins Publishers Ltd 2019

Collins® is a registered trademark of HarperCollins Publishers Limited

Mapping generated from Collins Bartholomew digital databases

Contains Ordnance Survey data © Crown copyright and database right (2019)

The grid on the maps is the National Grid used on Ordnance Survey mapping, except in Northern Ireland. The National Grid is taken from the Ordnance Survey map with the permission of the Controller of her Majesty's Stationery Office.

Please note that roads and other facilities which are proposed or due to open in 2019 or 2020 are shown as under construction unless they were officially opened before the book went to press.

Printed in China

Paperback   ISBN 978 0 00 831868 0   10 9 8 7 6 5 4 3 2 1
Spiral   ISBN 978 0 00 831869 7   10 9 8 7 6 5 4 3 2 1

e-mail: roadcheck@harpercollins.co.uk   facebook.com/collinsref   @collins_ref

© Natural England copyright. Contains Ordnance Survey data © Crown copyright and database right (2015)

Information for the alignment of the Wales Coast Path provided by © Natural Resources Wales. All rights reserved. Contains Ordnance Survey data. Ordnance Survey licence number 100019741. Crown copyright and database right (2013).

Information for the alignment of several Long Distance Trails in Scotland provided by © walkhighlands

Information on fixed speed camera locations provided by PocketGPSWorld.com

With thanks to the Wine Guild of the United Kingdom for help with researching vineyards.

For the latest information on Blue Flag award beaches visit www.blueflag.global

MIX
Paper from
responsible sources
FSC™ C007454

This book is produced from independently certified FSC™ paper to ensure responsible forest management.

For more information visit: www.harpercollins.co.uk/green

Promotional gifts and data sales
The mapping in this Collins Road Atlas is also available for use in promotional gifts or for sale as digital data. For details of products and services visit our website at www.collinsbartholomew.com or contact us at:
Promotional gift enquiries – collins.reference@harpercollins.co.uk
Data sales enquiries – collins.bartholomew@harpercollins.co.uk

Contents

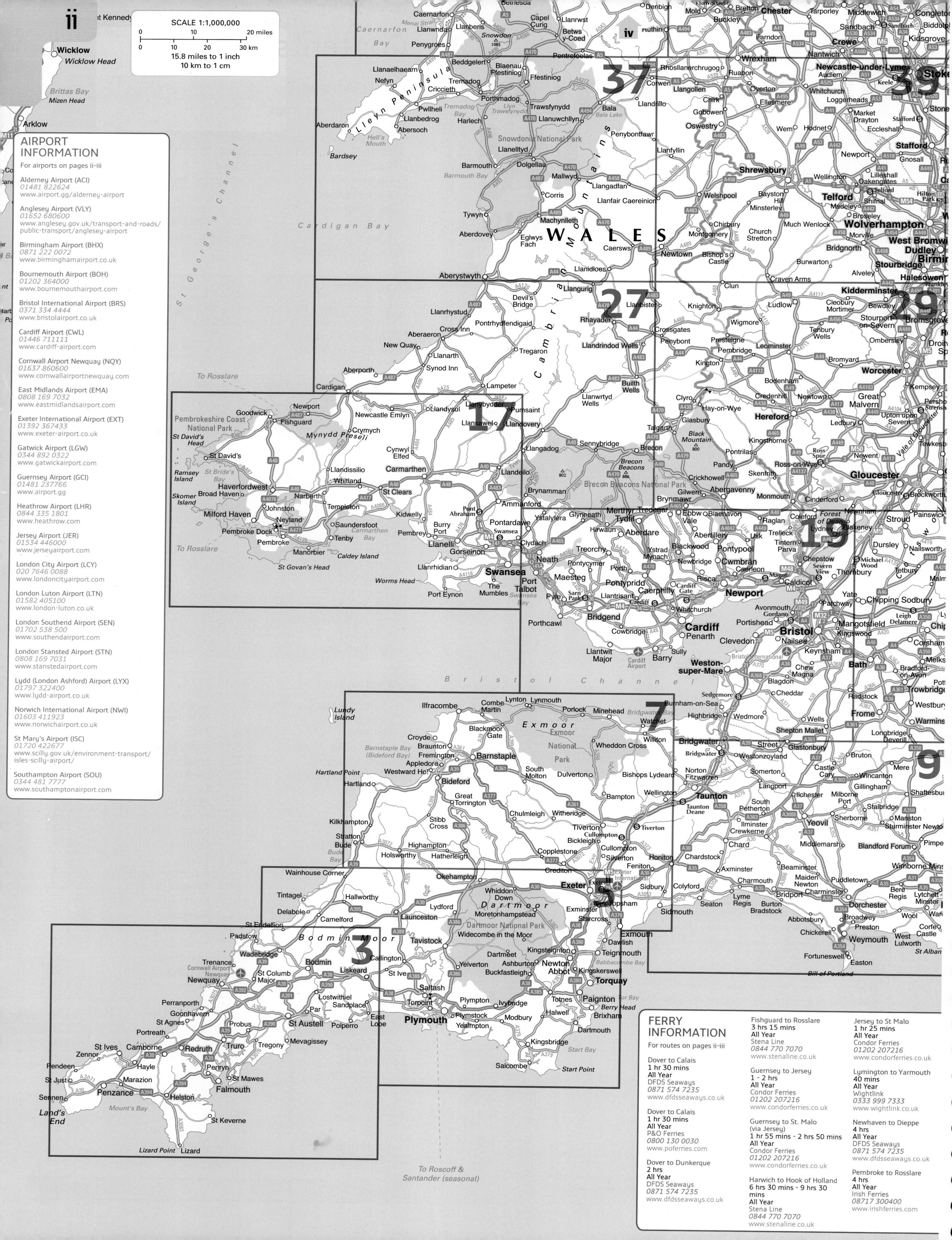

AIRPORT INFORMATION

For airports on pages ii-iii

Alderney Airport (ACI)
01481 822624
www.airport.gg/alderney-airport

Anglesey Airport (VLY)
01652 680600
www.anglesey.gov.uk/transport-and-roads/public-transport/anglesey-airport

Birmingham Airport (BHX)
0871 222 0072
www.birminghamairport.co.uk

Bournemouth Airport (BOH)
01202 364000
www.bournemouthairport.com

Bristol International Airport (BRS)
0371 334 4444
www.bristolairport.co.uk

Cardiff Airport (CWL)
01446 711111
www.cardiff-airport.com

Cornwall Airport Newquay (NQY)
01637 860600
www.cornwallairportnewquay.com

East Midlands Airport (EMA)
0808 169 7032
www.eastmidlandsairport.com

Exeter International Airport (EXT)
01392 367433
www.exeter-airport.co.uk

Gatwick Airport (LGW)
0344 892 0322
www.gatwickairport.com

Guernsey Airport (GCI)
01481 237766
www.airport.gg

Heathrow Airport (LHR)
0844 335 1801
www.heathrow.com

Jersey Airport (JER)
01534 446000
www.jerseyairport.com

London City Airport (LCY)
020 7646 0088
www.londoncityairport.com

London Luton Airport (LTN)
01582 405100
www.london-luton.co.uk

London Southend Airport (SEN)
01702 538 500
www.southendairport.com

London Stansted Airport (STN)
0808 169 7031
www.stanstedairport.com

Lydd (London Ashford) Airport (LYX)
01797 322400
www.lydd-airport.co.uk

Norwich International Airport (NWI)
01603 411923
www.norwichairport.co.uk

St Mary's Airport (ISC)
01720 422677
www.scilly.gov.uk/environment-transport/isles-scilly-airport/

Southampton Airport (SOU)
0344 481 7777
www.southamptonairport.com

FERRY INFORMATION

For routes on pages ii-iii

Dover to Calais
1 hr 30 mins
All Year
DFDS Seaways
0871 574 7235
www.dfdsseaways.co.uk

Dover to Calais
1 hr 30 mins
All Year
P&O Ferries
0800 130 0030
www.poferries.com

Dover to Dunkerque
2 hrs
All Year
DFDS Seaways
0871 574 7235
www.dfdsseaways.co.uk

Fishguard to Rosslare
3 hrs 15 mins
All Year
Stena Line
0844 770 7070
www.stenaline.co.uk

Guernsey to Jersey
1 - 2 hrs
All Year
Condor Ferries
01202 207216
www.condorferries.co.uk

Guernsey to St. Malo (via Jersey)
1 hr 55 mins - 2 hrs 50 mins
All Year
Condor Ferries
01202 207216
www.condorferries.co.uk

Harwich to Hook of Holland
6 hrs 30 mins - 9 hrs 30 mins
All Year
Stena Line
0844 770 7070
www.stenaline.co.uk

Jersey to St Malo
1 hr 25 mins
All Year
Condor Ferries
01202 207216
www.condorferries.co.uk

Lymington to Yarmouth
40 mins
All Year
Wightlink
0333 999 7333
www.wightlink.co.uk

Newhaven to Dieppe
4 hrs
All Year
DFDS Seaways
0871 574 7235
www.dfdsseaways.co.uk

Pembroke to Rosslare
4 hrs
All Year
Irish Ferries
08717 300400
www.irishferries.com

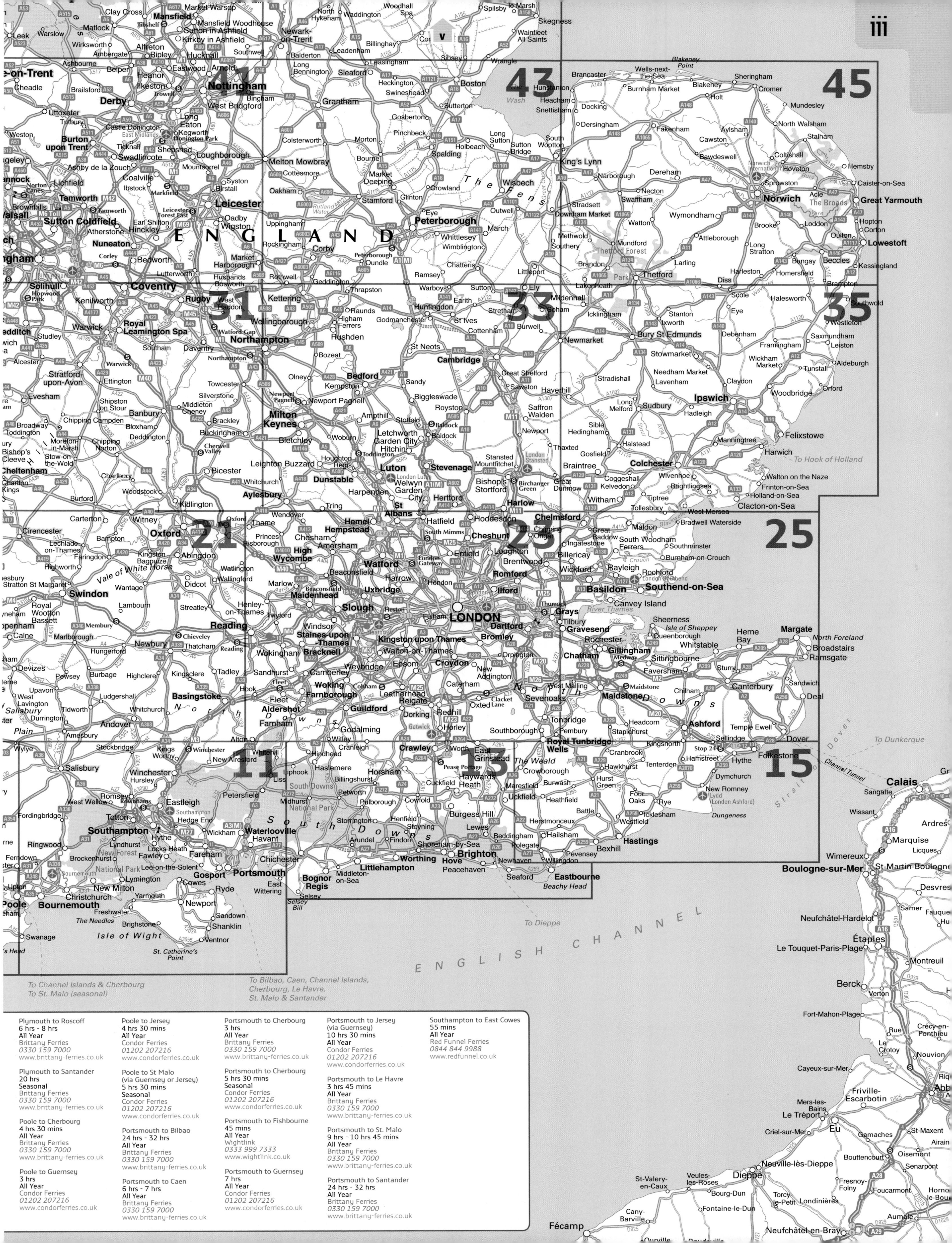

Grid references: 41, 43, 45, 31, 33, 35, 21, 23, 25, 11, 13, 15

E N G L A N D

ENGLISH CHANNEL

To Hook of Holland

To Dunkerque

To Dieppe

To Channel Islands & Cherbourg
To St. Malo (seasonal)

To Bilbao, Caen, Channel Islands,
Cherbourg, Le Havre,
St. Malo & Santander

Plymouth to Roscoff	Poole to Jersey	Portsmouth to Cherbourg	Portsmouth to Jersey (via Guernsey)	Southampton to East Cowes
6 hrs - 8 hrs All Year Brittany Ferries 0330 159 7000 www.brittany-ferries.co.uk	4 hrs 30 mins All Year Condor Ferries 01202 207216 www.condorferries.co.uk	3 hrs All Year Condor Ferries 01202 207216 www.condorferries.co.uk	10 hrs 30 mins All Year Condor Ferries 01202 207216 www.condorferries.co.uk	55 mins All Year Red Funnel Ferries 0844 844 9988 www.redfunnel.co.uk

Plymouth to Santander	Poole to St Malo (via Guernsey or Jersey)	Portsmouth to Cherbourg	Portsmouth to Le Havre	
20 hrs Seasonal Brittany Ferries 0330 159 7000 www.brittany-ferries.co.uk	5 hrs 30 mins Seasonal Condor Ferries 01202 207216 www.condorferries.co.uk	5 hrs 30 mins Seasonal Condor Ferries 01202 207216 www.condorferries.co.uk	3 hrs 45 mins All Year Brittany Ferries 0330 159 7000 www.brittany-ferries.co.uk	

Poole to Cherbourg	Portsmouth to Bilbao	Portsmouth to Fishbourne	Portsmouth to St. Malo	
4 hrs 30 mins All Year Brittany Ferries 0330 159 7000 www.brittany-ferries.co.uk	24 hrs - 32 hrs All Year Brittany Ferries 0330 159 7000 www.brittany-ferries.co.uk	45 mins All Year Wightlink 0333 999 7333 www.wightlink.co.uk	9 hrs - 10 hrs 45 mins All Year Brittany Ferries 0330 159 7000 www.brittany-ferries.co.uk	

Poole to Guernsey	Portsmouth to Caen	Portsmouth to Guernsey	Portsmouth to Santander	
3 hrs All Year Condor Ferries 01202 207216 www.condorferries.co.uk	6 hrs - 7 hrs All Year Brittany Ferries 0330 159 7000 www.brittany-ferries.co.uk	7 hrs All Year Condor Ferries 01202 207216 www.condorferries.co.uk	24 hrs - 32 hrs All Year Brittany Ferries 0330 159 7000 www.brittany-ferries.co.uk	

Channel Tunnel

To Dunkerque

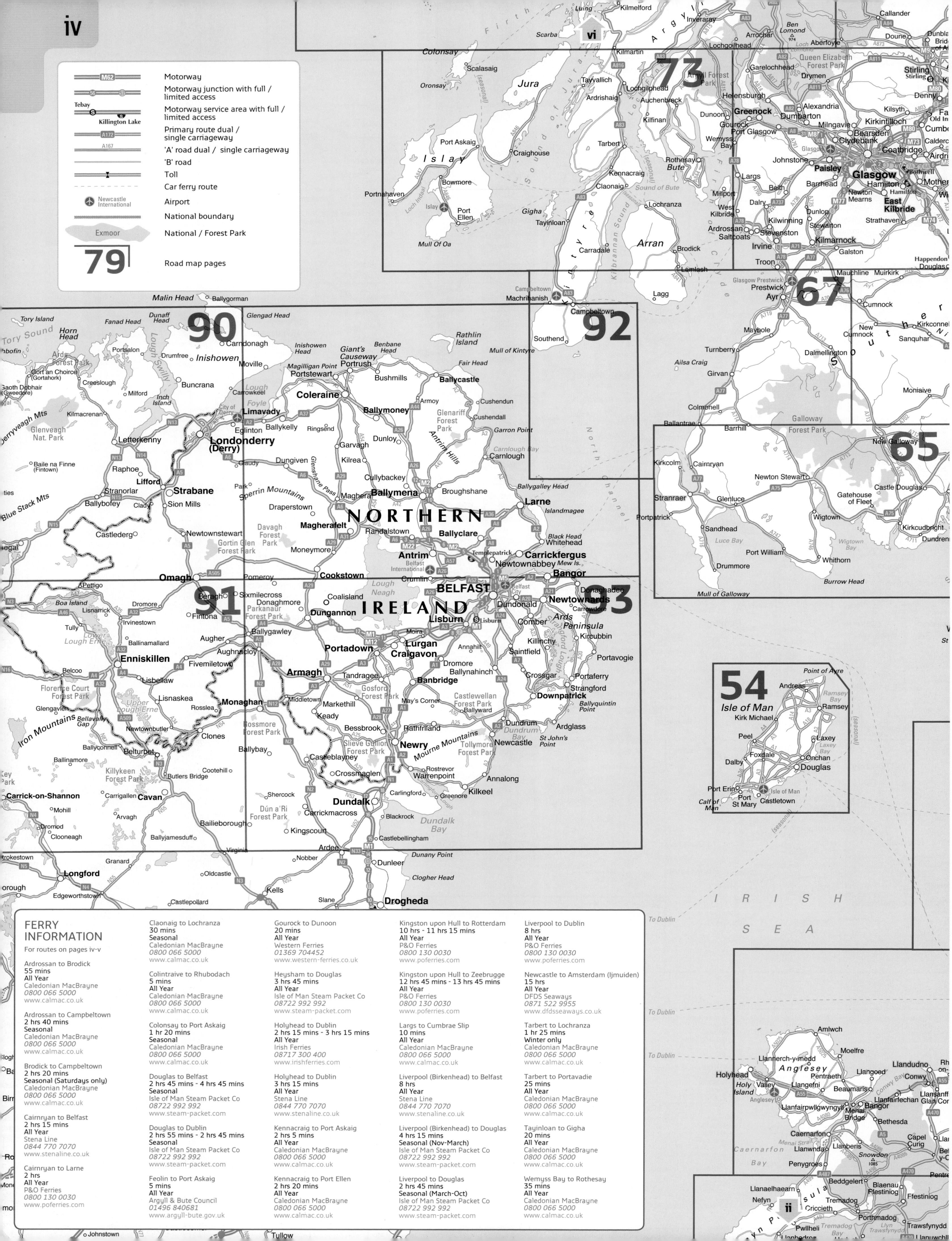

iv

Legend

M62	Motorway
	Motorway junction with full / limited access
Tebay / Killington Lake	Motorway service area with full / limited access
A12	Primary route dual / single carriageway
A167	'A' road dual / single carriageway
	'B' road
	Toll
	Car ferry route
Newcastle International	Airport
	National boundary
Exmoor	National / Forest Park
79	Road map pages

FERRY INFORMATION

For routes on pages iv-v

Ardrossan to Brodick
55 mins
All Year
Caledonian MacBrayne
0800 066 5000
www.calmac.co.uk

Ardrossan to Campbeltown
2 hrs 40 mins
Seasonal
Caledonian MacBrayne
0800 066 5000
www.calmac.co.uk

Brodick to Campbeltown
2 hrs 20 mins
Seasonal (Saturdays only)
Caledonian MacBrayne
0800 066 5000
www.calmac.co.uk

Cairnryan to Belfast
2 hrs 15 mins
All Year
Stena Line
0844 770 7070
www.stenaline.co.uk

Cairnryan to Larne
2 hrs
All Year
P&O Ferries
0800 130 0030
www.poferries.com

Claonaig to Lochranza
30 mins
Seasonal
Caledonian MacBrayne
0800 066 5000
www.calmac.co.uk

Colintraive to Rhubodach
5 mins
All Year
Caledonian MacBrayne
0800 066 5000
www.calmac.co.uk

Colonsay to Port Askaig
1 hr 20 mins
Seasonal
Caledonian MacBrayne
0800 066 5000
www.calmac.co.uk

Douglas to Belfast
2 hrs 45 mins - 4 hrs 45 mins
Seasonal
Isle of Man Steam Packet Co
08722 992 992
www.steam-packet.com

Douglas to Dublin
2 hrs 55 mins - 2 hrs 45 mins
Seasonal
Isle of Man Steam Packet Co
08722 992 992
www.steam-packet.com

Feolin to Port Askaig
5 mins
All Year
Argyll & Bute Council
01496 840681
www.argyll-bute.gov.uk

Gourock to Dunoon
20 mins
All Year
Western Ferries
01369 704452
www.western-ferries.co.uk

Heysham to Douglas
3 hrs 45 mins
All Year
Isle of Man Steam Packet Co
08722 992 992
www.steam-packet.com

Holyhead to Dublin
1 hr 20 mins
Seasonal
Caledonian MacBrayne
0800 066 5000
www.calmac.co.uk

Holyhead to Dublin
2 hrs 15 mins - 3 hrs 15 mins
All Year
Irish Ferries
08717 300 400
www.irishferries.com

Holyhead to Dublin
3 hrs 15 mins
All Year
Stena Line
0844 770 7070
www.stenaline.co.uk

Kennacraig to Port Askaig
2 hrs 5 mins
All Year
Caledonian MacBrayne
0800 066 5000
www.calmac.co.uk

Kennacraig to Port Ellen
2 hrs 20 mins
All Year
Caledonian MacBrayne
0800 066 5000
www.calmac.co.uk

Kingston upon Hull to Rotterdam
10 hrs - 11 hrs 15 mins
All Year
P&O Ferries
0800 130 0030
www.poferries.com

Kingston upon Hull to Zeebrugge
12 hrs 45 mins - 13 hrs 45 mins
All Year
P&O Ferries
0800 130 0030
www.poferries.com

Largs to Cumbrae Slip
10 mins
All Year
Caledonian MacBrayne
0800 066 5000
www.calmac.co.uk

Liverpool (Birkenhead) to Belfast
8 hrs
All Year
Stena Line
0844 770 7070
www.stenaline.co.uk

Liverpool (Birkenhead) to Douglas
4 hrs 15 mins
Seasonal (Nov-March)
Isle of Man Steam Packet Co
08722 992 992
www.steam-packet.com

Liverpool to Douglas
2 hrs 45 mins
Seasonal (March-Oct)
Isle of Man Steam Packet Co
08722 992 992
www.steam-packet.com

Liverpool to Dublin
8 hrs
All Year
P&O Ferries
0800 130 0030
www.poferries.com

Newcastle to Amsterdam (Ijmuiden)
15 hrs
All Year
DFDS Seaways
0871 522 9955
www.dfdsseaways.co.uk

Tarbert to Lochranza
1 hr 25 mins
Winter only
Caledonian MacBrayne
0800 066 5000
www.calmac.co.uk

Tarbert to Portavadie
25 mins
All Year
Caledonian MacBrayne
0800 066 5000
www.calmac.co.uk

Tayinloan to Gigha
20 mins
All Year
Caledonian MacBrayne
0800 066 5000
www.calmac.co.uk

Wemyss Bay to Rothesay
35 mins
All Year
Caledonian MacBrayne
0800 066 5000
www.calmac.co.uk

AIRPORT INFORMATION

For airports on pages iv-v

Anglesey Airport (VLY)
01652 680600
www.anglesey.gov.uk/transport-and-roads/
public-transport/anglesey-airport

Blackpool Airport (BLK)
01253 472525
www.blackpoolairport.com

Campbeltown Airport (CAL)
01586 553797
www.hial.co.uk/campbeltown-airport/

Doncaster Sheffield Airport (DSA)
01302 625050
www.flydsa.co.uk

Durham Tees Valley Airport (MME)
08712 242426
www.durhamteesvalleyairport.com

East Midlands Airport (EMA)
0808 169 7032
www.eastmidlandsairport.com

Edinburgh Airport (EDI)
0844 448 8833
www.edinburghairport.com

Glasgow Airport (GLA)
0344 481 5555
www.glasgowairport.com

Glasgow Prestwick Airport (PIK)
0871 223 0700
www.glasgowprestwick.com

Humberside Airport (HUY)
0844 887 7747
www.humbersideairport.com

Islay Airport (ILY)
01496 302361
www.hial.co.uk/islay-airport/

Isle of Man Airport (IOM)
01624 821600
to www.gov.im/airport

Leeds Bradford International Airport (LBA)
0871 288 2288
www.leedsbradfordairport.co.uk

Liverpool John Lennon Airport (LPL)
0871 521 8484
www.liverpoolairport.com

Manchester Airport (MAN)
0808 169 7030
www.manchesterairport.co.uk

Newcastle International Airport (NCL)
0871 882 1121
www.newcastleairport.com

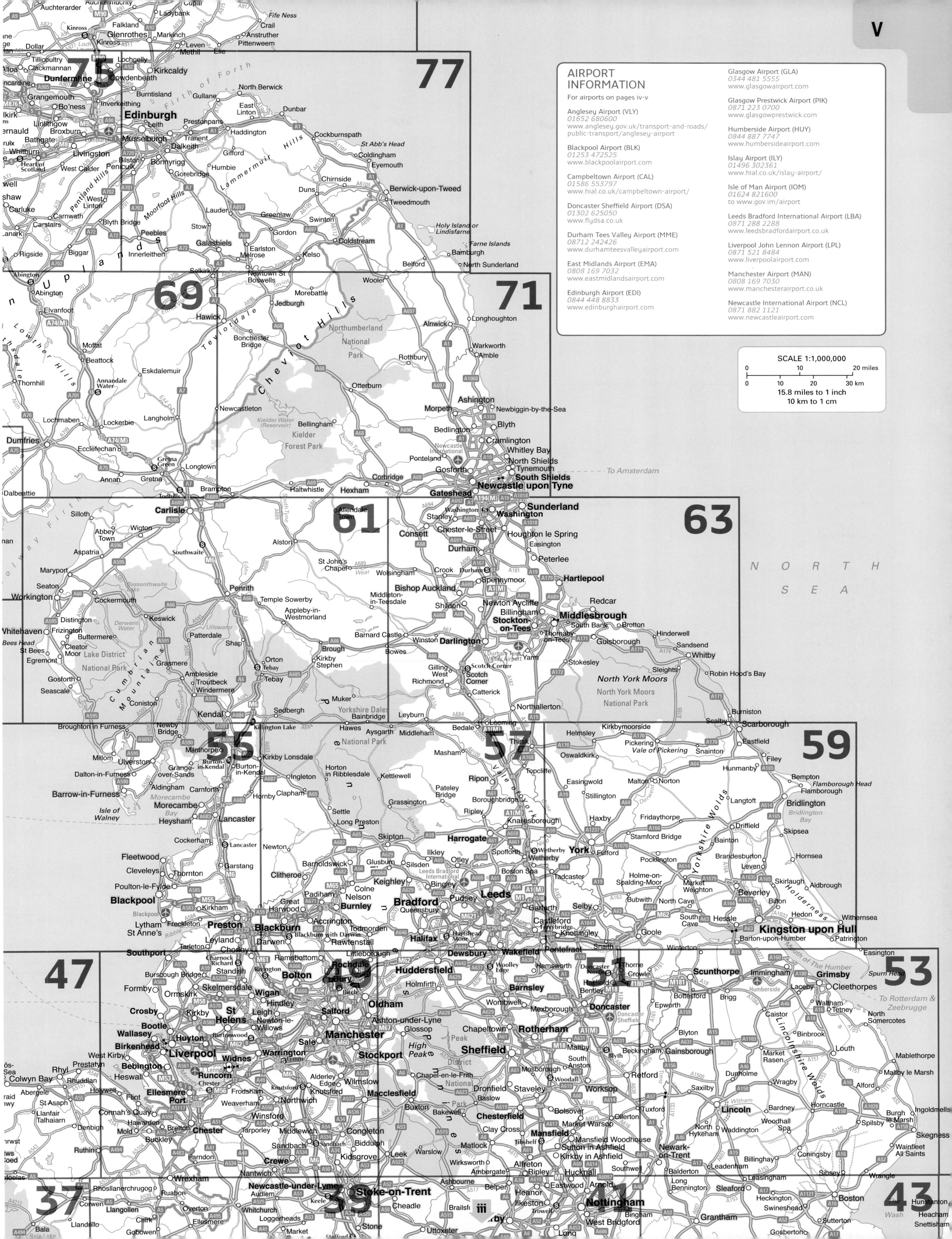

SCALE 1:1,000,000

0   10   20 miles
0   10   20   30 km
15.8 miles to 1 inch
10 km to 1 cm

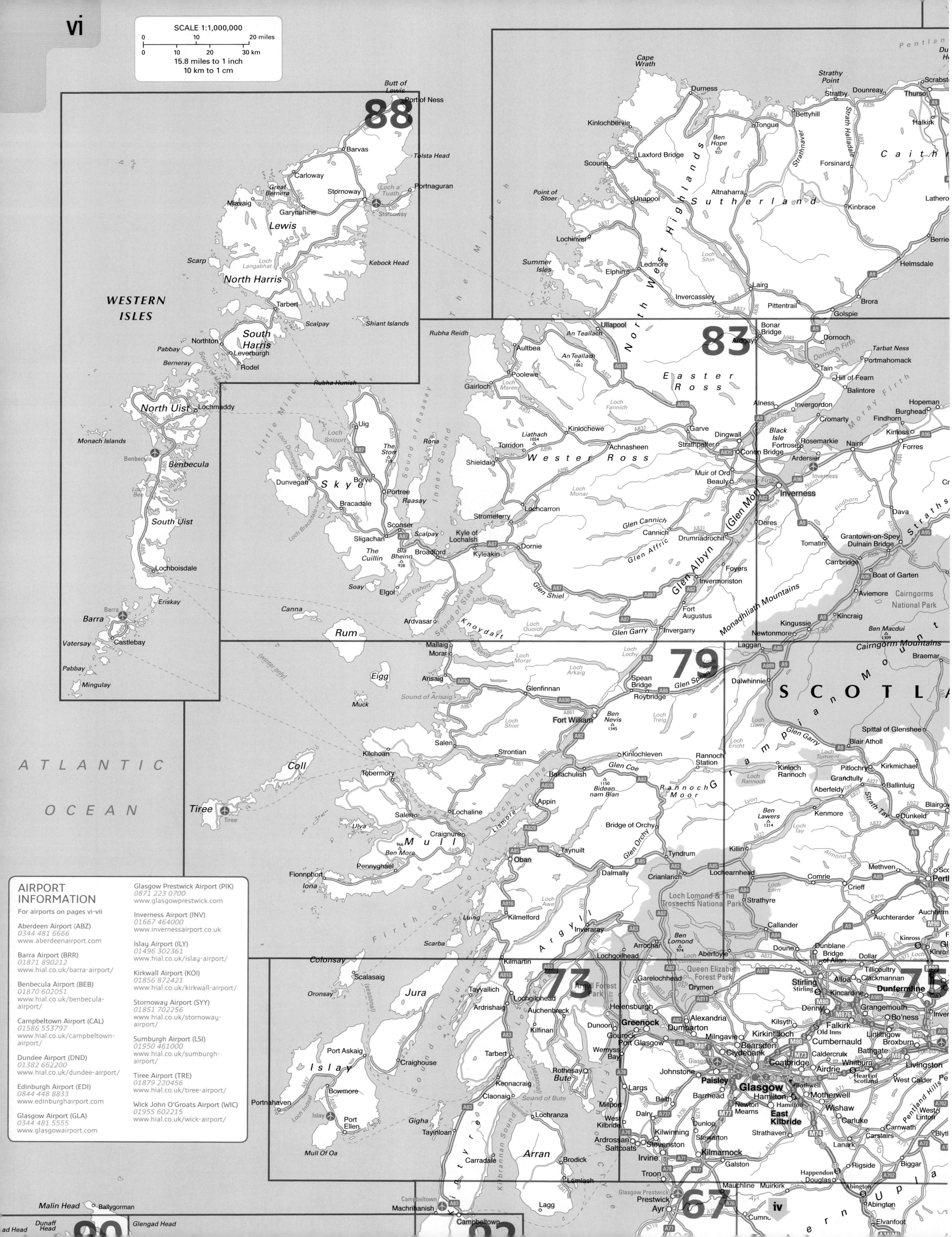

SCALE 1:1,000,000

0   10   20 miles

0   10   20   30 km

15.8 miles to 1 inch
10 km to 1 cm

AIRPORT INFORMATION

For airports on pages vi-vii

Aberdeen Airport (ABZ)
0344 481 6666
www.aberdeenairport.com

Barra Airport (BRR)
01871 890212
www.hial.co.uk/barra-airport/

Benbecula Airport (BEB)
01870 602051
www.hial.co.uk/benbecula-airport/

Campbeltown Airport (CAL)
01586 553797
www.hial.co.uk/campbeltown-airport/

Dundee Airport (DND)
01382 662200
www.hial.co.uk/dundee-airport/

Edinburgh Airport (EDI)
www.edinburghairport.com

Glasgow Airport (GLA)
0344 481 5555
www.glasgowairport.com

Glasgow Prestwick Airport (PIK)
0871 223 0700
www.glasgowprestwick.com

Inverness Airport (INV)
01667 464000
www.invernessairport.co.uk

Islay Airport (ILY)
01496 302361
www.hial.co.uk/islay-airport/

Kirkwall Airport (KOI)
01856 872421
www.hial.co.uk/kirkwall-airport/

Stornoway Airport (SYY)
01851 702256
www.hial.co.uk/stornoway-airport/

Sumburgh Airport (LSI)
01950 461000
www.hial.co.uk/sumburgh-airport/

Tiree Airport (TRE)
01879 220456
www.hial.co.uk/tiree-airport/

Wick John O'Groats Airport (WIC)
01955 602215
www.hial.co.uk/wick-airport/

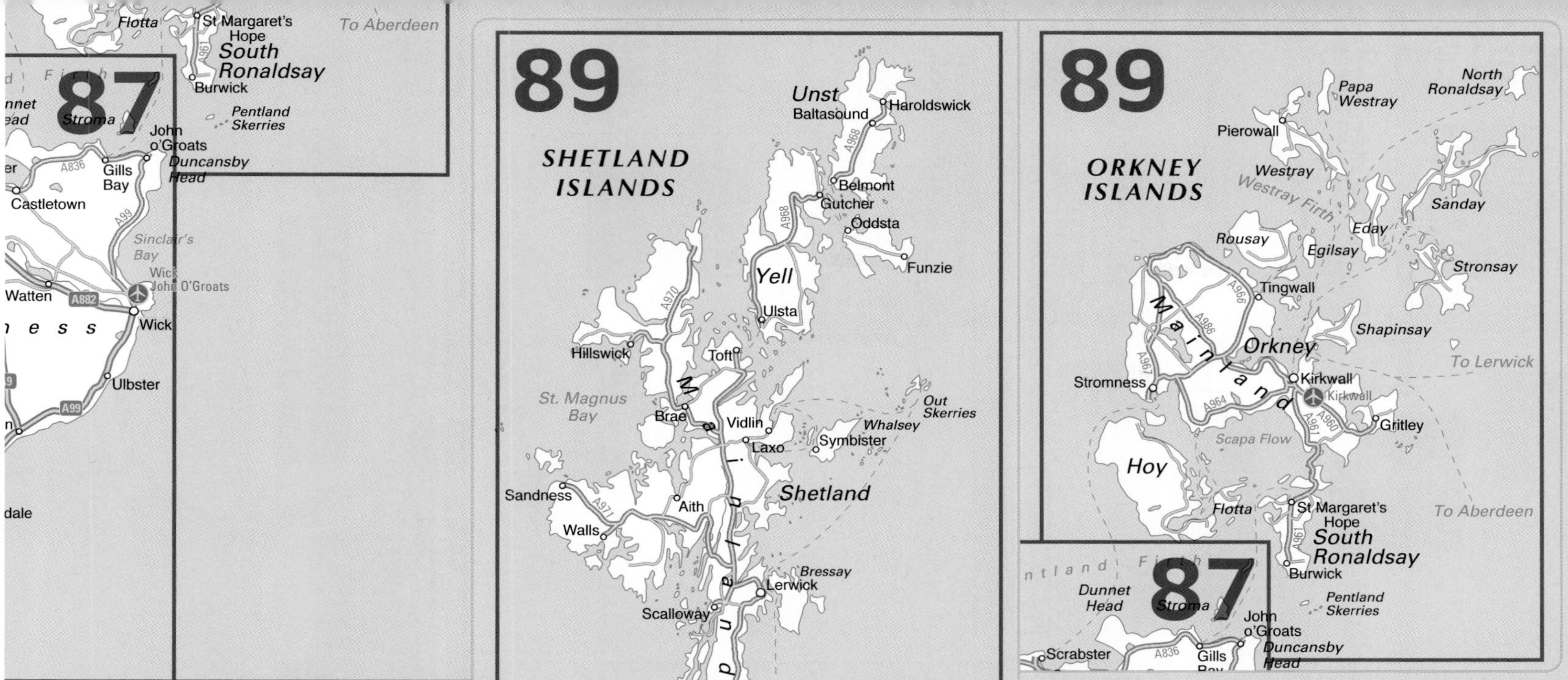

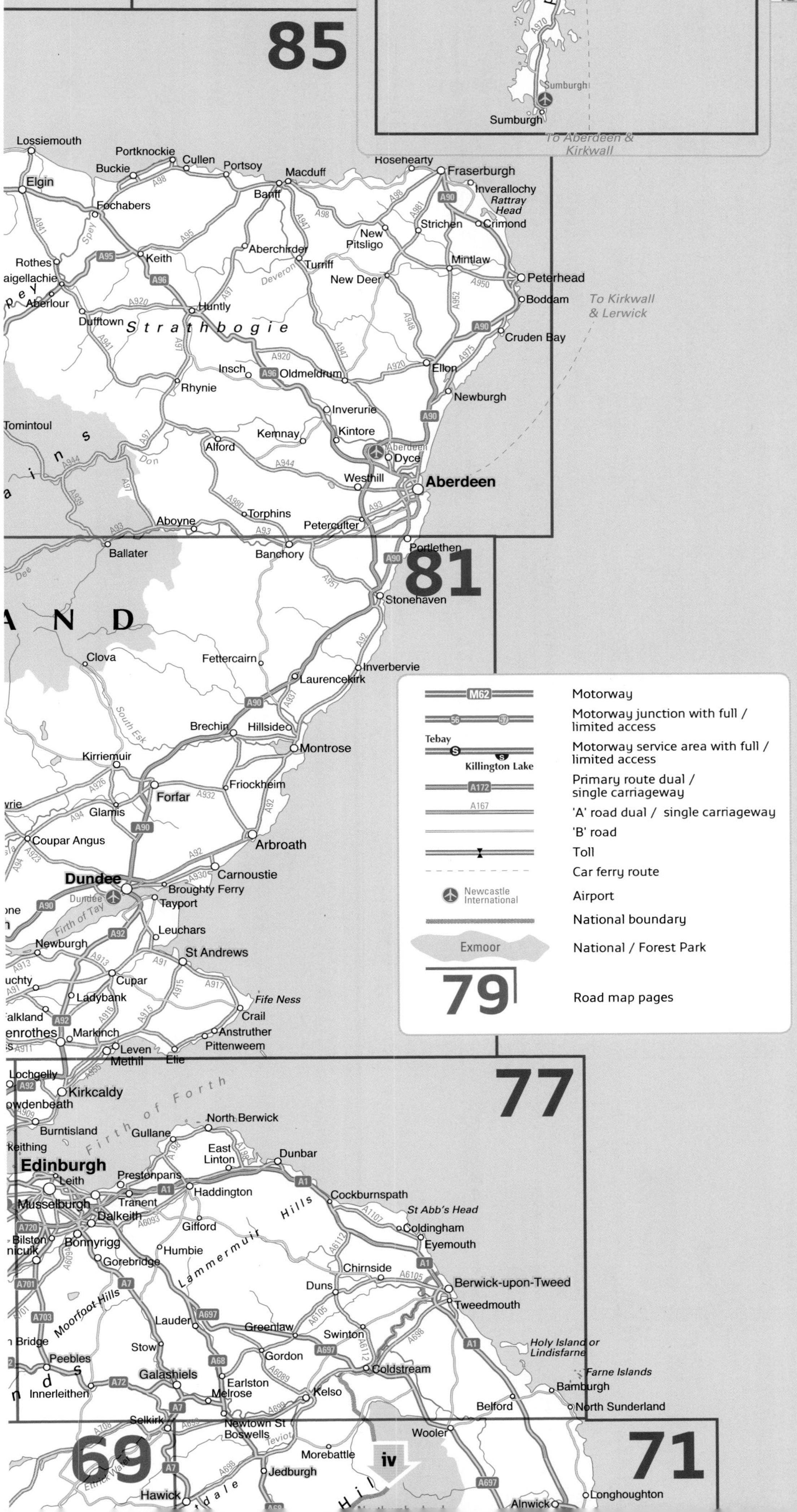

87

89
SHETLAND ISLANDS

89
ORKNEY ISLANDS

85

81

79 Road map pages

77

69

71

Legend

Motorway	
Motorway junction with full / limited access	
Motorway service area with full / limited access	
Primary route dual / single carriageway	
'A' road dual / single carriageway	
'B' road	
Toll	
Car ferry route	
Airport	
National boundary	
National / Forest Park	

FERRY INFORMATION

For routes on pages vi-vii

Aberdeen to Kirkwall
6 hrs - 7 hrs 15 mins
All Year
North Link Ferries
0845 6000 449
www.northlinkferries.co.uk

Aberdeen to Lerwick
12 hrs 30 mins
All Year
North Link Ferries
0845 6000 449
www.northlinkferries.co.uk

Ardrossan to Brodick
55 mins
All Year
Caledonian MacBrayne
0800 066 5000
www.calmac.co.uk

Ardrossan to Campbeltown
2 hrs 40 mins
Seasonal
Caledonian MacBrayne
0800 066 5000
www.calmac.co.uk

Barra to Eriskay
40 mins
All Year
Caledonian MacBrayne
0800 066 5000
www.calmac.co.uk

Belmont to Gutcher
10 mins
All Year
Shetland Islands Council
01806 244200
www.shetland.gov.uk/ferries/

Belmont to Hamars Ness
30 mins
All Year
Shetland Islands Council
01806 244200
www.shetland.gov.uk/ferries/

Brodick to Campbeltown
2 hrs 20 mins
Seasonal (Saturdays only)
Caledonian MacBrayne
0800 066 5000
www.calmac.co.uk

Claonaig to Lochranza
30 mins
Seasonal
Caledonian MacBrayne
0800 066 5000
www.calmac.co.uk

Coll to Tiree
55 mins - 1 hr
All Year
Caledonian MacBrayne
0800 066 5000
www.calmac.co.uk

Colonsay to Port Askaig
1 hr 20 mins
Seasonal
Caledonian MacBrayne
0800 066 5000
www.calmac.co.uk

Cromarty to Nigg
5 mins
Seasonal
Highland Ferries
07468 417137
www.highlandferries.co.uk

Eday to Sanday
20 mins
All Year
Orkney Ferries
01856 872044
www.orkneyferries.co.uk

Eday to Stronsay
35 mins
All Year
Orkney Ferries
01856 872044
www.orkneyferries.co.uk

Egilsay to Rousay
20 mins
All Year
Orkney Ferries
01856 872044
www.orkneyferries.co.uk

Egilsay to Wyre
15 mins
All Year
Orkney Ferries
01856 872044
www.orkneyferries.co.uk

Lerwick to Bressay
5 mins
All Year
Shetland Islands Council
01806 244200
www.shetland.gov.uk/ferries/

Gill's Bay to St. Margaret's Hope
1 hr
All Year
Pentland Ferries
01856 831226
www.pentlandferries.co.uk

Glenelg to Kylerhea
5 mins
Seasonal
Skye Ferry
01599 522273
www.skyeferry.co.uk

Gourock to Dunoon
20 mins
All Year
Western Ferries
01369 704452
www.western-ferries.co.uk

Gutcher to Hamars Ness
25 mins
All Year
Shetland Islands Council
01806 244200
www.shetland.gov.uk/ferries/

Houton to Flotta
35 mins
All Year
Orkney Ferries
01856 872044
www.orkneyferries.co.uk

Houton to Lyness
35 mins
All Year
Orkney Ferries
01856 872044
www.orkneyferries.co.uk

Kennacraig to Port Askaig
2 hrs 5 mins
All Year
Caledonian MacBrayne
0800 066 5000
www.calmac.co.uk

Kennacraig to Port Ellen
2 hrs 20 mins
All Year
Caledonian MacBrayne
0800 066 5000
www.calmac.co.uk

Kirkwall to Eday
1 hr 15 mins
All Year
Orkney Ferries
01856 872044
www.orkneyferries.co.uk

Kirkwall to North Ronaldsay
2 hrs 40 mins
All Year
Orkney Ferries
01856 872044
www.orkneyferries.co.uk

Kirkwall to Papa Westray
1 hr 50 mins
All Year
Orkney Ferries
01856 872044
www.orkneyferries.co.uk

Kirkwall to Sanday
1 hr 25 mins
All Year
Orkney Ferries
01856 872044
www.orkneyferries.co.uk

Kirkwall to Shapinsay
45 mins
All Year
Orkney Ferries
01856 872044
www.orkneyferries.co.uk

Kirkwall to Stronsay
1 hr 35 mins
All Year
Orkney Ferries
01856 872044
www.orkneyferries.co.uk

Kirkwall to Westray
1 hr 25 mins
All Year
Orkney Ferries
01856 872044
www.orkneyferries.co.uk

Largs to Cumbrae Slip
10 mins
All Year
Caledonian MacBrayne
0800 066 5000
www.calmac.co.uk

Laxo to Symbister
30 mins
All Year
Shetland Islands Council
01806 244200
www.shetland.gov.uk/ferries/

Lerwick to Kirkwall
5 hrs 30 mins - 7 hrs 45 mins
All Year
North Link Ferries
0845 6000 449
www.northlinkferries.co.uk

Lerwick to Skerries
2 hrs 30 mins
All Year
Shetland Islands Council
01806 244200
www.shetland.gov.uk/ferries/

Leverburgh to Berneray
1 hr
All Year
Caledonian MacBrayne
0800 066 5000
www.calmac.co.uk

Lochaline to Fishnish
15 mins
All Year
Caledonian MacBrayne
0800 066 5000
www.calmac.co.uk

Longhope to Flotta
30 mins
All Year
Orkney Ferries
01856 872044
www.orkneyferries.co.uk

Longhope to Lyness
30 mins
All Year
Orkney Ferries
01856 872044
www.orkneyferries.co.uk

Luing to Seil
5 mins
All Year
Argyll and Bute Council
01852 300382
www.argyll-bute.gov.uk

Lyness to Flotta
20 mins
All Year
Orkney Ferries
01856 872044
www.orkneyferries.co.uk

Mallaig to Armadale
30 mins
All Year
Caledonian MacBrayne
0800 066 5000
www.calmac.co.uk

Mallaig to Lochboisdale
3 hrs 30 mins
All Year
Caledonian MacBrayne
0800 066 5000
www.calmac.co.uk

Oban to Castlebay
4 hrs 45 mins
All Year
Caledonian MacBrayne
0800 066 5000
www.calmac.co.uk

Oban to Coll
2 hrs 45 mins
All Year
Caledonian MacBrayne
0800 066 5000
www.calmac.co.uk

Oban to Colonsay
2 hrs 20 mins
All Year
Caledonian MacBrayne
0800 066 5000
www.calmac.co.uk

Oban to Craignure
45 mins
All Year
Caledonian MacBrayne
0800 066 5000
www.calmac.co.uk

Oban to Lismore
55 mins
All Year
Caledonian MacBrayne
0800 066 5000
www.calmac.co.uk

Oban to Lochboisdale
5 hrs 20 mins
Winter only
Caledonian MacBrayne
0800 066 5000
www.calmac.co.uk

Oban to Tiree
3 hrs 30 mins - 4 hrs 15 mins
All Year
Caledonian MacBrayne
0800 066 5000
www.calmac.co.uk

Rousay to Wyre
5 mins
All Year
Orkney Ferries
01856 872044
www.orkneyferries.co.uk

Sconser to Raasay
25 mins
All Year
Caledonian MacBrayne
0800 066 5000
www.calmac.co.uk

Scrabster to Stromness
1 hr 30 mins
All Year
North Link Ferries
0845 6000 449
www.northlinkferries.co.uk

Tarbert to Lochranza
1 hr 25 mins
Winter only
Caledonian MacBrayne
0800 066 5000
www.calmac.co.uk

Tarbert to Portavadie
25 mins
All Year
Caledonian MacBrayne
0800 066 5000
www.calmac.co.uk

Tayinloan to Gigha
20 mins
All Year
Caledonian MacBrayne
0800 066 5000
www.calmac.co.uk

Tingwall to Rousay
25 mins
All Year
Orkney Ferries
01856 872044
www.orkneyferries.co.uk

Tobermory to Kilchoan
35 mins
All Year
Caledonian MacBrayne
0800 066 5000
www.calmac.co.uk

Toft to Ulsta
20 mins
All Year
Shetland Islands Council
01806 244200
www.shetland.gov.uk/ferries/

Uig to Lochmaddy
1 hr 45 mins
All Year
Caledonian MacBrayne
0800 066 5000
www.calmac.co.uk

Uig to Tarbert
1 hr 40 mins
All Year
Caledonian MacBrayne
0800 066 5000
www.calmac.co.uk

Ullapool to Stornoway
2 hrs 30 mins
All Year
Caledonian MacBrayne
0800 066 5000
www.calmac.co.uk

Vidlin to Skerries
1 hr 30 mins
All Year
Shetland Islands Council
01806 244200
www.shetland.gov.uk/ferries/

Vidlin to Symbister
45 mins
All Year
Shetland Islands Council
01806 244200
www.shetland.gov.uk/ferries/

Wemyss Bay to Rothesay
35 mins
All Year
Caledonian MacBrayne
0800 066 5000
www.calmac.co.uk

Westray to Papa Westray
40 mins - 1 hr 45 mins
All Year
Orkney Ferries
01856 872044
www.orkneyferries.co.uk

Wyre to Tingwall
45 mins
All Year
Orkney Ferries
01856 872044
www.orkneyferries.co.uk

M25 orbital map

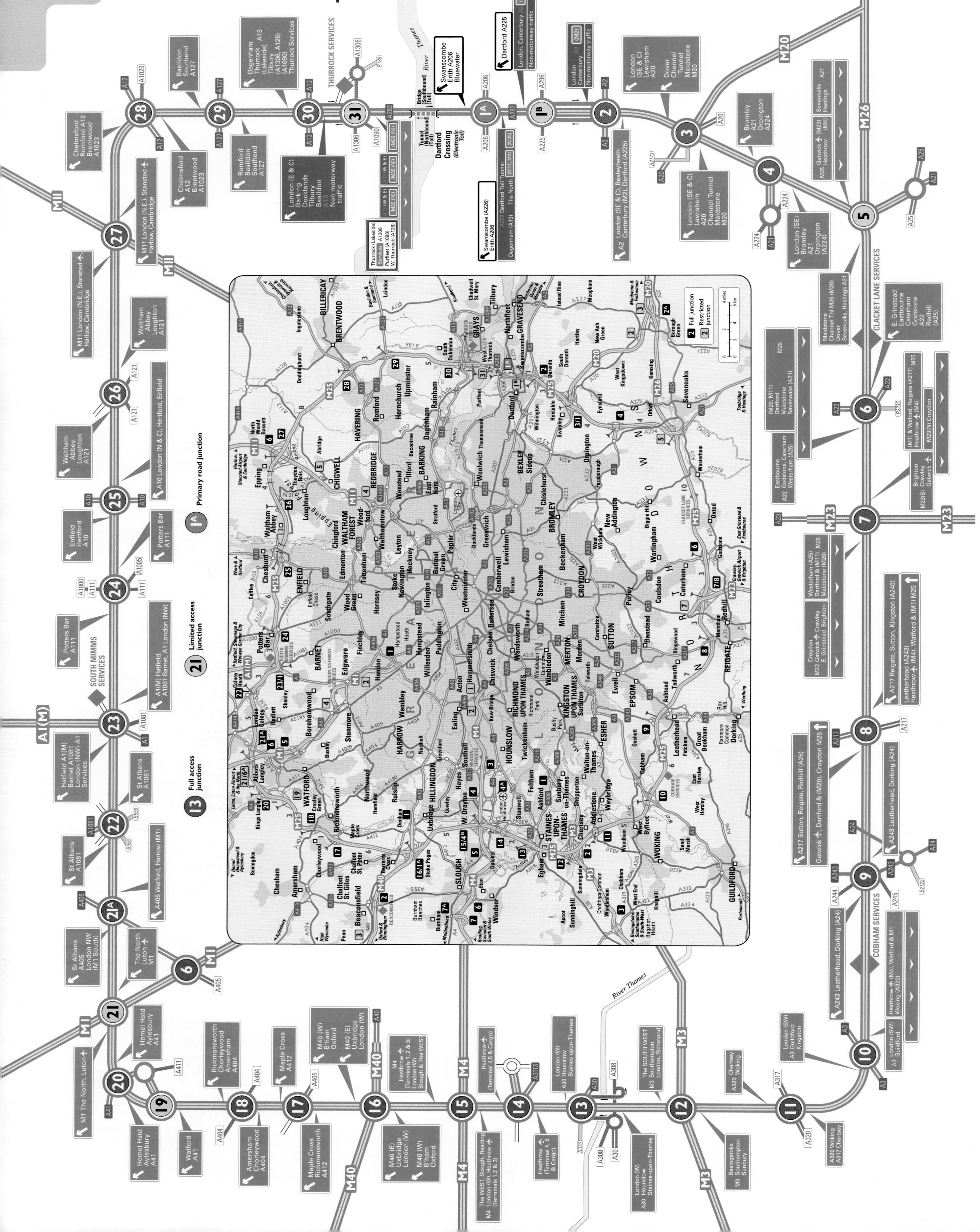
THURROCK SERVICES
SOUTH MIMMS SERVICES
CLACKET LANE SERVICES
COBHAM SERVICES
Dartford Crossing (Electronic Toll)
Bridge (Southbound) (Toll)
Tunnel (Northbound) (Toll)
River Thames
13 Full access junction
21 Limited access junction
1A Primary road junction
Full junction
Restricted junction

Birmingham motorways map

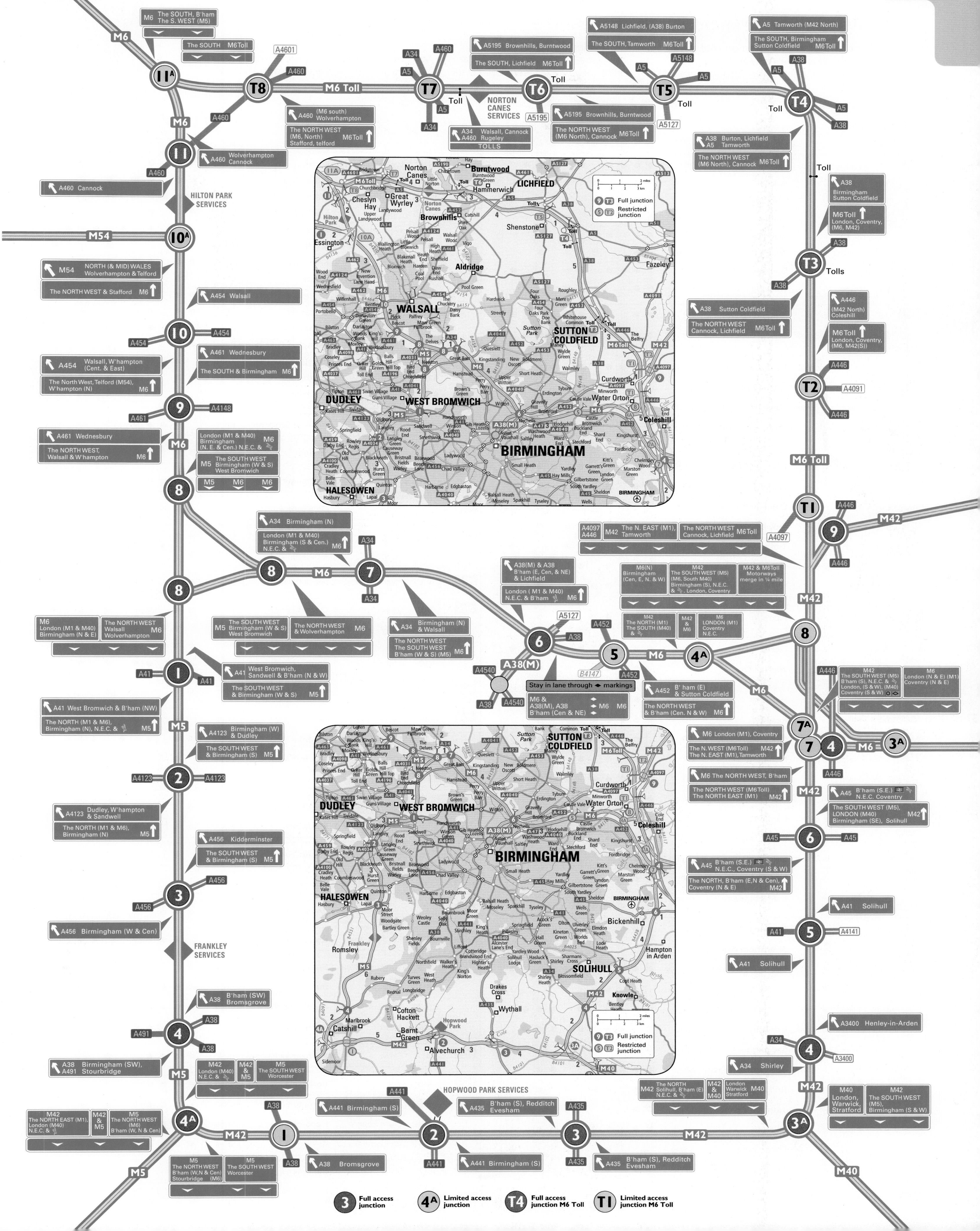
M6
The SOUTH, B'ham
The S. WEST (M5)
The SOUTH M6Toll
A4601
A460
M6 Toll
A34
A460
A5
A5195 Brownhills, Burntwood
The SOUTH, Lichfield M6Toll
A5148 Lichfield, (A38) Burton
The SOUTH, Tamworth M6Toll
A5148
A5
A5 Tamworth (M42 North)
The SOUTH, Birmingham
Sutton Coldfield M6Toll
A38
11A
T8
T7
T6
T5
T4
Toll
NORTON CANES SERVICES
A5195
A5127
A460 (M6 south) Wolverhampton
The NORTH WEST (M6, North) Stafford, telford M6Toll
A34 Walsall, Cannock
A460 Rugeley
TOLLS
A5195 Brownhills, Burntwood
The NORTH WEST (M6 North), Cannock M6Toll
A38 Burton, Lichfield
A5 Tamworth
The NORTH WEST (M6 North), Cannock M6Toll
11
A460 Wolverhampton Cannock
A460 Cannock
HILTON PARK SERVICES
M54
10A
M54 NORTH (& MID) WALES Wolverhampton & Telford
The NORTH WEST & Stafford M6
A454 Walsall
10
A454
A461 Wednesbury
The SOUTH & Birmingham M6
A454 Walsall, W'hampton (Cent. & East)
The North West, Telford (M54), W'hampton (N) M6
9
A4148
A461
A461 Wednesbury
The NORTH WEST, Walsall & W'hampton M6
London (M1 & M40) Birmingham (N. E. & Cen.) N.E.C. & M6
M5 The SOUTH WEST Birmingham (W & S) West Bromwich
8
A38 Birmingham Sutton Coldfield
M6Toll London, Coventry, (M6, M42)
T3
Tolls
A38 Sutton Coldfield
The NORTH WEST Cannock, Lichfield M6Toll
A446 (M42 North) Coleshill
M6Toll London, Coventry, (M6, M42(S))
T2
A4091
A446
M6 Toll
T1
A34 Birmingham (N)
London (M1 & M40) Birmingham (S & Cen.) N.E.C. & M6
7
M6
A34
A4097 A446
M42 The N. EAST (M1), Tamworth
The NORTH WEST Cannock, Lichfield M6Toll
A4097
M42
9
M6(N) Birmingham (Cen, E, N. & W)
M42 The SOUTH WEST (M5) (M6, South M40) Birmingham (S), N.E.C. & London, Coventry
M42 & M6Toll Motorways merge in ¼ mile
A38(M) & A38 B'ham (E, Cen, & NE) & Lichfield
London (M1 & M40) N.E.C. & B'ham M6
M6 London (M1 & M40) Birmingham (N & E)
The NORTH WEST Walsall Wolverhampton M6
M5 The SOUTH WEST Birmingham (W & S) West Bromwich
The NORTH WEST & Wolverhampton M6
A34 Birmingham (N) & Walsall
The NORTH WEST The SOUTH WEST B'ham (W & S) (M5) M6
A5127
A452
6
A38(M)
5
4A
A38
A4540
B4147
A452
Stay in lane through markings
M6 & A38(M), A38 B'ham (Cen & NE) M6 M6
A452 B'ham (E) & Sutton Coldfield
The NORTH WEST & B'ham (Cen. N & W) M6
M42 The NORTH (M1) The SOUTH (M40)
M42 & M6
M6 LONDON (M1) Coventry N.E.C.
M42 The SOUTH WEST (M5) B'ham (S), N.E.C. & London, (S & W), (M40) Coventry (S & W)
M6 London (N & E) (M1) Coventry (N & E)
A41
1
A41 West Bromwich, Sandwell & B'ham (N & W)
The SOUTH WEST & Birmingham (W & S) M5
A41 West Bromwich & B'ham (NW)
The NORTH (M1 & M6), Birmingham (N), N.E.C. & M5
M5
A4123 Birmingham (W) & Dudley
The SOUTH WEST & Birmingham (S) M5
2
A4123
A4123 Dudley, W'hampton & Sandwell
The NORTH (M1 & M6), Birmingham (N) M5
A456 Kidderminster
The SOUTH WEST & Birmingham (S) M5
3
A456
A456 Birmingham (W & Cen)
FRANKLEY SERVICES
A38 B'ham (SW) Bromsgrove
4
A491
A38 Birmingham (SW), A491 Stourbridge
M42 London (M40) N.E.C. &
M42 & M5
M5 The SOUTH WEST Worcester
M6 London (M1), Coventry
The N. WEST (M6Toll) The N. EAST (M1), Tamworth M42
7A
7
4
3A
A446
M6 The NORTH WEST, B'ham
The NORTH WEST (M6Toll) The NORTH EAST (M1) M42
A45 B'ham (S.E.) N.E.C. Coventry
The SOUTH WEST (M5), LONDON (M40) Birmingham (SE), Solihull M42
A45
A45 B'ham (S.E.) N.E.C., Coventry (S & W)
The NORTH, B'ham (E,N & Cen), Coventry (N & E) M42
A41 Solihull
5
A4141
A41 Solihull
A3400 Henley-in-Arden
A34
A3400
A34 Shirley
M42 Solihull, B'ham (E) N.E.C. &
The NORTH
M42 & M40
London Warwick Stratford M40
M40 London, Warwick, Stratford
M42 The SOUTH WEST Birmingham (S & W)
M42 The NORTH EAST (M1), London (M40) N.E.C. &
M42 & M5
M5 The NORTH WEST (M6) B'ham (W, N & Cen)
A441
HOPWOOD PARK SERVICES
A38
A441 Birmingham (S)
A435 B'ham (S), Redditch Evesham
A435
4A
1
2
3
3A
M42
M5
A38 Bromsgrove
A441 Birmingham (S)
A435 B'ham (S), Redditch Evesham
M5 The NORTH WEST B'ham (W,N & Cen) Stourbridge (M6)
M5 The SOUTH WEST Worcester
M40
WALSALL
WEST BROMWICH
DUDLEY
BIRMINGHAM
SUTTON COLDFIELD
HALESOWEN
LICHFIELD
SOLIHULL
Full junction
Restricted junction
Full access junction
Limited access junction
Full access junction M6 Toll
Limited access junction M6 Toll

Motorway services information

All motorway service areas have fuel, food, toilets, disabled facilities and free short-term parking

For further information on motorway services providers:
Moto www.moto-way.com   RoadChef www.roadchef.com   Welcome Break www.welcomebreak.co.uk
Euro Garages www.eurogarages.com   Extra www.extraservices.co.uk   Westmorland www.westmorland.com

Motorway Services · Petrol · ½ m

Motorway	Junction	Service provider	Service name	Fuel supplier	Information	Accommodation	Conference facilities	Showers	M&S Simply Food	Waitrose	Costa Coffee	Starbucks	Burger King	KFC	McDonalds
A1(M)	1	Welcome Break	South Mimms	BP	●	●	●	●			●		●	●	
	10	Extra	Baldock	Shell	●	●	●	●			●				●
	17	Extra	Peterborough	Shell	●	●	●	●			●			●	●
	34	Moto	Blyth	Esso	●	●		●			●	●			
	46	Moto	Wetherby	BP	●	●	●	●			●	●			
	53	Moto	Scotch Corner	Esso	●	●	●	●			●				
	61	RoadChef	Durham	Shell	●	●					●				●
	64	Moto	Washington	BP	●	●									
A74(M)	16	RoadChef	Annandale Water	BP	●	●			●					●	
	22	Welcome Break	Gretna Green	BP	●	●					●		●		
M1	2-4	Welcome Break	London Gateway	Shell	●	●	●	●			●		●		
	11-12	Moto	Toddington	BP	●	●	●	●		●	●				
	14-15	Welcome Break	Newport Pagnell	Shell	●	●		●			●		●		
	15A	RoadChef	Northampton	BP	●						●				
	16-17	RoadChef	Watford Gap	BP	●	●	●				●				
	21-21A	Welcome Break	Leicester Forest East	Shell	●	●					●		●		
	22	Euro Garages	Markfield	BP	●										
	23A	Moto	Donington Park	BP	●	●	●	●			●	●			
	25-26	Moto	Trowell	BP	●	●		●			●				
	28-29	RoadChef	Tibshelf	Shell	●	●	●				●				
	30-31	Welcome Break	Woodall	Shell	●	●		●			●		●		
	38-39	Moto	Woolley Edge	BP	●	●		●			●				
M2	4-5	Moto	Medway	BP		●	●	●			●				
M3	4A-5	Welcome Break	Fleet	Shell	●	●	●	●			●		●	●	
	8-9	Moto	Winchester	BP	●	●		●			●				
M4	3	Moto	Heston	BP	●	●	●	●			●	●			
	11-12	Moto	Reading	BP	●	●	●	●			●	●			
	13	Moto	Chieveley	BP	●	●	●	●			●				
	14-15	Welcome Break	Membury	BP	●	●					●		●	●	
	17-18	Moto	Leigh Delamere	BP	●	●	●	●			●	●			
	23A	RoadChef	Magor	Esso	●	●									●
	30	Welcome Break	Cardiff Gate	Shell	●	●					●				
	33	Moto	Cardiff West	Esso	●	●					●				
	36	Welcome Break	Sarn Park	Shell	●	●					●		●		
	47	Moto	Swansea	BP	●	●					●				
	49	RoadChef	Pont Abraham	Esso	●						●				●
M5	3-4	Moto	Frankley	BP		●		●	●		●				
	8	RoadChef	Strensham (South)	BP	●						●				
	8	RoadChef	Strensham (North)	Texaco	●	●	●				●				
	11-12	Westmorland	Gloucester	Texaco	●				●						
	13-14	Welcome Break	Michaelwood	BP	●	●					●		●		
	19	Welcome Break	Gordano	Shell	●	●	●	●			●		●		
	21-22	RoadChef	Sedgemoor (South)	Shell	●	●					●				
	21-22	Welcome Break	Sedgemoor (North)	Shell	●	●		●			●		●		
	24	Moto	Bridgwater	BP		●		●			●				
	25-26	RoadChef	Taunton Deane	Shell	●	●		●			●				
	27	Moto	Tiverton	Shell	●	●					●				
	28	Extra	Cullompton	Shell	●			●			●				
	29-30	Moto	Exeter	BP	●	●		●			●	●			
M6 Toll	T6-T7	RoadChef	Norton Canes	BP	●	●	●	●			●				●

Motorway	Junction	Service provider	Service name	Fuel supplier	Information	Accommodation	Conference facilities	Showers	M&S Simply Food	Waitrose	Costa Coffee	Starbucks	Burger King	KFC	McDonalds
M6	3-4	Welcome Break	Corley	Shell	●	●		●			●		●		
	10-11	Moto	Hilton Park	BP	●	●	●	●			●	●			
	14-15	RoadChef	Stafford (South)	Esso	●	●	●	●			●				●
	14-15	Moto	Stafford (North)	BP	●	●		●			●				
	15-16	Welcome Break	Keele	Shell	●	●					●		●		
	16-17	RoadChef	Sandbach	BP	●						●				●
	18-19	Moto	Knutsford	BP	●	●		●			●	●			
	20	Moto	Lymm	BP	●	●	●	●			●				
	27-28	Welcome Break	Charnock Richard	Shell	●	●		●			●		●		
	32-33	Moto	Lancaster	BP	●	●		●			●				
	35A-36	Moto	Burton-in-Kendal (N)	BP	●	●		●			●				
	36-37	RoadChef	Killington Lake (S)	BP	●	●					●				●
	38-39	Westmorland	Tebay	Total	●	●	●		●						
	41-42	Moto	Southwaite	BP	●	●		●			●				
	44-45	Moto	Todhills	BP/Shell	●										
M8	4-5	BP	Heart of Scotland	BP		●	●	●							
M9	9	Moto	Stirling	BP	●	●					●				
M11	8	Welcome Break	Birchanger Green	Shell	●	●	●	●		●	●		●	●	
M18	5	Moto	Doncaster North	BP	●	●					●				
M20	8	RoadChef	Maidstone	Esso	●	●					●				●
	11	Stop 24	Stop 24	Shell	●	●					●				
M23	11	Moto	Pease Pottage	BP	●			●			●	●			
M25	5-6	RoadChef	Clacket Lane	BP	●	●					●				●
	9-10	Extra	Cobham	Shell	●	●	●				●		●	●	
	23	Welcome Break	South Mimms	BP	●	●	●				●		●	●	
	30	Moto	Thurrock	Esso	●	●					●				
M27	3-4	RoadChef	Rownhams	BP	●	●					●				●
M40	2	Extra	Beaconsfield	Shell	●		●				●		●	●	
	8	Welcome Break	Oxford	BP	●	●					●		●		
	10	Moto	Cherwell Valley	Esso	●	●		●			●				
	12-13	Welcome Break	Warwick	BP	●	●	●	●			●		●	●	
M42	2	Welcome Break	Hopwood Park	Shell	●						●		●		
	10	Moto	Tamworth	Esso	●	●					●				
M48	1	Moto	Severn View	BP	●	●					●				
M54	4	Welcome Break	Telford	Shell	●	●					●				
M56	14	RoadChef	Chester	Shell	●	●	●				●				●
M61	6-7	Euro Garages	Rivington	BP		●	●	●							
M62	7-9	Welcome Break	Burtonwood	Shell	●						●		●		
	18-19	Moto	Birch	BP	●	●		●			●				
	25-26	Welcome Break	Hartshead Moor	Shell	●	●		●			●		●		
	33	Moto	Ferrybridge	BP	●	●					●				
M65	4	Extra	Blackburn with Darwen	Shell	●	●	●				●				●
M74	4-5	RoadChef	Bothwell (South)	Shell	●	●	●				●				
	5-6	RoadChef	Hamilton (North)	Shell	●	●	●				●				
	11-12	Cairn Lodge	Happendon	Shell											
	12-13	Welcome Break	Abington	Shell	●	●					●		●		
M80	6-7	Shell	Old Inns	Shell	●										
M90	6	Moto	Kinross	BP	●	●		●			●				

There are a number of operators of motorway service areas in Britain; RoadChef, Welcome Break and Moto being the biggest three. All motorway service areas are required by law to provide fuel, free toilets and free short term parking 24 hours a day. Details of other facilities provided at each service area are shown opposite, although most of these will not be open 24 hours a day.

As part of its *Think, don't drive tired* road safety campaign the Government has the following tips for drivers:

- If you are feeling tired, opening the window or turning up the radio does not work, instead find a safe place to stop.
- On long journeys take a 15 minute break every 2 hours.
- If feeling tired, a 15 minute nap will help as will drinking 2 cups of coffee or other high caffeine drink. The most effective solution is to have some caffeine and then take a short sleep which gives the caffeine time to kick in.
- Avoid making long trips between midnight and 6am when you are most susceptible to sleepiness.
- Don't begin a journey if you are already feeling tired.

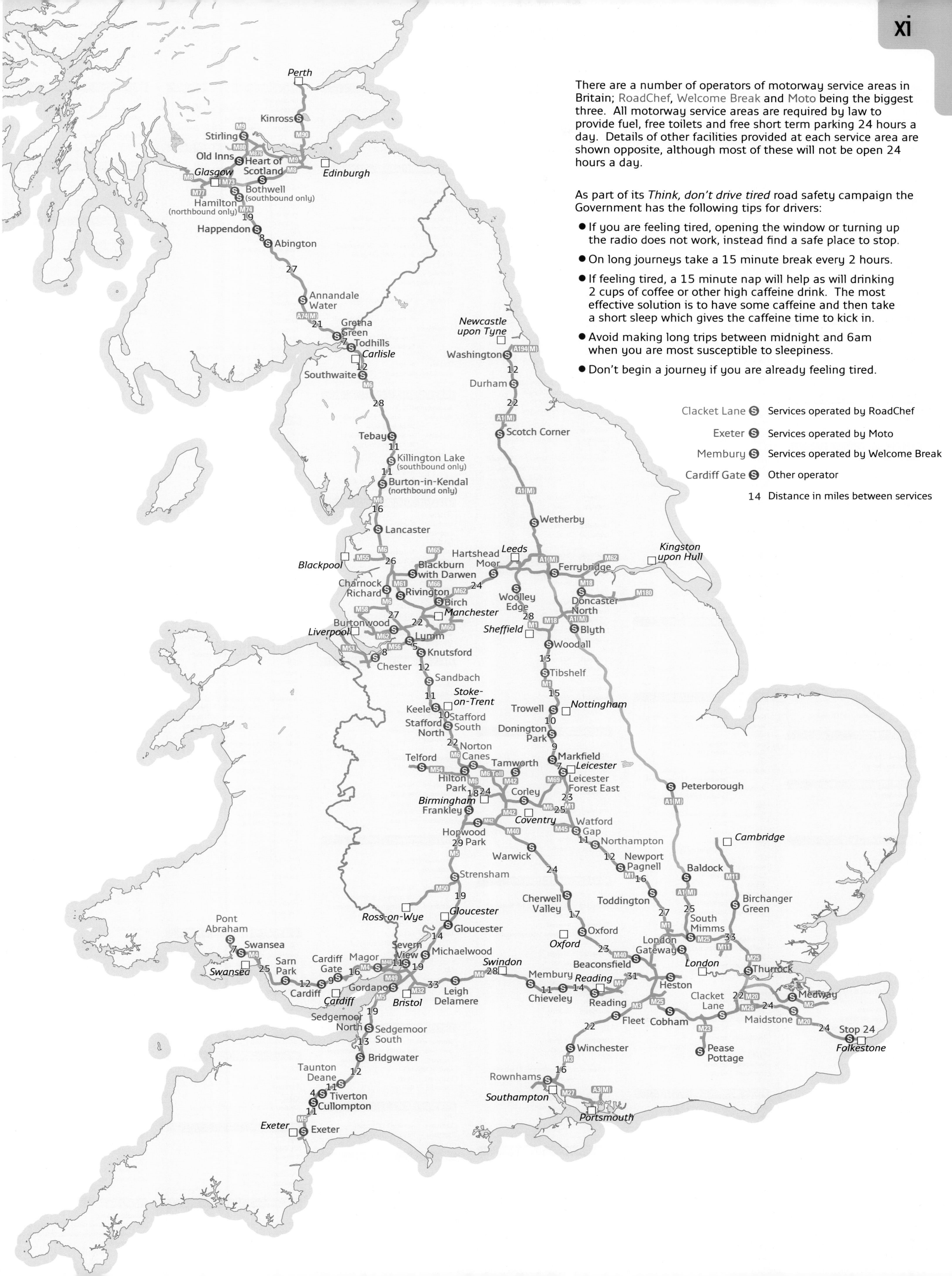

Clacket Lane Ⓢ Services operated by RoadChef
Exeter Ⓢ Services operated by Moto
Membury Ⓢ Services operated by Welcome Break
Cardiff Gate Ⓢ Other operator

14 Distance in miles between services

Restricted motorway junctions

Restricted motorway junctions are shown on the maps as 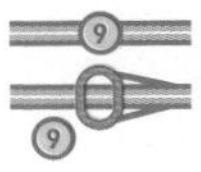

A1(M) LONDON TO NEWCASTLE

Junction	Direction	Restriction
2	Northbound	No access
	Southbound	No exit
3	Southbound	No access
5	Northbound	No exit
	Southbound	No access
		No exit
41	Northbound	No exit to M62 Eastbound
43	Northbound	No exit to M1 Westbound
Dishforth	Southbound	No access from A168 Eastbound
57	Northbound	No access
		Exit only to A66(M) Northbound
	Southbound	Access only from A66(M) Southbound
		No exit
65	Northbound	No access from A1
	Southbound	No exit to A1

A3(M) PORTSMOUTH

Junction	Direction	Restriction
1	Northbound	No exit
	Southbound	No access
4	Northbound	No access
	Southbound	No exit

A38(M) BIRMINGHAM

Junction	Direction	Restriction
Victoria Road	Northbound	No exit
	Southbound	No access

A48(M) CARDIFF

Junction	Direction	Restriction
Junction with M4	Westbound	No access from M4 29 Eastbound
	Eastbound	No exit to M4 29 Westbound
29A	Westbound	No exit to A48 Eastbound
	Eastbound	No access from A48 Westbound

A57(M) MANCHESTER

Junction	Direction	Restriction
Brook Street	Westbound	No exit
	Eastbound	No access

A58(M) LEEDS

Junction	Direction	Restriction
Westgate	Southbound	No access
Woodhouse Lane	Westbound	No exit

A64(M) LEEDS

Junction	Direction	Restriction
Claypit Lane	Eastbound	No access

A66(M) DARLINGTON

Junction	Direction	Restriction
Junction with A1(M)	Northbound	No access from A1(M) Southbound
		No exit
	Southbound	No access
		No exit to A1(M) Northbound

A74(M) LOCKERBIE

Junction	Direction	Restriction
18	Northbound	No access
	Southbound	No exit

A167(M) NEWCASTLE

Junction	Direction	Restriction
Campden Street	Northbound	No exit
	Southbound	No access
		No exit

M1 LONDON TO LEEDS

Junction	Direction	Restriction
2	Northbound	No exit
	Southbound	No access
4	Northbound	No exit
	Southbound	No access
6A	Northbound	Access only from M25 21
		No exit
	Southbound	No access
		Exit only to M25 21
7	Northbound	Access only from A414
		No exit
	Southbound	No access
		Exit only to A414
17	Northbound	No access
		Exit only to M45
	Southbound	Access only from M45
		No exit
19	Northbound	Exit only to M6
	Southbound	Access only from M6
21A	Northbound	No access
	Southbound	No exit
23A	Northbound	No access from A453
	Southbound	No exit to A453
24A	Northbound	No exit
	Southbound	No access
35A	Northbound	No access
	Southbound	No exit
43	Northbound	No access
		Exit only to M621
	Southbound	No exit
		Access only from M621
48	Northbound	No exit to A1(M) Southbound
		Access only from A1(M) Northbound
	Southbound	Exit only to A1(M) Southbound

M2 ROCHESTER TO CANTERBURY

Junction	Direction	Restriction
1	Westbound	No exit to A2 Eastbound
	Eastbound	No access from A2 Westbound

M3 LONDON TO WINCHESTER

Junction	Direction	Restriction
8	Westbound	No access
	Eastbound	No exit
10	Northbound	No access
	Southbound	No exit
13	Southbound	No exit to A335 Eastbound
		No access
14	Westbound	No access
	Eastbound	No exit

M4 LONDON TO SWANSEA

Junction	Direction	Restriction
1	Westbound	No access from A4 Eastbound
	Eastbound	No exit to A4 Westbound
2	Westbound	No access from A4 Eastbound
		No exit to A4 Eastbound
	Eastbound	No access from A4 Westbound
		No exit to A4 Westbound
21	Westbound	No access from M48 Eastbound
	Eastbound	No exit to M48 Westbound
23	Westbound	No exit to M48 Eastbound
	Eastbound	No access from M48 Westbound
25	Westbound	No access
	Eastbound	No exit
25A	Westbound	No access
	Eastbound	No exit
29	Westbound	No access
		Exit only to A48(M)
	Eastbound	Access only from A48(M) Eastbound
		No exit
38	Westbound	No access
39	Westbound	No exit
	Eastbound	No access
		No exit
41	Westbound	No exit
	Eastbound	No access
42	Westbound	No exit to A48
	Eastbound	No access from A48

M5 BIRMINGHAM TO EXETER

Junction	Direction	Restriction
10	Northbound	No exit
	Southbound	No access
11A	Northbound	No access from A417 Eastbound
	Southbound	No exit to A417 Westbound

M6 COVENTRY TO CARLISLE

Junction	Direction	Restriction
Junction with M1	Northbound	No access from M1 19 Southbound
	Southbound	No exit to M1 19 Northbound
3A	Northbound	No access from M6 Toll
	Southbound	No exit to M6 Toll
4	Northbound	No exit to M42 Northbound
		No access from M42 Southbound
	Southbound	No exit to M42
		No access from M42 Southbound
4A	Northbound	No access from M42 8 Northbound
		No exit
	Southbound	No access
		Exit only to M42 8
5	Northbound	No access
	Southbound	No exit
10A	Northbound	No access
		Exit only to M54
	Southbound	Access only from M54
		No exit
11A	Northbound	No exit to M6 Toll
	Southbound	No access from M6 Toll
24	Northbound	No exit
	Southbound	No access
25	Northbound	No access
	Southbound	No exit
30	Northbound	Access only from M61 Northbound
		No exit
	Southbound	No access
		Exit only to M61 Southbound
31A	Northbound	No access
	Southbound	No exit

M6 Toll BIRMINGHAM

Junction	Direction	Restriction
T1	Northbound	Exit only to M42
		Access only from A4097
	Southbound	No exit
		Access only from M42 Southbound
T2	Northbound	No exit
		No access
	Southbound	No access
T5	Northbound	No exit
	Southbound	No access
T7	Northbound	No access
	Southbound	No exit
T8	Northbound	No access
	Southbound	No exit

M8 EDINBURGH TO GLASGOW

Junction	Direction	Restriction
6A	Westbound	No exit
	Eastbound	No access
7	Westbound	No exit
	Eastbound	No access
7A	Westbound	No access
	Eastbound	No exit
8	Westbound	No access from M73 2 Southbound
		No access from A8 Eastbound
		No access from A89 Eastbound
	Eastbound	No access from A89 Westbound
		No exit to M73 2 Northbound
9	Westbound	No exit
	Eastbound	No access
13	Westbound	Access only from M80
	Eastbound	Exit only to M80
14	Westbound	No exit
	Eastbound	No access
16	Westbound	No access
	Eastbound	No exit
17	Eastbound	Access only from A82, not central Glasgow
		Exit only to A82, not central Glasgow
18	Westbound	No access
	Eastbound	No access
19	Westbound	Access only from A814 Eastbound
	Eastbound	Exit only to A814 Westbound, not central Glasgow
20	Westbound	No access
	Eastbound	No exit
21	Westbound	No exit
	Eastbound	No access
22	Westbound	No access
		Exit only to M77 Southbound
	Eastbound	Access only from M77 Northbound
		No exit
23	Westbound	No access
	Eastbound	No exit
25A	Eastbound	No exit
	Westbound	No access
28	Westbound	No access
	Eastbound	No exit
28A	Westbound	No access
	Eastbound	No exit

M9 EDINBURGH TO STIRLING

Junction	Direction	Restriction
2	Westbound	No exit
	Eastbound	No access
3	Westbound	No access
	Eastbound	No exit
6	Westbound	No exit
	Eastbound	No access
8	Westbound	No access
	Eastbound	No exit

M11 LONDON TO CAMBRIDGE

Junction	Direction	Restriction
4	Northbound	No access from A1400 Westbound
		No exit
	Southbound	No access
		No exit to A1400 Eastbound
5	Northbound	No access
	Southbound	No exit
8A	Northbound	No access
	Southbound	No exit
9	Northbound	No access
	Southbound	No exit
13	Northbound	No access
	Southbound	No exit
14	Northbound	No access from A428 Eastbound
		No exit to A428 Westbound
		No exit to A1307
	Southbound	No access from A428 Eastbound
		No access from A1307
		No exit

M20 LONDON TO FOLKESTONE

Junction	Direction	Restriction
2	Westbound	No exit
	Eastbound	No access
3	Westbound	No access
		Exit only to M26 Westbound
	Eastbound	Access only from M26 Eastbound
		No exit
11A	Westbound	No exit
	Eastbound	No access

M23 LONDON TO CRAWLEY

Junction	Direction	Restriction
7	Northbound	No exit to A23 Southbound
	Southbound	No access from A23 Northbound
10A	Southbound	No access from B2036
	Northbound	No exit to B2036

M25 LONDON ORBITAL MOTORWAY

Junction	Direction	Restriction
1B	Clockwise	No access
	Anticlockwise	No exit
5	Clockwise	No exit to M26 Eastbound
	Anticlockwise	No access from M26 Westbound
Spur of M25 5	Clockwise	No access from M26 Westbound
	Anticlockwise	No exit to M26 Eastbound
19	Clockwise	No access
	Anticlockwise	No exit
21	Clockwise	No access from M1 6A Northbound
		No exit to M1 6A Southbound
	Anticlockwise	No access from M1 6A Northbound
		No exit to M1 6A Southbound
31	Clockwise	No exit
	Anticlockwise	No access

M26 SEVENOAKS

Junction	Direction	Restriction
Junction with M25 5	Westbound	No exit to M25 Anticlockwise
		No exit to M25 spur
	Eastbound	No access from M25 Clockwise
		No access from M25 spur
Junction with M20	Westbound	No access from M20 3 Eastbound
	Eastbound	No exit to M20 3 Westbound

M27 SOUTHAMPTON TO PORTSMOUTH

Junction	Direction	Restriction
4 West	Westbound	No exit
	Eastbound	No access
4 East	Westbound	No access
	Eastbound	No exit
10	Westbound	No access
	Eastbound	No exit
12 West	Westbound	No exit
	Eastbound	No access
12 East	Westbound	No access from A3
	Eastbound	No exit

M40 LONDON TO BIRMINGHAM

Junction	Direction	Restriction
3	Westbound	No access
	Eastbound	No exit
7	Eastbound	No exit
8	Northbound	No access
	Southbound	No exit
13	Northbound	No access
	Southbound	No exit
14	Northbound	No exit
	Southbound	No access
16	Northbound	No exit
	Southbound	No access

M42 BIRMINGHAM

Junction	Direction	Restriction
1	Northbound	No exit
	Southbound	No access
7	Northbound	No access
		Exit only to M6 Northbound
	Southbound	Access only from M6 Northbound
		No exit
7A	Northbound	No access
		Exit only to M6 Eastbound
	Southbound	No access
		No exit
8	Northbound	Access only from M6 Southbound
		No exit
	Southbound	Access only from M6 Southbound
		Exit only to M6 Northbound

M45 COVENTRY

Junction	Direction	Restriction
Junction with M1	Westbound	No access from M1 17 Southbound
	Eastbound	No exit to M1 17 Northbound
Junction with A45	Westbound	No exit
	Eastbound	No access

M48 CHEPSTOW

Junction	Direction	Restriction
M4	Westbound	No exit to M4 Eastbound
	Eastbound	No access from M4 Westbound

M49 BRISTOL

Junction	Direction	Restriction
18A	Northbound	No access from M5 Southbound
	Southbound	No access from M5 Northbound

M53 BIRKENHEAD TO CHESTER

Junction	Direction	Restriction
11	Northbound	No access from M56 15 Eastbound
		No exit to M56 15 Westbound
	Southbound	No access from M56 15 Eastbound
		No exit to M56 15 Westbound

M54 WOLVERHAMPTON TO TELFORD

Junction	Direction	Restriction
Junction with M6	Westbound	No access from M6 10A Southbound
	Eastbound	No exit to M6 10A Northbound

M56 STOCKPORT TO CHESTER

Junction	Direction	Restriction
1	Westbound	No access from M60 Eastbound
		No access from A34 Northbound
	Eastbound	No exit to M60 Westbound
		No exit to A34 Southbound
2	Westbound	No access
	Eastbound	No exit
3	Westbound	No exit
	Eastbound	No access
4	Westbound	No access
	Eastbound	No exit
7	Westbound	No access
	Eastbound	No exit
8	Westbound	No exit
	Eastbound	No access
9	Westbound	No exit to M6 Southbound
	Eastbound	No access from M6 Northbound
15	Westbound	No access
		No access from M53 11
	Eastbound	No exit
		No exit to M53 11

M57 LIVERPOOL

Junction	Direction	Restriction
3	Northbound	No exit
	Southbound	No access
5	Northbound	Access only from A580 Westbound
		No exit
	Southbound	No access
		Exit only to A580 Eastbound

M58 LIVERPOOL TO WIGAN

Junction	Direction	Restriction
1	Westbound	No access
	Eastbound	No exit

M60 MANCHESTER

Junction	Direction	Restriction
2	Westbound	No exit
	Eastbound	No access
3	Westbound	No access from M56 1
		No access from A34 Southbound
		No exit to A34 Northbound
	Eastbound	No access from A34 Southbound
		No exit to M56 1
		No exit to A34 Northbound
4	Westbound	No access
	Eastbound	No exit to M56
5	Westbound	No access from A5103 Southbound
		No exit to A5103 Southbound
	Eastbound	No access from A5103 Northbound
		No exit to A5103 Northbound
14	Westbound	No access from A580
		No exit to A580 Eastbound
	Eastbound	No access from A580 Westbound
		No exit to A580
16	Westbound	No access
	Eastbound	No exit
20	Westbound	No access
	Eastbound	No exit
22	Westbound	No access
25	Westbound	No access
26	Eastbound	No access
		No exit
27	Westbound	No exit
	Eastbound	No access

M61 MANCHESTER TO PRESTON

Junction	Direction	Restriction
2	Northbound	No access from A580 Eastbound
		No access from A666
	Southbound	No exit to A580 Westbound
3	Northbound	No access from A580 Eastbound
		No access from A666
	Southbound	No exit to A580 Westbound
Junction with M6	Northbound	No exit to M6 30 Southbound
	Southbound	No access from M6 30 Northbound

M62 LIVERPOOL TO HULL

Junction	Direction	Restriction
23	Westbound	No exit
	Eastbound	No access
32A	Westbound	No exit to A1(M) Southbound

M65 BURNLEY

Junction	Direction	Restriction
9	Westbound	No exit
	Eastbound	No access
11	Westbound	No access
	Eastbound	No exit

M66 MANCHESTER TO EDENFIELD

Junction	Direction	Restriction
1	Northbound	No access
	Southbound	No exit
Junction with A56	Northbound	Exit only to A56 Northbound
	Southbound	Access only from A56 Southbound

M67 MANCHESTER

Junction	Direction	Restriction
1	Westbound	No exit
	Eastbound	No access
2	Westbound	No access
	Eastbound	No exit

M69 COVENTRY TO LEICESTER

Junction	Direction	Restriction
2	Northbound	No exit
	Southbound	No access

M73 GLASGOW

Junction	Direction	Restriction
1	Northbound	No access from A721 Eastbound
	Southbound	No exit to A721 Eastbound
2	Northbound	No access from M8 8 Eastbound
	Southbound	No exit to M8 8 Westbound

M74 GLASGOW

Junction	Direction	Restriction
1	Westbound	No exit to M8 Kingston Bridge
	Eastbound	No access from M8 Kingston Bridge
3	Westbound	No access
	Eastbound	No exit
3A	Westbound	No exit
	Eastbound	No access
7	Northbound	No exit
	Southbound	No access
9	Northbound	No access
		No exit
	Southbound	No access
10	Southbound	No exit
11	Northbound	No exit
	Southbound	No access
12	Northbound	Access only from A70 Northbound
	Southbound	Exit only to A70 Southbound

M77 GLASGOW

Junction	Direction	Restriction
Junction with M8	Northbound	No exit to M8 22 Westbound
	Southbound	No access from M8 22 Eastbound
4	Northbound	No exit
	Southbound	No access
6	Northbound	No exit to A77
	Southbound	No access from A77
7	Northbound	No access
		No exit
8	Northbound	No access
	Southbound	No access

M80 STIRLING

Junction	Direction	Restriction
4A	Northbound	No access
	Southbound	No exit
6A	Northbound	No exit
	Southbound	No access
8	Northbound	No access from M876
	Southbound	No exit to M876

M90 EDINBURGH TO PERTH

Junction	Direction	Restriction
1	Northbound	No exit to A90
2A	Northbound	No access
	Southbound	No exit
7	Northbound	No exit
	Southbound	No access
8	Northbound	No access
	Southbound	No exit
10	Northbound	No access from A912
		No exit to A912 Southbound
	Southbound	No access from A912 Northbound
		No exit to A912

M180 SCUNTHORPE

Junction	Direction	Restriction
1	Westbound	No exit
	Eastbound	No access

M606 BRADFORD

Junction	Direction	Restriction
Straithgate Lane	Northbound	No access

M621 LEEDS

Junction	Direction	Restriction
2A	Northbound	No exit
	Southbound	No access
5	Northbound	No access
	Southbound	No exit
6	Northbound	No exit
	Southbound	No access

M876 FALKIRK

Junction	Direction	Restriction
Junction with M80	Westbound	No exit to M80 8 Northbound
	Eastbound	No access from M80 8 Southbound
Junction with M9	Westbound	No access
	Eastbound	No exit

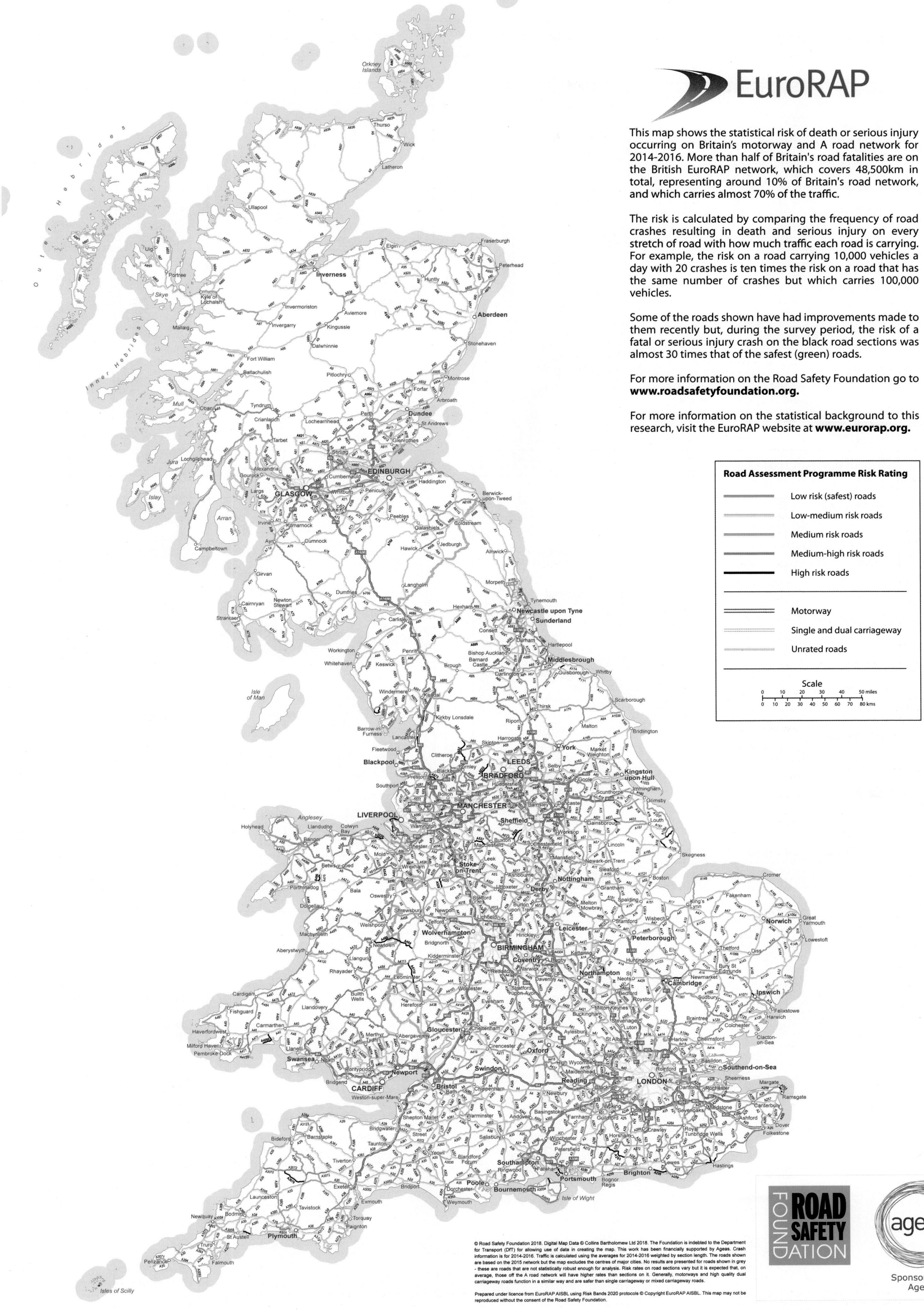

EuroRAP

This map shows the statistical risk of death or serious injury occurring on Britain's motorway and A road network for 2014-2016. More than half of Britain's road fatalities are on the British EuroRAP network, which covers 48,500km in total, representing around 10% of Britain's road network, and which carries almost 70% of the traffic.

The risk is calculated by comparing the frequency of road crashes resulting in death and serious injury on every stretch of road with how much traffic each road is carrying. For example, the risk on a road carrying 10,000 vehicles a day with 20 crashes is ten times the risk on a road that has the same number of crashes but which carries 100,000 vehicles.

Some of the roads shown have had improvements made to them recently but, during the survey period, the risk of a fatal or serious injury crash on the black road sections was almost 30 times that of the safest (green) roads.

For more information on the Road Safety Foundation go to **www.roadsafetyfoundation.org.**

For more information on the statistical background to this research, visit the EuroRAP website at **www.eurorap.org.**

Road Assessment Programme Risk Rating

——	Low risk (safest) roads
——	Low-medium risk roads
——	Medium risk roads
——	Medium-high risk roads
——	High risk roads
═══	Motorway
┈┈┈	Single and dual carriageway
——	Unrated roads

Scale

0 10 20 30 40 50 miles
0 10 20 30 40 50 60 70 80 kms

ROAD SAFETY FOUNDATION

ageas

Sponsored by Ageas

xiv Airport plans

Stansted

Manchester

Heathrow

Glasgow

Gatwick

Birmingham

Key to map symbols   P Short stay car park   P Mid stay car park   P Long stay car park   P Other car park   ▢ Airport terminal building

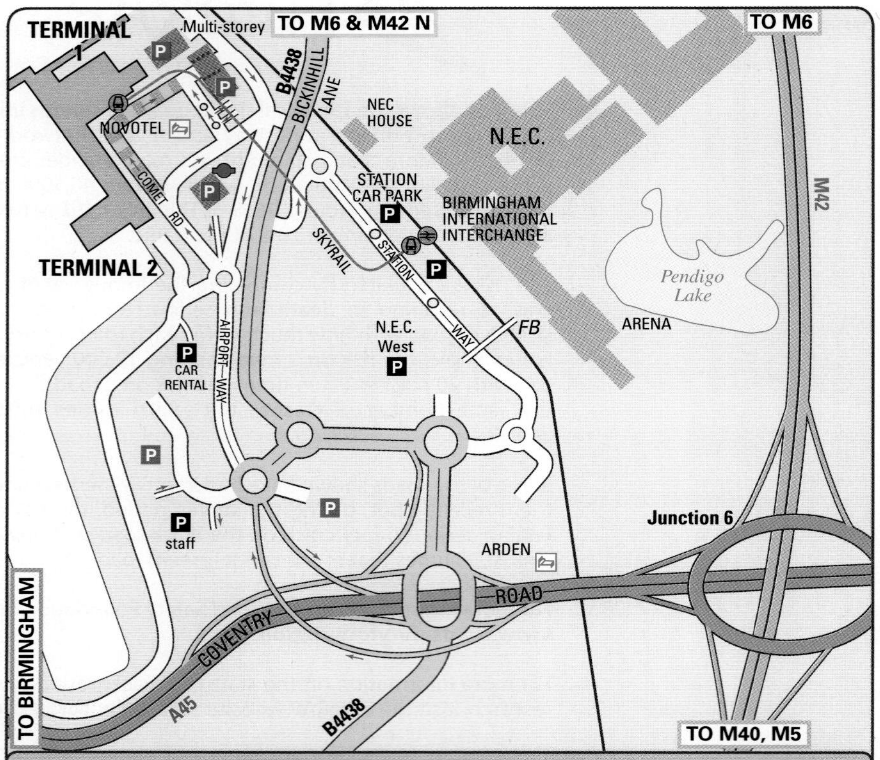

BIRMINGHAM (BHX)

Appears on main
map page 40

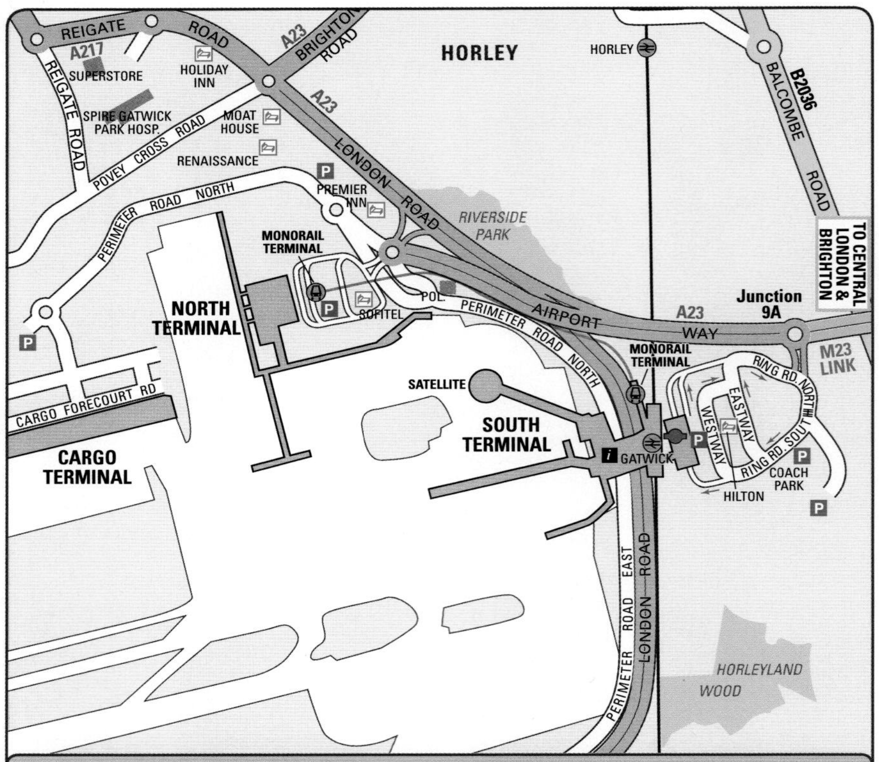

GATWICK (LGW)

Appears on main
map page 23

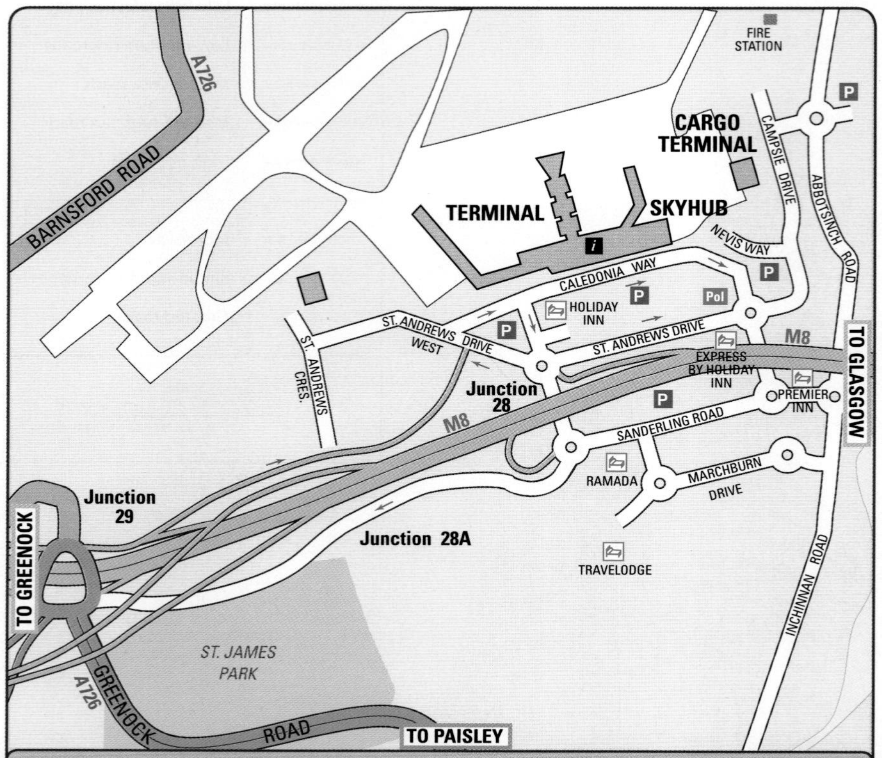

GLASGOW (GLA)

Appears on main
map page 74

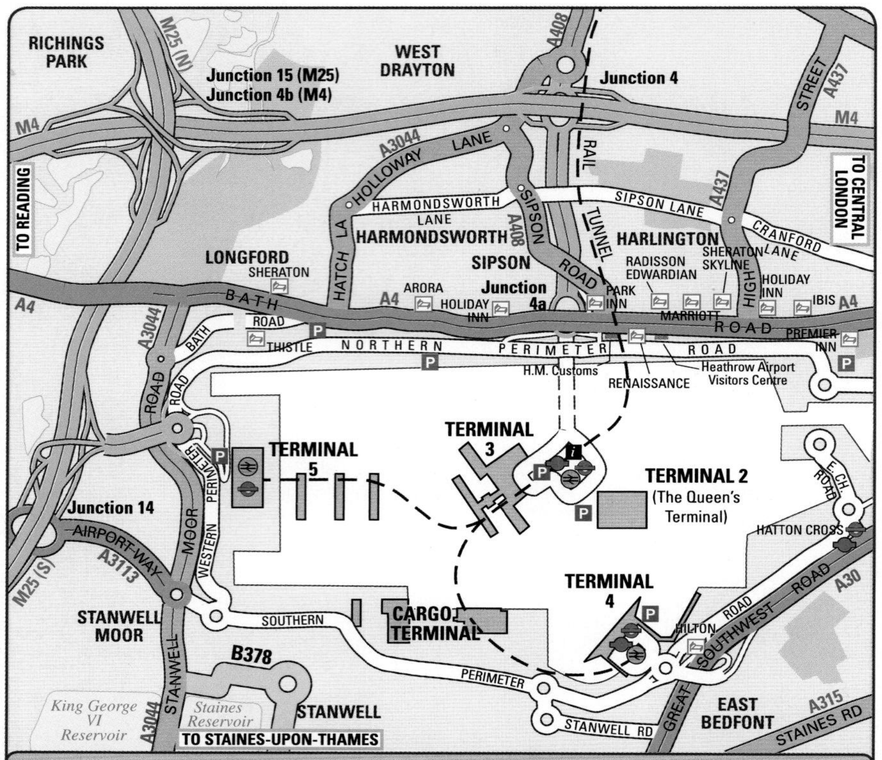

HEATHROW (LHR)

Appears on main
map page 22

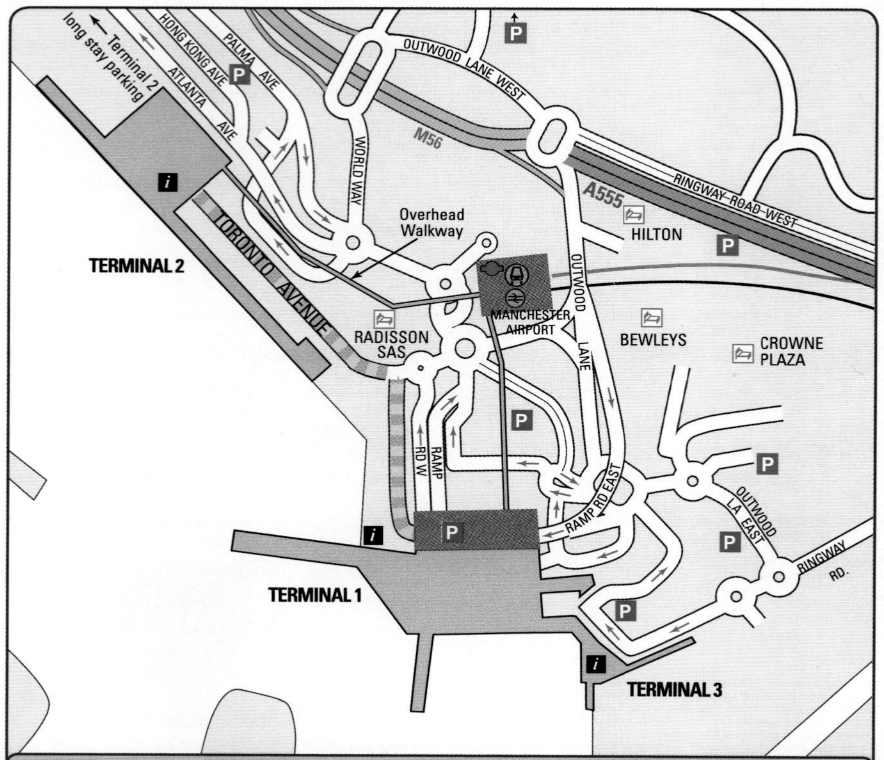

MANCHESTER (MAN)

Appears on main
map page 49

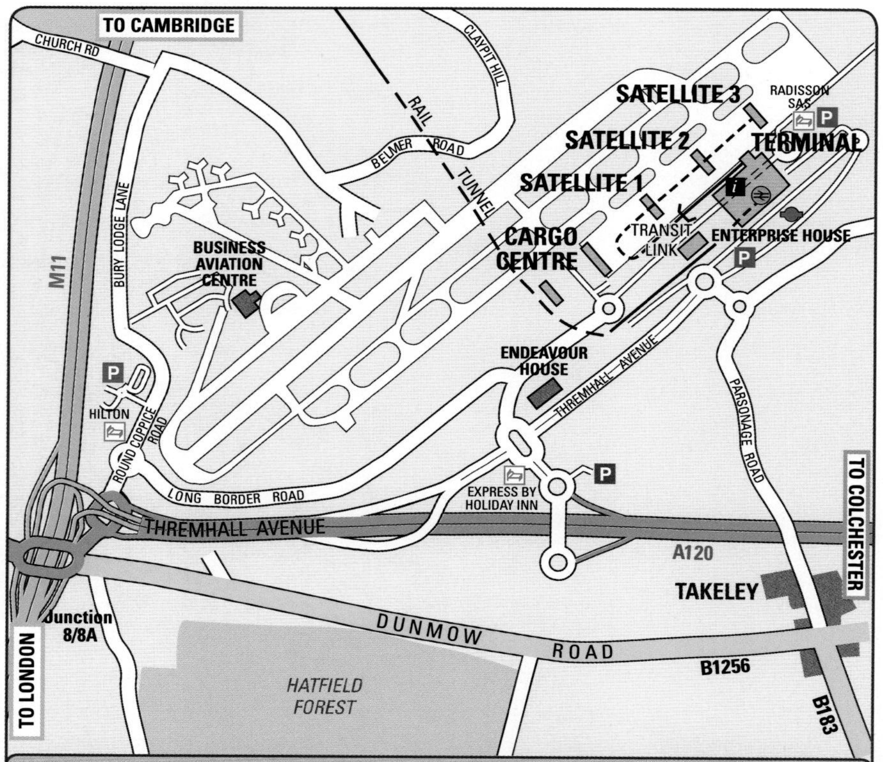

STANSTED (STN)

Appears on main
map page 33

Map scale

A scale bar appears at the bottom of every page to help with measurements.

0	2	4	6 miles
0	2	4	6	8	10 km

England, Wales & Southern Scotland are at a scale of 1:200,000 or 3.2 miles to 1 inch.
Northern Scotland & Northern Ireland are at a scale of 1:316,800 or 5 miles to 1 inch.
Orkney & Shetland are at a scale of 1:411,840 or 6.5 miles to 1 inch.

Symbols used on the map

M5	Motorway
M6 Toll	Toll motorway
8 9	Motorway junction with full / limited access (in congested areas there is just a numbered symbol)
Maidstone Birch Sarn	Motorway service area with off road / full / limited access
A556	Primary route dual / single carriageway
S	24 hour service area on primary route
Peterhead	Primary route destination. Primary route destinations are places of major traffic importance linked by the primary route network. They are shown on a green background on direction signs.
A30	'A' road dual / single carriageway
B1403	'B' road dual / single carriageway
	Minor road
	Road with restricted access
	Roads with passing places
	Road proposed or under construction
33	Multi-level junction with full / limited access (with junction number)
	Roundabout
4	Road distance in miles between markers
	Road tunnel
	Steep hill (arrows point downhill)
Toll / Electronic Toll	Toll / Electronic Toll
	Level crossing
St. Malo 8hrs	Car ferry route with journey times
	Railway line / station / tunnel
Wales Coast Path	National Trail / Long Distance Route
50 V	Fixed safety camera / fixed average-speed safety camera. Speed shown by number within camera, a V indicates a variable limit.
50 50	
✈ ✈	Airport with / without scheduled services
H	Heliport
P&R P&R	Park and Ride site operated by bus / rail (runs at least 5 days a week)
	Built up area
□ □ □	Town / Village / Other settlement
Hythe	Seaside destination
—··—··—	International boundary
—·—·—·—	National boundary
KENT	County / Unitary Authority boundary and name
	Heritage Coast
	National Park
	Regional / Forest Park boundary
	Woodland
Danger Zone	Military range
468 ▲941	Spot / Summit height (in metres)
	Lake / Dam / River / Waterfall
	Canal / Dry canal / Canal tunnel
	Lighthouse
	Beach
SEE PAGE 91	Area covered by urban area map
190	National Grid reference figures
SY	National Grid reference letters

Places of interest

A selection of tourist detail is shown on the mapping. It is advisable to check with the local tourist information centre regarding opening times and facilities available.

Any of the following symbols may appear on the map in maroon ★ which indicates that the site has World Heritage status.

ℹ	Tourist information centre (open all year)	⚽	Major football club
ℹ	Tourist information centre (open seasonally)	£	Major shopping centre / Outlet village
m	Ancient monument		Major sports venue
	Aquarium		Motor racing circuit
	Aqueduct / Viaduct		Mountain bike trail
	Arboretum	🏛	Museum / Art gallery
1643	Battlefield		Nature reserve (NNR indicates a National Nature Reserve)
	Blue flag beach		Racecourse
▲	Camp site / Caravan site		Rail Freight Terminal
	Castle		Ski slope (artificial / natural)
	Cave		Spotlight nature reserve (Best sites for access to nature)
	Country park		Steam railway centre / preserved railway
	County cricket ground		Surfing beach
	Distillery		Theme park
†	Ecclesiastical feature		University
	Event venue		Vineyard
	Farm park		Wildlife park / Zoo
	Garden		Wildlife Trust nature reserve
	Golf course	★	Other interesting feature
	Historic house	(NT) (NTS)	National Trust / National Trust for Scotland property
	Historic ship		

Reading our maps

Safety Camera The number inside the camera shows the speed limit at the camera location.

Multi-level junctions Non-motorway junctions where slip roads are used to access the main roads.

Distances Blue numbers give distances in miles between junctions shown with a blue marker.

Park & Ride Sites are shown that operate at least 5 days a week. Bus operated sites have a yellow symbol and rail operated sites a pink symbol.

Motorway service area

World Heritage site Places of interest defined by UNESCO as special on a world scale.

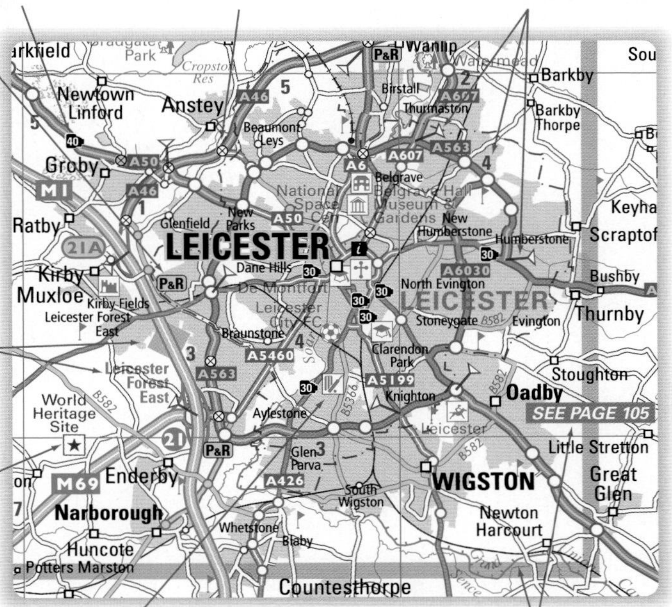

Places of interest Blue symbols indicate places of interest. See the section at the bottom of the page for the different types of feature represented on the map.

More detailed maps Green boxes indicate busy built-up areas. More detailed mapping is available.

Map pages

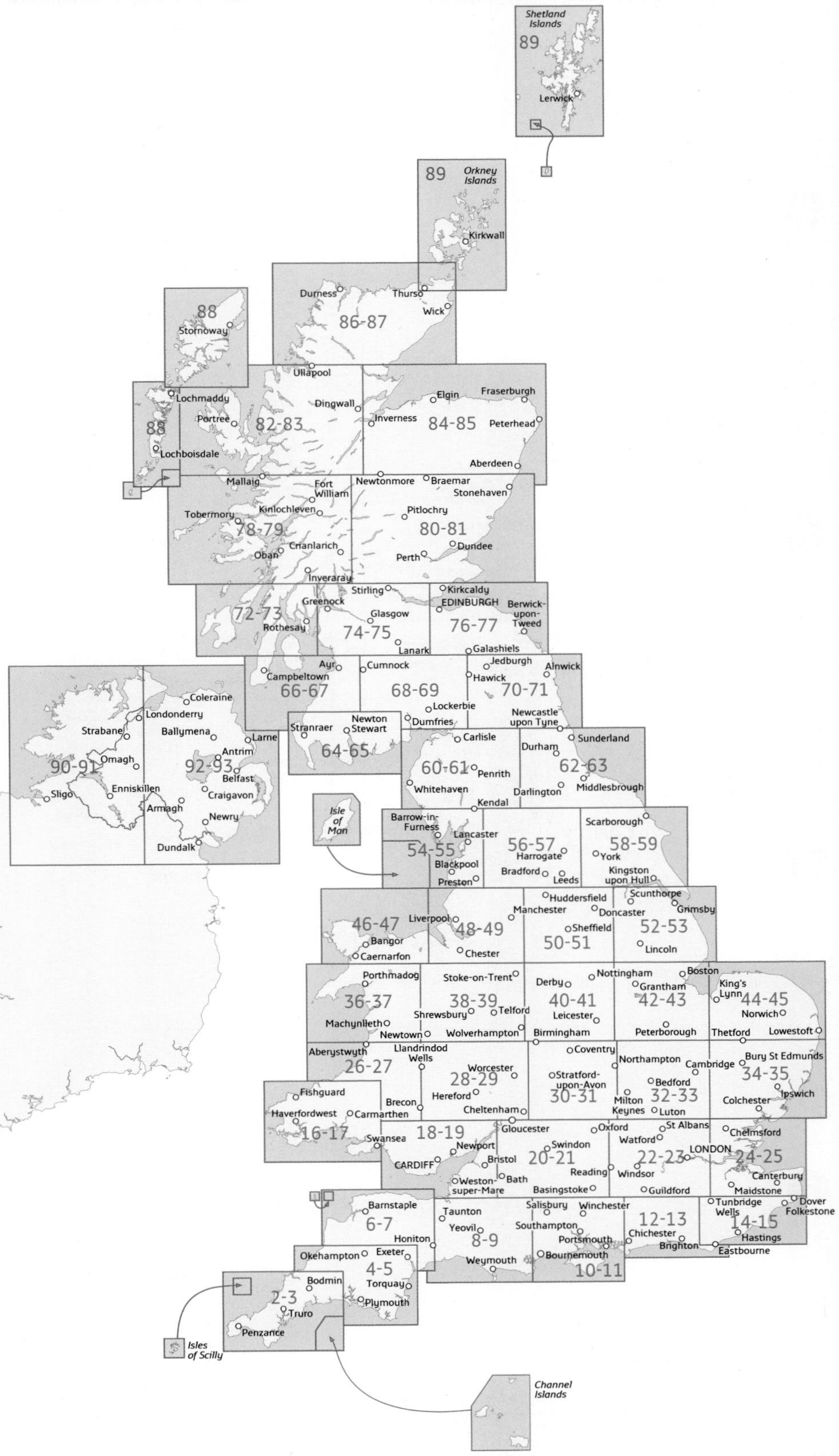

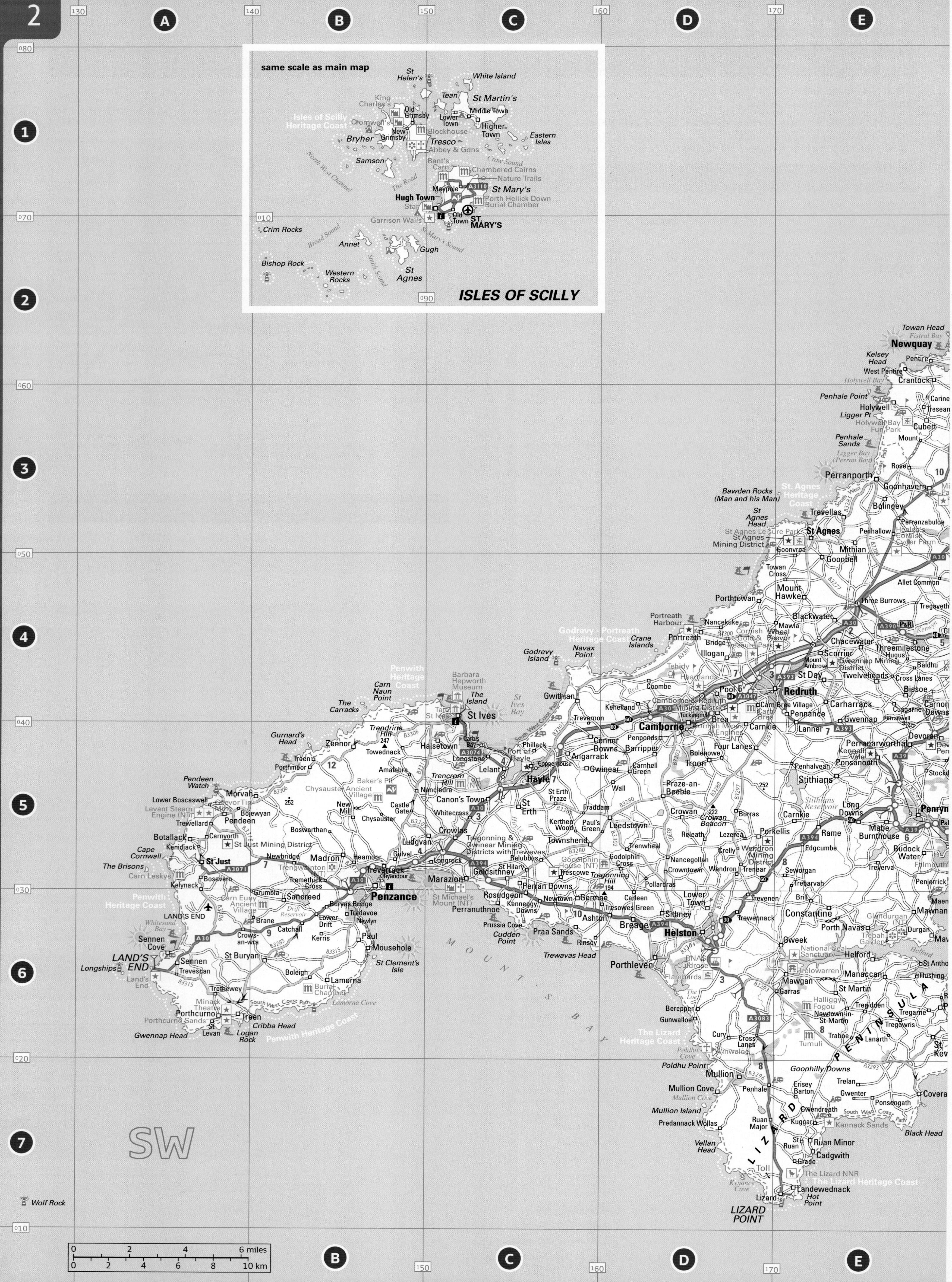

ISLES OF SCILLY

same scale as main map

St Helen's · White Island · Tean · St Martin's · King Charles's · Old Grimsby · Middle Town · Cromwell's · Lower Town · Isles of Scilly Heritage Coast · New Grimsby · Blockhouse' · Higher Town · Bryher · Tresco · Abbey & Gdns · Eastern Isles · Samson · Bant's Carn · Chambered Cairns · Nature Trails · Maypole · A3110 · St Mary's · Hugh Town · Porth Hellick Down Burial Chamber · Star · ST MARY'S · Old Town · Garrison Walls · Crim Rocks · Broad Sound · Annet · Gugh · Bishop Rock · Western Rocks · St Agnes

North West Channel · The Road · Crow Sound · St Mary's Sound · Smith Sound

SW

Wolf Rock

Newquay · Towan Head · Fistral Bay · Kelsey Head · Pentire · West Pentire · Crantock · Penhale Point · Holywell · Holywell Bay · Ligger Pt · Holywell Bay Fun Park · Cubert · Carine · Tresean · Mount · Penhale Sands · Rose · Ligger Bay (Perran Bay) · Perranporth · Goonhavern · Goonhoon · 10 · Bawden Rocks (Man and his Man) · St Agnes Heritage Coast · Trevellas · Bolingey · Perranzabuloe · St Agnes Head · Penhallow · St Agnes · Mithian · Cox Farm · St Agnes Leisure Park · St Agnes Mining District · Goonvrea · Goonbell · Towan Cross · Mount Hawke · Allet Common · Tregaveth · Porthtowan · Blackwater · Three Burrows · Nancekuke · Cornish Mawla · Wheel · A30 · A390 · P&R · Godrevy - Portreath Heritage Coast · Crane Islands · Portreath · Bridge · Scorrier · Gwennap Mining District · Navax Point · Tehidy · Heartland · Mount Ambrose · Twelveheads · Cross Lanes · Godrevy Island · Coombe · Camborne & Redruth · Pool · Redruth · Carharrack · Cusgarne · Carnon Downs · Devoran · Gwithian · Trevarnon · A30 Mining District · Carn Brea Village · Pennance · Lanner · A393 · St Day · Keheland · Cornish Moor · Carn Brea · Carnkie · Perranarworthal · The Carracks · Carn Naun Point · Penwith Heritage Coast · Barbara Hepworth Museum · The Island · St Ives Bay · Camborne · Brea · Four Lanes · Penhalvean · Stithians · Kennall Vale · Ponsanooth · Trendrine Hill 247 · St Ives · Phillack · Connor Downs · Barripper · Carnhell Green · Troon · Praze-an-Beeble · Penryn · Gurnard's Head · Zennor · Towednack · Halsetown · Carbis Bay · Port of Hayle · Gwinear · Wall · B3280 · Crowan · Burras · Carnkie · Lowin Downs · Mabe Burnthouse · Budock Water · Treen · Porthmeor · 12 · Longstone · Lelant · Hayle 7 · St Erth Praze · Praddam · Crowan Beacon 222 · Lezerea · Porkellis · Rame · Treverva · Pendeen Watch · Baker's Pit · Nancledra · Canon's Town · St Erth · Kerthen Wood · Paul's Green · Leedstown · Trenwheal · Nancegollan · Wendron Mining District · Edgcumbe · Penjerrick · Lower Boscaswell · Morvah · Chysauster Ancient Village · New Mill · Castle Gate · Whitecross · Townshend · Godolphin Cross · Crowntown · Wendron · Trenear · Sithney · Treverva · Levant Steam Engine (NT) · Bojewyan · 252 · Chysauster · Tregonning & Gwinear Mining Districts with Trewavas · Belubbus · Godolphin House (NT) · Trescowe · Tregonning Hill 194 · Seworgan · Trelowarren · Trewellard · Pendeen · Boswarthen · Ludgvan · Crowlas · Gulval · St Hilary · Goldsithney · Pollardras · Lower Town · Trevenen · Brill · Constantine · Botallack · Carnyorth · St Just Mining District · Newbridge · Madron · Heamoor · Trewennack · Porth Navas · Glendurgan (NT) · Mawnan · Cape Cornwall · Kenidjack · Tremethick Cross · Trevarrack · Longrock · Marazion · Rosudgeon · Newtown · Gerthoe · Carleen · Helston · 30 · Gweek · Mawnan Smith · The Brisons · St Just · Bosaven · Tregavarah · A30 · Gulval · St Michael's Mount (NT) · Perranuthnoe · Kenneggy Downs · Ashton · Tresowes Green · Breage · National Seal Sanctuary · Helford · Carn Leskys · Kelynack · Sancreed · Penzance · Perranuthnoe · 10 · Prussia Cove · Praa Sands · Rinsey · Sithney · Porthleven · RNAS Culdrose · Mawgan · Garras · St Anthony · Penwith Heritage Coast · Carn Euny Ancient Village · Buryas Bridge · Lower Drift · Tredavoe · Newlyn · Paul · Cudden Point · Trewavas Head · Flambards · Halligye Fogou · Tregidden · Newtown-in-St-Martin · Tregarne · Flushing · LAND'S END · Brane · Catchall · Kerris · Mousehole · MOUNT'S BAY · Porthleven · The Loe · 3 · Mawgan · St Martin · Tregowris · Sennen Cove · Crows-an-wra · St Buryan · Boleigh · Lamorna · St Clement's Isle · Berepper · Cury · Cross Lanes · Lanarth · St Kev · Longships · Sennen · Trevescan · Boleigh · Lamorna Cove · Gunwalloe · Poldhu · 8 · Tumuli · Land's End · Trethewey · Lamorna · Cove · The Lizard Heritage Coast · Goonhilly Downs · Minack Theatre · Treen · Cribba Head · South West Coast Path · Poldhu Point · Mullion · Trelan · Porthcurno · South West Coast Path · Mullion Cove · Penhale · Erisey Barton · Gwenter · Ponsongath · Coverack · Gwennap Head · Levan · Logan Rock · Penwith Heritage Coast · Mullion Cove · Gwendreath · South West Coast Path · Mullion Island · Predannack Wollas · Ruan Major · Kuggar · Kennack Sands · Black Head · Vellan Head · LIZARD PENINSULA · Ruan Minor · Cadgwith · Toll · Grade · Ruan · LIZARD · The Lizard NNR · The Lizard Heritage Coast · Kynance Cove · Landewednack · Lizard · Hot Point · LIZARD POINT

0 2 4 6 miles
0 2 4 6 8 10 km

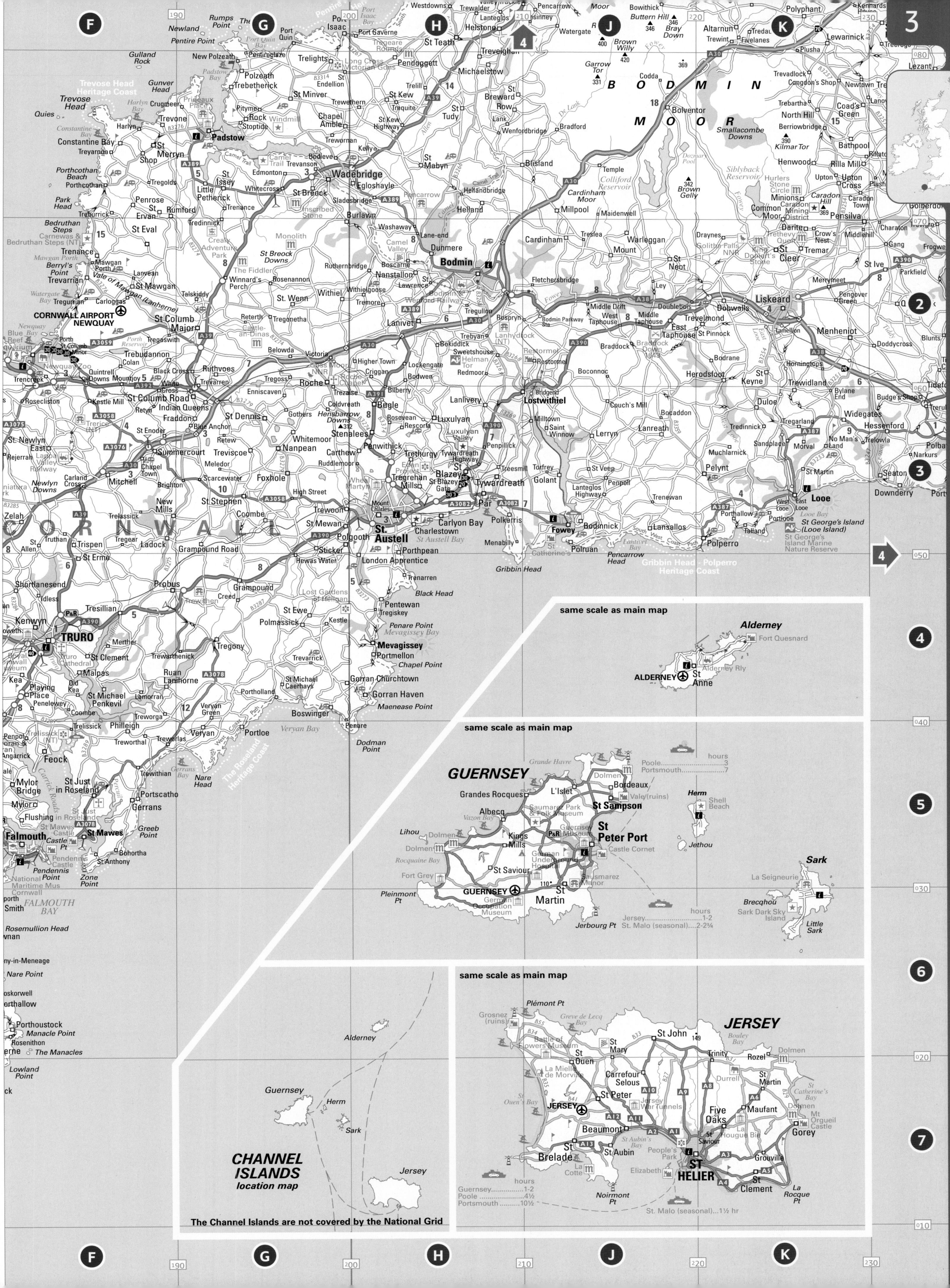
F
G
H
J
K
BODMIN MOOR
CORNWALL
Padstow
Wadebridge
Bodmin
Liskeard
Looe
Lostwithiel
Fowey
St. Austell
Mevagissey
TRURO
Falmouth
St Mawes
Newquay
CORNWALL AIRPORT NEWQUAY
Camelford
Port Isaac
St Teath
Helstone
Tintagel
Polzeath
Rock
Trevose Head
Constantine Bay
St Merryn
St Columb Major
St Columb Road
Indian Queens
Summercourt
Mitchell
St Dennis
Roche
Bugle
Luxulyan
Par
St Blazey
Tywardreath
Charlestown
Polperro
Lanreath
Pelynt
Duloe
Menheniot
St Cleer
St Neot
Dobwalls
Warleggan
Cardinham
Blisland
St Mabyn
St Kew
St Tudy
Michaelstow
Altarnun
Five Lanes
Lewannick
Bolventor
Brown Willy
Rough Tor
St Stephen
Grampound
Probus
Tresillian
Tregony
St Mewan
Polgooth
Gorran Haven
Dodman Point
Veryan
Portloe
Gerrans
Portscatho
St Just in Roseland
Feock
Mylor Bridge
Flushing
Pendennis Point
FALMOUTH BAY
Rosemullion Head
Nare Point
Porthallow
The Manacles
Lowland Point
Manacle Point
Porthoustock
Rosenithon
Penryn
Kea
Playing Place
Malpas
St Clement
St Michael Penkevil
Ruan Lanihorne
Philleigh
Black Head
Pentewan
Chapel Point
Maenease Point
Veryan Bay
Gribbin Head
Gribbin Head - Polperro Heritage Coast
The Roseland Heritage Coast
Trevose Head Heritage Coast
St George's Island (Looe Island)
St George's Island Marine Nature Reserve
Seaton
Downderry
Looe Bay
Polruan
Bodinnick
Lansallos
Talland
Menabilly
Polkerris
Carlyon Bay
St Austell Bay
same scale as main map
Alderney
ALDERNEY
St Anne
Fort Quesnard
Alderney Rly
GUERNSEY
Grande Havre
Grandes Rocques
L'Islet
Bordeaux
Dolmen
Vale (ruins)
St Sampson
Albecq
Vazon Bay
Saumarez Park & Folk Museum
Kings Mills
Lihou
Rocquaine Bay
Fort Grey
St Saviour
St Peter Port
Castle Cornet
German Underground Hospital
GUERNSEY
St Martin
Sausmarez Manor
German Occupation Museum
Pleinmont Pt
Jerbourg Pt
Herm
Shell Beach
Jethou
Sark
La Seigneurie
Brecqhou
Sark Dark Sky Island
Little Sark
hours
Poole....................3
Portsmouth....................7
Jersey....................1-2
St. Malo (seasonal)....2-2¼
CHANNEL ISLANDS
location map
Alderney
Guernsey
Herm
Sark
Jersey
The Channel Islands are not covered by the National Grid
JERSEY
Plémont Pt
Grosnez (ruins)
Greve de Lecq Bay
St Mary
St John
Bouley Bay
Trinity
Rozel
St Ouen
Battle of Flowers Museum
La Mielle de Morville
St Ouen's Bay
St Peter
Carrefour Selous
Jersey War Tunnels
JERSEY
Durrell
St Martin
St Catherine's Bay
Maufant
Five Oaks
Mt Orgueil Castle
Gorey
Beaumont
St Aubin's Bay
St Saviour
La Hougue Bie
St Brelade
St Aubin
People's Park
Elizabeth Castle
ST HELIER
Grouville
St Clement
La Rocque Pt
Noirmont Pt
La Cotte
Guernsey....................1-2
Poole....................4½
Portsmouth....................10½
St. Malo (seasonal)....1½ hr
190
200
210
220
230
050
040
030
020
010
080
070
060
2
3
4
5
6
7

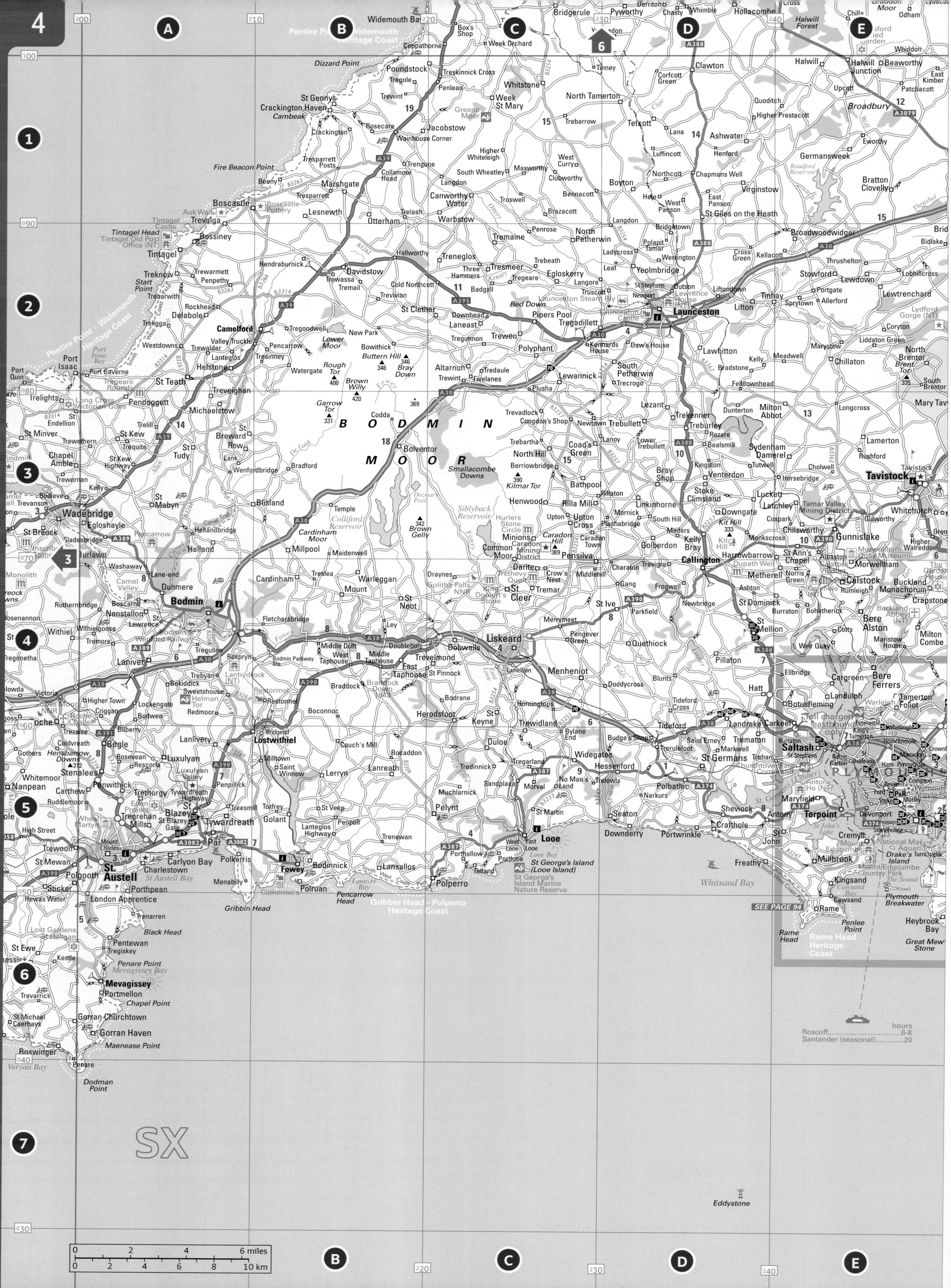
A
B
C
D
E
1
2
3
4
5
6
7
BODMIN MOOR
SX
Pentire Point - Widemouth Heritage Coast
Gribbin Head - Polperro Heritage Coast
Rame Head Heritage Coast
SEE PAGE 94
Launceston
Bodmin
Camelford
Wadebridge
Liskeard
Looe
Fowey
Lostwithiel
St Austell
Mevagissey
Callington
Tavistock
Saltash
Torpoint
Tintagel
Boscastle
Whitsand Bay
Eddystone
hours
Roscoff.......................................6-8
Santander (seasonal)..............20
0 2 4 6 miles
0 2 4 6 8 10 km

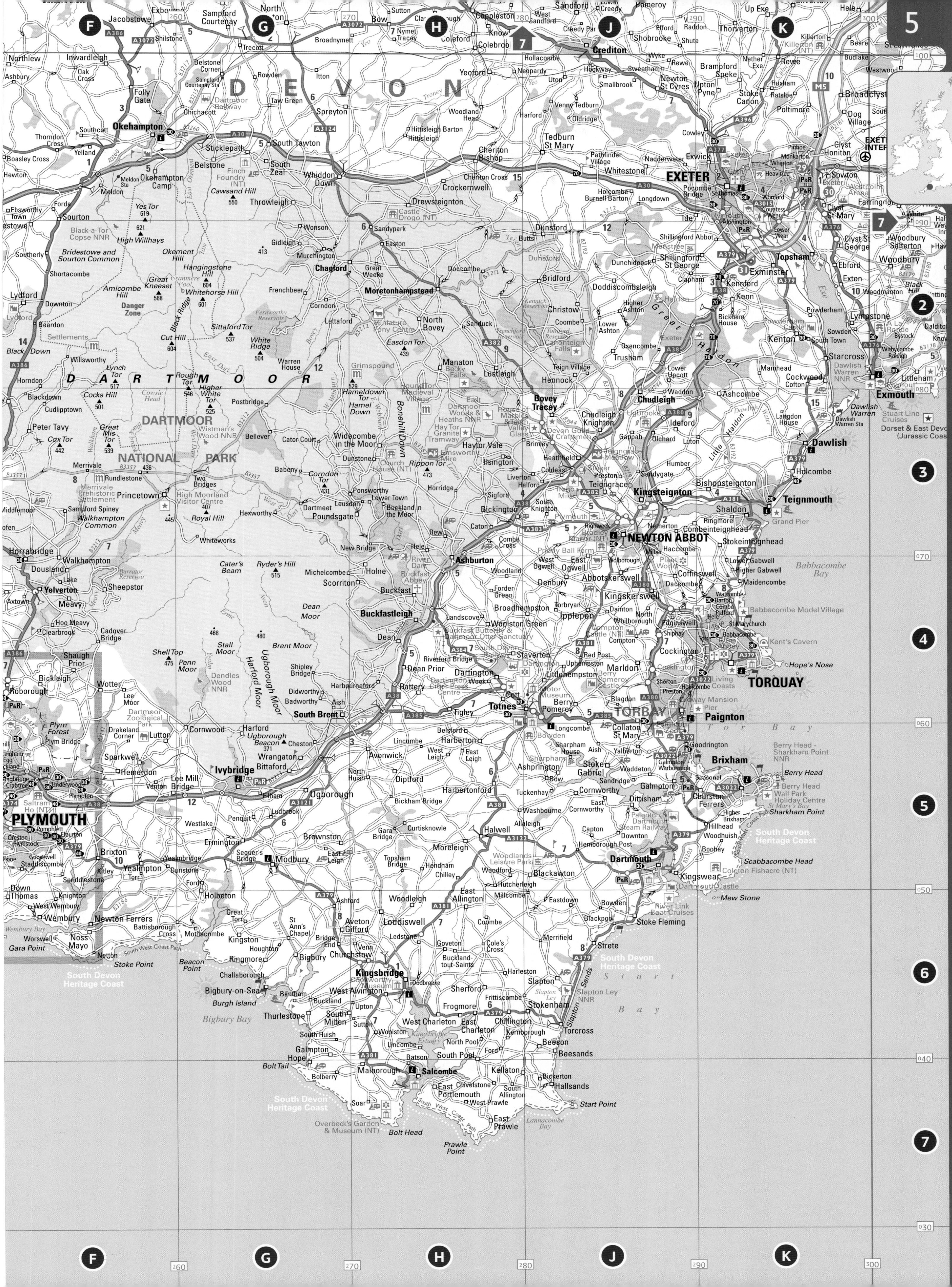
DEVON
DARTMOOR
DARTMOOR NATIONAL PARK
EXETER
PLYMOUTH
TORQUAY
NEWTON ABBOT
TORBAY
Crediton
Okehampton
Chagford
Moretonhampstead
Bovey Tracey
Chudleigh
Dawlish
Teignmouth
Exmouth
Topsham
Kingsteignton
Ashburton
Buckfastleigh
Totnes
Paignton
Brixham
Dartmouth
Kingswear
Ivybridge
South Brent
Princetown
Yelverton
Modbury
Kingsbridge
Salcombe
Tavistock
Lydford
Dartmouth Castle
Start Point
Bolt Head
Bolt Tail
Prawle Point
Hope's Nose
Berry Head
Babbacombe Bay
Tor Bay
Start Bay
Bigbury Bay
South Devon Heritage Coast
Dorset & East Devon (Jurassic Coast)
Haldon
Yes Tor
High Willhays
Cut Hill
Hameldown Tor
Haytor Vale
Castle Drogo (NT)
Dartmoor Railway
Paignton & Dartmouth Steam Railway
Babbacombe Model Village
Kent's Cavern
Start Point
F
G
H
J
K
2
3
4
5
6
7
260
270
280
290
300
030
040
050
060
070
080
090
100

For a more detailed map of Plymouth see page 94

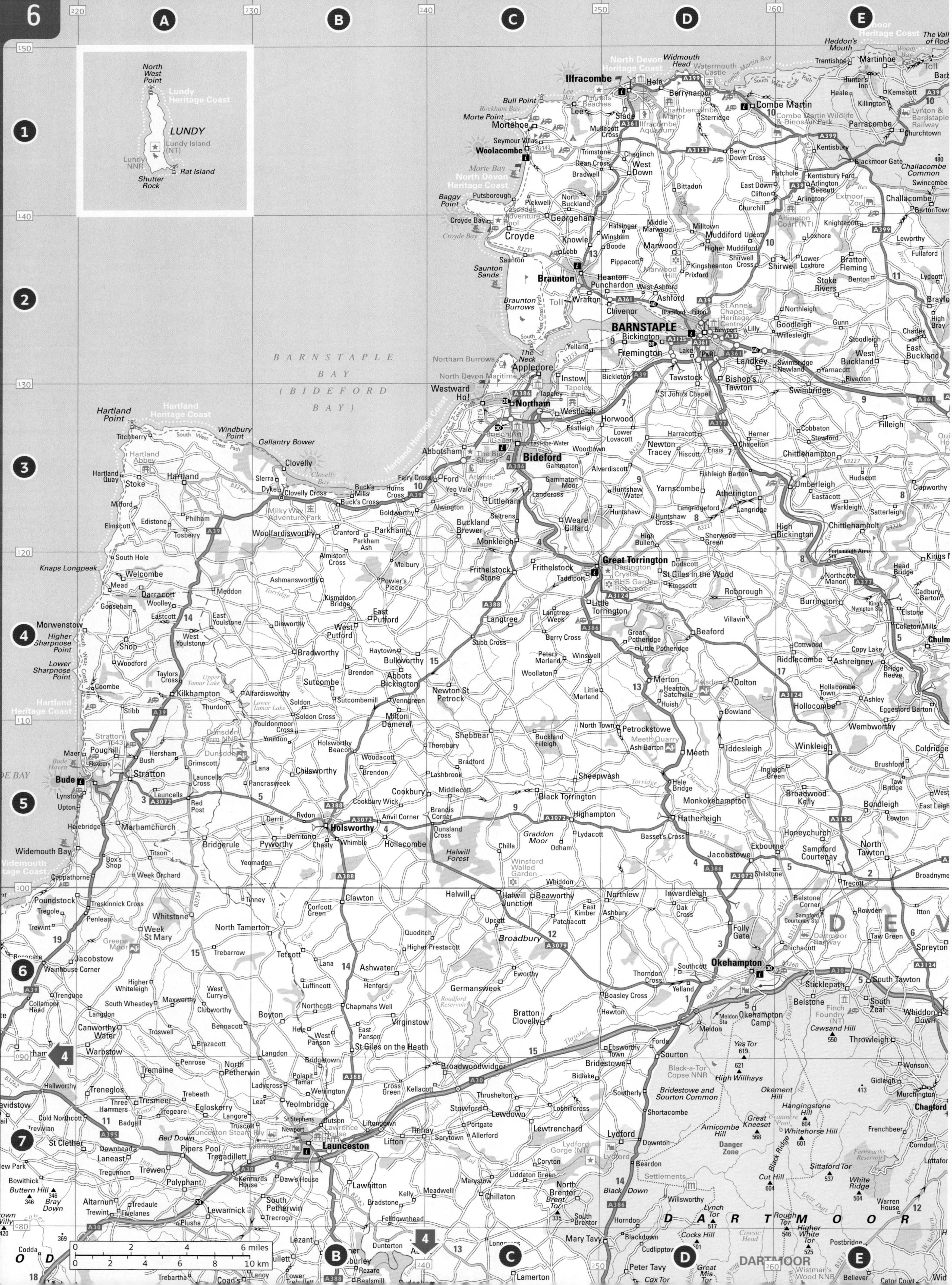
A
B
C
D
E
1
2
3
4
5
6
7
LUNDY
North West Point
Lundy Heritage Coast
Lundy Island (NT)
Lundy NNR
Rat Island
Shutter Rock
BARNSTAPLE BAY (BIDEFORD BAY)
North Devon Heritage Coast
Hartland Heritage Coast
Hartland Point
Ilfracombe
Combe Martin
Woolacombe
Croyde
Braunton
BARNSTAPLE
Appledore
Northam
Westward Ho!
Bideford
Clovelly
Hartland
Great Torrington
Holsworthy
Bude
Stratton
Okehampton
Launceston
Lydford
Chagford
Mary Tavy
Lynton & Barnstaple Railway
Exmoor Zoo
Tarka Trail
Milky Way Adventure Park
Dartington Crystal
RHS Garden Rosemoor
Meeth Quarry
Halwill Forest
Dartmoor Railway
Lydford Gorge (NT)
Launceston Steam Rly
Black-a-Tor Copse NNR
High Willhays
Yes Tor
Cawsand Hill
DARTMOOR
DEVON
0 2 4 6 miles
0 2 4 6 8 10 km

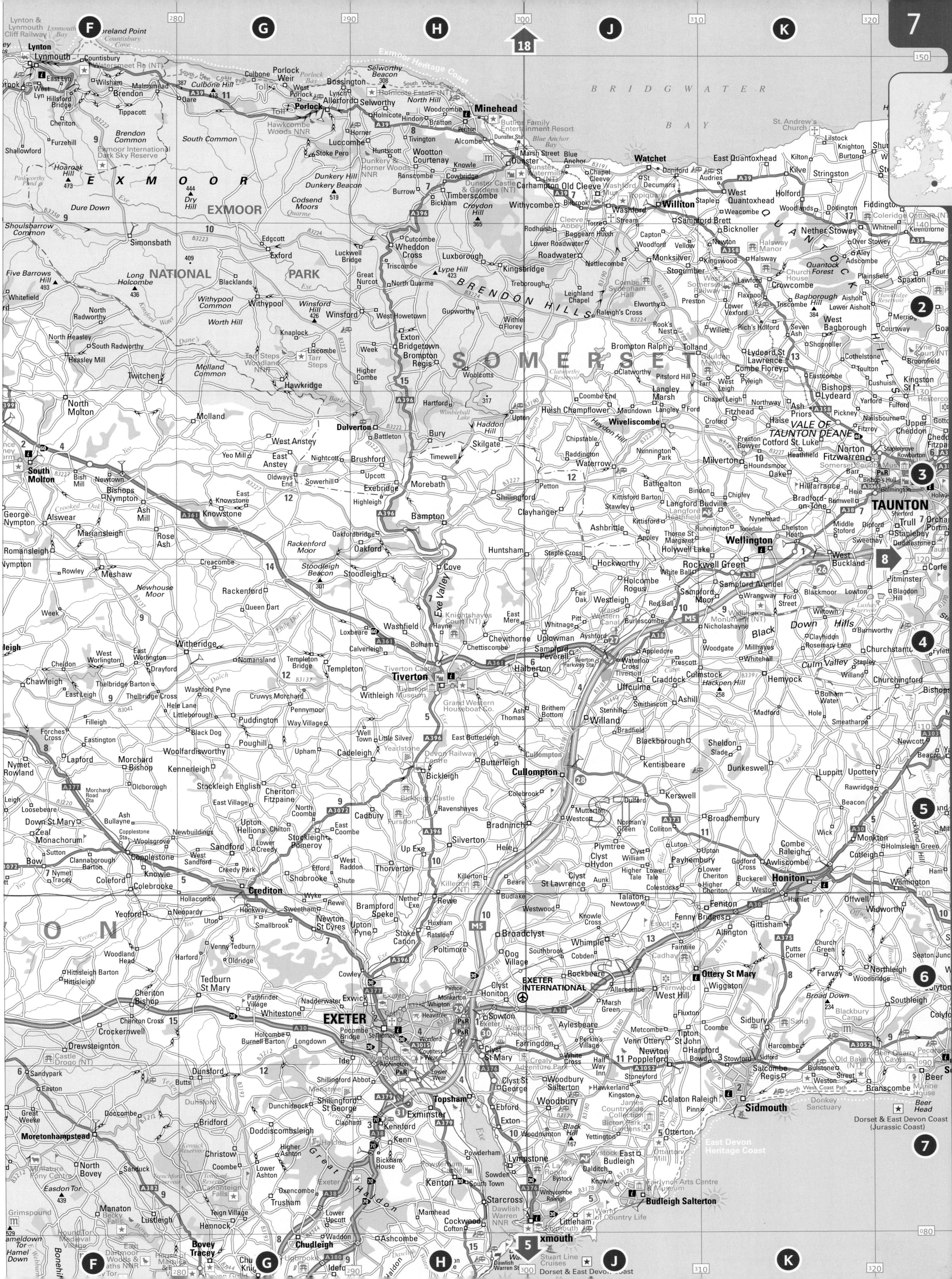
F
G
H
J
K
18
BRIDGWATER BAY
Lynton & Lynmouth Cliff Railway
Lynton
Lynmouth
Countisbury
Porlock
Porlock Weir
Minehead
Dunster
Watchet
Williton
Washford
Stogumber
Bishops Lydeard
Wiveliscombe
Dulverton
Exmoor Heritage Coast
EXMOOR
EXMOOR NATIONAL PARK
BRENDON HILLS
SOMERSET
QUANTOCK HILLS
VALE OF TAUNTON DEANE
TAUNTON
Wellington
Milverton
Bampton
Tiverton
Cullompton
Willand
Uffculme
Hemyock
Honiton
Crediton
South Molton
North Molton
Witheridge
Bickleigh
Silverton
Bradninch
Ottery St Mary
Sidmouth
Budleigh Salterton
Exmouth
EXETER
EXETER INTERNATIONAL
Topsham
Starcross
Dawlish Warren
Kenton
Chudleigh
Bovey Tracey
Moretonhampstead
Cheriton Bishop
Crockernwell
Sandford
Copplestone
Bow
Colebrooke
Lapford
Morchard Bishop
Beer
Branscombe
Sidbury
Dunkeswell
Upottery
Clyst St Mary
Woodbury
Lympstone
Haldon
East Devon Heritage Coast
Dorset & East Devon Coast (Jurassic Coast)
Exe Valley
8
5
280
290
300
310
320
150
140
130
120
110
100
090
080
2
3
4
5
6
7

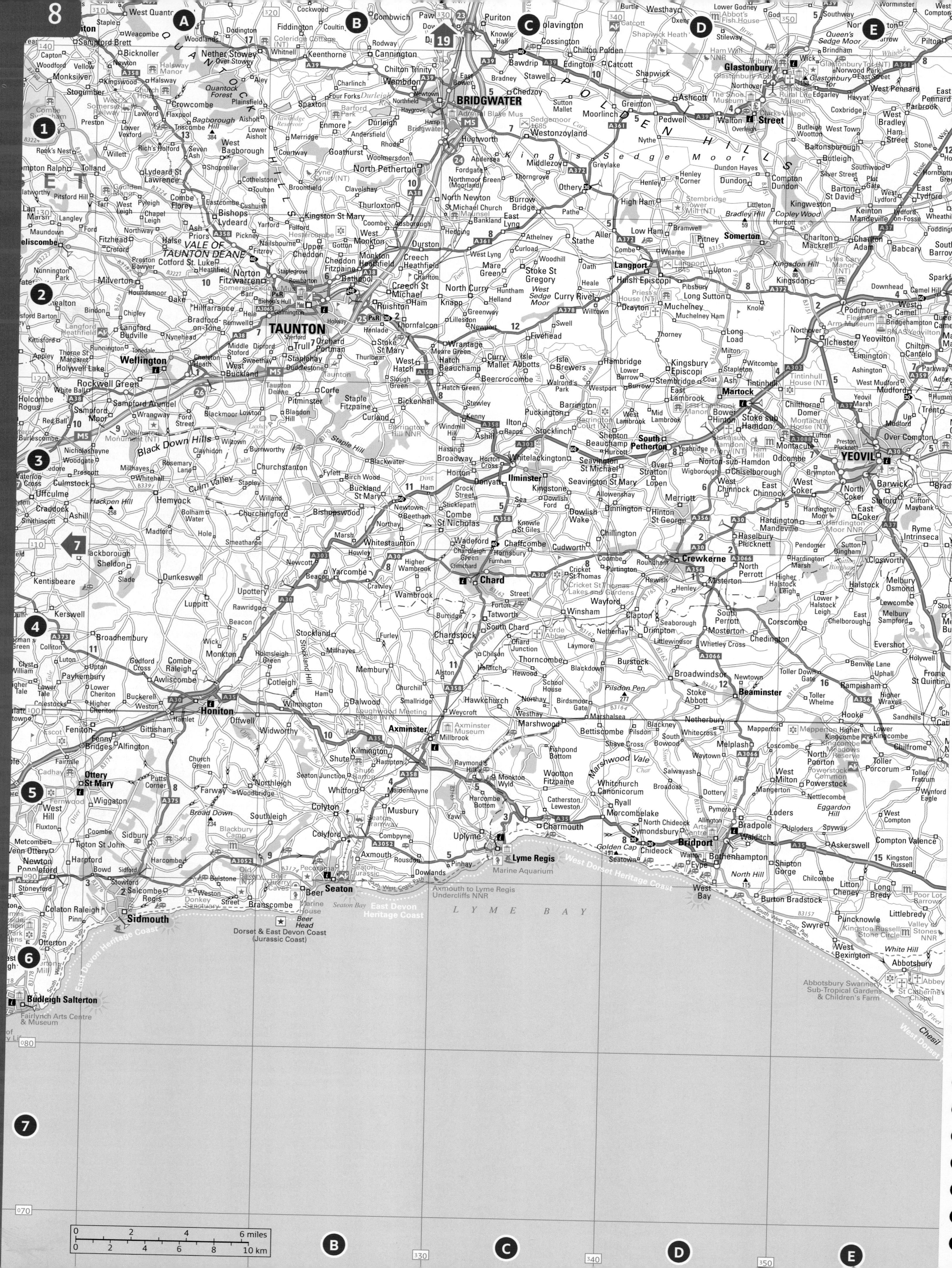
A
B
C
D
E
1
2
3
4
5
6
7
19
BRIDGWATER
TAUNTON
Wellington
Honiton
Axminster
Chard
Ilminster
Crewkerne
YEOVIL
Martock
Langport
Somerton
Glastonbury
Street
South Petherton
Beaminster
Bridport
Lyme Regis
Seaton
Sidmouth
Budleigh Salterton
Ottery St Mary
Abbotsbury
VALE OF TAUNTON DEANE
Black Down Hills
Culm Valley
King's Sedge Moor
POLDEN HILLS
QUANTOCK HILLS
Marshwood Vale
LYME BAY
West Dorset Heritage Coast
East Devon Heritage Coast
Dorset & East Devon Coast (Jurassic Coast)
Axmouth to Lyme Regis Undercliffs NNR
Chesil
0 2 4 6 miles
0 2 4 6 8 10 km

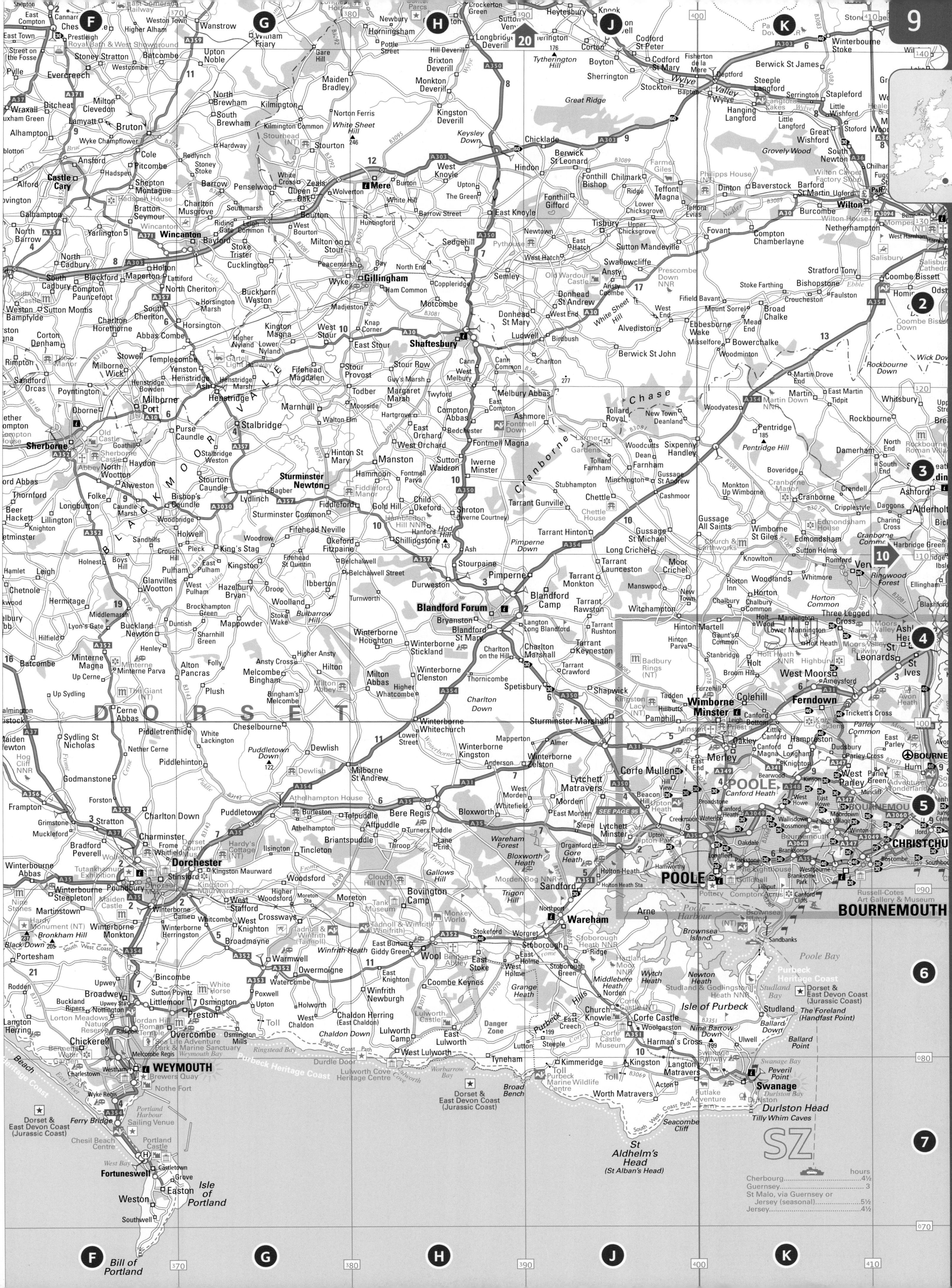

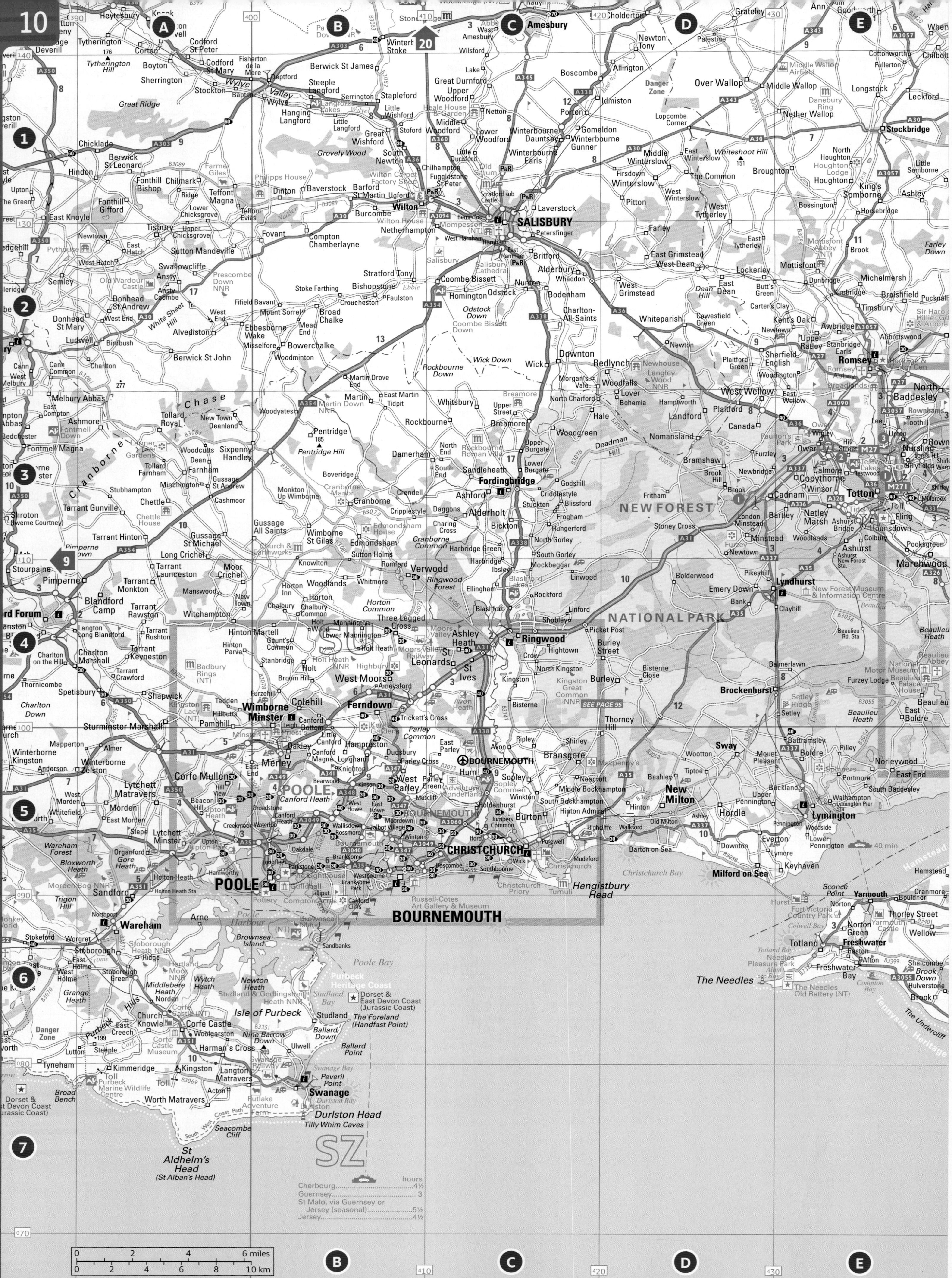

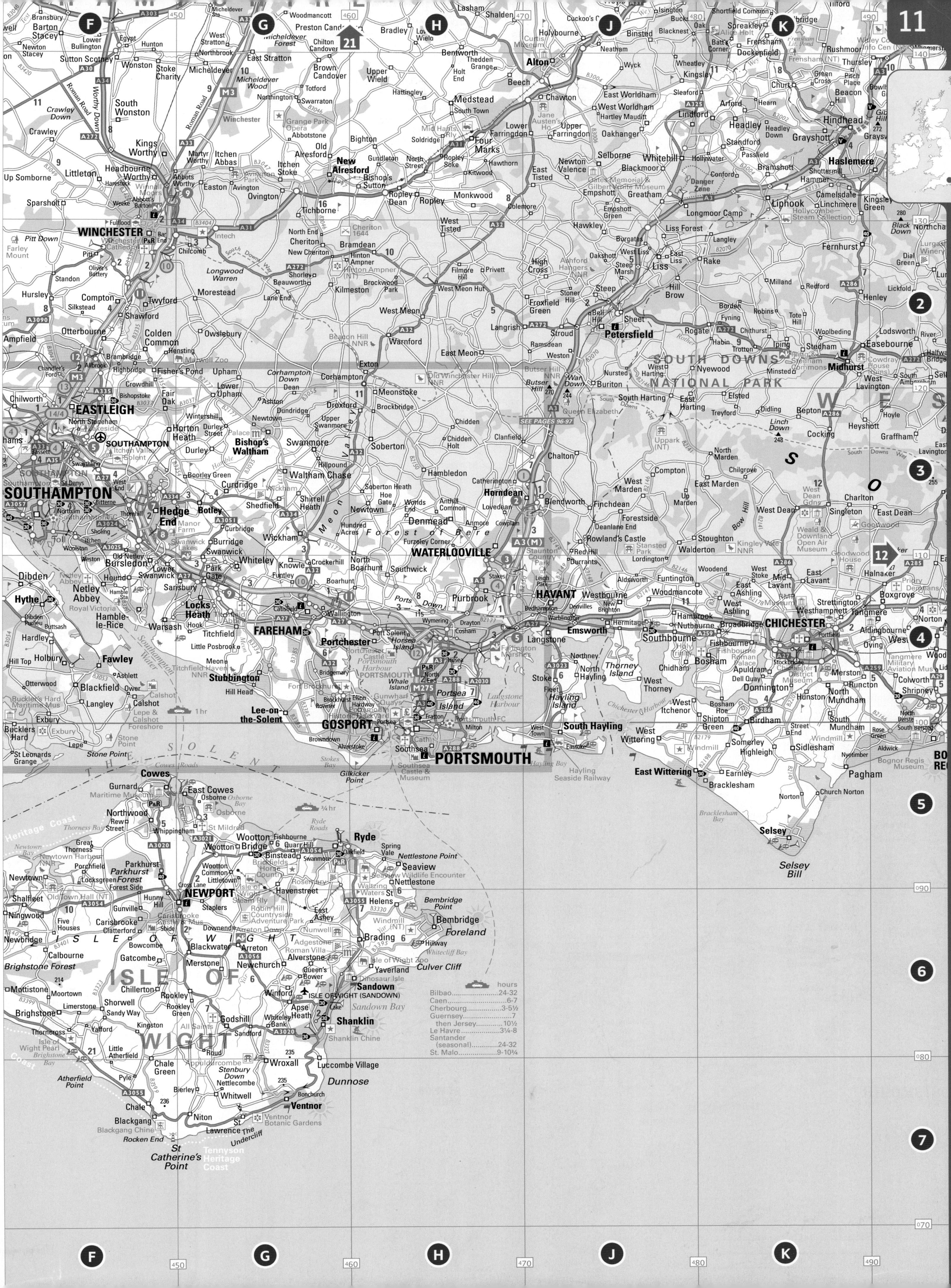

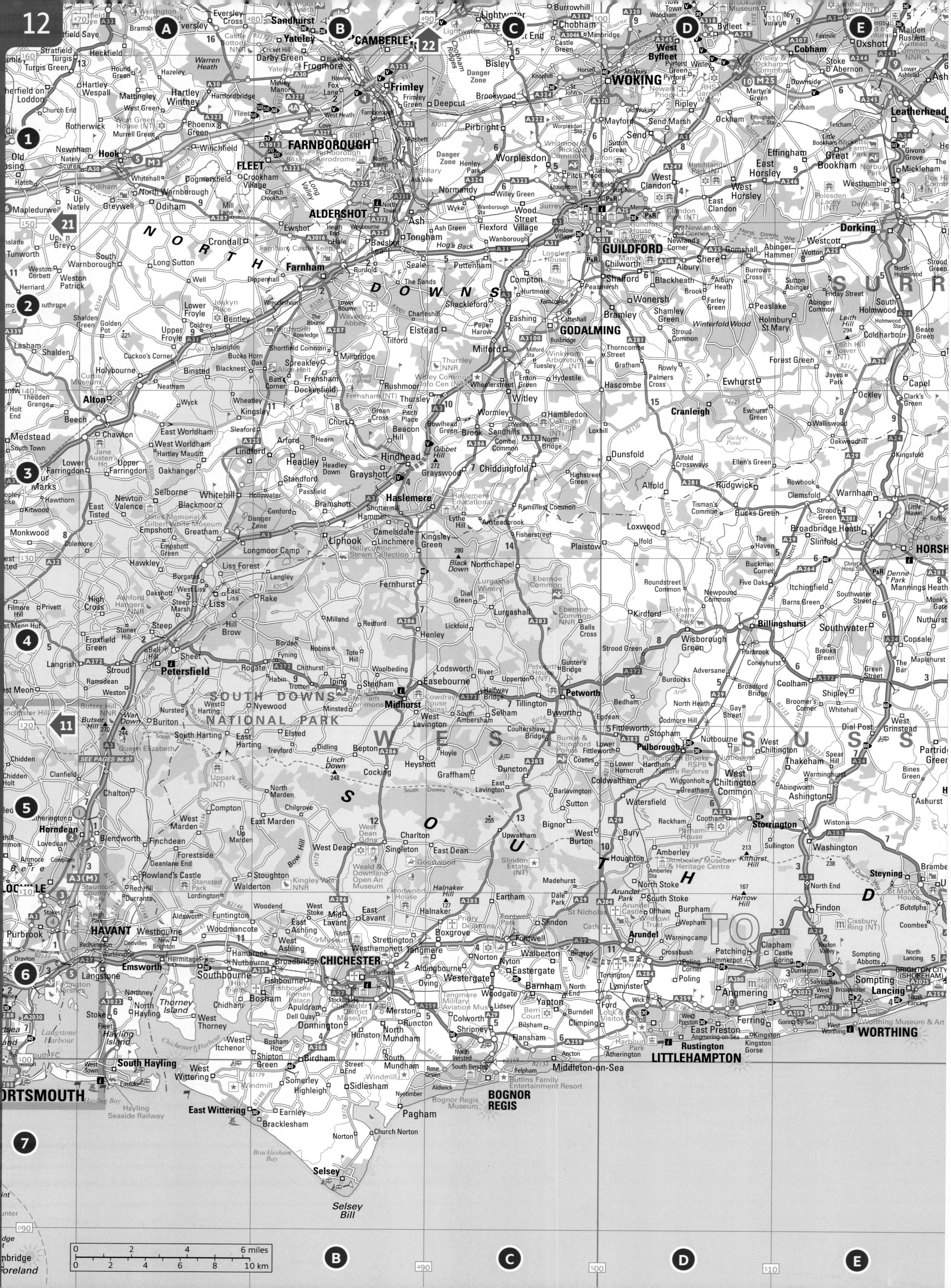

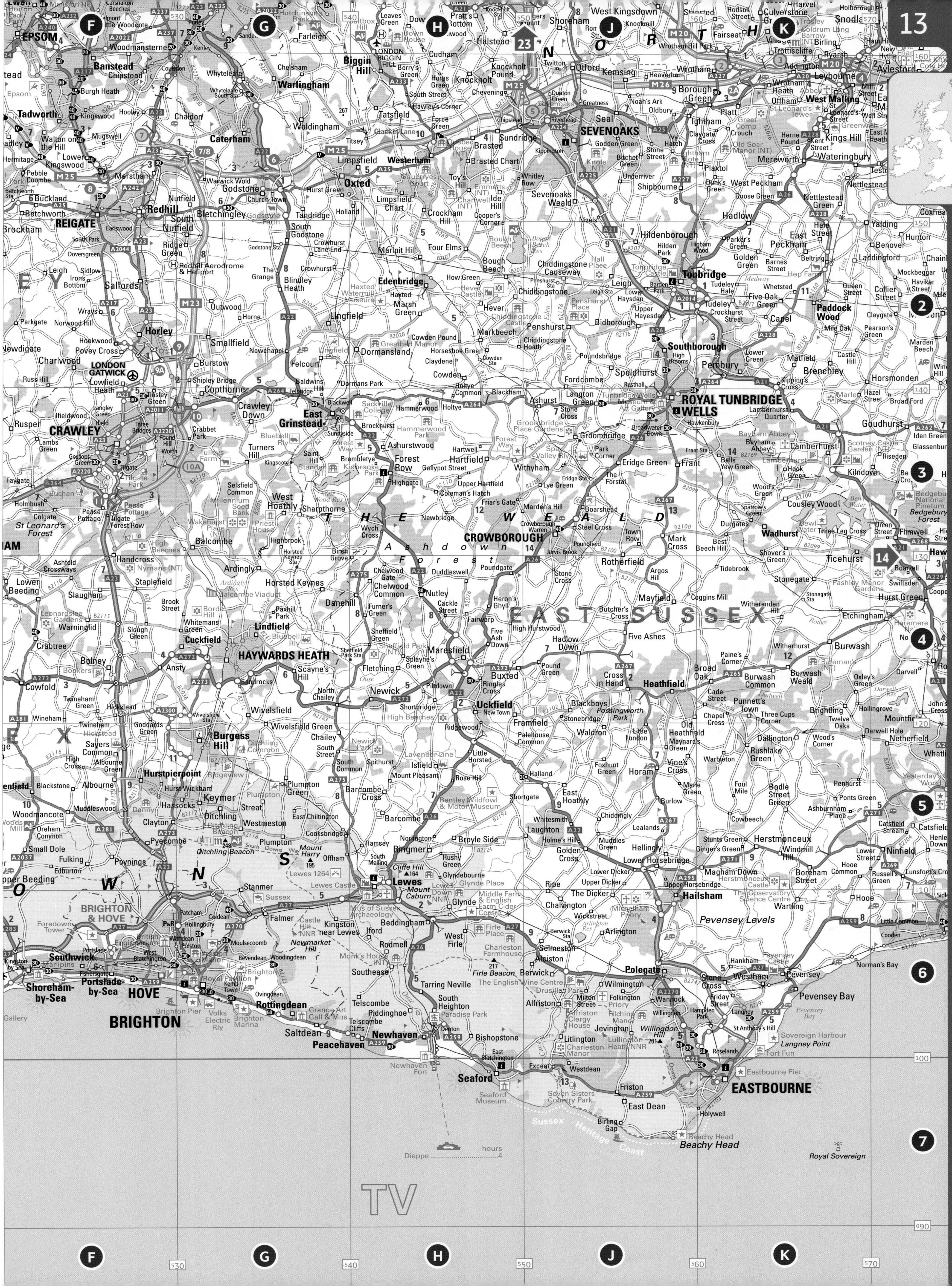
F
G
H
J
K
EPSOM
Banstead
Tadworth
Caterham
Warlingham
Biggin Hill
Westerham
Oxted
Redhill
REIGATE
Horley
LONDON GATWICK
CRAWLEY
East Grinstead
Edenbridge
Lingfield
SEVENOAKS
Tonbridge
Southborough
ROYAL TUNBRIDGE WELLS
Paddock Wood
West Malling
Aylesford
Leybourne
Wrotham
Kemsing
Otford
Shoreham
West Kingsdown
Halstead
Knockholt
Chiddingstone
Hildenborough
Penshurst
Pembury
Brenchley
Horsmonden
Goudhurst
Lamberhurst
Wadhurst
Ticehurst
Flimwell
Hawkhurst
Crowborough
THE WEALD
Ashdown Forest
EAST SUSSEX
Mayfield
Rotherfield
Heathfield
Burwash
Uckfield
Maresfield
Nutley
Forest Row
Hartfield
Haywards Heath
Lindfield
Cuckfield
Burgess Hill
Hurstpierpoint
Keymer
Ditchling
Hassocks
Plumpton
Lewes
Ringmer
Newick
Chailey
Wivelsfield
Hailsham
Herstmonceux
Horam
Polegate
Wilmington
Alfriston
Seaford
Newhaven
Peacehaven
Saltdean
Rottingdean
BRIGHTON
BRIGHTON & HOVE
HOVE
Portslade-by-Sea
Southwick
Shoreham-by-Sea
EASTBOURNE
Pevensey
Pevensey Bay
Pevensey Levels
Westham
Beachy Head
Birling Gap
East Dean
Friston
Sussex Heritage Coast
Royal Sovereign
Dieppe hours 4
TV
Dartmouth
M25
M23
M20
M26
A22
A23
A26
A27
A21
A259
A264
A272
A275
1
2
3
4
5
6
7

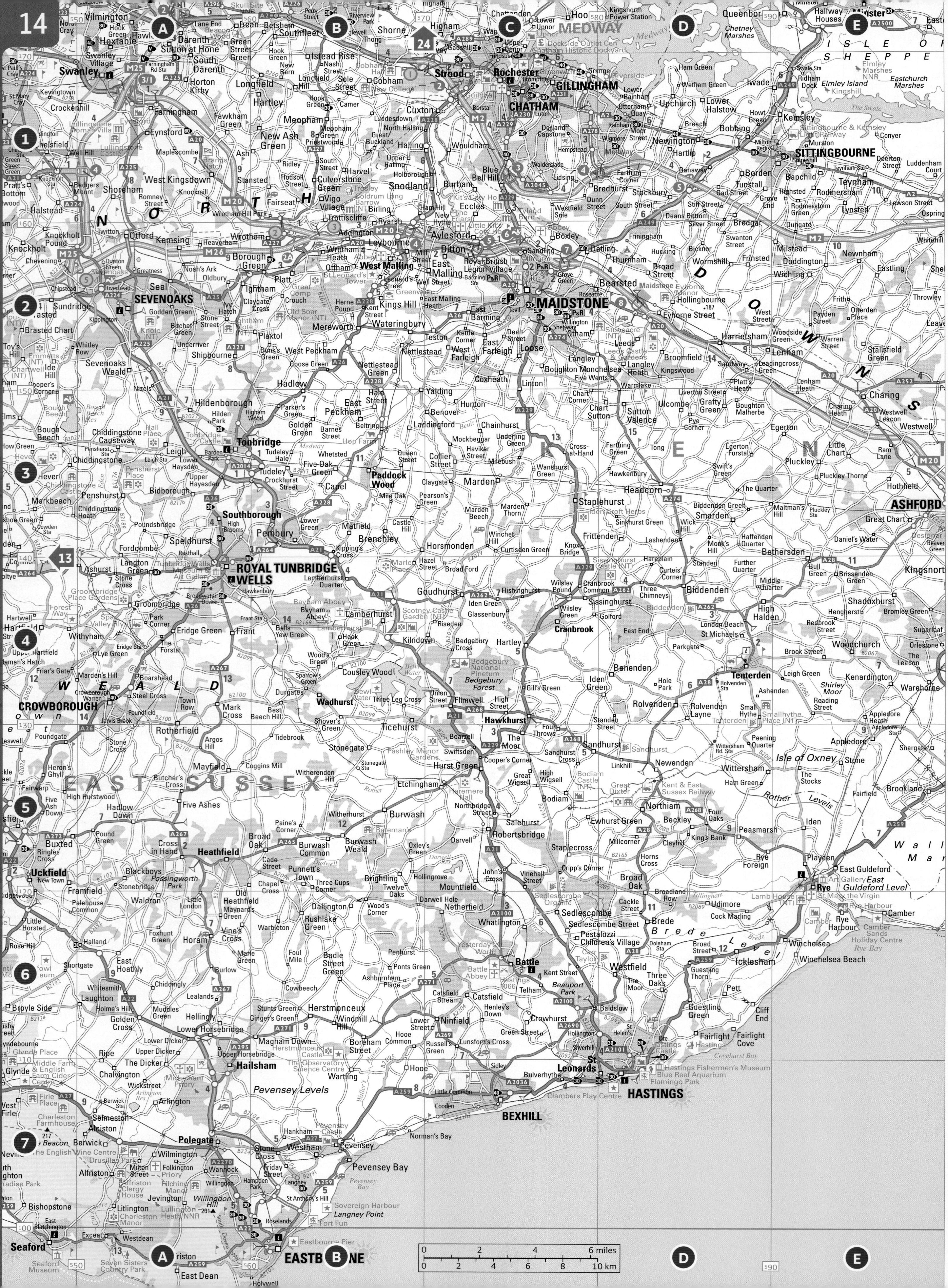
MEDWAY
ISLE OF SHEPPEY
Swanley
Strood
Rochester
GILLINGHAM
CHATHAM
SITTINGBOURNE
SEVENOAKS
MAIDSTONE
NORTH DOWNS
West Malling
Kings Hill
Tonbridge
Southborough
ROYAL TUNBRIDGE WELLS
Paddock Wood
Staplehurst
Headcorn
ASHFORD
KENT
Cranbrook
Tenterden
Hawkhurst
CROWBOROUGH
WEALD
EAST SUSSEX
Heathfield
Uckfield
Hailsham
Battle
Rye
Isle of Oxney
Winchelsea
Brede Level
Pevensey Levels
Pevensey Bay
BEXHILL
HASTINGS
Polegate
Seaford
EASTBOURNE
Langney Point
0 2 4 6 miles
0 2 4 6 8 10 km

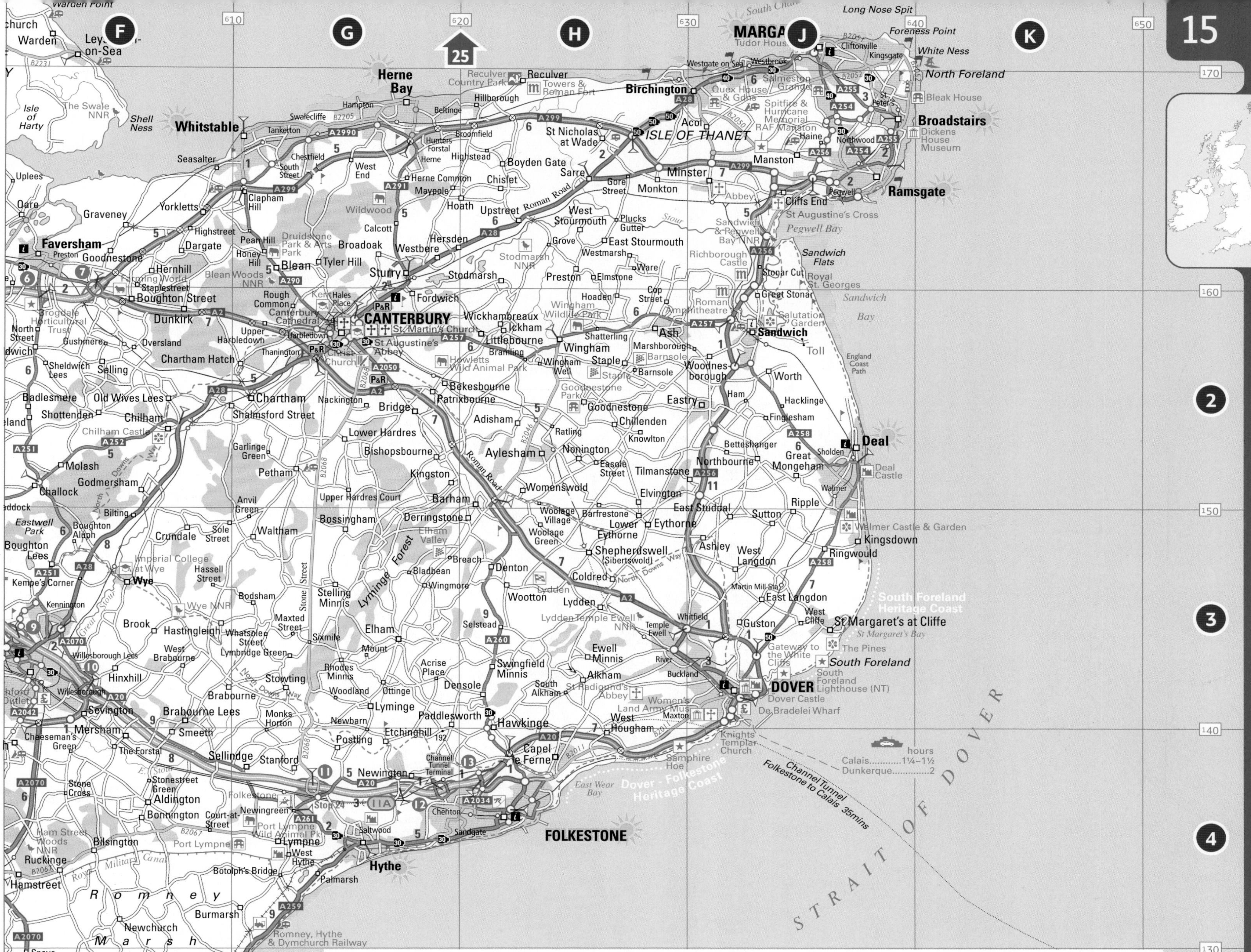

Channel Tunnel terminal maps

Eurotunnel: Access from the UK

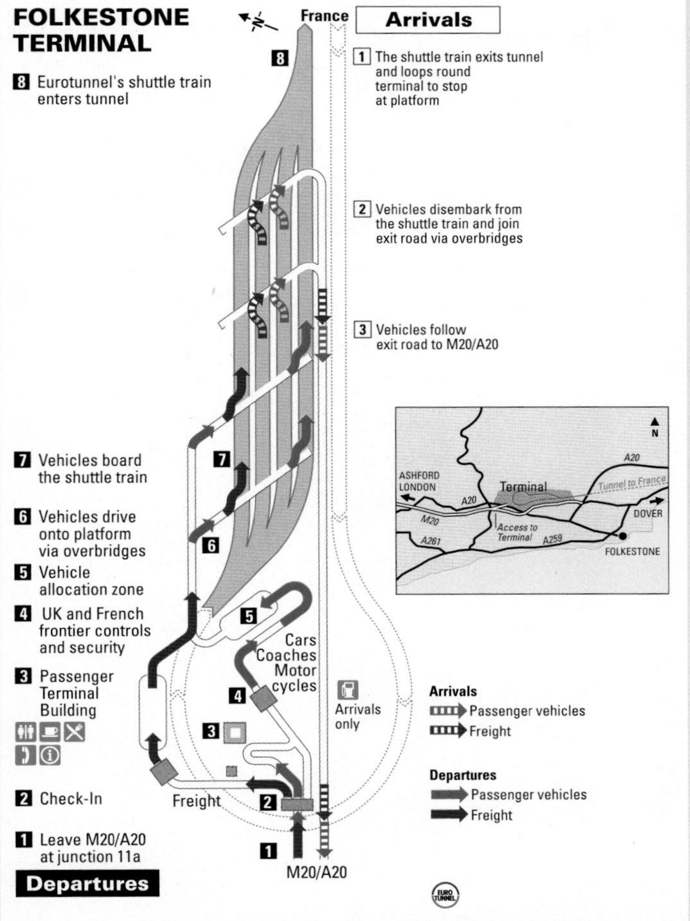

Eurotunnel: Access from France

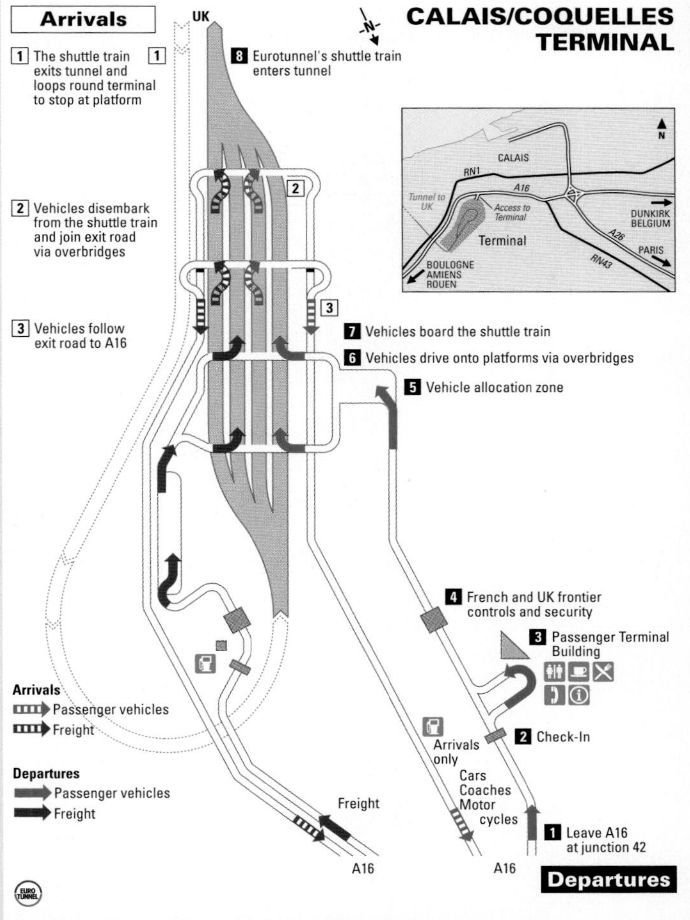

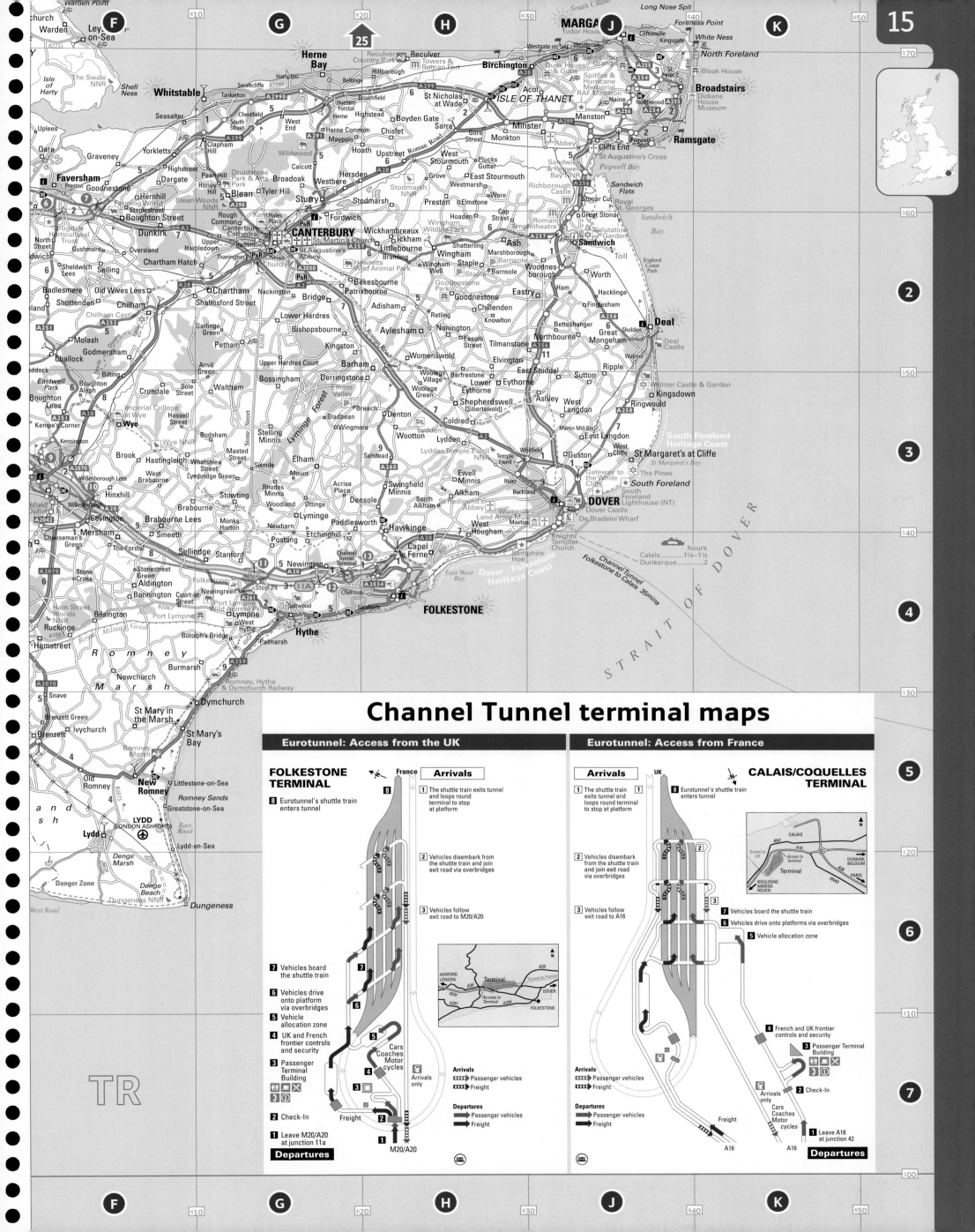

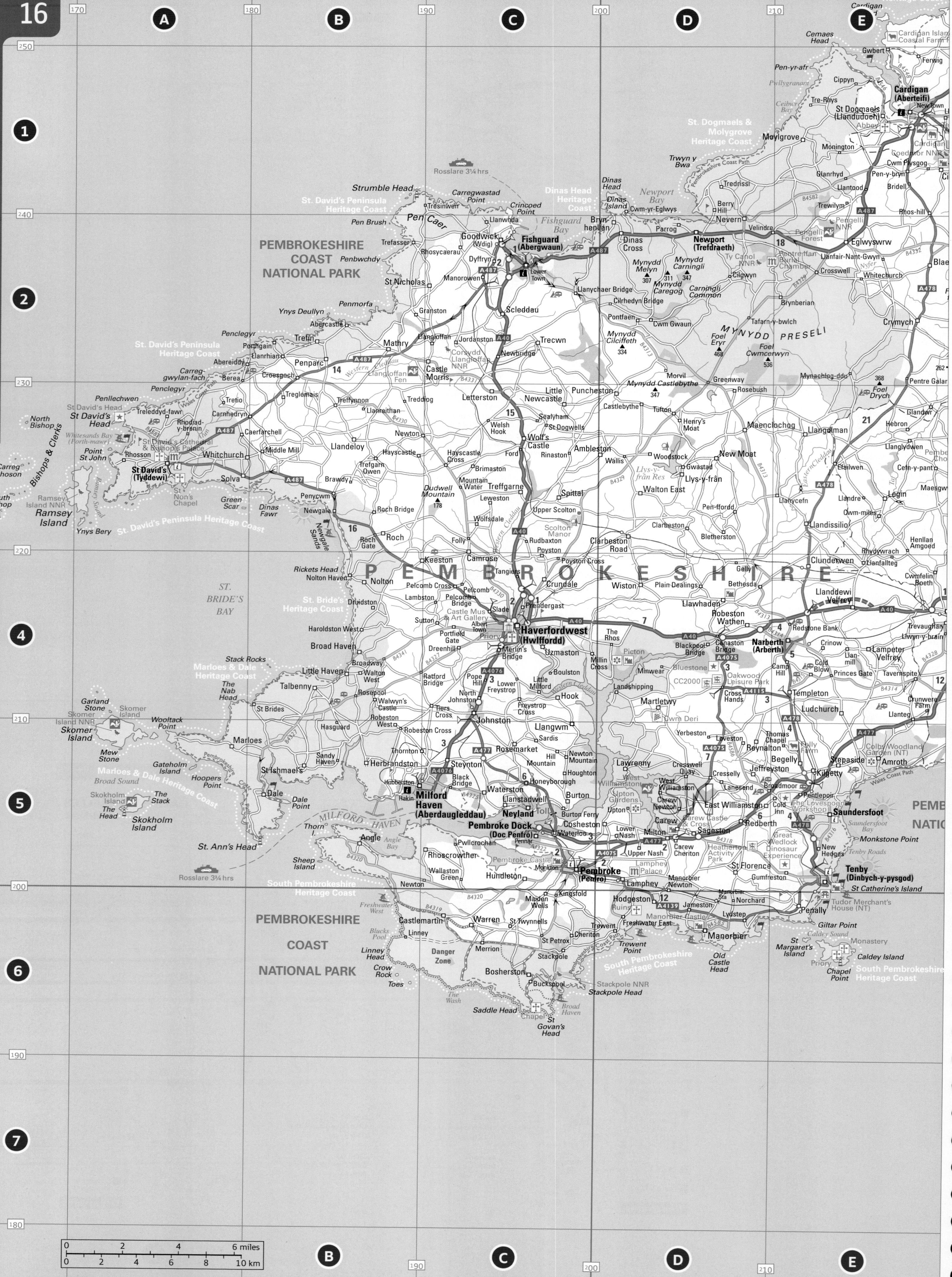

PEMBROKESHIRE COAST NATIONAL PARK
PEMBROKESHIRE
PEMBROKESHIRE COAST NATIONAL PARK
St. David's Peninsula Heritage Coast
Dinas Head Heritage Coast
St. Dogmaels & Moylgrove Heritage Coast
St. Bride's Heritage Coast
Marloes & Dale Heritage Coast
South Pembrokeshire Heritage Coast
Cardigan Heritage Coast
Strumble Head
Pen Caer
Pen Brush
Carregwastad Point
Crincoed Point
Fishguard Bay
Rosslare 3¼ hrs
Goodwick (Wdig)
Fishguard (Abergwaun)
Lower Town
Dinas Head
Dinas Island
Cwm-yr-Eglwys
Newport Bay
Bryn-henllan
Dinas Cross
Newport (Trefdraeth)
Nevern
Cardigan (Aberteifi)
St Dogmaels (Llandudoch)
Abbey
Moylgrove
Cemaes Head
Gwbert
Ferwig
Pen-yr-afr
Cippyn
Tre-Rhys
Trwyn y Bwa
Eglwyswrw
Velindre
Pentre Ifan Burial Chamber
Crosswell
Whitechurch
Crymych
MYNYDD PRESELI
Foel Eryr 468
Foel Cwmcerwyn 536
Mynydd Cilciffeth 334
Mynydd Castlebythe 347
Mynydd Melyn 307
Mynydd Carningli 347
Mynydd Caregog 311
Carningli Common
Cilgwyn
Llanychaer Bridge
Cilrhedyn Bridge
Pontfaen
Cwm Gwaun
Tafarn-y-bwlch
Brynberian
Rosebush
Greenway
Morvil
Puncheston
Little Newcastle
Castlebythe
Tufton
Henry's Moat
Maenclochog
Llangolman
Mynachlog-ddu
Foel Drych
Pentre Galar
Glandwr
Hebron
Llanglydwen
Efailwen
Cefn-y-pant
Llandre
Login
Llanycefn
Llandissilio
Clunderwen
Rhydwyrach
Llanfallteg
Henllan Amgoed
Cwmfelin Boeth
Llanddewi Velfrey
Redstone Bank
Trevaughan
Llwyn-y-brain
Crinow
Lampeter Velfrey
Llan-mill
Princes Gate
Tavernspite
Narberth (Arberth)
Templeton
Ludchurch
Crunwere Farm
Llanteg
Colby Woodland Garden (NT)
Amroth
Stepaside
Kilgetty
Begelly
Reynalton
Jeffreyston
Thomas Chapel
Saundersfoot
Saundersfoot Bay
Monkstone Point
Tenby (Dinbych-y-pysgod)
St Catherine's Island
Tudor Merchant's House (NT)
Penally
Giltar Point
Caldey Sound
Monastery
Caldey Island
Priory
St Margaret's Island
Chapel Point
New Hedges
Manorbier
Jameston
Lydstep
Manorbier Castle
Old Castle Head
Lamphey
Lamphey Palace
Hodgeston
Freshwater East
Trewent
Trewent Point
Stackpole
Stackpole Head
Stackpole NNR
Bosherston
Broad Haven
St Govan's Head
Chapel
Saddle Head
Merrion
Danger Zone
St Petrox
St Twynnells
Warren
Castlemartin
Linney
Linney Head
Crow Rock
Toes
Blucks Pool
Freshwater West
Maiden Wells
Kingsfold
Pembroke (Penfro)
Monkton
Pembroke Castle
Hundleton
Wallaston Green
Rhoscrowther
Pwllcrochan
Pembroke Dock (Doc Penfro)
Pennar
Waterloo
Angle
Angle Bay
Thorn I.
Newton
Sheep Island
St. Ann's Head
MILFORD HAVEN
Dale
Dale Point
St Ishmael's
Hoopers Point
Gateholm Island
Marloes
Wooltack Point
Skomer Island
Skomer Island NNR
Garland Stone
Mew Stone
Skokholm Island
Skokholm Island
The Head
The Stack
Broad Sound
Milford Haven (Aberdaugleddau)
Hakin
Hubberston
Herbrandston
Thornton
Steynton
Neyland
Llanstadwell
Waterston
Honeyborough
Burton
Burton Ferry
Cosheston
Upton
Upton Gardens
Lower Nash
Upper Nash
Milton
Carew
Carew Castle & Cross
Carew Cheriton
Carew Newton
Sageston
Redberth
Cold Inn
East Williamston
West Williamston
Cresswell Quay
Cresselly
Lawrenny
Yerbeston
Loveston
Martletwy
Cwm Deri
Heatherton Activity Park
Great Wedlock Dinosaur Experience
St Florence
Gumfreston
Manorbier Newton
Oakwood Leisure Park
CC2000
Bluestone
Cross Hands
Landshipping
Minwear
Millin Cross
Picton
Blackpool Bridge
Canaston Bridge
Robeston Wathen
Llawhaden
Bethesda
Gelly
Plain Dealings
Wiston
The Rhos
Uzmaston
Boulston
Little Milford
Hook
Freystrop
Lower Freystrop
Freystrop Cross
Llangwm
Sardis
Rosemarket
Hill Mountain
Newton Mountain
Houghton
Johnston
North Johnston
Tiers Cross
Robeston West
Robeston Cross
Walwyn's Castle
Rosepool
Walton West
Little Haven
Broad Haven
Broadway
Haroldston West
Druidston
Nolton Haven
Nolton
Rickets Head
Stack Rocks
Talbenny
The Nab Head
St Brides
Hasguard
Sandy Haven
ST. BRIDE'S BAY
Newgale
Newgale Sands
Roch
Roch Gate
Roch Bridge
Penycwm
Dinas Fawr
Green Scar
Solva
Whitchurch
Middle Mill
Caerfarchell
St David's (Tyddewi)
St Non's Chapel
St David's Cathedral & Bishop's Palace
Rhosson
Whitesands Bay (Porth-mawr)
St David's Head
Point St John
North Bishop
Bishops & Clerks
Carreg Rhoson
South Bishop
Ramsey Island NNR
Ramsey Island
Ramsey Sound
Ynys Bery
Treleddyd-fawr
Rhodiad-y-brenin
Carnhedryn
Tretio
Penllechwen
Penclegyr
Carreg-gwylan-fach
Abereiddy
Berea
Llanrhian
Porthgain
Trefin
Abercastle
Ynys Deullyn
Penmorfa
Croesgoch
Treglemais
Llanreithan
Treffynnon
Penparc
Mathry
Llangloffan
Llangloffan Fen
Castle Morris
Corsydd Llangloffan NNR
Jordanston
Granston
St Nicholas
Penbwchdy
Trefasser
Rhosycaerau
Tresinwen
Llanwnda
Manorowen
Dyffryn
Scleddau
Trecwn
Newbridge
Letterston
Treddiog
Llandeloy
Newton
Hayscastle
Hayscastle Cross
Trefgarn Owen
Brawdy
Brimaston
Dudwell Mountain 178
Mountain Water
Treffgarne
Leweston
Wolfsdale
Welsh Hook
Wolf's Castle
Sealyham
St Dogwells
Ford
Rinaston
Ambleston
Walton East
Woodstock
Wallis
Llys-y-frân
Llys-y-frân Res
Gwastad
New Moat
Pen-ffordd
Bletherston
Clarbeston
Clarbeston Road
Spittal
Upper Scolton
Scolton Manor
Rudbaxton
Poyston
Poyston Cross
Crundale
Tangiers
Folly
Camrose
Keeston
Pelcomb Cross
Pelcomb
Pelcomb Bridge
Lambston
Slade
Prendergast
Castle Mus Art Gallery
Albert Town
Sutton
Portfield Gate
Dreenhill
Priory
Haverfordwest (Hwlffordd)
Merlin's Bridge
Pope Hill
Ratford Bridge
Black Bridge
Newcastle
Penrhiw
Llantood
Glanrhyd
Monington
Bridell
Pen-y-bryn
Cwm Plysgog
Coedmor NNR
Pengelli Forest
Pengelli NNR
Trewilym
Rhos-hill
Llanfair-Nant-Gwyn
Tredrissi
Berry Hill
Parrog
Ty Canol NNR
Cardigan Island Coastal Farm Park
Cardigan Island
Pwllygranant
Ceibwr Bay
Pembrokeshire Coast Path
Wales Coast Path
Western Cleddau
Eastern Cleddau
Tenby Roads
The Wash
A40
A487
A477
A478
A4076
A4075
A4115
A4139
B4329
B4313
B4330
B4331
B4341
B4327
B4320
B4319
B4318
B4585
B4584
B4588
B4582
B4546
B4548
B4332
B4314
B4328
B4586
B4322
262
368
A
B
C
D
E
1
2
3
4
5
6
7
170
180
190
200
210
250
240
230
220
210
200
190
180
0 2 4 6 miles
0 2 4 6 8 10 km

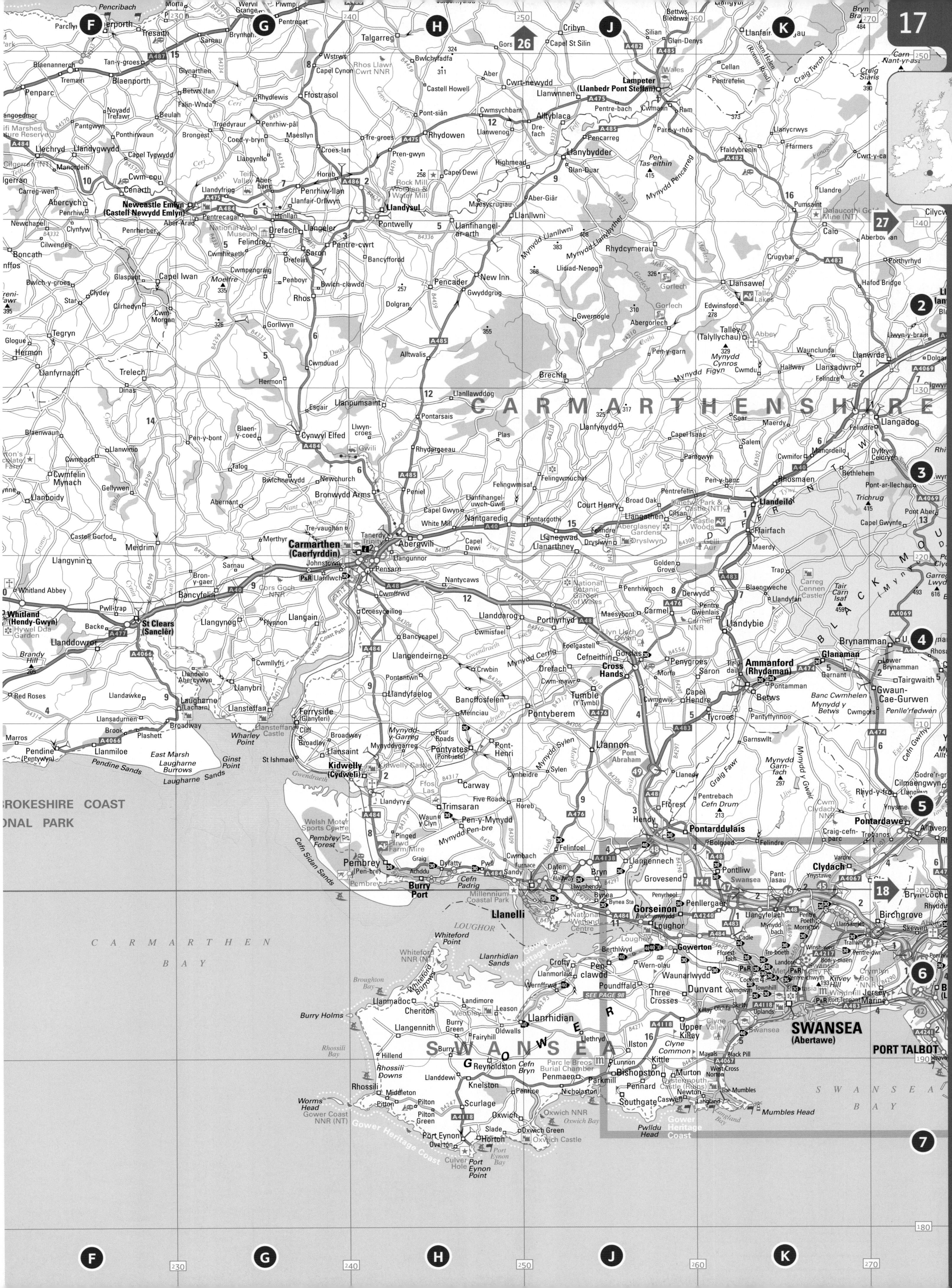
F
G
H
J
K
CARMARTHENSHIRE
CARMARTHEN BAY
SWANSEA
SWANSEA BAY
BROKESHIRE COAST
ONAL PARK
LOUGHOR
Newcastle Emlyn
(Castell Newydd Emlyn)
Llandysul
Lampeter
(Llanbedr Pont Steffan)
Llanybydder
Carmarthen
(Caerfyrddin)
Abergwili
St Clears
(Sanclêr)
Whitland
(Hendy-Gwyn)
Laugharne
(Lacharn)
Kidwelly
(Cydweli)
Llandeilo
Ammanford
(Rhydaman)
Llandybie
Cross Hands
Pontarddulais
Llanelli
Burry Port
Pembrey
(Pen-bre)
Gorseinon
Loughor
Gowerton
SWANSEA
(Abertawe)
PORT TALBOT
Pontardawe
Clydach
Llangadog
Llanrhidian
Penclawdd
Pendine
(Pentywyn)
Ferryside
(Glanyferi)
Llansteffan
Rhossili
Port Eynon
Oxwich
Mumbles Head
Pendine Sands
Laugharne Sands
Cefn Sidan Sands
Burry Holms
Worms Head
Gower Heritage Coast
Glanaman
Brynamman
Talley
(Talyllychau)
Llansawel
Brechfa
Cynwyl Elfed
Llanpumsaint
Pencader
New Inn
Cenarth
Drefach
Felindre
Saron
Llangeler
Pentre-cwrt
Rhos
Meidrim
Bancyfelin
Llanboidy
Cwmfelin Mynach
Trelech
Tegryn
Llanfyrnach
Hermon
Capel Iwan
Llanddarog
Porthyrhyd
Pontyberem
Pontyates
(Pont-iets)
Trimsaran
Llangennech
Bynea
Penllergaer
Morriston
Skewen
Birchgrove
Dunvant
Killay
Sketty
Upper Killay
Bishopston
Murton
Southgate
Pennard
Mumbles
Newton
Langland
Caswell
Reynoldston
Knelston
Scurlage
Horton
Llangennith
Llanmadoc
Cheriton
Three Crosses
Waunarlwydd
Gwaun-Cae-Gurwen
Tycroes
Betws
Saron
Llangathen
Ffairfach
Llanwrda
Pumsaint
Caio
Dolaucothi Gold Mine (NT)
National Botanic Garden of Wales
Aberglasney Gardens
Dinefwr Park & Castle (NT)
Carreg Cennen Castle
National Wool Museum
Millennium Coastal Park
National Wetland Centre
Welsh Motor Sports Centre
Pembrey Forest
Mynydd Llanllwni
Mynydd Pencarreg
Mynydd Sylen
Mynydd Cerrig
BLACK MOUNTAIN
Tair Carn Isaf
Trichrug
SEE PAGE 98
26
27
18
230
240
250
260
270
180
190
200
210
220
230
240
250

For a more detailed map of Swansea see page 98

For a more detailed map of Swansea see page 98

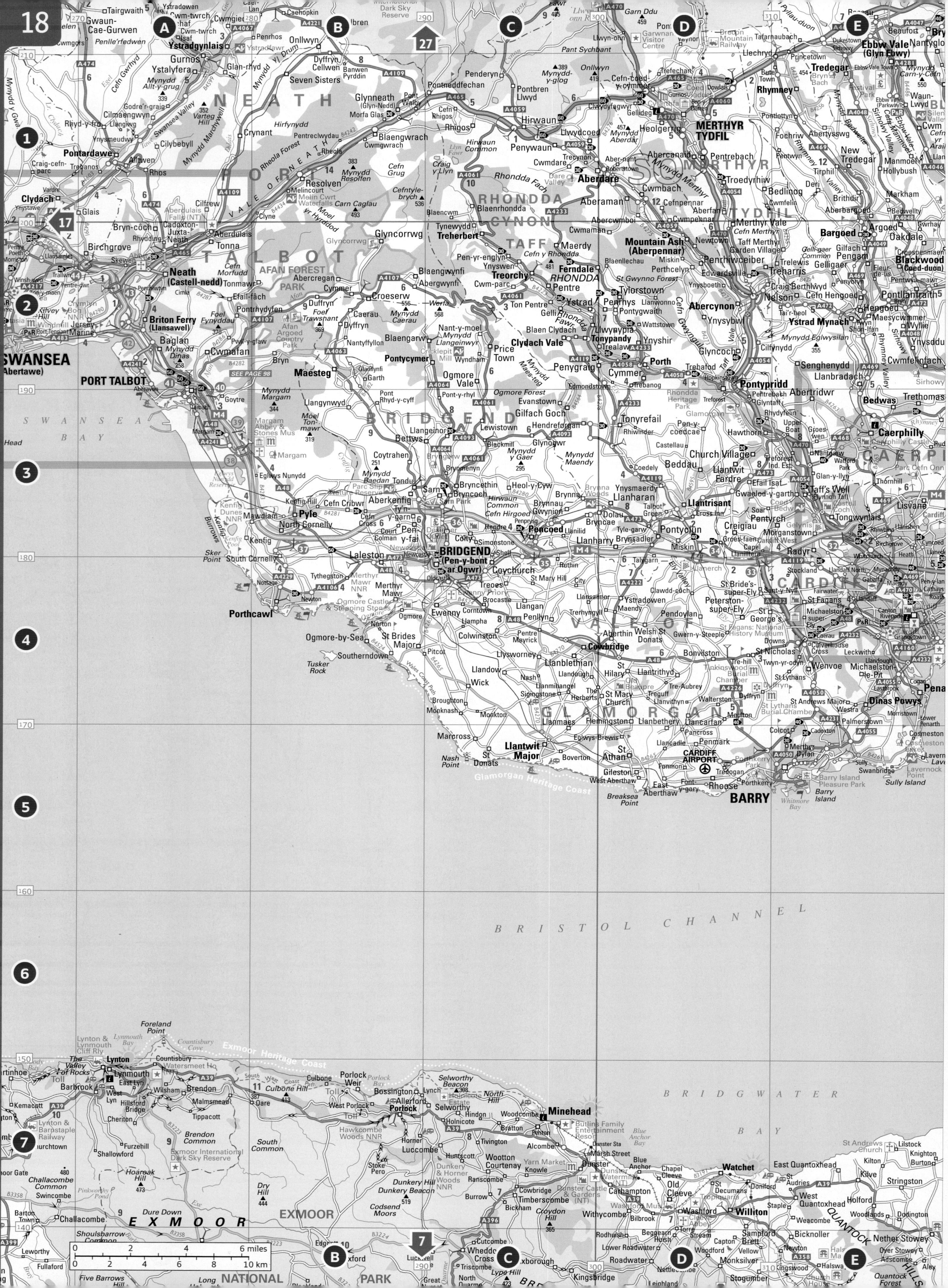
A
B
C
D
E
1
2
3
4
5
6
7
27
17
7
NEATH
PORT
TALBOT
RHONDDA
CYNON
TAFF
MERTHYR
TYDFIL
BRIDGEND
VALE OF
GLAMORGAN
SWANSEA
(Abertawe)
PORT TALBOT
Neath
(Castell-nedd)
Briton Ferry
(Llansawel)
Ystradgynlais
Pontardawe
Clydach
Maesteg
Pyle
Porthcawl
BRIDGEND
(Pen-y-bont
ar Ogwr)
Llantwit
Major
Cowbridge
Aberdare
Mountain Ash
(Aberpennar)
Treorchy
Ferndale
Tonypandy
Porth
Pontypridd
Llantrisant
Pontyclun
Caerphilly
MERTHYR
TYDFIL
Ebbw Vale
(Glyn Ebwy)
Tredegar
Rhymney
Bargoed
Blackwood
(Coed-duon)
Ystrad Mynach
Nelson
Abercynon
Pencoed
Dinas Powys
BARRY
Barry Island
Sully Island
CARDIFF
AIRPORT
SWANSEA BAY
BRISTOL CHANNEL
BRIDGWATER BAY
Glamorgan Heritage Coast
Exmoor Heritage Coast
Foreland
Point
Lynton
Lynmouth
Porlock
Minehead
Dunster
Watchet
Williton
EXMOOR
EXMOOR NATIONAL PARK
QUANTOCK HILLS
Tusker
Rock
Nash
Point
Breaksea
Point
Sker
Point
0 2 4 6 miles
0 2 4 6 8 10 km

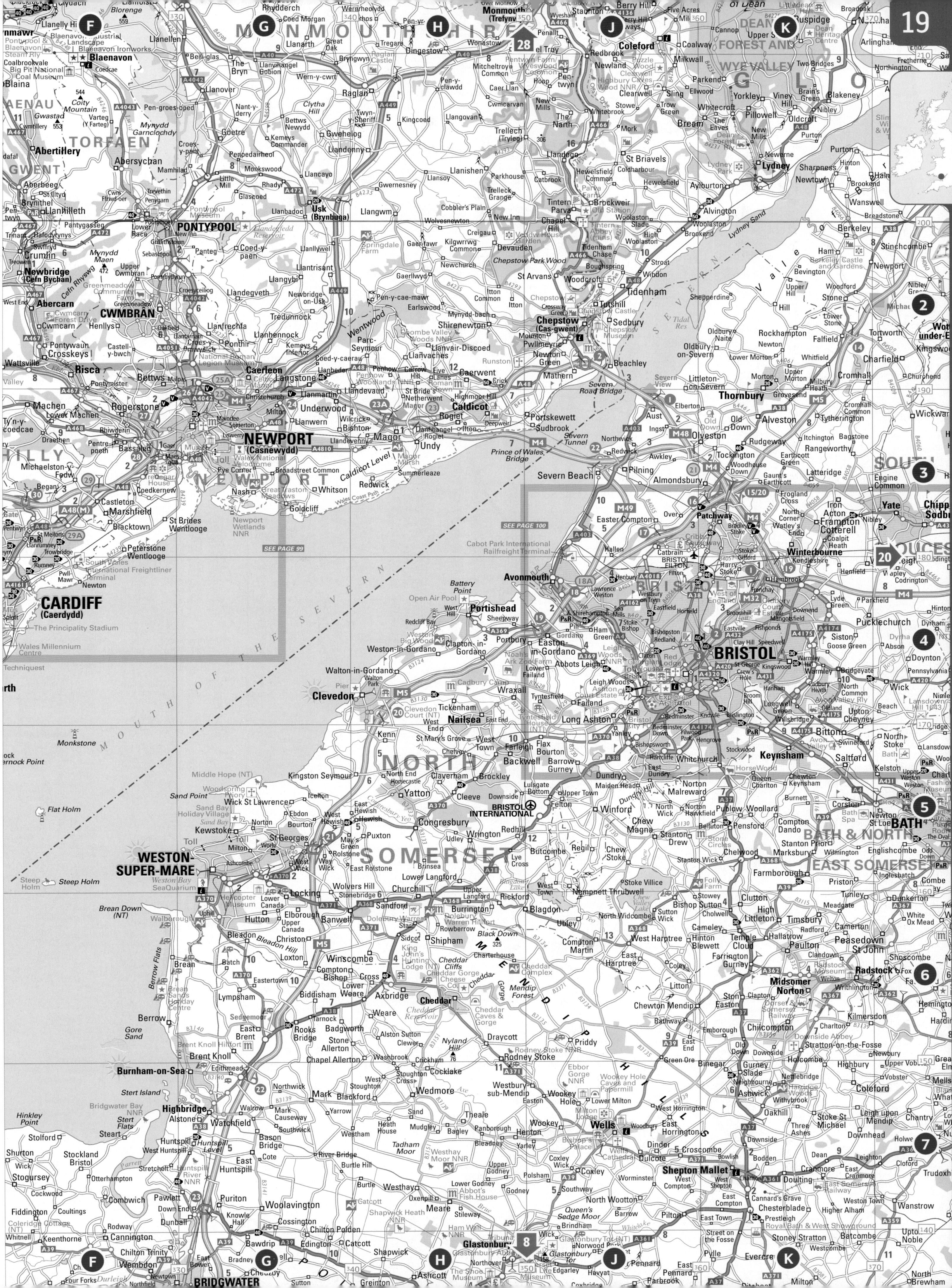

For a more detailed map of Cardiff & Newport see page 99 and of Bristol see page 100

SEE PAGE 99

SEE PAGE 100

CARDIFF (Caerdydd)

NEWPORT (Casnewydd)

CWMBRAN

PONTYPOOL

Blaenavon

Abertillery

BRISTOL

BATH

WESTON-SUPER-MARE

Burnham-on-Sea

BRIDGWATER

Chepstow (Cas-gwent)

Coleford

Lydney

Thornbury

Yate

Keynsham

Clevedon

Nailsea

Portishead

Avonmouth

Shepton Mallet

Midsomer Norton

Radstock

Wells

Cheddar

Glastonbury

TORFAEN

GWENT

NEWPORT

NORTH SOMERSET

SOMERSET

BATH & NORTH EAST SOMERSET

MONMOUTHSHIRE

WYE VALLEY

DEAN FOREST AND

GLOUCESTERSHIRE

MOUTH OF THE SEVERN

MENDIP HILLS

Severn Road Bridge

Prince of Wales Bridge

Severn Beach

Steep Holm

Flat Holm

Brean Down (NT)

GLOUCESTERSHIRE

WILTSHIRE

SOUTH GLOUCESTERSHIRE

BATH & NORTH EAST SOMERSET

Major towns:
STROUD, Cirencester, Nailsworth, Dursley, Wotton-under-Edge, Tetbury, Malmesbury, SWINDON, Royal Wootton Bassett, Wroughton, Chippenham, Calne, Corsham, Melksham, Devizes, Marlborough, Chipping Sodbury, Yate, BATH, Bradford-on-Avon, TROWBRIDGE, Westbury, Frome, Radstock, Warminster, Amesbury, Pewsey, Cricklade, Fairford

0   2   4   6 miles
0   2   4   6   8   10 km

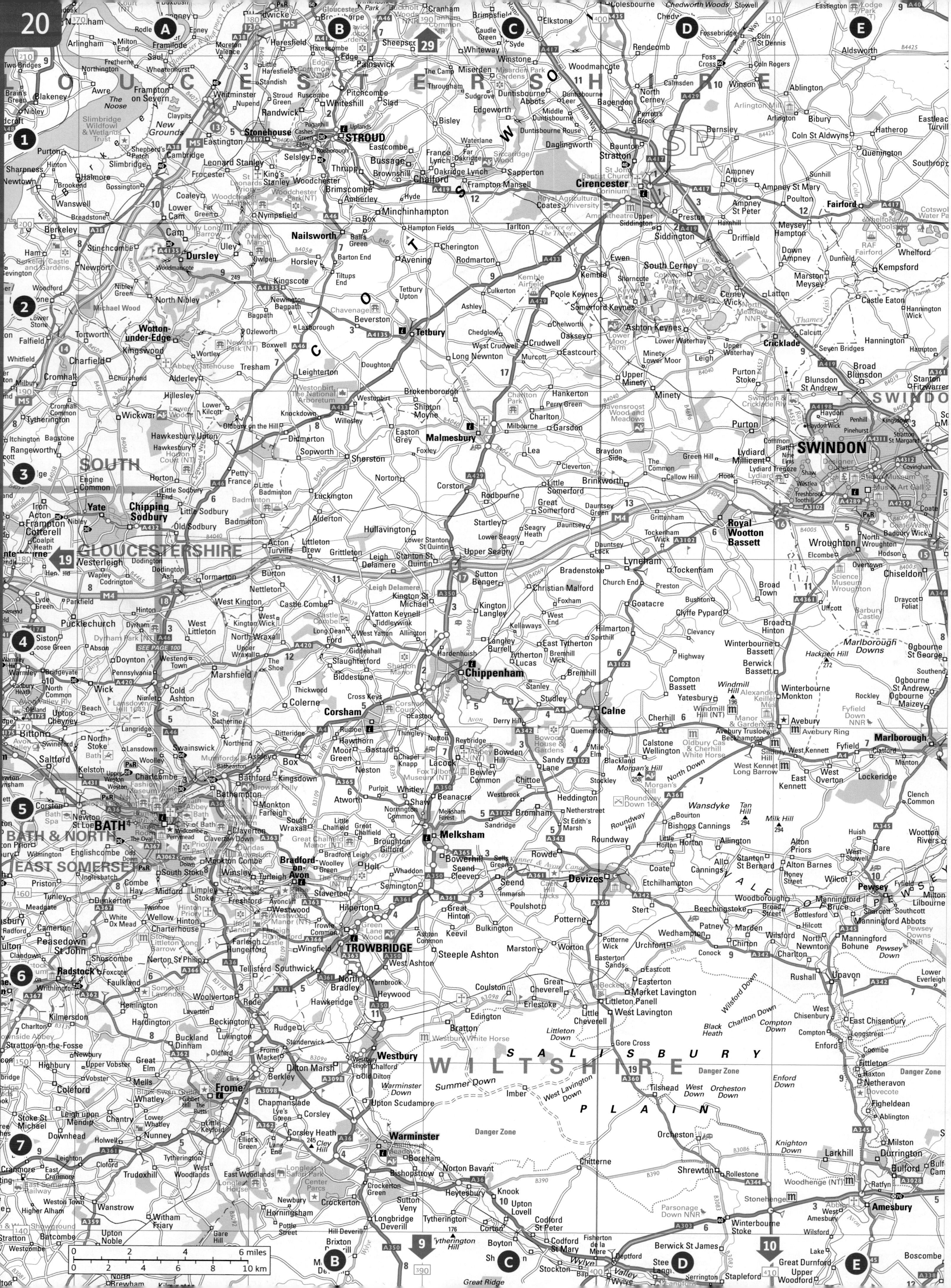

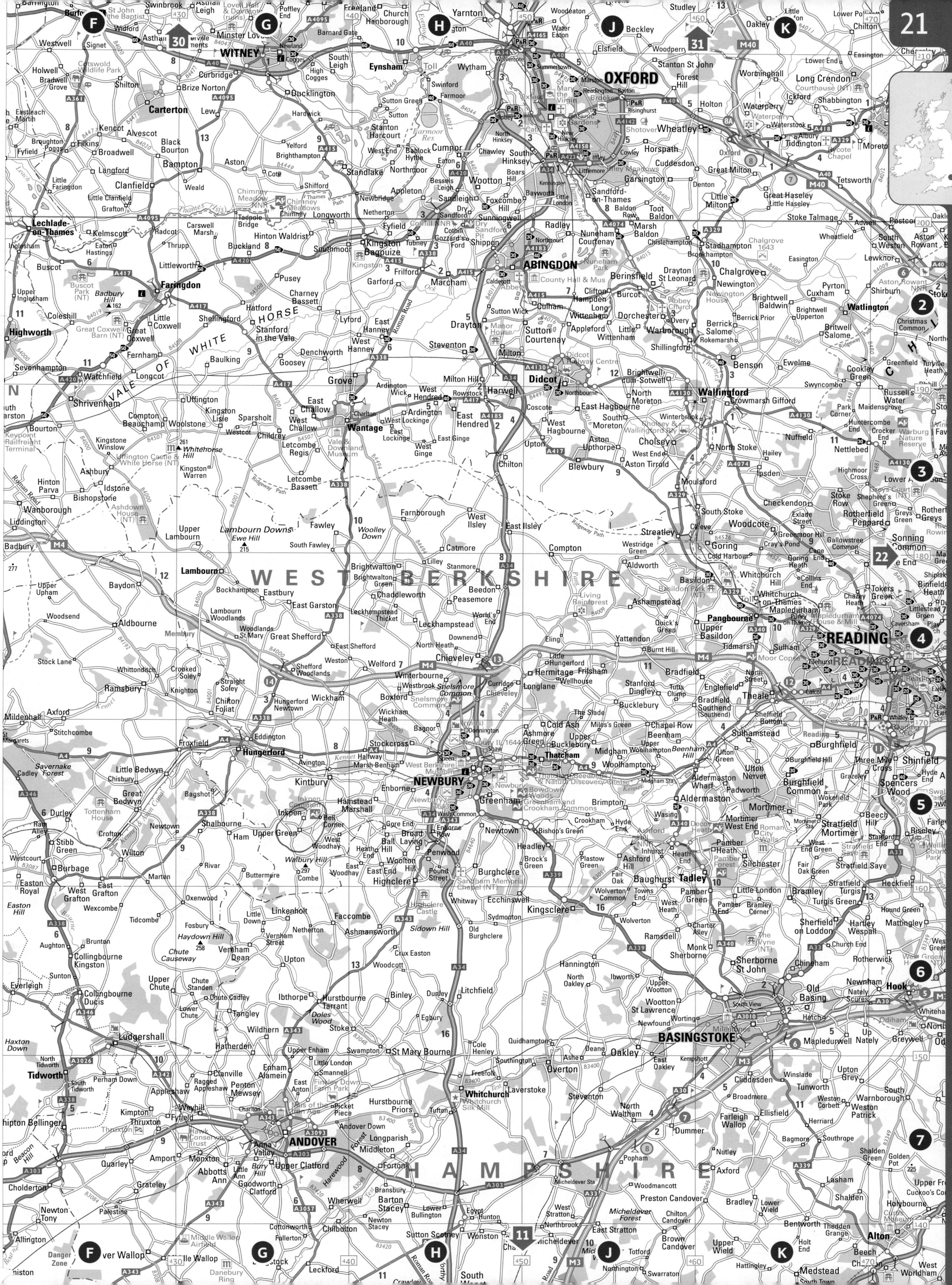
WITNEY
OXFORD
ABINGDON
Didcot
Wallingford
Wantage
Faringdon
Carterton
Highworth
Lechlade-on-Thames
Eynsham
Wheatley
Thame
Watlington
READING
Pangbourne
Theale
NEWBURY
Hungerford
Thatcham
Lambourn
WEST BERKSHIRE
BASINGSTOKE
ANDOVER
Whitchurch
Tadley
Kingsclere
Tidworth
Ludgershall
Hook
Alton
HAMPSHIRE
VALE OF WHITE HORSE
Lambourn Downs
Savernake Forest
Micheldever Forest
M4
M40
M3
A34
A4
A303
A338
A339
A40
A417
A420
30
31
22
11

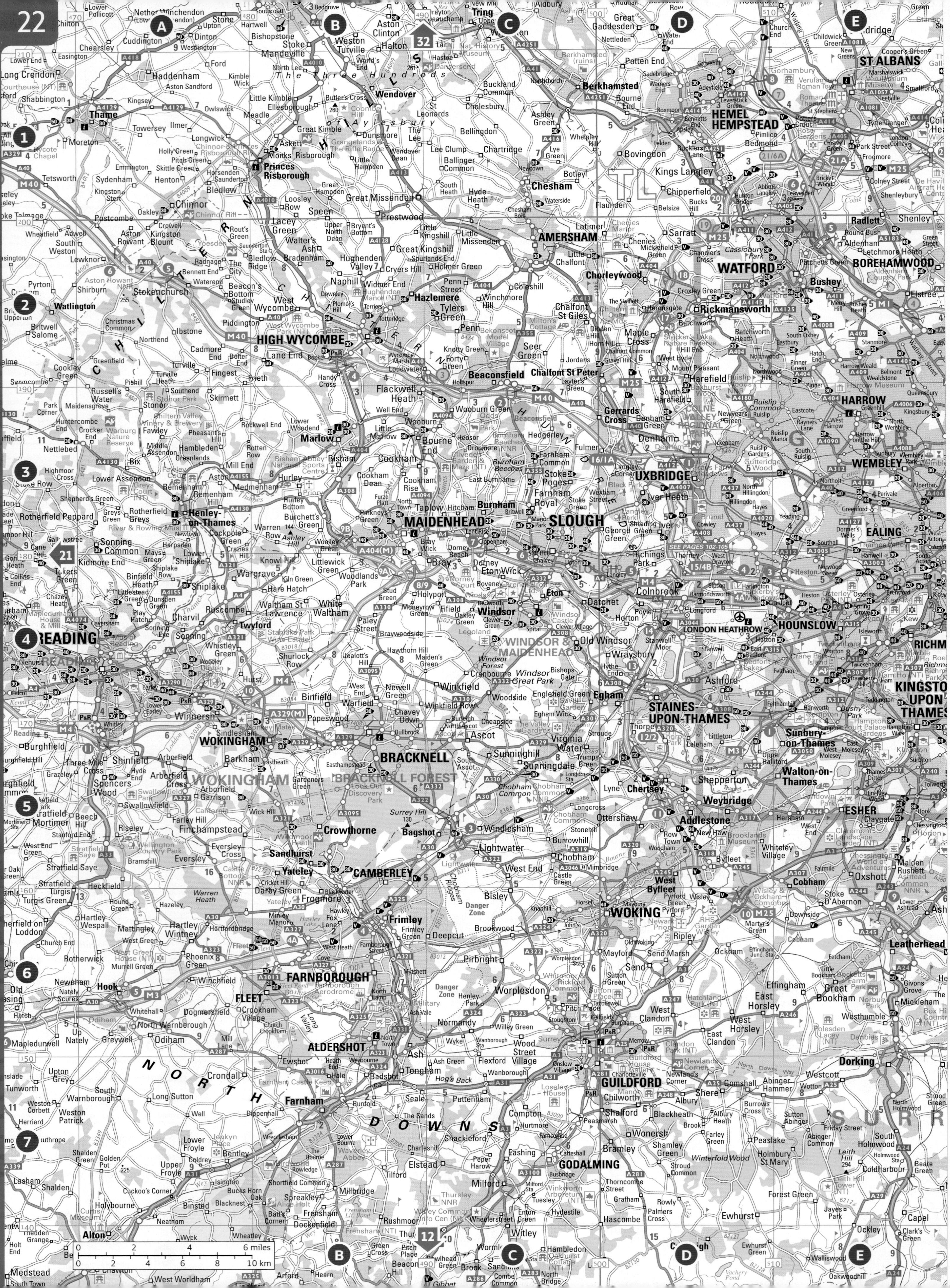
32
21
12
A
B
C
D
E
1
2
3
4
5
6
7
Thame
Princes Risborough
Wendover
Tring
Berkhamsted
HEMEL HEMPSTEAD
ST ALBANS
Watlington
Chinnor
Chesham
AMERSHAM
WATFORD
BOREHAMWOOD
Rickmansworth
HIGH WYCOMBE
Beaconsfield
Marlow
Henley-on-Thames
MAIDENHEAD
SLOUGH
UXBRIDGE
HARROW
WEMBLEY
EALING
HOUNSLOW
LONDON HEATHROW
READING
Twyford
Windsor
Eton
Egham
STAINES-UPON-THAMES
WOKINGHAM
BRACKNELL
Ascot
Crowthorne
Sandhurst
CAMBERLEY
Frimley
FARNBOROUGH
FLEET
Hook
ALDERSHOT
Farnham
Alton
WOKING
Weybridge
Chertsey
Addlestone
Walton-on-Thames
ESHER
Cobham
Leatherhead
GUILDFORD
GODALMING
Dorking
KINGSTON UPON THAMES
CHILTERN HILLS
NORTH DOWNS
WOKINGHAM
BRACKNELL FOREST
WINDSOR & MAIDENHEAD
SEE PAGES 102-105
0 2 4 6 miles
0 2 4 6 8 10 km

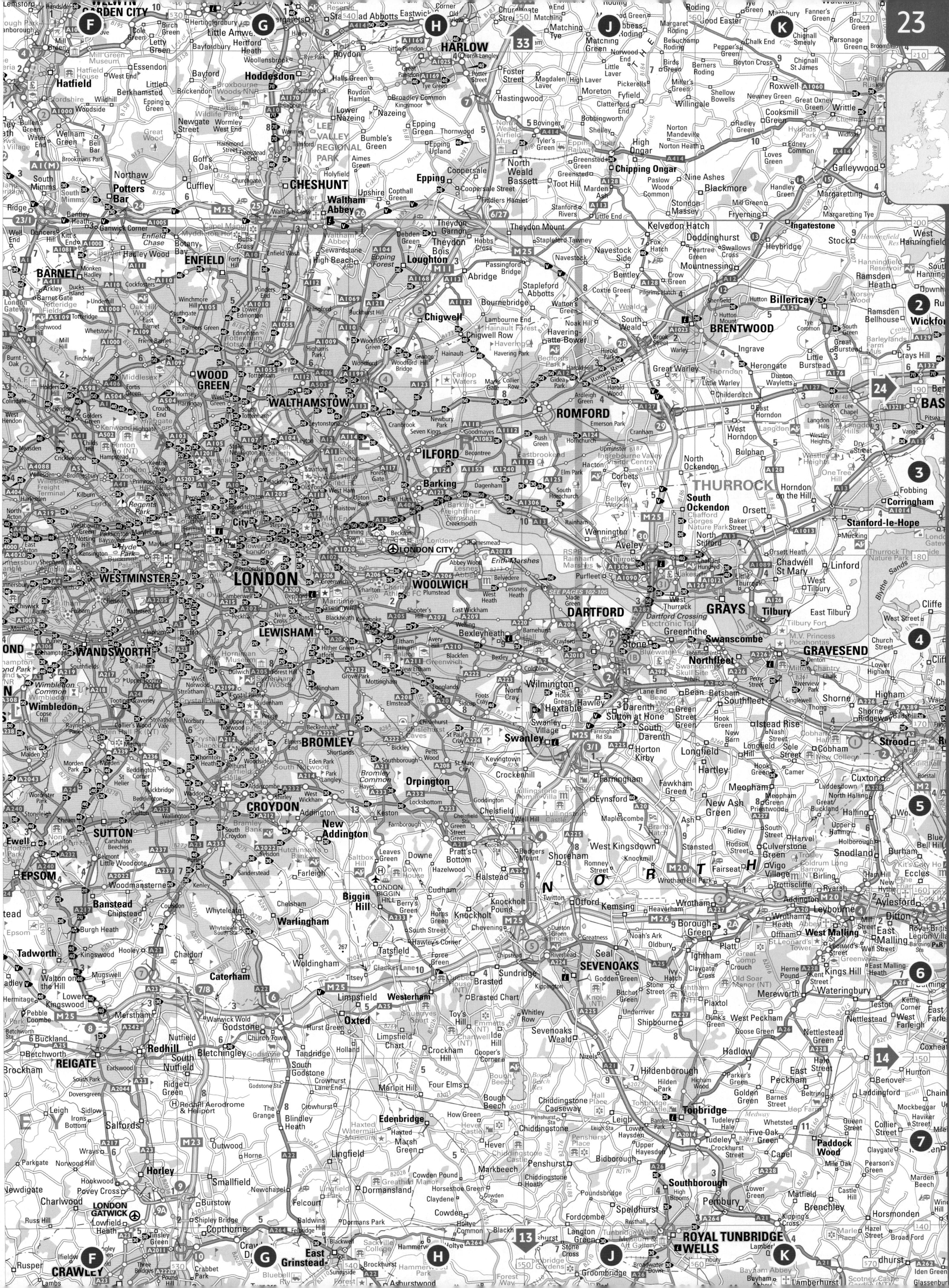

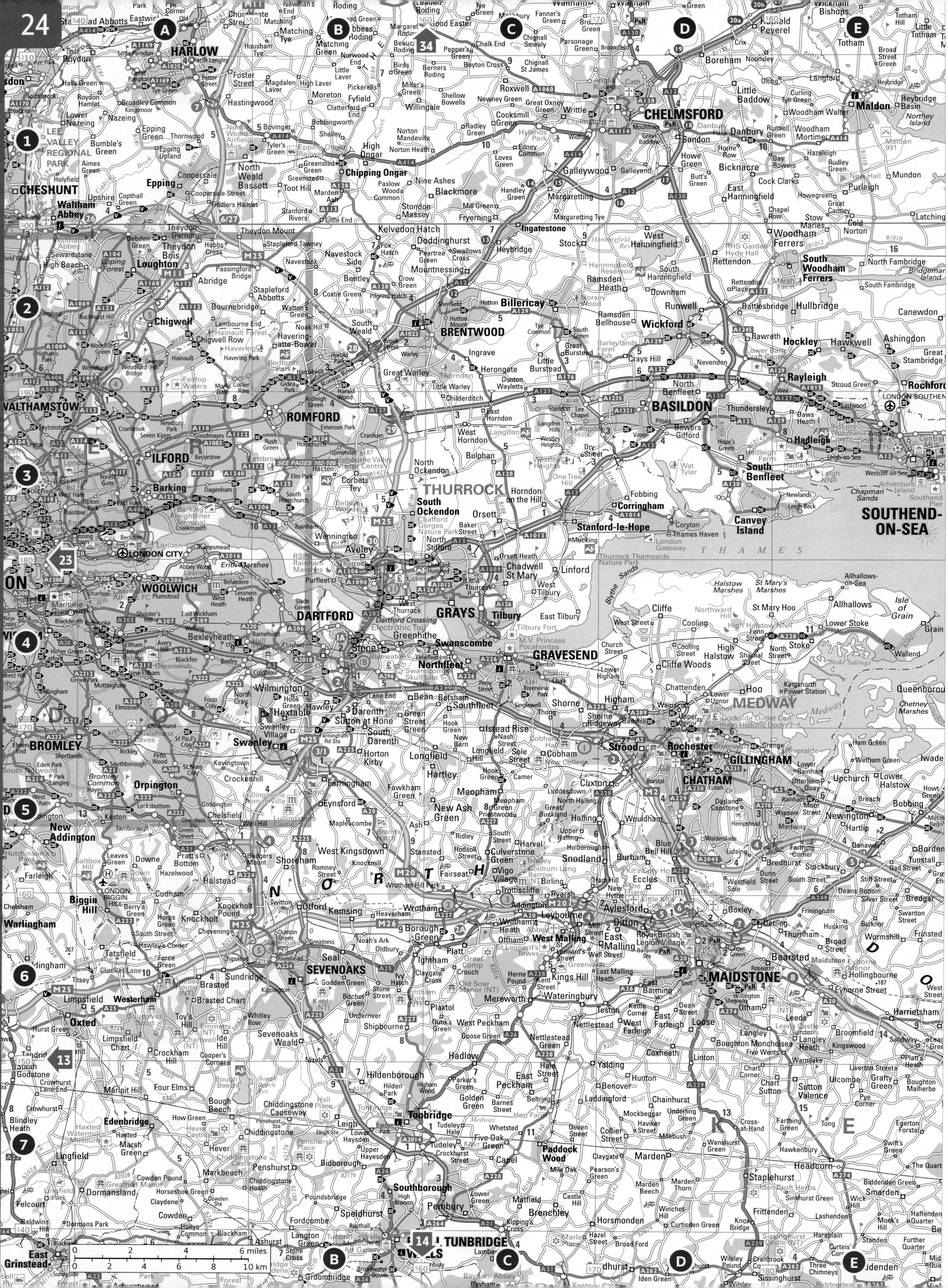

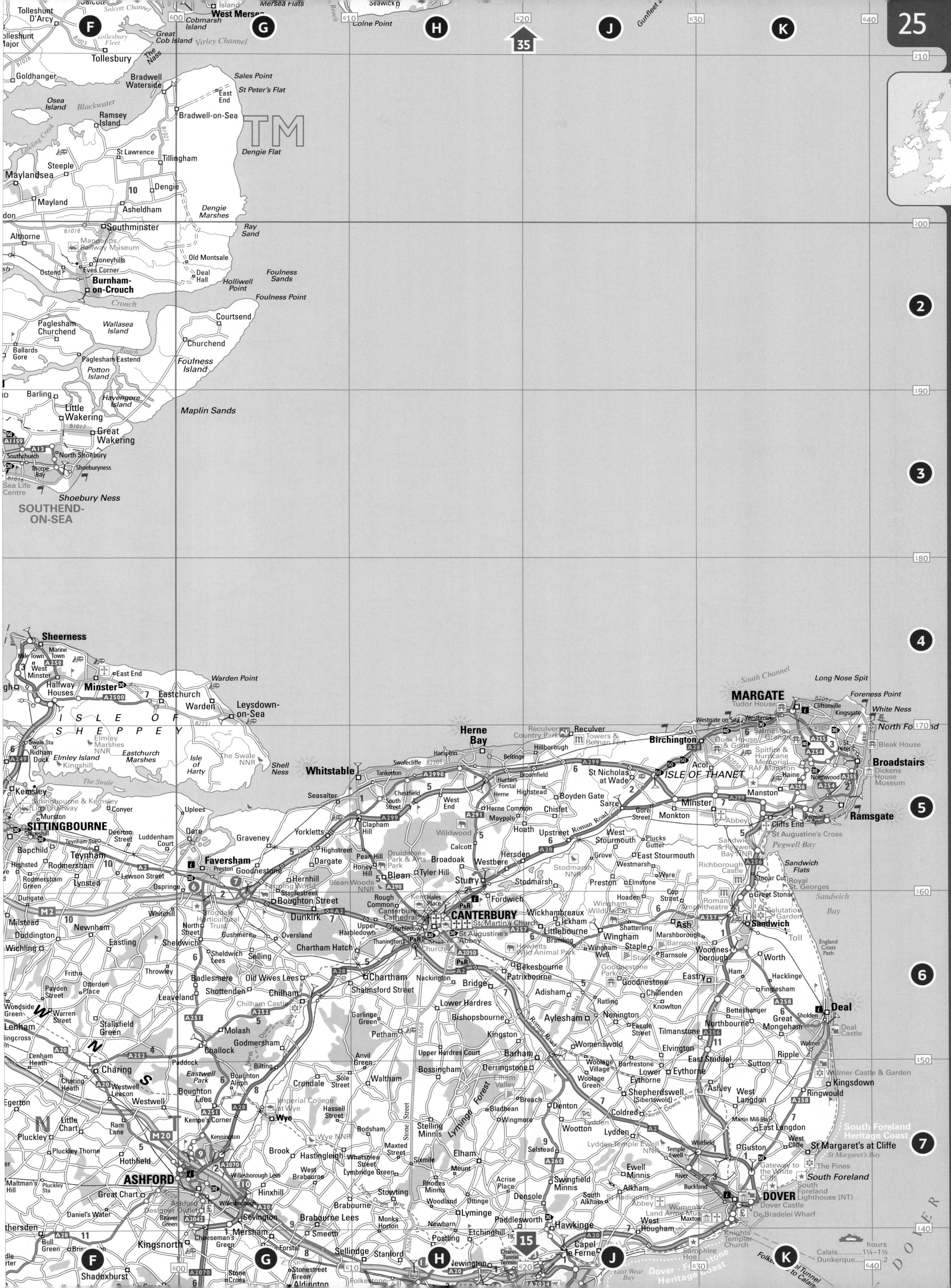

F
G
H
J
K
35
15
TM
2
3
4
5
6
7
Tolleshunt D'Arcy
Tollesbury
Goldhanger
Osea Island
Blackwater
Bradwell Waterside
Bradwell-on-Sea
Ramsey Island
Sales Point
St Peter's Flat
East End
West Mersea
Mersea Flats
Cobmarsh Island
Great Cob Island
Virley Channel
Colne Point
Seawick
Gunfleet
Dengie Flat
St Lawrence
Tillingham
Steeple
Maylandsea
Mayland
Dengie
Asheldham
Dengie Marshes
Southminster
Althorne
Mangapps Railway Museum
Stoneyhills
Ostend
Eves Corner
Burnham-on-Crouch
Old Montsale
Deal Hall
Ray Sand
Holliwell Point
Foulness Sands
Foulness Point
Crouch
Courtsend
Paglesham Churchend
Wallasea Island
Ballards Gore
Churchend
Paglesham Eastend
Foulness Island
Potton Island
Barling
Havengore Island
Little Wakering
Maplin Sands
Great Wakering
Southchurch
North Shoebury
Thorpe Bay
Shoeburyness
Sea Life Centre
Shoebury Ness
SOUTHEND-ON-SEA
Sheerness
Marine Town
Mile Town
West Minster
East End
Halfway Houses
Minster
Eastchurch
Warden Point
Warden
Leysdown-on-Sea
ISLE OF SHEPPEY
Elmley Marshes NNR
Elmley Island
Kingshill
Eastchurch Marshes
Isle of Harty
The Swale NNR
Shell Ness
The Swale
Kemsley
Sittingbourne & Kemsley Light Railway
Conyer
Murston
SITTINGBOURNE
Bapchild
Teynham
Rodmersham
Lynsted
Highsted
Deerton Street
Luddenham Court
Uplees
Oare
Graveney
Faversham
Preston
Goodnestone
Ospringe
Lewson Street
Milstead
Doddington
Newnham
Eastling
Wichling
Whitehill
Brogdale Horticultural Trust
North Street
Sheldwich
Sheldwich Lees
Throwley
Badlesmere
Shottenden
Leaveland
Frith
Otterden Place
Payden Street
Woodside Green
Warren Street
Lenham
Stalisfield Green
Molash
Challock
Charing
Charing Heath
Lenham Heath
Westwell
Westwell Leacon
Egerton
Little Chart
Pluckley
Pluckley Thorne
Hothfield
Ram Lane
Maltman's Hill
Pluckley Sta
Great Chart
Daniel's Water
ASHFORD
Ashford Designer Outlet
Kennington
Kempe's Corner
Boughton Lees
Boughton Aluph
Eastwell Park
Paddock
Godmersham
Bilting
Chilham
Chilham Castle
Old Wives Lees
Selling
Gushmere
Hernhill
Staplestreet
Boughton Street
Dunkirk
Yorkletts
Whitstable
Seasalter
Highstreet
Dargate
Blean Woods NNR
Oversland
Chartham Hatch
Chartham
Shalmsford Street
Garlinge Green
Petham
Crundale
Sole Street
Waltham
Wye
Imperial College at Wye
Hassell Street
Wye NNR
Bodsham
Brook
Hastingleigh
Whatsole Street
Lymbridge Green
West Brabourne
Brabourne
Brabourne Lees
Willesborough Lees
Willesborough
Hinxhill
Sevington
Mersham
Smeeth
Kingsnorth
Cheeseman's Green
Beaver Green
Bull Green
Brisley
Shadoxhurst
Stone Cross
Forstal
Stonestreet Green
Aldington
Sellindge
Stanford
Newington
Postling
Etchinghill
Paddlesworth
Hawkinge
Capel-le-Ferne
Folkestone
Channel Tunnel Terminal
Herne Bay
Reculver
Reculver Country Park
Towers & Roman Fort
Hillborough
Beltinge
Hampton
Swalecliffe
Tankerton
Chestfield
South Street
Clapham Hill
West End
Herne
Hunters Forstal
Broomfield
Highstead
Herne Common
Maypole
Wildwood
Hoath
Calcott
Broadoak
Westbere
Hersden
Tyler Hill
Blean
Rough Common
Hales Place
Sturry
Fordwich
Canterbury Cathedral
CANTERBURY
St Martin's Church
St Augustine's Abbey
Harbledown
Upper Harbledown
Thanington
Nackington
Bridge
Bekesbourne
Patrixbourne
Lower Hardres
Upper Hardres Court
Bishopsbourne
Kingston
Barham
Derringstone
Bossingham
Stelling Minnis
Elham
Elham Valley
Lyminge Forest
Breach
Bladbean
Wingmore
Denton
Wootton
Selstead
Swingfield Minnis
Densole
Acrise Place
Ottinge
Lyminge
Woodland
Rhodes Minnis
Sixmile
Maxted Street
Stowting
Monks Horton
Newbarn
Hermitage
Stone Street
Wickhambreaux
Ickham
Littlebourne
Bramling
Wingham
Wingham Wildlife Park
Wingham Well
Howletts Wild Animal Park
Goodnestone Park
Goodnestone
Adisham
Aylesham
Nonington
Ratling
Chillenden
Knowlton
Easole Street
Womenswold
Woolage Village
Woolage Green
Barfrestone
Eythorne
Lower Eythorne
Elvington
Tilmanstone
Shepherdswell (Sibertswold)
Coldred
Lydden
Lydden Temple Ewell NNR
Temple Ewell
Ewell Minnis
Alkham
St Radigund's Abbey
South Alkham
West Hougham
River
Buckland
Whitfield
DOVER
Dover Castle
De Bradelei Wharf
Women's Land Army Museum
Maxton
Knights Templar Church
Samphire Hoe
Dover - Folkestone Heritage Coast
East Wear Bay
Folkestone to Calais
Channel Tunnel
hours
Calais 1¼–1½
Dunkerque 2
DOVER
South Foreland Heritage Coast
South Foreland
South Foreland Lighthouse (NT)
The Pines
Gateway to the White Cliffs
St Margaret's at Cliffe
St Margaret's Bay
West Cliffe
Guston
East Langdon
Martin Mill Sta
West Langdon
Ashley
East Studdal
Sutton
Ripple
Ringwould
Kingsdown
Walmer
Walmer Castle & Garden
Deal
Deal Castle
Sholden
Great Mongeham
Northbourne
Betteshanger
Finglesham
Hacklinge
Worth
Ham
Eastry
Barnsole
Staple
Shatterling
Marshborough
Woodnesborough
Ash
Sandwich
Salutation Garden
Sandwich Bay
England Coast Path
Toll
Royal St. Georges
Great Stonar
Stonar Cut
Sandwich Flats
Richborough Castle
Roman Amphitheatre
Cop Street
Hoaden
Elmstone
Preston
Westmarsh
Ware
Stodmarsh
Stodmarsh NNR
Grove
East Stourmouth
West Stourmouth
Plucks Gutter
Stour
Upstreet
Roman Road
Chislet
Boyden Gate
St Nicholas at Wade
Sarre
Gore Street
Monkton
Minster
Abbey
ISLE OF THANET
Acol
Manston
Spitfire & Hurricane Memorial
RAF Manston
Quex House & Gdns
Birchington
Westgate on Sea
Westbrook
Salmestone Grange
MARGATE
Tudor House
Cliftonville
Kingsgate
Foreness Point
White Ness
North Foreland
Long Nose Spit
South Channel
Bleak House
Broadstairs
Dickens House Museum
St Peter's
Haine
Northwood
Pegwell
Ramsgate
Cliffs End
St Augustine's Cross
Pegwell Bay
Sandwich & Pegwell Bay NNR
A2
A20
A28
A249
A250
A251
A252
A256
A257
A258
A260
A290
A291
A299
A2990
A2500
M2
M20
A13
A1159
B1018
B1021
B1023
B1026
B2008
B2205
B2231
B2068
B2046
600
610
620
630
640
140
150
160
170
180
190
200
210

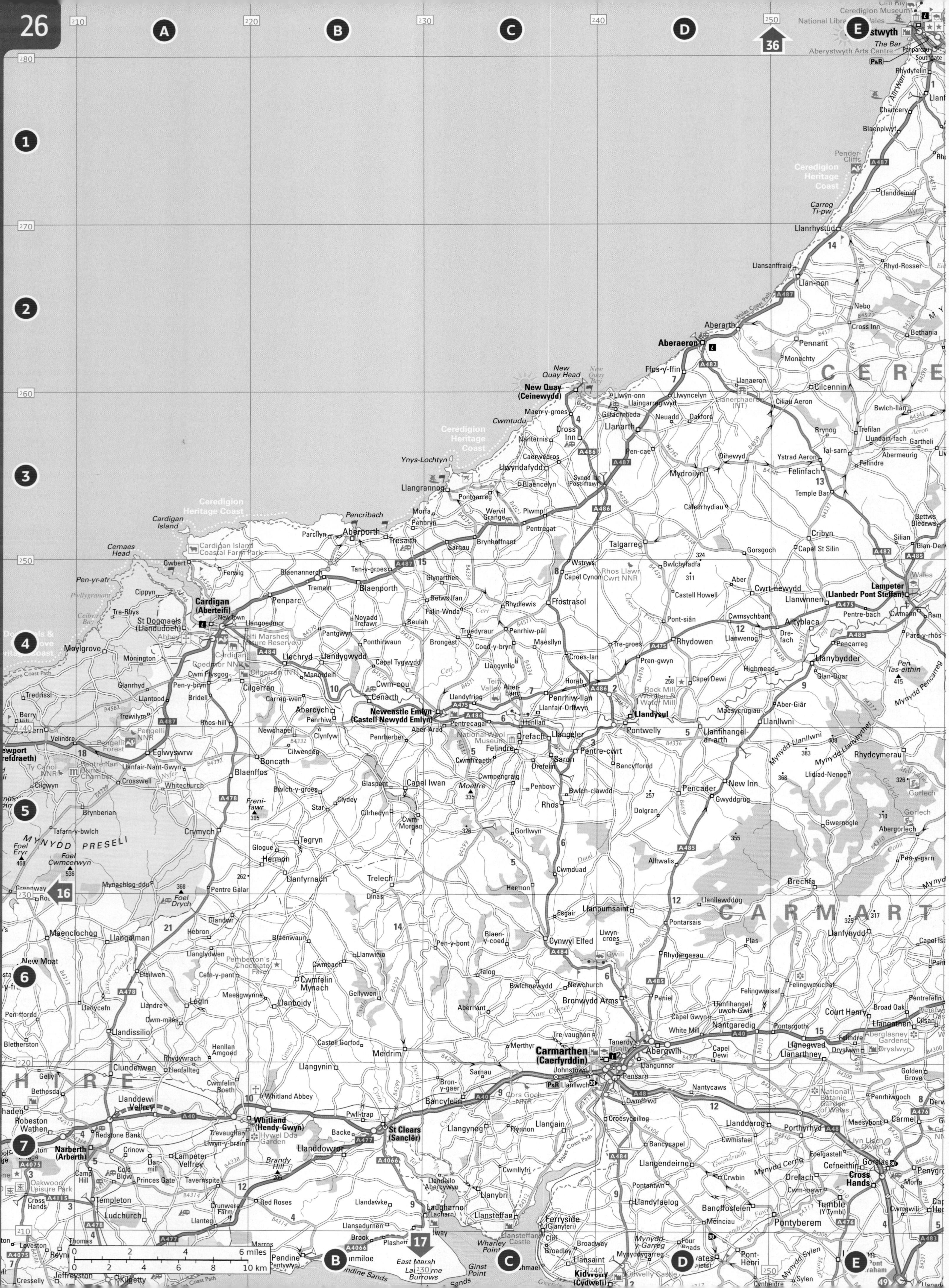
A
B
C
D
E
1
2
3
4
5
6
7
36
16
17
Aberystwyth
Ceredigion Museum
National Library of Wales
The Bar
Aberystwyth Arts Centre
Rhydyfelin
Chancery
Blaenplwyf
Penderi Cliffs
Ceredigion Heritage Coast
Llanddeiniol
Carreg Ti-pw
Llanrhystud
Llansanffraid
Llan-non
Rhyd-Rosser
Nebo
Cross Inn
Bethania
Aberarth
Aberaeron
Pennant
Monachty
CERE
Ffos-y-ffin
Llanerchaeron (NT)
Cilcennin
New Quay Head
New Quay Bay
New Quay (Ceinewydd)
Llwyn-onn
Llaingarreglwyd
Llwyncelyn
Gilfachreda
Maen-y-groes
Neuadd
Oakford
Ciliau Aeron
Bwlch-llan
Cwmtudu
Cross Inn
Llanarth
Trefilan
Nanternis
Pen-cae
Brynog
Llundain-fach
Gartheli
Tal-sarn
Dihewyd
Ystrad Aeron
Abermeurig
Felinfach
Caerwedros
Llwyndafydd
Synod Inn (Post-mawr)
Mydroilyn
Ynys-Lochtyn
Blaencelyn
Temple Bar
Llangrannog
Pontgarreg
Caerdrhydiau
Morfa
Penbryn
Wervil Grange
Plwmp
Pentregat
Bettws Bledrws
Cardigan Island
Pencribach
Aberporth
Parcllyn
Tresaith
Sarnau
Brynhoffnant
Cribyn
Silian
Talgarreg
Gorsgoch
Capel St Silin
Cemaes Head
Cardigan Island Coastal Farm Park
Gwbert
Ferwig
Blaenannerch
Tan-y-groes
Glynarthen
Wstrws
Capel Cynon
Rhos Llawr Cwrt NNR
Bwlchyfadfa
Aber
Cwrt-newydd
Lampeter (Llanbedr Pont Steffan)
Pen-yr-afr
Pwllgranant
Ceibwr Bay
Cippyn
Tremain
Blaenporth
Betws Ifan
Ffostrasol
Castell Howell
Llanwnnen
Tre-Rhys
Cardigan (Aberteifi)
Penparc
Falin-Wnda
Rhydlewis
Pont-siân
Cwmsychbant
Alltyblaca
Pentre-bach
Cwmann
Ram
St Dogmaels (Llandudoch)
New Town
Llangoedmor
Noyadd Trefawr
Pantgwyn
Beulah
Troedyraur
Penrhiw-pâl
Llanwenog
Dre-fach
Pare-y-rhôs
Moylgrove
Abbey
Teifi Marshes Nature Reserve
Ponthirwaun
Brongest
Coed-y-bryn
Maesllyn
Tre-groes
Rhydowen
Pencarreg
Monington
Coedmor NNR
Llechryd
Llandygwydd
Capel Tygwydd
Croes-lan
Pren-gwyn
Llanybydder
Pembrokeshire Coast Path
Cwm Plysgog
Cilgerran (NT)
Manordeifi
Llangynllo
Pen Tas-eithin
Glanrhyd
Pen-y-bryn
Cilgerran
Cwm-cou
Teifi Valley
Horeb
Rock Mill Woollen & Water Mill
Capel Dewi
Highmead
Glan-Duar
Tredrissi
Llantood
Bridell
Carreg-wen
Cenarth
Llandyfriog
Aber-banc
Penrhiw-llan
Llanfair-Orllwyn
Llandysul
Maesycrugiau
Aber-Giâr
Mynydd Pencarreg
Berry Hill
Trewilym
Abercych
Penrhiw
Newcastle Emlyn (Castell Newydd Emlyn)
Pentrecagal
Henllan
Pontwelly
Llanllwni
Rhos-hill
Newchapel
Clynfyw
Aber-Arad
Penrherber
National Wool Museum
Drefach
Llangeler
Llanfihangel-ar-arth
Mynydd Llanllwni
Mynydd Llanybyther
Velindre
Newport (Trefdraeth)
Pengelli Forest
Pengelli NNR
Eglwyswrw
Cilwendeg
Boncath
Felindre
Cwmhiraeth
Saron
Pentre-cwrt
Bancyffordd
Rhydcymerau
Ty Canol NNR
Pentre Ifan Burial Chamber
Llanfair-Nant-Gwyn
Blaenffos
Drefelin
Cwmpengraig
Penboyr
Pencader
New Inn
Llidiad-Nenog
Gorlech
Cilgwyn
Crosswell
Whitechurch
Nyfer
Glaspant
Capel Iwan
Moelfre
Bwlch-clawdd
Gwyddgrug
Bwlch-y-groes
Clydey
Star
Cilrhedyn
Cwm-Morgan
Rhos
Dolgran
Brynberian
Frenni-fawr
Gorllwyn
Gwernogle
Abergorlech
Tafarn-y-bwlch
Crymych
MYNYDD PRESELI
Foel Eryr
Foel Cwmcerwyn
Tegryn
Glogue
Hermon
Cothi
Pen-y-garn
Alltwalis
Brechfa
Greenway
Rosebush
Mynachlog-ddu
Foel Drych
Pentre Galar
Llanfyrnach
Trelech
Dinas
Hermon
Cwmduad
Llanllawddog
Esgair
Llanpumsaint
CARMART
Llanfynydd
Maenclochog
Glandwr
Hebron
Llangolman
Blaenwaun
Pen-y-bont
Blaen-y-coed
Cynwyl Elfed
Llwyn-croes
Pontarsais
Capel Isaac
Plas
Rhydargaeau
Gwili
New Moat
Llanglydwen
Pemberton's Chocolate Farm
Llanwinio
Efailwen
Cefn-y-pant
Cwmbach
Talog
Cwmfelin Mynach
Bwlchnewydd
Newchurch
Felingwmisaf
Felingwmuchaf
Pentrefelin
Llandre
Login
Maesgwynne
Llanboidy
Gellywen
Bronwydd Arms
Peniel
Llanfihangel-uwch-Gwili
Broad Oak
Court Henry
Llangathen
Cilsan
Pen-ffordd
Llanycefn
Cwm-miles
Abernant
Capel Gwyn
Nant Cynnen
Aberglasney Gardens
Llandissilio
Tre-vaughan
White Mill
Nantgaredig
Pontargothi
Felindre
Dryslwyn
Llangadog
Llanarthney
Bletherston
Henllan Amgoed
Castell Gorfod
Meidrim
Merthyr
Carmarthen (Caerfyrddin)
Tanerdy
Trinity
Abergwili
Capel Dewi
Rhydywrach
Llanfallteg
Llangynin
Johnstown
Llangunnor
Clunderwen
Pensarn
Golden Grove
Gelly
Cwmfelin Boeth
Sarnau
Bron-y-gaer
Cwmffrwd
Nantycaws
National Botanic Garden of Wales
Bethesda
Llanddewi Velfrey
Whitland Abbey
Bancyfelin
Cors Goch NNR
Penrhiwgoch
Robeston Wathen
Whitland (Hendy-Gwyn)
Pwll-trap
St Clears (Sanclêr)
Croesyceiliog
Llanddarog
Porthyrhyd
Maesybont
Carmel
Redstone Bank
Trevaughan
Hywel Dda Garden
Backe
Llangynog
Ffynnon
Llangain
Bancycapel
Cwmisfael
Llyn Llech Owain
Narberth (Arberth)
Crinow
Llwyn-y-brain
Llanddowror
Foelgastell
Lampeter Velfrey
Llan-mill
Brandy Hill
Cwmllyfri
Llangendeirne
Mynydd Cerrig
Cefneithin
Gorslas
Cold Blow
Princes Gate
Tavernspite
Llandeilo Abercywyn
Crwbin
Drefach
Cross Hands
Oakwood Leisure Park
Camp Hill
Pontantwn
Cwm-mawr
Cross Hands
Templeton
Red Roses
Llandawke
Llanybri
Llandyfaelog
Tumble (Y Tymbl)
Cwmgwili
Ludchurch
Crunwere Farm
Laugharne (Talacharn)
Llansteffan
Ferryside (Glanyferi)
Bancffosfelen
Pontyberem
Llanteg
Llansadurnen
Llansteffan Castle
Meinciau
Thomas Chapel
Marros
Brook
Plashett
Wharfley Point
Cliff
Broadway
Mynydd-y-Garreg
Four Roads
Pont-Henri
Loveston
Reynalton
Pendine (Pentywyn)
Pendine Sands
East Marsh
Laugharne Burrows
Ginst Point
Broadlay
Llansaint
Mynyddygarreg
Mynydd Sylen
Jeffreyston
Cresselly
Kilgetty
Kidwelly (Cydweli)
Kidwelly Castle
Sylen
Carway
Ponthenri
A487
A482
A485
A486
A475
A484
A478
A40
A477
A4066
A4075
A4115
A48
A476
A4138
0 2 4 6 miles
0 2 4 6 8 10 km

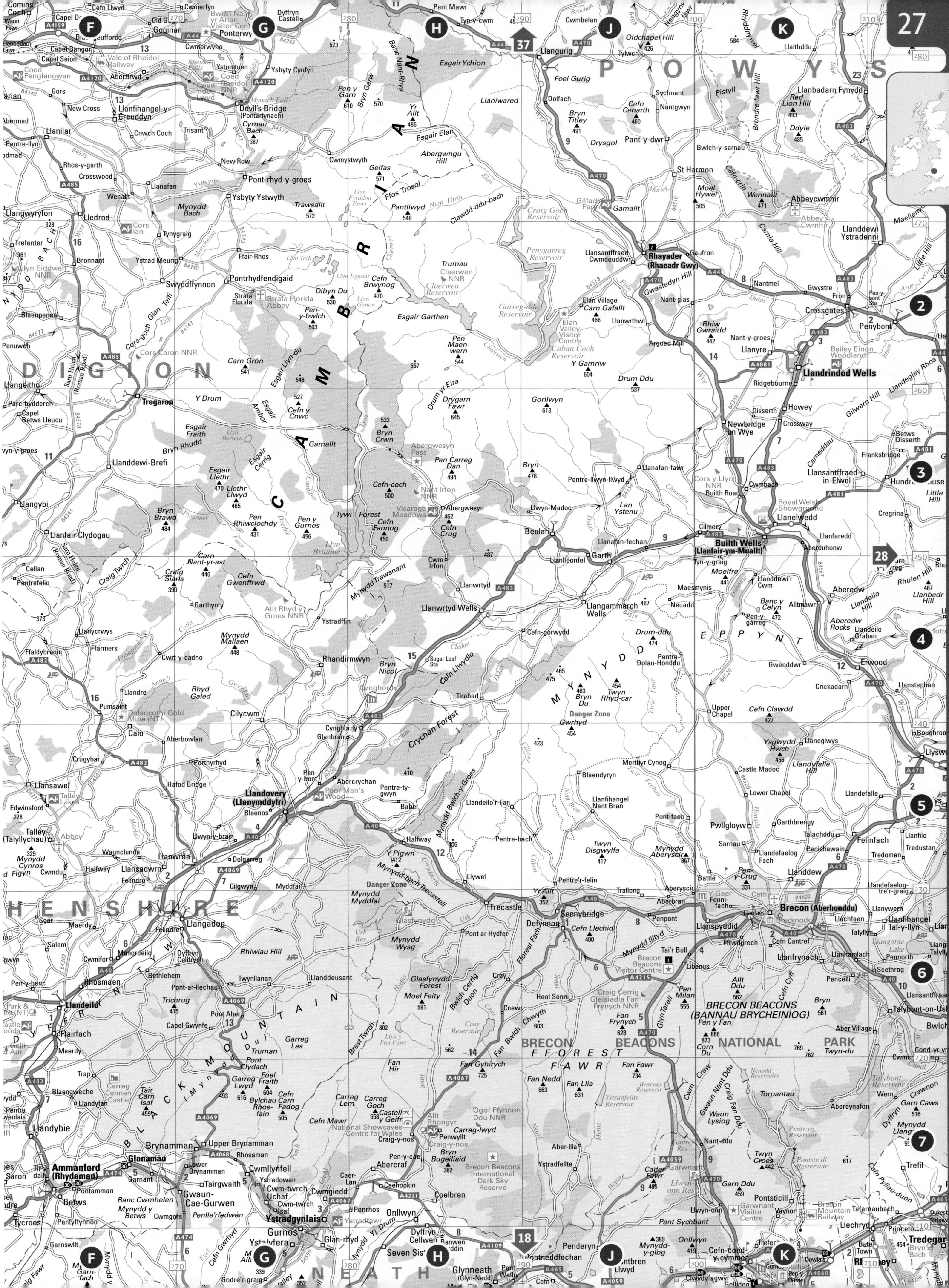

P O W Y S
CAMBRIAN
DIGION
HENSHIRE
MYNYDD EPPYNT
BLACK MOUNTAIN
BRECON BEACONS NATIONAL PARK
BRECON BEACONS (BANNAU BRYCHEINIOG)
FFOREST FAWR
NEATH
37
28
18
Aberystwyth
Capel Bangor
Capel Seion
Vale of Rheidol Railway
Ponterwyd
Goginan
Devil's Bridge (Pontarfynach)
Llanfihangel-y-Creuddyn
Ysbyty Ystwyth
Pont-rhyd-y-groes
Cwmystwyth
Llangurig
Llanidloes
Rhayader (Rhaeadr Gwy)
Elan Valley Visitor Centre
Craig Goch Reservoir
Penygarreg Reservoir
Claerwen Reservoir
Caban Coch Reservoir
Garreg-ddu Reservoir
St Harmon
Abbeycwmhir
Llanbadarn Fynydd
Crossgates
Penybont
Llandrindod Wells
Newbridge on Wye
Howey
Llanelwedd
Royal Welsh Showground
Builth Wells (Llanfair-ym-Muallt)
Garth
Beulah
Abergwesyn
Llanwrtyd Wells
Llangammarch Wells
Tregaron
Pontrhydfendigaid
Strata Florida Abbey
Cors Caron NNR
Llanddewi-Brefi
Lampeter
Llandovery (Llanymddyfri)
Rhandirmwyn
Llyn Brianne
Cilycwm
Pumsaint
Dolaucothi Gold Mine (NT)
Caio
Cynghordy
Halfway
Llanwrda
Llangadog
Llandeilo
Ffairfach
Trecastle
Sennybridge
Defynnog
Brecon (Aberhonddu)
Llanfaes
Libanus
Brecon Beacons Visitor Centre
Talybont-on-Usk
Llangynidr
Pen y Fan
Corn Du
Fan Fawr
Fan Gyhirych
Fan Brycheiniog
Craig-y-nos
Penwyllt
Abercraf
Ystradgynlais
Brynamman
Ammanford (Rhydaman)
Glanaman
Gwaun-Cae-Gurwen
Llandybie
Tycroes
Garnant
Cwmllynfell
Seven Sisters
Glynneath (Glyn-Nedd)
Pontneddfechan
Penderyn
Ystradfellte
Merthyr Tydfil
Pontsticill
Brecon Mountain Railway
Tredegar
Rhymney
Dowlais
Cefn-coed-y-cymmer
Usk Reservoir
Cray Reservoir
Neuadd Reservoirs
Talybont Reservoir
Pentwyn Reservoir
Pontsticill Reservoir
Llwyn-onn Res
Beacons Reservoir
Danger Zone

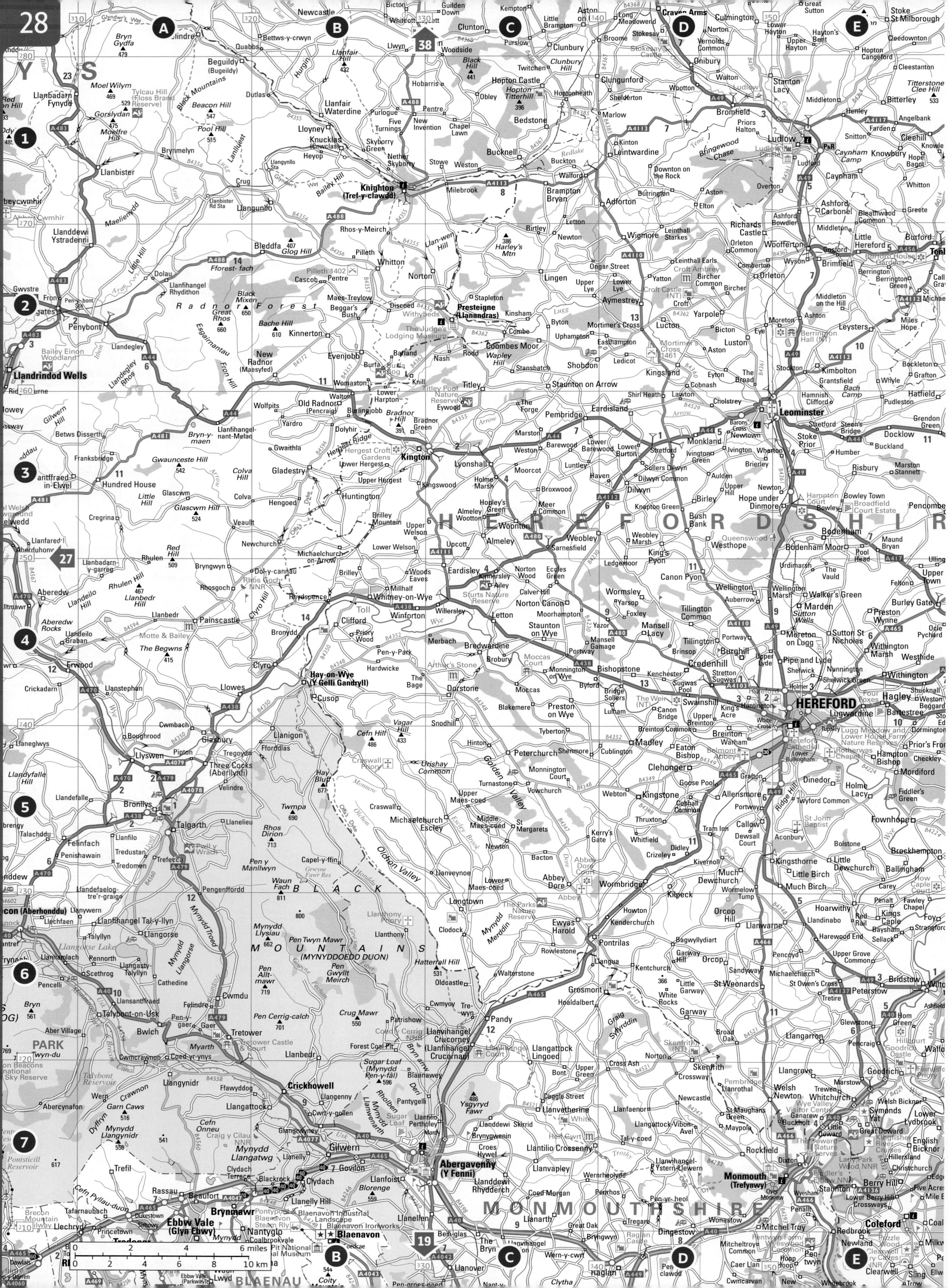

Map page — Herefordshire / Monmouthshire / Powys borders.

Grid references: A B C D E (top and bottom); 1 2 3 4 5 6 7 (sides).

Major places:
Knighton (Tref-y-clawdd), Presteigne (Llanandras), Kington, Leominster, Hereford, Hay-on-Wye (Y Gelli Gandryll), Talgarth, Crickhowell, Abergavenny (Y Fenni), Brynmawr, Ebbw Vale (Glyn Ebwy), Blaenavon, Monmouth (Trefynwy), Craven Arms, Ludlow, Llandrindod Wells, Brecon (Aberhonddu).

Counties: HEREFORDSHIRE, MONMOUTHSHIRE, POWYS.

Features: Radnor Forest, BLACK MOUNTAINS (MYNYDDOEDD DUON), Brecon Beacons National Park, Hatterall Hill, Sugar Loaf (Mynydd Pen-y-fâl), Hergest Ridge, Golden Valley, Llangorse Lake, Talybont Reservoir, Offa's Dyke.

Scale: 0 2 4 6 miles / 0 2 4 6 8 10 km

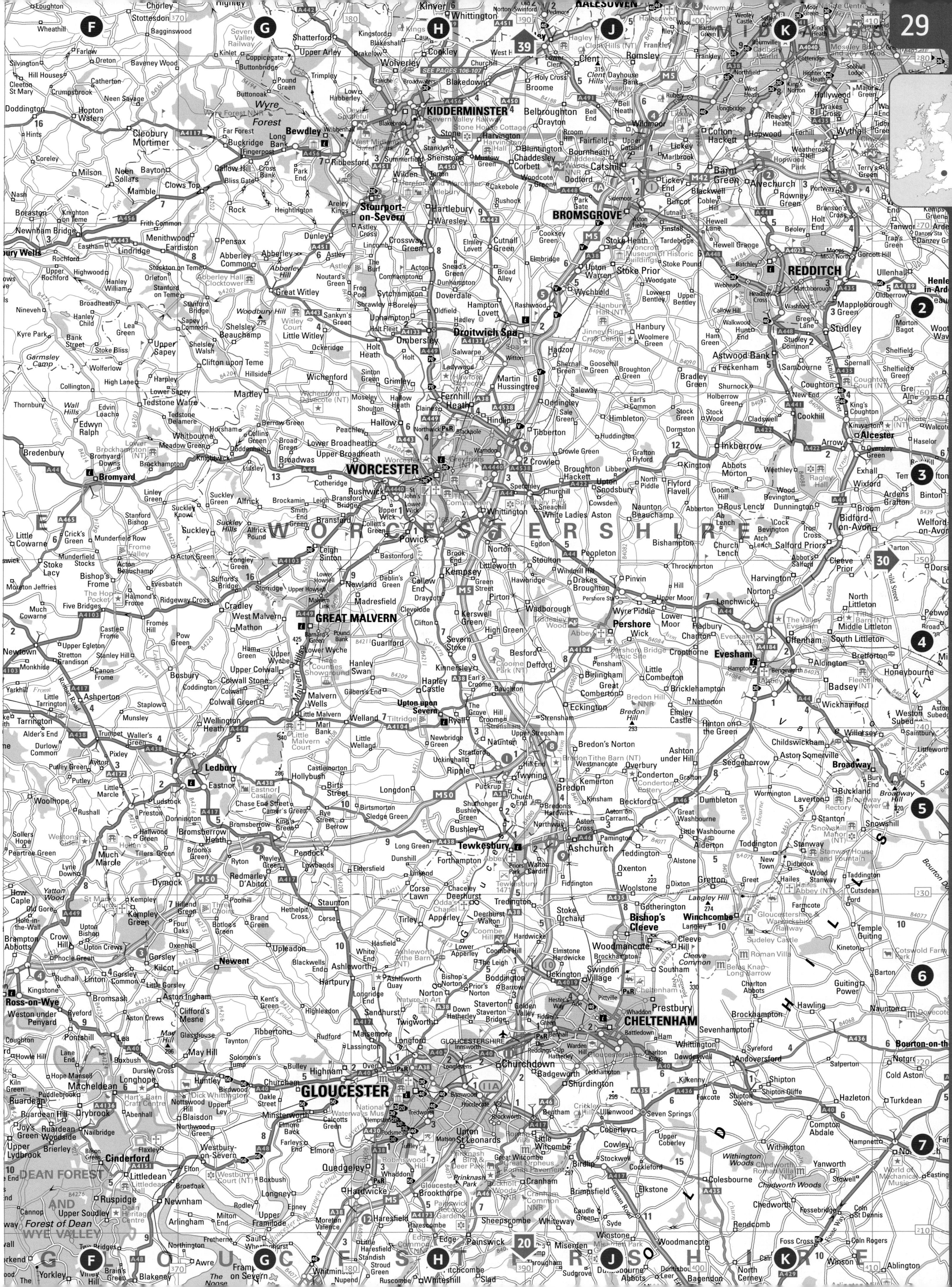

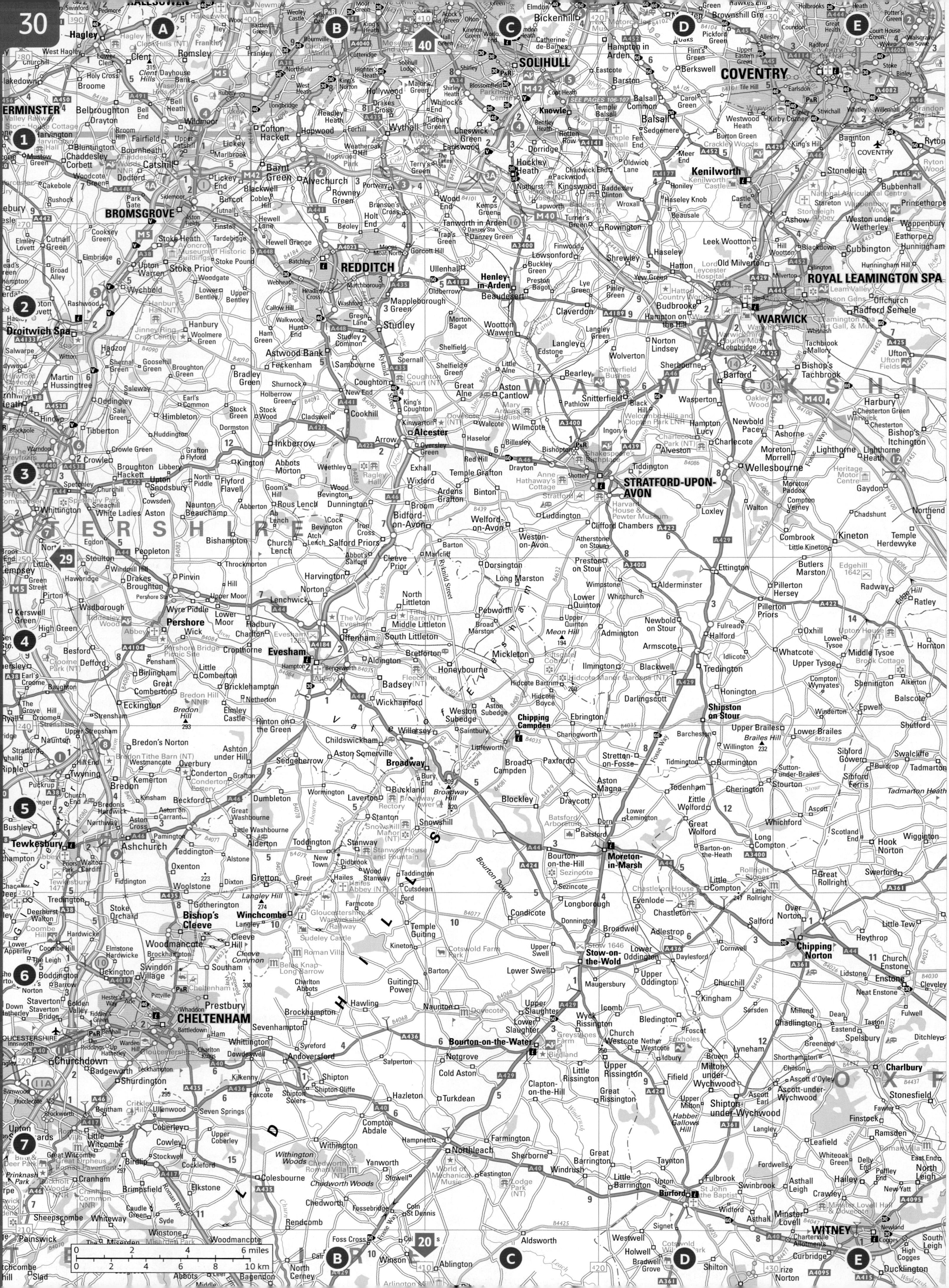

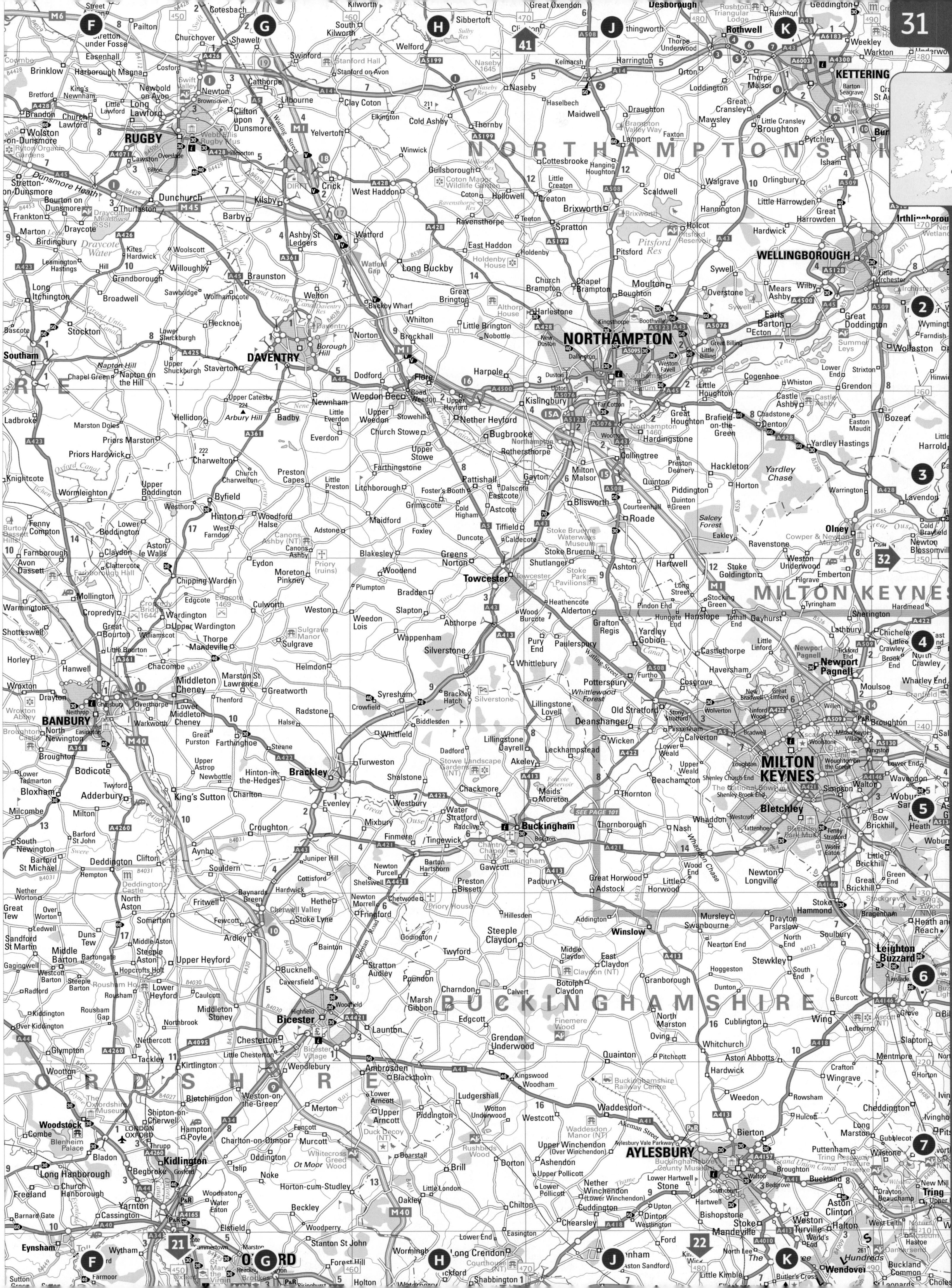

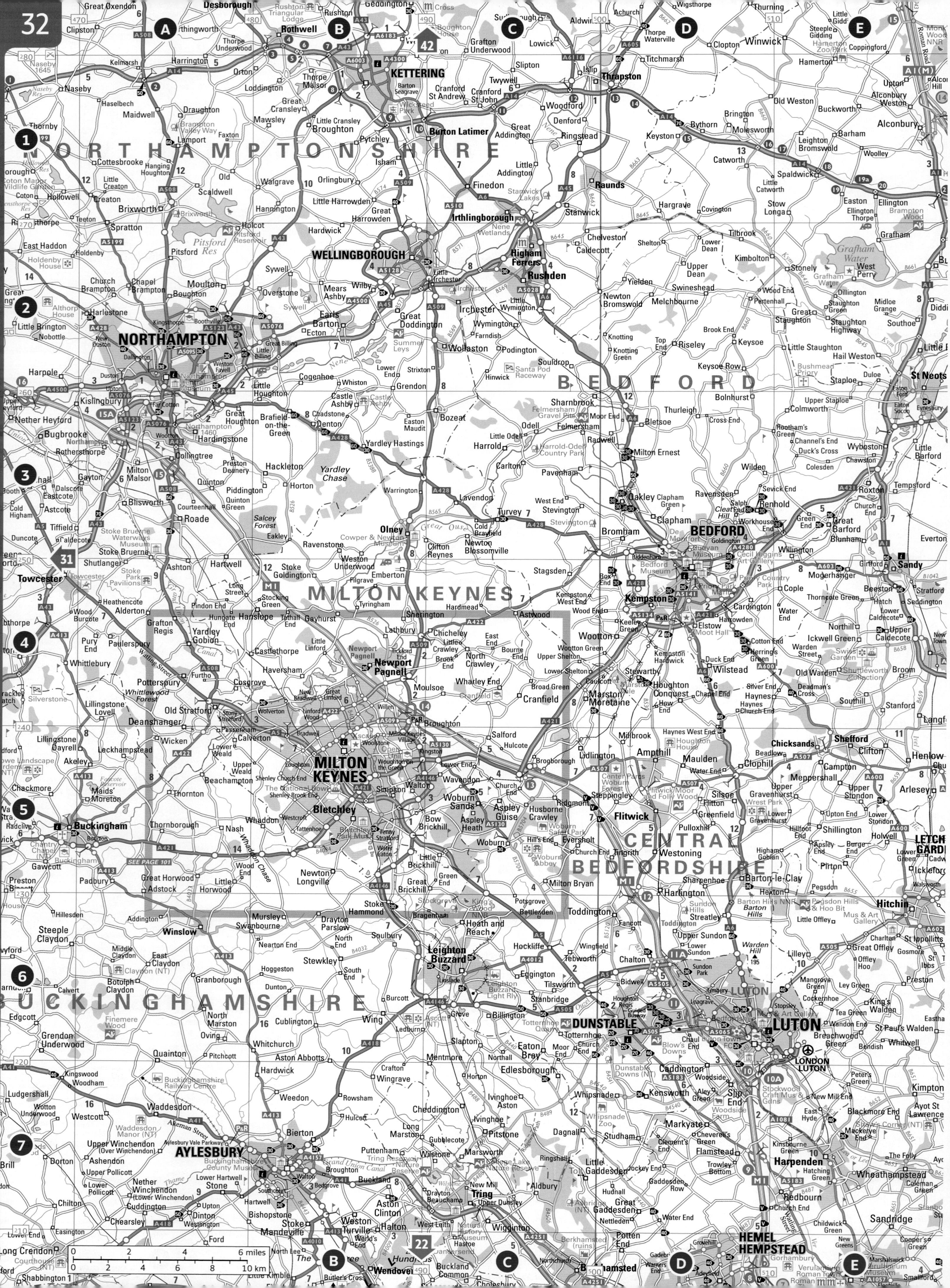

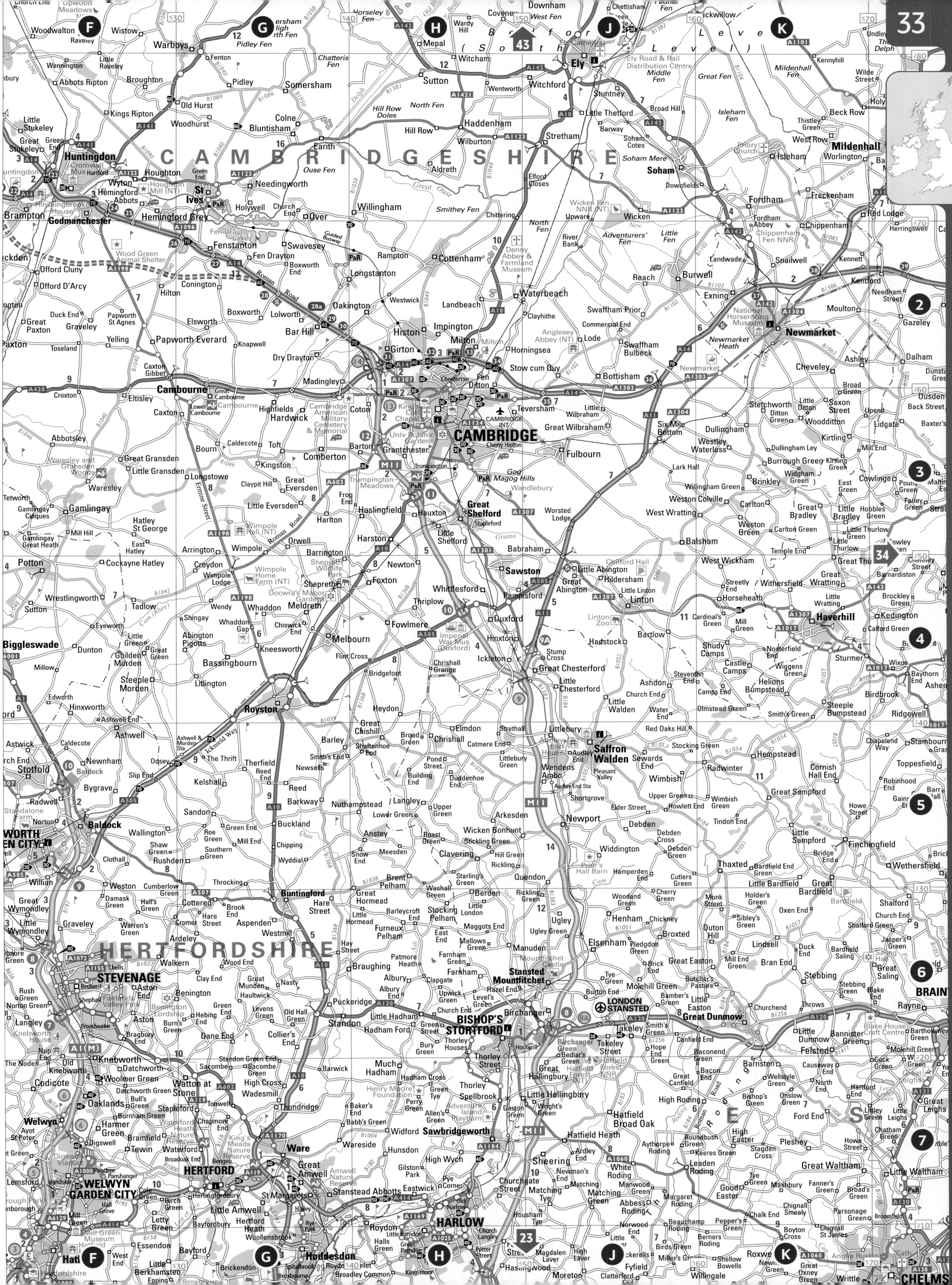
CAMBRIDGESHIRE
HERTFORDSHIRE
CAMBRIDGE
Huntingdon
Godmanchester
St Ives
Ely
Soham
Newmarket
Mildenhall
Haverhill
Royston
Saffron Walden
Baldock
STEVENAGE
HERTFORD
Ware
BISHOP'S STORTFORD
Sawbridgeworth
HARLOW
Hoddesdon
WELWYN GARDEN CITY
Great Dunmow
Thaxted
Cambourne
Sawston
Linton
Buntingford
Stansted Mountfitchet
LONDON STANSTED
Gamlingay
Biggleswade
Warboys
Chatteris Fen
Bedford Level (South Level)
Burwell
Bottisham
Great Shelford
Melbourn
Bassingbourn
Ashwell
Letchworth Garden City
Welwyn
Knebworth
Standon
Puckeridge
Great Chesterford
Newport
Elsenham
Takeley
Hatfield Broad Oak
Sheering
Roxwell
Great Waltham
Felsted
Braintree
Chelmsford
Great Bardfield
Finchingfield
Steeple Bumpstead
Kedington
Papworth Everard
Bar Hill
Histon
Cottenham
Waterbeach
Fulbourn
Milton
Girton
Teversham
Fen Ditton
Impington
Longstanton
Willingham
Over
Somersham
Sutton
Haddenham
Witchford
Stretham
Fordham
Chippenham
Cheveley
Kirtling
West Wratting
Balsham
Great Abington
Hinxton
Duxford
Whittlesford
Ickleton
Fowlmere
Barkway
Barley
Sandon
Walkern
Benington
Much Hadham
Hunsdon
Great Amwell
Stanstead Abbotts
Matching Tye
Good Easter
High Easter
Pleshey
Little Waltham
33
34
43
23

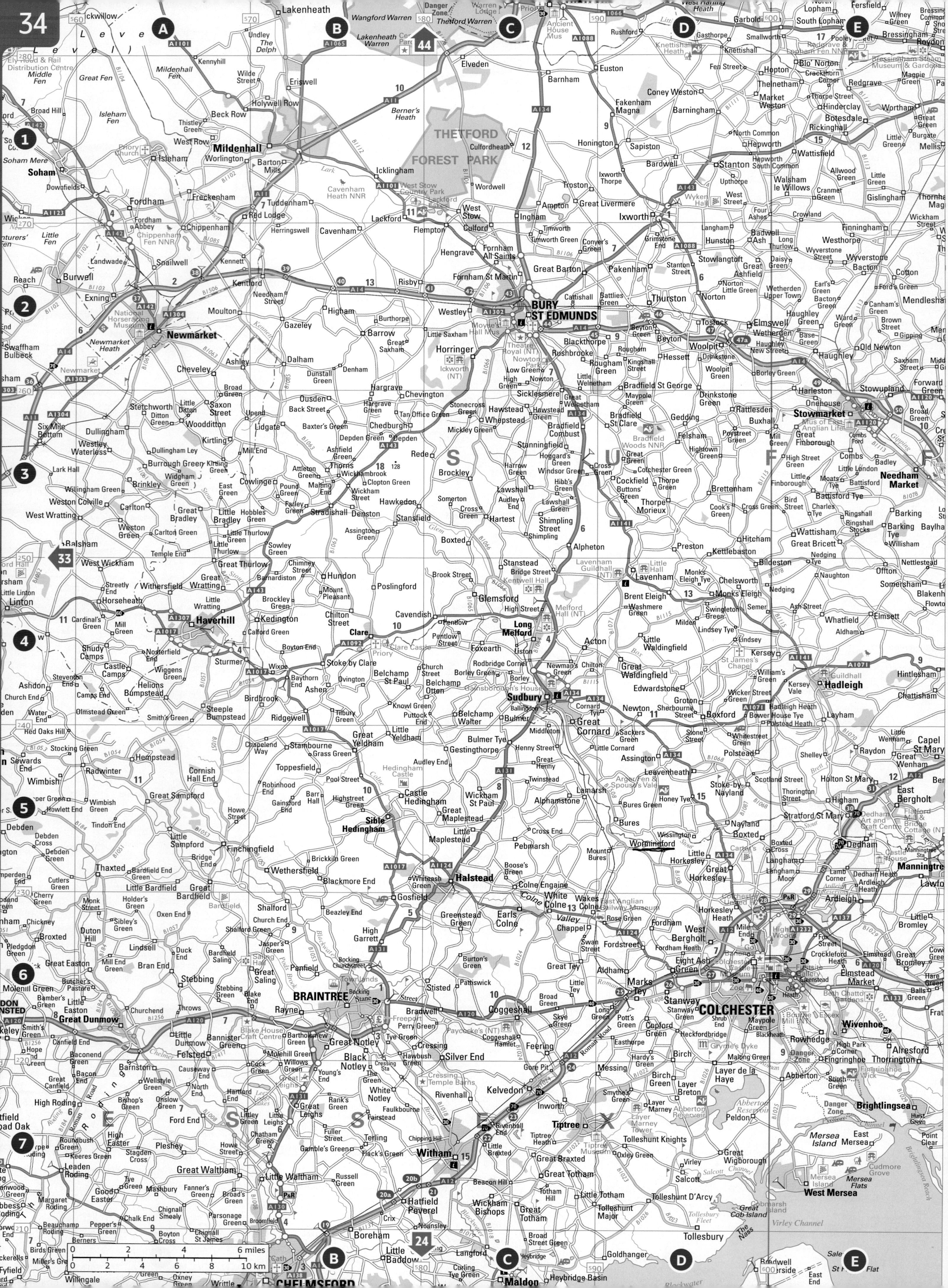
Mildenhall
Soham
Newmarket
BURY ST EDMUNDS
THETFORD FOREST PARK
Haverhill
Long Melford
Sudbury
Hadleigh
Stowmarket
Needham Market
Clare
Sible Hedingham
Halstead
BRAINTREE
Great Dunmow
COLCHESTER
Coggeshall
Witham
Tiptree
Maldon
CHELMSFORD
Wivenhoe
Brightlingsea
West Mersea
Mersea Island
Dedham
Manningtree
Lavenham
Ixworth
Botesdale
Lakenheath
Elveden
Thurston
Woolpit
Kelvedon
Hatfield Peverel
Tollesbury
S U F F
E S S E X
33
44
24
0 2 4 6 miles
0 2 4 6 8 10 km

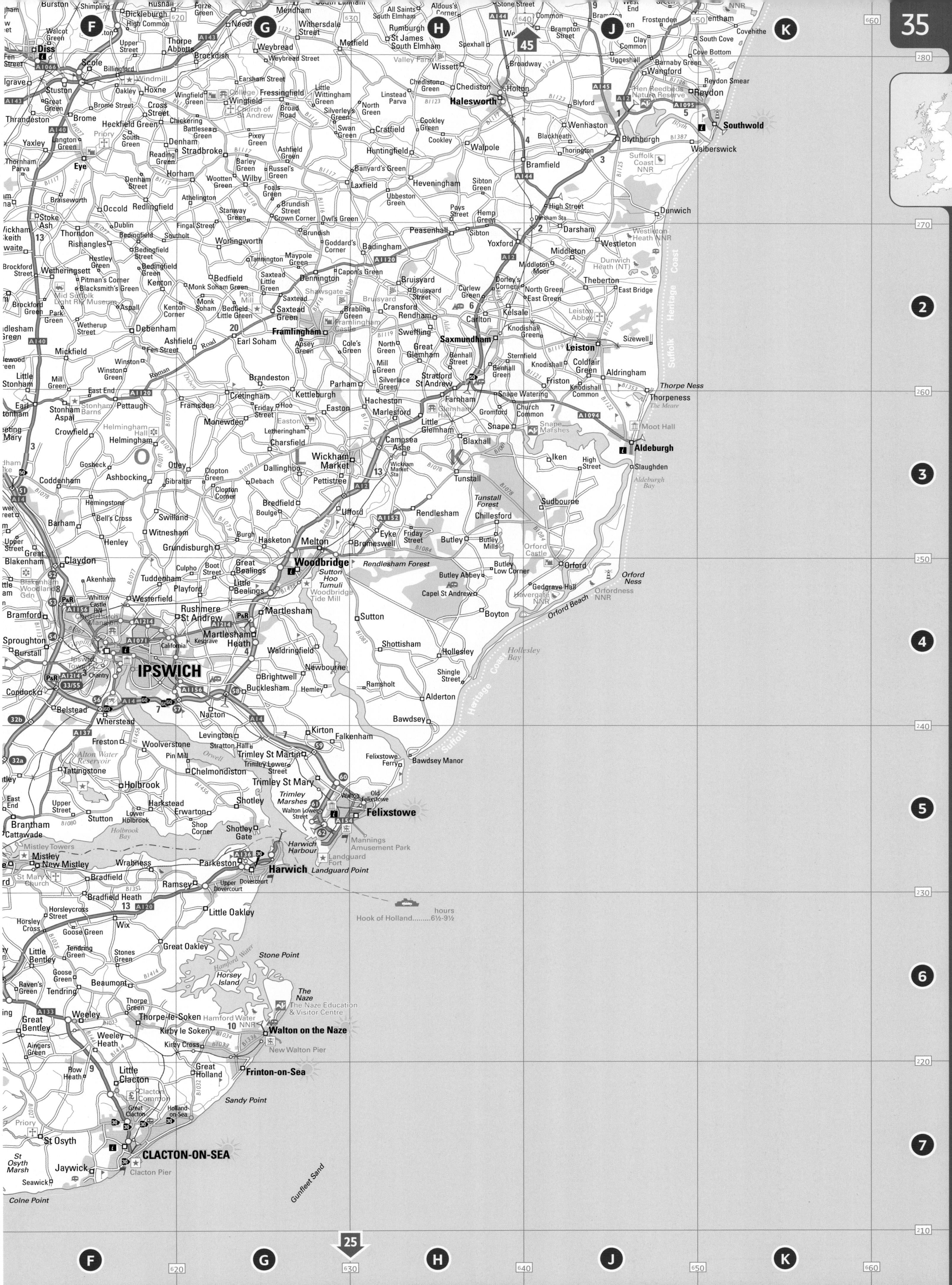
F
G
H
J
K
2
3
4
5
6
7
45
25
620
630
640
650
660
280
270
260
250
240
230
220
210
Diss
Scole
Hoxne
Eye
Brome
Yaxley
Stradbroke
Wilby
Horham
Denham
Occold
Redlingfield
Thorndon
Rishangles
Bedingfield
Worlingworth
Kenton
Debenham
Mickfield
Stonham Aspal
Pettaugh
Crowfield
Helmingham
Coddenham
Ashbocking
Otley
Framsden
Monewden
Cretingham
Brandeston
Kettleburgh
Earl Soham
Saxtead
Framlingham
Dennington
Badingham
Laxfield
Weybread
Mendham
Metfield
Withersdale Street
St James South Elmham
Rumburgh
Wissett
Halesworth
Holton
Chediston
Walpole
Huntingfield
Heveningham
Cratfield
Ubbeston Green
Peasenhall
Sibton
Yoxford
Bramfield
Blythburgh
Wenhaston
Thorington
Wangford
Reydon
Southwold
Walberswick
Dunwich
Darsham
Westleton
Middleton
Theberton
Eastbridge
Leiston
Sizewell
Aldringham
Knodishall
Friston
Thorpeness
Aldeburgh
Snape
Saxmundham
Kelsale
Carlton
Benhall Street
Stratford St Andrew
Farnham
Great Glemham
Little Glemham
Parham
Hacheston
Marlesford
Campsea Ashe
Wickham Market
Blaxhall
Tunstall
Iken
Sudbourne
Chillesford
Orford
Orford Ness
Orford Beach
Butley
Eyke
Rendlesham
Ufford
Melton
Woodbridge
Rendlesham Forest
Sutton Hoo Tumuli
Sutton
Shottisham
Hollesley
Hollesley Bay
Shingle Street
Alderton
Bawdsey
Bawdsey Manor
Ramsholt
Boyton
Martlesham
Martlesham Heath
Rushmere St Andrew
Kesgrave
IPSWICH
Claydon
Bramford
Sproughton
Copdock
Belstead
Wherstead
Freston
Woolverstone
Holbrook
Tattingstone
Chelmondiston
Shotley
Shotley Gate
Nacton
Levington
Kirton
Falkenham
Trimley St Martin
Trimley St Mary
Felixstowe
Landguard Point
Harwich
Dovercourt
Parkeston
Wrabness
Mistley
Manningtree
Bradfield
Ramsey
Little Oakley
Great Oakley
Wix
Beaumont
Thorpe-le-Soken
Kirby le Soken
Walton on the Naze
The Naze
Frinton-on-Sea
Great Holland
Weeley
Little Clacton
Great Clacton
St Osyth
Jaywick
CLACTON-ON-SEA
Clacton Pier
Colne Point
Gunfleet Sand
Sandy Point
Stone Point
Hamford Water
Horsey Island
Holbrook Bay
Alton Water Reservoir
Hook of Holland........6½-9½ hours
Suffolk Heritage Coast
Suffolk Coast NNR
Orfordness NNR
Havergate NNR
Tunstall Forest
Minsmere
Dunwich Heath (NT)
Westleton Heath NNR
Hen Reedbeds Nature Reserve
The Naze Education & Visitor Centre
New Walton Pier
Mannings Amusement Park
Landguard Fort
Moot Hall
A12
A14
A140
A143
A144
A145
A1120
A1094
A1152
A1156
A1214
A137
A120
A133
A136
A1095
A1071
A1066

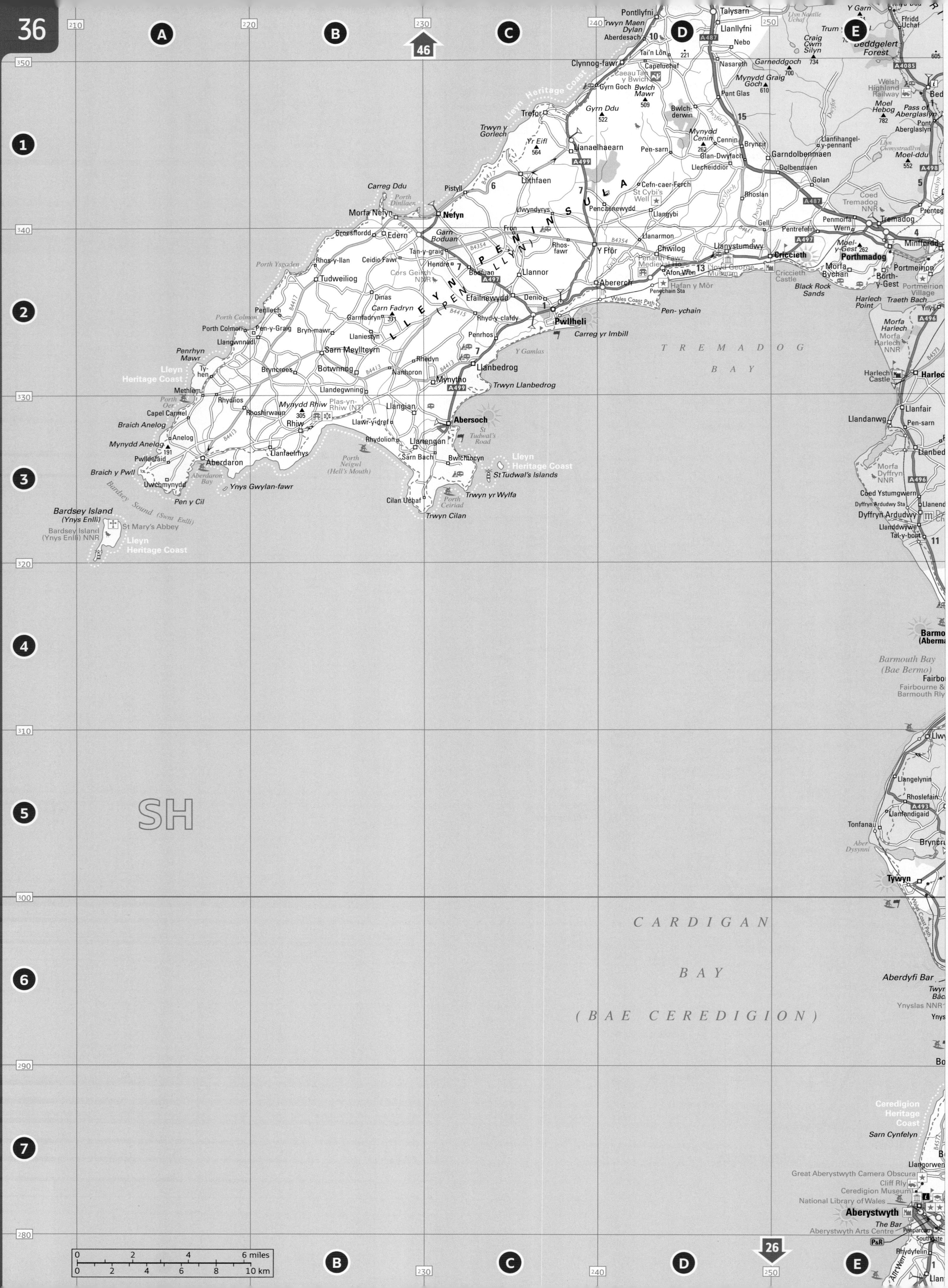

A
B
C
D
E
46
26
1
2
3
4
5
6
7
SH
LLEYN PENINSULA
(PEN LLŶN)
TREMADOG
BAY
CARDIGAN
BAY
(BAE CEREDIGION)
Pontllyfni
Talysarn
Trwyn Maen Dylan
Aberdesach
Llanllyfni
Nebo
Clynnog-fawr
Tai'n Lôn
Capeluchaf
Nasareth
Garneddgoch
Beddgelert Forest
Craig Cwm Silyn
Mynydd Graig Goch
Pant Glas
Gyrn Goch
Bwlch Mawr
Gyrn Ddu
Bwlch-derwin
Welsh Highland Railway
Moel Hebog
Pass of Aberglaslyn
Aberglaslyn
Trefor
Lleyn Heritage Coast
Trwyn y Gorlech
Yr Eifl
Llanaelhaearn
Pen-sarn
Mynydd Cenin
Cennin
Bryncir
Garndolbenmaen
Dolbenmaen
Glan-Dwyfach
Llecheiddior
Llanfihangel-y-pennant
Moel-ddu
Golan
Llithfaen
Pistyll
Carreg Ddu
Porth Dinllaen
Morfa Nefyn
Nefyn
Cefn-caer-Ferch
St Cybi's Well
Pencaenewydd
Llangybi
Llwyndyrys
Rhoslan
Coed Tremadog NNR
Prenteg
Tremadog
Penmorfa
Wern
Gell
Pentrefelin
Minffordd
Porthmadog
Moel-y-Gest
Garn Boduan
Groesffordd
Edern
Fron
Rhos-fawr
Y Ffôr
Llanarmon
Chwilog
Llanystumdwy
Criccieth
Criccieth Castle
Porth Ysgaden
Rhos-y-llan
Ceidio Fawr
Tan-y-graig
Hendre
Boduan
Cors Geirch NNR
Llannor
Penarth Fawr Medieval Ho
Afon Wen
Lloyd George Museum
Hafan y Môr
Penychain Sta
Morfa Bychan
Borth-y-Gest
Portmeirion
Portmeirion Village
Black Rock Sands
Harlech Point
Traeth Bach
Tudweiliog
Dinas
Carn Fadryn
Garnfadryn
Efailnewydd
Denio
Abererch
Wales Coast Path
Pen-ychain
Pwllheli
Carreg yr Imbill
Penllech
Porth Colmon
Pen-y-Graig
Bryn-mawr
Llaniestyn
Rhyd-y-clafdy
Penrhos
Morfa Harlech
Morfa Harlech NNR
Penrhyn Mawr
Llangwnnadl
Sarn Meyllteyrn
Y Gamlas
Ty-hen
Bryncroes
Botwnnog
Rhedyn
Nanhoron
Mynytho
Llanbedrog
Trwyn Llanbedrog
Harlech Castle
Harlech
Methlem
Porth Oer
Capel Carmel
Rhydlios
Llandegwning
Mynydd Rhiw
Plas-yn-Rhiw (NT)
Llangian
Rhoshirwaun
Rhiw
Llawr-y-dref
Abersoch
Llanfair
Llandanwg
Pen-sarn
Braich Anelog
Anelog
Mynydd Anelog
Rhydolion
Llanengan
St Tudwal's Road
Llanbedr
Pwlldefaid
Aberdaron
Llanfaelrhys
Sarn Bach
Bwlchtocyn
Lleyn Heritage Coast
St Tudwal's Islands
Porth Neigwl (Hell's Mouth)
Braich y Pwll
Aberdaron Bay
Uwchmynydd
Ynys Gwylan-fawr
Morfa Dyffryn NNR
Trwyn yr Wylfa
Coed Ystumgwern
Pen y Cil
Bardsey Sound (Swnt Enlli)
Cilan Uchaf
Porth Ceiriad
Trwyn Cilan
Dyffryn Ardudwy
Bardsey Island (Ynys Enlli)
St Mary's Abbey
Bardsey Island (Ynys Enlli) NNR
Llanddwywe
Tal-y-bont
Barmo (Aberma
Barmouth Bay (Bae Bermo)
Fairbourne & Barmouth Rly
Llangelynin
Rhoslefain
Llanfendigaid
Tonfanau
Aber Dysynni
Bryncru
Tywyn
Aberdyfi Bar
Ynyslas NNR
Ceredigion Heritage Coast
Sarn Cynfelyn
Llangorwen
Great Aberystwyth Camera Obscura
Cliff Rly
Ceredigion Museum
National Library of Wales
Aberystwyth
The Bar
Aberystwyth Arts Centre
Penparcau
Southgate
Rhydyfelin
A487
A499
A497
A4085
A498
A496
A493
B4354
B4417
B4413
B4415
B4411
0 2 4 6 miles
0 2 4 6 8 10 km

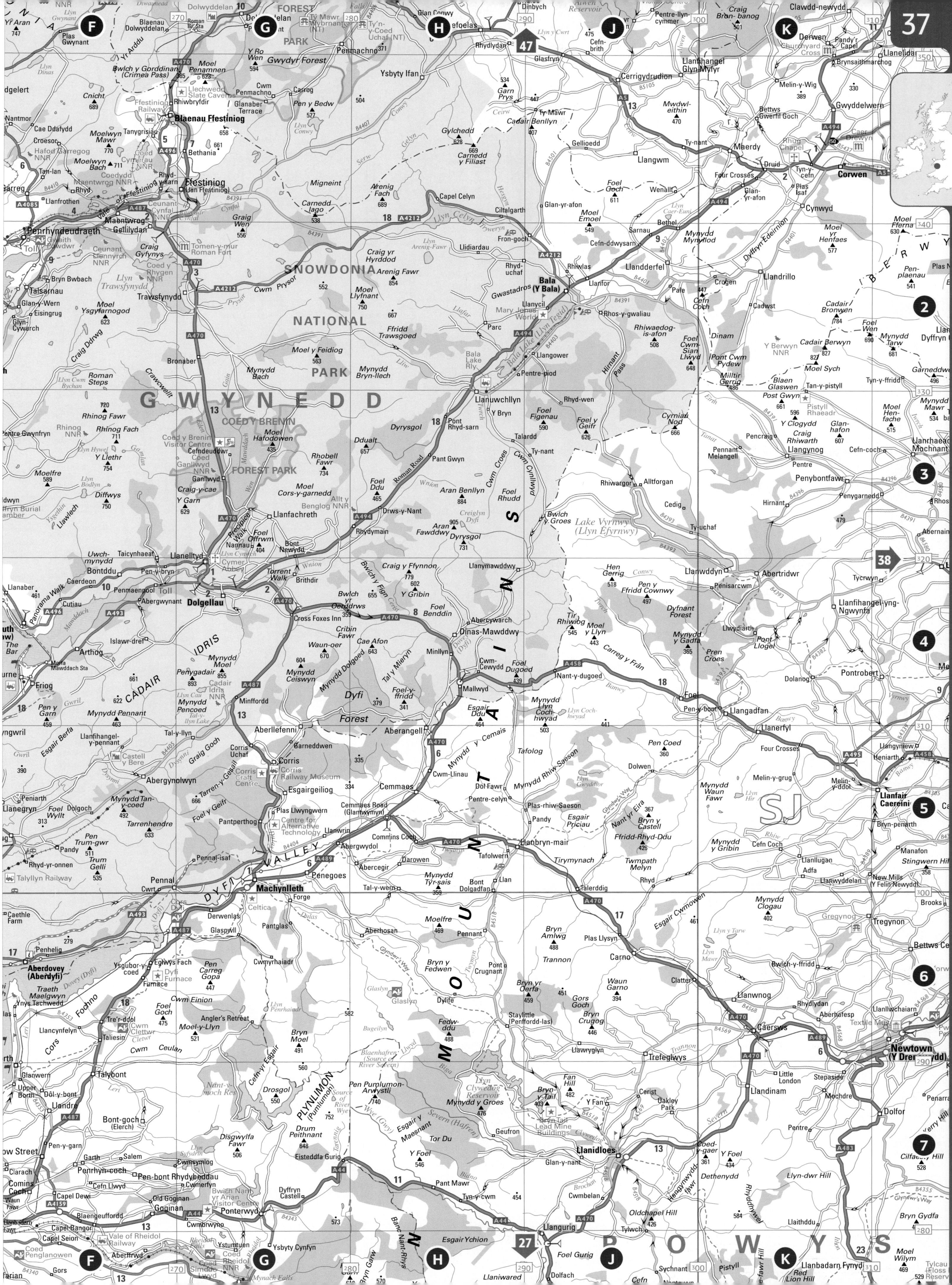

F
G
H
J
K
2
3
4
5
6
7
38
47
27
SNOWDONIA
NATIONAL
PARK
GWYNEDD
COED Y BRENIN
FOREST PARK
CADAIR
IDRIS
Dyfi
Forest
MOUNTAINS
PLYNLIMON (Pumlumon)
POWYS
SJ
BERWYN
Blaenau Ffestiniog
Ffestiniog
Penrhyndeudraeth
Maentwrog
Trawsfynydd
Talsarnau
Harlech
Dolgellau
Llanelltyd
Bontddu
Barmouth
Arthog
Friog
Tywyn
Abergynolwyn
Corris
Aberllefenni
Machynlleth
Pennal
Aberdovey (Aberdyfi)
Talybont
Bow Street
Ponterwyd
Goginan
Capel Bangor
Ysbyty Ifan
Penmachno
Dolwyddelan
Pentrefoelas
Cerrigydrudion
Corwen
Maerdy
Druid
Cynwyd
Llandrillo
Bala (Y Bala)
Bala Lake (Llyn Tegid)
Llanuwchllyn
Llangower
Rhos-y-gwaliau
Llandderfel
Sarnau
Frongoch
Capel Celyn
Llyn Celyn
Llangynog
Penybontfawr
Llanrhaeadr-ym-Mochnant
Lake Vyrnwy (Llyn Efyrnwy)
Llanwddyn
Abertridwr
Llanfihangel-yng-Ngwynfa
Pontrobert
Dolanog
Llangadfan
Llanerfyl
Llanfair Caereinion
Dinas-Mawddwy
Mallwyd
Cemmaes
Cemmaes Road (Glantwymyn)
Llanbrynmair
Talerddig
Carno
Clatter
Llanwnog
Caersws
Newtown (Y Drenewydd)
Llandinam
Trefeglwys
Llanidloes
Llangurig
Staylittle (Penffordd-las)
Dylife
Tregynon
Bettws Cedewain
Dolfor
Tan-y-pistyll
Pistyll Rhaeadr
Cwm Cynllwyd
Bwlch y Groes
Cross Foxes Inn
Minffordd
Tal-y-llyn
Corris Railway Museum
Centre for Alternative Technology
Talyllyn Railway
Vale of Rheidol Railway
Devil's Bridge
Clywedog Reservoir
Bryn Tail Lead Mine Buildings
Eisteddfa Gurig
Blaenhafren (Source of River Severn)
Dyfi Furnace
Cymer Abbey
Llechwedd Slate Caverns
Tomen-y-mur Roman Fort
Arenig Fawr
Aran Fawddwy
Aran Benllyn
Cadair Berwyn
Moel Sych
Pen Pumlumon Arwystli
A5
A470
A487
A493
A494
A496
A4212
A458
A495
A489
A44
A4159
A483

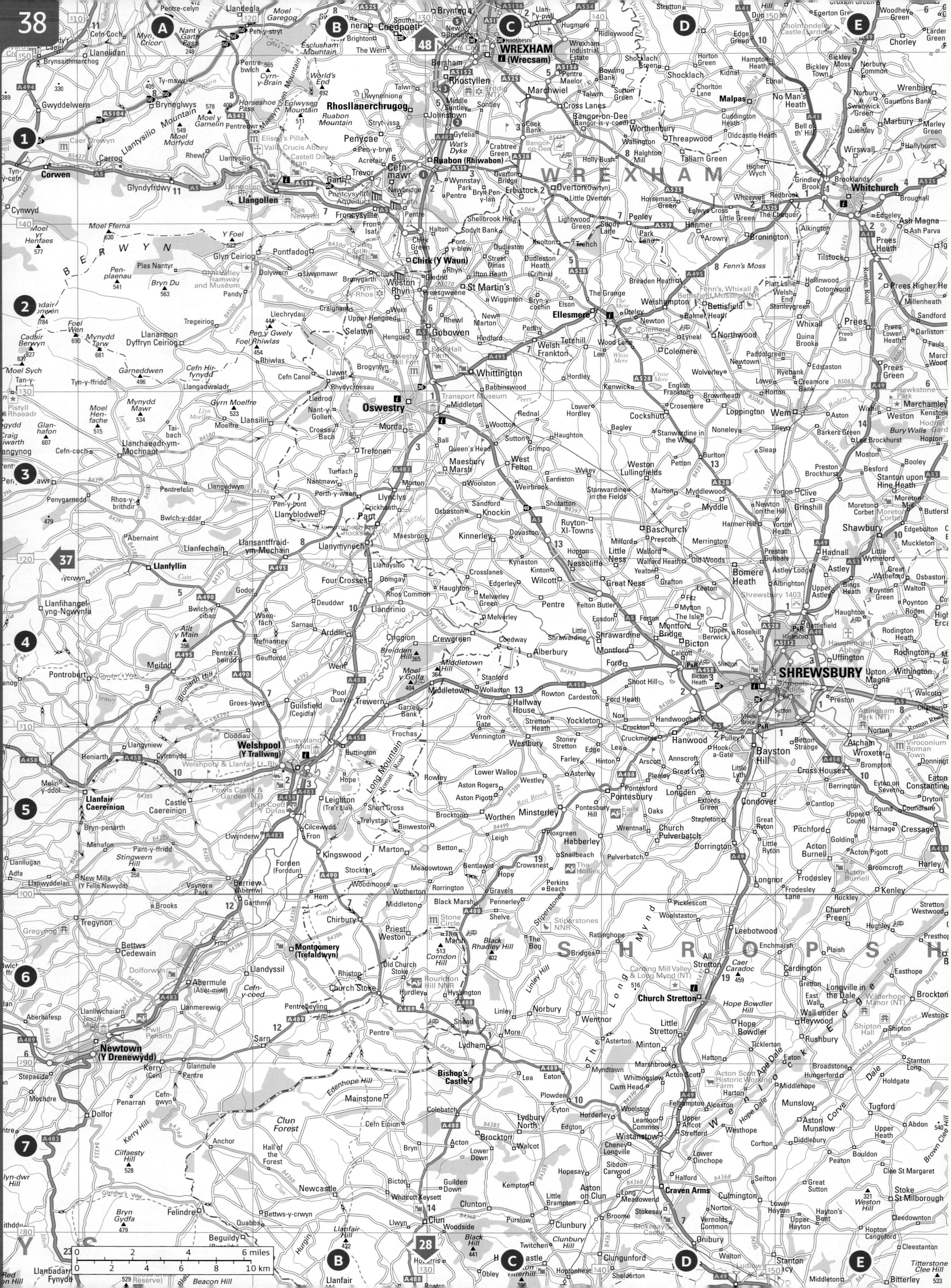
A
B
C
D
E
1
2
3
4
5
6
7
48
37
28
WREXHAM
WREXHAM (Wrecsam)
Rhosllanerchrugog
Ruabon (Rhiwabon)
Llangollen
Corwen
Chirk (Y Waun)
Oswestry
Ellesmere
Whitchurch
Whittington
Gobowen
St Martin's
Overton
Bangor-on-Dee
Malpas
Wem
Prees
Shawbury
BERWYN
Llanfyllin
Welshpool (Y Trallwng)
Llanfair Caereinion
Montgomery (Trefaldwyn)
Newtown (Y Drenewydd)
SHREWSBURY
Pontesbury
Minsterley
Church Stretton
Bishop's Castle
Craven Arms
Clun
Clun Forest
Long Mountain
SHROPSHIRE
Wenlock Edge
The Long Mynd
0 2 4 6 miles
0 2 4 6 8 10 km

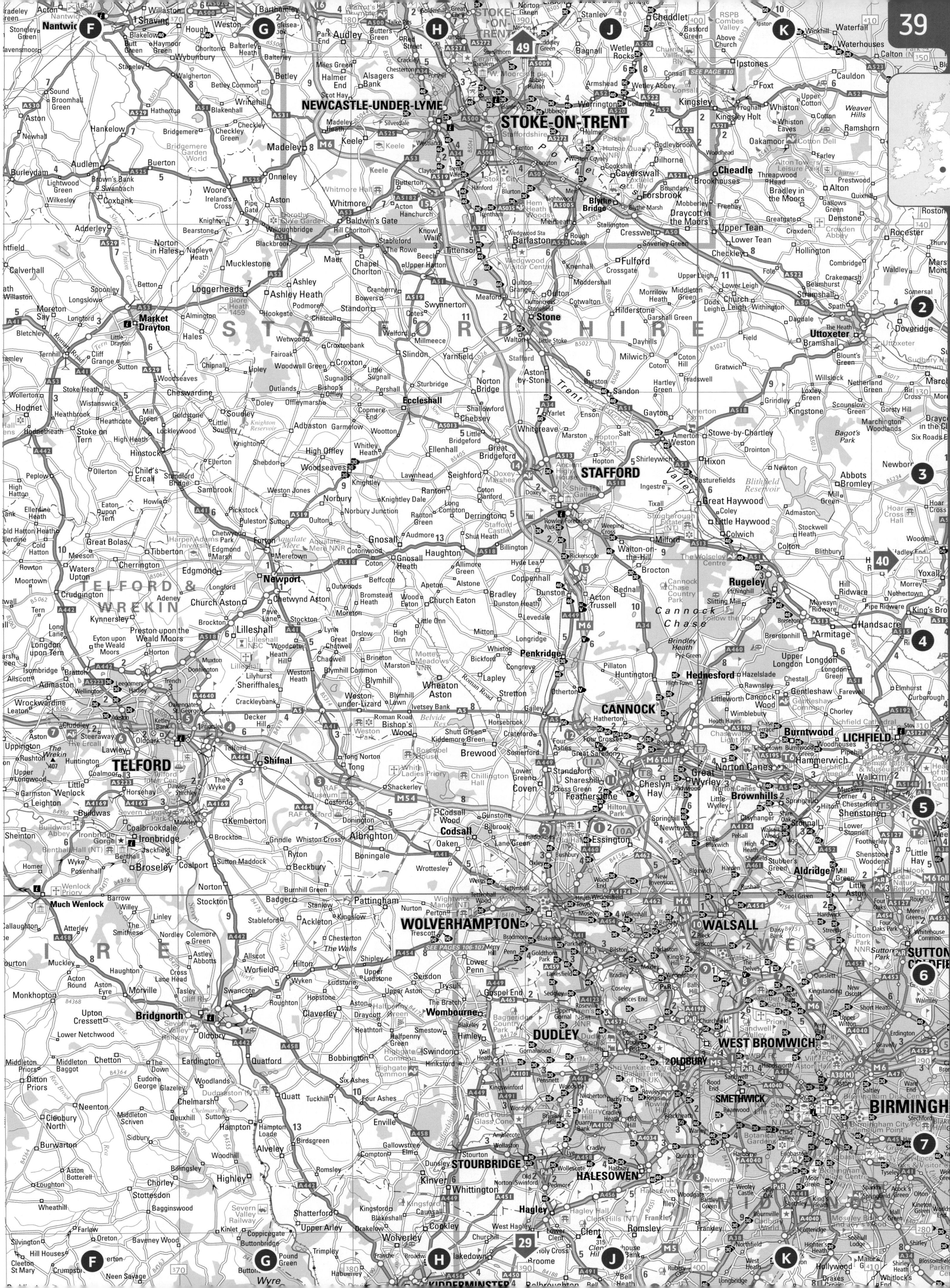

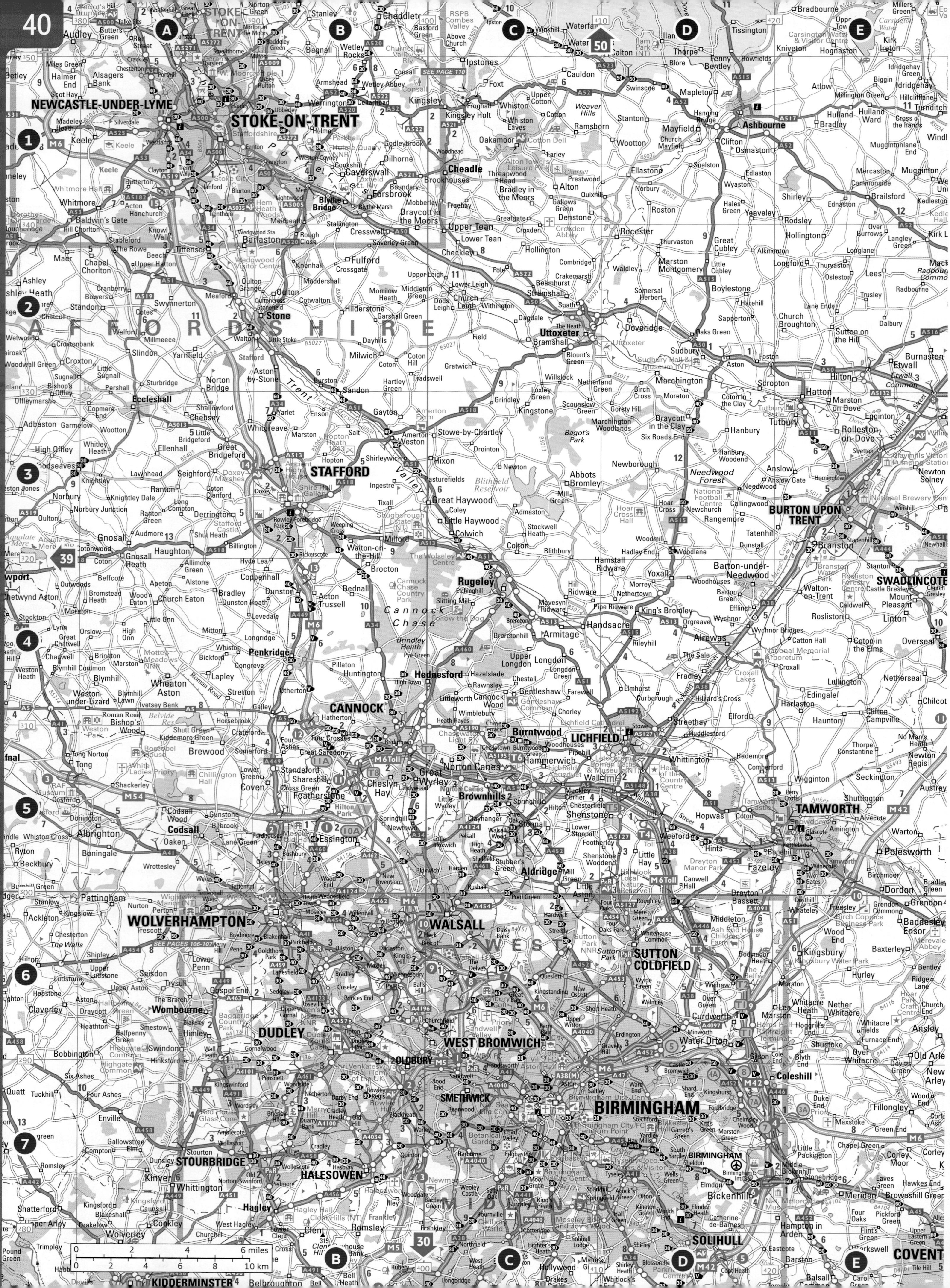

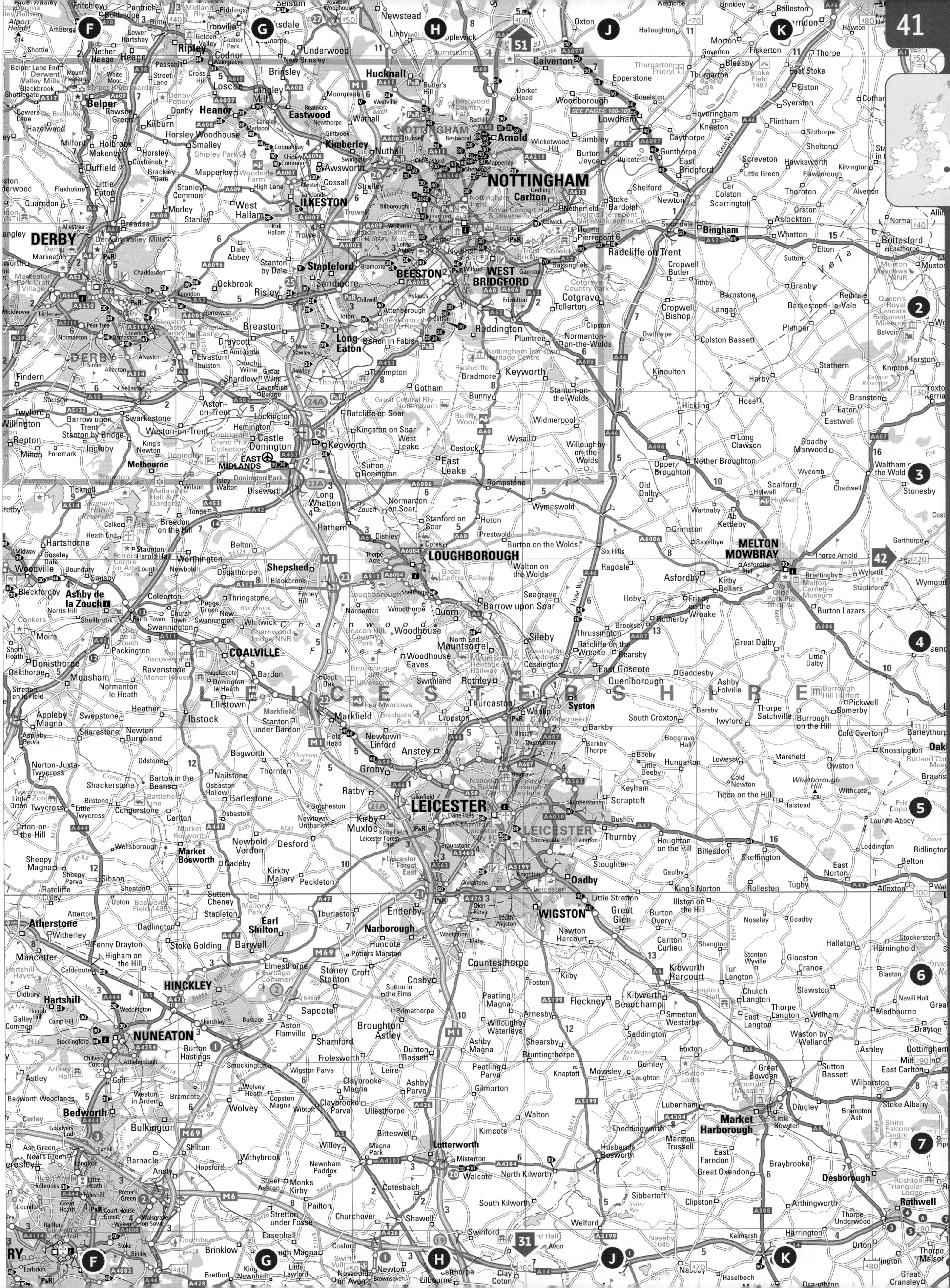

For a more detailed map of Derby & Nottingham see pages 108-109

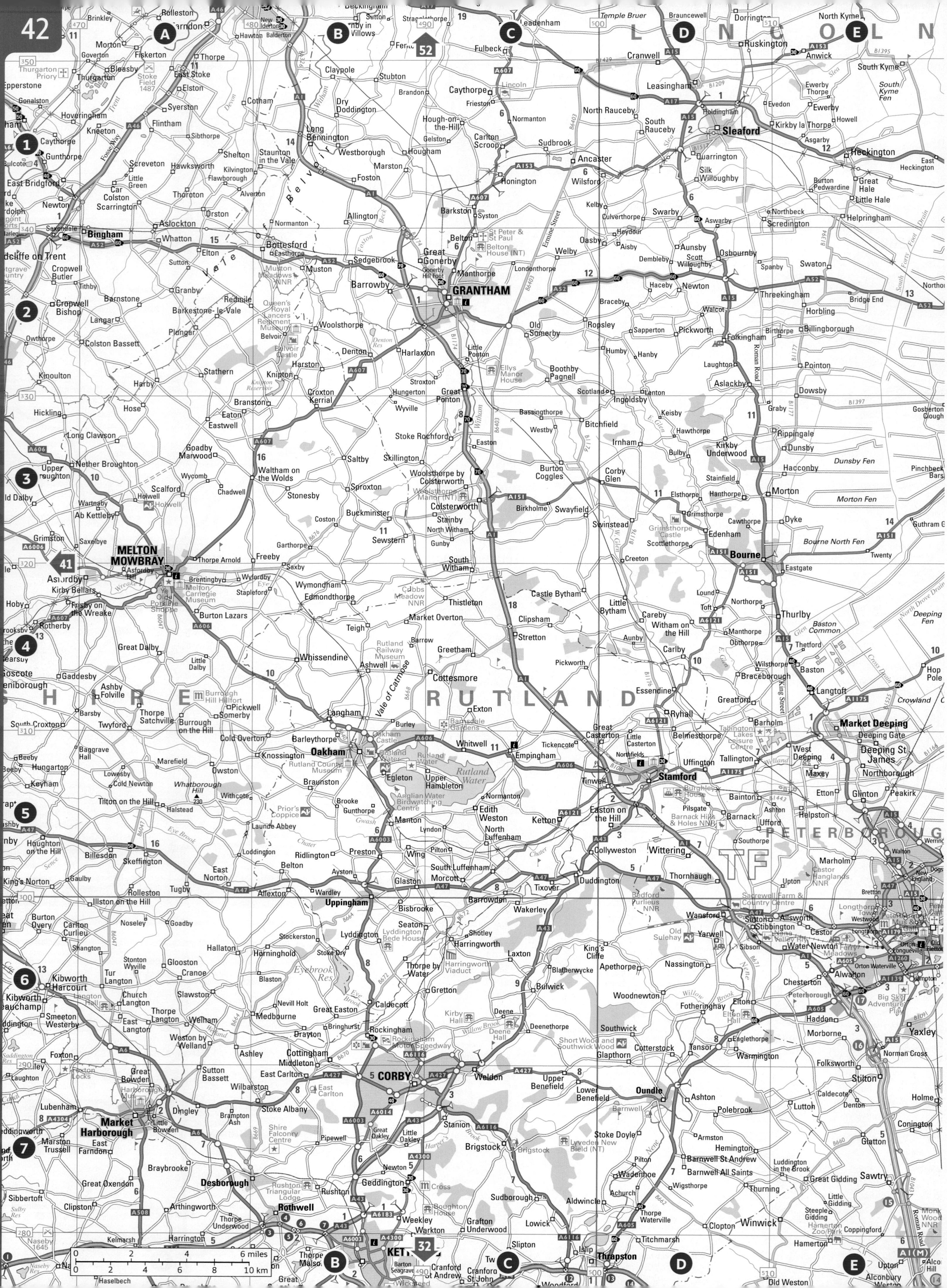

LINCOLN

RUTLAND

SHIRE

Major towns: Grantham, Sleaford, Heckington, Bingham, Melton Mowbray, Oakham, Stamford, Bourne, Market Deeping, Deeping St James, Uppingham, Corby, Market Harborough, Desborough, Rothwell, Kettering, Oundle, Thrapston, Peterborough

Selected places:
Rolleston, Brinkley, Morton, Fiskerton, Goverton, Bleasby, Thurgarton Priory, Thurgarton, Epperstone, Gonalston, Hoveringham, Kneeton, East Stoke, Elston, Flintham, Sibthorpe, Syerston, Thoroton, Cotham, Claypole, Stubton, Brandon, Caythorpe, Frieston, Normanton, North Rauceby, South Rauceby, Cranwell, Ruskington, Leasingham, Holdingham, Evedon, Ewerby, Howell, Kirkby la Thorpe, Asgarby, Anwick, South Kyme, North Kyme, Ewerby Thorpe

East Bridgford, Newton, Car Colston, Scarrington, Aslockton, Whatton, Orston, Thoroton, Alverton, Kilvington, Staunton in the Vale, Long Bennington, Westborough, Marston, Hougham, Hough-on-the-Hill, Carlton Scroop, Normanton, Honington, Barkston, Syston, Ancaster, Wilsford, Kelby, Culverthorpe, Heydour, Aunsby, Aswarby, Scott Willoughby, Spanby, Swaton, Threekingham, Horbling, Billingborough, Bridge End

Bottesford, Muston, Barrowby, Sedgebrook, Great Gonerby, Manthorpe, Londonthorpe, Welby, Oasby, Aisby, Dembleby, Osbournby, Pointon, Sapperton, Pickworth, Folkingham, Birthorpe, Aslackby, Dowsby, Graby, Rippingale, Dunsby, Haconby, Morton, Morton Fen, Dunsby Fen

Belvoir Castle, Harlaxton, Denton, Harston, Knipton, Croxton Kerrial, Branston, Eaton, Eastwell, Stroxton, Great Ponton, Hungerton, Wyville, Boothby Pagnell, Ingoldsby, Keisby, Hawthorpe, Bulby, Irnham, Corby Glen, Swayfield, Swinstead, Grimsthorpe, Grimsthorpe Castle, Edenham, Scottlethorpe, Edenham

Colston Bassett, Hickling, Long Clawson, Hose, Goadby Marwood, Waltham on the Wolds, Stonesby, Sproxton, Buckminster, Sewstern, North Witham, South Witham, Gunby, Skillington, Stoke Rochford, Easton, Woolsthorpe by Colsterworth, Colsterworth, Stainby, Birkholme, Burton Coggles, Bitchfield, Westby, Bassingthorpe

Melton Mowbray, Asfordby, Kirby Bellars, Frisby on the Wreake, Rotherby, Brooksby, Thorpe Arnold, Freeby, Saxby, Wymondham, Edmondthorpe, Thistleton, Market Overton, Teigh, Whissendine, Ashwell, Langham, Barleythorpe, Cottesmore, Greetham, Stretton, Clipsham, Castle Bytham, Little Bytham, Careby, Witham on the Hill, Manthorpe, Obthorpe, Baston, Langtoft, Thurlby, Northorpe, Toft, Lound

Oakham, Barnsdale, Egleton, Braunston, Brooke, Gunthorpe, Hambleton, Upper Hambleton, Normanton, Edith Weston, North Luffenham, South Luffenham, Ketton, Tinwell, Stamford, Burghley House, Great Casterton, Little Casterton, Tickencote, Empingham, Whitwell, Exton, Ryhall, Belmesthorpe, Essendine, Greatford, Braceborough, Wilsthorpe, Barholm, West Deeping, Maxey, Northborough, Etton, Glinton, Peakirk, Helpston

Knossington, Owston, Cold Overton, Marefield, Lowesby, Cold Newton, Whatborough Hill, Withcote, Launde Abbey, Loddington, Belton, Ridlington, Preston, Ayston, Wing, Pilton, Lyndon, Manton, Morcott, Glaston, Barrowden, Wakerley, Duddington, Collyweston, Wittering, Thornhaugh, Wansford, Sutton, Stibbington, Sibson, Water Newton, Castor, Ailsworth

Billesdon, Skeffington, Tilton on the Hill, Halstead, Tugby, East Norton, Allexton, Wardley, Uppingham, Bisbrooke, Seaton, Lyddington, Stoke Dry, Harringworth, Shotley, Laxham, King's Cliffe, Apethorpe, Nassington, Yarwell, Sutton, Alwalton, Chesterton, Haddon, Morborne, Yaxley, Stilton

Kibworth Harcourt, Kibworth Beauchamp, Church Langton, Thorpe Langton, Welham, Slawston, Nevill Holt, Medbourne, Drayton, Bringhurst, Great Easton, Caldecott, Rockingham, Gretton, Harringworth Viaduct, Deene, Deenethorpe, Bulwick, Blatherwycke, Woodnewton, Fotheringhay, Elton, Warmington, Southwick, Cotterstock, Tansor, Glapthorn, Oundle, Ashton, Polebrook, Luddington in the Brook, Coningby

Foxton, Lubenham, Market Harborough, Great Bowden, Sutton Bassett, Wilbarston, Middleton, Cottingham, East Carlton, Corby, Weldon, Upper Benefield, Lower Benefield, Brigstock, Stanion, Stoke Doyle, Barnwell, Pilton, Wadenhoe, Achurch, Thorpe Waterville, Aldwincle, Clopton, Thurning, Winwick

Naseby, Sibbertoft, Clipston, Great Oxendon, Braybrooke, Desborough, Arthingworth, Rushton, Thorpe Underwood, Rothwell, Kettering, Geddington, Weekley, Grafton Underwood, Warkton, Slipton, Sudborough, Lowick, Islip, Thrapston, Titchmarsh, Hemington, Barnwell St Andrew, Barnwell All Saints, Hamerton, Steeple Gidding, Great Gidding, Little Gidding

Scale:
0   2   4   6 miles
0 2 4 6 8 10 km

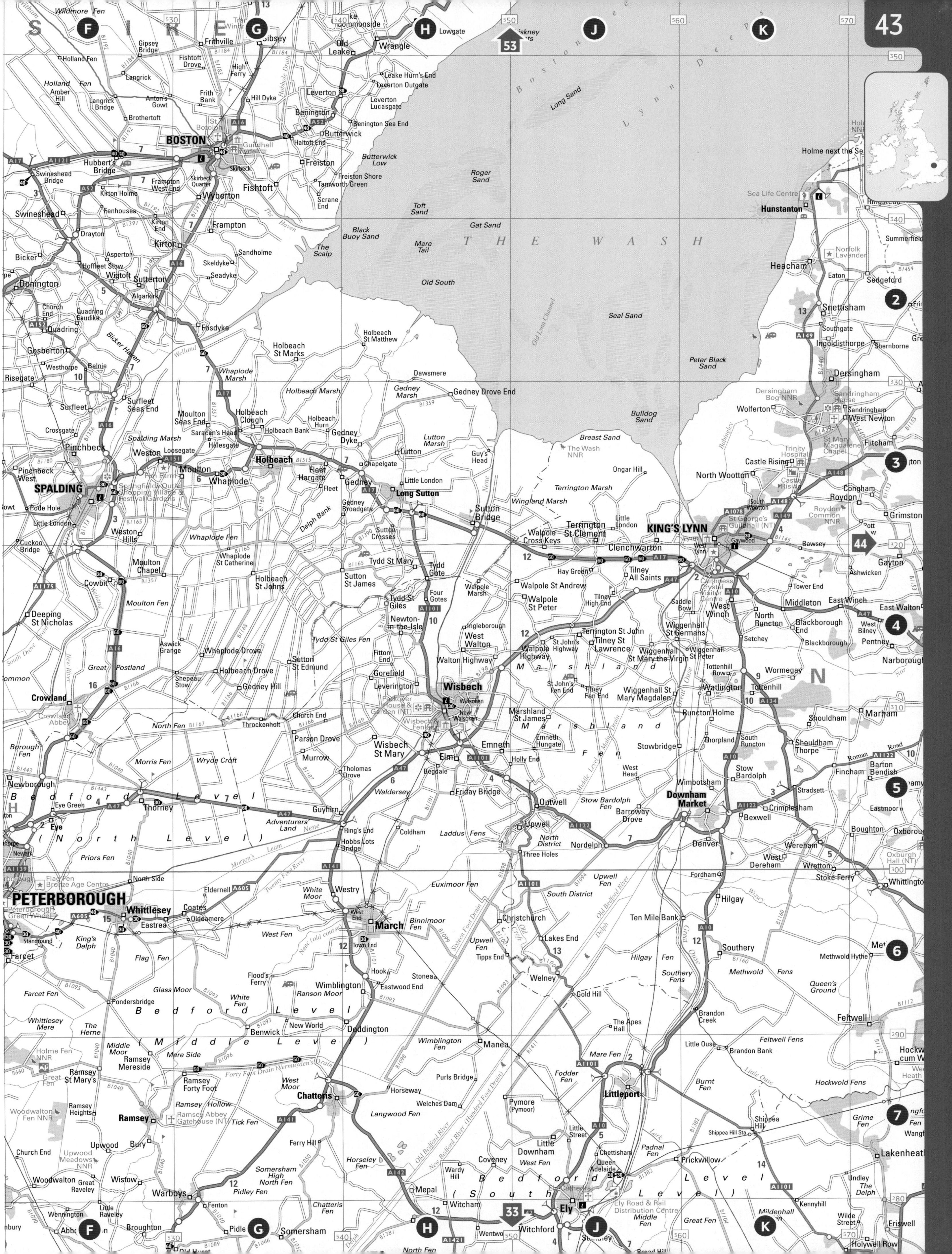

THE WASH
Boston
Long Sand
Lynn Deeps
Roger Sand
Toft Sand
Gat Sand
Black Buoy Sand
Mare Tail
The Scalp
Old South
Seal Sand
Peter Black Sand
Bulldog Sand
Breast Sand
The Wash NNR
Old Lynn Channel
BOSTON
Sibsey
Frithville
Old Leake
Wrangle
Lowgate
Leverton
Benington
Butterwick
Freiston
Fishtoft
Wyberton
Frampton
Kirton
Sutterton
Wigtoft
Swineshead
Donington
Gosberton
Quadring
Surfleet
Pinchbeck
SPALDING
Weston
Moulton
Whaplode
Holbeach
Fleet Hargate
Gedney
Long Sutton
Sutton Bridge
Terrington St Clement
Clenchwarton
KING'S LYNN
Hunstanton
Heacham
Snettisham
Dersingham
Wolferton
Sandringham
Castle Rising
North Wootton
Gaywood
Roydon
Grimston
Gayton
Middleton
East Winch
West Winch
North Runcton
Crowland
Thorney
Eye
PETERBOROUGH
Whittlesey
Coates
Eastrea
March
Wisbech
Emneth
Elm
Friday Bridge
Outwell
Upwell
Nordelph
Downham Market
Denver
Stow Bardolph
Wimbotsham
Marham
Shouldham
Wereham
Stoke Ferry
Hilgay
Southery
Methwold
Feltwell
Littleport
Ely
Manea
Chatteris
Doddington
Benwick
Ramsey
Warboys
Somersham
Witchford
Lakenheath
Bedford Level (North Level)
Bedford Level (Middle Level)
Bedford Level (South Level)
Marshland Fen

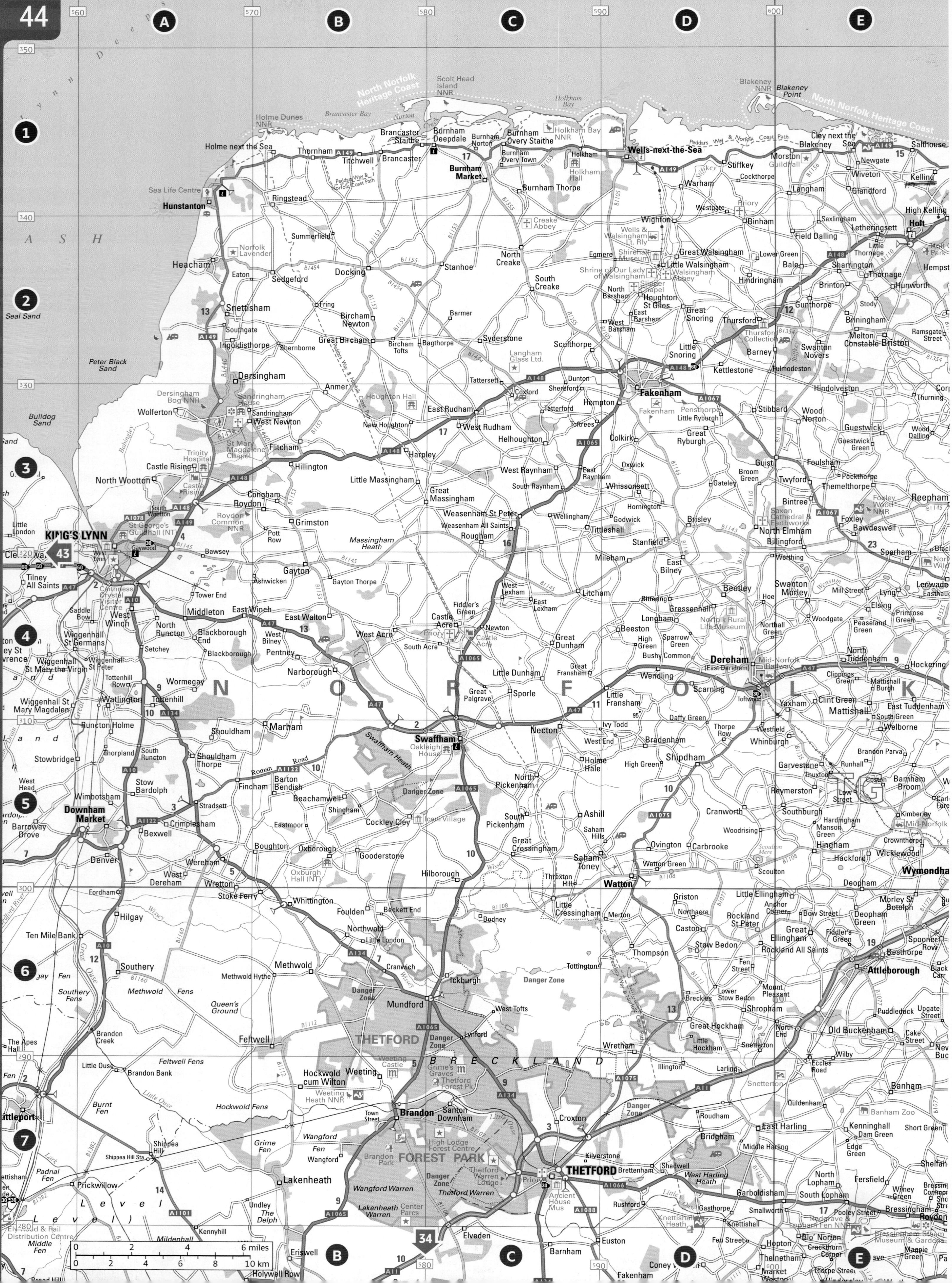
A
B
C
D
E
1
2
3
4
5
6
7
North Norfolk Heritage Coast
Scolt Head Island NNR
Blakeney NNR
Blakeney Point
Holme Dunes NNR
Brancaster Bay
Holkham Bay
Holme next the Sea
Thornham
Titchwell
Brancaster
Brancaster Staithe
Burnham Deepdale
Burnham Norton
Burnham Overy Staithe
Burnham Overy Town
Burnham Market
Holkham
Holkham Hall
Holkham Bay NNR
Wells-next-the-Sea
Stiffkey
Morston
Blakeney
Cley next the Sea
Salthouse
Kelling
Newgate
Wiveton
Glandford
Langham
High Kelling
Holt
Letheringsett
Sea Life Centre
Hunstanton
Ringstead
Burnham Thorpe
Warham
Cockthorpe
Binham
Priory
Wighton
Wells & Walsingham Lt. Rly
Creake Abbey
Summerfield
Norfolk Lavender
Heacham
Eaton
Sedgeford
Docking
Stanhoe
North Creake
South Creake
Egmere
Great Walsingham
Little Walsingham
Walsingham Abbey
Shrine of Our Lady of Walsingham
Field Dalling
Saxlingham
Lower Green
Bale
Hindringham
Sharrington
Thornage
Brinton
Hunworth
Hempstead
Seal Sand
Snettisham
Fring
Bircham Newton
Barmer
North Barsham
Houghton St Giles
East Barsham
West Barsham
Great Snoring
Thursford
Thursford Collection
Gunthorpe
Stody
Briningham
Southgate
Ingoldisthorpe
Shernborne
Great Bircham
Bircham Tofts
Bagthorpe
Syderstone
Sculthorpe
Little Snoring
Barney
Melton Constable
Briston
Swanton Novers
Ramsgate Street
Peter Black Sand
Langham Glass Ltd.
Dersingham
Anmer
Kettlestone
Fulmodeston
Dersingham Bog NNR
Sandringham House
Sandringham
West Newton
Houghton Hall
Tattersett
Coxford
Dunton
Shereford
Fakenham
Hempton
Hindolveston
Bulldog Sand
Wolferton
New Houghton
East Rudham
West Rudham
Tatterford
Toftrees
Pensthorpe
Little Ryburgh
Stibbard
Wood Norton
Thurning
Flitcham
St Mary Magdalene Chapel
Harpley
Helhoughton
Colkirk
Great Ryburgh
Guestwick
Wood Dalling
Guestwick Green
Trinity Hospital
Castle Rising
Hillington
West Raynham
East Raynham
Oxwick
Guist
Foulsham
North Wootton
Little Massingham
South Raynham
Whissonsett
Broom Green
Gateley
Twyford
Themelthorpe
Pockthorpe
Congham
Roydon
Great Massingham
Horningtoft
Bintree
Reepham
Little London
South Wootton
St George's Guildhall (NT)
KING'S LYNN
Roydon Common NNR
Grimston
Weasenham St Peter
Weasenham All Saints
Wellingham
Godwick
Brisley
Saxon Cathedral & Earthworks
North Elmham
Foxley
Foxley Wood NNR
Bawdeswell
Pott Row
Massingham Heath
Rougham
Tittleshall
Stanfield
Billingford
Gaywood
Bawsey
43
Tilney All Saints
Gayton
Ashwicken
Gayton Thorpe
Mileham
East Bilney
Worthing
Sparham
Caithness Crystal Visitor Centre
Tower End
West Lexham
East Lexham
Litcham
Beetley
Swanton Morley
Mill Street
Lyng
Lenwade
Saddle Bow
West Winch
Middleton
East Winch
East Walton
Fiddler's Green
Castle Acre
Newton
Bittering
Gressenhall
Norfolk Rural Life Museum
Hoe
Elsing
Peaseland Green
Primrose Green
North Runcton
Blackborough End
Blackborough
West Bilney
Pentney
West Acre
Priory
South Acre
Great Dunham
Longham
Beeston
High Green
Sparrow Green
Bushy Common
Woodgate
Northall Green
Wiggenhall St Germans
Setchey
Wiggenhall St Mary the Virgin
Wiggenhall St Peter
Narborough
Little Dunham
Great Fransham
Dereham (East Dereham)
Mid-Norfolk Railway
North Tuddenham
Hockering
Tottenhill Row
Wormegay
NORFOLK
Great Palgrave
Sporle
Wendling
Scarning
Clippings Green
Mattishall Burgh
Wiggenhall St Mary Magdalen
Watlington
Tottenhill
Little Fransham
Toftwood
Yaxham
Clint Green
Mattishall
East Tuddenham
Runcton Holme
Shouldham
Marham
Swaffham
Oakleigh House
Necton
Ivy Todd
Daffy Green
Thorpe Row
Westfield
Whinburgh
South Green
Welborne
Stowbridge
Thorpland
South Runcton
Shouldham Thorpe
Swaffham Heath
West End
Bradenham
Shipdham
Brandon Parva
Runhall
Garvestone
Thuxton
Coston
Barnham Broom
West Head
Wimbotsham
Stow Bardolph
Roman Road
Fincham
Barton Bendish
Beachamwell
Danger Zone
Holme Hale
High Green
North Pickenham
Reymerston
Low Street
Downham Market
Stradsett
Crimplesham
Shingham
Cockley Cley
Iceni Village
South Pickenham
Ashill
Cranworth
Southburgh
Kimberley
Hardingham
Mid-Norfolk
Barroway Drove
Bexwell
Eastmoor
Saham Hills
Woodrising
Mansion Green
Denver
Boughton
Oxborough
Gooderstone
Great Cressingham
Ovington
Carbrooke
Hingham
Crownthorpe
Wicklewood
Hackford
Wereham
West Dereham
Wretton
Oxburgh Hall (NT)
Hilborough
Saham Toney
Watton Green
Scoulton Mere
Scoulton
Wymondham
Stoke Ferry
Threxton Hill
Watton
Deopham
Fordham
Whittington
Foulden
Beckett End
Bodney
Little Cressingham
Merton
Griston
Northacre
Little Ellingham
Anchor Corner
Bow Street
Morley St Botolph
Hilgay
Northwold
Little London
Rockland St Peter
Caston
Deopham Green
Ten Mile Bank
Stow Bedon
Great Ellingham
Fiddler's Green
Spooner Row
Rockland All Saints
Besthorpe
Thompson
Fen Street
Methwold
Cranwich
Tottington
Attleborough
Southery
Methwold Hythe
Ickburgh
Danger Zone
Mount Pleasant
Southery Fens
Methwold Fens
Queen's Ground
Mundford
West Tofts
Breckles
Lower Stow Bedon
Shropham
Puddledock
Upgate Street
Brandon Creek
THETFORD
Feltwell
Lynford
Great Hockham
Little Hockham
North End
Old Buckenham
Cake Street
The Apes Hall
Wretham
Snetterton
New Buckenham
BRECKLAND
Weeting Castle
Grime's Graves
Thetford Forest Pk
Illington
Larling
Wilby
Eccles Road
Little Ouse
Brandon Bank
Feltwell Fens
Hockwold cum Wilton
Weeting
Weeting Heath NNR
Snetterton
Banham
Fen
Burnt Fen
Hockwold Fens
Town Street
Brandon
Santon Downham
Danger Zone
Croxton
Roudham
Quidenham
Banham Zoo
Littleport
Wangford
Grime Fen
High Lodge Forest Centre
East Harling
Kenninghall
Dam Green
Short Green
Shippea Hill
Shippea Hill Sta
Brandon Park
FOREST PARK
Bridgham
Middle Harling
Edge Green
Kilverstone
Shadwell
Shelfanger
Padnal Fen
Prickwillow
Lakenheath
Thetford Warren Lodge
Priory
THETFORD
Brettenham
West Harling Heath
North Lopham
Fersfield
Wangford Warren
Thetford Warren
Ancient House Mus
Garboldisham
South Lopham
Winfarthing
Level
Undley
The Delph
Lakenheath Warren
Center Parcs
Rushford
Gasthorpe
Smallworth
Pooley Street
Bressingham
Roydon
Ely Road & Rail Distribution Centre
Kennyhill
Mildenhall
Elveden
Knettishall Heath
Knettishall
Redgrave & Lopham Fen NNR
Bressingham Steam Museum & Gardens
Middle Fen
34
Euston
Fen Street
Hopton
Blo' Norton
Crackthorn Corner
Mappie Green
Eriswell
Barnham
Coney Weston
Thelnetham
Holywell Row
Fakenham
Thorpe Street
0 2 4 6 miles
0 2 4 6 8 10 km

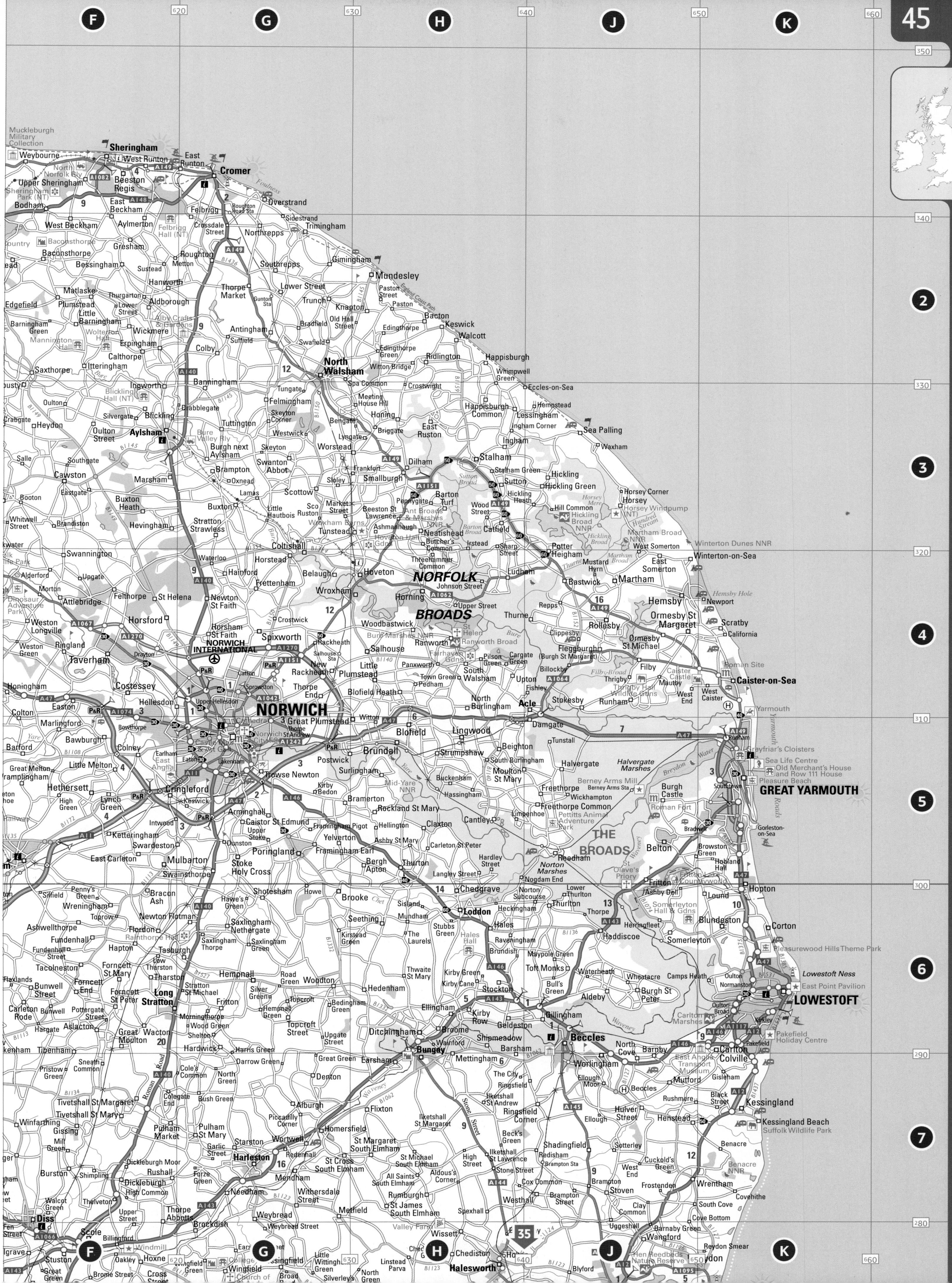
F
G
H
J
K
2
3
4
5
6
7
620
630
640
650
660
350
340
330
320
310
300
290
280
Muckleburgh Military Collection
Weybourne
Sheringham
West Runton
East Runton
Cromer
North Norfolk Rly
Upper Sheringham
Sheringham Park (NT)
Beeston Regis
Bodham
East Beckham
Felbrigg
Overstrand
Sidestrand
Trimingham
West Beckham
Aylmerton
Felbrigg Hall (NT)
Crossdale Street
Northrepps
Baconsthorpe
Gresham
Roughton
Bessingham
Metton
Southrepps
Gimingham
Mundesley
Sustead
Hanworth
Thorpe Market
Lower Street
Matlaske
Thurgarton
Aldborough
Plumstead
Little Barningham
Edgefield
Barningham Green
Alby Crafts & Gardens
Wolterton Hall
Wickmere
Trunch
Paston Street
Knapton
Paston
Old Hall Street
Bacton
Keswick
Walcott
Antingham
Suffield
Bradfield
Edingthorpe
Swafield
Mannington Hall
Erpingham
Colby
Calthorpe
Itteringham
Saxthorpe
North Walsham
Edingthorpe Green
Witton Bridge
Ridlington
Happisburgh
Whimpwell Green
Eccles-on-Sea
Banningham
Ingworth
Blickling Hall (NT)
Tungate
Felmingham
Spa Common
Crostwight
Meeting House Hill
Happisburgh Common
Hempstead
Lessingham
Oulton
Brabblegate
Skeyton Corner
Honing
Sea Palling
Ingham Corner
Waxham
Heydon
Silvergate
Blickling
Tuttington
Bengate
Briggate
East Ruston
Ingham
Oulton Street
Aylsham
Bure Valley Rly
Westwick
Lyngate
Worstead
Burgh next Aylsham
Skeyton
Swanton Abbot
Dilham
Stalham
Salle
Southgate
Frankfort
Smallburgh
Stalham Green
Hickling
Cawston
Brampton
Oxnead
Marsham
Sutton
Hickling Green
Horsey Corner
Horsey
Booton
Eastgate
Lamas
Scottow
Sloley
Barton Turf
Hickling Heath
Buxton Heath
Buxton
Little Hautbois
Sco Ruston
Market Street
Beeston St Lawrence
Pennygate
Ant Broads & Marshes NNR
Wood Street
Hill Common
Hickling Broad NNR
Horsey Windpump (NT)
Whitwell Street
Brandiston
Hevingham
Stratton Strawless
Wroxham Barns
Ashmanhaugh
Tunstead
Neatishead
Catfield
Martham Broad NNR
West Somerton
Winterton Dunes NNR
Coltishall
Hoveton Hall Gdns
Butcher's Common
Irstead
Sharp Street
Potter Heigham
Swannington
Waterloo
Horstead
Threehammer Common
Mustard Hyrn
East Somerton
Winterton-on-Sea
Alderford
Upgate
Hainford
Belaugh
Hoveton
NORFOLK
BROADS
Ludham
Bastwick
Martham
Frettenham
Wroxham
Horning
Johnson Street
Hemsby
Hemsby Hole
Newport
Morton
Felthorpe
St Helena
Newton St Faith
Repps
Thurne
Ormesby St Margaret
Attlebridge
Dinosaur Adventure Park
Upper Street
Rollesby
Scratby
California
Weston Longville
Horsford
Crostwick
Woodbastwick
Clippesby
Ormesby St Michael
Horsham St Faith
Spixworth
Rackheath
Burr Marshes NNR
Ranworth
St Helen
Ranworth Broad
Fleggburgh (Burgh St Margaret)
Weston Green
Ringland
NORWICH INTERNATIONAL
Salhouse
Salhouse Sta
Little Plumstead
Panxworth
Fairhaven Gdns
Pilson Green
Cargate Green
South Walsham
Billockby
Filby
Thrigby
Thrigby Hall Wildlife Gdns
Caister Castle
Mautby
Roman Site
Caister-on-Sea
Taverham
Drayton
Catton
New Rackheath
Town Green
Pedham
Upton
Fishley
West End
West Caister
Honingham
Costessey
Hellesdon
Sprowston
Thorpe End
Blofield Heath
North Burlingham
Acle
Stokesby
Runham
Yarmouth
Easton
Colton
NORWICH
Upper Hellesdon
Great Plumstead
Witton
Damgate
Marlingford
Bowthorpe
Thorpe St Andrew
Blofield
Lingwood
Tunstall
Greyfriar's Cloisters
Sea Life Centre
Old Merchant's House and Row 111 House
Pleasure Beach
Barford
Bawburgh
Colney
Earlham
Castle Mus & Art Gall
Norwich Cathedral
Brundall
Strumpshaw
Beighton
South Burlingham
Halvergate
Halvergate Marshes
Breydon Water
Little Melton
Eaton
East Anglia
Lakenham
Postwick
Moulton St Mary
Berney Arms Mill
Great Melton
Ramplingham
Cringleford
Trowse Newton
Surlingham
Buckenham
Berney Arms Sta
Burgh Castle
GREAT YARMOUTH
Southtown
Hethersett
Keswick
Kirby Bedon
Mid-Yare NNR
Hassingham
Freethorpe
Wickhampton
Roman Fort
High Green
Lynch Green
Intwood
Arminghall
Caistor St Edmund
Bramerton
Rockland St Mary
Limpenhoe
Freethorpe Common
Pettitts Animal Adventure Park
Gorleston-on-Sea
Ketteringham
Upper Stoke
Framingham Pigot
Hellington
Claxton
Cantley
Bradwell
Swardeston
Dunston
Yelverton
Ashby St Mary
Carleton St Peter
THE BROADS
Belton
Browston Green
East Carleton
Mulbarton
Poringland
Framingham Earl
Hardley Street
Reedham
Hobland Hall
Stoke Holy Cross
Bergh Apton
Thurton
Norton Marshes
St Olave's Priory
Swainsthorpe
Langley Street
Nogdam End
Fritton
Fritton Lake Countryworld
Silfield
Penny's Green
Bracon Ash
Shotesham
Howe
Brooke
Chedgrave
Norton Subcourse
Lower Thurlton
Ashby Dell
Lound
Hopton
Wreningham
Hawe's Green
Sisland
Loddon
Heckingham
Thurlton
Thorpe
Somerleyton Hall & Gdns
Toprow
Newton Flotman
Saxlingham Nethergate
Mundham
Blundeston
Corton
Ashwellthorpe
Flordon
Seething
Hales
Herringfleet
Haddiscoe
Fundenhall
Rainthorpe Hall
Saxlingham Thorpe
Saxlingham Green
Kirstead Green
The Laurels
Stubbs Green
Hales Hall
Raveningham
Somerleyton
Fundenhall Street
Hapton
Tasburgh
Pleasurewood Hills Theme Park
Tacolneston
Forncett St Mary
Low Tharston
Brundish
Maypole Green
Tharston
Toft Monks
Flaxlands
Forncett End
Stratton St Michael
Hempnall
Road Green
Woodton
Thwaite St Mary
Kirby Green
Waterheath
Wheatacre
Camps Heath
Oulton
Lowestoft Ness
Bunwell Street
Forncett St Peter
Long Stratton
Silver Green
Topcroft
Hedenham
Kirby Cane
Stockton
Bull's Green
Burgh St Peter
Normanston
East Point Pavilion
LOWESTOFT
Carleton Rode
Bunwell
Pottergate Street
Fritton
Hempnall Green
Bedingham Green
Ellingham
Aldeby
Oulton Broad
Hargate
Aslacton
Morningthorpe
Wood Green
Topcroft Street
Upgate Street
Ditchingham
Kirby Row
Geldeston
Gillingham
Carlton Marshes
Great Moulton
Wacton
Shelton
Broome
Beccles
Pakefield
Pakefield Holiday Centre
Tibenham
Hardwick
Harris Green
Bungay
Wainford
Shipmeadow
Barsham
North Cove
Barnby
Carlton Colville
Darrow Green
Great Green
Earsham
Mettingham
Worlingham
East Anglia Transport Museum
Sneath Common
Pristow Green
Cole's Common
North Green
Denton
The City
Ringsfield
Ellough Moor
Mutford
Gisleham
Colegate End
Bush Green
Alburgh
Ilketshall St Andrew
Rushmere
Black Street
Kessingland
Tivetshall St Margaret
Tivetshall St Mary
Flixton
Ringsfield Corner
Ellough
Hulver Street
Henstead
Kessingland Beach
Suffolk Wildlife Park
Winfarthing
Gissing
Pulham Market
Pulham St Mary
Piccadilly Corner
Homersfield
Ilketshall St Margaret
Beck's Green
Shadingfield
Sotterley
Benacre
Mill Green
Garlic Street
Starston
Wortwell
Redenhall
St Margaret South Elmham
Ilketshall St Lawrence
Redisham
Brampton Sta
Cuckold's Green
Dickleburgh Moor
Harleston
St Cross South Elmham
St Michael South Elmham
High Street
Stone Street
West End
Benacre NNR
Burston
Shimpling
Rushall
Dickleburgh
Mendham
All Saints South Elmham
Aldous's Corner
Cox Common
Brampton
Stoven
Frostenden
Wrentham
Walcot Green
Thelveton
High Common
Needham
Withersdale Street
Rumburgh
Westhall
Brampton Street
Covehithe
Upper Street
Thorpe Abbotts
Metfield
St James South Elmham
Spexhall
Clay Common
South Cove
Diss
Weybread
Weybread Street
Cove Bottom
Scole
Brockdish
Valley Farm
Wissett
Uggeshall
Barnaby Green
Wangford
Billingford
Windmill
Chediston
Reydon Smear
Stuston
Oakley
Hoxne
Wingfield
Withersfield
Linstead Parva
Halesworth
Blyford
Hen Reedbeds Nature Reserve
Brome Street
Cross Street
Silverley's Green
North Green
Great Green
35

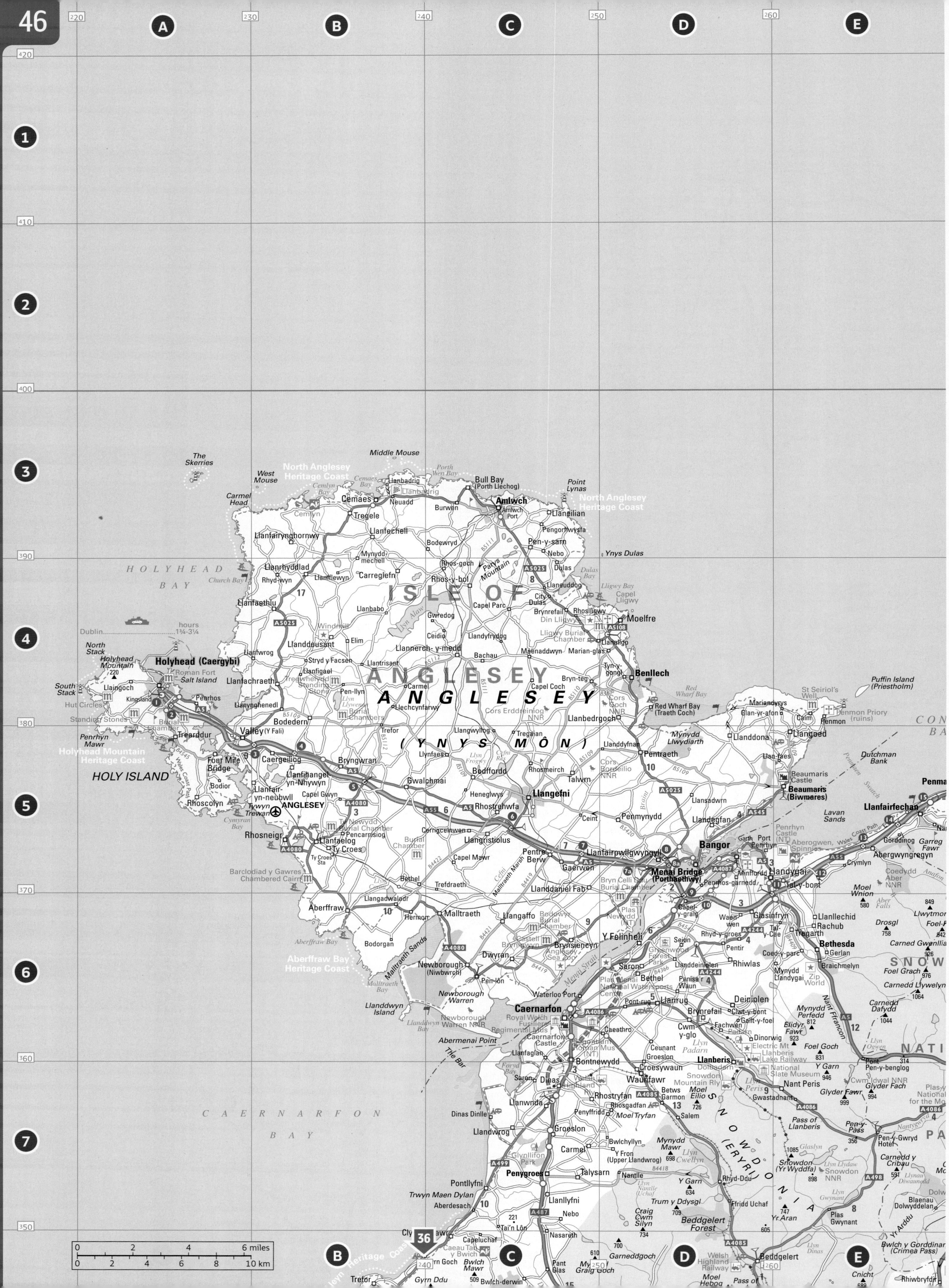

A
B
C
D
E
1
2
3
4
5
6
7
ISLE OF ANGLESEY
ANGLESEY
(YNYS MÔN)
HOLY ISLAND
HOLYHEAD BAY
CAERNARFON BAY
SNOWDONIA
(ERYRI)
The Skerries
Middle Mouse
West Mouse
Carmel Head
North Anglesey Heritage Coast
Cemaes Bay
Cemaes
Llanbadrig
Porth Wen Bay
Bull Bay (Porth Llechog)
Amlwch
Amlwch Port
Point Lynas
Llaneilian
Tregele
Llanfechell
Llanfairynghornwy
Llanrhyddlad
Rhyd-wyn
Church Bay
Carreglefn
Rhos-y-bol
Parys Mountain
Penysarn
Nebo
Dulas
Ynys Dulas
Dulas Bay
Lligwy Bay
Moelfre
Llanfaethlu
Llanbabo
Capel Parc
Llanddeusant
Elim
Llannerch-y-medd
Llandyfrydog
Maenaddwyn
Marian-glas
Benllech
Red Wharf Bay
Dublin
hours 1¾-3¼
North Stack
Holyhead Mountain
Holyhead (Caergybi)
Roman Fort
Salt Island
South Stack
Llaingoch
Kingsland
Penrhos
Llanfachraeth
Llanynghenedl
Bodedern
Valley (Y Fali)
Trearddur
Four Mile Bridge
Bodior
Rhoscolyn
Holyhead Mountain Heritage Coast
Penrhyn Mawr
Caergeiliog
Bryngwran
Gwalchmai
Llanfihangel-yn-Nhywyn
Llanfair-yn-neubwll
Capel Gwyn
Tywyn Trewan
ANGLESEY
Rhosneigr
Cymyran Bay
Llanfaelog
Ty Croes
Barclodiad y Gawres Chambered Cairn
Aberffraw
Aberffraw Bay
Aberffraw Bay Heritage Coast
Bodorgan
Malltraeth
Malltraeth Sands
Hermon
Llangadwaladr
Bethel
Trefdraeth
Llangefni
Rhostrehwfa
Bodffordd
Heneglwys
Cerrigceinwen
Llangristiolus
Capel Mawr
Pentre Berw
Gaerwen
Llanfairpwllgwyngyll
Menai Bridge (Porthaethwy)
Bangor
Llandegfan
Pentraeth
Talwrn
Rhosmeirch
Penmynydd
Llansadwrn
Beaumaris Castle
Beaumaris (Biwmares)
Llangoed
Penmon
Penmon Priory (ruins)
Puffin Island (Priestholm)
Dutchman Bank
Lavan Sands
Llanfairfechan
Llanddaniel Fab
Llangaffo
Brynsiencyn
Dwyran
Newborough (Niwbwrch)
Newborough Warren
Llanddwyn Island
Y Felinheli
Caernarfon
Waterloo Port
Abermenai Point
The Bar
Llanfaglan
Saron
Dinas
Bontnewydd
Llanwnda
Dinas Dinlle
Llandwrog
Groeslon
Carmel
Penygroes
Talysarn
Nantlle
Pontllyfni
Trwyn Maen Dylan
Aberdesach
Llanllyfni
Nebo
Nasareth
Tai'n Lôn
Capeluchaf
Llanrug
Deiniolen
Brynrefail
Cwm-y-glo
Llanberis
Llyn Padarn
Ceunant
Waunfawr
Betws Garmon
Rhostryfan
Rhosgadfan
Moel Tryfan
Moel Eilio
Snowdon (Yr Wyddfa)
Pass of Llanberis
Pen-y-Pass
Nant Peris
Rhyd-Ddu
Beddgelert
Beddgelert Forest
Yr Aran
Plas Gwynant
Bethesda
Rachub
Llanllechid
Tregarth
Glasinfryn
Llandygai
Tal-y-bont
Abergwyngregyn
Penrhyn Castle
Nant Ffrancon
Pen-y-benglog
Y Garn
Glyder Fawr
Glyder Fach
Tryfan
Carnedd Llywelyn
Carnedd Dafydd
Foel Grach
Pen-y-Gwryd Hotel
Yr Arddu
Garnedd Goch
Mynydd Mawr
Y Garn
Trum y Ddysgl
Craig Cwm Silyn
0
2
4
6 miles
0
2
4
6
8
10 km
36

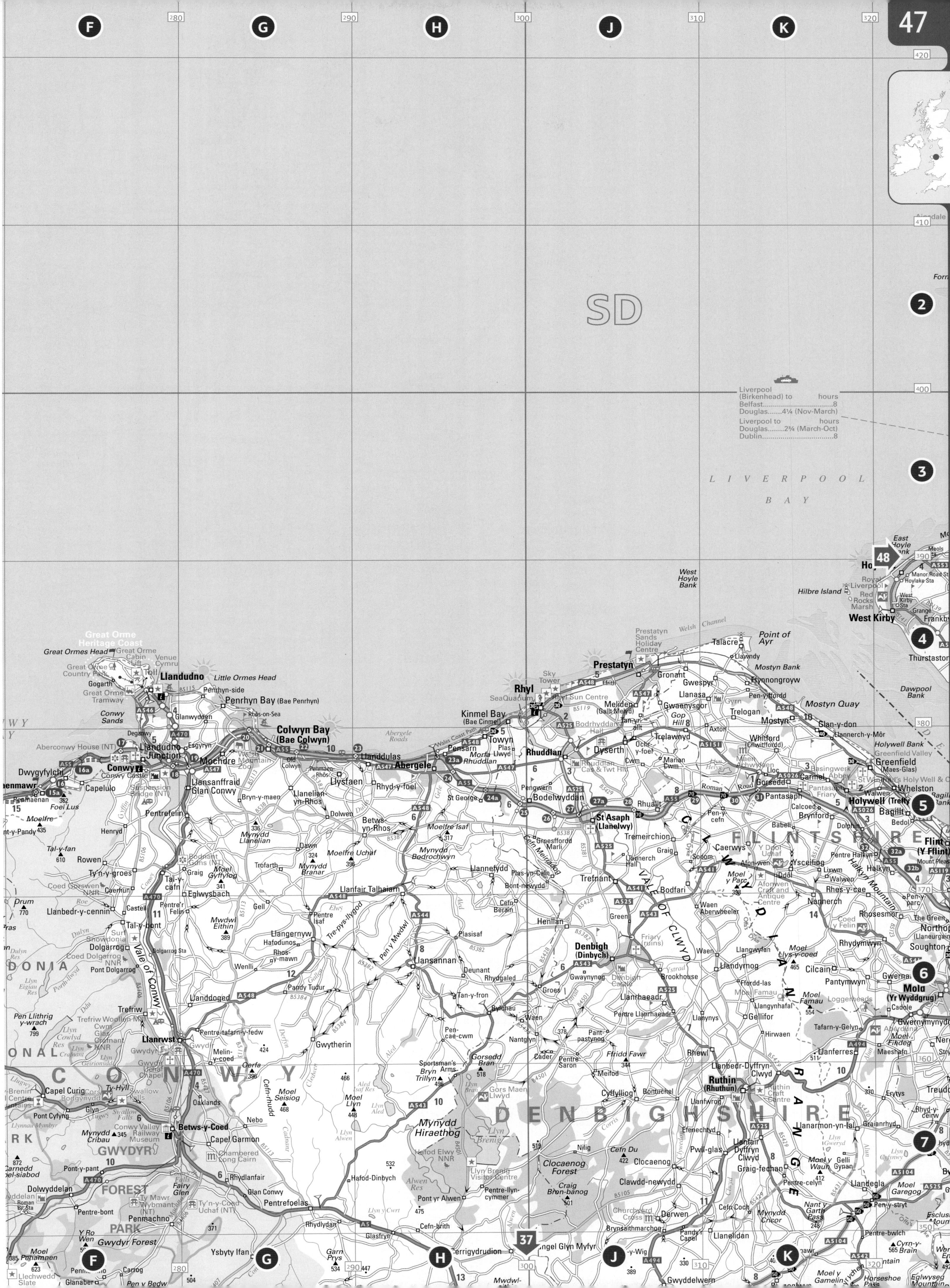
F
G
H
J
K
280
290
300
310
320
420
410
400
390
380
370
360
350
SD
2
3
4
5
6
7
Liverpool
(Birkenhead) to hours
Belfast 8
Douglas 4¼ (Nov-March)
Liverpool to hours
Douglas 2¾ (March-Oct)
Dublin 8
LIVERPOOL
BAY
West Hoyle Bank
East Hoyle Bank
48
Hilbre Island
West Kirby
Point of Ayr
Talacre
Mostyn Bank
Mostyn Quay
Dawpool Bank
Thurstaston
Great Orme Heritage Coast
Great Ormes Head
Llandudno
Little Ormes Head
Penrhyn Bay (Bae Penrhyn)
Colwyn Bay (Bae Colwyn)
Abergele Roads
Abergele
Kinmel Bay (Bae Cinmel)
Towyn
Rhyl
Prestatyn
Gronant
Gwespyr
Ffynnongroyw
Mostyn
Whitford (Chwitffordd)
Greenfield (Maes-Glas)
Holywell (Treffynnon)
Flint (Y Fflint)
Dyserth
Rhuddlan
Meliden (Gallt Melyd)
St Asaph (Llanelwy)
Bodelwyddan
Conwy
Llandudno Junction
Mochdre
Deganwy
Dwygyfylchi
Penmaenmawr
Llansanffraid Glan Conwy
Llanddulas
Llysfaen
Betws-yn-Rhos
Llanfair Talhaiarn
Llangernyw
Llansannan
Denbigh (Dinbych)
Trefnant
Henllan
Bodfari
Caerwys
Ysceifiog
Halkyn
Northop
Mold (Yr Wyddgrug)
Cilcain
Llanferres
Ruthin (Rhuthun)
Llanarmon-yn-Ial
Clocaenog Forest
Clawdd-newydd
Derwen
Cerrigydrudion
Pentrefoelas
Betws-y-Coed
Llanrwst
Trefriw
Capel Curig
Dolwyddelan
Gwydyr Forest
Ysbyty Ifan
Mynydd Hiraethog
Llyn Brenig
Llyn Alwen
Alwen Res
Gwytherin
Pandy Tudur
Llanddoged
Eglwysbach
Tal-y-cafn
Rowen
Dolgarrog
Capelulo
Vale of Conwy
VALE OF CLWYD
CLWYDIAN RANGE
FLINTSHIRE
DENBIGHSHIRE
CONWY
GWYDYR
FOREST
PARK
37

For a more detailed map of Merseyside see pages 112-113

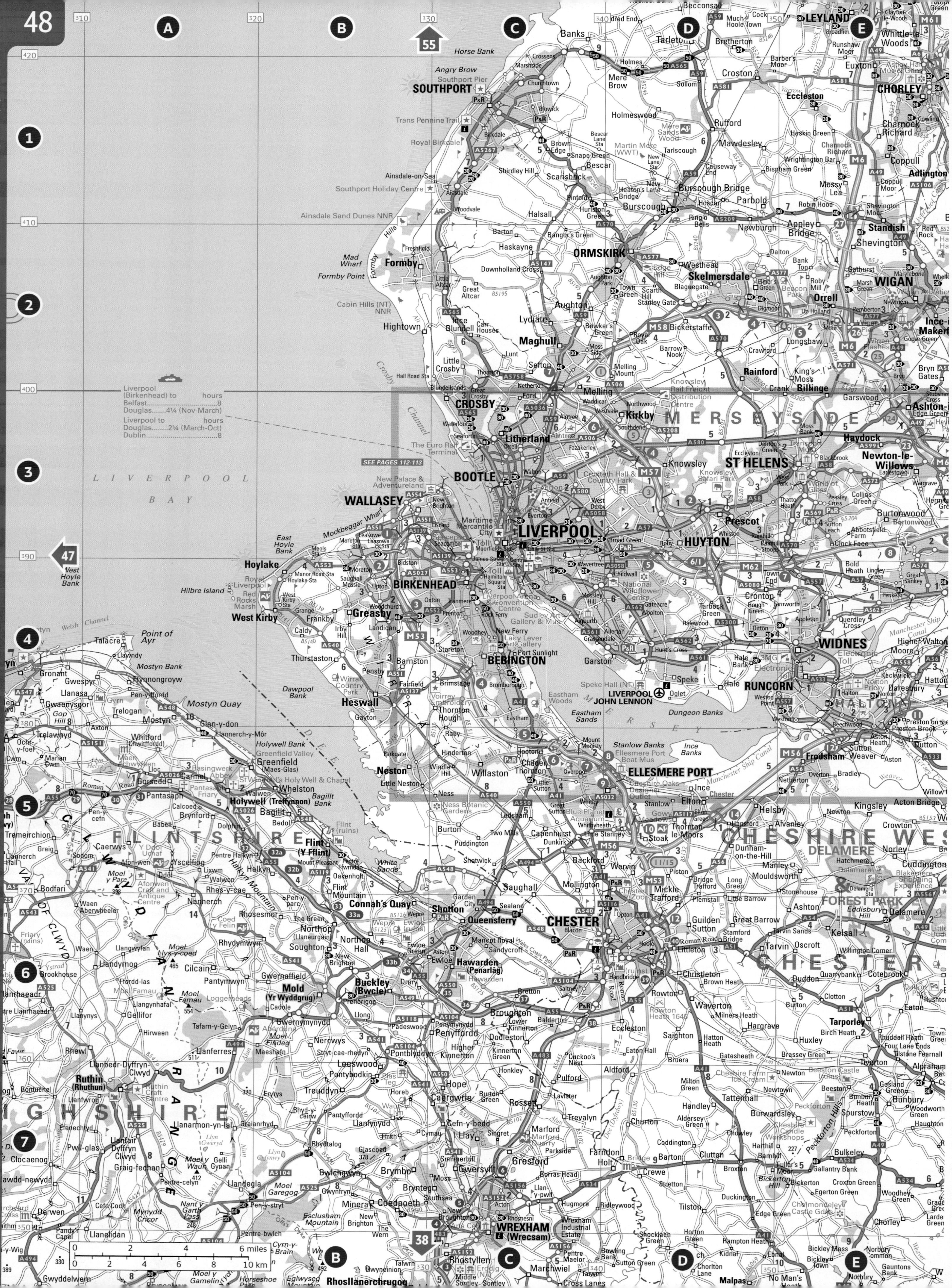

310 320 330 340 350

A   B   C   D   E

55

Horse Bank

Banks

LEYLAND

Becconsall

Much Hoole Town

CHORLEY

1

SOUTHPORT

Southport Pier

Angry Brow

Churchtown

Tarleton

Bretherton

Eccleston

Croston

Euxton

Whittle-le-Woods

Runshaw Moor

Royal Birkdale

Birkdale

Holmeswood

Mere Sands Wood

Rufford

Charnock Richard

Coppull

Adlington

2

Ainsdale-on-Sea

Southport Holiday Centre

Ainsdale Sand Dunes NNR

Martin Mere (WWT)

Burscough Bridge

Parbold

Appley Bridge

Standish

Shevington

Freshfield

Formby

Formby Point

Halsall

ORMSKIRK

Westhead

SKELMERSDALE

Bickerstaffe

WIGAN

Orrell

Mad Wharf

Haskayne

Downholland Cross

Aughton

Town Green

Up Holland

3

Cabin Hills (NT) NNR

Hightown

Maghull

Lydiate

Sefton

Rainford

King's Moss

Billinge

Garswood

Ashton

LIVERPOOL BAY

Liverpool (Birkenhead) to Belfast.......8 hours
Douglas.......4¼ (Nov-March)
Liverpool to
Douglas.......2¾ (March-Oct)
Dublin.......8 hours

CROSBY

Kirkby

Knowsley

ST HELENS

Haydock

Newton-le-Willows

WALLASEY

BOOTLE

LIVERPOOL

Prescot

HUYTON

47

West Hoyle Bank

Hoylake

BIRKENHEAD

Huyton

Broad Green

Whiston

Burtonwood

Hilbre Island

West Kirby

Greasby

Wavertree

4

Point of Ayr

Talacre

Thurstaston

Barnston

BEBINGTON

Garston

WIDNES

RUNCORN

Bromborough

5

Mostyn

Greenfield

Holywell (Treffynnon)

Neston

Willaston

ELLESMERE PORT

Frodsham

FLINTSHIRE

Flint (Y Fflint)

Burton

CHESHIRE WEST

DELAMERE

6

Mold (Yr Wyddgrug)

Buckley (Bwcle)

Hawarden (Penarlâg)

Broughton

CHESTER

FOREST PARK

Ruthin (Rhuthun)

Connah's Quay

Queensferry

Saltney

Tarporley

7

Hope

Caergwrle

Rossett

DENBIGHSHIRE

Llanferres

Gresford

38

WREXHAM (Wrecsam)

Rhosllanerchrugog

0 2 4 6 miles
0 2 4 6 8 10 km

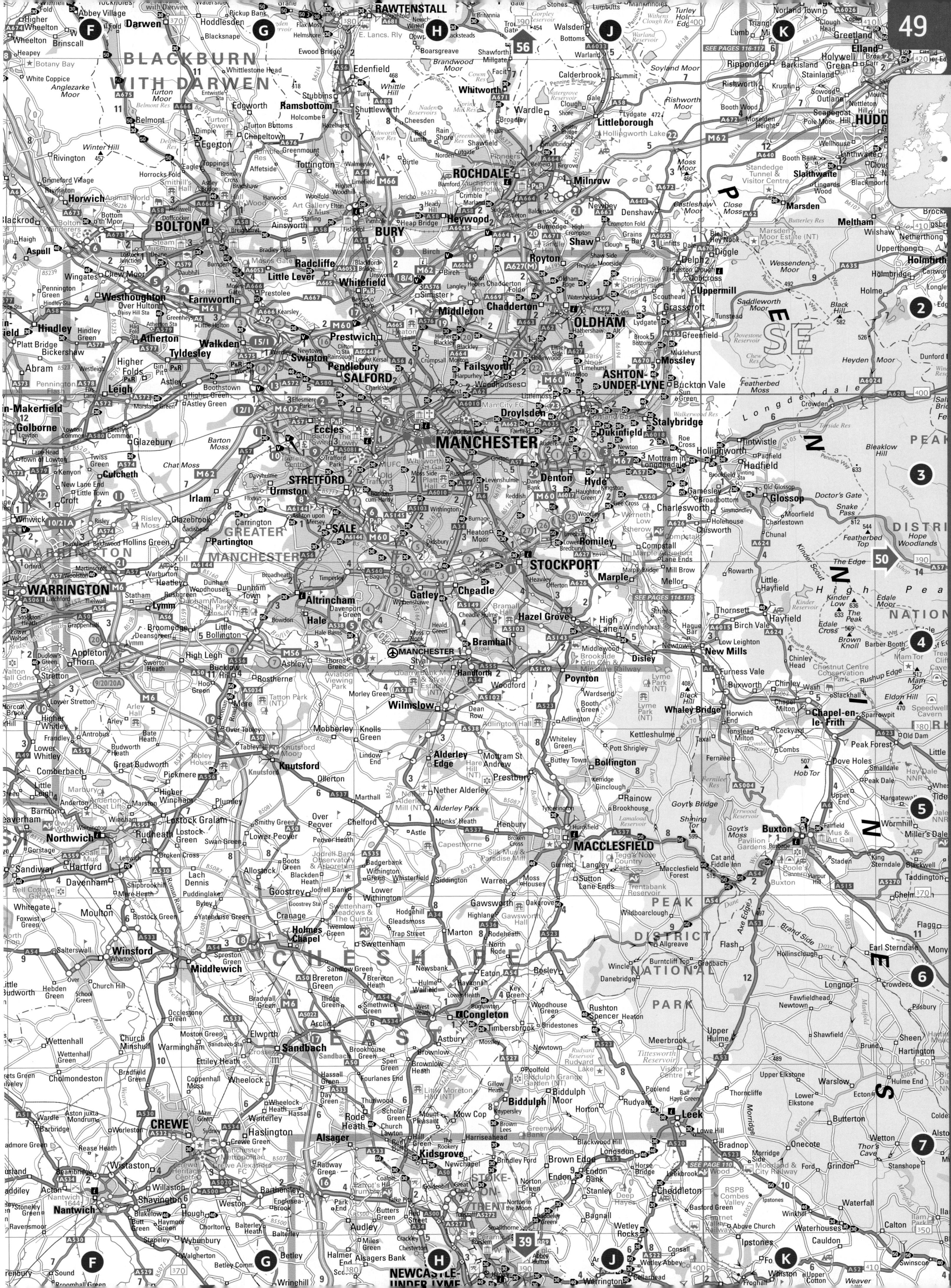

For a more detailed map of Stoke-on-Trent see page 110, Greater Manchester see pages 114-115 and Leeds & Bradford see pages 116-117

RAWTENSTALL

DEWSBURY

Heckmondwike

Mirfield

Ossett

Horbury

Middlestown

HUDDERSFIELD

Ramsbottom

Whitworth

Littleborough

Marsden

Meltham

Holmfirth

Denby Dale

Skelmanthorpe

Penistone

ROCHDALE

Milnrow

BURY

Heywood

Shaw

Uppermill

Stocksbridge

Radcliffe

Whitefield

Middleton

Chadderton

OLDHAM

Mossley

Prestwich

Failsworth

ASHTON-UNDER-LYNE

Glossop

SALFORD

Swinton

Droylsden

Stalybridge

Dukinfield

Hyde

Hadfield

PEAK DISTRICT

Eccles

MANCHESTER

Denton

Romiley

Charlesworth

Bradfield

Sale

STOCKPORT

Marple

New Mills

Hayfield

Edale

Bamford

Altrincham

Hale

Cheadle

Hazel Grove

Bramhall

Disley

Hope

Hathersage

Whaley Bridge

Chapel-en-le-Frith

Castleton

Bradwell

Wilmslow

Poynton

Buxworth

Chinley

HIGH PEAK

Knutsford

Alderley Edge

Bollington

Peak Forest

Tideswell

Eyam

Grindleford

Prestbury

Rainow

Dove Holes

Calver

PEAK DISTRICT NATIONAL PARK

Macclesfield

Buxton

Bakewell

Holmes Chapel

Congleton

Leek

Matlock

Sandbach

Biddulph

Alsager

Kidsgrove

NATIONAL PARK

STOKE-ON-TRENT

Waterhouses

NEWCASTLE-UNDER-LYME

CHESHIRE

DERBYSHIRE

0 2 4 6 miles
0 2 4 6 8 10 km

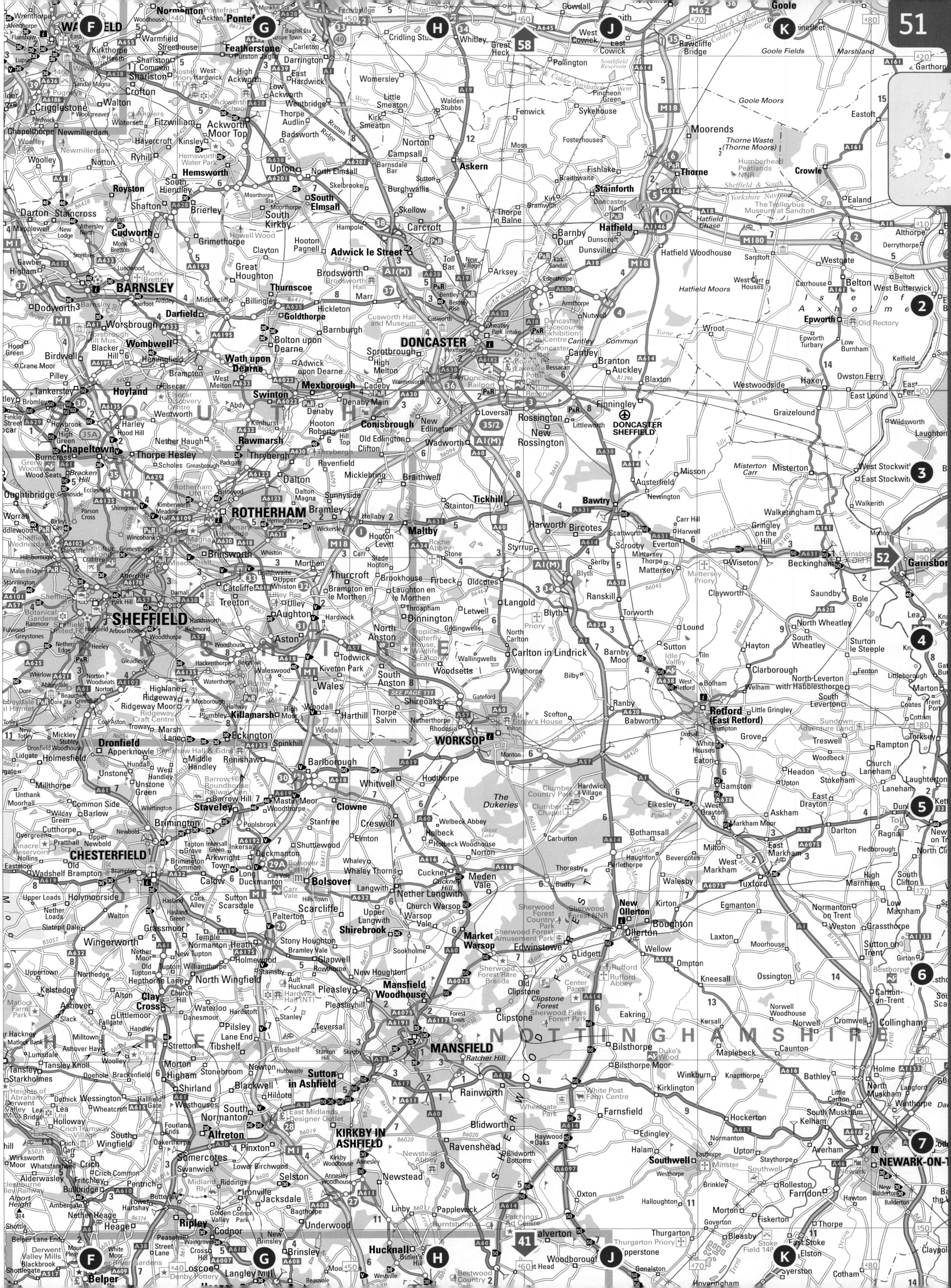
Goole
Thorne
Crowle
Hatfield
Askern
South Elmsall
BARNSLEY
DONCASTER
DONCASTER SHEFFIELD
Epworth
Isle of Axholme
Mexborough
Conisbrough
Rossington
Bawtry
ROTHERHAM
Maltby
Tickhill
SHEFFIELD
Retford (East Retford)
Dronfield
WORKSOP
Staveley
Bolsover
CHESTERFIELD
Clowne
Ollerton
Tuxford
Market Warsop
Mansfield Woodhouse
MANSFIELD
NOTTINGHAMSHIRE
Sutton in Ashfield
KIRKBY IN ASHFIELD
Alfreton
Ripley
Southwell
NEWARK-ON-T
Hucknall
Belper
SOUTH YORKSHIRE
DERBYSHIRE
SHERWOOD FOREST
The Dukeries
SEE PAGE 111

For a more detailed map of Sheffield see page 111

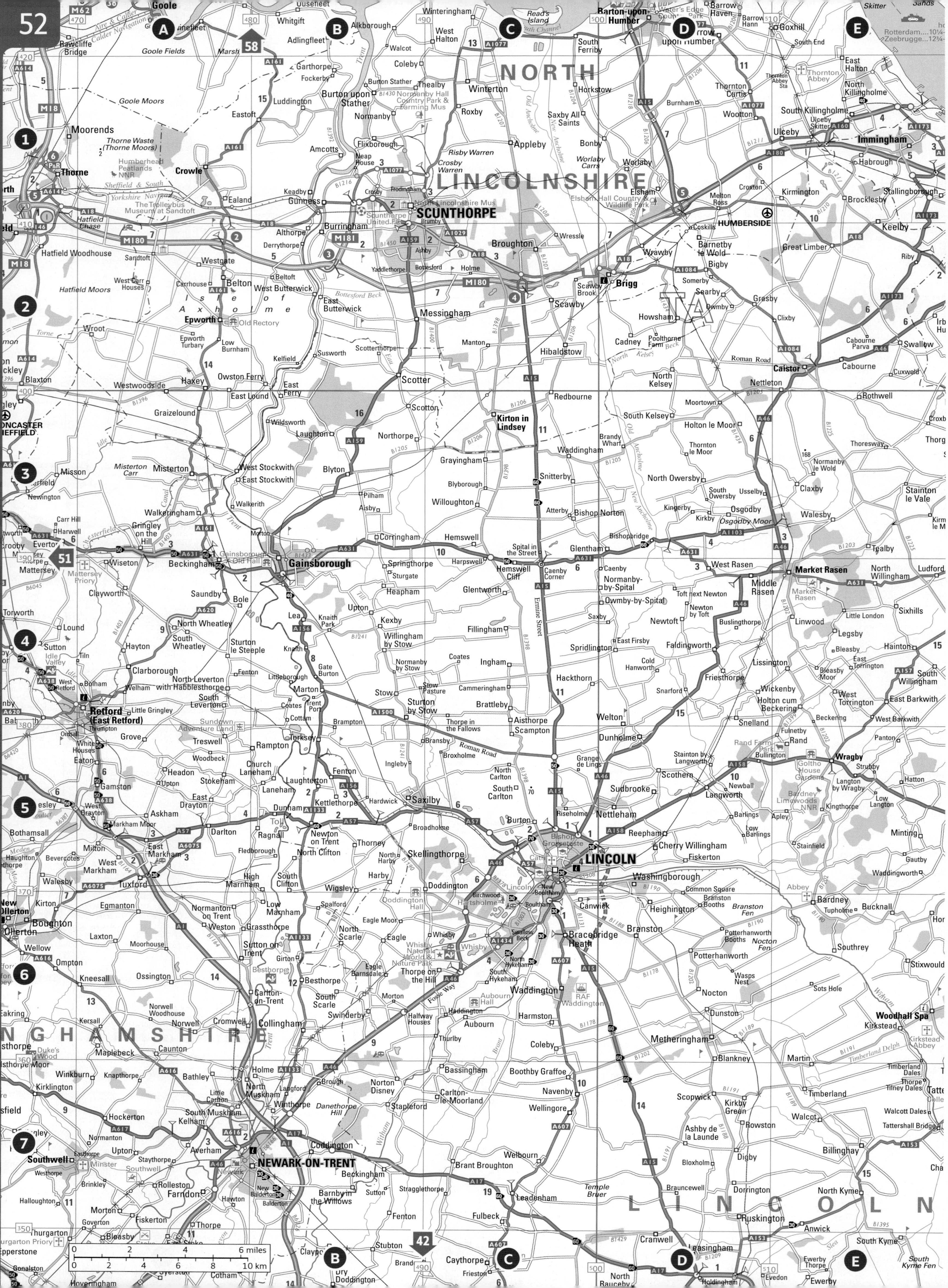
NORTH LINCOLNSHIRE
LINCOLNSHIRE
NGHAMSHIRE
LINCOLN
Goole
Goole Fields
Goole Moors
Rawcliffe Bridge
Thorne
Moorends
Thorne Waste (Thorne Moors)
Humberhead Peatlands NNR
Crowle
Eastoft
Luddington
Garthorpe
Fockerby
Whitgift
Adlingfleet
Alkborough
Winteringham
West Halton
Whitton
Read's Island
Barton-upon-Humber
Barrow upon Humber
Barrow Haven
Goxhill
South Ferriby
Horkstow
Winterton
Burton upon Stather
Normanby Hall Country Park & Farming Mus
Thealby
Coleby
Roxby
Saxby All Saints
Bonby
Worlaby
Appleby
Risby Warren
Crosby Warren
Flixborough
Amcotts
Neap House
Keadby
Gunness
Frodingham
Crosby
North Lincolnshire Mus
SCUNTHORPE
Scunthorpe United FC
Brumby
Burringham
Althorpe
Derrythorpe
Ashby
Bottesford
Yaddlethorpe
Holme
Broughton
Wressle
Elsham
Elsham Hall Country & Wildlife Park
Melton Ross
Croxton
Kirmington
HUMBERSIDE
Barnetby le Wold
Bigby
Brigg
Wrawby
Scawby Brook
Scawby
Somerby
Searby
Owmby
Howsham
Grasby
Clixby
Cadney
Poolthorpe Farm
Hibaldstow
Manton
Messingham
Ealand
The Trolleybus Museum at Sandtoft
Sandtoft
Hatfield Chase
Hatfield Woodhouse
Hatfield Moors
Westgate
Belton
West Butterwick
East Butterwick
Carrhouse
West Carr Houses
Isle of Axholme
Epworth
Old Rectory
Epworth Turbary
Low Burnham
Kelfield
Susworth
Scotterthorpe
Scotter
Scotton
Wroot
Owston Ferry
East Ferry
Haxey
Westwoodside
Blaxton
East Lound
Graizelound
DONCASTER SHEFFIELD
Misson
Misterton
Misterton Carr
West Stockwith
East Stockwith
Walkerith
Walkeringham
Gringley on the Hill
Wildsworth
Laughton
Blyton
Northorpe
Pilham
Aisby
Corringham
Morton
Gainsborough
Gainsborough Old Hall
Beckingham
Wiseton
Mattersey
Mattersey Priory
Everton
Harwell
Carr Hill
Newington
Clayworth
Saundby
Bole
Lea
Knaith Park
Knaith
Springthorpe
Sturgate
Heapham
Upton
Kexby
Willingham by Stow
Gate Burton
Marton
Stow
Stow Pasture
Littleborough
North Wheatley
South Wheatley
Sturton le Steeple
Fenton
Hayton
Clarborough
North Leverton with Habblesthorpe
South Leverton
Welham
Retford (East Retford)
Ordsall
Thrumpton
Little Gringley
Grove
Sundown Adventure Land
Treswell
Woodbeck
Rampton
Coates
Cottam
Torksey
Brampton
Church Laneham
Laneham
Laughterton
Kettlethorpe
Fenton
Dunham
Ragnall
Newton on Trent
Hardwick
Saxilby
Broadholme
Thorney
North Clifton
South Clifton
Headon
Upton
Stokeham
East Drayton
Askham
Darlton
Gamston
Eaton
West Drayton
Markham Moor
Bothamsall
Milton
West Markham
East Markham
Tuxford
Egmanton
Haughton
Bevercotes
Walesby
Kirton
New Ollerton
Ollerton
Boughton
Wellow
Laxton
Moorhouse
Ompton
Kneesall
Ossington
Normanton on Trent
Weston
Grassthorpe
High Marnham
Low Marnham
Fledborough
Sutton on Trent
Carlton-on-Trent
Besthorpe
Girton
South Scarle
North Scarle
Spalford
Eagle
Eagle Moor
Eagle Barnsdale
Swinderby
Morton
Collingham
Cromwell
Norwell
Norwell Woodhouse
Kersall
Caunton
Maplebeck
Bathley
Winkburn
Knapthorpe
Kirklington
Hockerton
Normanton
Upton
Southwell
Southwell Minster
Staythorpe
Averham
Kelham
South Muskham
North Muskham
Little Carlton
Holme
Langford
Winthorpe
Coddington
NEWARK-ON-TRENT
Newark
Balderton
New Balderton
Hawton
Farndon
Rolleston
Fiskerton
Morton
Thorpe
Bleasby
Thurgarton
Halloughton
Brinkley
Barnby in the Willows
Beckingham
Sutton
Stragglethorpe
Fenton
Stubton
Claypole
Dry Doddington
Brant Broughton
Danethorpe Hill
Stapleford
Norton Disney
Carlton-le-Moorland
Bassingham
Thurlby
Halfway Houses
Haddington
Aubourn
Aubourn Hall
Thorpe on the Hill
Whisby
Whisby Nature Park
Doddington
Doddington Hall
Skellingthorpe
North Harby
Harby
Wigsley
Birchwood
Hartsholme
Boultham
New Boultham
Bracebridge Heath
North Hykeham
South Hykeham
Swallow Beck
Waddington
RAF Waddington
Harmston
Coleby
Boothby Graffoe
Navenby
Wellingore
Welbourn
Leadenham
Fulbeck
Caythorpe
Brandon
Cranwell
Temple Bruer
Leasingham
North Rauceby
Sleaford
Ruskington
Dorrington
Digby
Bloxholm
Brauncewell
Ashby de la Launde
Rowston
Kirkby Green
Scopwick
Blankney
Metheringham
Dunston
Nocton
Potterhanworth
Potterhanworth Booths
Nocton Fen
Wasps Nest
Branston
Branston Booths
Branston Fen
Heighington
Canwick
Washingborough
Fiskerton
Cherry Willingham
Reepham
Nettleham
Riseholme
Burton
Bishop Grosseteste
Sudbrooke
Scothern
Langworth
Dunholme
Welton
Grange de Lings
Scampton
Aisthorpe
Thorpe in the Fallows
Brattleby
Cammeringham
Ingham
Hackthorn
Spridlington
Fillingham
Saxby
Glentworth
Harpswell
Hemswell
Hemswell Cliff
Spital in the Street
Caenby Corner
Caenby
Glentham
Owmby-by-Spital
Normanby-by-Spital
Ermine Street
Bishopbridge
Willoughton
Blyborough
Grayingham
Kirton in Lindsey
Snitterby
Atterby
Bishop Norton
Waddingham
Brandy Wharf
Redbourne
South Kelsey
North Kelsey
Moortown
Holton le Moor
Thornton le Moor
North Owersby
South Owersby
Usselby
Kingerby
Kirkby
Osgodby
Osgodby Moor
Claxby
Walesby
Middle Rasen
Market Rasen
West Rasen
Toft next Newton
Newton by Toft
Newtoft
Faldingworth
East Firsby
Cold Hanworth
Friesthorpe
Snarford
Buslingthorpe
Lissington
Wickenby
Holton cum Beckering
Snelland
Stainton by Langworth
Rand
Rand Farm Park
Fulnetby
Bullington
Goltho House Gardens
Wragby
Newball
Barlings
Low Barlings
Apley
Bardney Limewoods NNR
Kingthorpe
Stainfield
Bardney
Tupholme
Bucknall
Southrey
Stixwould
Woodhall Spa
Kirkstead
Kirkstead Abbey
Martin
Timberland
Timberland Dales
Thorpe Tilney Dales
Walcott
Walcott Dales
Tattershall Bridge
Billinghay
North Kyme
South Kyme
South Kyme Fen
Anwick
Evedon
Ewerby
Ewerby Thorpe
Holdingham
Strubby
Langton by Wragby
Low Langton
Minting
Hatton
Panton
Gautby
Waddingworth
Sots Hole
West Barkwith
East Barkwith
West Torrington
East Torrington
Beckering
Bleasby
Bleasby Moor
Legsby
Linwood
Little London
Sixhills
Hainton
South Willingham
North Willingham
Ludford
Tealby
Stainton le Vale
Normanby le Wold
Thoresway
Rothwell
Nettleton
Caistor
Cabourne
Cabourne Parva
Cuxwold
Swallow
Grasby
Great Limber
Keelby
Riby
Brocklesby
Stallingborough
Habrough
Immingham
Ulceby
Ulceby Skitter
Thornton Abbey
Thornton Curtis
Wootton
Burnham
South Killingholme
North Killingholme
East Halton
South End
Skitter
Rotterdam...10¼
Zeebrugge...12¾
0 2 4 6 miles
0 2 4 6 8 10 km
A B C D E
1 2 3 4 5 6 7
58
51
42
M62 M18 M180 M181 A18 A161 A1077 A15 A46 A57 A631 A156 A1133 A17 A1500 A158 A607 A153 A1084 A1173 A1103 A1434 A614 A616 A617 A6075 A638 A620 A1

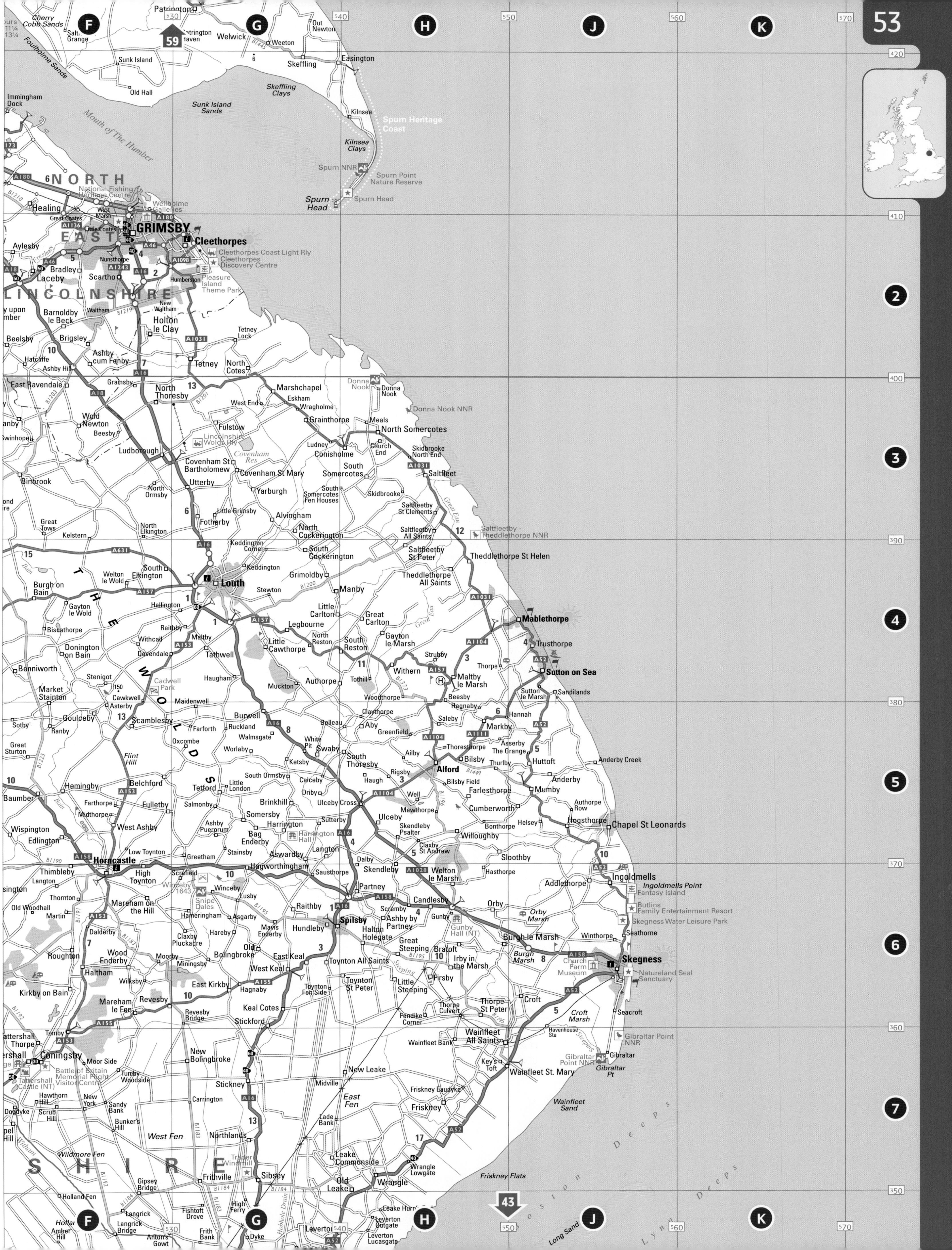

Patrington
Cherry Cobb Sands
Patrington Haven
Welwick
Out Newton
Weeton
Skeffling
Easington
Sunk Island
Old Hall
Skeffling Clays
Sunk Island Sands
Kilnsea
Spurn Heritage Coast
Kilnsea Clays
Spurn NNR
Spurn Point Nature Reserve
Spurn Head
Foulholme Sands
Immingham Dock
Mouth of The Humber
NORTH
National Fishing Heritage Centre
Healing
Wellholme Galleries
GRIMSBY
Cleethorpes
Cleethorpes Coast Light Rly
Cleethorpes Discovery Centre
Pleasure Island Theme Park
Aylesby
EAST
Bradley
Laceby
Scartho
Nunsthorpe
Humberston
LINCOLNSHIRE
New Waltham
Waltham
Barnoldby le Beck
Holton le Clay
Tetney Lock
Beelsby
Brigsley
Ashby cum Fenby
Hatcliffe
Ashby Hill
Tetney
North Cotes
East Ravendale
Grainsby
North Thoresby
Marshchapel
Donna Nook
Donna Nook NNR
West End
Eskham
Wragholme
Grainthorpe
Wold Newton
Beesby
Fulstow
Lincolnshire Wolds Rly
Covenham Res
Meals
North Somercotes
Ludney
Conisholme
Church End
Skidbrooke North End
Ludborough
Covenham St Bartholomew
Covenham St Mary
South Somercotes
Saltfleet
Binbrook
Utterby
North Ormsby
Yarburgh
South Somercotes Fen Houses
Skidbrooke
Saltfleetby St Clements
Little Grimsby
Alvingham
Great Tows
Kelstern
North Elkington
Fotherby
North Cockerington
Saltfleetby All Saints
Saltfleetby - Theddlethorpe NNR
Great Eau
Keddington Corner
South Cockerington
Saltfleetby St Peter
Theddlethorpe St Helen
Keddington
South Elkington
Welton le Wold
Louth
Burgh on Bain
Grimoldby
Theddlethorpe All Saints
Stewton
Manby
Gayton le Wold
Hallington
Little Carlton
Great Carlton
Mablethorpe
Biscathorpe
Raithby
Legbourne
Trusthorpe
Withcall
Maltby
Little Cawthorpe
North Reston
South Reston
Gayton le Marsh
Donington on Bain
Tathwell
Sutton on Sea
Strubby
Benniworth
Thorpe
Withern
Maltby le Marsh
Stenigot
Cadwell Park
Haugham
Authorpe
Tothill
Market Stainton
Muckton
Sandilands
Sutton le Marsh
Cawkwell
Woodthorpe
Beesby
Asterby
Maidenwell
Hagnaby
Goulceby
Scamblesby
Burwell
Claythorpe
Saleby
Hannah
Ranby
Farforth
Ruckland
Belleau
Aby
Markby
Sotby
Walmsgate
Greenfield
Oxcombe
White Pit
Swaby
Thoresthorpe
Asserby
Great Sturton
Worlaby
The Grange
Flint Hill
Ketsby
South Thoresby
Ailby
Bilsby
Huttoft
Anderby Creek
Thurlby
Alford
Rigsby
South Ormsby
Calceby
Haugh
Bilsby Field
Anderby
Hemingby
Belchford
Little London
Tetford
Driby
Farlesthorpe
Mumby
Baumber
Farthorpe
Fulletby
Salmonby
Brinkhill
Ulceby Cross
Well
Mawthorpe
Cumberworth
Authorpe Row
Midthorpe
Somersby
Ulceby
Hogsthorpe
Chapel St Leonards
Wispington
West Ashby
Ashby Puerorum
Harrington
Skendleby
Helsey
Bonthorpe
Edlington
Bag Enderby
Harrington Hall
Sutterby
Skendleby Psalter
Willoughby
Low Toynton
Stainsby
Langton
Claxby St Andrew
Horncastle
Greetham
Aswardby
Sloothby
Thimbleby
High Toynton
Scrafield
Hagworthingham
Dalby
Skendleby
Welton le Marsh
Hasthorpe
Ingoldmells
Langton
Winceby 1643
Winceby
Sausthorpe
Addlethorpe
Ingoldmells Point
Fantasy Island
Thornton
Snipe Dales
Lusby
Partney
Candlesby
Butlins Family Entertainment Resort
Old Woodhall
Mareham on the Hill
Raithby
Scremby
Orby
Martin
Hameringham
Asgarby
Ashby by Partney
Gunby
Orby Marsh
Skegness Water Leisure Park
Spilsby
Gunby Hall (NT)
Dalderby
Claxby Pluckacre
Hareby
Mavis Enderby
Hundleby
Halton Holegate
Burgh le Marsh
Winthorpe
Seathorne
Great Steeping
Bratoft
Roughton
Wood Enderby
Moorby
Old Bolingbroke
East Keal
Irby in the Marsh
Burgh Marsh
Church Farm Museum
Skegness
Haltham
Miningsby
West Keal
Toynton All Saints
Natureland Seal Sanctuary
Wilksby
Steeping
Firsby
Kirkby on Bain
East Kirkby
Toynton Fen Side
Toynton St Peter
Little Steeping
Croft
Mareham le Fen
Revesby
Hagnaby
Thorpe Culvert
Thorpe St Peter
Croft Marsh
Revesby Bridge
Keal Cotes
Fendike Corner
Seacroft
Stickford
Havenhouse Sta
Tattershall Thorpe
Tumby
Wainfleet All Saints
Gibraltar Point NNR
Coningsby
New Bolingbroke
Wainfleet Bank
Moor Side
Battle of Britain Memorial Flight Visitor Centre
Tumby Woodside
Key's Toft
Gibraltar Point NNR
Gibraltar
Gibraltar Pt
Tattershall Castle (NT)
New Leake
Wainfleet St. Mary
Stickney
Midville
Hawthorn Hill
New York
Carrington
Friskney Eaudyke
Wainfleet Sand
Dogdyke
Scrub Hill
Sandy Bank
East Fen
Friskney
Bunker's Hill
Lade Bank
West Fen
Northlands
Boston Deeps
Wildmore Fen
Trader Windmill
Leake Commonside
Wrangle Lowgate
SHIRE
Frithville
Sibsey
Wrangle
Friskney Flats
Lynn Deeps
Gipsey Bridge
Old Leake
Holland Fen
Langrick
Fishtoft Drove
High Ferry
Hobhole Drain
Leake Hurn's End
Leverton Outgate
Langrick Bridge
Frith Bank
Leverton
Leverton Lucasgate
Amber Hill
Anton's Gowt
Dyke
Long Sand
THE WOLDS
Witham
Bain
Steeping

59
43

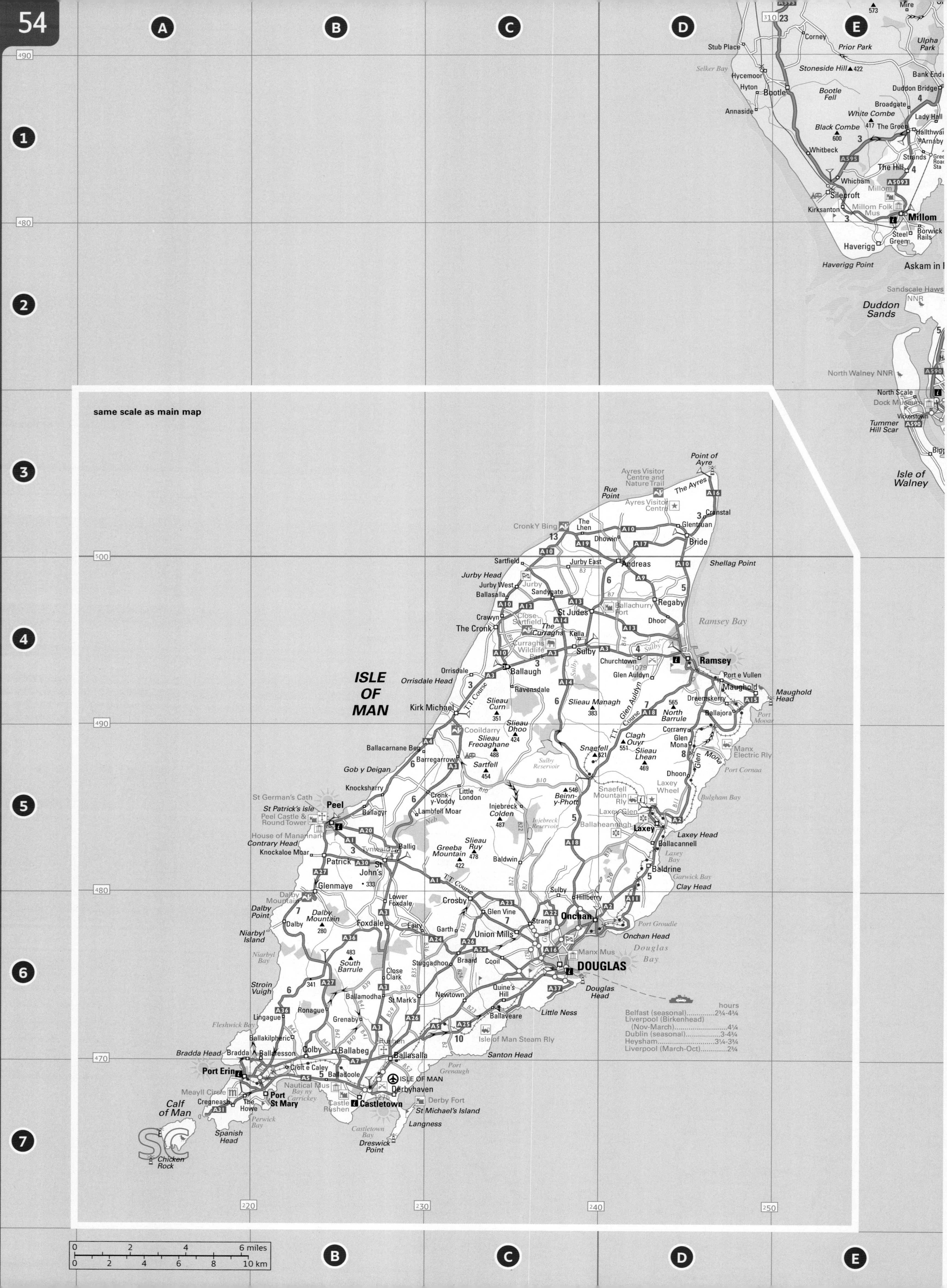

ISLE
OF
MAN

same scale as main map

Point of
Ayre

Ayres Visitor
Centre and
Nature Trail

The Ayres

Rue
Point

Ayres Visitor
Centre

Cranstal

The Lhen

Glentruan

Cronk Y Bing

Bride

Shellag Point

Sartfield

Jurby East
Andreas

Jurby Head
Jurby West
Ballasalla
Jurby
Sandygate

Ballachurry
Fort

Regaby

Crawyn

St Judes

Dhoor

Ramsey Bay

Close
Sartfield

Kella

The Cronk

The
Curraghs

Ballacarnell

Sulby

Churchtown

Ramsey

Curraghs
Wildlife
Park

Orrisdale

Ballaugh

Sulby

Glen Auldyn

Port e Vullen
Maughold

Orrisdale Head

Ravensdale

Maughold
Head

Slieau Managh
383

Dreemskerry

Kirk Michael

Slieau
Curn
351

North
Barrule
565

Ballajora

Port
Mooar

Slieau
Dhoo
424

Clagh
Ouyr
551

Corrany

Cooildarry

Glen Mona

Slieau
Freoaghane
488

Snaefell
621

Slieau
Lhean
469

Manx
Electric Rly

Ballacarnane Beg

Barregarrow

Sartfell
454

Sulby Reservoir

Dhoon

Gob y Deigan

Knocksharry

Cronk
y-Voddy

Little
London

Beinn-
y-Phott
546

Laxey
Wheel

Port Cornaa

St German's Cath

Laxey
Mountain
Rly

Bulgham Bay

St Patrick's Isle
Peel Castle &
Round Tower

Peel

Lambfell Moar

Injebreck
Colden
487

Laxey Glen

House of Manannan
Contrary Head

Ballagyr

Snaefell
Mountain

Laxey

Injebreck
Reservoir

Laxey Head

Knockaloe Moar

Tynwald

Ballig

Slieau
Ruy
478

Ballaheannagh

Ballacannell

Patrick

St
John's

Greeba
Mountain
422

Baldwin

Laxey
Bay

Glenmaye

Garwick Bay

Dalby
Mountain

Lower
Foxdale

Crosby

Sulby

Clay Head

Dalby
Point

Glen Vine

Hillberry

Niarbyl
Island

Dalby
280

Foxdale

Fairy

Garth

Union Mills

Strang

Onchan

Port Groudle

Niarbyl
Bay

483

Onchan Head

South
Barrule

Stuggadhoo

Braaid

Cooil

Manx Mus

Douglas
Bay

Stroin
Vuigh

341

Ronague

St Mark's

Newtown

Quine's
Hill

DOUGLAS

Douglas
Head

Lingague

Ballamodha

Grenaby

Ballaveare

Little Ness

hours
Belfast (seasonal)..............2¾-4¾
Liverpool (Birkenhead)
(Nov-March)...................4¼
Dublin (seasonal)...............3-4¼
Heysham..........................3¼-3¾
Liverpool (March-Oct)........2¾

Fleshwick Bay

Ballakilpheric

Rushen

Isle of Man Steam Rly

Bradda Head

Bradda

Ballafesson

Colby

Ballabeg

Ballasalla

Santon Head

Port Erin

Ballakilpheric

Port
Grenaugh

Croit e Caley

Ballasalla

Meayll Circle

Nautical Mus
Bay ny
Carrickey

Balladoole

ISLE OF MAN

Derbyhaven

Creganeash

The
Howe

Port
St Mary

Castle
Rushen

Castletown

Derby Fort

Calf
of Man

A31

St Michael's Island

Spanish
Head

Perwick
Bay

Castletown
Bay

Langness

Chicken
Rock

Dreswick
Point

0   2   4   6 miles
0 2 4 6 8 10 km

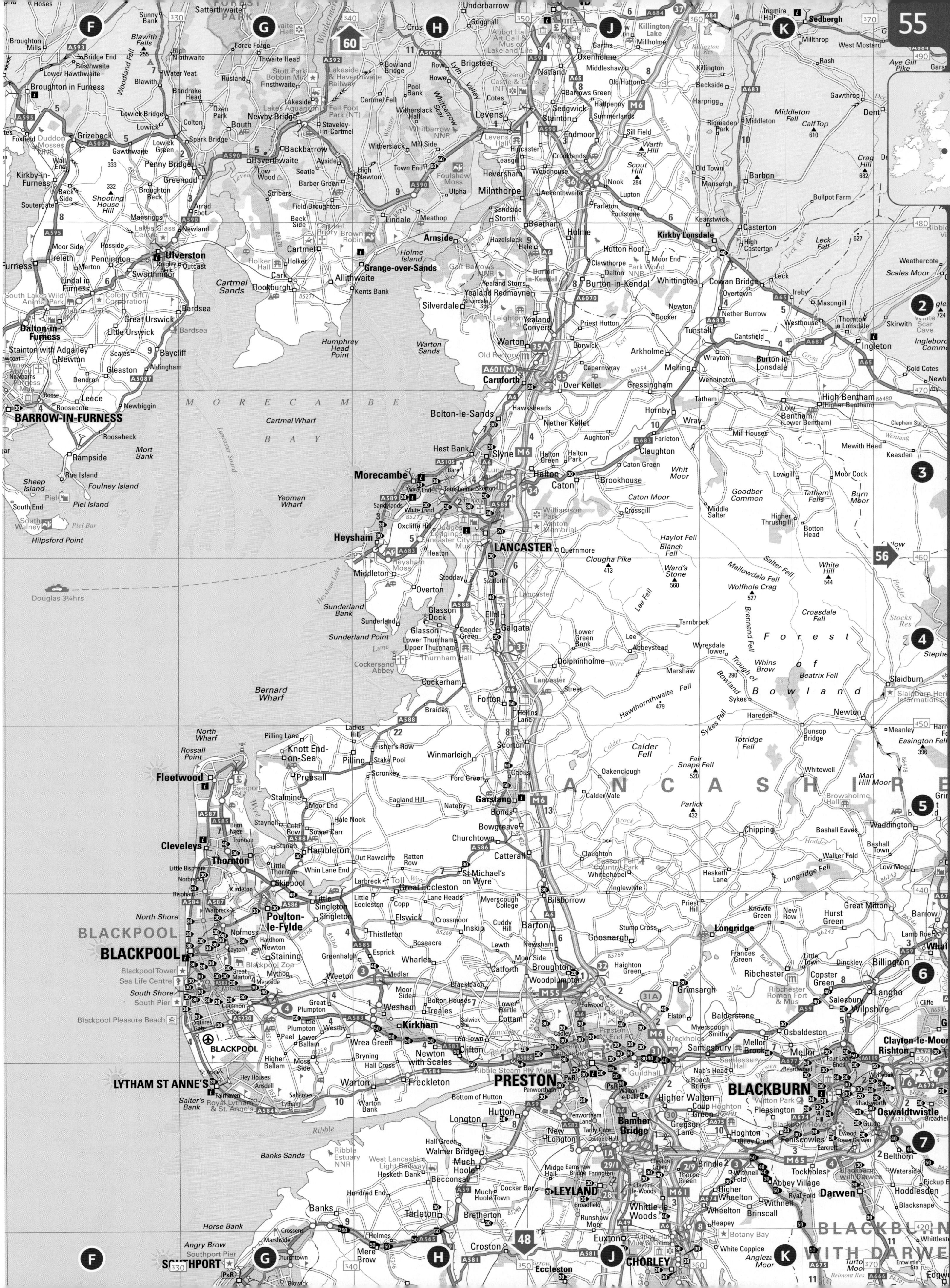
BARROW-IN-FURNESS
Ulverston
Dalton-in-Furness
Kirkby-in-Furness
Broughton in Furness
Grange-over-Sands
Cartmel
Newby Bridge
Lakeside
Levens
Milnthorpe
Arnside
Silverdale
Carnforth
Kirkby Lonsdale
Sedbergh
Ingleton
High Bentham
Morecambe
Heysham
LANCASTER
Galgate
Garstang
Fleetwood
Cleveleys
Thornton
Poulton-le-Fylde
BLACKPOOL
LYTHAM ST ANNE'S
Kirkham
Longridge
Clitheroe
PRESTON
BLACKBURN
Darwen
LEYLAND
CHORLEY
SOUTHPORT
Oswaldtwistle
M O R E C A M B E
B A Y
Forest of Bowland
L A N C A S H I R E
BLACKBURN WITH DARWEN
Douglas 3¼hrs
Ribble
60
56
48

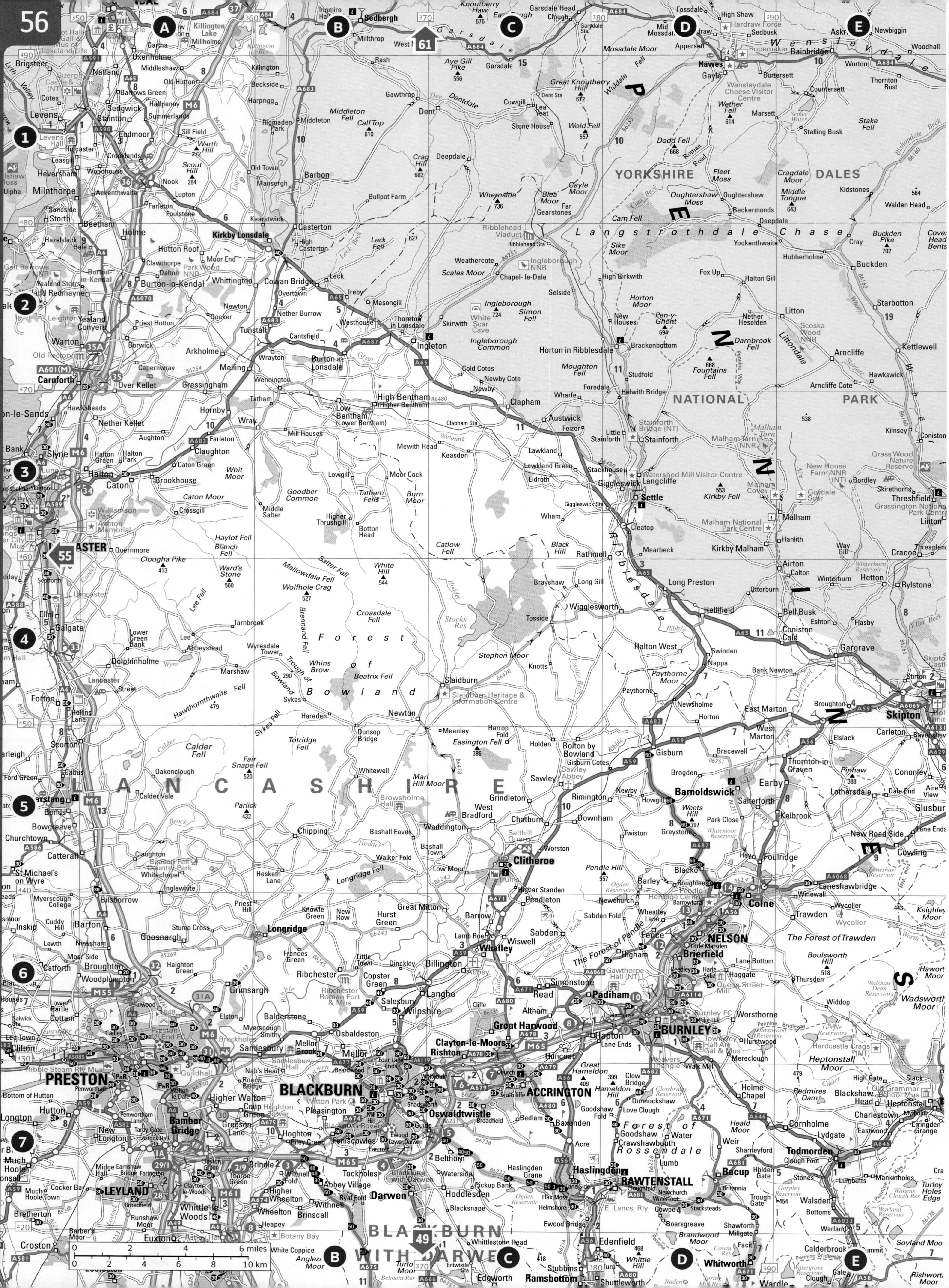
A
B
C
D
E
1
2
3
4
5
6
7
61
55
49
YORKSHIRE DALES
NATIONAL PARK
PENNINES
LANCASHIRE
Forest of Bowland
Langstrothdale Chase
Wensleydale
Ribblesdale
Garsdale
Dentdale
Forest of Rossendale
The Forest of Pendle
PRESTON
BLACKBURN
BURNLEY
ACCRINGTON
NELSON
RAWTENSTALL
LEYLAND
Kirkby Lonsdale
Sedbergh
Hawes
Settle
Clitheroe
Skipton
Colne
Carnforth
Garstang
Longridge
Darwen
Oswaldtwistle
Haslingden
Bacup
Todmorden
Whitworth
Padiham
Brierfield
Barnoldswick
Ingleton
High Bentham
Kendal
Milnthorpe
Whalley
Great Harwood
Clayton-le-Moors
Rishton
Bamber Bridge
Chorley
BLACKBURN WITH DARWEN
0 2 4 6 miles
0 2 4 6 8 10 km

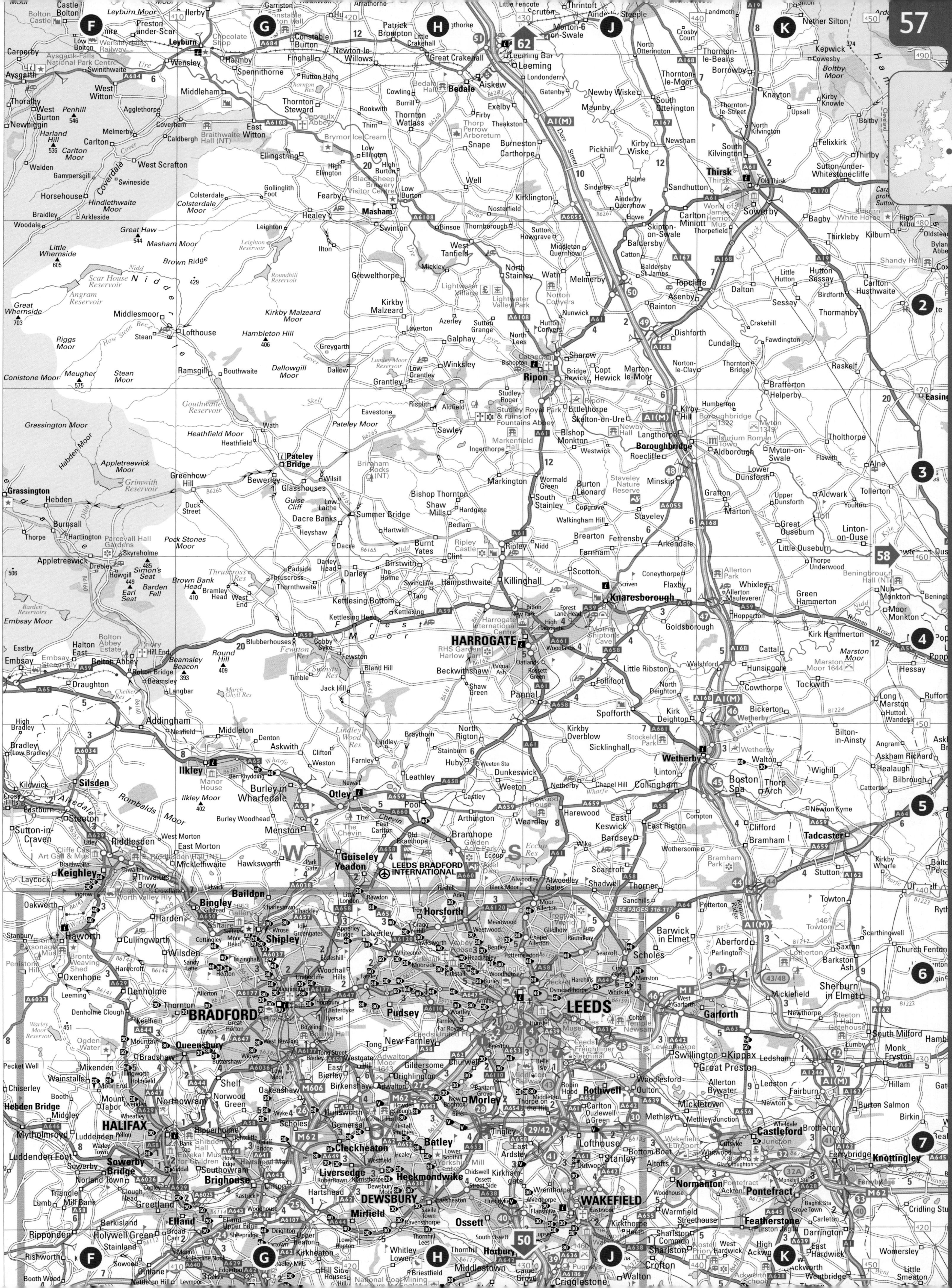

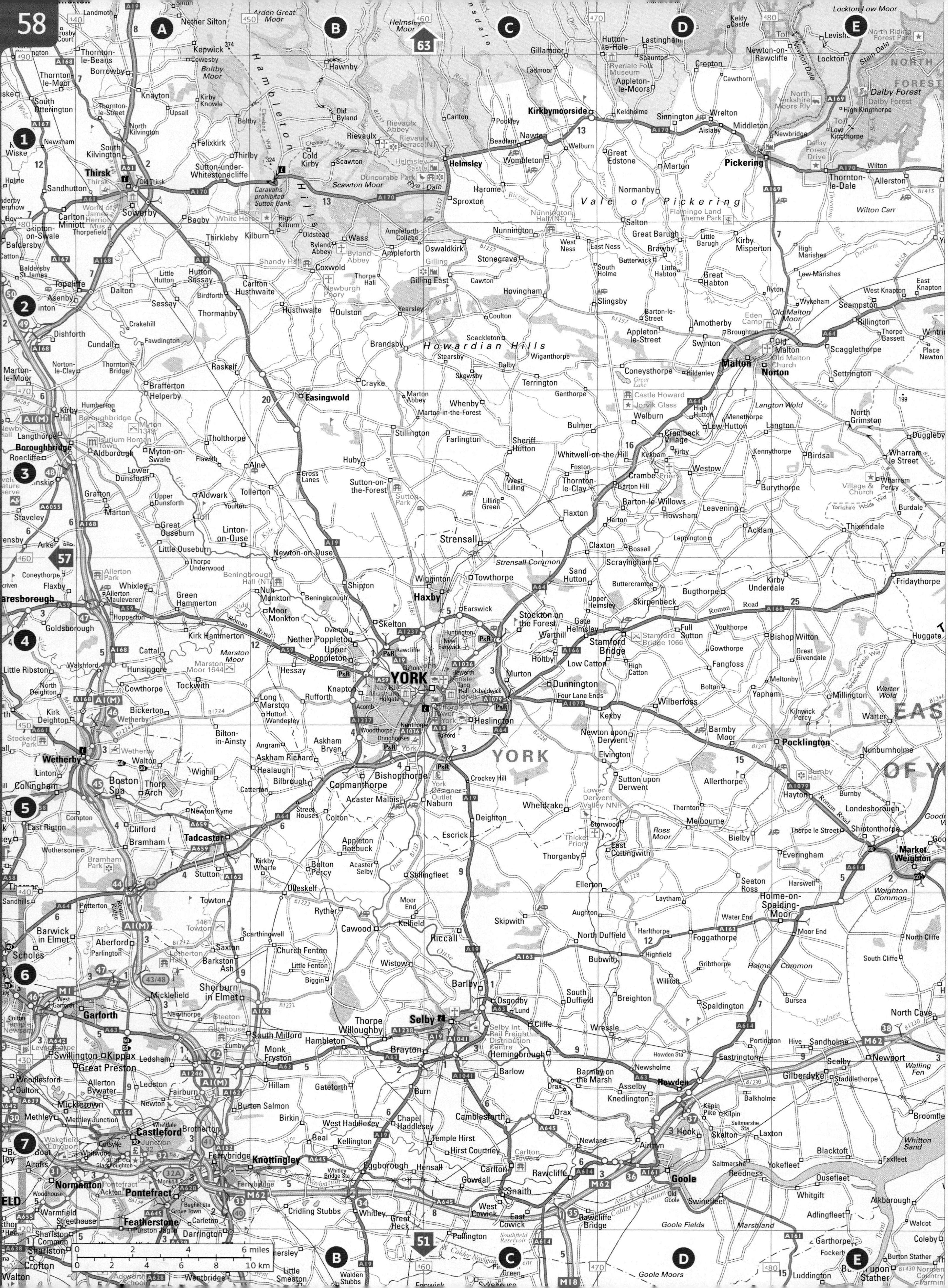
A
B
C
D
E
1
2
3
4
5
6
7
63
57
51
Arden Great Moor
Helmsley Moor
Lockton Low Moor
Nether Silton
Landmoth
Thornton-le-Beans
Borrowby
Thornton-le-Moor
Kepwick
Cowesby
Boltby Moor
Hawnby
Gillamoor
Fadmoor
Hutton-le-Hole
Lastingham
Spaunton
Ryedale Folk Museum
Appleton-le-Moors
Keldy Castle
Cropton
Cawthorn
Newton-on-Rawcliffe
Levisham
Lockton
North Riding Forest Park
NORTH
FOREST
Dalby Forest
High Kingthorpe
Stain Dale
Newton Dale
Hambleton Hills
South Otterington
Knayton
Upsall
Kirby Knowle
Thornton-le-Street
North Kilvington
Old Byland
Rievaulx Abbey
Rievaulx Terrace (NT)
Carlton
Pockley
Kirkbymoorside
Keldholme
Sinnington
Wrelton
Aislaby
Middleton
North Yorkshire Moors Rly
Newbridge
Low Kingthorpe
Dalby Forest Drive
Newsham
Felixkirk
Thirlby
Rievaulx
Cold Kirby
Scawton
Helmsley Castle
Helmsley
Beadlam
Nawton
Welburn
Wombleton
Great Edstone
Marton
Pickering
Thornton-le-Dale
Wilton
Allerston
South Kilvington
Thirsk
Sutton-under-Whitestonecliffe
Old Thirsk
Caravans prohibited Sutton Bank
Duncombe Park
Rye Dale
Scawton Moor
Harome
Sandhutton
Sowerby
Carlton Miniott
World of James Herriot
Bagby
Kilburn White Horse
High Kilburn
Sproxton
Riccal
Normanby
Vale of Pickering
Flamingo Land Theme Park
Wilton Carr
Nunnington Hall (NT)
Salton
Skipton-on-Swale
Baldersby
Thorpefield
Thirkleby
Kilburn
Oldstead
Wass
Ampleforth College
Byland Abbey
Oswaldkirk
Nunnington
Great Barugh
Little Barugh
Kirby Misperton
West Ness
East Ness
Brawby
Butterwick
High Marishes
Low Marishes
Baldersby St James
Ampleforth
Coxwold
Stonegrave
Gilling
Gilling East
Shandy Hall
Thorpe Hall
South Holme
Little Habton
Great Habton
Topcliffe
Asenby
Dalton
Little Hutton
Hutton Sessay
Carlton Husthwaite
Birdforth
Newburgh Priory
Cawton
Hovingham
Slingsby
Ryton
Wykeham
West Knapton
East Knapton
Scampston
Sessay
Thormanby
Husthwaite
Oulston
Yearsley
Coulton
Barton-le-Street
Amotherby
Eden Camp
Old Malton Moor
Rillington
Dishforth
Crakehill
Fawdington
Scackleton
Appleton-le-Street
Broughton
Thorpe Bassett
Wintringham
Cundall
Brandsby
Howardian Hills
Stearsby
Dalby
Skewsby
Wiganthorpe
Swinton
Old Malton
Old Malton Church
Malton
Norton
Scagglethorpe
Place Newton
Marton-le-Moor
Norton-le-Clay
Thornton Bridge
Raskelf
Crayke
Terrington
Coneysthorpe
Great Lake
Hildenley
Settrington
Brafferton
Helperby
Easingwold
Ganthorpe
Castle Howard
Jorvik Glass
Kirby Hill
Humberton
Marton Abbey
Whenby
Marton-in-the-Forest
Welburn
High Hutton
Menethorpe
Langton Wold
North Grimston
Boroughbridge
Myton
Isurium Roman Town
Langthorpe
Aldborough
Myton-on-Swale
Tholthorpe
Stillington
Farlington
Sheriff Hutton
Bulmer
Crambeck Village
Low Hutton
Langton
Duggleby
Kennythorpe
Wharram le Street
Roecliffe
Flawith
Alne
Huby
Whitwell-on-the-Hill
Kirkham
Firby
Birdsall
Westow
Wharram Percy
Village & Church
Minskip
Grafton
Lower Dunsforth
Upper Dunsforth
Aldwark
Tollerton
Youlton
Cross Lanes
Sutton-on-the-Forest
Sutton Park
West Lilling
Lilling Green
Foston
Thornton-le-Clay
Crambe
Barton Hill
Barton-le-Willows
Howsham
Leavening
Burythorpe
Burdale
Yorkshire Wolds Way
Staveley
Marton
Great Ouseburn
Linton-on-Ouse
Flaxton
Harton
Acklam
Thixendale
Little Ouseburn
Strensall
Claxton
Bossall
Leppington
Arkendale
Thorpe Underwood
Newton-on-Ouse
Strensall Common
Scrayingham
Kirby Underdale
Fridaythorpe
Allerton Park
Coneythorpe
Flaxby
Whixley
Allerton Mauleverer
Beningbrough Hall (NT)
Shipton
Wigginton
Towthorpe
Sand Hutton
Buttercrambe
Bugthorpe
Knaresborough
Green Hammerton
Nun Monkton
Beningbrough
Haxby
Upper Helmsley
Skirpenbeck
Roman Road
Goldsborough
Hopperton
Moor Monkton
Earswick
Stockton on the Forest
Gate Helmsley
Full Sutton
Youlthorpe
Bishop Wilton
Huggate
Kirk Hammerton
Marston Moor
Overton
Skelton
Huntington
New Earswick
Warthill
Stamford Bridge
Stamford Bridge 1066
Gowthorpe
Great Givendale
Cattal
Nether Poppleton
Upper Poppleton
Rawcliffe
Holtby
Low Catton
High Catton
Fangfoss
Little Ribston
Walshford
Hunsingore
Marston Moor 1644
Hessay
Clifton
YORK
Heworth
Minster
Murton
Dunnington
Bolton
Meltonby
Warter Wold
North Deighton
Cowthorpe
Tockwith
Long Marston
Rufforth
Knapton
Nat Rly Museum
Holgate
Jorvik
Osbaldwick
Four Lane Ends
Wilberfoss
Yapham
Millington
Kirk Deighton
Bickerton
Wetherby
Hutton Wandesley
Acomb
Clifford's Tower
Heslington
Kexby
Kilnwick Percy
Warter
EAST
Stockeld Park
Bilton-in-Ainsty
Angram
Askham Bryan
Woodthorpe
Dringhouses
Fulford
Newton upon Derwent
Barmby Moor
Pocklington
Nunburnholme
Askham Richard
Walton
Healaugh
Bishopthorpe
Elvington
Wighill
Bilbrough
York Designer Outlet
Crockey Hill
Sutton upon Derwent
Allerthorpe
Burnby Hall
Boston Spa
Thorp Arch
Linton
Collingham
Catterton
Copmanthorpe
Acaster Malbis
Naburn
Wheldrake
Lower Derwent Valley NNR
Thornton
Hayton
Burnby
Londesborough
Goodmanham
Newton Kyme
Street Houses
Colton
Deighton
Melbourne
Ross Moor
Thorpe le Street
Shiptonthorpe
East Rigton
Compton
Clifford
Bramham
Tadcaster
Appleton Roebuck
Escrick
Storwood
Thicket Priory
East Cottingwith
Bielby
Market Weighton
Wothersome
Kirkby Wharfe
Bolton Percy
Acaster Selby
Stillingfleet
Thorganby
Everingham
Bramham Park
Stutton
Ellerton
Seaton Ross
Harswell
Weighton Common
Thorner
Sandhills
Towton
Ulleskelf
Laytham
Holme-on-Spalding-Moor
Potterton
Ryther
Moor End
Kelfield
Skipwith
Aughton
Water End
Barwick in Elmet
1461 Towton
Scarthingwell
Cawood
Riccall
North Duffield
Harlthorpe
Foggathorpe
Moor End
North Cliffe
Aberford
Saxton
Church Fenton
Highfield
South Cliffe
Scholes
Parlington
Lotherton Hall
Barkston Ash
Little Fenton
Wistow
Bubwith
Gribthorpe
Holme
Common
Biggin
Willitoft
Sherburn in Elmet
Barlby
Micklefield
South Duffield
Breighton
Bursea
West Garforth
Garforth
Newthorpe
Steeton Hall Gatehouse
Thorpe Willoughby
Selby
Osgodby
Lund
Cliffe
Spaldington
North Cave
Selby Int. Rail Freight Distribution Centre
Wressle
Foulness
Colton
Temple Newsam
South Milford
Lumby
Hambleton
Brayton
Hemingbrough
Portington
Hive
Sandholme
Newport
Levensthorpe
Swillington
Kippax
Ledsham
Monk Fryston
Howden Sta
Eastrington
Scalby
Walling Fen
Great Preston
Newsholme
Barmby on the Marsh
Gilberdyke
Staddlethorpe
Woodlesford
Allerton Bywater
Ledston
Hillam
Barlow
Long Drax
Asselby
Howden
Oulton
Fairburn
Gateforth
Burn
Knedlington
Balkholme
Mickletown
Newton
Burton Salmon
Camblesforth
Drax
Kilpin Pike
Kilpin
Broomfleet
Methley
Methley Junction
Birkin
Chapel Haddlesey
Saltmarshe Sta
Castleford
Brotherton
West Haddlesey
Temple Hirst
Newland
3 Hook
Skelton
Laxton
Whitton Sand
Wakefield Europort
Whitwood
Xscape
Glasshoughton
Junction 32
Beal
Kellington
Hirst Courtney
Carlton Towers
Airmyn
Blacktoft
Altofts
Ferrybridge
Knottingley
Eggborough
Hensall
Carlton
Rawcliffe
Saltmarshe
Yokefleet
Faxfleet
Normanton
Pontefract
Whitley Bridge Sta
Gowdall
Goole
Reedness
Ousefleet
Woodhouse
Ackton
Ferrybridge
Aire & Calder Navigation
Snaith
Old Goole
Swinefleet
Whitgift
Alkborough
Warmfield
Baghill Sta
Grove Town
Cridling Stubbs
Whitley
West Cowick
East Cowick
Rawcliffe Bridge
Goole Fields
Marshland
Adlingfleet
Walcot
Streethouse
Featherstone
Carleton
Great Heck
Purston Jaglin
Darrington
Pollington
Southfield Reservoir
Garthorpe
Coleby
Sharlston Common
Sharlston
Fockerby
Burton Stather
Crofton
Goole Moors
Luddington
Burton upon Stather
Normanby
Walton
Ackworth
Wentbridge
Little Smeaton
Walden Stubbs
Fenwick
Sykehouse
0 2 4 6 miles
0 2 4 6 8 10 km

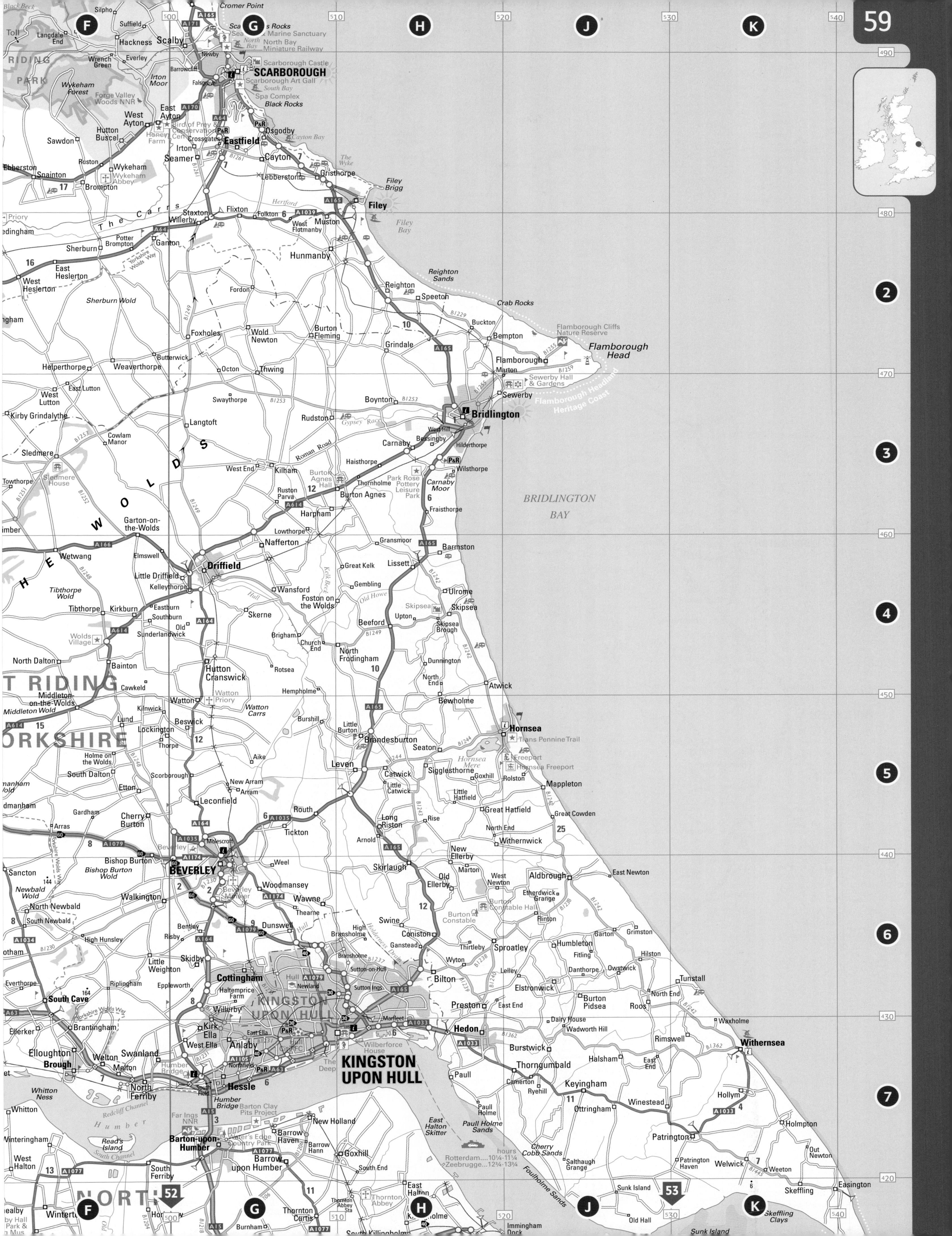
F
G
H
J
K
500
510
520
530
540
490
480
470
460
450
440
430
420
2
3
4
5
6
7
Cromer Point
Scalby
Hackness
Suffield
Silpho
Langdale End
Toll
Wrench Green
Everley
Irton Moor
Wykeham Forest
Forge Valley Woods NNR
North Bay Miniature Railway
Sea Life Marine Sanctuary
Scarborough Castle
SCARBOROUGH
Scarborough Art Gall
South Bay
Spa Complex
Black Rocks
Newby
Barrowcliff
Falsgrave
East Ayton
West Ayton
Hutton Buscel
Sawdon
Bird of Prey & Conservation Cen
Honey Farm
Crossgates
Eastfield
Osgodby
Cayton Bay
Irton
Seamer
Cayton
Ruston
Wykeham
Wykeham Abbey
Ebberston
Snainton
Brompton
Lebberston
Gristhorpe
The Wyke
Filey Brigg
Filey
Filey Bay
The Carrs
Priory
Staxton
Willerby
Flixton
Folkton
Hertford
West Flotmanby
Muston
Potter Brompton
Sherburn
Ganton
Hunmanby
East Heslerton
West Heslerton
Yorkshire Wolds Way
Sherburn Wold
Reighton Sands
Reighton
Speeton
Crab Rocks
Fordon
Foxholes
Wold Newton
Burton Fleming
Grindale
Buckton
Bempton
Flamborough Cliffs Nature Reserve
Flamborough Head
Flamborough
Marton
Sewerby Hall & Gardens
Sewerby
Flamborough Headland Heritage Coast
Helperthorpe
Weaverthorpe
Butterwick
Octon
Thwing
West Lutton
East Lutton
Swaythorpe
Boynton
Kirby Grindalythe
Langtoft
Rudston
Gypsey Race
Bridlington
Sledmere
Sledmere House
Cowlam Manor
Roman Road
Carnaby
West Hill
Bessingby
Hilderthorpe
Haisthorpe
Wilsthorpe
Towthorpe
West End
Kilham
Burton Agnes Hall
Thornholme
Park Rose Pottery Leisure Park
Carnaby Moor
Ruston Parva
Burton Agnes
Fraisthorpe
THE WOLDS
BRIDLINGTON BAY
Harpham
Garton-on-the-Wolds
Lowthorpe
Nafferton
Gransmoor
Barmston
Wetwang
Elmswell
Driffield
Little Driffield
Kelleythorpe
Great Kelk
Lissett
Gembling
Wansford
Kelk Beck
Ulrome
Foston on the Wolds
Old Howe
Skipsea
Upton
Skipsea Brough
Tibthorpe Wold
Tibthorpe
Kirkburn
Eastburn
Southburn
Old
Sunderlandwick
Skerne
Beeford
Wolds Village
Brigham
Church End
North Frodingham
North Dalton
Bainton
Rotsea
Dunnington
Hutton Cranswick
Cawkeld
Watton Priory
North End
Atwick
EAST RIDING OF YORKSHIRE
Middleton-on-the-Wolds
Middleton Wold
Hempholme
Watton
Watton Carrs
Bewholme
Kilnwick
Lund
Beswick
Burshill
Little Burton
Hornsea
Lockington
Brandesburton
Trans Pennine Trail
Thorpe
Seaton
Holme on the Wolds
Aike
Freeport
Hornsea Mere
Hornsea Freeport
South Dalton
Scorborough
Leven
Catwick
Sigglesthorne
Goxhill
Rolston
Etton
New Arram
Arram
Little Catwick
Little Hatfield
Mappleton
Leconfield
Gardham
Cherry Burton
Routh
Long Riston
Rise
Great Hatfield
Great Cowden
Arras
Tickton
North End
Withernwick
Molescroft
Beverley
Arnold
New Ellerby
Bishop Burton
Weel
Skirlaugh
Marton
West Newton
Aldbrough
East Newton
Sancton
Bishop Burton Wold
BEVERLEY
Old Ellerby
Etherdwick Grange
Newbald Wold
Walkington
Woodmansey
Beverley Minster
Wawne
Thearne
Burton Constable Hall
Burton Constable
Flinton
North Newbald
South Newbald
Bentley
Dunswell
High Hunsley
Risby
Swine
Coniston
Bransholme
Ganstead
Thirtleby
Sproatley
Humbleton
Garton
Grimston
Fitling
Hilston
Little Weighton
Skidby
Wyton
Lelley
Danthorpe
Owstwick
Everthorpe
Riplingham
Cottingham
Eppleworth
Bilton
Elstronwick
Tunstall
South Cave
Haltemprice Farm
Hull
Newland
Sutton-on-Hull
Sutton Ings
Preston
East End
Burton Pidsea
Roos
North End
Brantingham
Willerby
KINGSTON UPON HULL
Marfleet
Dairy House
Waxholme
Ellerker
Kirk Ella
East Ella
Wadworth Hill
Hedon
Rimswell
Withernsea
Elloughton
West Ella
Anlaby
Hull City FC
Wilberforce House
Burstwick
Halsham
East End
Brough
Welton
Swanland
Melton
Newington
Humber Bridge
The Deep
Paull
Thorngumbald
Whitton Ness
North Ferriby
South Field
Hessle
KINGSTON UPON HULL
Camerton
Ryehill
Keyingham
Hollym
Redcliff Channel
Humber Bridge
Barton Clay Pits Project
Paull Holme
Ottringham
Winestead
Whitton
Far Ings NNR
Humber
New Holland
East Halton Skitter
Paull Holme Sands
Holmpton
Read's Island
South Channel
Winteringham
Barton-upon-Humber
Water's Edge Country Park
Barrow Haven
Barrow Hann
Patrington
Goxhill
hours
Rotterdam....10¼-11¼
Zeebrugge....12¼-13¼
Cherry Cobb Sands
Salthaugh Grange
Patrington Haven
Welwick
Out Newton
Weeton
West Halton
South Ferriby
Barrow upon Humber
South End
Foulholme Sands
Sunk Island
Easington
Skeffling
NORTH LINCOLNSHIRE
East Halton
Thornton Abbey
Thornton Curtis
Thornton Abbey Sta
Old Hall
Skeffling Clays
Burnham
Immingham Dock
Sunk Island
52
53

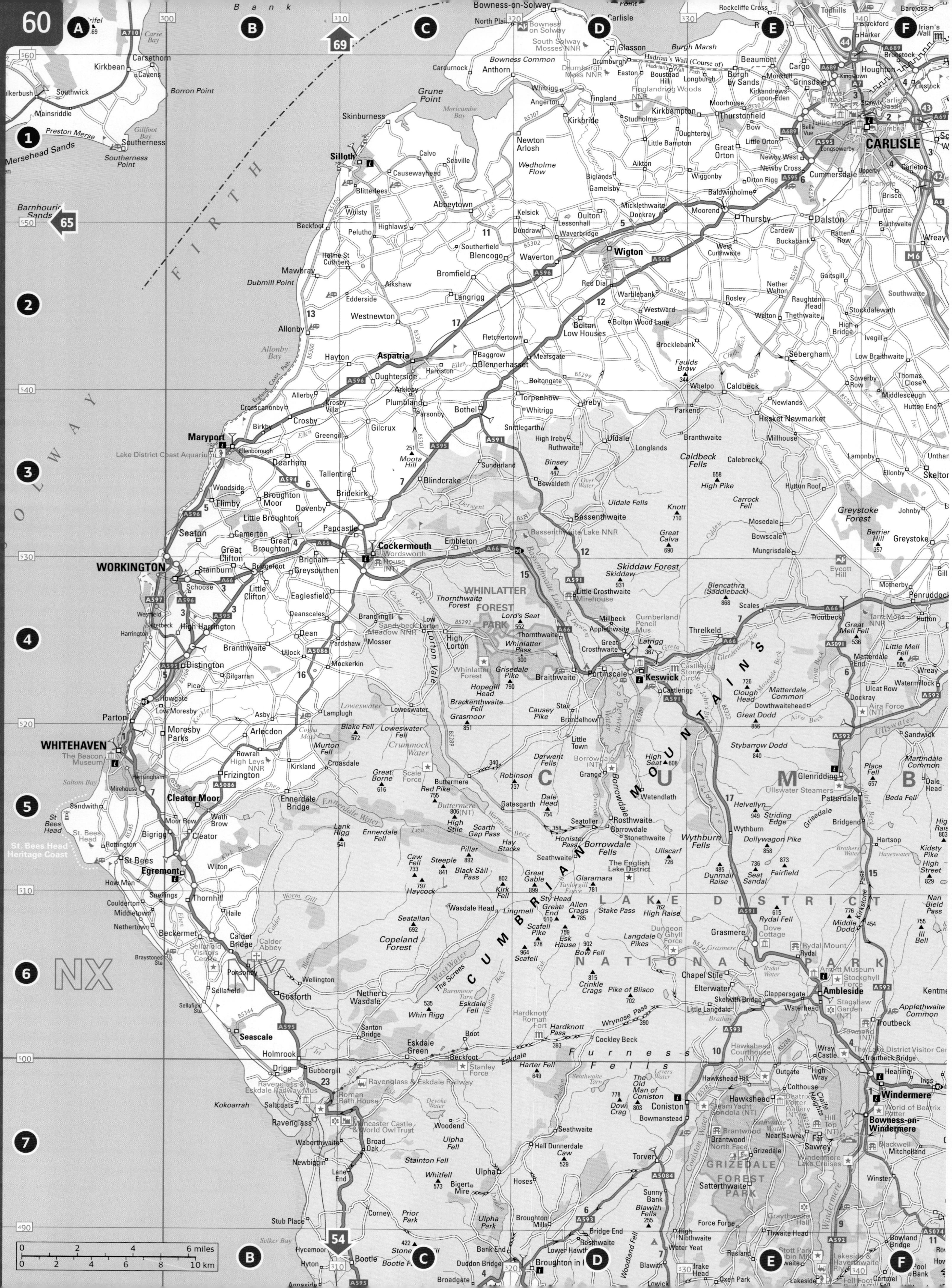
Bowness-on-Solway
North Plain
Carlisle
Rockcliffe Cross
Todhills
Blackford
Harker
Kirkbean
Carsethorn
Cavens
Southwick
Mainsriddle
Borron Point
Preston Merse
Southerness
Southerness Point
Mersehead Sands
Barnhourie Sands
Cardurnock
Anthorn
Bowness Common
Glasson
Burgh Marsh
Drumburgh
Easton
Hadrian's Wall (Course of)
Beaumont
Cargo
Houghton
Burgh by Sands
Monkhill
Grinsdale
Kingstown
Linstock
Whitrigg
Finglandrigg Woods
Fingland
Angerton
Kirkbampton
Moorhouse
Thurstonfield
Grune Point
Moricambe Bay
Skinburness
Kirkbride
Studholme
Newton Arlosh
Oughterby
Little Bampton
Little Orton
Great Orton
CARLISLE
Belle Vue
Newby West
Newby Cross
Cummersdale
Carleton
Silloth
Calvo
Seaville
Causewayhead
Wedholme Flow
Aikton
Biglands
Wiggonby
Orton Rigg
Blitterlees
Gamelsby
Baldwinholme
Abbeytown
Micklethwaite
Dockray
Moorend
Thursby
Dalston
Brisco
Durdar
Kelsick
Oulton
Lessonhall
Waverbridge
Wolsty
Beckfoot
Pelutho
Highlaws
Dundraw
Cardew
Buckabank
Ratten Row
Burthwaite
Wreay
Southerfield
Blencogo
Waverton
Wigton
West Curthwaite
Holme St Cuthbert
Mawbray
Dubmill Point
Bromfield
Red Dial
Gaitsgill
Aikshaw
Edderside
Langrigg
Warblebank
Nether Welton
Raughton Head
Southwaite
Westnewton
Allonby
Allonby Bay
Bolton Low Houses
Bolton Wood Lane
Westward
Rosley
Welton
Thethwaite
Stockdalewath
High Bridge
Ivegill
Fletchertown
Brocklebank
Sebergham
Low Braithwaite
Hayton
Aspatria
Baggrow
Blennerhasset
Mealsgate
Faulds Brow
Oughterside
Harriston
Boltongate
Whelpo
Caldbeck
Sowerby Row
Thomas Close
Allerby
Crosscanonby
Arkleby
Plumbland
Crosby Villa
Crosby
Parsonby
Torpenhow
Whitrigg
Ireby
Parkend
Newlands
Middlesceugh
Hutton End
Hesket Newmarket
Bothel
Birkby
Gilcrux
Greengill
Maryport
Ellenborough
Lake District Coast Aquarium
Snittlegarth
High Ireby
Ruthwaite
Uldale
Longlands
Branthwaite
Millhouse
Caldbeck Fells
Calebreck
Lamonby
Unthank
Moota Hill
Sunderland
Binsey
Bewaldeth
High Pike
Ellonby
Skelton
Dearham
Tallentire
Blindcrake
Hutton Roof
Woodside
Broughton Moor
Bridekirk
Uldale Fells
Carrock Fell
Knott
Greystoke Forest
Johnby
Flimby
Dovenby
Bassenthwaite
Mosedale
Little Broughton
Papcastle
Bassenthwaite Lake NNR
Great Calva
Bowscale
Berrier Hill
Greystoke
Seaton
Camerton
Great Broughton
Cockermouth
Wordsworth House (NT)
Embleton
Mungrisdale
Great Clifton
WORKINGTON
Stainburn
Bridgefoot
Brigham
Greysouthen
Skiddaw Forest
Skiddaw
Eycott Hill
Schoose
Little Clifton
Eaglesfield
WHINLATTER FOREST PARK
Thornthwaite Forest
Little Crosthwaite
Mirehouse
Blencathra (Saddleback)
Motherby
Penruddock
Westfield
Salterbeck
Harrington
High Harrington
Deanscales
Brandlingill
Lord's Seat
Millbeck
Applethwaite
Cumberland Pencil Mus
Scales
Troutbeck
Tarn Moss NNR
Hutton
Great Mell Fell
Sandybeck Meadow NNR
Low Lorton
Dean
Branthwaite
Pardshaw
Mosser
High Lorton
Thornthwaite
Whinlatter Pass
Great Crosthwaite
Latrigg
Threlkeld
Matterdale End
Little Mell Fell
Distington
Ullock
Mockerkin
Lorton Vale
Whinlatter Forest
Grisedale Pike
Braithwaite
Portinscale
Keswick
Castlerigg Stone Circle
Wreay
Watermillock
Gilgarran
Pica
Hopegill Head
Clough Head
Matterdale Common
Ulcat Row
Dockray
Howgate
Low Moresby
Brackenthwaite Fell
Grasmoor
Causey Pike
Stair
Castlerigg
Dowthwaitehead
Aira Force (NT)
Parton
Asby
Loweswater
Lamplugh
Brandelhow
Great Dodd
WHITEHAVEN
The Beacon Museum
Moresby Parks
Arlecdon
Blake Fell
Loweswater Fell
Crummock Water
Little Town
Sandwick
Stybarrow Dodd
Rowrah
High Leys NNR
Murton Fell
Croasdale
Derwent Fells
Borrowdale (NT)
High Seat
Martindale Common
Frizington
Kirkland
Scale Force
Grange
Glenridding
Place Fell
Saltom Bay
Hensingham
Mirehouse
Great Borne
Robinson
Watendlath
Dale Head
Cleator Moor
Ennerdale Bridge
Buttermere
Red Pike
Ullswater Steamers
Patterdale
Beda Fell
Sandwith
Ennerdale Water
Gatesgarth
Buttermere (NT)
Helvellyn
Wath Brow
Moor Row
Dale Head
Seatoller
Rosthwaite
Borrowdale
Striding Edge
Bridgend
St Bees Head
High Stile
Scarth Gap Pass
Honister Pass
Stonethwaite
Wythburn
Grisedale
Bigrigg
Cleator
Lank Rigg
Ennerdale Fell
Borrowdale Fells
Wythburn Fells
Hartsop
St. Bees Head Heritage Coast
Rottington
Pillar
Hay Stacks
Dollywagon Pike
St Bees
Wilton
Caw Fell
Steeple
Seathwaite
Ullscarf
The English Lake District
Fairfield
Kidsty Pike
High Street
Egremont
Black Sail Pass
Great Gable
Glaramara
Dunmail Raise
Seat Sandal
How Man
Haycock
Kirk Fell
Sty Head
Allen Crags
High Raise
Nan Bield Pass
Snellings
Thornhill
Wasdale Head
Lingmell
Great End
Stake Pass
Rydal Fell
Coulderton
Haile
Middletown
Seatallan
Scafell Pike
Esk Hause
Middle Dodd
Ill Bell
Nethertown
Dungeon Ghyll Force
Grasmere
Dove Cottage
Beckermet
Calder Bridge
Calder Abbey
Copeland Forest
Scafell
Bow Fell
Langdale Pikes
Rydal Mount
Rydal
Sellafield Visitors Centre
Braystones
NX
NY
Ponsonby
The Screes
Crinkle Crags
Chapel Stile
Armitt Museum
Stockghyll Force
Kentmere
Wellington
Sellafield
Nether Wasdale
Pike of Blisco
Elterwater
Ambleside
Gosforth
Burnmoor Tarn
Eskdale Fell
Skelwith Bridge
Clappersgate
Stagshaw Garden (NT)
Applethwaite Common
Whin Rigg
Hardknott Roman Fort
Wrynose Pass
Little Langdale
Waterhead
Troutbeck
Seascale
Santon Bridge
Boot
Hardknott Pass
Cockley Beck
Hawkshead Courthouse (NT)
Wray Castle
The Lake District Visitor Centre
Troutbeck Bridge
Holmrook
Eskdale Green
Beckfoot
Furness Fells
Drigg
Gubbergill
Stanley Force
Harter Fell
Seathwaite Tarn
The Old Man of Coniston
Levers Water
Hawkshead Hill
Outgate
High Wray
Colthouse
Claife Heights
Ravenglass & Eskdale Railway
Ravenglass & Eskdale Railway Mus
Roman Bath House
Devoke Water
Dow Crag
Coniston
Hawkshead
Beatrix Potter Gallery
Windermere
World of Beatrix Potter
Kokoarrah
Saltcoats
Bowmanstead
Steam Yacht Gondola (NT)
Ravenglass
Muncaster Castle & World Owl Trust
Woodend
Seathwaite
Brantwood
Near Sawrey
Hill Top (NT)
Bowness-on-Windermere
Waberthwaite
Broad Oak
Ulpha Fell
Hall Dunnerdale
Caw
North Face
Grizedale
Far Sawrey
Blackwell
Mitchelland
Newbiggin
Stainton Fell
Torver
GRIZEDALE FOREST PARK
Windermere Lake Cruises
Lane End
Whitfell
Ulpha
Bigert Mire
Hoses
Satterthwaite
Winster
Sunny Bank
Blawith Fells
Corney
Prior Park
Stub Place
Ulpha Park
Broughton Mills
Force Forge
Graythwaite Hall
Bridge End
Rosthwaite
High Nibthwaite
Thwaite Head
Bowland Bridge
Selker Bay
Hycemoor
Stoneside Hill
Bank End
Lower Hawthwaite
Water Yeat
Rusland
Stott Park Bobbin Mill
Lakeside & Haverthwaite Railway
Hyton
Bootle
Bootle Fell
Duddon Bridge
Broughton in Furness
Blawith
Woodland Fell
Brake Head
Oxen Park
Lakeside
Fell Foot Park
Cartmel Fell
Annaside
Broadgate
Lowick
Solway Firth
CUMBRIAN MOUNTAINS
LAKE DISTRICT NATIONAL PARK
CUMBRIA
0 2 4 6 miles
0 2 4 6 8 10 km
69
65
54

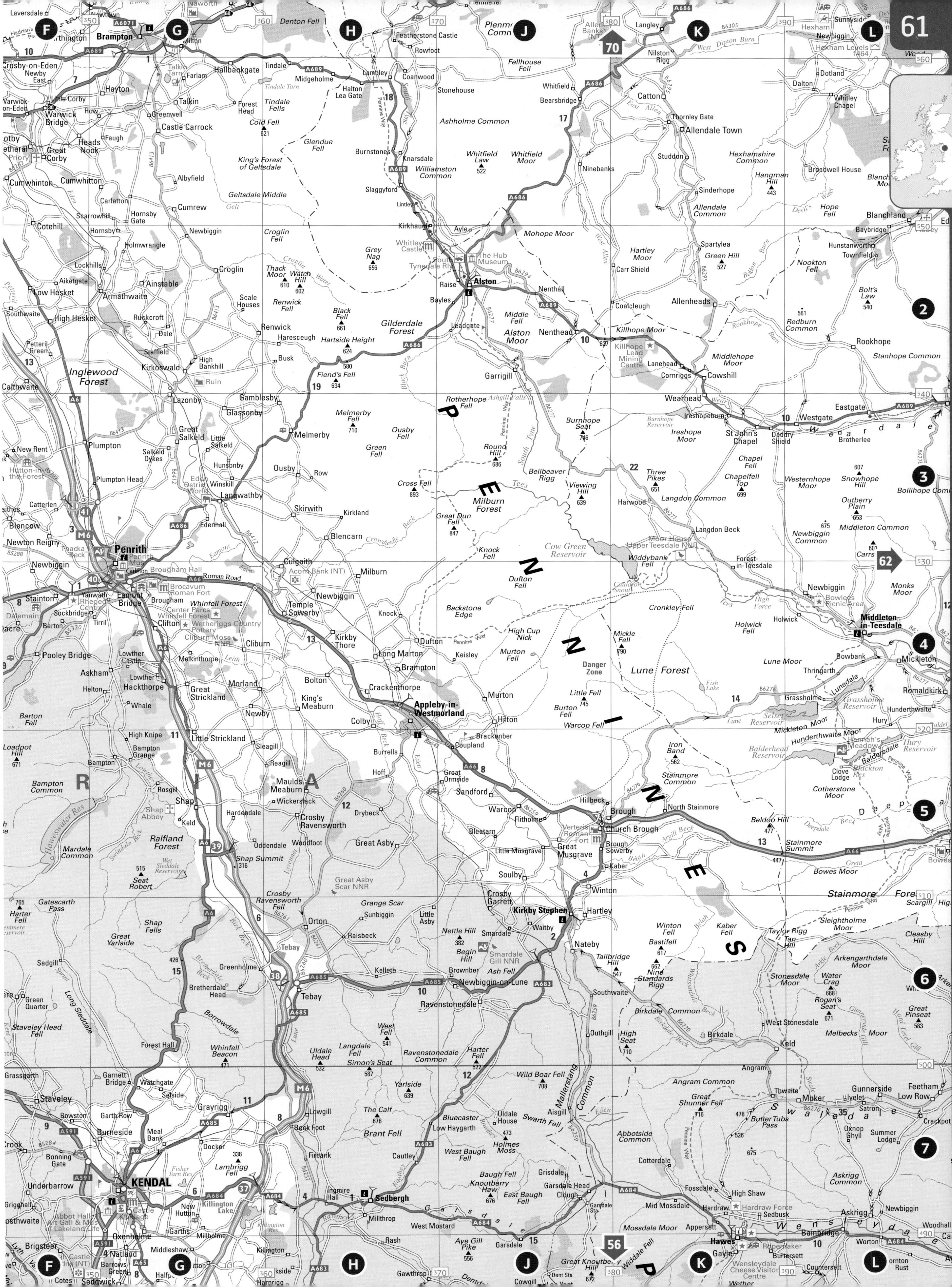

Brampton
Denton Fell
Featherstone Castle
Rowfoot
Plenmeller Common
Allen Banks (NT)
Langley
Hexham
Newbiggin
Hexham Levels
Sunnyside
Crosby-on-Eden
Hallbankgate
Tindale
Midgeholme
Lambley
Coanwood
Halton Lea Gate
Fellhouse Fell
Nilston Rigg
West Dipton Burn
Dotland
Dalton
Hayton
Talkin Tarn
Farlam
Talkin
Stonehouse
Whitfield
Bearsbridge
Catton
Whitley Chapel
Little Corby
Warwick-on-Eden
Warwick Bridge
How
Forest Head
Tindale Fells
Cold Fell
Ashholme Common
Thornley Gate
Allendale Town
Greenwell
Castle Carrock
Great Corby
Heads Nook
Faugh
Glendue Fell
Burnstones
Knarsdale
Whitfield Law
Whitfield Moor
Ninebanks
Studdon
Hexhamshire Common
Hangman Hill
Broadwell House
King's Forest of Geltsdale
Williamston Common
Slaggyford
Cumwhinton
Cumwhitton
Albyfield
Geltsdale Middle
Sinderhope
Allendale Common
Carlatton
Hornsby Gate
Cumrew
Linitley
Hope Fell
Blanchland
Scarrowhill
Hornsby
Cotehill
Newbiggin
Croglin Fell
Kirkhaugh
Ayle
Mohope Moor
Baybridge
Holmwrangle
Whitley Castle
Grey Nag
The Hub Museum
South Tynedale Rly
Hartley Moor
Spartylea
Green Hill
Hunstanworth
Townfield
Nookton Fell
Lockhills
Croglin
Thack Moor
Watch Hill
Raise
Alston
Carr Shield
Aiketgate
Ainstable
Armathwaite
Low Hesket
Scale Houses
Renwick Fell
Bayles
Nenthall
Coalcleugh
Allenheads
Bolt's Law
Southwaite
High Hesket
Ruckcroft
Dale
Renwick
Black Fell
Gilderdale Forest
Middle Fell
Leadgate
Alston Moor
Nenthead
Killhope Moor
Redburn Common
Petteril Green
Staffield
Harescough
Hartside Height
Killhope Lead Mining Centre
Middlehope Moor
Rookhope
Stanhope Common
Inglewood Forest
High Bankhill
Busk
Kirkoswald
Fiend's Fell
Garrigill
Lanehead
Cornriggs
Cowshill
Calthwaite
Ruin
Lazonby
Gamblesby
Glassonby
Rotherhope Fell
Ashgill Falls
Burnhope Seat
Burnhope Reservoir
Wearhead
Ireshopeburn
Ireshope Moor
St John's Chapel
Daddry Shield
Westgate
Eastgate
Brotherlee
Weardale
Melmerby Fell
Melmerby
Ousby Fell
Green Fell
Round Hill
Great Salkeld
Little Salkeld
Salkeld Dykes
Plumpton
New Rent
Hutton-in-the-Forest
Hunsonby
Ousby
Row
Bellbeaver Rigg
Three Pikes
Chapel Fell
Chapelfell Top
Westernhope Moor
Snowhope Hill
Bollihope Common
Plumpton Head
Eden Ostrich World
Winskill
Langwathby
Cross Fell
Viewing Hill
Harwood
Langdon Common
Outberry Plain
Catterlen
Skirwith
Kirkland
Milburn Forest
Great Dun Fell
Middleton Common
Newbiggin Common
Langdon Beck
Blencow
Newton Reigny
Edenhall
Blencarn
Crowdundle Beck
Knock Fell
Cow Green Reservoir
Moor House Upper Teesdale NNR
Carrs
Penrith
Thacka Beck
Penrith Museum
Culgaith
Acorn Bank (NT)
Milburn
Dufton Fell
Widdybank Fell
Forest-in-Teesdale
Newbiggin
Brougham Hall
Roman Road
Cauldron Snout
Monks Moor
Stainton
Yanwath
Eamont Bridge
Rheged Centre
Brocavum Roman Fort
Brougham
Newbiggin
Temple Sowerby
Backstone Edge
Cronkley Fell
Bowlees Picnic Area
High Force
Dalemain
Sockbridge
Whinfell Forest
Center Parcs Whinfell Forest
Knock
Holwick Fell
Holwick
Middleton-in-Teesdale
Barton
Tirril
Clifton
Wetheriggs Country Pottery
Cliburn Moss NNR
Cliburn
Kirkby Thore
High Cup Nick
Pennine Way
Mickle Fell
Pooley Bridge
Lowther Castle
Melkinthorpe
Long Marton
Dufton
Keisley
Murton Fell
Danger Zone
Lune Forest
Lune Moor
Bowbank
Mickleton
Askham
Lowther
Hackthorpe
Great Strickland
Morland
Brampton
Bolton
Crackenthorpe
Thringarth
Lunedale
Helton
Whale
King's Meaburn
Appleby-in-Westmorland
Murton
Little Fell
Fish Lake
Grassholme
Grassholme Reservoir
Romaldkirk
Barton Fell
Newby
Colby
Hilton
Burton Fell
Warcop Fell
Selset Reservoir
Mickleton Moor
Hunderthwaite
Hunderthwaite Moor
Hury
High Knipe
Little Strickland
Brackenber
Coupland
Hury Reservoir
Loadpot Hill
Bampton Grange
Sleagill
Burrells
Iron Band
Balderhead Reservoir
Hannah's Meadow
Baldersdale
Bampton
Reagill
Hoff
Great Ormside
Stainmore Common
Clove Lodge
Blackton Res
Bampton Common
Rosgill
Maulds Meaburn
Sandford
Cotherstone Moor
Shap
Shap Abbey
Wickerslack
Crosby Ravensworth
Hardendale
Drybeck
Warcop
Flitholme
Hillbeck
Brough
North Stainmore
Keld
Bleatarn
Verteris Roman Fort
Church Brough
Argill Beck
Beldoo Hill
Deepdale
Ralfland Forest
Mardale Common
Haweswater Res
Oddendale
Woodfoot
Great Asby
Little Musgrave
Brough Sowerby
Great Musgrave
Kaber
Stainmore Summit
Bowes
Shap Summit
Wet Sleddale Reservoir
Seat Robert
Great Asby Scar NNR
Soulby
Winton
Bowes Moor
Stainmore Forest
Harter Fell
Gatescarth Pass
Crosby Ravensworth Fell
Grange Scar
Sunbiggin
Little Asby
Crosby Garrett
Kirkby Stephen
Hartley
Scargill
Great Yarlside
Shap Fells
Orton
Raisbeck
Nettle Hill
Smardale
Waitby
Winton Fell
Kaber Fell
Taylor Rigg
Tan Hill
Sleightholme Moor
Cleasby Hill
Tebay
Begin Hill
Smardale Gill NNR
Nateby
Bastifell
Tailbridge Hill
Arkengarthdale Moor
Sadgill
Greenholme
Brownber
Ash Fell
Nine Standards Rigg
Stonesdale Moor
Water Crag
Bretherdale Head
Kelleth
Newbiggin-on-Lune
Southwaite
Rogan's Seat
Great Pinseat
Green Quarter
Long Sleddale
Tebay
Ravenstonedale
Birkdale Common
West Stonesdale
Melbecks Moor
Staveley Head Fell
Borrowdale
West Fell
High Seat
Outhgill
Birkdale
Keld
Forest Hall
Whinfell Beacon
Uldale Head
Langdale Fell
Simon's Seat
Ravenstonedale Common
Harter Fell
Angram
Grassgarth
Garnett Bridge
Watchgate
Selside
Wild Boar Fell
Mallerstang Common
Angram Common
Thwaite
Muker
Gunnerside
Feetham
Low Row
Staveley
Grayrigg
Lowgill
Yarlside
The Calf
Aisgill
Great Shunner Fell
Ivelet
Satron
Crackpot
Bowston
Garth Row
Beck Foot
Bluecaster
Uldale House
Low Haygarth
Swarth Fell
Butter Tubs Pass
Oxnop Ghyll
Summer Lodge
Crook
Burneside
Meal Bank
Brant Fell
Holmes Moss
Abbotside Common
Bonning Gate
Docker
Firbank
West Baugh Fell
Cautley
Cotterdale
Askrigg Common
Kendal
Underbarrow
Fisher Tarn Res
Lambrigg Fell
Baugh Fell
Knoutberry Haw
Grisdale
Garsdale Head
Clough
Fossdale
High Shaw
Crosthwaite
Abbot Hall Art Gall & Mus of Lakeland Life
Castle
Kirkby
New Hutton
Killington Lake
Ingmire Hall
Sedbergh
East Baugh Fell
Garsdale Sta.
Mid Mossdale
Hardraw
Hardraw Force
Sedbusk
Askrigg
Newbiggin
Garths
Millholme
Killington Res
Millthrop
West Mostard
Mossdale Moor
Appersett
Bainbridge
Wensleydale
Woodhall
Oxenholme
Brigsteer
Sizergh Castle (NT)
Natland
Middleshaw
Killington
Rash
Aye Gill Pike
Garsdale
Great Knoutberry Hill
Widdale Fell
Hawes
Gayle
Wensleydale Cheese Visitor Centre
Burtersett
Worton
Thornton Rust
Countersett
Barrows Green
Sedgwick
Halfpenny
Gawthrop
Cowgill
Dent Sta
Dentdale
PENNINES
62
56
70

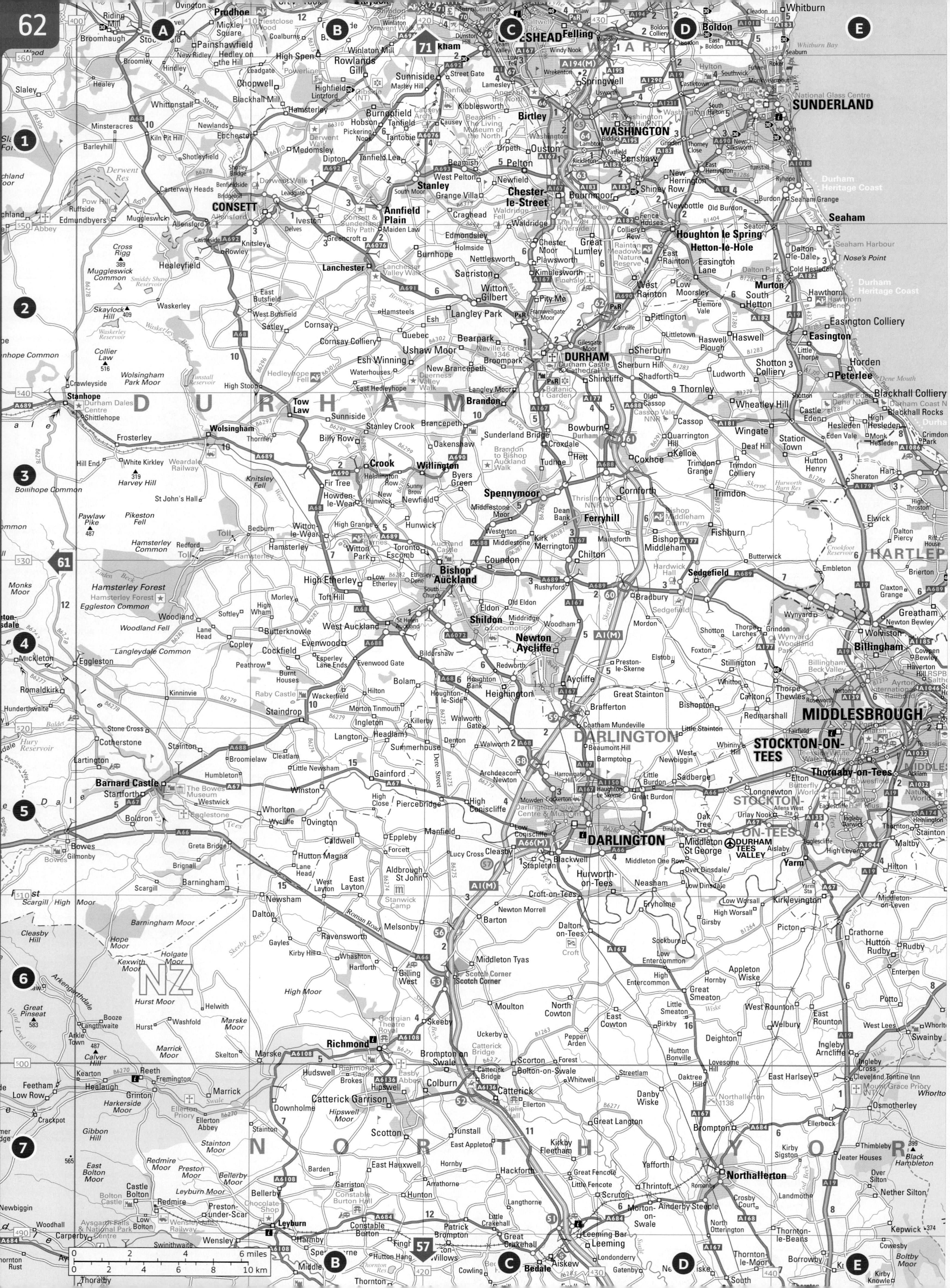

DURHAM
NORTH YOR
NZ
HARTLEP
SUNDERLAND
WASHINGTON
GATESHEAD
Felling
Boldon
Whitburn
Prudhoe
CONSETT
Stanley
Chester-le-Street
Houghton le Spring
Hetton-le-Hole
Seaham
Murton
Easington
Peterlee
Horden
DURHAM
Annfield Plain
Lanchester
Tow Law
Stanhope
Wolsingham
Crook
Willington
Spennymoor
Ferryhill
Bishop Auckland
Shildon
Newton Aycliffe
Sedgefield
Billingham
MIDDLESBROUGH
STOCKTON-ON-TEES
Thornaby-on-Tees
Yarm
DARLINGTON
Barnard Castle
Richmond
Catterick Garrison
Catterick
Leyburn
Bedale
Northallerton
Hurworth-on-Tees
Scotch Corner
Staindrop
Middleton St George
DURHAM TEES VALLEY
Durham Heritage Coast
Hamsterley Forest
Derwent Res
Wear
Tees
A1(M)
A19
A66
A68
A167
A688
A689
A690
A691
A692
A693
A6108
A684
71
61
57
0 2 4 6 miles
0 2 4 6 8 10 km

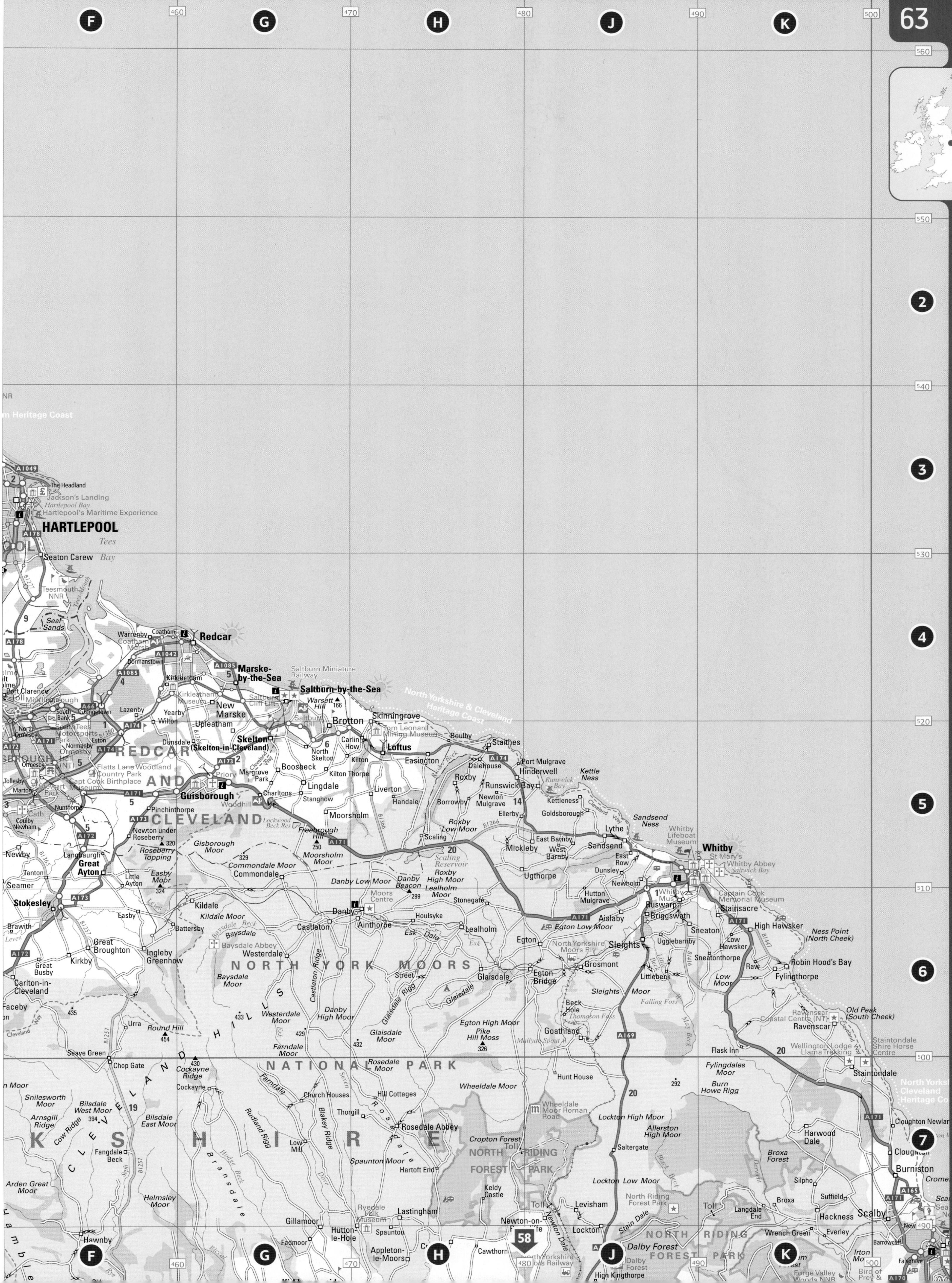
F
G
H
J
K
460
470
480
490
500
560
550
540
530
520
510
500
2
3
4
5
6
7
HARTLEPOOL
The Headland
Jackson's Landing
Hartlepool Bay
Hartlepool's Maritime Experience
Tees Bay
Seaton Carew
Teesmouth NNR
Seal Sands
Heritage Coast
Redcar
Coatham
Warrenby
Coatham Marsh
Dormanstown
Marske-by-the-Sea
Saltburn Miniature Railway
Saltburn-by-the-Sea
Warsett Hill
166
North Yorkshire & Cleveland Heritage Coast
Kirkleatham
Kirkleatham Museum
New Marske
Yearby
Wilton
Lazenby
Port Clarence
Upleatham
Skelton
Skelton-in-Cleveland
Dunsdale
Brotton
Skinningrove
Tom Leonard Mining Museum
Carlin How
Loftus
North Skelton
Kilton
Kilton Thorpe
Boulby
Staithes
Easington
Port Mulgrave
Hinderwell
Kettle Ness
Runswick Bay
Dalehouse
Roxby
Borrowby
Newton Mulgrave
Ellerby
Kettleness
Goldsborough
Sandsend Ness
Lythe
Sandsend
Whitby Lifeboat Museum
Whitby
St Mary's
Whitby Abbey
Saltwick Bay
East Barnby
West Barnby
Mickleby
Ugthorpe
Dunsley
Newholm
Captain Cook Memorial Museum
Stainsacre
High Hawsker
Ness Point (North Cheek)
Low Hawsker
Robin Hood's Bay
Fylingthorpe
Raw
Old Peak (South Cheek)
Ravenscar
Coastal Centre (NT)
Wellington Lodge Llama Trekking
Staintondale Shire Horse Centre
Staintondale
REDCAR AND CLEVELAND
Guisborough
Priory
Margrove Park
Boosbeck
Lingdale
Charltons
Stanghow
Liverton
Handale
Woodhill
Lockwood Beck Res
Moorsholm
Freebrough Hill
250
Scaling
Scaling Reservoir
Roxby Low Moor
Pinchinthorpe
Newton under Roseberry
Roseberry Topping
320
Gisborough Moor
329
Commondale Moor
Commondale
Moorsholm Moor
Danby Low Moor
Danby Beacon
299
Roxby High Moor
Lealholm Moor
Moors Centre
Danby
Ainthorpe
Castleton
Houlsyke
Lealholm
Stonegate
Egton Low Moor
Aislaby
Ruswarp
Briggswath
Sneaton
Sleights
Ugglebarnby
Sneatonthorpe
Littlebeck
Egton
Grosmont
Egton Bridge
Glaisdale
North Yorkshire Moors Rly
Hutton Mulgrave
Great Ayton
Little Ayton
Langbaurgh
Newby
Tanton
Seamer
Stokesley
Easby
Easby Moor
324
Kildale
Kildale Moor
Battersby
Baysdale Abbey
Baysdale
Westerdale
Great Broughton
Ingleby Greenhow
Kirkby
Great Busby
Carlton-in-Cleveland
Brawith
Faceby
NORTH YORK MOORS
NATIONAL PARK
CLEVELAND HILLS
Baysdale Moor
Westerdale Moor
Danby High Moor
Glaisdale Moor
Glaisdale Rigg
Castleton Ridge
Street
Farndale Moor
Rosedale Moor
Egton High Moor
Pike Hill Moss
326
Sleights Moor
Falling Foss
Beck Hole
Goathland
Mallyan Spout
Thomason Foss
Low Moor
Flask Inn
Fylingdales Moor
Burn Howe Rigg
Hunt House
Wheeldale Moor
Wheeldale Moor Roman Road
292
Lockton High Moor
Allerston High Moor
Saltergate
Cropton Forest
NORTH RIDING FOREST PARK
Toll
Kelly Castle
Levisham
Lockton
Lockton Low Moor
North Riding Forest Park
Newton-on-Rawcliffe
58
Newton Dale
North Yorkshire Moors Railway
Dalby Forest
Stain Dale
Langdale End
Broxa
Broxa Forest
Silpho
Suffield
Hackness
Harwood Dale
Cloughton
Cloughton Newlands
Burniston
Scalby
Wrench Green
Everley
Irton Moor
Forge Valley Woods NNR
Barrowcliff
Urra
Round Hill
454
435
433
429
432
430
Cockayne Ridge
Cockayne
Chop Gate
Seave Green
Church Houses
Hill Cottages
Thorgill
Rosedale Abbey
Rosedale
Farndale
Rudland Rigg
Blakey Ridge
Low Mill
Spaunton Moor
Hartoft End
Bransdale
Snilesworth Moor
Bilsdale West Moor
Bilsdale East Moor
Arnsgill Ridge
Cow Ridge
394
Fangdale Beck
Arden Great Moor
Helmsley Moor
Hawnby
Gillamoor
Fadmoor
Hutton-le-Hole
Ryedale Folk Museum
Spaunton
Lastingham
Appleton-le-Moors
Cawthorn
High Kingthorpe
Dalby Forest
A1049
A178
A1042
A1085
A174
A171
A173
A172
A169
A170
A165
B1257
B1266
B1366
B1365
B1447
B1416
CLEVELAND
YORKSHIRE

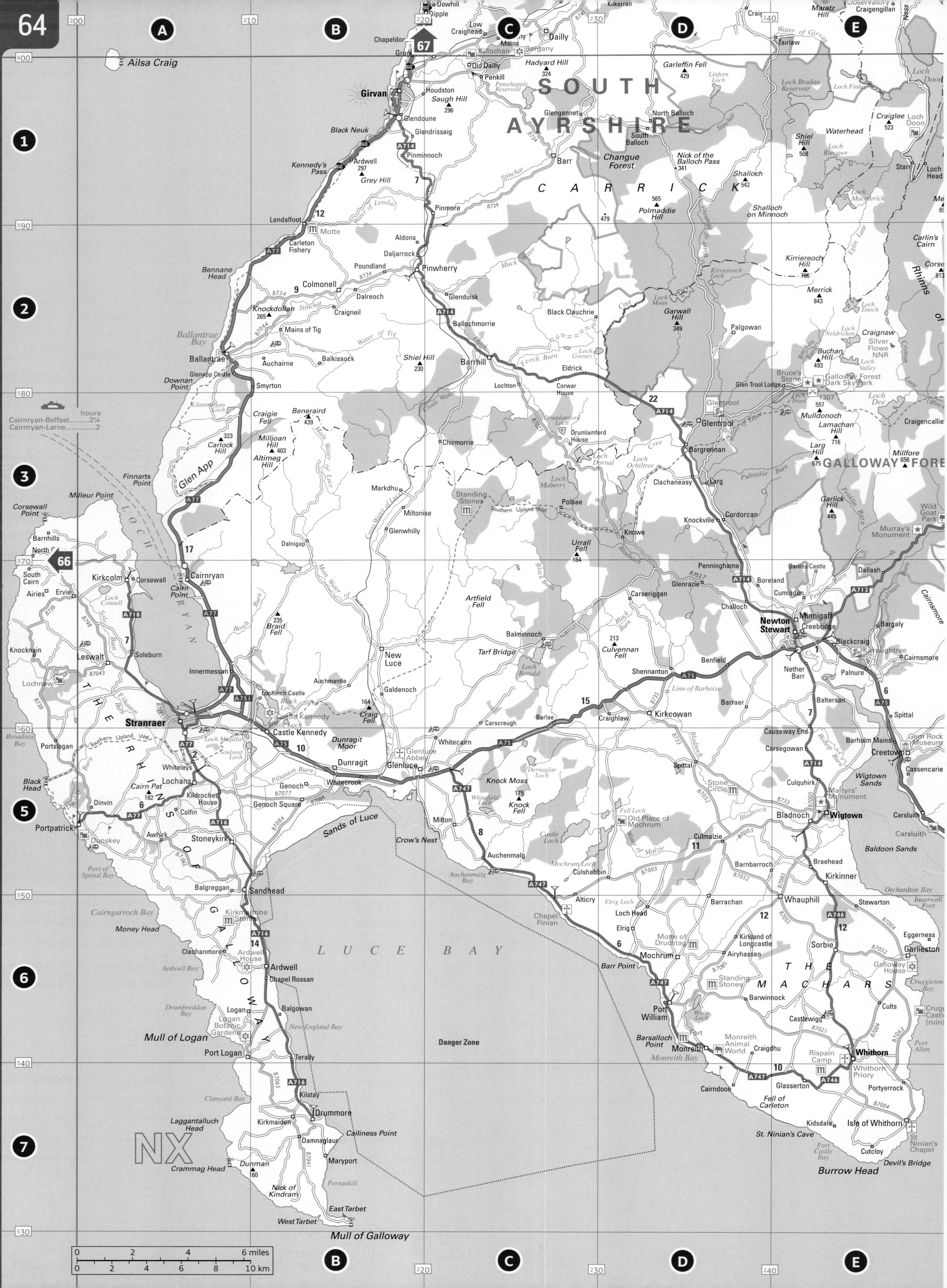
A
B
C
D
E
1
2
3
4
5
6
7
67
66
Ailsa Craig
Girvan
Dailly
Old Dailly
Penkill
Hadyard Hill
Garleffin Fell
SOUTH AYRSHIRE
CARRICK
Water of Girvan
Tairlaw
Loch Bradan Reservoir
Loch Finlas
Loch Doon
Houston Saugh Hill
Glendoune
Black Neuk
Glendrissaig
Glengennet
North Balloch
South Balloch
Changue Forest
Barr
Nick of the Balloch Pass
Shalloch
Shalloch on Minnoch
Craiglee
Waterhead
Shiel Hill
Loch Riecawr
Starr
Loch Head
Kennedy's Pass
Ardwell
Grey Hill
Pinminnoch
Pinmore
Polmaddie Hill
Loch Macaterick
Lendalfoot
Motte
Carleton Fishery
Aldons
Daljarrock
Poundland
Pinwherry
Bennane Head
Colmonell
Dalreoch
Knockdolian
Craigneil
Kirriereoch Hill
Kirriereoch Loch
Carlin's Cairn
Corserine
Rhinns of Kells
Merrick
Loch Enoch
Glenduisk
Black Clauchrie
Garwall Hill
Loch Moan
Ballochmorrie
Mains of Tig
Water of Tig
Ballantrae Bay
Ballantrae
Auchairne
Balkissock
Shiel Hill
Barrhill
Feoch Burn
Loch Goosey
Eldrick
Palgowan
Craignaw
Silver Flowe NNR
Buchan Hill
Loch Valley
Glenapp Castle
Downan Point
Smyrton
Lochton
Corwar House
Bruce's Stone
Glen Trool Lodge
Galloway Forest Dark Sky Park
Loch Trool
Loch Dee
Cairnryan-Belfast hours 2¼
Cairnryan-Larne 2
Kilantringan Loch
Craigie Fell
Beneraird
Drumlamford Loch
Drumlamford House
Glentrool
Mulldonoch
Lamachan Hill
Craigencallie
Carlock Hill
Milljoan Hill
Altimeg Hill
Glen App
Chirmorrie
Bargrennan
Loch Dornal
Loch Ochiltree
Larg Hill
Millfore
GALLOWAY FOREST
Finnarts Point
Milleur Point
Markdhu
Clachaneasy
Larg
Loch Maberry
Standing Stones
Southern Upland Way
Polbae
Corsewall Point
Miltonise
Cordorcan
Knockville
Garlick Hill
Wild Goat Park
Murray's Monument
Glenwhilly
Knowe
Barnhills
North Cairn
Dalnigap
Urrall Fell
Loch Ryan
South Cairn
Kirkcolm
Corsewall
Cairnryan
Cairn Point
Penninghame
Garlies Castle
Dallash
Airies
Ervie
Loch Connell
Glenrazie
Boreland
Cumloden
Carseriggan
Artfield Fell
Challoch
Cairnsmore
Braid Fell
Newton Stewart
Minnigaff
Creebridge
Bargaly
Blackcraig
Knocknain
Leswalt
Soleburn
Innermessan
Balminnoch
Tarf Bridge
Culvennan Fell
New Luce
Kirroughtree
Cairnsmore
Nether Barr
Benfield
Palnure
Lochnaw
THE RHINNS
Auchmantle
Loch Ronald
Shennanton
Linn of Barhoise
Gaidenoch
Baltersan
Stranraer
Lochinch Castle
Castle Kennedy
Craig Fell
Barlae
Craighlaw
Kirkcowan
Barraer
Spittal
Broadsea Bay
Portslogan
Castle Kennedy
Dunragit Moor
Carscreugh
Whitecairn
Causeway End
Barholm Mains
Gem Rock Museum
Creetown
Soulseat Loch
Glenluce Abbey
Carsegowan
Cassencarie
Whiteleys
Lochans
Dunragit
Glenluce
Dernaglar Loch
Knock Moss
Black Head
Genoch
Whitecrook
Culquhirk
Martyrs' Monument
Wigtown Sands
Cairn Pat
Kildrochet House
Genoch Square
Stone Circle
Dinvin
Colfin
Whitefield Loch
Knock Fell
Fell Loch
Old Place of Mochrum
Bladnoch
Wigtown
Carsluith
Portpatrick
Awhirk
Sands of Luce
Milton
Carsluith
Dunskey
Stoneykirk
Crow's Nest
Castle Loch
Culmalzie
Baldoon Sands
Port of Spittal Bay
Auchenmalg
Auchenmalg Bay
Mochrum Loch
Culshabbin
Braehead
Barnbarroch
Kirkinner
Balgreggan
Sandhead
Orchardton Bay
Cairngarroch Bay
Alticry
Elrig Loch
Barrachan
Whauphill
Stewarton
Innerwell Port
Money Head
Kirkmadrine Stones
Chapel Finian
Loch Head
Elrig
Motte of Druchtag
Kirkland of Longcastle
Airyhassen
Sorbie
Eggerness
Garlieston
Clachanmore
Ardwell House
Ardwell Bay
LUCE BAY
Mochrum
Barr Point
Galloway House
Cruggleton Bay
Ardwell
Chapel Rossan
Standing Stones
Barwinnock
THE MACHARS
Drumbreddan Bay
Port William
White Loch
Castlewigg
Cults
Cruggleton Castle (ruin)
Logan
Logan Botanic Gardens
Balgowan
New England Bay
Barsalloch Point
Monreith
Monreith Animal World
Craigdhu
Rispain Camp
Port Allen
Mull of Logan
Port Logan
Danger Zone
Monreith Bay
Whithorn
Whithorn Priory
Terally
Cairndoon
Glasserton
Portyerrock
Clanyard Bay
Kilstay
Fell of Carleton
Laggantalluch Head
Drummore
Kirkmaiden
Kidsdale
Isle of Whithorn
Cailiness Point
St. Ninian's Cave
Damnaglaur
St Ninian's Chapel
NX
Crammag Head
Dunman
Maryport
Port Castle Bay
Cutcloy
Devil's Bridge
Burrow Head
Portankill
Nick of Kindram
East Tarbet
West Tarbet
Mull of Galloway
0 2 4 6 miles
0 2 4 6 8 10 km
200
210
220
230
240
600
590
580
570
560
550
540
530
A77
A714
A75
A747
A716
A718
A751
A712
A746
B734
B7044
B7027
B7005
B7052
B7065
B7041
B7004
B7063
B7021
B7085
B7084
B7077
B733
B735
B7043
B738
B798
B7042

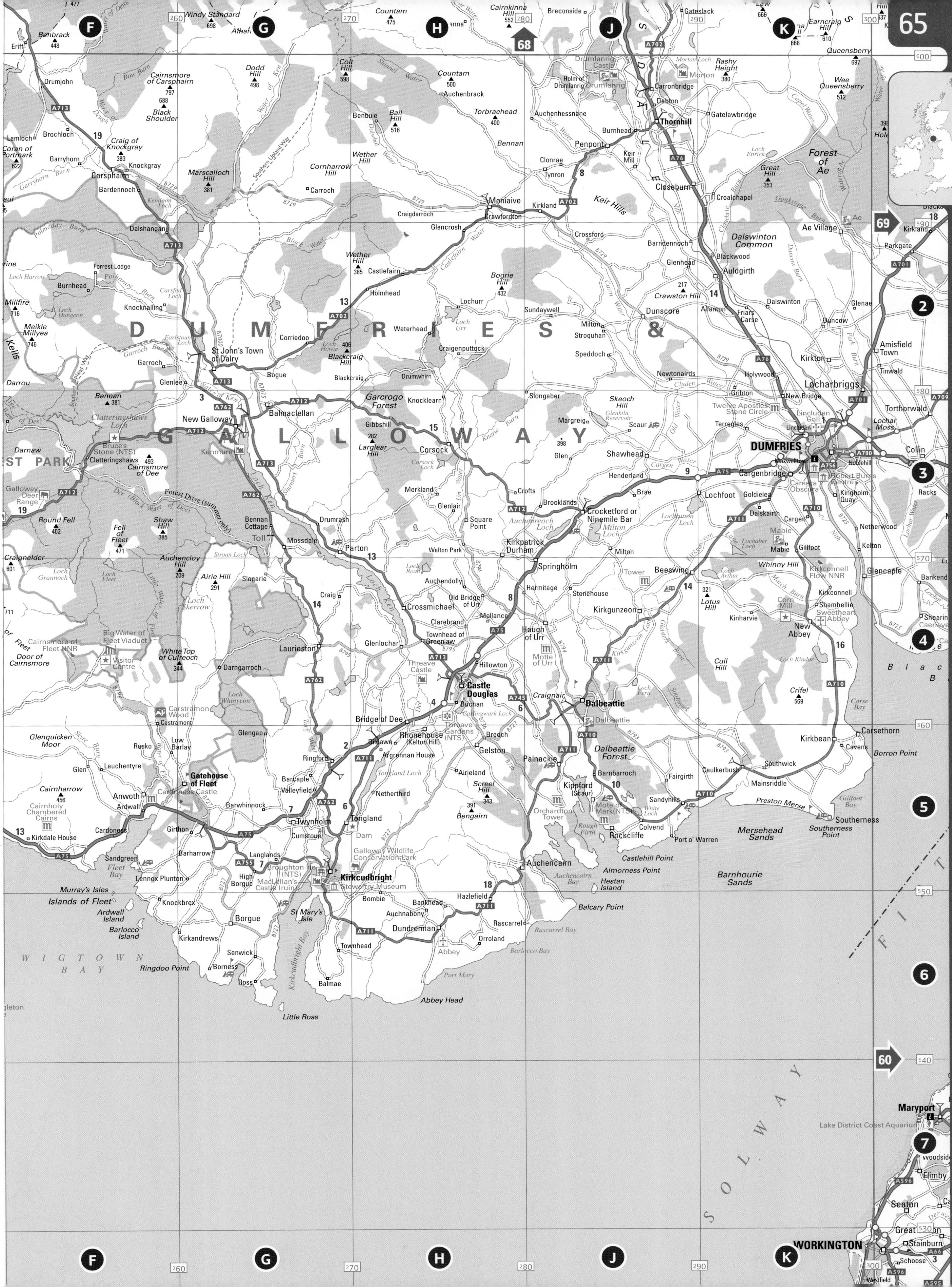
DUMFRIES & GALLOWAY
DUMFRIES
Castle Douglas
Dalbeattie
Kirkcudbright
Gatehouse of Fleet
New Galloway
St John's Town of Dalry
Thornhill
Moniaive
Carsphairn
Maryport
WORKINGTON
Locharbriggs
Crocketford or Ninemile Bar
Springholm
Auldgirth
Closeburn
Penpont
Dunscore
Lochfoot
Beeswing
Kirkbean
Southerness
New Abbey
Rockcliffe
Kippford (Scaur)
Palnackie
Auchencairn
Dundrennan
Borgue
Twynholm
Tongland
Laurieston
Crossmichael
Corsock
Balmaclellan
Parton
Mossdale
Kenmure
Clatteringshaws Loch
Bruce's Stone (NTS)
Threave Castle
Threave Gardens (NTS)
Cardoness Castle
Stewartry Museum
Galloway Wildlife Conservation Park
Abbey
Sweetheart Abbey
Drumlanrig Castle
Forest of Ae
Dalswinton Common
Dalbeattie Forest
Garcrogo Forest
Keir Hills
Galloway Forest Park
Forest Drive (summer only)
Carsphairn
Cairnsmore of Carsphairn 797
Cairnsmore of Fleet NNR
Cairnsmore of Dee
Screel Hill 343
Bengairn
Criffel 569
Lotus Hill
Cuil Hill
Mersehead Sands
Barnhourie Sands
Preston Merse
Hestan Island
Balcary Point
Abbey Head
Little Ross
Ringdoo Point
Islands of Fleet
Murray's Isles
Ardwall Island
Barlocco Island
WIGTOWN BAY
SOLWAY
Lake District Coast Aquarium
Loch Ken
Carlingwark Loch
Auchenreoch Loch
Milton Loch
Lochrutton Loch
Kirkconnell Flow NNR
Caerlaverock
A75
A76
A701
A702
A710
A711
A712
A713
A745
A755
A762
A596
A66
B729
B794
B795
B727
B796
B7000
B725
F G H J K
68
69
60
2 3 4 5 6 7
260 270 280 290 300
600 590 580 570 560 550 540 530

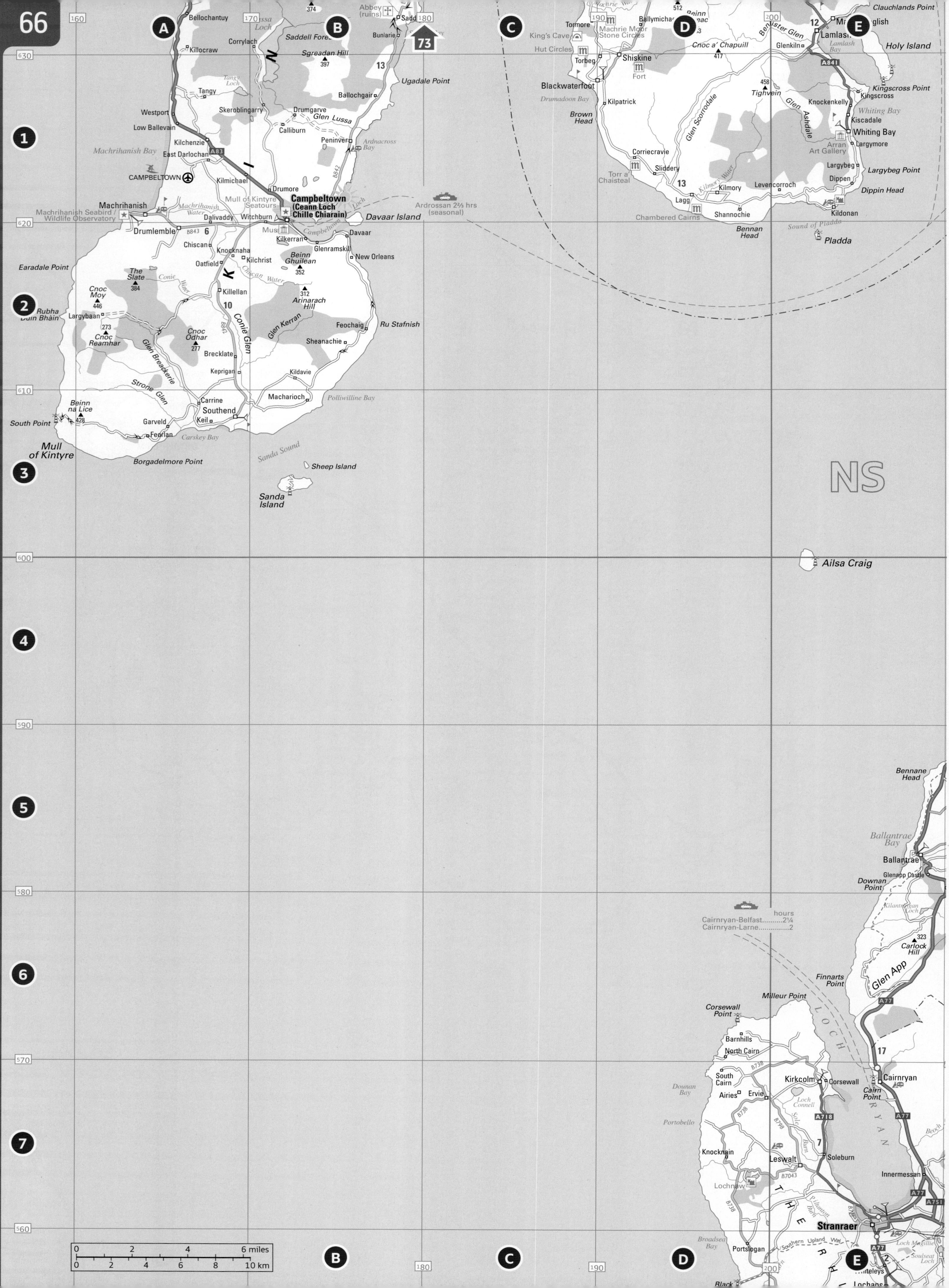

A
B
C
D
E
1
2
3
4
5
6
7
73
Bellochantuy
Killocraw
Corrylach
Saddell Forest
Sgreadan Hill
397
Bunlarie
Saddell
Abbey (ruins)
Ugadale Point
Ballochgair
Tangy
Westport
Low Ballevain
Skeroblingarry
Drumgarve
Glen Lussa
Calliburn
Kilchenzie
Machrihanish Bay
East Darlochan
A83
Peninver
Ardnacross Bay
B842
CAMPBELTOWN
Kilmichael
Drumore
Campbeltown
(Ceann Loch
Chille Chiarain)
Mull of Kintyre Seatours
Machrihanish
Machrihanish Seabird / Wildlife Observatory
Machrihanish Water
Dalivaddy
Witchburn
Ardrossan 2½ hrs (seasonal)
Davaar Island
Drumlemble
B843
Chiscan
Kilkerran
Davaar
Campbeltown Loch
Glenramskill
Knocknaha
Kilchrist
Oatfield
Beinn Ghuilean
352
New Orleans
Earadale Point
The Slate
384
Conie Water
Chiscan Water
Cnoc Moy
446
Killellan
312
Arinarach Hill
Rubha Dùin Bhàin
Largybaan
273
Cnoc Reamhar
Cnoc Odhar
277
B842
Conie Glen
Glen Kerran
Feochaig
Ru Stafnish
Sheanachie
Glen Breackerie
Brecklate
Kepirgan
Kildavie
Strone Glen
Machariach
Polliwilline Bay
Carrine
Southend
Beinn na Lice
428
South Point
Garveld
Keil
Feorlan
Carskey Bay
Mull of Kintyre
Borgadelmore Point
Sanda Sound
Sheep Island
Sanda Island
Tormore
Ballymichael
King's Cave
Machrie Moor Stone Circles
Hut Circles
Torbeg
Shiskine
Fort
Blackwaterfoot
Drumadoon Bay
Brown Head
Kilpatrick
Cnoc a' Chapuill
417
Benlister Glen
Glenkiln
Lamlash
Lamlash Bay
Holy Island
Clauchlands Point
A841
458
Tighvein
Glen Scorrodale
Glen Ashdale
Knockenkelly
Kingscross Point
Kingscross
Whiting Bay
Kiscadale
Arran Art Gallery
Largymore
Corriecravie
Sliddery
Torr a' Chaisteal
Kilmory Water
Kilmory
Levencorroch
Largybeg
Largybeg Point
Dippen
Dippen Head
Lagg
Shannochie
Chambered Cairns
Kildonan
Bennan Head
Sound of Pladda
Pladda
NS
Ailsa Craig
Bennane Head
Ballantrae Bay
Ballantrae
Glenapp Castle
Downan Point
Kilantringan Loch
323
Carlock Hill
Cairnryan-Belfast..........2¼
Cairnryan-Larne...............2
hours
Finnarts Point
Glen App
Milleur Point
A77
Corsewall Point
Barnhills
North Cairn
B738
South Cairn
Kirkcolm
Corsewall
Dounan Bay
Airies
Ervie
Loch Connell
Cairnryan
Cairn Point
A718
Portobello
LOCH RYAN
Knocknain
Leswalt
Soleburn
Innermessan
B7043
Lochnaw
THE RHINS
Stranraer
A751
Broadsea Bay
Portslogan
Southern Upland Way
Loch Magillie
Soulseat Loch
Lochans
0 2 4 6 miles
0 2 4 6 8 10 km
160
170
180
190
200
630
620
610
600
590
580
570
560

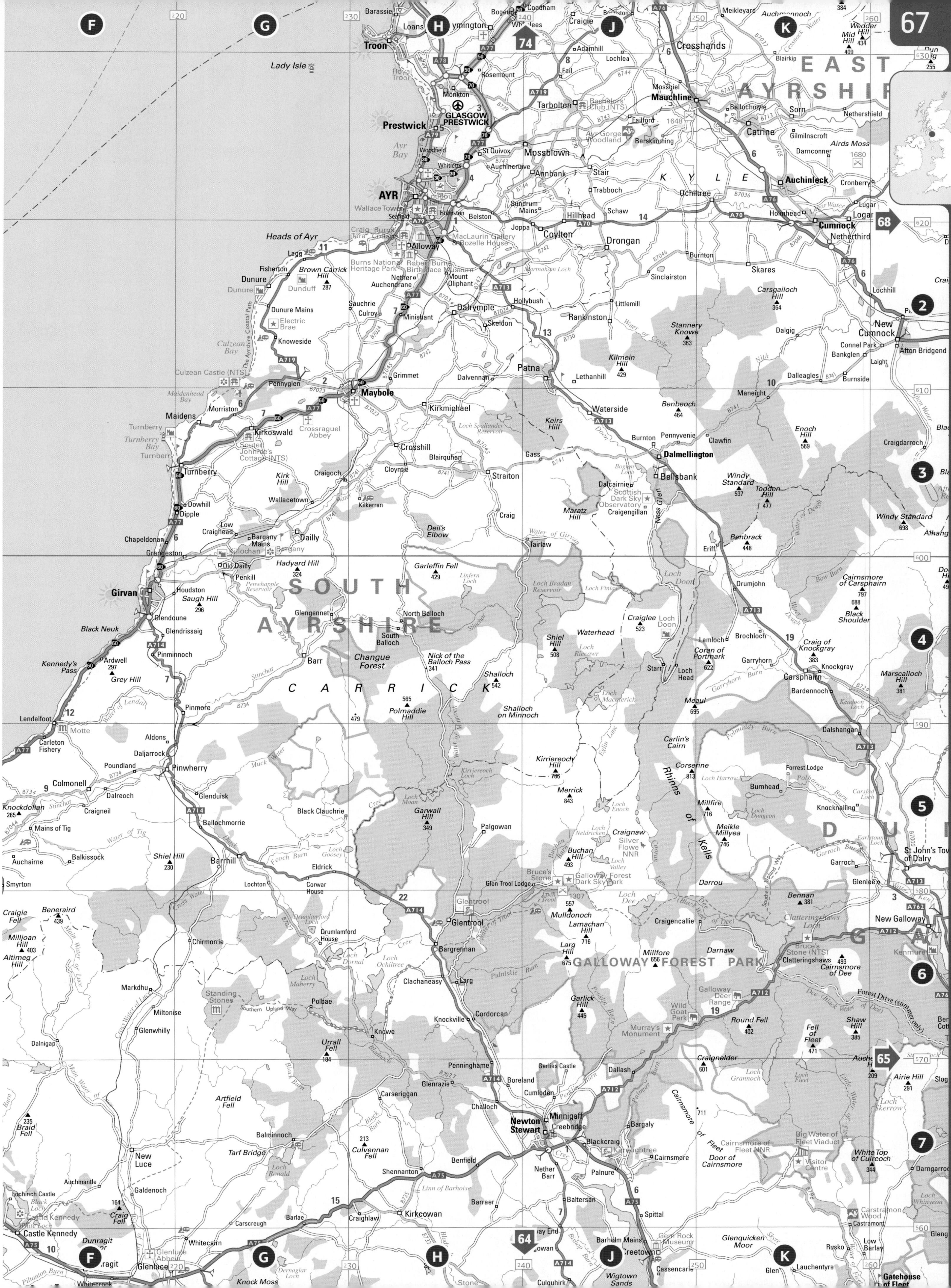

EAST AYRSHIRE
SOUTH AYRSHIRE
CARRICK
KYLE
GALLOWAY FOREST PARK
Troon
Lady Isle
Prestwick
Glasgow Prestwick
Monkton
Ayr Bay
AYR
Alloway
Heads of Ayr
Dunure
Maybole
Culzean Castle (NTS)
Culzean Bay
Maidens
Turnberry
Turnberry Bay
Kirkoswald
Crossraguel Abbey
Girvan
Dailly
Kennedy's Pass
Lendalfoot
Colmonell
Pinwherry
Barrhill
Barr
Straiton
Crosshill
Kirkmichael
Dalrymple
Patna
Dalmellington
Bellsbank
Carsphairn
Dalry
St John's Town of Dalry
New Galloway
Glentrool
Newton Stewart
Minnigaff
Creebridge
Kirkcowan
New Luce
Glenluce
Castle Kennedy
Mauchline
Catrine
Sorn
Auchinleck
Cumnock
New Cumnock
Drongan
Coylton
Tarbolton
Mossblown
Crosshands
Stair
Ochiltree
Lugar
Craigie
Symington
Loans
Barassie
Dundonald
Merrick
843
Shalloch on Minnoch
Kirriereoch Hill
Mullwharchar
Corserine
813
Rhinns of Kells
Cairnsmore of Fleet
Cairnsmore of Carsphairn
797
Loch Doon
Loch Bradan Reservoir
Changue Forest
Nick of the Balloch Pass
Glen Trool Lodge
Bruce's Stone
Galloway Forest Dark Sky Park
Scottish Dark Sky Observatory
Clatteringshaws Loch
Murray's Monument
Wild Goat Park
Galloway Deer Range
Forest Drive (summer only)
Creetown
Gem Rock Museum
Wigtown Sands
74
68
65
64

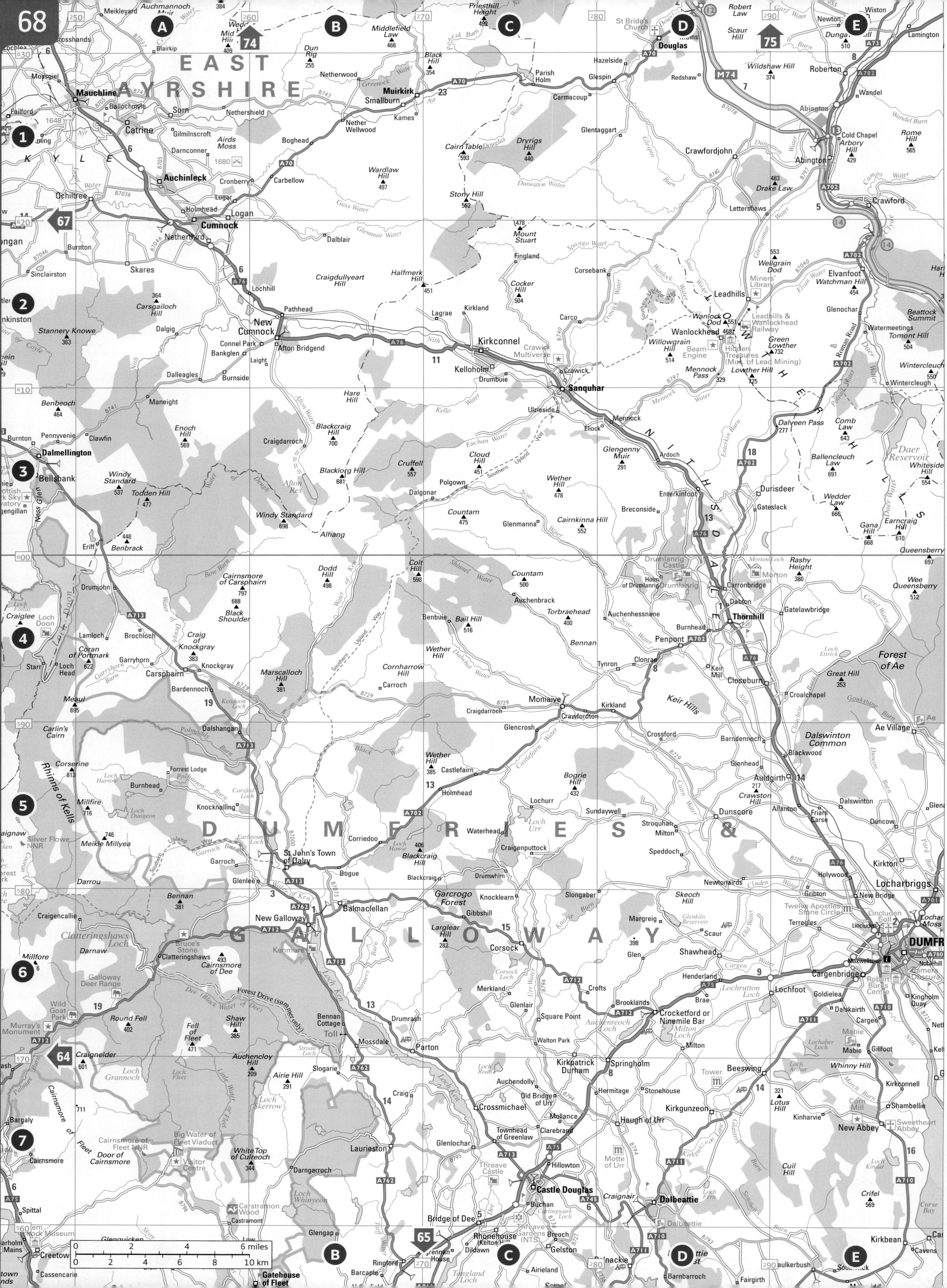

A
B
C
D
E
74
75
67
64
65
1
2
3
4
5
6
7
EAST AYRSHIRE
KYLE
DUMFRIES & GALLOWAY
NITHSDALE
LOWTHER HILLS
Meikleyard
Auchmannoch Muir
Crosshands
Blairkip
Mossgiel
Mauchline
Ballochmyle
Sorn
Failford
Catrine
Gilmilnscroft
Nethershield
Darnconner
Airds Moss
Auchinleck
Ochiltree
Cronberry
Lugar
Logan
Holmhead
Cumnock
Netherthird
Burnton
Skares
Sinclairston
Dalblair
Carsgailoch Hill
Stannery Knowe
Dalgig
Connel Park
Bankglen
New Cumnock
Pathhead
Lochhill
Afton Bridgend
Laight
Burnside
Dalleagles
Benbeoch
Maneight
Pennyvenie
Clawfin
Burnton
Dalmellington
Bellsbank
Enoch Hill
Windy Standard
Todden Hill
Benbrack
Eriff
Drumjohn
Craiglee
Loch Doon
Lamloch
Brochloch
Coran of Portmark
Starr
Loch Head
Garryhorn
Carsphairn
Knockgray
Craig of Knockgray
Bardennoch
Meaul
Carlin's Cairn
Corserine
Rhinns of Kells
Millfire
Meikle Millyea
Silver Flowe NNR
Darrou
Bennan
Craigencallie
Clatteringshaws Loch
Darnaw
Bruce's Stone
Clatteringshaws
Cairnsmore of Dee
Galloway Deer Range
Wild Goat Park
Murray's Monument
Round Fell
Craignelder
Loch Grannoch
Shaw Hill
Fell of Fleet
Auchencloy Hill
Airie Hill
Loch Skerrow
Cairnsmore of Fleet
Bargaly
Cairnsmore
Cairnsmore of Fleet NNR
Door of Cairnsmore
Big Water of Fleet Viaduct
Visitor Centre
White Top of Culreoch
Laurieston
Darngarroch
Loch Whinyeon
Carstramon Wood
Castramont
Spittal
Creetown
Glenquicken
Gatehouse of Fleet
Gatehouse
Glengap
Ringford
Barcaple
Tongland Loch
Wedder Hill
Dun Rig
Middlefield Law
Netherwood
Muirkirk
Smallburn
Kames
Nether Wellwood
Boghead
Carbellow
Wardlaw Hill
Black Hill
Priesthill Height
Parish Holm
Cairn Table
Dryrigs Hill
Stony Hill
Glenmuir Water
Craigdullyeart Hill
Halfmerk Hill
Mount Stuart
Fingland
Cocker Hill
Lagrae
Kirkland
Kirkconnel
Kelloholm
Drumbuie
Crawick Multiverse
Crawick
Sanquhar
Hare Hill
Blackcraig Hill
Craigdarroch
Blacklorg Hill
Cruffell
Cloud Hill
Polgown
Dalgonar
Countam
Windy Standard
Afton Res
Alhang
Glenmanna
Cairnkinna Hill
Wether Hill
Breconside
Ulzieside
Eliock
Mennock
Ardoch
Glengenny Muir
Enterkinfoot
Durisdeer
Gateslack
Dodd Hill
Colt Hill
Cairnsmore of Carsphairn
Black Shoulder
Countam
Auchenbrack
Torbraehead
Auchenhessnane
Benbuie
Bail Hill
Wether Hill
Cornharrow Hill
Carroch
Marscalloch Hill
Kendoon Loch
Dalshangan
Craigdarroch
Moniaive
Glencrosh
Crawfordton
Kirkland
Tynron
Clonrae
Penpont
Bennan
Burnhead
Thornhill
Keir Mill
Keir Hills
Closeburn
Crossford
Forrest Lodge
Loch Harrow
Burnhead
Carsfad Loch
Knocknalling
Loch Dungeon
Earlstoun Loch
Wether Hill
Castlefairn
Holmhead
Bogrie Hill
Lochurr
Sundaywell
Loch Urr
Corriedoo
Waterhead
Craigenputtock
Stroquhan
Milton
Dunscore
Speddoch
St John's Town of Dalry
Garroch
Glenlee
Bogue
Blackcraig Hill
Loch Howie
Blackcraig
Drumwhirn
Garcrogo Forest
Knocklearn
Gibbshill
Slongaber
Skeoch Hill
Margreig
Glenkiln Reservoir
Scaur
Balmaclellan
New Galloway
Kenmure
Larglear Hill
Corsock
Glen
Shawhead
Corsock Loch
Merkland
Glenlair
Crofts
Brooklands
Square Point
Crocketford or Ninemile Bar
Auchenreoch Loch
Milton Loch
Milton
Walton Park
Bennan Cottage
Toll
Mossdale
Drumrash
Parton
Slogarie
Stroan Loch
Kirkpatrick Durham
Springholm
Loch Roan
Auchendolly
Old Bridge of Urr
Crossmichael
Hermitage
Stonehouse
Kirkgunzeon
Haugh of Urr
Mollance
Clarebrand
Townhead of Greenlaw
Glenlochar
Threave Castle
Motte of Urr
Hillowton
Castle Douglas
Carlingwark Loch
Buchan
Bridge of Dee
Threave Gardens (NTS)
Rhonehouse (Kelton Hill)
Dildawn
Gelston
Breoch
Airieland
Craignair
Dalbeattie
Palnackie
Barnbarroch
Craig
Douglas
St Bride's Church
Hazelside
Glespin
Carmacoup
Glentaggart
Crawfordjohn
Duneaton Water
Redshaw
Robert Law
Scaur Hill
Wildshaw Hill
Roberton
Drake Law
Lettershaws
Wiston
Newton
Dungavel Hill
Lamington
Wandel
Abington
Cold Chapel
Arbory Hill
Rome Hill
Crawford
Wellgrain Dod
Elvanfoot
Watchman Hill
Miners' Library
Leadhills
Leadhills & Wanlockhead Railway
Wanlock Dod
Wanlockhead
Willowgrain Hill
Beam Engine
Hidden Treasures (Mus. of Lead Mining)
Green Lowther
Lowther Hill
Mennock Pass
Glenochar
Watermeetings
Tomont Hill
Beattock Summit
Wintercleuch
Dalveen Pass
Comb Law
Daer Reservoir
Ballencleuch Law
Whiteside Hill
Wedder Law
Gana Hill
Earncraig Hill
Queensberry
Morton Loch
Morton
Rashy Height
Wee Queensberry
Drumlanrig Castle
Holm of Drumlanrig
Carronbridge
Dabton
Gatelawbridge
Loch Ettrick
Great Hill
Forest of Ae
Croalchapel
Ae Village
Barndennoch
Dalswinton Common
Blackwood
Glenhead
Auldgirth
Crawston Hill
Allanton
Friars Carse
Dalswinton
Duncow
Kirkton
Holywood
Newtonairds
Locharbriggs
New Bridge
Gribton
Twelve Apostles Stone Circle
Lincluden Coll
Lochar Moss
Terregles
DUMFRIES
Maxwelltown
Cargenbridge
Robert Burns Centre
Camera Obscura
Henderland
Lochfoot
Lochrutton Loch
Goldielea
Kingholm Quay
Dalskairth
Cargen
Mabie
Gillfoot
Beeswing
Whinny Hill
Kirkconnell
Lotus Hill
Kinharvie
Shambellie
Corn Mill
New Abbey
Sweetheart Abbey
Cuil Hill
Loch Kindar
Criffel
Carse Bay
Kirkbean
Cavens
Southwick
Caulkerbush
Fairgirth
Dalbeattie Forest
0 2 4 6 miles
0 2 4 6 8 10 km

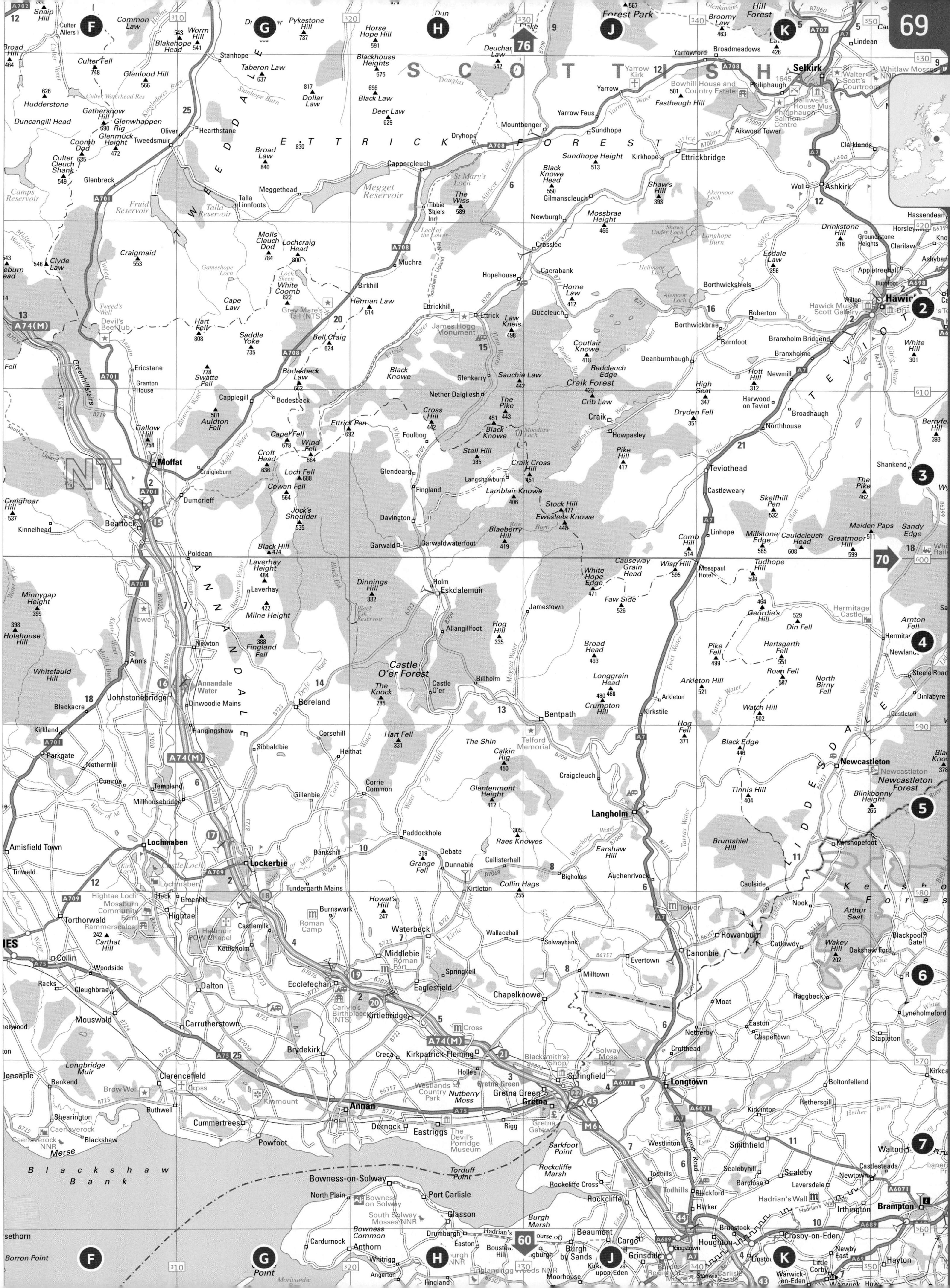

S C O T T I S H
E T T R I C K F O R E S T
T W E E D D A L E
A N N A N D A L E
T E V I O T D A L E
L I D D E S D A L E
B l a c k s h a w
B a n k
Kershope Forest
Forest Park
Castle O'er Forest
Craik Forest
Newcastleton Forest
Selkirk
Hawick
Moffat
Lockerbie
Lochmaben
Langholm
Annan
Gretna
Gretna Green
Longtown
Brampton
Newcastleton
Ecclefechan
Johnstonebridge
Beattock
Eskdalemuir
Ettrick
Ettrickbridge
Yarrow
Tweedsmuir
Talla Reservoir
Fruid Reservoir
Megget Reservoir
St Mary's Loch
Loch of the Lowes
Tibbie Shiels Inn
Cappercleuch
Teviothead
Canonbie
Rowanburn
Kirtlebridge
Kirkpatrick-Fleming
Eaglesfield
Middlebie
Waterbeck
Springfield
Eastriggs
Dornock
Cummertrees
Powfoot
Ruthwell
Clarencefield
Carrutherstown
Dalton
Collin
Torthorwald
Tinwald
Amisfield Town
Parkgate
Kirkland
Boreland
Bentpath
Craik
Ashkirk
Philiphaugh
Bowness-on-Solway
Port Carlisle
Glasson
Drumburgh
Burgh by Sands
Rockcliffe
Houghton
Crosby-on-Eden
Irthington
Smithfield
Scaleby
Westlinton
Kirklinton
Hethersgill
Walton
Newtown
Netherby
Grey Mare's Tail (NTS)
Devil's Beef Tub
Ettrick Pen 692
Broad Law 840
Dollar Law 817
Hart Fell 808
White Coomb 822
Telford Memorial
Carlyle's Birthplace (NTS)
Annandale Water
NT
A7
A74(M)
A701
A708
A709
A75
A6071
A689
A69
M6
76
70
60
F G H J K
2 3 4 5 6 7

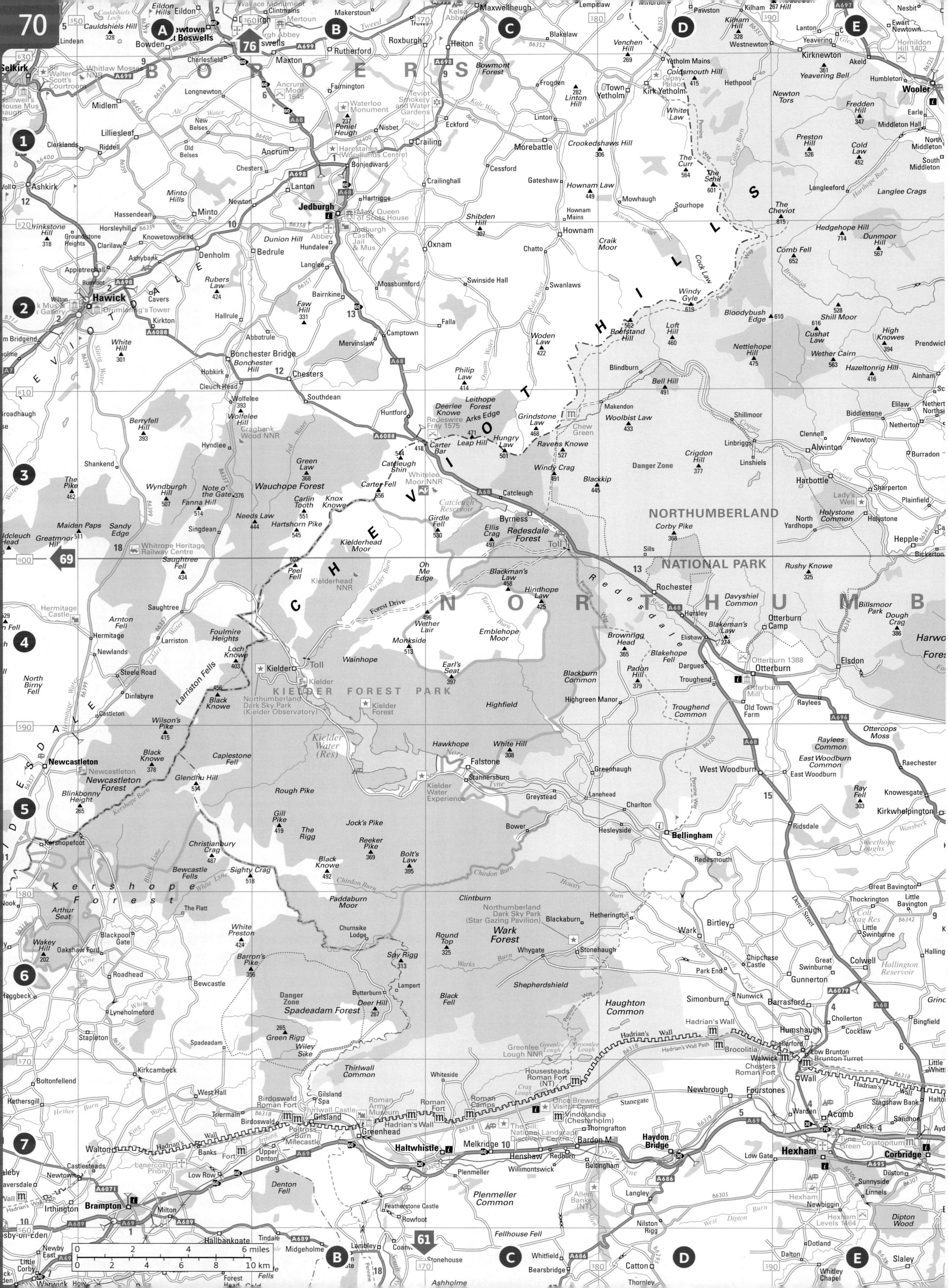
A
B
C
D
E
1
2
3
4
5
6
7
76
69
61
BORDERS
CHEVIOT HILLS
NORTHUMBERLAND
NORTHUMBERLAND NATIONAL PARK
NORTHUMB
KIELDER FOREST PARK
TEVIOTDALE
LIDDESDALE
Kershope Forest
Selkirk
Hawick
Jedburgh
Newtown St Boswells
Eildon
Eildon Hills
Cauldshiels Hill 328
Bowden
Melrose
Makerstoun
Rutherford
Maxton
Roxburgh
Heiton
Kelso Abbey
Maxwellheugh
Lempitlaw
Pawston
Kilham
Kilham Hill 328
Westnewton
Nesbit
Lanton
Ewart Newtown
Yeavering
Kirknewton
Akeld
Homildon Hill 1402
Yeavering Bell 361
Humbleton
Wooler
Earle
Middleton Hall
North Middleton
South Middleton
Fredden Hill 347
Cold Law 452
Preston Hill 526
Langleeford
Langlee Crags
The Cheviot 815
Hedgehope Hill 714
Dunmoor Hill 567
Comb Fell 652
Newton Tors
Hethpool
Yetholm Mains
Coldsmouth Hill
Gipsy Palace
Kirk Yetholm
Town Yetholm
Vencher Hill 269
Blakelaw
Bowmont Forest
Frogden
Linton Hill 282
Linton
White Law
The Curr 564
The Schil 601
Crookedshaws Hill 306
Morebattle
Cessford
Eckford
Crailing
Crailinghall
Teviot Smokery and Water Gardens
Waterloo Monument
Peniel Heugh 237
Nisbet
Harestanes (Woodlands Centre)
Bonjedward
Ancrum
Ancrum Moor 1545
Fairnington
Charlesfield
Whitlaw Mosses NNR
Sir Walter Scott's Courtroom
Longnewton
Midlem
Lilliesleaf
New Belses
Old Belses
Riddell
Clerklands
Ashkirk
Chesters
Lanton
Hartrigge
Mary Queen of Scots House
Jedburgh Castle Jail & Mus
Abbey
Newton
Minto Hills
Minto
Hassendean
Horsleyhill
Drinkstone Hill 318
Groundistone Heights
Clarilaw
Knowetownhead
Ashybank
Denholm
Appletreehall
Burnfoot
Rubers Law 424
Cavers
Drumlanrig's Tower
Wilton
Museum & Gallery
Kirkton
Hallrule
Dunion Hill
Bedrule
Hundalee
Langlee
Oxnam
Shibden Hill 307
Gateshaw
Hownam Law 449
Mowhaugh
Hownam Mains
Hownam
Sourhope
Chatto
Craik Moor
Swinside Hall
Swanlaws
Mossburnford
Bairnkine
Faw Hill 331
Camptown
Falla
Abbotrule
Bonchester Bridge
Bonchester Hill
Hobkirk
Chesters
Cleuch Head
Mervinslaw
White Hill 301
Southdean
Wolfelee 393
Wolfelee Hill
Huntford
Berryfell Hill 393
Cragbank Wood NNR
Hyndlee
Broadhaugh
Shankend
The Pike 462
Wyndburgh Hill 507
Note o' the Gate 376
Fanna Hill 514
Wauchope Forest
Green Law 368
Carlin Tooth 551
Needs Law 444
Knox Knowe
Hartshorn Pike 545
Maiden Paps 511
Sandy Edge
Singdean
Greatmoor Hill
Whitrope Heritage Railway Centre
Saughtree Fell 434
Saughtree
Hermitage Castle
Hermitage
Arnton Fell
Newlands
Larriston
Foulmire Heights
Loch Knowe 403
Larriston Fells
Steele Road
Dinlabyre
Castleton
North Birny Fell
Black Knowe 456
Wilson's Pike 415
Black Knowe 378
Newcastleton
Newcastleton Forest
Glendhu Hill 514
Blinkbonny Height 265
Kershopefoot
Christianbury Crag 487
Bewcastle Fells
Sighty Crag 518
Arthur Seat
The Flatt
Wakey Hill 202
Oakshaw Ford
Blackpool Gate
White Preston 424
Roadhead
Bewcastle
Barron's Pike 356
Haggbeck
Lyneholmeford
Stapleton
Spadeadam
Danger Zone
Spadeadam Forest
Green Rigg
Wiley Sike
Deer Hill 267
Butterburn
Lampert
Kirkcambeck
Boltonfellend
Hethersgill
West Hall
Birdoswald Roman Fort
Gilsland Spa
Gilsland
Thirlwall Castle
Roman Army Museum
Greenhead
Poltross Burn Milecastle
Banks
Hadrian's Wall
Walton
Upper Denton
Lanercost Priory
Castlesteads
Newtown
Low Row
Denton Fell
Brampton
Irthington
Milton
Hallbankgate
Tindale
Midgeholme
Lambley
Coanwood
Featherstone Castle
Rowfoot
Stonehouse
Haltwhistle
Melkridge
Plenmeller
Plenmeller Common
Henshaw
Willimontswick
Bardon Mill
Redburn
Beltingham
Haydon Bridge
Allen Banks (NT)
Langley
Nilston Rigg
Fellhouse Fell
Whitfield
Bearsbridge
Catton
Thornley
Ashholme
Hexham
Corbridge
Acomb
Anick
Sandhoe
Warden
Low Gate
Dilston
Linnels
Sunnyside
Newbiggin
Hexham Levels 1464
Dipton Wood
Dotland
Dalton
Whitley Chapel
Slaley
The Sill: National Landscape Discovery Centre
Vindolanda (Chesterholm)
Once Brewed Visitor Centre
Thorngrafton
Housesteads Roman Fort (NT)
Roman Fort
Roman Camps
Whiteside
Thirlwall Common
Greenlee Lough NNR
Haughton Common
Stanegate
Newbrough
Fourstones
Walwick
Chesters Roman Fort
Wall
Chollerford
Humshaugh
Low Brunton
Brunton Turret
Brocolitia
Stagshaw Bank
Halton
Cocklaw
Chollerton
Barrasford
Simonburn
Nunwick
Gunnerton
Great Swinburne
Colwell
Hallington Reservoir
Bingfield
Park End
Chipchase Castle
Birtley
Wark
Little Swinburne
Colt Crag Res
Thockrington
Little Bavington
Great Bavington
Sweethope Loughs
Ridsdale
Kirkwhelpington
Knowesgate
Ray Fell 303
Raechester
East Woodburn
East Woodburn Common
West Woodburn
Raylees Common
Ottercops Moss
Raylees
Old Town Farm
Otterburn Mill
Otterburn
Otterburn 1388
Elsdon
Troughend
Troughend Common
Dargues
Blakehope Fell
Brownrigg Head 365
Padon Hill 379
Blakeman's Law 274
Otterburn Camp
Elishaw
Horsley
Rochester
Davyshiel Common
Billsmoor Park
Dough Crag 386
Rushy Knowe 325
Sills
Corby Pike 368
North Yardhope
Holystone Common
Holystone
Lady's Well
Hepple
Bickerton
Sharperton
Plainfield
Harbottle
Crigdon Hill 377
Danger Zone
Linbriggs
Linshiels
Alwinton
Clennell
Netherton
Burradon
Newton
Biddlestone
Elilaw
Shillmoor
Woolbist Law 433
Makendon
Chew Green
Ravens Knowe 527
Windy Crag 491
Blackkip 445
Bell Hill 491
Blindburn
Nettlehope Hill 475
Wether Cairn 563
Hazeltonrig Hill 416
Alnham
High Knowes 394
Cushat Law 616
Shill Moor 528
Bloodybush Edge 610
Loft Hill 460
Windy Gyle 619
Beefstand Hill 562
Cock Law
Woden Law 422
Philip Law 414
Grindstone Law 468
Hungry Law 501
Leap Hill 471
Arks Edge
Leithope Forest
Deerlee Knowe
Redeswire Fray 1575
Carter Bar 418
Catcleugh Shin 544
Whitelee Moor NNR
Carter Fell 556
Catcleugh
Catcleugh Reservoir
Byrness
Redesdale Forest
Ellis Crag 497
Girdle Fell 530
Kielderhead Moor
Peel Fell 602
Kielderhead NNR
Oh Me Edge
Blackman's Law 458
Hindhope Law 425
Forest Drive
Wether Lair 496
Emblehope Moor
Monkside 513
Wainhope
Earl's Seat 397
Kielder
Toll
Northumberland Dark Sky Park (Kielder Observatory)
Kielder Forest
Highfield
Blackburn Common
Highgreen Manor
Kielder Water (Res)
Hawkhope
White Hill 308
Falstone
Stannersburn
Kielder Water Experience
Greystead
Lanehead
Greenhaugh
Charlton
Hesleyside
Bellingham
Bower
Redesmouth
Caplestone Fell
Rough Pike
Gill Pike 419
Jock's Pike
The Rigg
Reeker Pike 369
Bolt's Law 395
Black Knowe 492
Paddaburn Moor
Clintburn
Northumberland Dark Sky Park (Star Gazing Pavilion)
Blackaburn
Hetherington
Wark Forest
Churnsike Lodge
Round Top 325
Whygate
Stonehaugh
Spy Rigg 313
Shepherdshield
Black Fell
Pennine Way
Redesdale
Dere Street
Tweed
Teviot
Kale Water
Jed Water
Liddel Water
Kielder Burn
Chirdon Burn
Coquet
North Tyne
South Tyne
Rede
0 2 4 6 miles
0 2 4 6 8 10 km

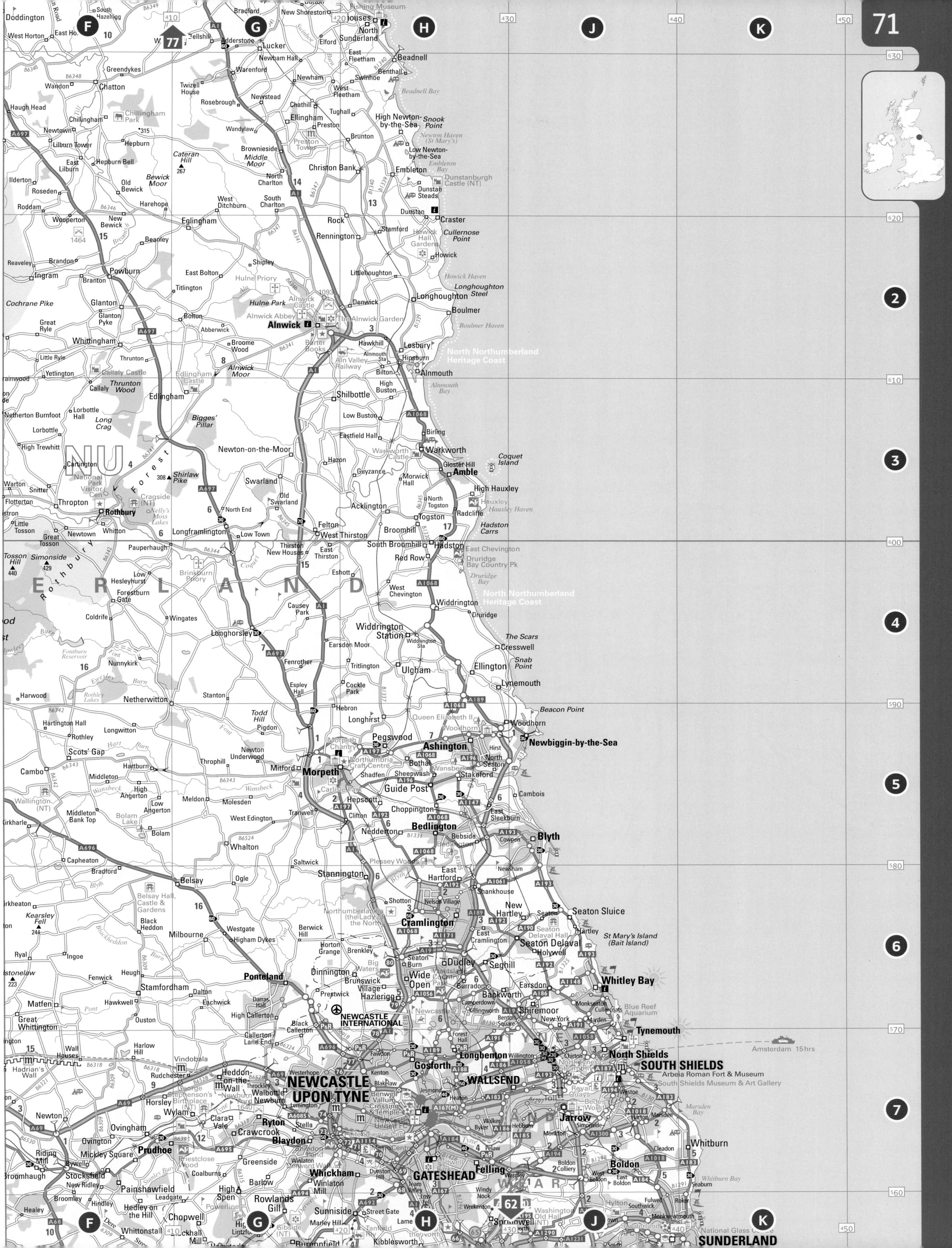
F
G
H
J
K
1
2
3
4
5
6
7
NU
NORTHUMBERLAND
Alnwick
Amble
Warkworth
Rothbury
Morpeth
Ashington
Bedlington
Blyth
Cramlington
Seaton Delaval
Whitley Bay
Tynemouth
North Shields
SOUTH SHIELDS
WALLSEND
NEWCASTLE UPON TYNE
GATESHEAD
Felling
Jarrow
Boldon
Whitburn
SUNDERLAND
Ponteland
Prudhoe
Ryton
Blaydon
Whickham
Gosforth
Longbenton
Newbiggin-by-the-Sea
Cresswell
Lynemouth
Ellington
Widdrington
Hadston
Craster
Embleton
Beadnell
North Sunderland
Lesbury
Alnmouth
Shilbottle
Longhoughton
Powburn
Coquet Island
North Northumberland Heritage Coast
Dunstanburgh Castle (NT)
Druridge Bay Country Pk
NEWCASTLE INTERNATIONAL
Amsterdam 15hrs
Arbeia Roman Fort & Museum
South Shields Museum & Art Gallery
Hadrian's Wall
Wylam
Stamfordham
Belsay
Whalton
Longhorsley
Longframlington
Felton
Seaton Sluice
St Mary's Island (Bait Island)
Blue Reef Aquarium
Beacon Point
77
62

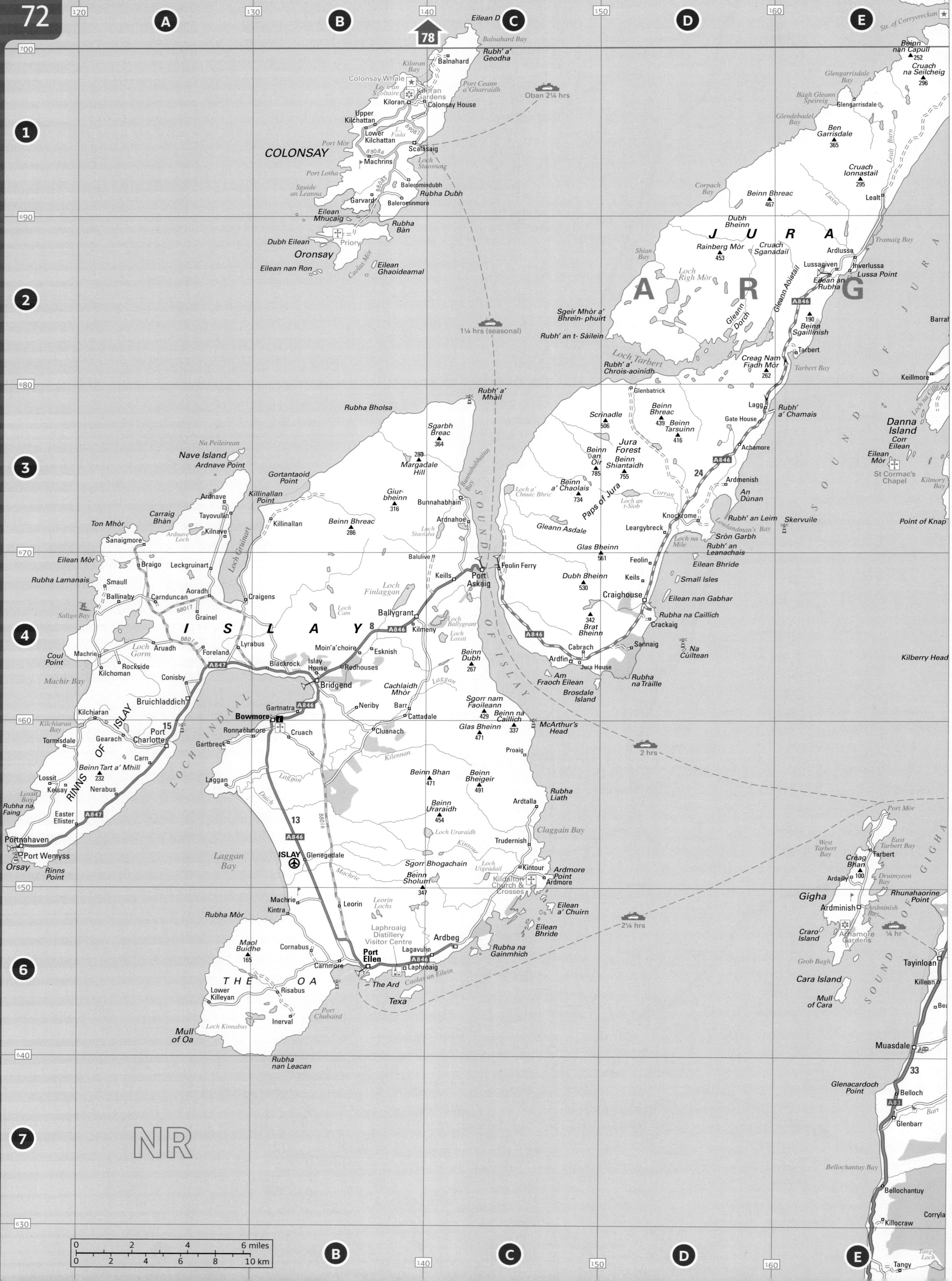
A
B
C
D
E
1
2
3
4
5
6
7
120
130
140
150
160
700
690
680
670
660
650
640
630
78
Eilean D
Balnahard Bay
Balnahard
Rubh' a' Geodha
Kiloran Bay
Colonsay Whale
Loch an Sgoltaire
Kiloran Gardens
Kiloran
Colonsay House
Port Ceann a' Gharraidh
Oban 2¼ hrs
Upper Kilchattan
Lower Kilchattan
L. Fada
B8087
Port Mòr
B8086
Scalasaig
COLONSAY
Machrins
Loch Staosnaig
Port Lotha
B8085
Balerominduhb
Squide an Leanna
Garvard
Rubha Dubh
Baleromindmore
Eilean Mhucaig
Rubha Bàn
Dubh Eilean
Priory
Oronsay
Caolas Mòr
Eilean Ghaoideamal
Eilean nan Ron
Sgeir Mhòr a' Bhrein- phuirt
1¼ hrs (seasonal)
Rubh' an t- Sàilein
Str. of Corryvreckan
Beinn nan Capull
252
Cruach na Seilcheig
296
Glengarrisdale Bay
Bàgh Gleann Speireig
Glengarrisdale
Glendebadel Bay
Ben Garrisdale
365
Cruach Ionnastail
295
Corpach Bay
Beinn Bhreac
467
Lealt
Dubh Bheinn
J U R A
Tramaig Bay
Shian Bay
Rainberg Mòr
453
Cruach Sganadail
Ardlussa
Loch Righ Mòr
Lussagiven
Inverlussa
Lussa Point
Eilean an Rubha
A R G
Gleann Dorch
Gleann Aoistail
A846
190
Beinn Sgaillinish
Barrah
Loch Tarbert
Tarbert
Creag Nam Fiadh Mòr
262
Tarbert Bay
Rubh' a' Chrois-aoinidh
Keillmore
Rubh' a' Mhàil
Glenbatrick
Rubha Bholsa
Scrinadle
506
Beinn Bhreac
439
Beinn Tarsuinn
416
Lagg
Gate House
Rubh' a' Chamais
Danna Island
Corr Eilean
Sgarbh Breac
364
Jura Forest
Achamore
Na Peileirean
Nave Island
Ardnave Point
283
Margadale Hill
Beinn an Oir
785
Beinn Shiantaidh
755
24
Eilean Mòr
Gortantaoid Point
Loch a' Chnuic Bhric
Beinn a' Chaolais
734
Ardmenish
St Cormac's Chapel
Kilmory Bay
Killinallan Point
Giur-bheinn
316
Bunnahabhain
Bunnahabhain Bay
Paps of Jura
Loch an t-Siob
Corran
An Dùnan
Ardnave
Carraig Bhàn
Tayovullin
Killinallan
Beinn Bhreac
286
Ardnahoe
Loch Staoisha
Gleann Asdale
Knockrome
Leargybreck
Lowlandman's Bay
Rubh' an Leim
Skervuile
Point of Knap
Ton Mhòr
Ardnave Loch
Kilnave
Loch Gruinart
Sròn Garbh
Loch na Mile
Rubh' an Leanachais
Sanaigmore
Glas Bheinn
561
Eilean Mòr
Balulive
Feolin
Eilean Bhride
Braigo
Leckgruinart
Feolin Ferry
Dubh Bheinn
530
Keills
Small Isles
Rubha Lamanais
Smaull
Keills
Port Askaig
Aoradh
Loch Finlaggan
Craighouse
Eilean nan Gabhar
Ballinaby
Carnduncan
Craigens
Saligo Bay
B8017
Loch Cam
Ballygrant
Rubha na Caillich
I S L A Y
Grainel
8
Loch Ballygrant
342
Brat Bheinn
Crackaig
Loch Gorm
B8018
A846
Kilmeny
Moin'a'choire
Loch Lossit
A846
Aruadh
Lyrabus
Sannaig
Coul Point
Machrie
Foreland
Esknish
Beinn Dubh
267
Cabrach
Na Cùiltean
Rockside
Blackrock
Islay House
Redhouses
Ardfin
Jura House
Kilberry Head
Kilchoman
A847
Am Fraoch Eilean
Rubha na Tràille
Machir Bay
Conisby
Bridgend
Cachlaidh Mhòr
Laggan
Brosdale Island
Bruichladdich
Gartnatra
A846
Neriby
Barr
Sgorr nam Faoileann
429
Kilchiaran
Bowmore
Cattadale
Beinn na Caillich
337
McArthur's Head
Kilchiaran Bay
15
Ronnachmore
Cruach
Glas Bheinn
471
Tormisdale
Gearach
Port Charlotte
Cluanach
Gartbreck
Proaig
2 hrs
Carn
LOCH INDAAL
RINNS OF ISLAY
Kilennan
Beinn Tart a' Mhill
232
Lossit
Laggan
Beinn Bhan
471
Beinn Bheigeir
491
Rubha Liath
Kelsay
Nerabus
Lossit Bay
Ardtalla
Port Mòr
Rubha na Faing
Duich
B8016
Beinn Uraraidh
454
Easter Ellister
A847
13
Claggain Bay
East Tarbert Bay
Loch Uraraidh
Kintour
West Tarbert Bay
Creag Bhan
Tarbert
Portnahaven
A846
Trudernish
100
Port Wemyss
Laggan Bay
ISLAY
Glenegedale
Sgorr Bhogachain
Loch Uigeadail
Kintour
Ardaily
Druimyeon Bay
Orsay
Beinn Sholum
Kildalton Church & Crosses
Ardmore Point
Ardmore
Rinns Point
Machrie
347
Gigha
Rhunahaorine Point
Machrie
Leorin
Leorin Lochs
Eilean a' Chùirn
Ardminish
Ardminish Bay
Rubha Mòr
Kintra
2¼ hrs
¼ hr
Laphroaig Distillery Visitor Centre
Eilean Bhride
Craro Island
Achamore Gardens
Maol Buidhe
165
Cornabus
Ardbeg
Rubha na Gainmhich
Tayinloan
Port Ellen
Lagavulin
A846
Grob Bagh
Carnmore
Laphroaig
THE OA
Caolas an Eilein
Cara Island
Killean
Lower Killeyan
Risabus
The Ard
SOUND OF GIGHA
Texa
Mull of Cara
Port Chubaird
Inerval
Loch Kinnabus
Mull of Oa
Muasdale
33
Rubha nan Leacan
Glenacardoch Point
Belloch
A83
Barr
Glenbarr
NR
Bellochantuy Bay
Bellochantuy
Corryla
Killocraw
Tangy Loch
Tangy
SOUND OF ISLAY
SOUND OF JURA
0
2
4
6 miles
0
2
4
6
8
10 km

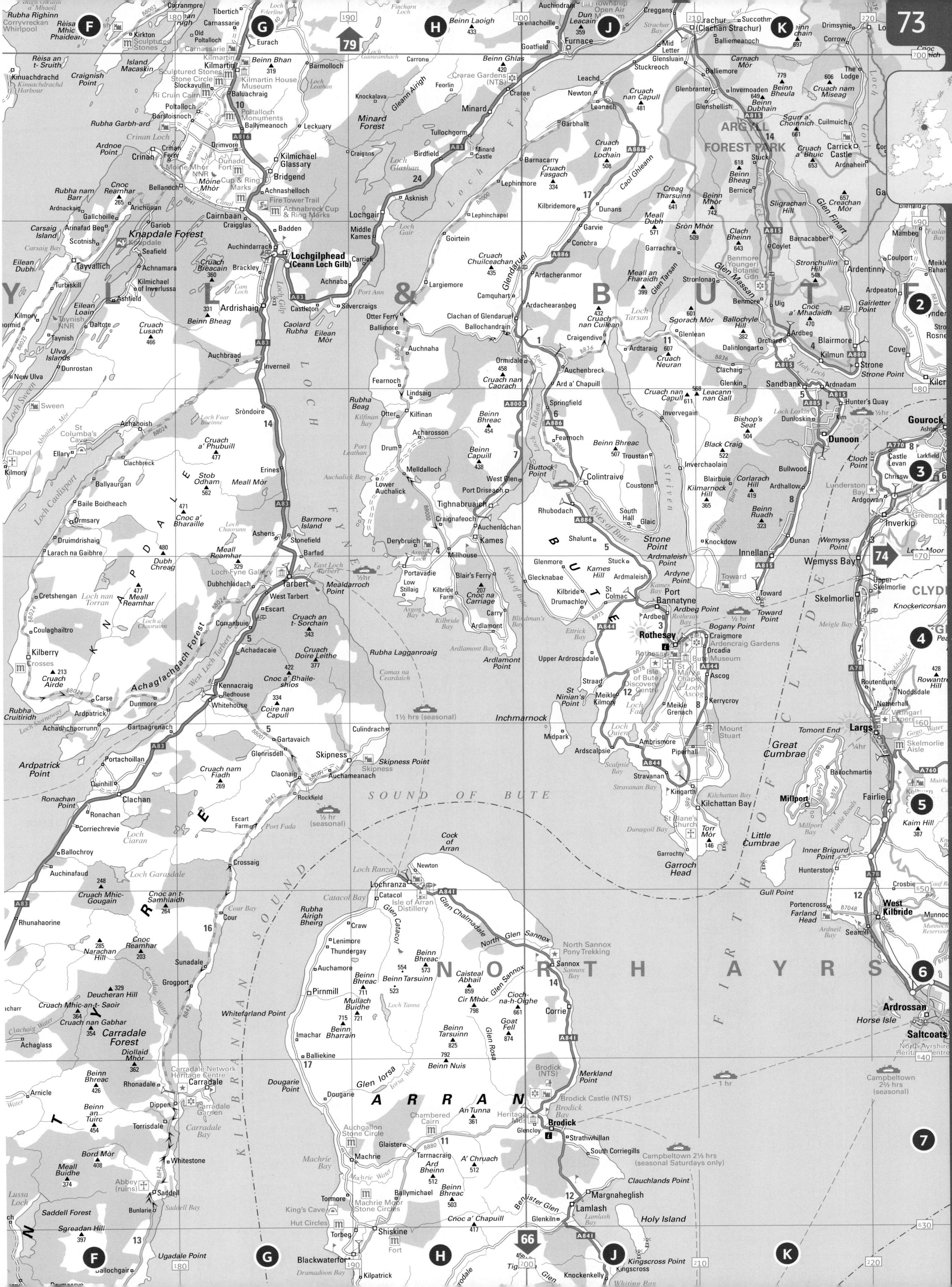

79
74
66
ARGYLL FOREST PARK
Knapdale Forest
Lochgilphead (Ceann Loch Gilb)
Ardrishaig
Tarbert
Kilmartin
Crinan
Tayvallich
Inveraray
Minard
Furnace
Strachur (Clachan Strachur)
Dunoon
Gourock
Kilmun
Sandbank
Tighnabruaich
Colintraive
Portavadie
Rothesay
Port Bannatyne
Kilchattan Bay
Wemyss Bay
Largs
Great Cumbrae
Millport
Little Cumbrae
Fairlie
West Kilbride
Ardrossan
Saltcoats
Skipness
Claonaig
Carradale
Carradale Forest
Saddell
Lochranza
Brodick
Lamlash
Holy Island
Corrie
Shiskine
Blackwaterfoot
Machrie
Inchmarnock
LOCH FYNE
SOUND OF BUTE
KILBRANNAN SOUND
FIRTH OF CLYDE
A R R A N
B U T E
K N A P D A L E
NORTH AYRS
ARGYLL & BUTE
Campbeltown 2½ hrs (seasonal Saturdays only)
Campbeltown 2¾ hrs (seasonal)
1½ hrs (seasonal)

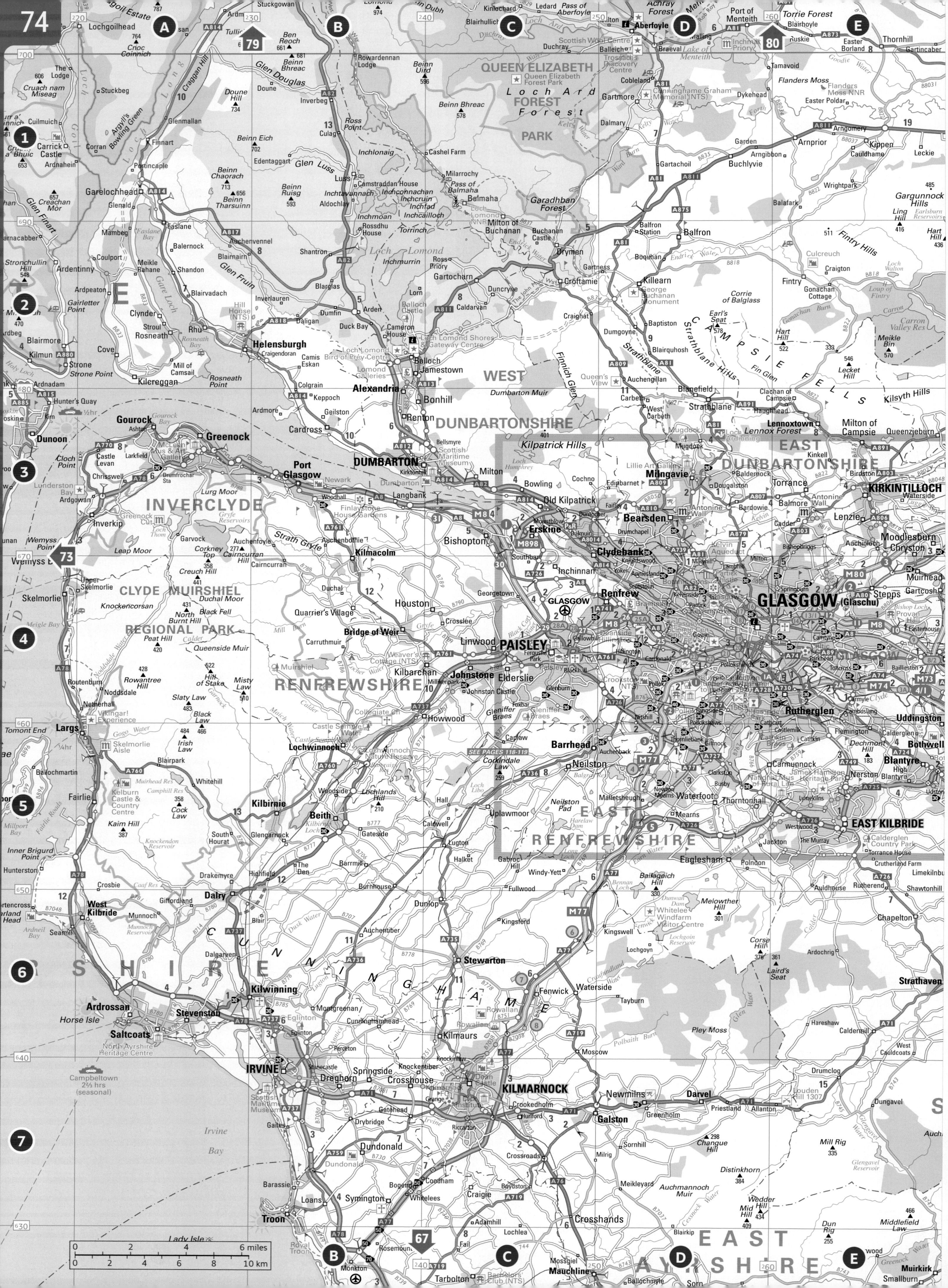

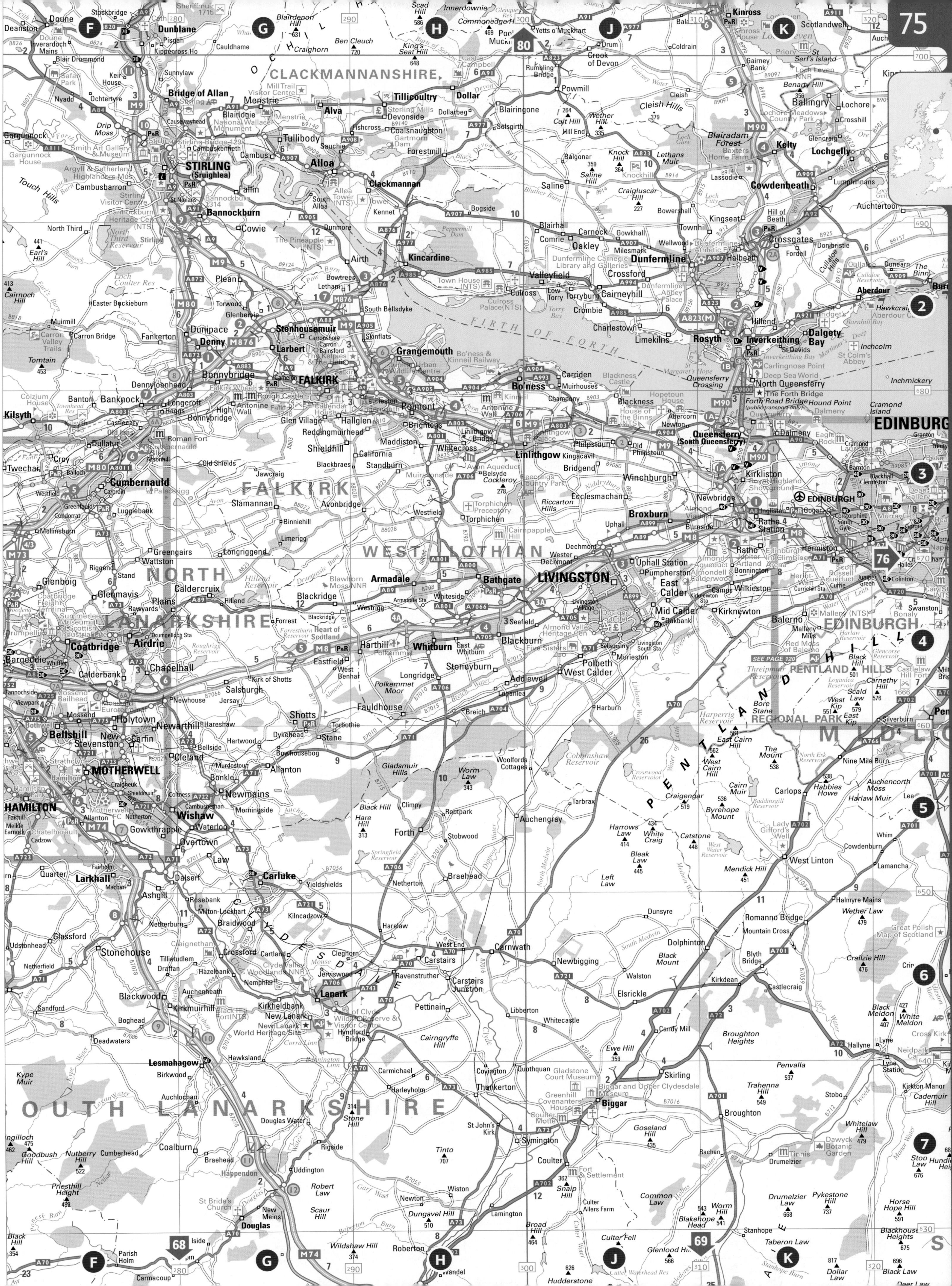
CLACKMANNANSHIRE
STIRLING
(Sruighlea)
FALKIRK
WEST LOTHIAN
NORTH LANARKSHIRE
SOUTH LANARKSHIRE
PENTLAND HILLS
REGIONAL PARK
EDINBURGH
LIVINGSTON
FIRTH OF FORTH
Dunblane
Bridge of Allan
Alloa
Tillicoultry
Dollar
Clackmannan
Dunfermline
Kincardine
Grangemouth
Bo'ness
Linlithgow
Bathgate
Whitburn
Broxburn
Queensferry
(South Queensferry)
Cumbernauld
Coatbridge
Airdrie
Motherwell
Hamilton
Wishaw
Carluke
Lanark
Biggar
Lesmahagow
Douglas
West Linton
Dalkeith
Cowdenbeath
Kelty
Lochgelly
Inverkeithing
Rosyth
Dalgety Bay
Aberdour
Kinross
Stenhousemuir
Larbert
Denny
Bonnybridge
Kilsyth
Armadale
Shotts
Bellshill
Larkhall
Carnwath
Carstairs
Stonehouse
Blackburn
Mid Calder
West Calder
East Calder
Balerno
Penicuik
Kirkliston
Ratho
Currie

For a more detailed map of Edinburgh see page 120

For a more detailed map of Edinburgh see page 120

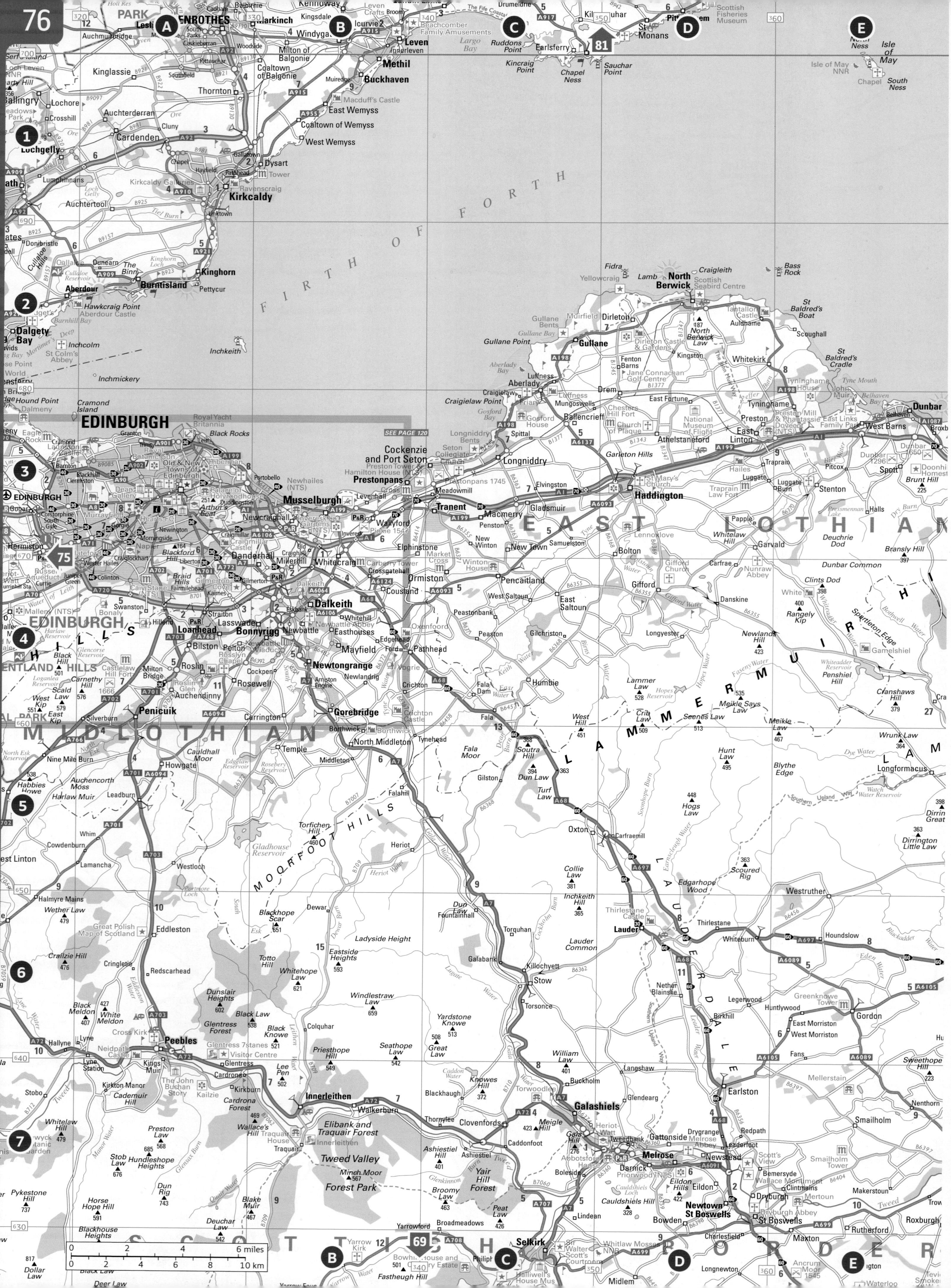
A
B
C
D
E
1
2
3
4
5
6
7
GLENROTHES
Markinch
Leven
Methil
Buckhaven
Kinglassie
Thornton
Lochgelly
Cardenden
Dysart
Kirkcaldy
Kinghorn
Burntisland
Aberdour
Dalgety Bay
Inchcolm
Inchkeith
Inchmickery
Cramond Island
FIRTH OF FORTH
Largo Bay
Ruddons Point
Earlsferry
Kincraig Point
Chapel Ness
Saucher Point
St Monans
81
Isle of May
Isle of May NNR
North Ness
South Ness
Fidra
Lamb
North Berwick
Craigleith
Bass Rock
Dirleton
Gullane
Gullane Point
Aberlady
Drem
Tantallon Castle
Whitekirk
Tyninghame
Dunbar
East Linton
Athelstaneford
Haddington
Longniddry
Cockenzie and Port Seton
Prestonpans
EDINBURGH
SEE PAGE 120
Musselburgh
Tranent
Macmerry
Dalkeith
Bonnyrigg
Loanhead
Penicuik
Gorebridge
Newtongrange
Mayfield
Pathhead
75
EAST LOTHIAN
Gifford
Pencaitland
Ormiston
Garvald
LAMMERMUIR HILLS
MIDLOTHIAN
PENTLAND HILLS
MOORFOOT HILLS
Lauder
LAUDERDALE
Stow
Oxton
Westruther
Gordon
Earlston
Galashiels
Melrose
Newtown St Boswells
St Boswells
Selkirk
Peebles
Innerleithen
Walkerburn
Tweed Valley Forest Park
West Linton
Eddleston
Longformacus
69
SCOTTISH BORDERS

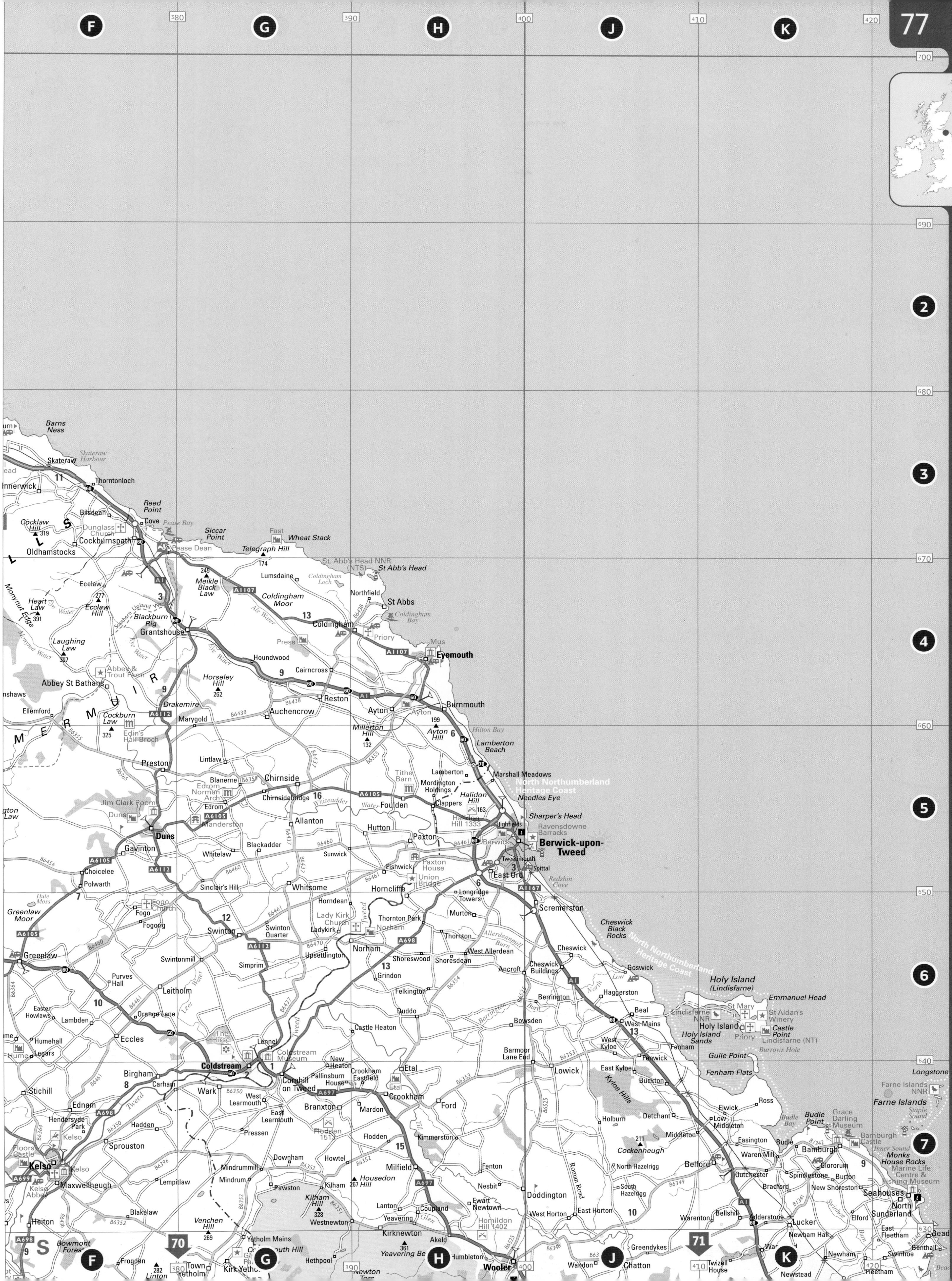

F
G
H
J
K
2
3
4
5
6
7
Barns Ness
Skateraw
Skateraw Harbour
Thorntonloch
Innerwick
Reed Point
Bilsdean
Cocklaw Hill
319
Dunglass Church
Cove
Pease Bay
Siccar Point
Fast
Wheat Stack
Cockburnspath
Oldhamstocks
Pease Dean
Telegraph Hill
174
St. Abb's Head NNR (NTS)
St Abb's Head
Lumsdaine
Coldingham Loch
Ecclaw
245
Meikle Black Law
A1107
Coldingham Moor
Northfield
St Abbs
Coldingham Bay
Monynut Edge
Heart Law
391
277
Ecclaw Hill
Blackburn Rig
Grantshouse
13
Coldingham
Priory
Laughing Law
307
Press
Mus
Eyemouth
Houndwood
Abbey & Trout Farm
Horseley Hill
262
9
Cairncross
Abbey St Bathans
Reston
Burnmouth
Ayton
Drakemire
Auchencrow
Ellemford
Cockburn Law
325
Edin's Hall Broch
Marygold
Millerton Hill
132
199
Ayton Hill
Hilton Bay
Lamberton Beach
Preston
Lintlaw
Lamberton
Marshall Meadows
Blanerne
Chirnside
Edrom
Norman Arch
Mordington Holdings
North Northumberland Heritage Coast
Needles Eye
Chirnsidebridge
16
A6105
Foulden
Halidon Hill
Clappers
Jim Clark Room
Duns
Edrom
Manderston
Allanton
Hutton
Halidon Hill 1333
163
Sharper's Head
Ravensdowne Barracks
Highfields
Berwick-upon-Tweed
Paxton
Berwick
Gavinton
Blackadder
Whitelaw
Sunwick
Paxton House
Tweedmouth
Spittal
East Ord
Fishwick
Union Bridge
Choicelee
Polwarth
Sinclair's Hill
Whitsome
Horncliffe
Redshin Cove
Longridge Towers
Scremerston
Hule Moss
Greenlaw Moor
Fogo Church
Fogo
Fogorig
12
Horndean
Lady Kirk Church
Ladykirk
Thornton Park
Murton
Swinton
Swinton Quarter
Norham
Thornton
Cheswick Black Rocks
Greenlaw
Swintonmill
Upsettlington
Shoreswood
Shoresdean
West Allerdean
Cheswick
Simprim
Grindon
Ancroft
Cheswick Buildings
Goswick
Holy Island (Lindisfarne)
Emmanuel Head
Purves Hall
Leitholm
Felkington
Haggerston
Easter Howlaws
Lambden
Orange Lane
Duddo
Berrington
Beal
St Mary
St Aidan's Winery
Lindisfarne NNR
Holy Island
Castle Point
West Mains
Humehall
Eccles
The Hirsel
Lennel
Castle Heaton
Bowsden
Holy Island Sands
Priory
Lindisfarne (NT)
Hume
Legars
Coldstream Museum
Coldstream
West Kyloe
Fenham
Burrows Hole
Guile Point
Barmoor Lane End
Fenwick
Birgham
New Heaton
Crookham Eastfield
Etal
Lowick
East Kyloe
Fenham Flats
Longstone
Stichill
Carham
Wark
Pallinsburn House
Cornhill on Tweed
Kyloe Hills
Buckton
Farne Islands NNR
Farne Islands
West Learmouth
Crookham
Ednam
Branxton
Ford
Staple Sound
Mardon
Detchant
Elwick
Ross
Hendersyde Park
East Learmouth
Holburn
Low Middleton
Budle Bay
Budle Point
Grace Darling Museum
Hadden
Pressen
Flodden 1513
Flodden
Kimmerston
211
Middleton
Easington
Bamburgh Castle
Floors Castle
Kelso
Sprouston
Cockenheugh
Budle
Bamburgh
Inner Sound
Downham
Howtel
Milfield
Waren Mill
Monks House Rocks
Mindrummill
Fenton
North Hazelrigg
Belford
Glororum
Maxwellheugh
Kelso Abbey
Lempitlaw
Mindrum
Pawston
Kilham
Housedon Hill
267
Outchester
Spindlestone
Burton
Marine Life Centre & Fishing Museum
Kilham Hill
328
Nesbit
Ewart Newtown
Doddington
South Hazelrigg
Bradford
New Shoreston
Seahouses
Blakelaw
Lanton
Coupland
Roman Road
East Horton
West Horton
10
Warenton
Bellshill
North Sunderland
Westnewton
Yeavering
Homildon Hill 1402
Adderstone
Lucker
Elford
Heiton
Venchen Hill
269
Glen
East Fleetham
Yetholm Mains
Kirknewton
Akeld
Greendykes
Newham Hall
Beadnell
Bowmont Forest
Yeavering Bell
361
Humbleton
Chatton
Newham
Swinhoe
Benthall
Frogden
282
Linton
Town Yetholm
Kirk Yetholm
Hethpool
Newton Tors
Wooler
Wandon
Twizell House
Newstead
Fleetham
70
71
A1
A1107
A1167
A6112
A6105
A697
A698
A699
A6105
B6438
B6355
B6437
B6460
B6461
B6470
B6350
B6352
B6351
B6353
B6354
B6525
B6348
B6349
B1341
B1342
B6396
B6364
B6461
B6456
B6365
Tweed
Whiteadder Water
Eye Water
Ale Water
Leet Water
Southern Upland Way
Till
Allerdeanmill Burn
Barrington Burn
Low
380
390
400
410
420
700
690
680
670
660
650
640
630

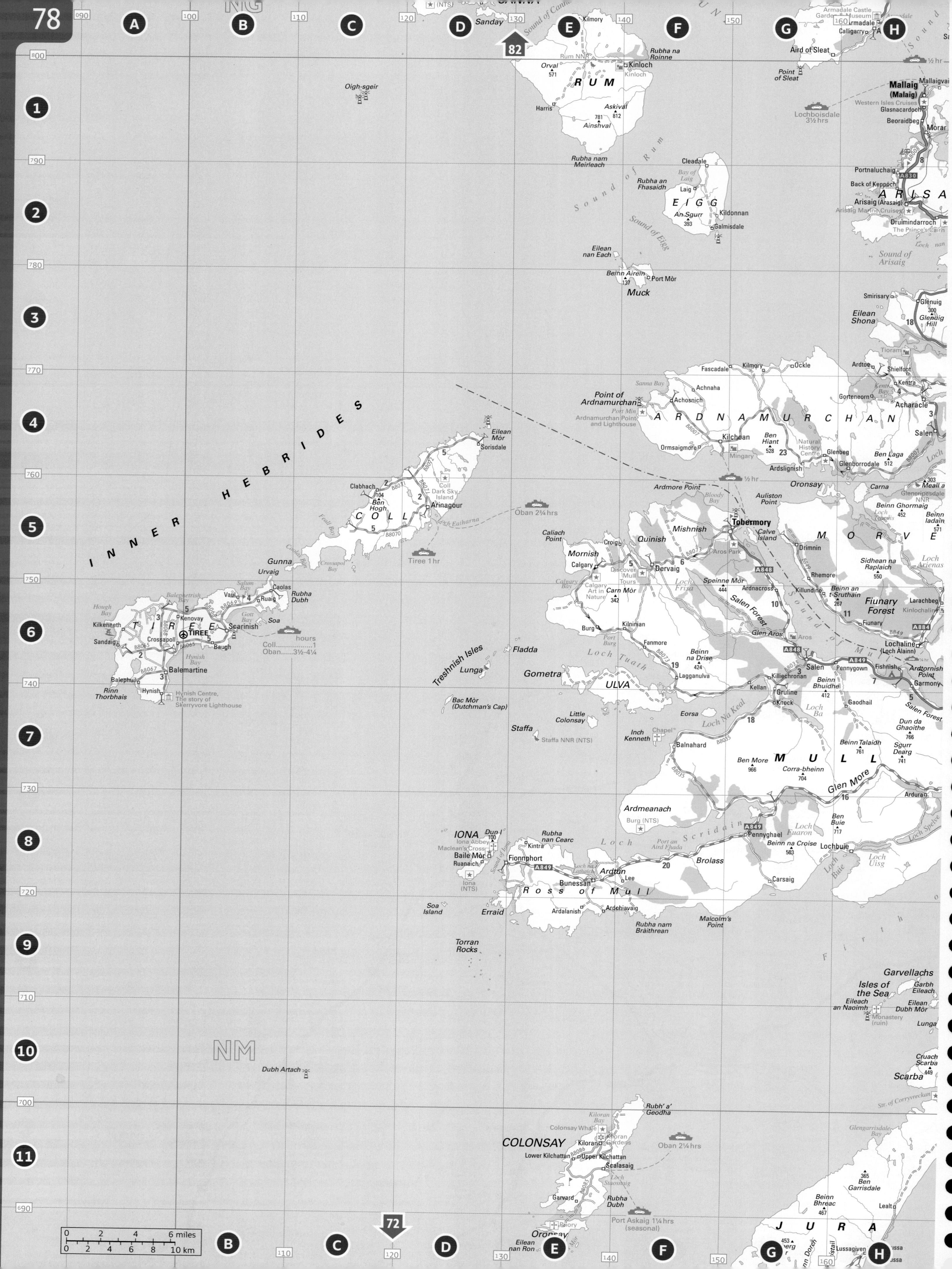

A
B
C
D
E
F
G
H
NG
NM
RUM
Rum NNR
Kilmory
Kinloch
Orval
571
Askival
812
781
Ainshval
Harris
Rubha na Rinne
Rubha nam Meirleach
Sanday
Sound of Canna
Sound of Rum
82
Oigh-sgeir
Armadale Castle Gardens & Museum
Armadale
Calligarry
Aird of Sleat
Point of Sleat
Mallaig (Malaig)
Mallaigvaig
Western Isles Cruises
Glasnacardoch
Lochboisdale 3½ hrs
Beoraidbeg
Morar
Portnaluchaig
Back of Keppoch
Arisaig (Arasaig)
Arisaig Marine Cruises
Druimindarroch
The Prince's Cairn
Sound of Arisaig
A830
½ hr
EIGG
Cleadale
Bay of Laig
Laig
Rubha an Fhasaidh
Kildonnan
An Sgurr
393
Galmisdale
Sound of Eigg
Eilean nan Each
Beinn Airein
137
Port Mòr
Muck
Smirisary
Glenuig
300
Glenuig Hill
Eilean Shona
18
Tioram
Ardtoe
Shielfoot
Kentra
Kentra Bay
Gorteneorn
Acharacle
Salen
Fascadale
Kilmory
Ockle
Sanna Bay
Achnaha
Achosnich
Point of Ardnamurchan
Port Min
Ardnamurchan Point and Lighthouse
ARDNAMURCHAN
B8007
Kilchoan
Mingary
Ormsaigmore
Ben Hiant
528
23
Natural History Centre
Glenbeg
Glenborrodale
Ben Laga
512
Ardslignish
Oronsay
Carna
Meall a' Chaorainn
Ardmore Point
Bloody Bay
Auliston Point
Tobermory
Calve Island
Aros Park
Mishnish
Quinish
Caliach Point
Mornish
Calgary
Croig
Dervaig
Discover Mull Tours
Calgary Bay
Calgary Art in Nature
Carn Mòr
342
Loch Frisa
Speinne Mòr
444
Salen Forest
Glen Aros
Aros
Ardnacross
Killundine
MORVERN
Drimnin
Rhemore
Beinn Ghormaig
452
Beinn Iadain
571
Sidhean na Raplaich
550
Beinn an t-Sruthain
267
Fiunary Forest
Fiunary
Larachbeg
Kinlochaline
Lochaline (Loch Alainn)
A884
Ardtornish Point
Garmony
Fishnish
B849
A848
A849
Salen
Pennygown
Burg
Port Burg
Kilninian
Fanmore
Beinn na Drise
424
B8073
Loch Tuath
Gometra
ULVA
Lagganulva
Killiechronan
Kellan
Gruline
Knock
Beinn Bhuidhe
412
Gaodhail
Loch Ba
Salen Forest
Dun da Ghaoithe
766
Sgurr Dearg
741
Beinn Talaidh
761
Eorsa
Loch Na Keal
Inch Kenneth
Chapel
Little Colonsay
Staffa
Staffa NNR (NTS)
Balnahard
B8035
Ben More
966
MULL
Corra-bheinn
704
Glen More
Ardura
16
Ben Buie
717
Ardmeanach
Burg (NTS)
Loch Scridain
Port an Aird Fhada
Pennyghael
Beinn na Croise
503
Lochbuie
Loch Uisg
Loch Fuaron
20
Brolass
Carsaig
Loch Spelve
IONA
Dun I
100
Iona Abbey
Maclean's Cross
Baile Mòr
Ruanaich
Iona (NTS)
Sound of Iona
Fionnphort
Kintra
Rubha nan Cearc
Ardtun
Lee
Bunessan
Ross of Mull
Ardalanish
Ardchiavaig
Erraid
Soa Island
Rubha nam Bràithrean
Malcolm's Point
Torran Rocks
Firth of Lorn
Garvellachs
Isles of the Sea
Garbh Eileach
Eileach an Naoimh
Monastery (ruin)
Eilean Dubh Mòr
Lunga
Cruach Scarba
449
Scarba
Str. of Corryvreckan
Dubh Artach
INNER HEBRIDES
COLL
Eilean Mòr
Sorisdale
Clabhach
Ben Hogh
104
Coll Dark Sky Island
Arinagour
Loch Eatharna
B8071
B8070
Feall Bay
Crossapol Bay
Oban 2¾ hrs
Tiree 1 hr
Gunna
Urvaig
Caolas
Salum Bay
Vaul
Ruaig
Rubha Dubh
Balephetrish Bay
Gott Bay
Soa
TIREE
Hough Bay
Kilkenneth
Kenovay
Sandaig
Crossapoll
Scarinish
Baugh
Hynish Bay
Balemartine
Balephuil
Hynish
Hynish Centre, The story of Skerryvore Lighthouse
Rinn Thorbhais
B8065
B8067
B8068
B8069
hours
Coll..................1
Oban......3½-4¼
Treshnish Isles
Fladda
Lunga
Bac Mòr (Dutchman's Cap)
COLONSAY
Rubh' a' Geodha
Kiloran Bay
Colonsay Whale
Kiloran
Kiloran Gardens
Lower Kilchattan
Upper Kilchattan
Scalasaig
Loch Staosnaig
B8086
B8085
Garvard
Rubha Dubh
Oban 2¼ hrs
Port Askaig 1¼ hrs (seasonal)
Priory
Oronsay
Eilean nan Ron
72
Glengarrisdale Bay
365
Ben Garrisdale
Beinn Bhreac
467
Lealt
JURA
Lussagiven
0 2 4 6 miles
0 2 4 6 8 10 km

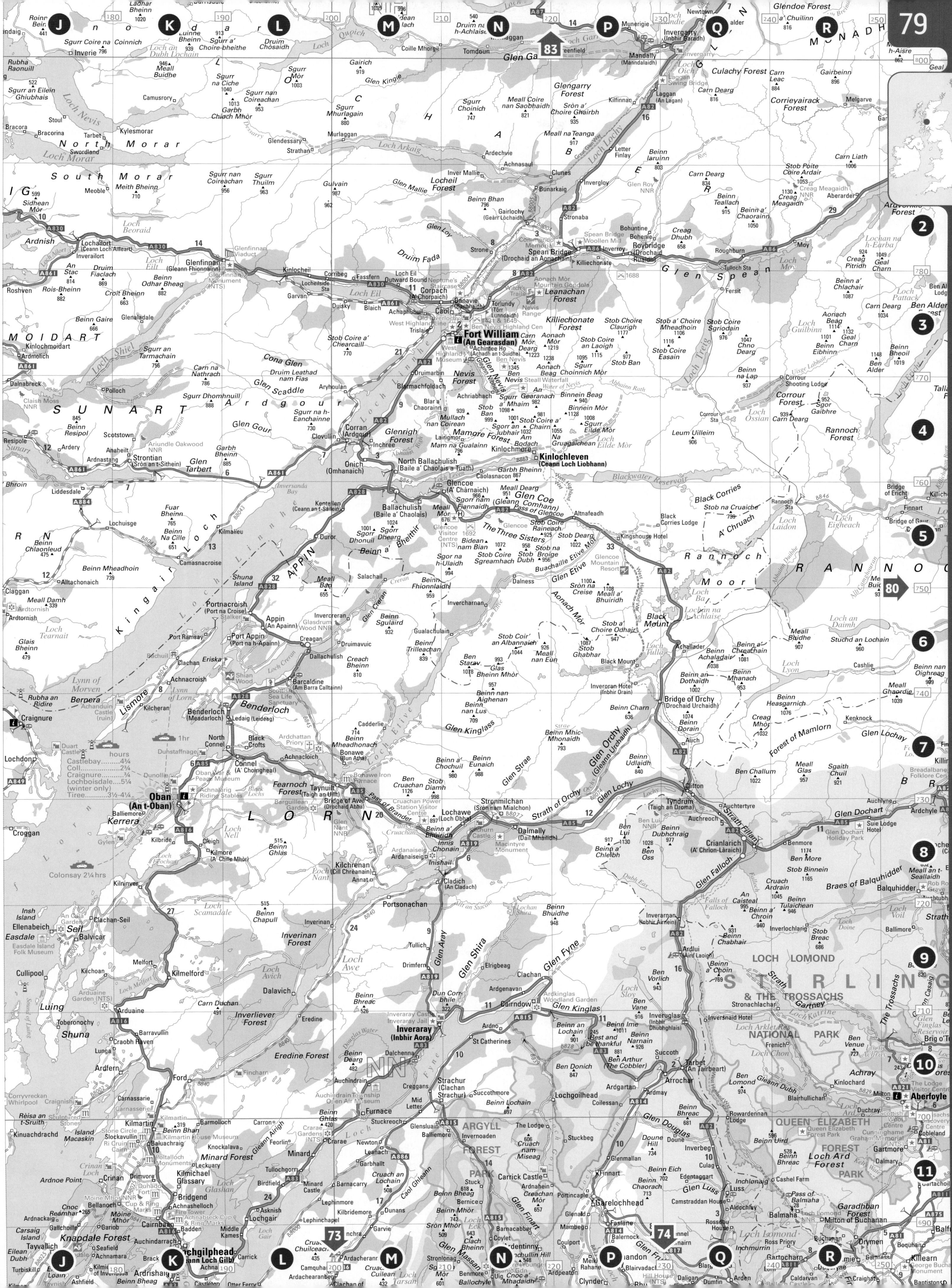

Fort William (An Gearasdan)
Oban (An t-Oban)
Inveraray (Inbhir Aora)
Kinlochleven (Ceann Loch Liobhann)
Aberfoyle
Lochgilphead
Ballachulish (Baile a' Chaolais)
Glencoe (A' Chàrnaich)
Spean Bridge (Drochaid an Aonachain)
Glenfinnan (Gleann Fhionnainn)
Tyndrum (Taigh an Droma)
Crianlarich (A' Chrìon-Làraich)
Bridge of Orchy (Drochaid Urchaidh)
Dalmally (Dail Mhàilidh)
Arrochar
Tarbet (An Tairbeart)
Invergarry (Inbhir Garadh)
Mallaig
North Morar
South Morar
MOIDART
SUNART
Ardgour
APPIN
LORN
Rannoch Moor
Glen Coe
Glen Spean
Loch Lochy
Loch Eil
Loch Linnhe
Loch Etive
Loch Awe
Loch Fyne
Loch Lomond
LOCH LOMOND & THE TROSSACHS NATIONAL PARK
STIRLING
ARGYLL FOREST PARK
QUEEN ELIZABETH FOREST PARK
Knapdale Forest
Ben Nevis 1345
Kerrera
Lismore
Luing
Shuna
Seil
Craignure
Colonsay 2¼ hrs
Castlebay.........4¾
Coll................2¾
Craignure..........¾
Lochboisdale.....5¼
(winter only)
Tiree............3½-4¼
83
80
73
74
J K L M N P Q R
2 3 4 5 6 7 8 9 10 11

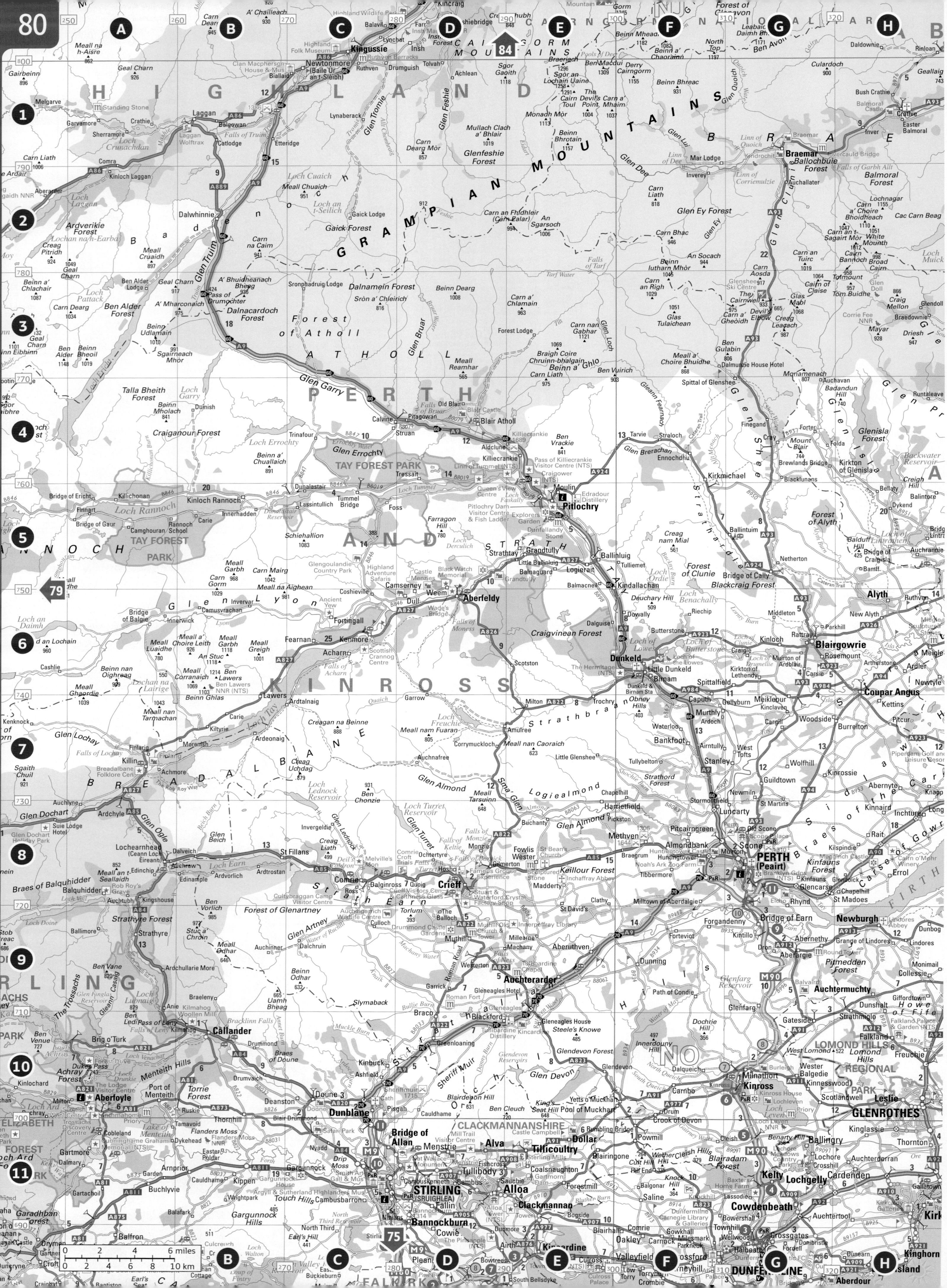
HIGHLAND
GRAMPIAN MOUNTAINS
CAIRNGORM MOUNTAINS
PERTH AND KINROSS
STIRLING
CLACKMANNANSHIRE
BREADALBANE
ATHOLL
Forest of Atholl
Kingussie
Newtonmore
Laggan
Dalwhinnie
Braemar
Blair Atholl
Pitlochry
Aberfeldy
Kenmore
Killin
Dunkeld
Blairgowrie
Alyth
Coupar Angus
PERTH (Peairt)
Crieff
Comrie
Auchterarder
Callander
Aberfoyle
Dunblane
Bridge of Allan
STIRLING (SRUIGHLEA)
Alloa
Tillicoultry
Dollar
Kinross
Lochgelly
Cowdenbeath
GLENROTHES
DUNFERMLINE
Bannockburn
Kincardine
Loch Rannoch
Loch Tay
Loch Earn
Loch Tummel
TAY FOREST PARK
Newburgh
Auchtermuchty
Strathyre
Lochearnhead
Glen Almond
Glen Lyon
Glen Garry
Glen Shee
Glen Devon
Ochil Hills
Sidlaw Hills
LOMOND HILLS REGIONAL PARK
84
79
75
A B C D E F G H
1 2 3 4 5 6 7 8 9 10 11
0 2 4 6 miles
0 2 4 6 8 10 km

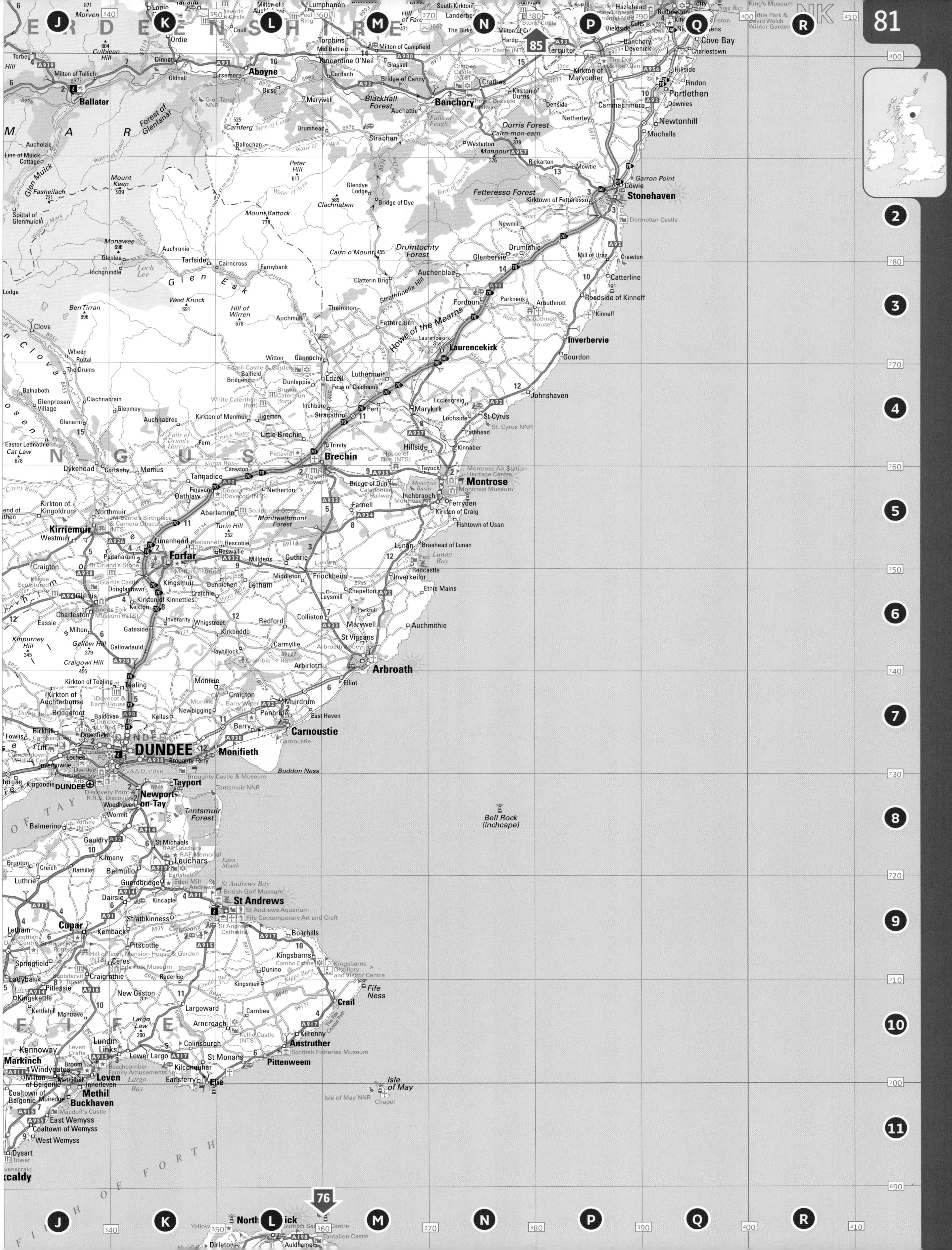
ABERDEENSHIRE
ANGUS
FIFE
FIRTH OF TAY
FIRTH OF FORTH
NK
J
K
L
M
N
P
Q
R
2
3
4
5
6
7
8
9
10
11
800
780
770
760
750
740
730
720
710
700
690
340
350
360
370
380
390
400
410
85
76
Aboyne
Ballater
Banchory
Crathes
Stonehaven
Cove Bay
Portlethen
Newtonhill
Muchalls
Cowie
Garron Point
Dunnottar Castle
Kirktown of Fetteresso
Fetteresso Forest
Durris Forest
Blackhall Forest
Forest of Glentanar
Glen Muick
Mount Keen
Mount Battock
Clachnaben
Drumtochty Forest
Cairn o'Mount
Glen Esk
Tarfside
Auchenblae
Fordoun
Fettercairn
Howe of the Mearns
Laurencekirk
Inverbervie
Gourdon
Catterline
Johnshaven
St Cyrus
Marykirk
Edzell
Brechin
Montrose
Hillside
Ferryden
Inchbraoch
Kirriemuir
Forfar
Letham
Friockheim
Inverkeilor
Lunan Bay
Ethie Mains
Auchmithie
Arbroath
Carnoustie
Monifieth
DUNDEE
Broughty Ferry
Buddon Ness
Tayport
Newport-on-Tay
Tentsmuir Forest
Bell Rock (Inchcape)
Leuchars
St Andrews
St Andrews Bay
Cupar
Crail
Fife Ness
Anstruther
Pittenweem
St Monans
Elie
Leven
Methil
Buckhaven
East Wemyss
West Wemyss
Dysart
Markinch
Isle of May
Isle of May NNR
North Berwick
Tantallon Castle
Dirleton
Auldhame

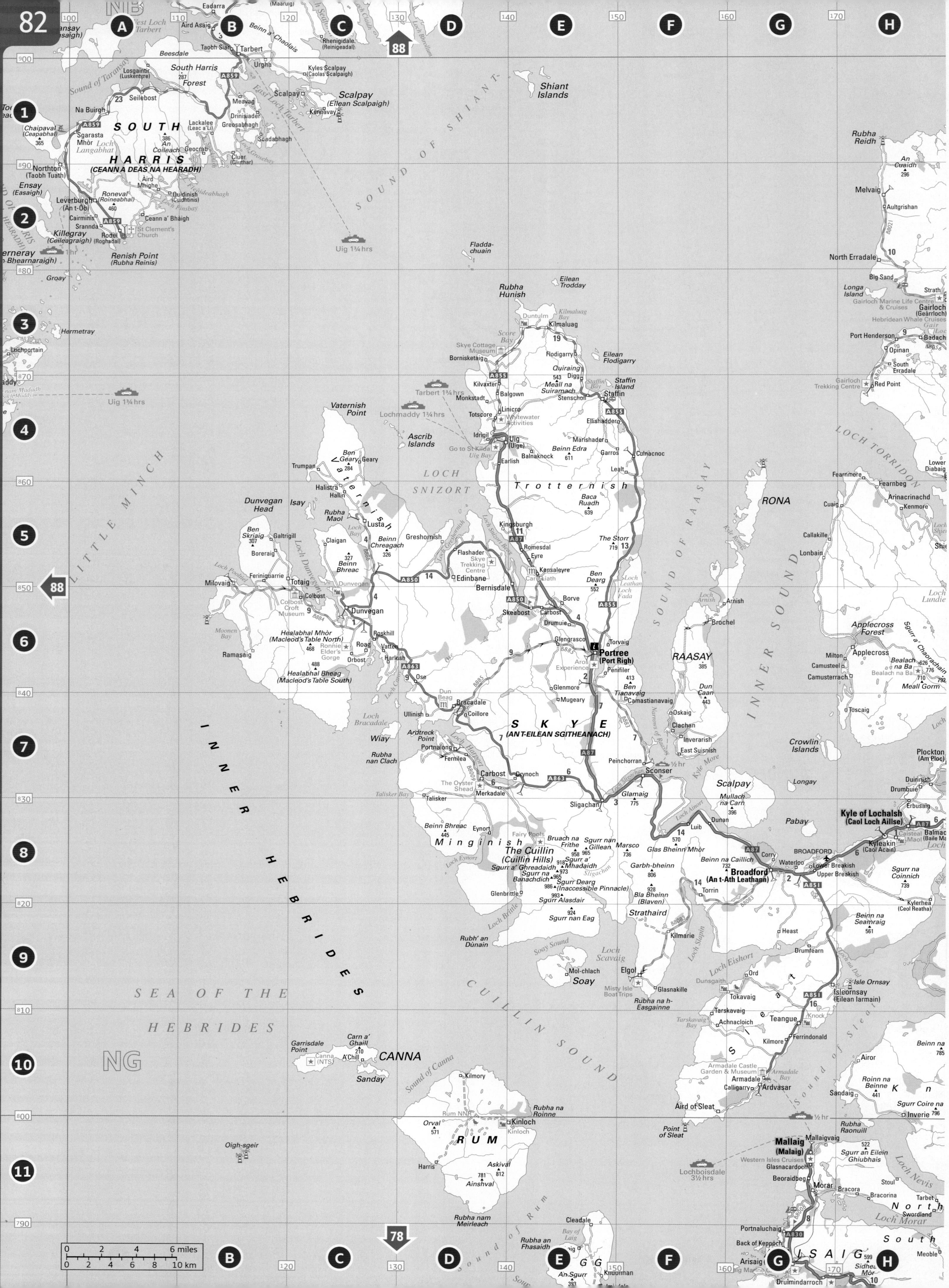

A
B
C
D
E
F
G
H
1
2
3
4
5
6
7
8
9
10
11
NB
NG
88
78
Tarbert
South Harris Forest
SOUTH HARRIS
(CEANN A DEAS NA HEARADH)
Sound of Taransay
Seilebost
Na Buirgh
Chaipaval (Ceapabhal)
Sgarasta Mhòr
Northton (Taobh Tuath)
Ensay (Easaigh)
Leverburgh (An t-Òb)
Roneval (Roineabhal)
Killegray (Ceileagraigh)
Rodel (Roghadal)
St Clement's Church
Renish Point (Rubha Reinis)
Groay
Hermetray
Lochportain
Scalpay (Eilean Scalpaigh)
Kyles Scalpay (Caolas Scalpaigh)
East Loch Tarbert
Rhenigidale (Reinigeadal)
Shiant Islands
SOUND OF SHIANT
Uig 1¾ hrs
Fladda-chuain
Eilean Trodday
Rubha Hunish
Duntulm
Kilmaluag
Score Bay
Skye Cottage Museum
Flodigarry
Eilean Flodigarry
Quiraing
Staffin
Staffin Island
Tarbert 1¾ hrs
Lochmaddy 1¾ hrs
Uig (Uige)
Ascrib Islands
Vaternish Point
Waternish
LOCH SNIZORT
Trotternish
Beinn Edra
Baca Ruadh
The Storr
Kingsburgh
LITTLE MINCH
Dunvegan Head
Isay
Dunvegan
Edinbane
Skeabost
Portree (Port Righ)
Healabhal Mhòr (Macleod's Table North)
Healabhal Bheag (Macleod's Table South)
Ramasaig
Bracadale
SKYE (AN T-EILEAN SGITHEANACH)
INNER HEBRIDES
Wiay
Carbost
Drynoch
Sligachan
Sconser
Glamaig
Minginish
The Cuillin (Cuillin Hills)
Sgurr Alasdair
Sgurr nan Eag
Bla Bheinn (Blaven)
Strathaird
Elgol
Soay
Loch Scavaig
CUILLIN SOUND
SOUND OF RAASAY
RAASAY
RONA
INNER SOUND
Scalpay
Pabay
Longay
Crowlin Islands
Broadford (An t-Ath Leathann)
Kyle of Lochalsh (Caol Loch Aillse)
Kyleakin (Caol Acain)
Plockton (Am Ploc)
Applecross
Applecross Forest
LOCH TORRIDON
Rubha Reidh
Melvaig
North Erradale
Gairloch (Gearrloch)
Badachro
Isle Ornsay
Isleornsay (Eilean Iarmain)
Sleat
Teangue
Armadale
Ardvasar
Aird of Sleat
Point of Sleat
Sound of Sleat
SEA OF THE HEBRIDES
CANNA
Sanday
Garrisdale Point
RUM
Kinloch
Harris
Askival
Ainshval
Rubha nam Meirleach
Oigh-sgeir
Lochboisdale 3½ hrs
Mallaig (Malaig)
Morar
Arisaig
Loch Nevis
Loch Morar
Knoydart
EIGG
0 2 4 6 miles
0 2 4 6 8 10 km

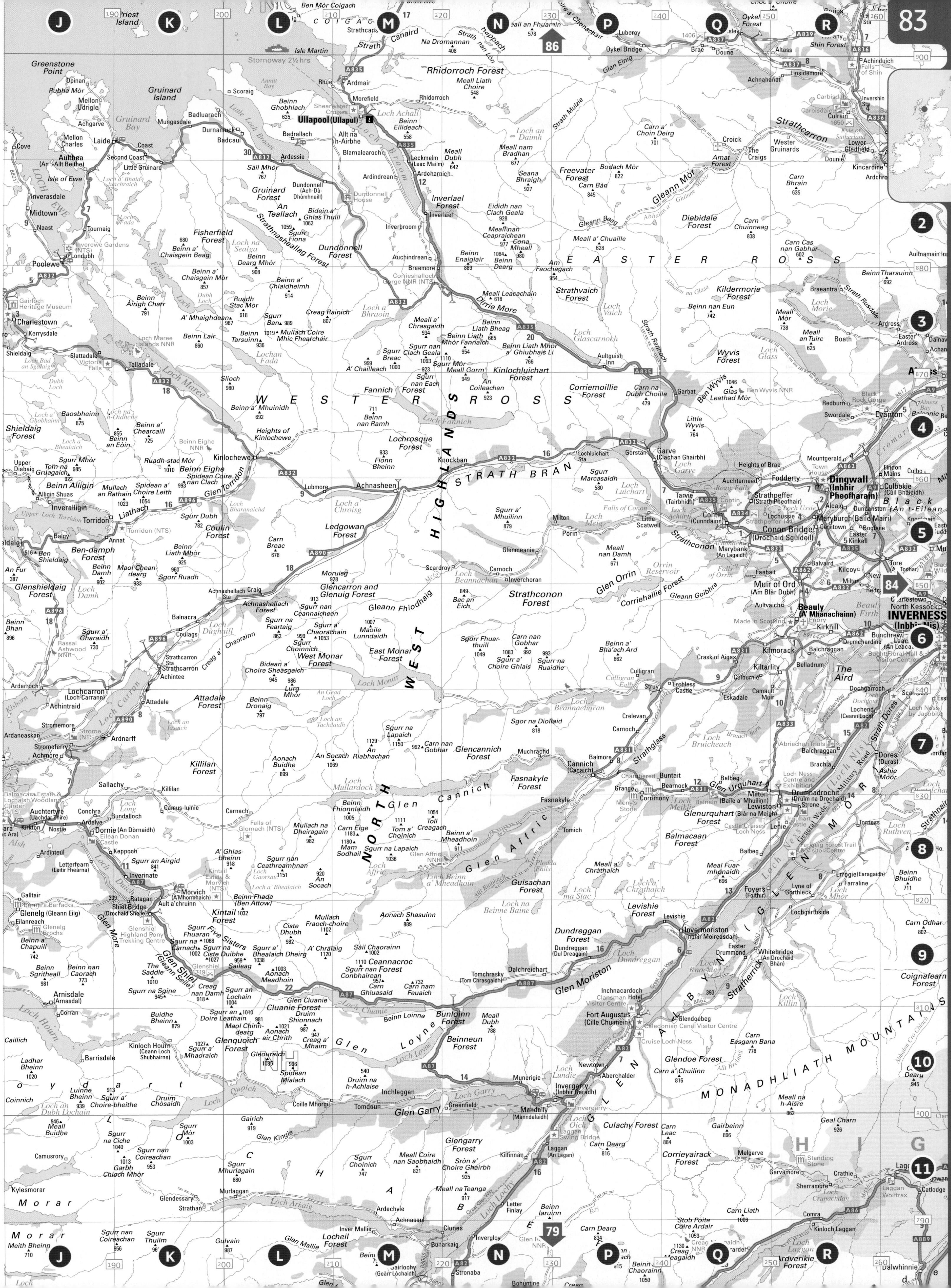
Ullapool (Ullapool)
Isle Martin
Stornoway 2½ hrs
Greenstone Point
Gruinard Island
Gruinard Bay
Laide
Aultbea
Isle of Ewe
Poolewe
Inverewe Gardens
Gairloch
Charlestown
Loch Maree
Kinlochewe
Torridon
Glen Torridon
Shieldaig
Annat
Lochcarron (Loch Carrann)
Loch Carron
Stromeferry
Strathcarron
Achnasheen
Ledgowan Forest
Strath Bran
Garve (Clachan Ghairbh)
Dirrie More
Rhidorroch Forest
Inverlael Forest
Fisherfield Forest
Dundonnell Forest
An Teallach
Fannich Forest
Kinlochluichart Forest
Strathvaich Forest
Freevater Forest
Strathcarron
Easter Ross
Wester Ross
North West Highlands
Glen Orrin
Strathconon Forest
Strathconon
Contin (Cunndainn)
Strathpeffer (Strath Pheofhair)
Dingwall (Inbhir Pheofharain)
Maryburgh (Baile Mairi)
Conon Bridge (Drochaid Sgùideil)
Muir of Ord (Am Blàr Dubh)
Beauly (A' Mhanachainn)
Inverness (Inbhir Nis)
Kiltarlity
The Aird
Glen Affric
Glen Cannich
Cannich (Canaich)
Strathglass
Loch Mullardoch
Loch Affric
Drumnadrochit (Druim na Drochaid)
Glen Urquhart
Loch Ness
Glen Mòr
Dores (Duras)
Foyers (Fothir)
Invermoriston (Inbhir Moireasdan)
Glen Moriston
Fort Augustus (Cille Chuimein)
Monadhliath Mountains
Invergarry (Inbhir Garadh)
Glen Garry
Loch Garry
Loch Quoich
Loch Cluanie
Glen Shiel
Five Sisters
Shiel Bridge
Glenelg (Gleann Eilg)
Ratagan
Dornie (An Dòrnaidh)
Eilean Donan Castle
Kyle of Lochalsh
Loch Duich
Loch Hourn
Knoydart
Loch Arkaig
Laggan (An Lagan)
Glen Loyne
Spean Bridge
Gairlochy (Geàrr Lòchaidh)
Loch Lochy
Kinloch Laggan
Dalwhinnie
Corrieyairack Forest
Laggan
A835
A832
A890
A896
A87
A887
A82
A831
A833
A862
A834
A86
A9
A889
A836
A837
A839
86
84
79
1
2
3
4
5
6
7
8
9
10
11
J
K
L
M
N
P
Q
R
NH

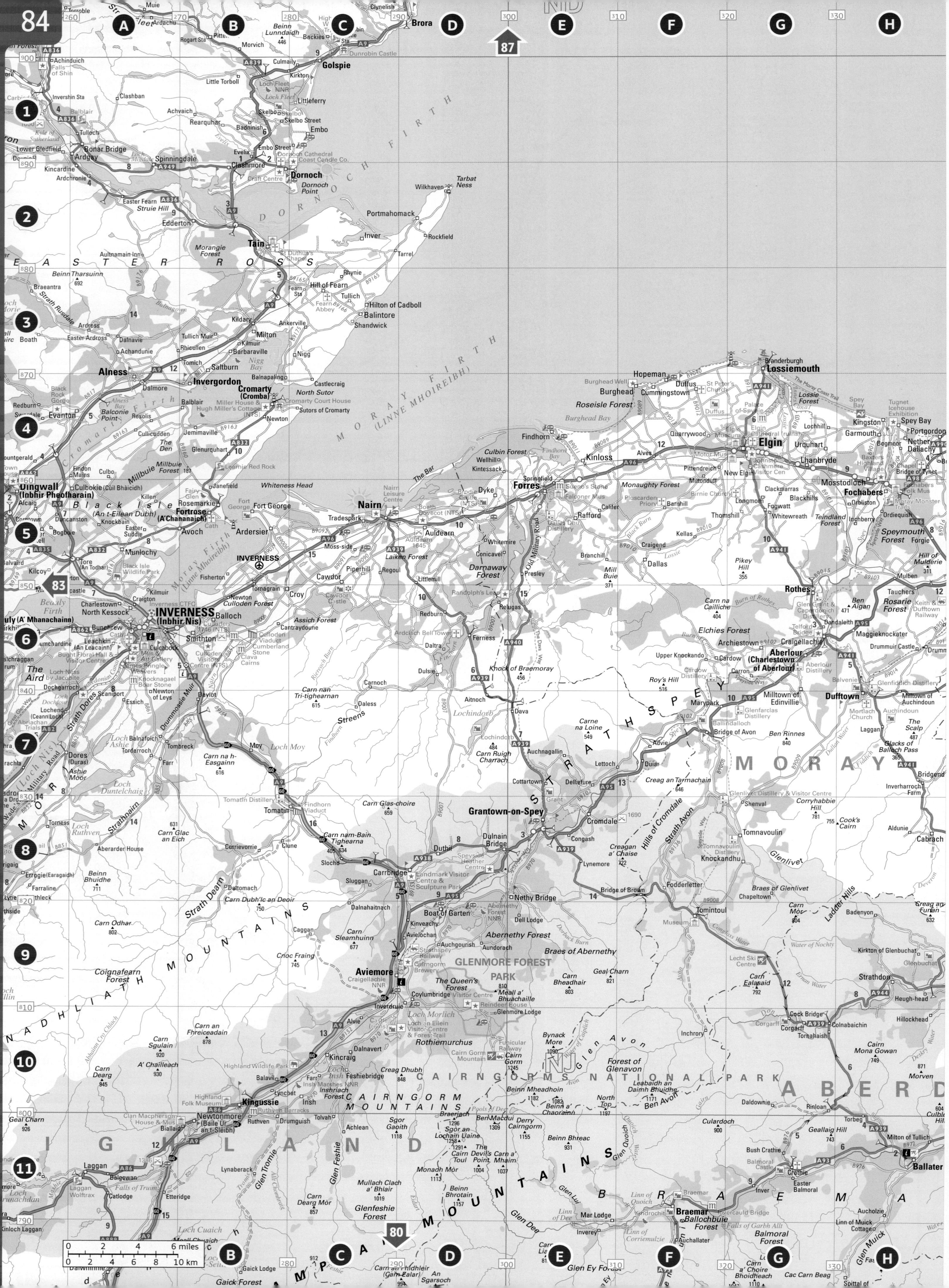

87
83
80
ND
NJ
Brora
Golspie
Dornoch
Tain
Embo
Bonar Bridge
Ardgay
Spinningdale
Clashmore
Edderton
Tarbat Ness
Portmahomack
Inver
Rockfield
Tarrel
DORNOCH FIRTH
EASTER ROSS
Hill of Fearn
Hilton of Cadboll
Balintore
Shandwick
Alness
Invergordon
Cromarty (Cromba)
Evanton
MORAY FIRTH (LINNE MHOIREIBH)
Dingwall (Inbhir Pheofharain)
Fortrose (A'Chananaich)
Black Isle (An t-Eilean Dubh)
Avoch
Munlochy
Ardersier
Fort George
Nairn
Auldearn
INVERNESS (Inbhir Nis)
INVERNESS
Culloden Forest
Cawdor
Croy
Balloch
Smithton
Forres
Kinloss
Burghead
Hopeman
Lossiemouth
Elgin
Lhanbryde
Fochabers
Spey Bay
Portgordon
Garmouth
Kingston
Rothes
Dallas
Findhorn
Culbin Forest
Darnaway Forest
Elchies Forest
Aberlour (Charlestown of Aberlour)
Craigellachie
Dufftown
MORAY
STRATHSPEY
Grantown-on-Spey
Cromdale
Nethy Bridge
Boat of Garten
Carrbridge
Aviemore
GLENMORE FOREST PARK
Abernethy Forest
Rothiemurchus
Kincraig
Kingussie
Newtonmore (Baile Ur an t-Sleibh)
Laggan
Tomintoul
Tomnavoulin
Glenlivet
Braemar
Ballater
Crathie
CAIRNGORMS NATIONAL PARK
CAIRNGORM MOUNTAINS
MONADHLIATH MOUNTAINS
GRAMPIAN MOUNTAINS
HIGHLAND
ABERDEENSHIRE
Strathdon
Cock Bridge
Ben Macdui 1309
Cairn Gorm 1245
Braeriach 1296
Ben Avon
Glenfeshie Forest
Tomatin
Dores
Loch Ness
Loch Moy
0 2 4 6 miles
0 2 4 6 8 10 km

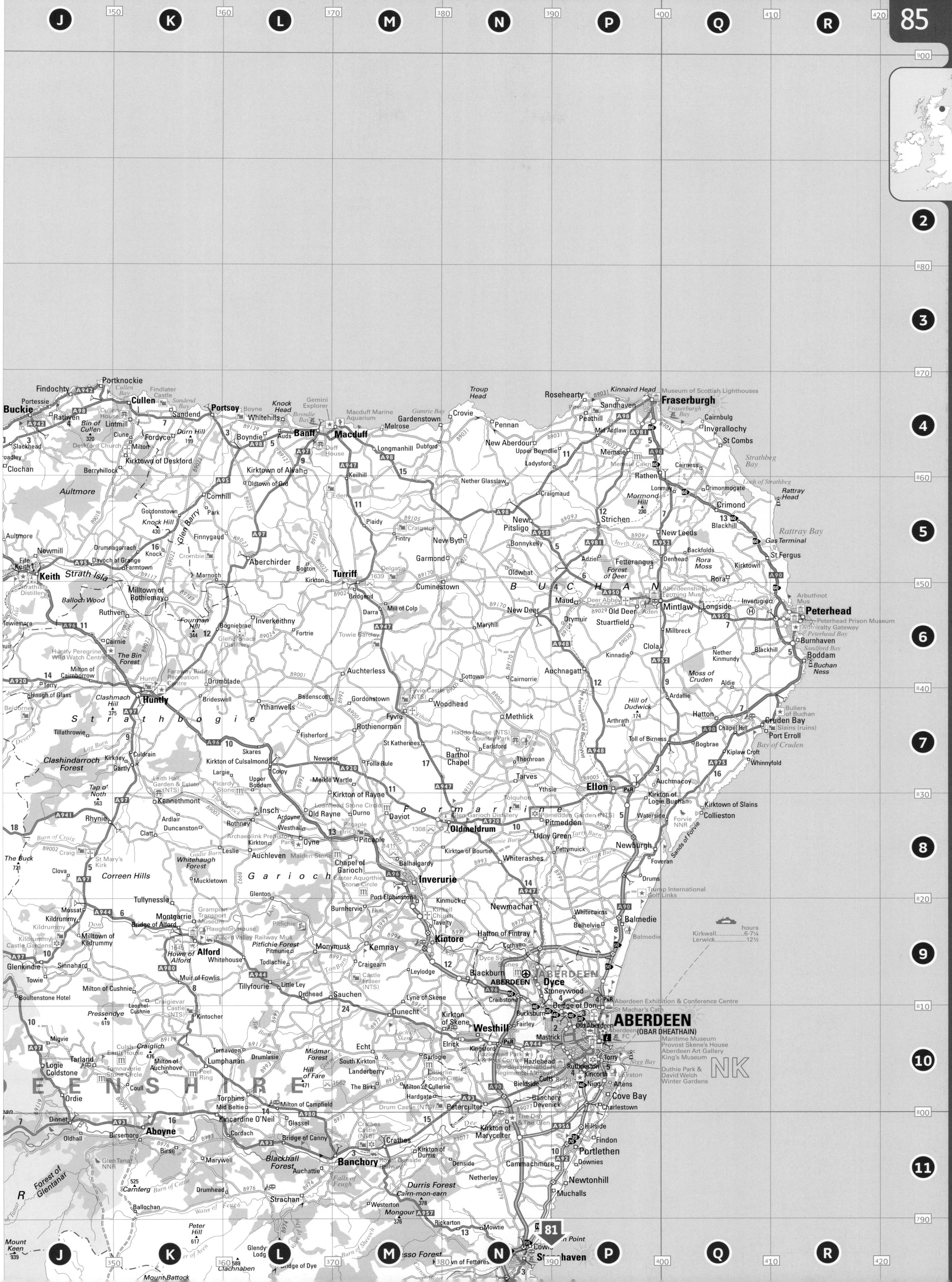
J
K
L
M
N
P
Q
R
350
360
370
380
390
400
410
420
900
880
870
860
850
840
830
820
810
800
790
2
3
4
5
6
7
8
9
10
11
Portknockie
Findochty
Portessie
Buckie
Cullen
Sandend
Portsoy
Whitehills
Knock Head
Gemini Explorer
Macduff Marine Aquarium
Banff
Macduff
Gardenstown
Crovie
Troup Head
Pennan
New Aberdour
Rosehearty
Kinnaird Head
Museum of Scottish Lighthouses
Fraserburgh
Sandhaven
Peathill
Cairnbulg
Inverallochy
St Combs
Strathbeg Bay
Rathen
Memsie
Crimond
Rattray Head
Rattray Bay
Gas Terminal
St Fergus
Strichen
New Pitsligo
New Leeds
Fetterangus
Mintlaw
Longside
Peterhead
Peterhead Prison Museum
Admiralty Gateway
Burnhaven
Boddam
Buchan Ness
Maud
New Deer
Old Deer
Stuartfield
Deer Abbey
Aberdeenshire Farming Mus
B U C H A N
Aultmore
Keith
Strath Isla
Milltown of Rothiemay
Ruthven
Balloch Wood
Huntly
The Bin Forest
Strathbogie
Clashindarroch Forest
Tap o' Noth
563
Rhynie
Kennethmont
Leith Hall, Garden & Estate (NTS)
Insch
Oyne
Old Rayne
Daviot
Oldmeldrum
Pitmedden
Pitmedden Garden (NTS)
Udny Green
Ellon
Newburgh
Collieston
Cruden Bay
Port Erroll
Bay of Cruden
Slains (ruins)
Hatton
Auchnagatt
Methlick
Haddo House (NTS) & Country Park
Tarves
Fyvie
Fyvie Castle (NTS)
Woodhead
Turriff
Cuminestown
Aberchirder
Cornhill
Portsoy
Auchterless
Rothienorman
Inverurie
Kintore
Kemnay
Monymusk
Alford
Grampian Transport Museum
Alford Valley Railway Mus
Bridge of Alford
Montgarrie
Whitehouse
Muir of Fowlis
Tillyfourie
Sauchen
Echt
Dunecht
Westhill
Kingswells
Blackburn
Dyce
ABERDEEN
Aberdeen
Bridge of Don
Stoneywood
Bucksburn
Old Aberdeen
ABERDEEN (OBAR DHEATHAIN)
Maritime Museum
Provost Skene's House
Aberdeen Art Gallery
King's Museum
Duthie Park & David Welch Winter Gardens
Aberdeen Exhibition & Conference Centre
St Machar's Cath
Balmedie
Trump International Golf Links
Newmachar
Kirkwall 6-7¼
Lerwick 12½
hours
NK
Torry
Nigg
Altens
Cove Bay
Charlestown
Cults
Bieldside
Peterculter
Milltimber
Drum Castle (NTS)
Crathes
Crathes Castle (NTS)
Banchory
Durris Forest
Cairn-mon-earn
378
Mongour
376
Portlethen
Findon
Newtonhill
Muchalls
Stonehaven
Cowie
Garron Point
Fetteresso Forest
Aboyne
Dinnet
Kincardine O'Neil
Torphins
Lumphanan
Tarland
Logie Coldstone
Forest of Glentanar
Glen Tanar NNR
Mount Keen
939
Peter Hill
617
Mount Battock
Clachnaben
589
Bridge of Dye
Strachan
Glendye Lodg
Ballochan
Birse
Finzean
Craigievar Castle (NTS)
Pressendye
619
Corrennie Forest
Correen Hills
Gordonstown
Knock Hill
430
Fourman Hill
344
Clashmach Hill
375
Whitehaugh Forest
Garioch
Formartine
Bennachie
Leslie
Auchleven
Oyne
Chapel of Garioch
Pitcaple
Kildrummy
Kildrummy Castle Gardens
Glenkindie
Towie
Mossat
Clova
The Buck
721
Lumsden
Strathbogie
Durn Hill
199
Fordyce
Deskford
Kirktown of Deskford
Clochan
Berryhillock
Auldearn
Kirktown of Alvah
Delgatie
Fintry
New Byth
Garmond
Fyvie
Maryculter
Kirkton of Maryculter
Netherley
Cammachmore
Kirkton of Durris
Balmedie
Toll of Birness
Mormond Hill
230
Hill of Dudwick
174
Forvie NNR
Sands of Forvie
Moss of Cruden
81
A98
A97
A95
A96
A947
A920
A948
A950
A952
A90
A975
A944
A93
A980
A956
A957
A941
A920
A942
A981
ABERDEENSHIRE

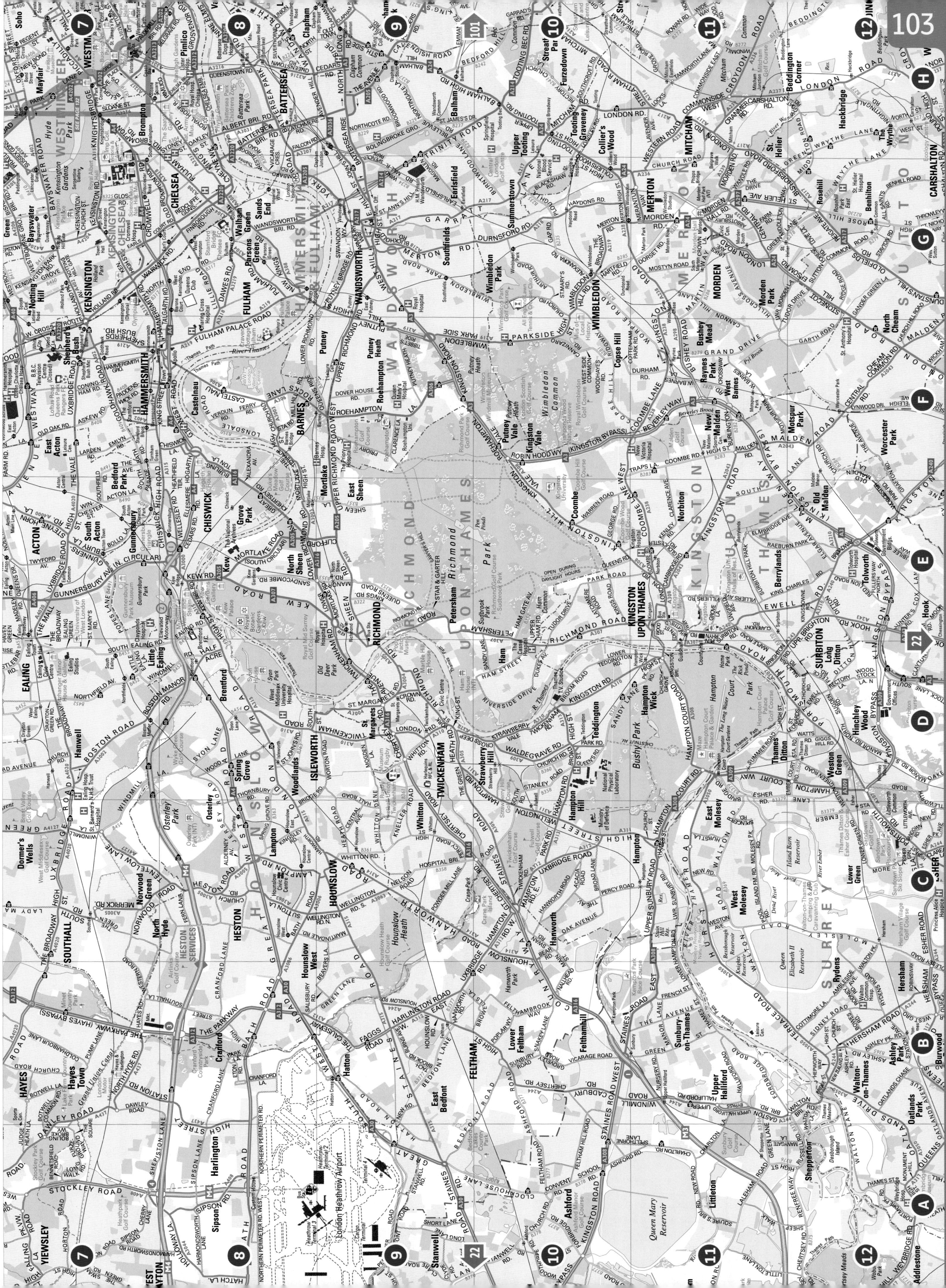

For a more detailed map of Central London see page 132

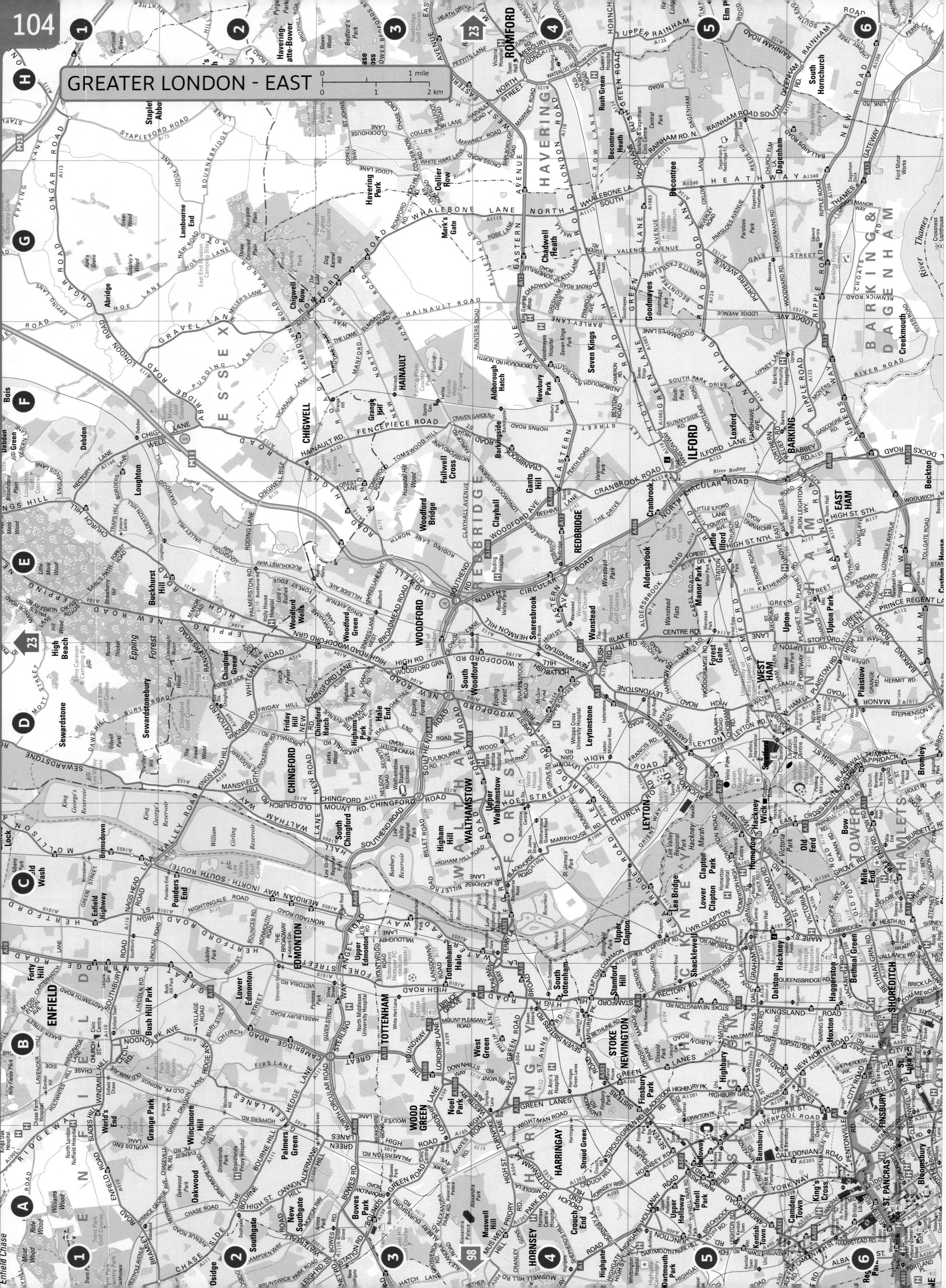

GREATER LONDON - EAST

For a more detailed map of Central London see page 132

0   1 mile
0   1   2 km

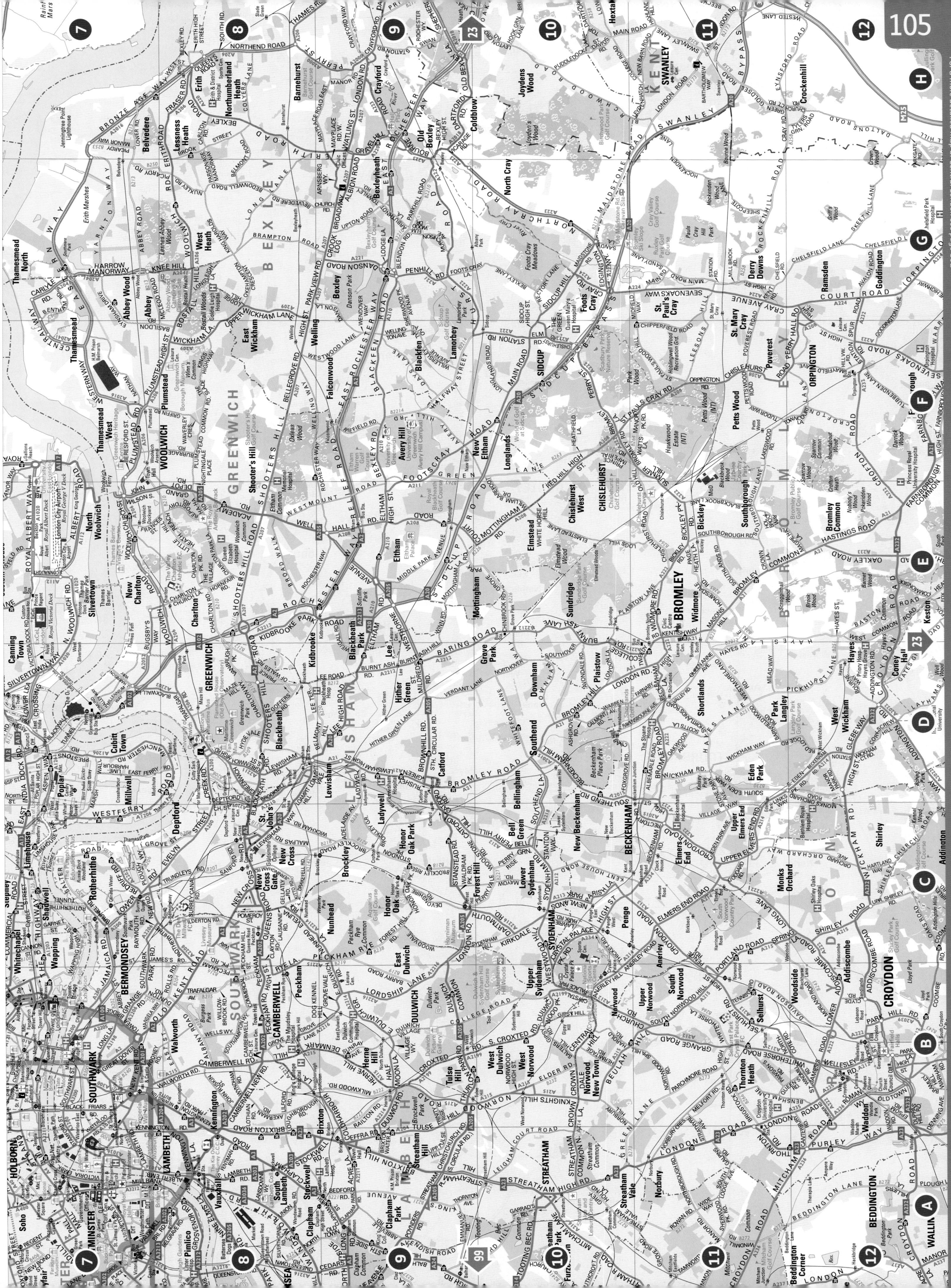

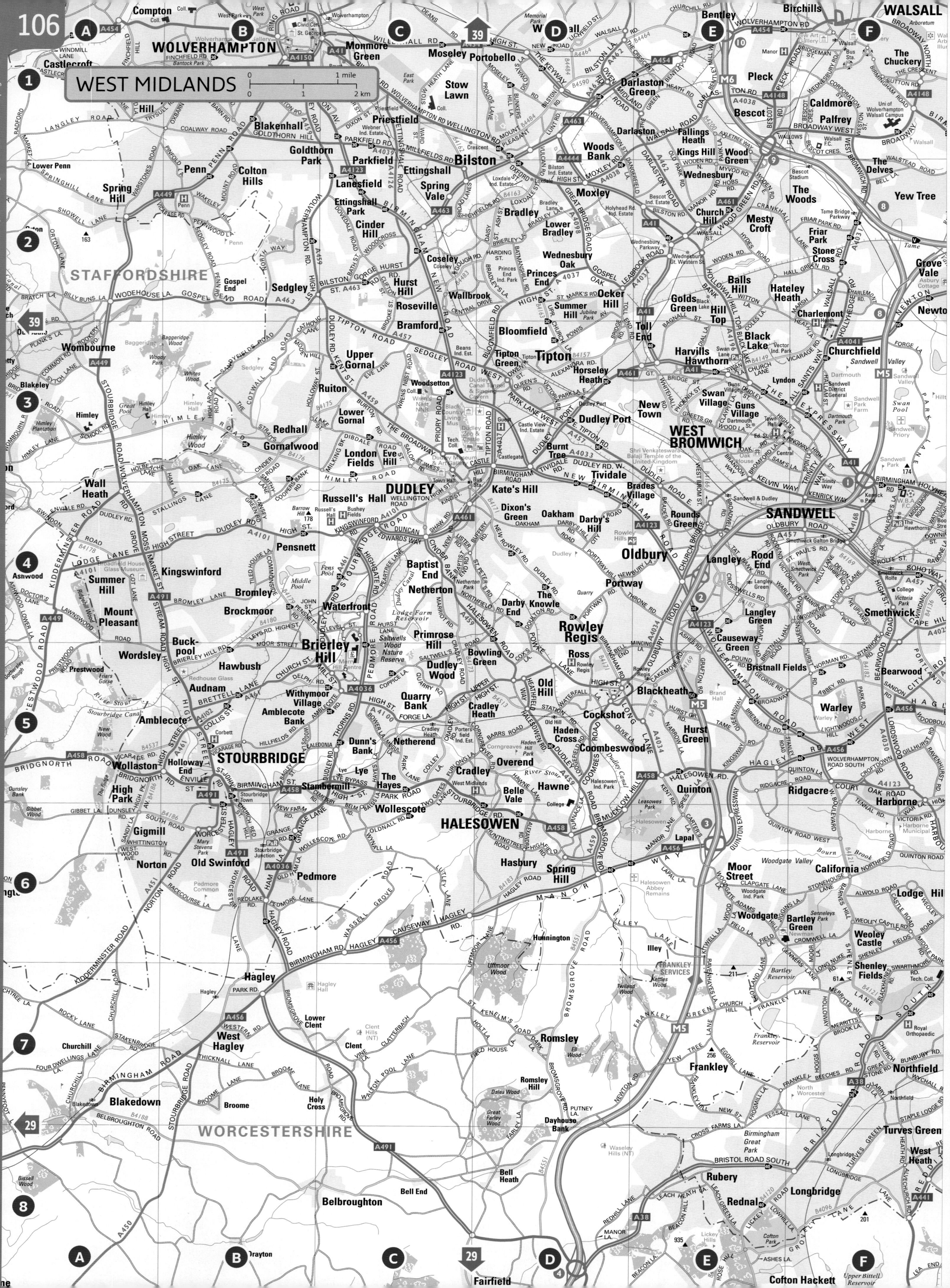

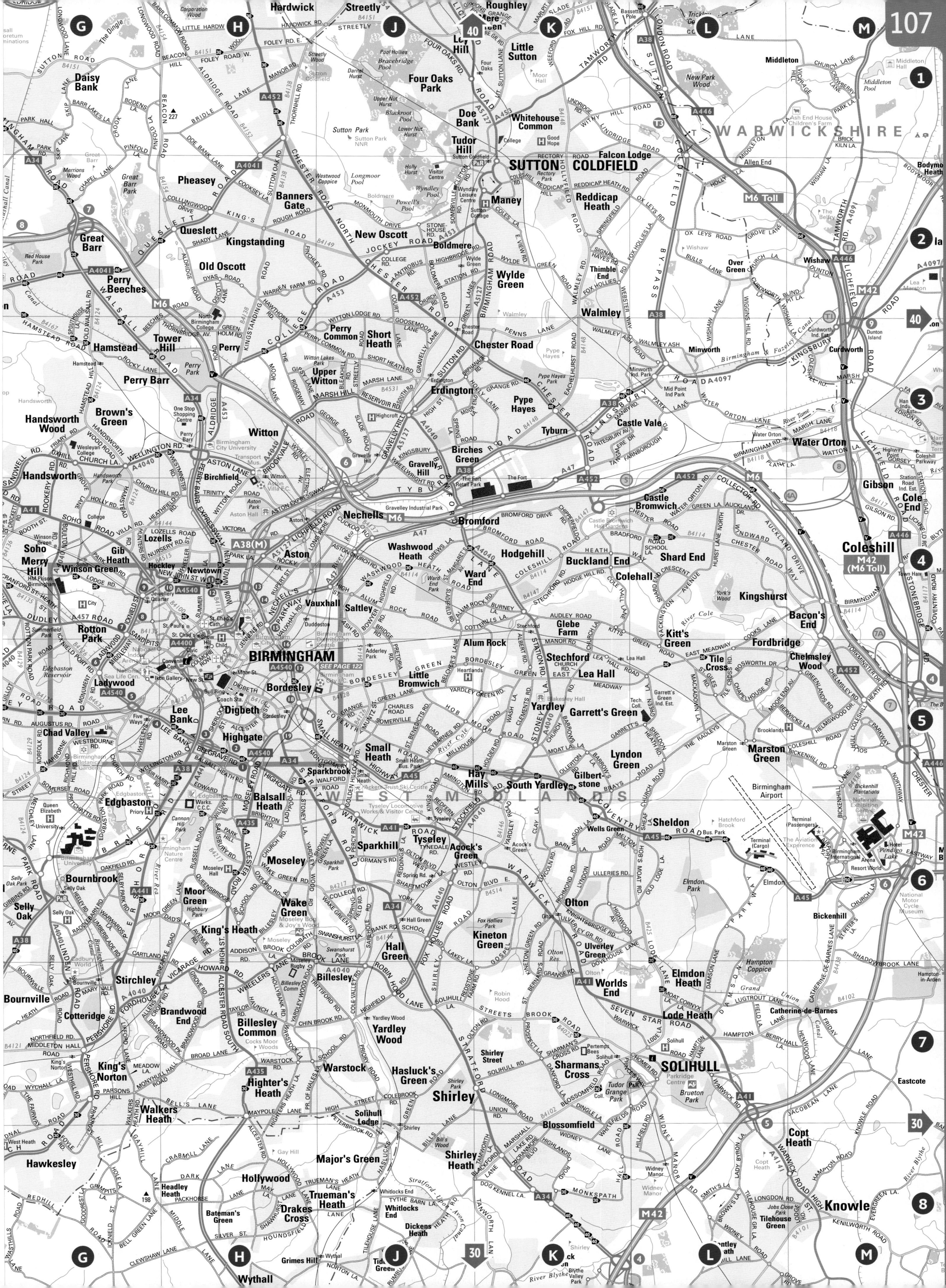

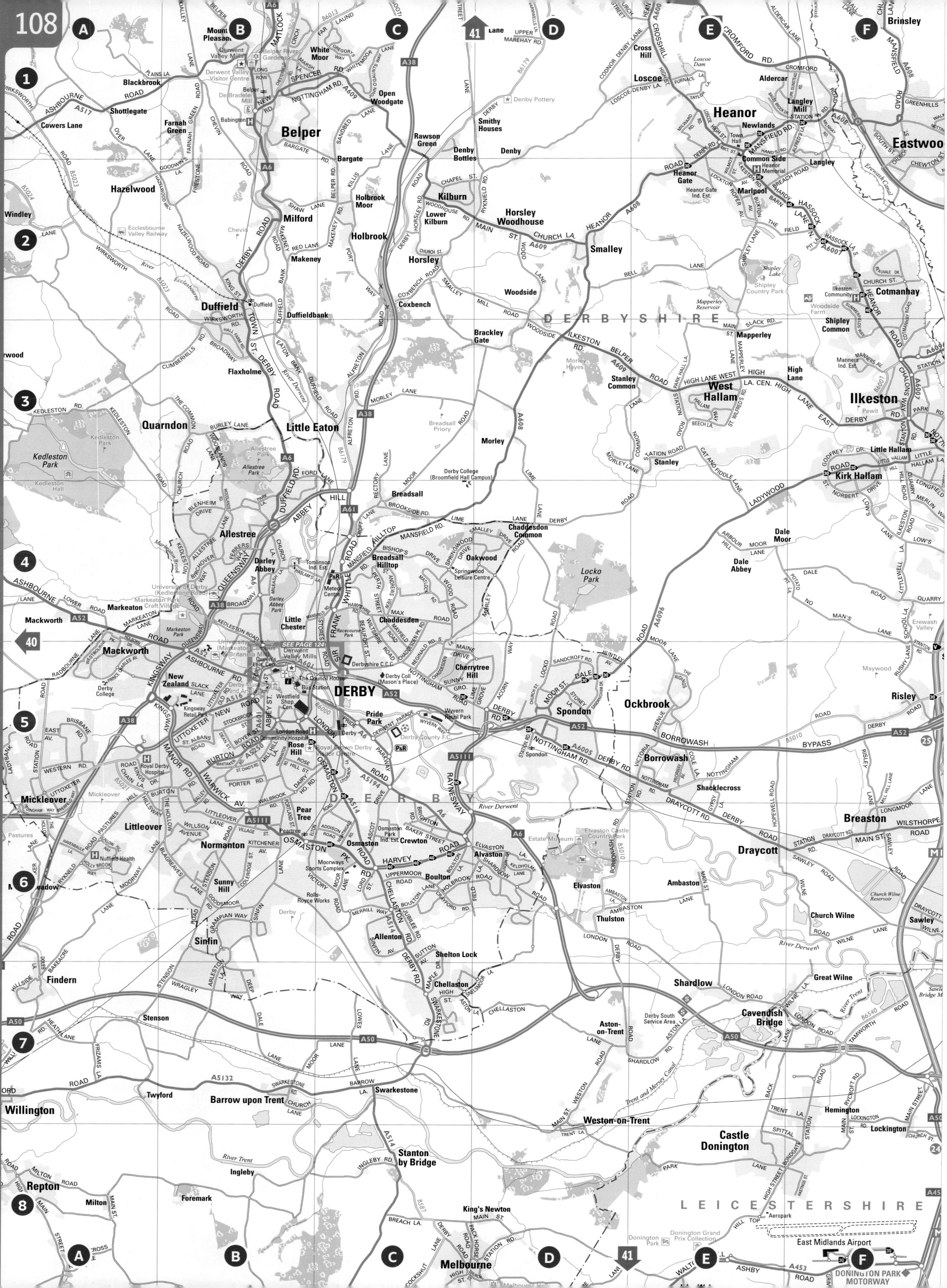

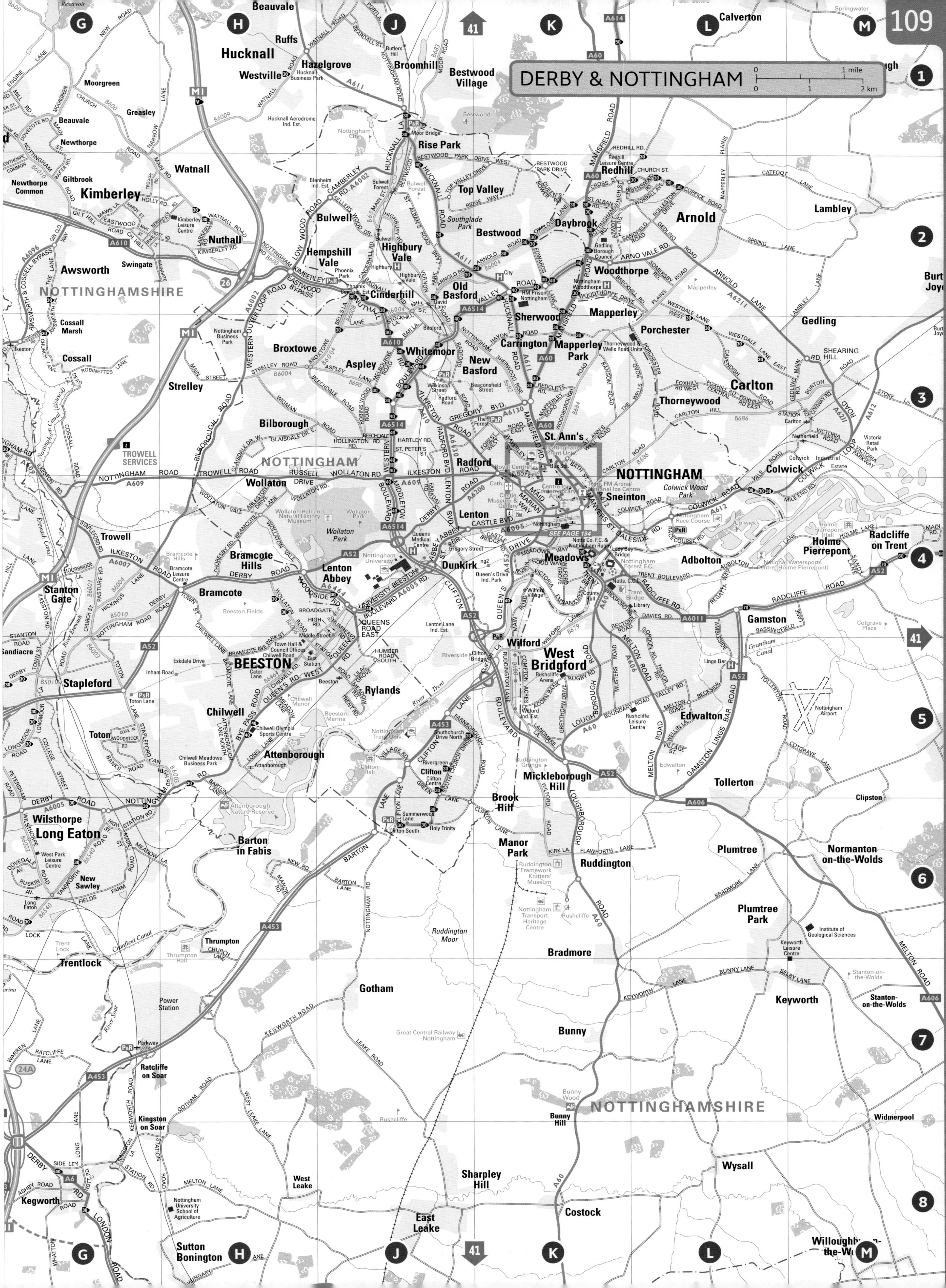

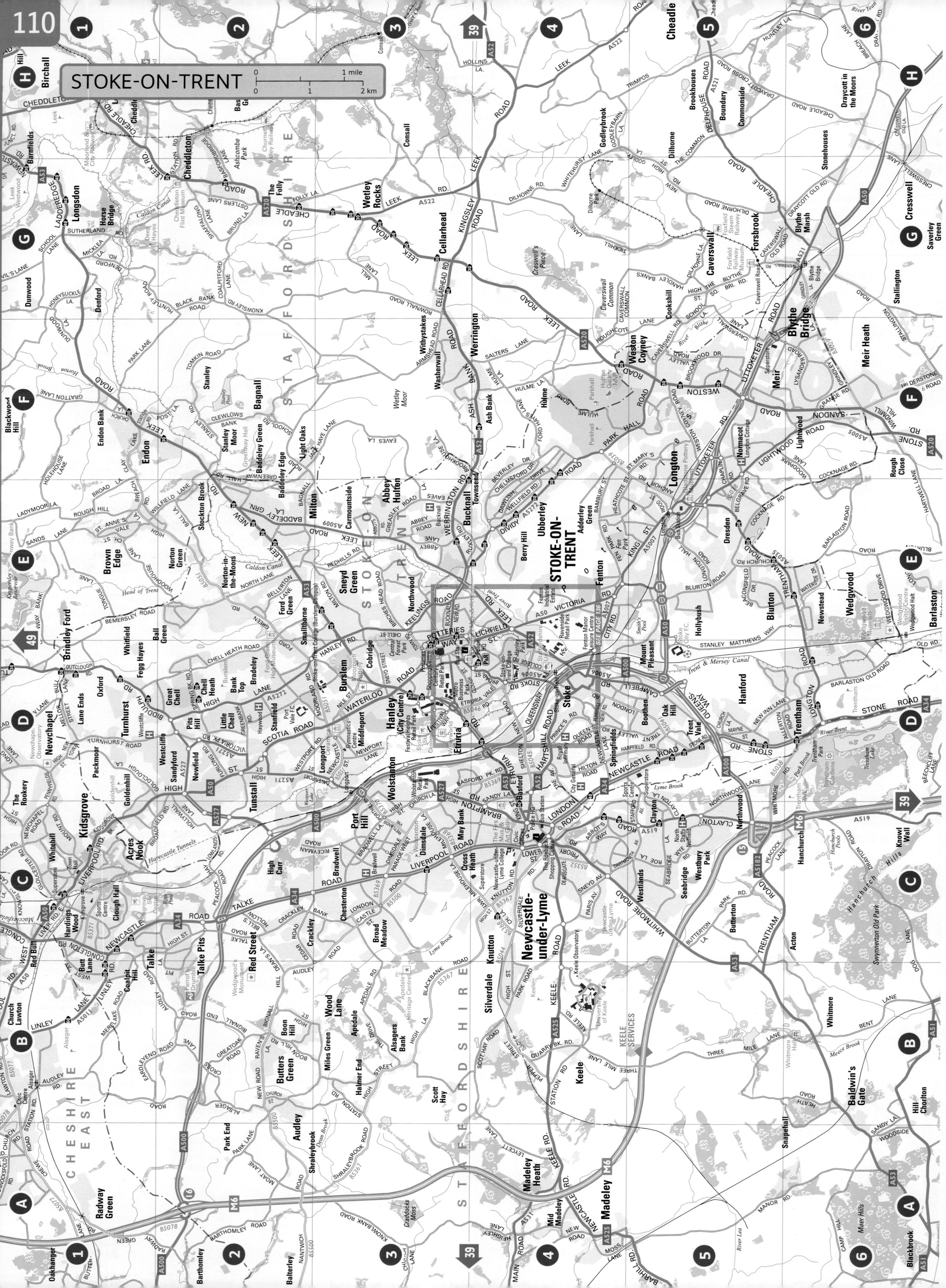

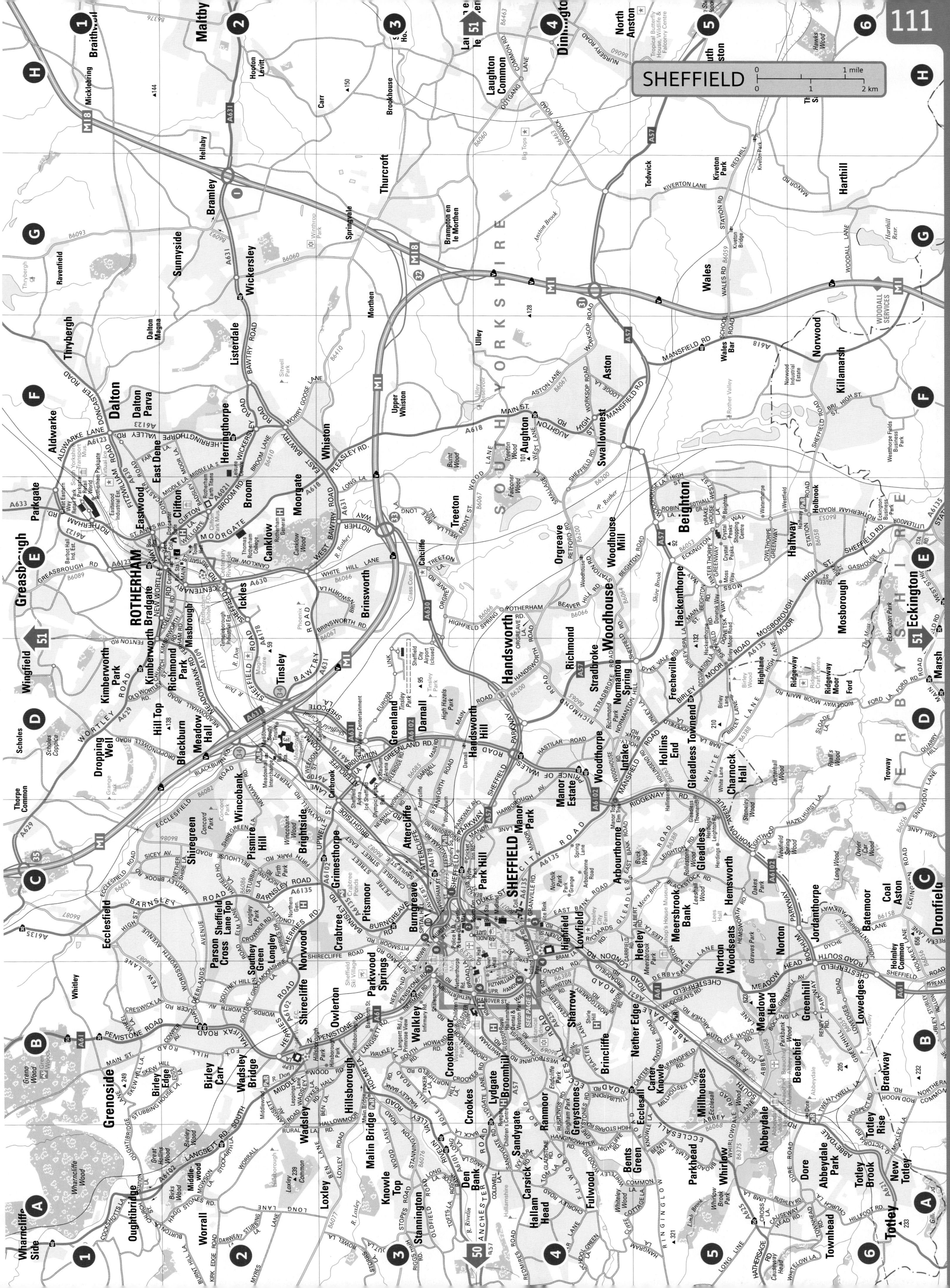

SHEFFIELD

SOUTH YORKSHIRE

DERBYSHIRE

For a more detailed map of Sheffield town centre see page 135

0 ___ 1 mile
0 ___ 1 ___ 2 km

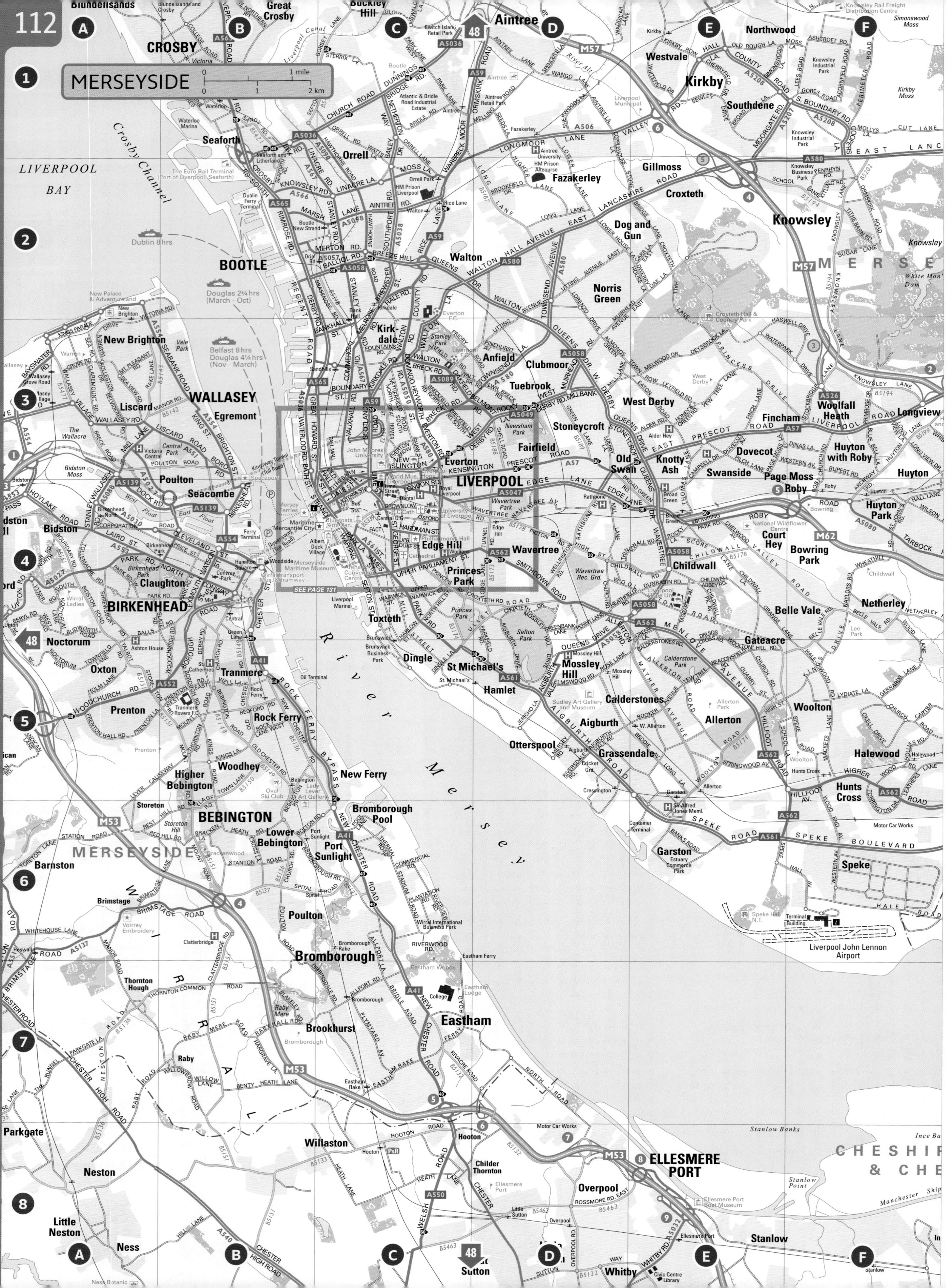

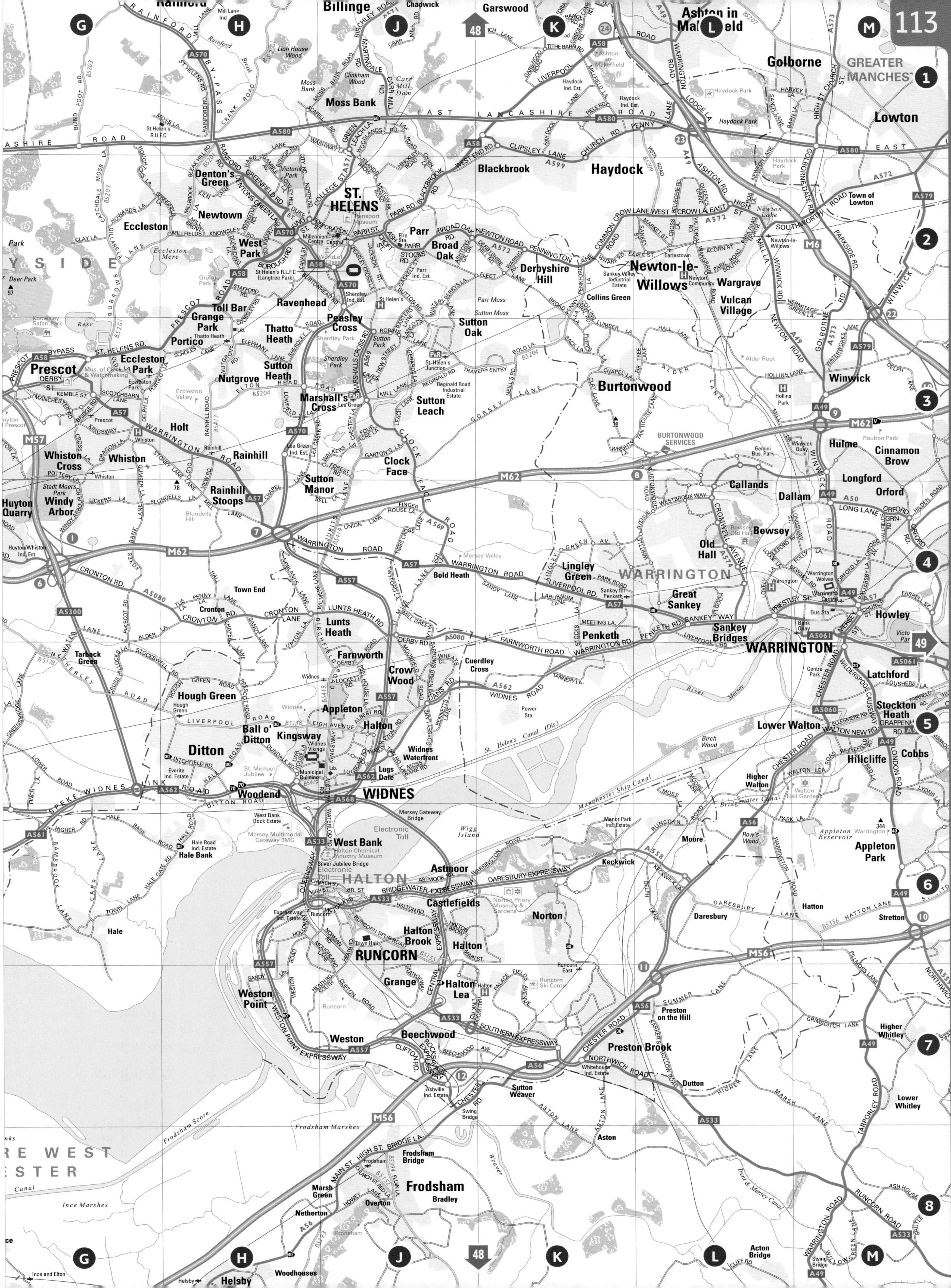

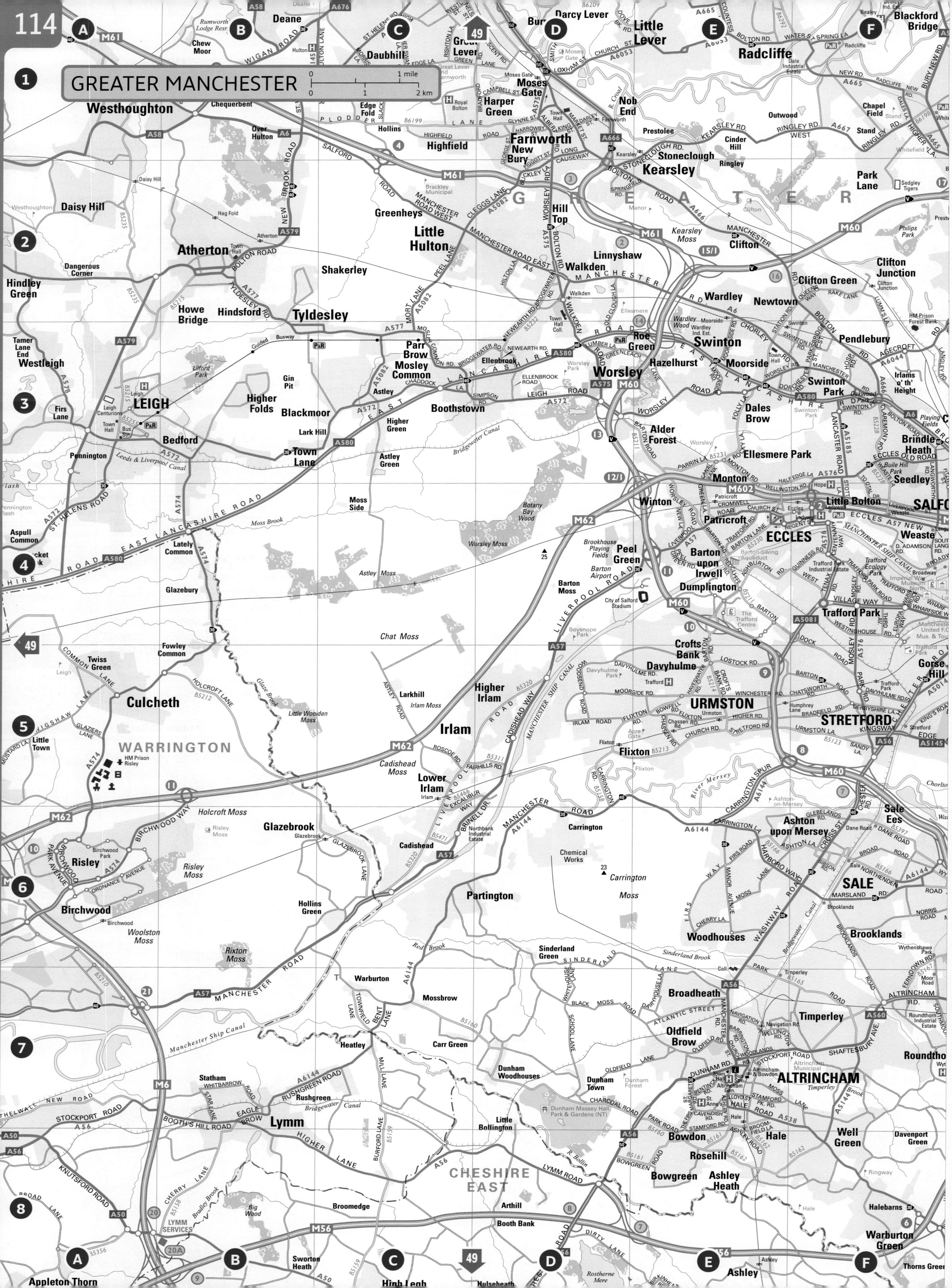

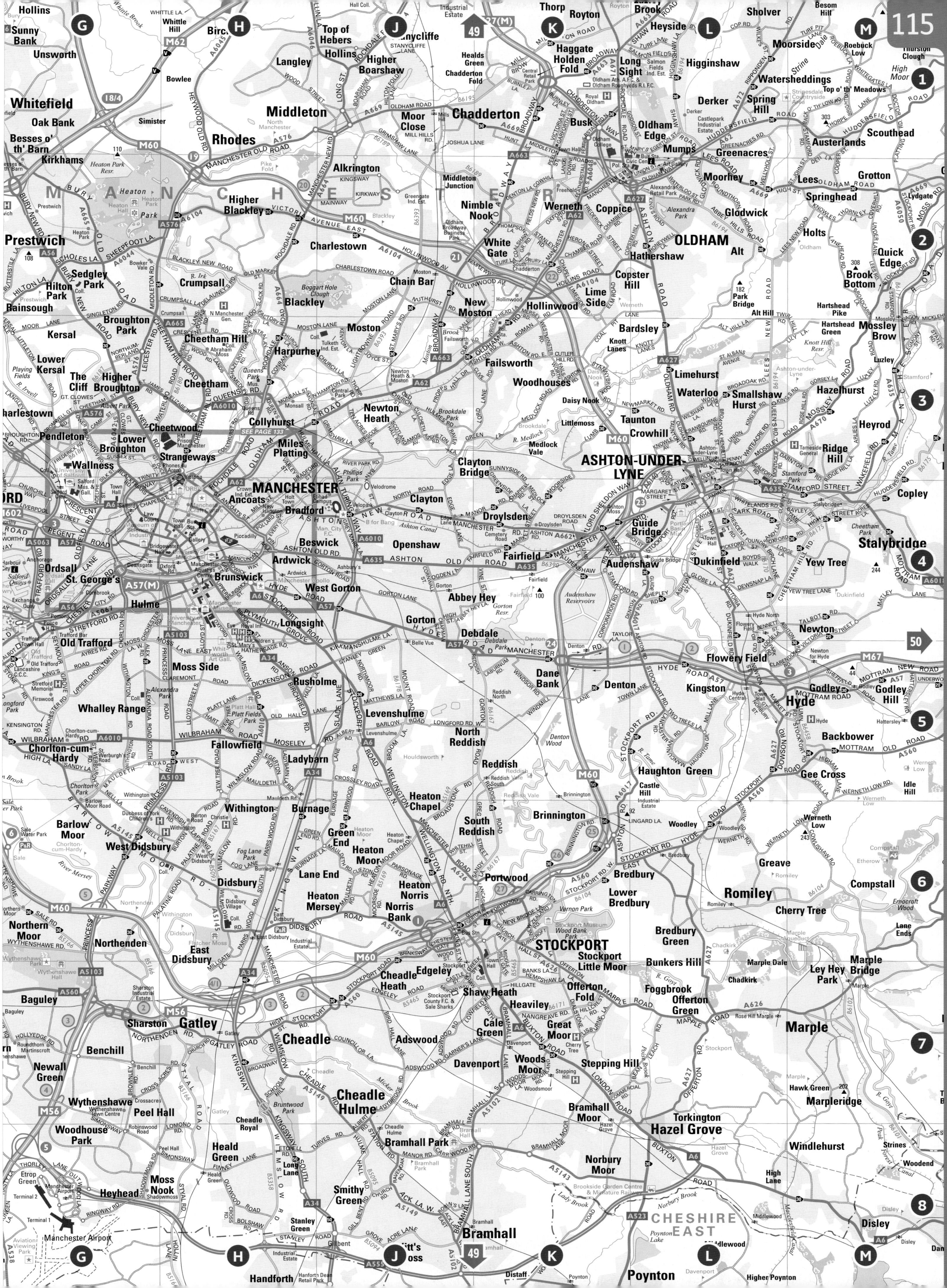

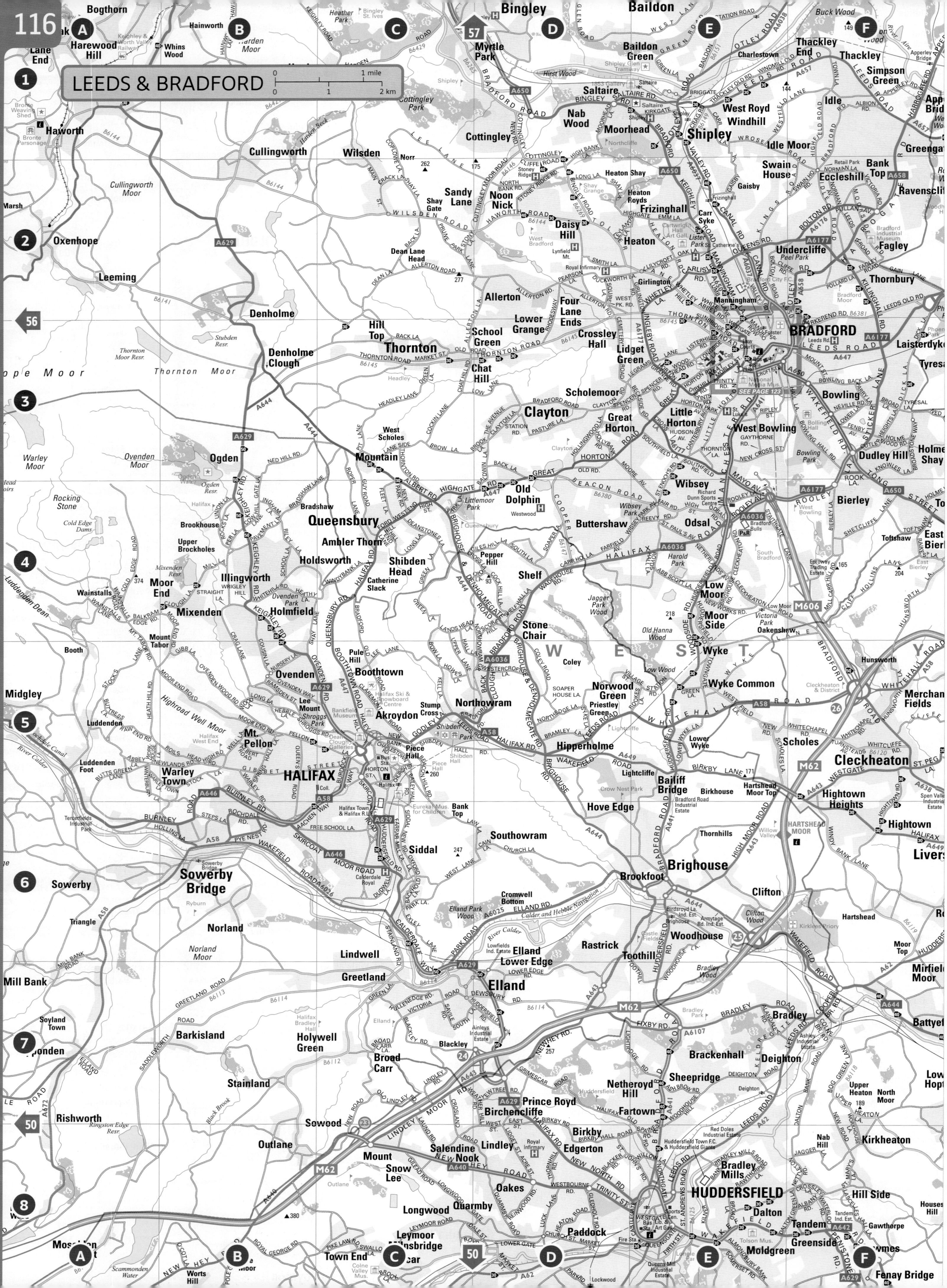

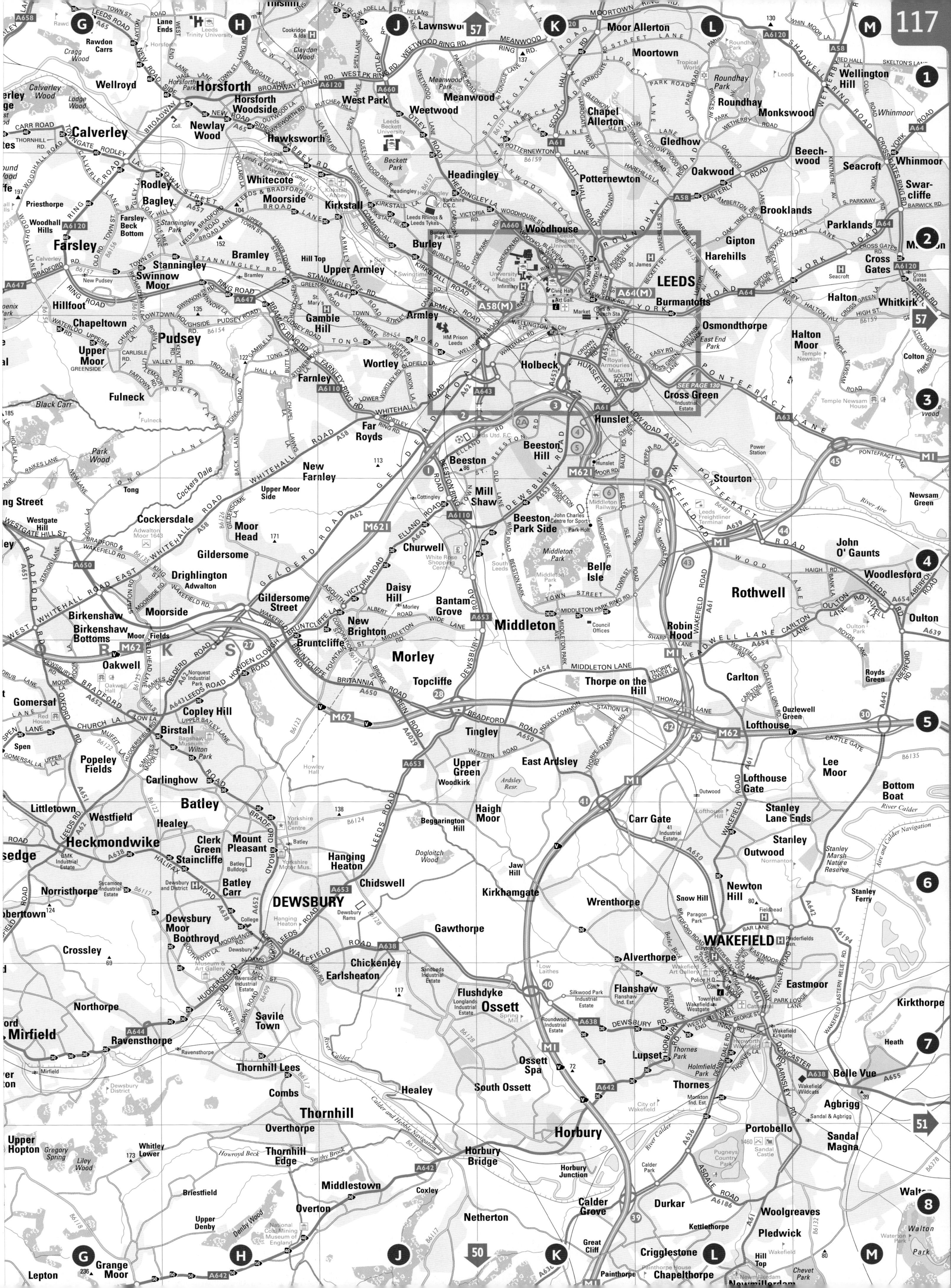

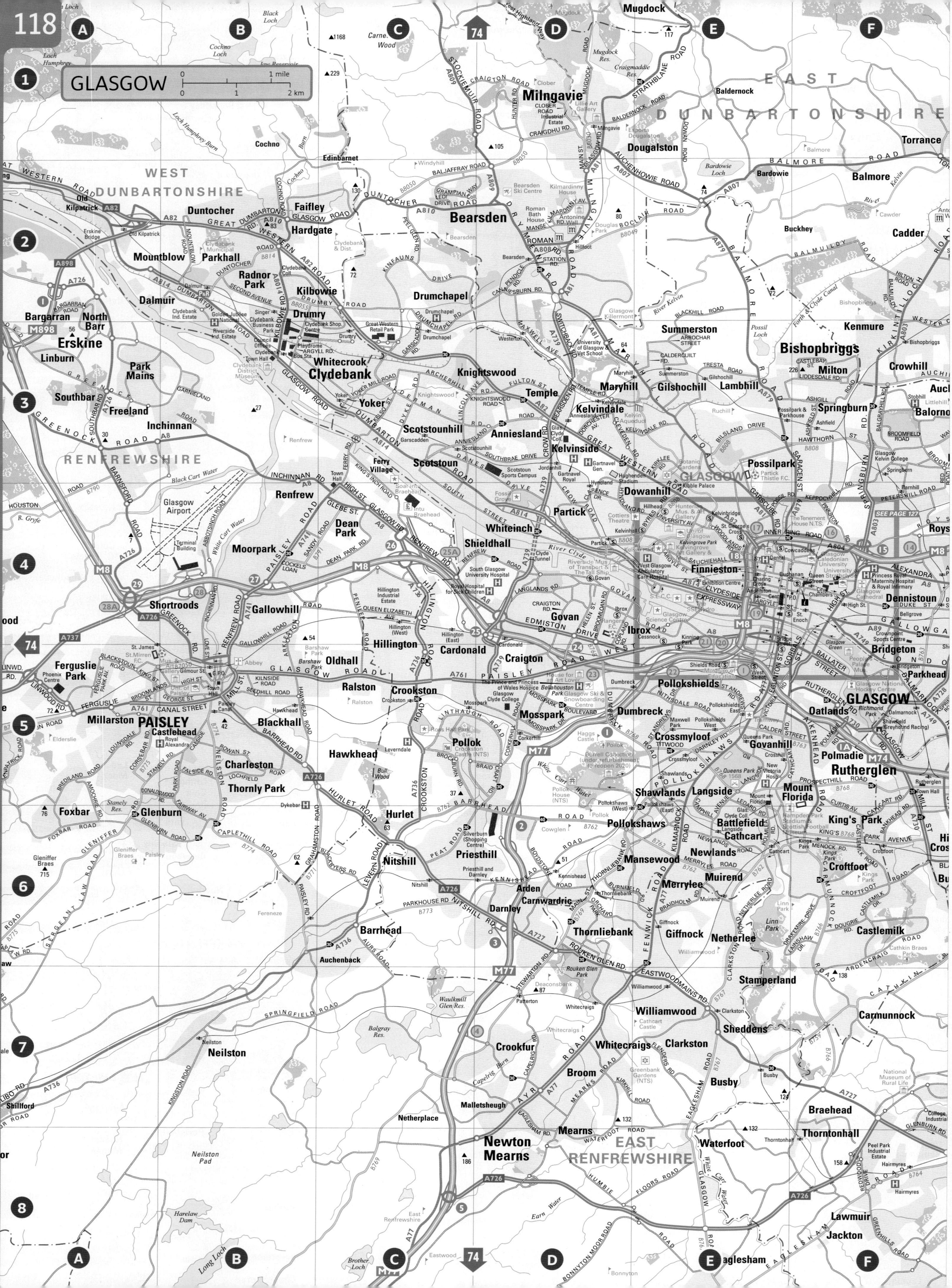

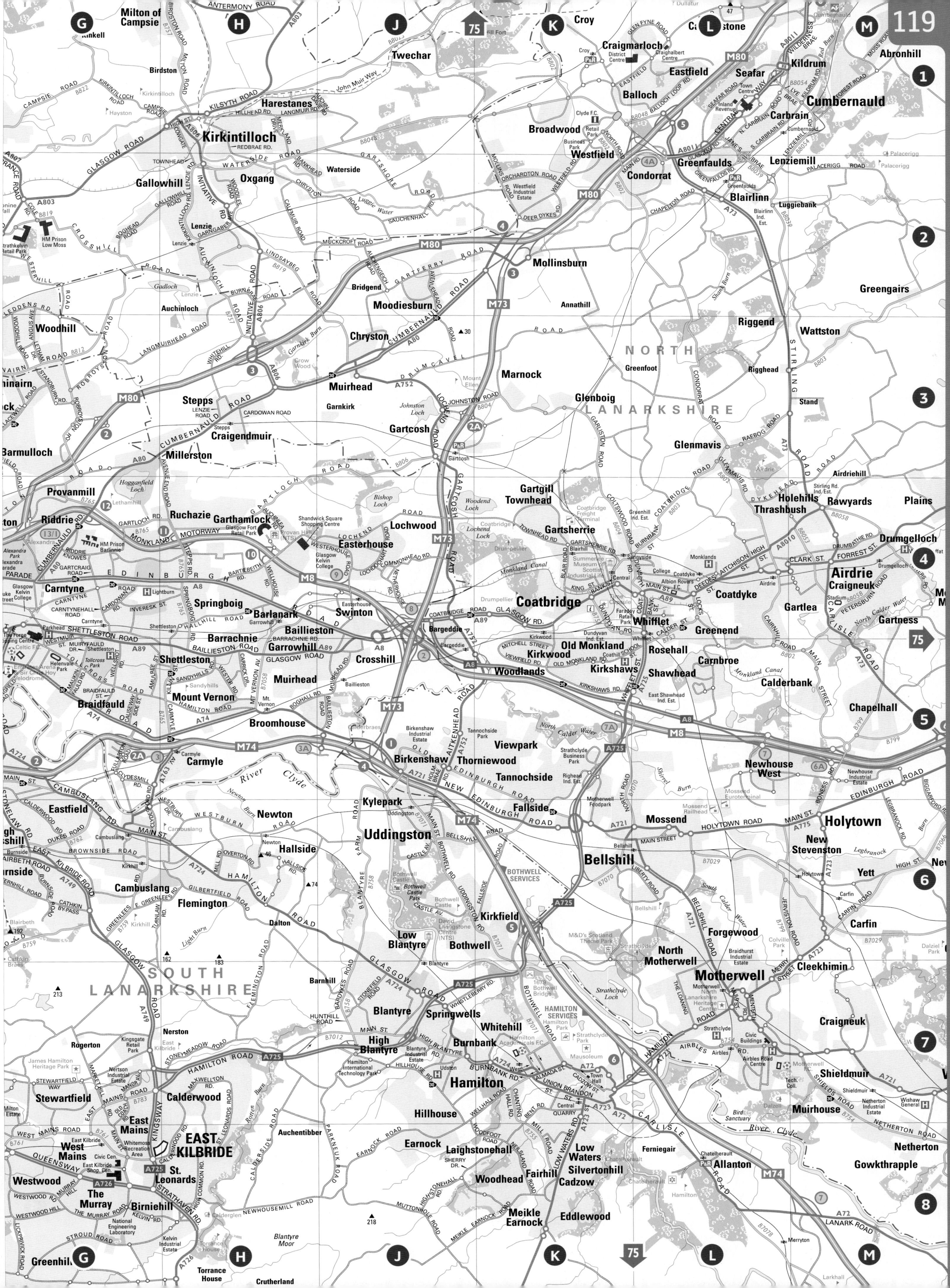

For a more detailed map of Edinburgh town centre see page 126

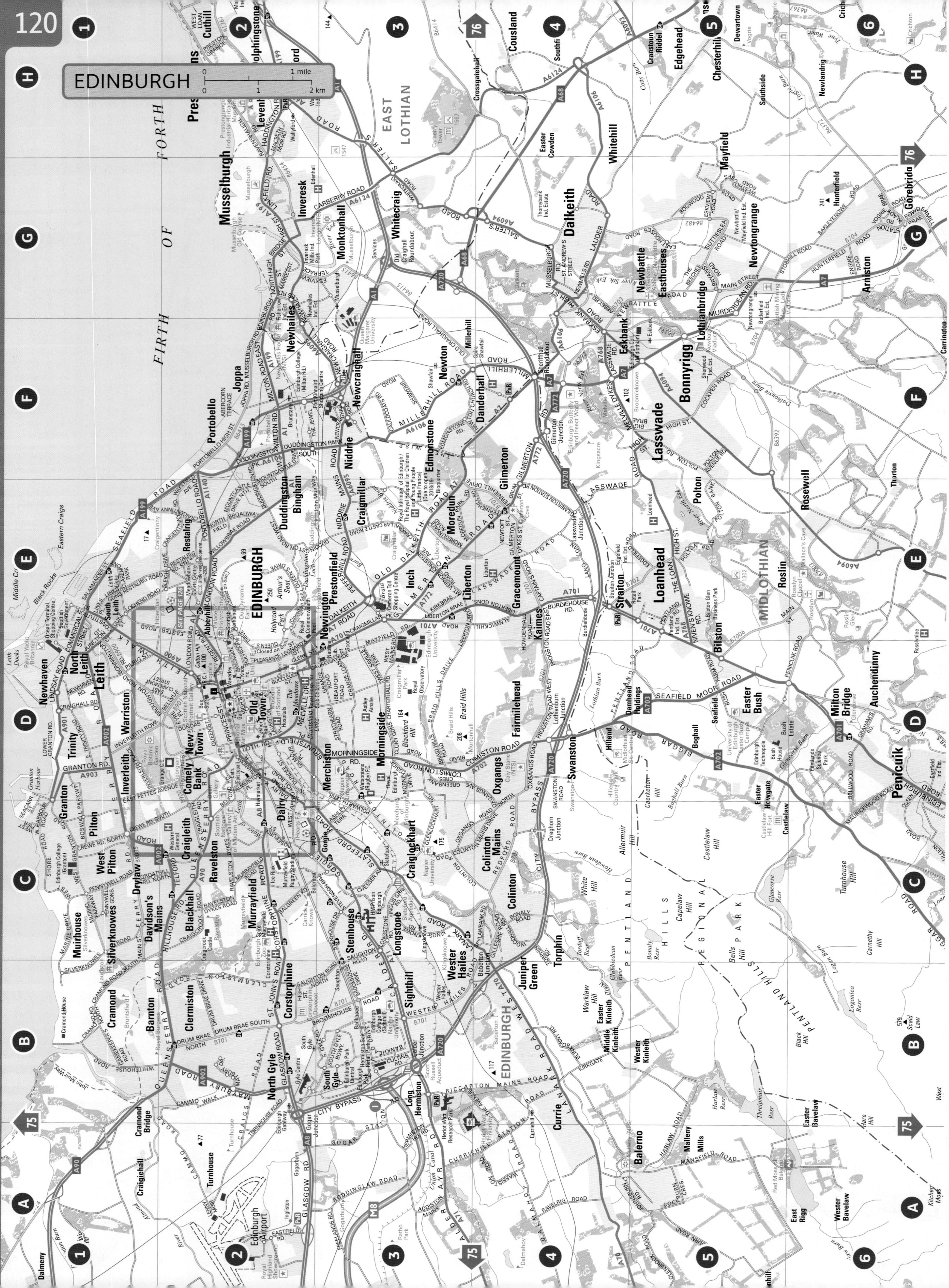

EDINBURGH

1 mile
1
2 km

EAST LOTHIAN

MIDLOTHIAN

FIRTH OF FORTH

Musselburgh, Inveresk, Monktonhall, Whitecraig, Newhailes, Newcraighall, Newton, Millerhill, Danderhall, Dalkeith, Easter Cowden, Whitehill, Mayfield, Cousland, Southfield, Edgehead, Chesterhill, Dewartown, Southside, Newlandrig, Newbattle, Easthouses, Newtongrange, Bonnyrigg, Lasswade, Lothianbridge, Eskbank, Arniston, Gorebridge

Portobello, Joppa, Leith, Newhaven, Trinity, Newington, Prestonfield, Niddrie, Craigmillar, Duddingston, Bingham, Edmonstone, Gilmerton, Moredun, Liberton, Inch, Gracemount, Kaimes, Burdiehouse, Straiton, Loanhead, Polton, Rosewell, Roslin, Bilston

North Leith, Warriston, Inverleith, Comely Bank, New Town, Old Town, EDINBURGH, Merchiston, Morningside, Fairmilehead, Damhead Holdings, Easter Bush, Milton Bridge, Auchendinny, Penicuik

Granton, Pilton, West Pilton, Drylaw, Davidson's Mains, Blackhall, Craigleith, Ravelston, Murrayfield, Dalry, Gorgie, Craiglockhart, Oxgangs, Colinton Mains, Swanston, Hillend, Boghall, Seafield, Castlelaw, Easter Howgate

Muirhouse, Silverknowes, Barnton, Cramond, Clermiston, Corstorphine, Stenhouse, Longstone, Sighthill, Wester Hailes, Juniper Green, Colinton, Torphin, Balerno, Currie, Hermiston, North Gyle, South Gyle

Cramond Bridge, Edinburgh Airport, Long Hermiston, Riccarton, Dalmeny, Craigiehall, Turnhouse

PENTLAND HILLS, PENTLAND HILLS REGIONAL PARK

A1, A7, A68, A701, A702, A703, A720, A900, A901, A902, A903, A904, A1140, A199, A6095, A6106, A6124, A772, M8, City Bypass

75, 76

Aberdeen Belfast Blackpool
Birmingham street map on page 122

Symbols used on the map

- M8 Motorway
- A4 Primary route dual / single carriageway / Junction
- A40 'A' road dual / single carriageway
- B507 'B' road dual / single carriageway
- Toll Other road dual / single carriageway / Toll
- One way street / Orbital route
- Access restriction
- Pedestrian street / Street market
- Minor road / Track
- FB Footpath / Footbridge
- Road under construction
- Extent of London congestion charging zone
- Main / other National Rail station
- London Underground / Overground station
- Light Rail / Station
- Bus / Coach station
- P&R Park and Ride site - rail operated (runs at least 5 days a week)
- Dublin 8hrs Vehicle / Pedestrian ferry
- Car park
- Theatre
- Major hotel
- Public House
- Pol Police station
- Lib Library
- PO Post Office
- Visitor information centre (open all year / seasonally)
- Toilet
- JAPAN Embassy
- Cinema
- Cathedral / Church
- Mormon Mosque / Synagogue / Other place of worship
- Park / Garden / Sports ground
- Cemetery
- Leisure & tourism
- Shopping
- Administration & law
- Health & welfare
- Education
- Industry / Office
- Other notable building

Street maps

Aberdeen	121
Belfast	121
Birmingham	122
Blackpool	121
Bournemouth	123
Bradford	123
Brighton	123
Bristol	123
Cambridge	123
Canterbury	123
Cardiff	124
Carlisle	124
Cheltenham	124
Chester	124
Coventry	124
Derby	124
Dover	125
Dundee	125
Durham	125
Eastbourne	125
Edinburgh	126
Exeter	125
Folkestone	125
Glasgow	127
Gloucester	128
Guildford	128
Harrogate	128
Hastings	128
Hereford	128
Hull (Kingston upon Hull)	128
Inverness	129
Leeds	130
Leicester	129
Lincoln	129
Liverpool	131
London	132
Manchester	133
Middlesbrough	129
Milton Keynes	129
Newcastle upon Tyne	129
Norwich	134
Nottingham	134
Oxford	134
Perth	134
Peterborough	134
Plymouth	134
Portsmouth	135
Reading	135
Salisbury	135
Scarborough	135
Sheffield	135
Southampton	135
Stoke-on-Trent	136
Stratford-upon-Avon	136
Sunderland	136
Swansea	136
Swindon	136
Torquay	136
Watford	137
Weston-super-Mare	137
Winchester	137
Windsor	137
Worcester	137
York	137

Locator map

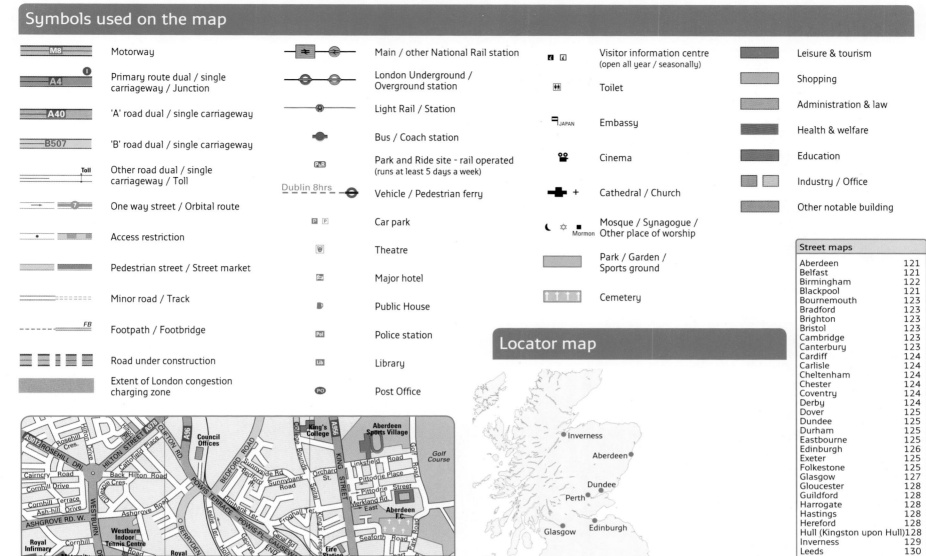
Inverness
Aberdeen
Dundee
Perth
Glasgow
Edinburgh
Newcastle upon Tyne
Belfast
Carlisle
Durham
Sunderland
Middlesbrough
Scarborough
Harrogate
York
Bradford
Blackpool
Leeds
Hull
Liverpool
Manchester
Lincoln
Chester
Sheffield
Nottingham
Stoke-on-Trent
Derby
Leicester
Norwich
Birmingham
Coventry
Peterborough
Worcester
Stratford-upon-Avon
Cambridge
Hereford
Cheltenham
Milton Keynes
Gloucester
Oxford
Watford
Swansea
Cardiff
Swindon
Windsor
LONDON
Weston-super-Mare
Bristol
Reading
Guildford
Canterbury
Dover
Salisbury
Winchester
Folkestone
Southampton
Brighton
Hastings
Exeter
Portsmouth
Eastbourne
Bournemouth
Torquay
Plymouth

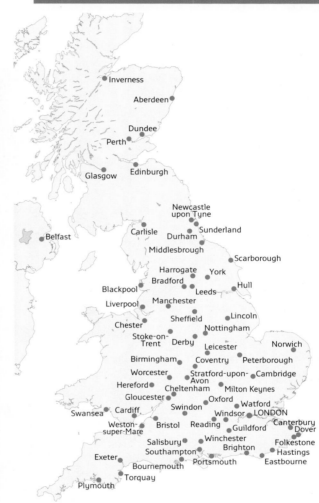
500 yds
500m

ABERDEEN

Appears on main map page 85

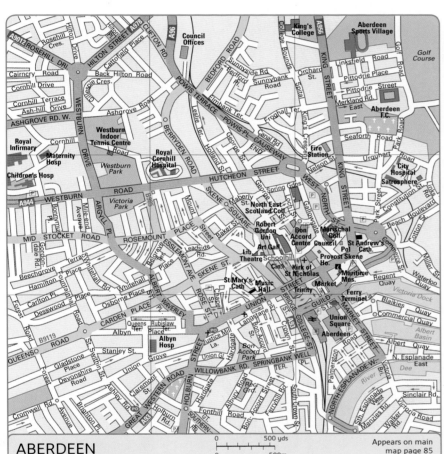
300 yds
300 m

BELFAST

Appears on main map page 93

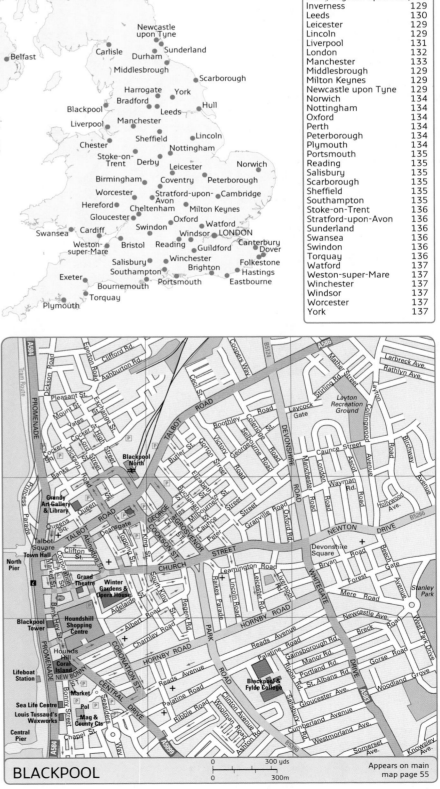
300 yds
300m

BLACKPOOL

Appears on main map page 55

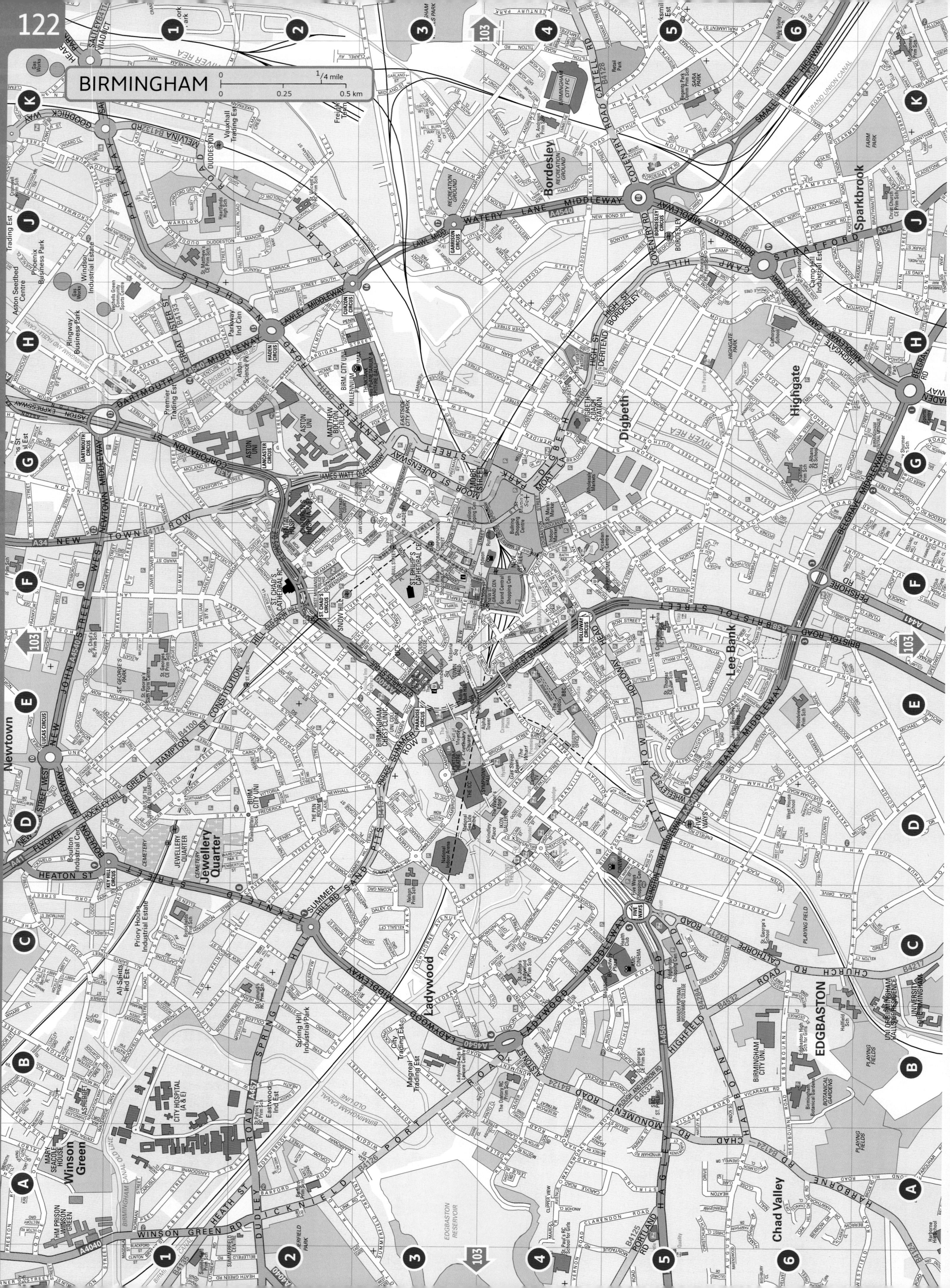
BIRMINGHAM
0 1/4 mile
0 0.25 0.5 km
Bordesley
Digbeth
Highgate
Sparkbrook
Lee Bank
Newtown
Jewellery Quarter
Ladywood
EDGBASTON
Chad Valley
Winson Green
MIDDLEWAY
BRISTOL STREET
BRISTOL ROAD
HAGLEY ROAD
STRATFORD ROAD
WATERY LANE MIDDLEWAY
DARTMOUTH MIDDLEWAY
LADYWOOD MIDDLEWAY
BELGRAVE MIDDLEWAY
CAMP HILL
COVENTRY ROAD
HOLLOWAY HEAD
BATH ROW
HARBORNE ROAD
MONUMENT ROAD
SPRING HILL
DUDLEY ROAD
WINSON GREEN RD
GREAT HAMPTON ST
CONSTITUTION HILL
CORPORATION ST
MOOR ST QUEENSWAY
FIVE WAYS
CITY HOSPITAL (A & E)
ST CHAD'S CATHEDRAL
ST PHILIP'S CATHEDRAL
ASTON UNI
BIRMINGHAM CITY FC
EDGBASTON RESERVOIR
BOTANICAL GARDENS
UNIVERSITY OF BIRMINGHAM
103

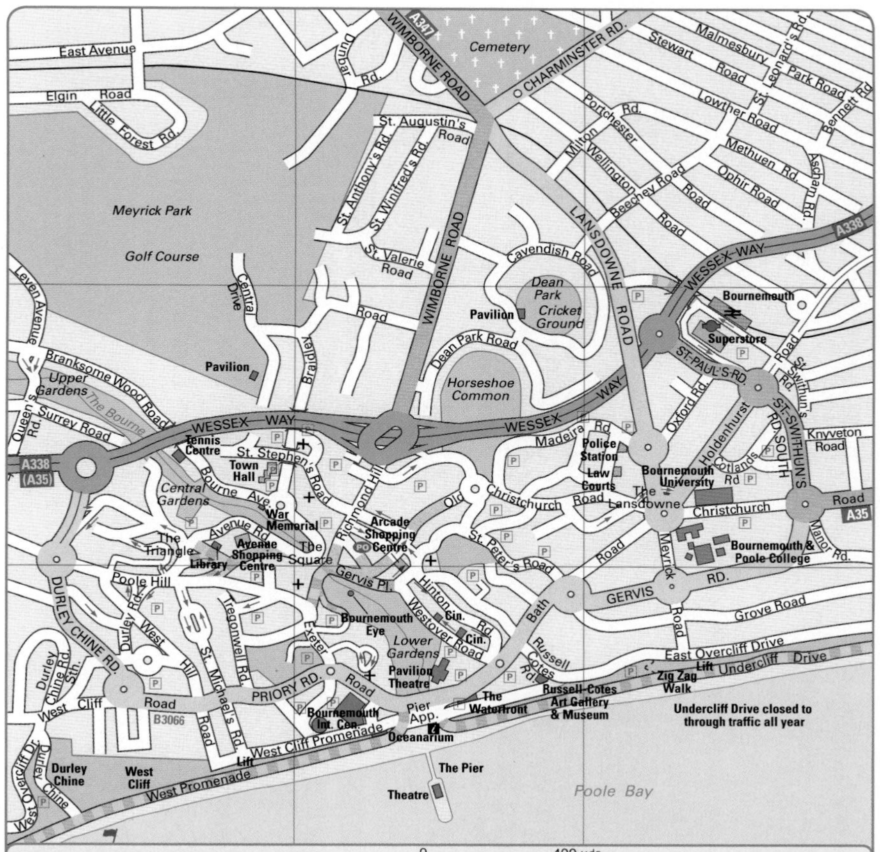

BOURNEMOUTH

Appears on main map page 10

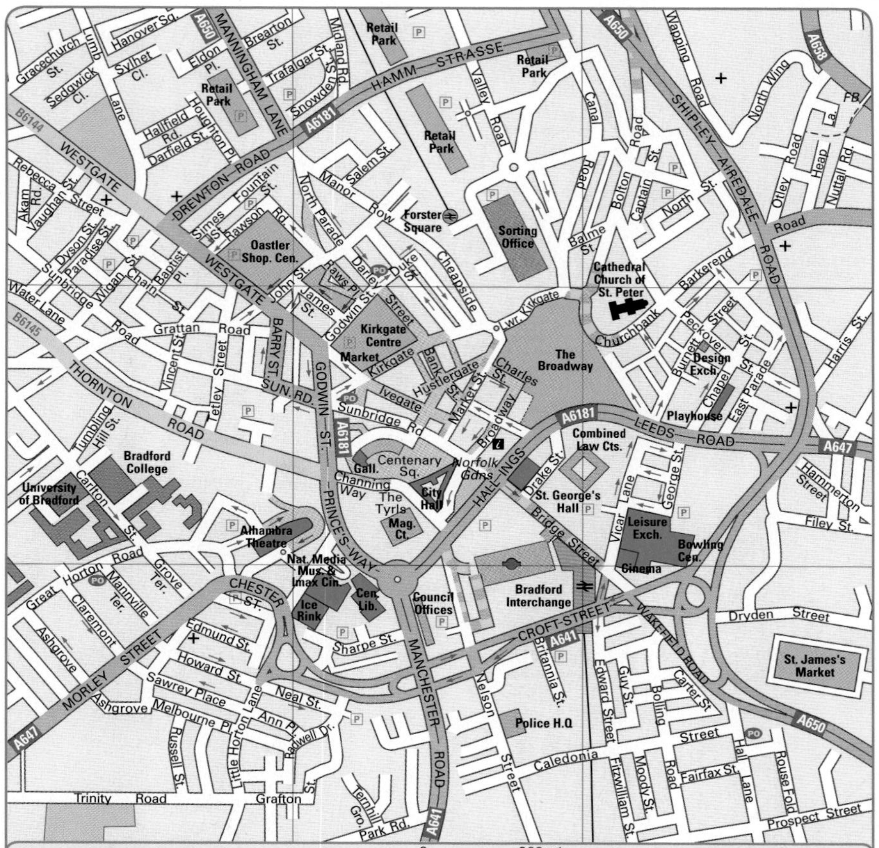

BRADFORD

Appears on main map page 57

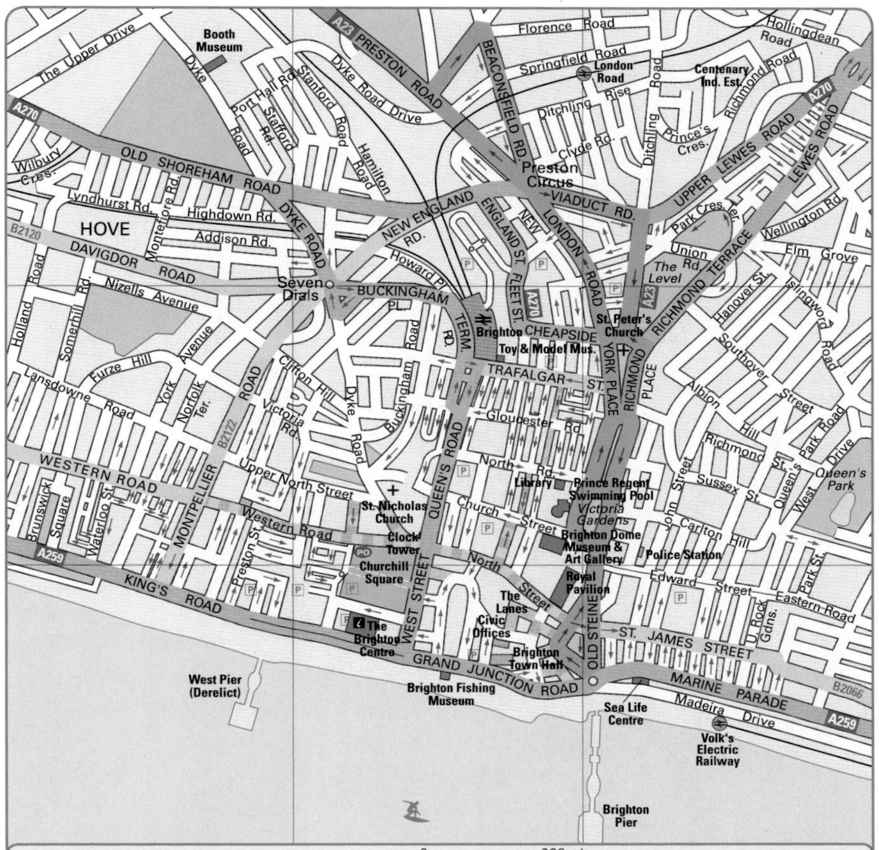

BRIGHTON

Appears on main map page 13

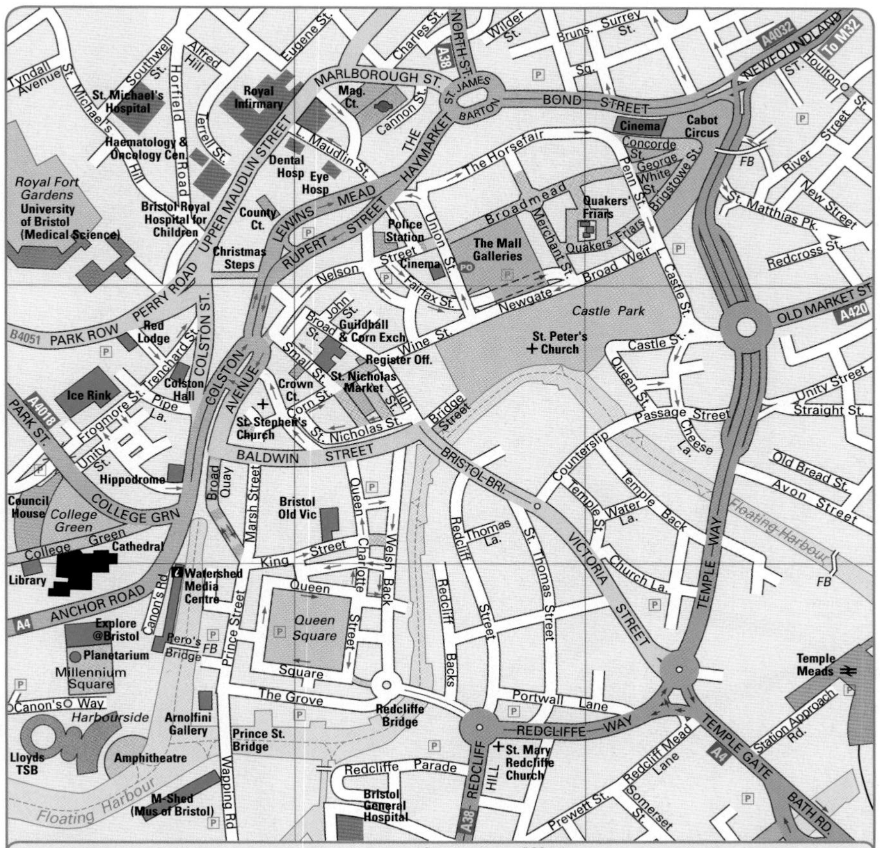

BRISTOL

Appears on main map page 19

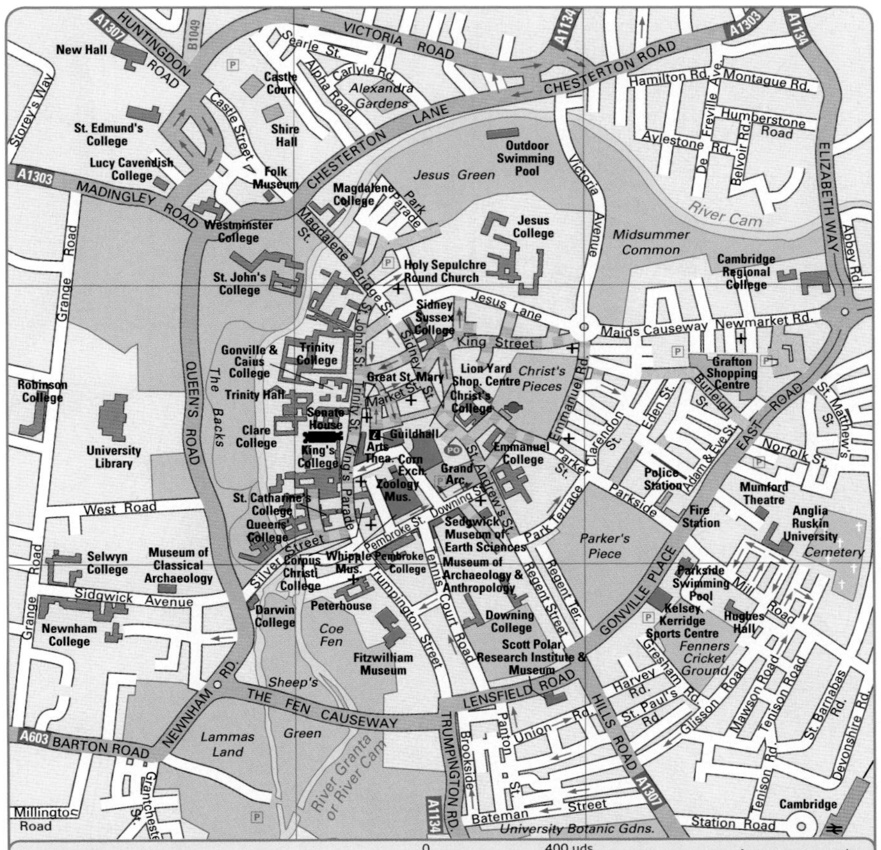

CAMBRIDGE

Appears on main map page 33

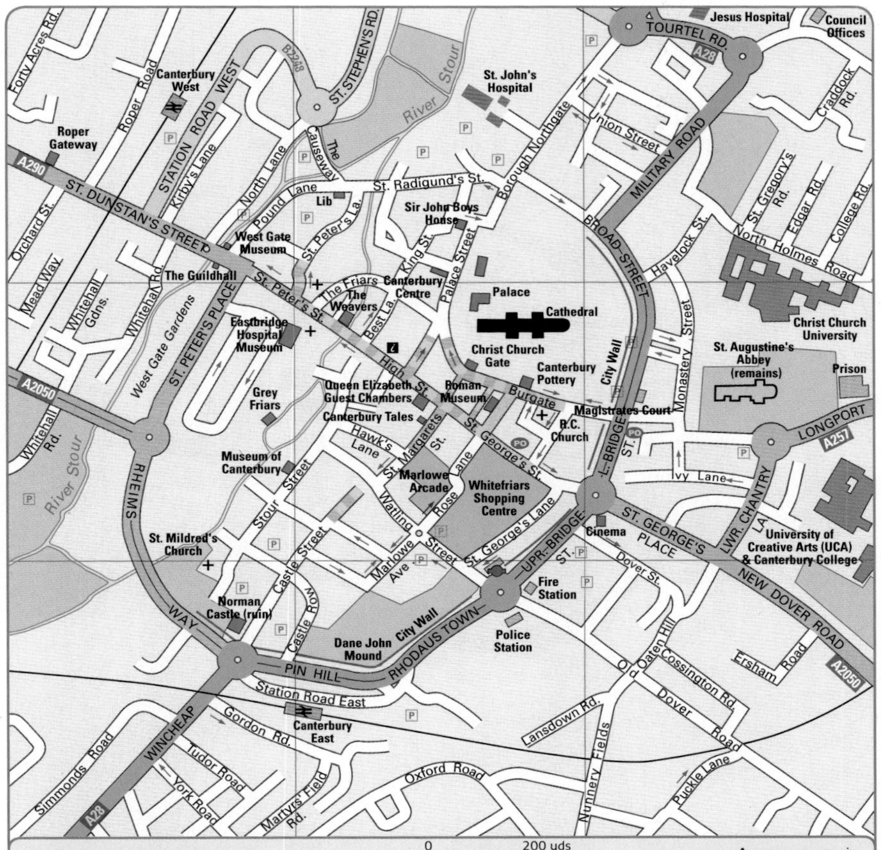

CANTERBURY

Appears on main map page 15

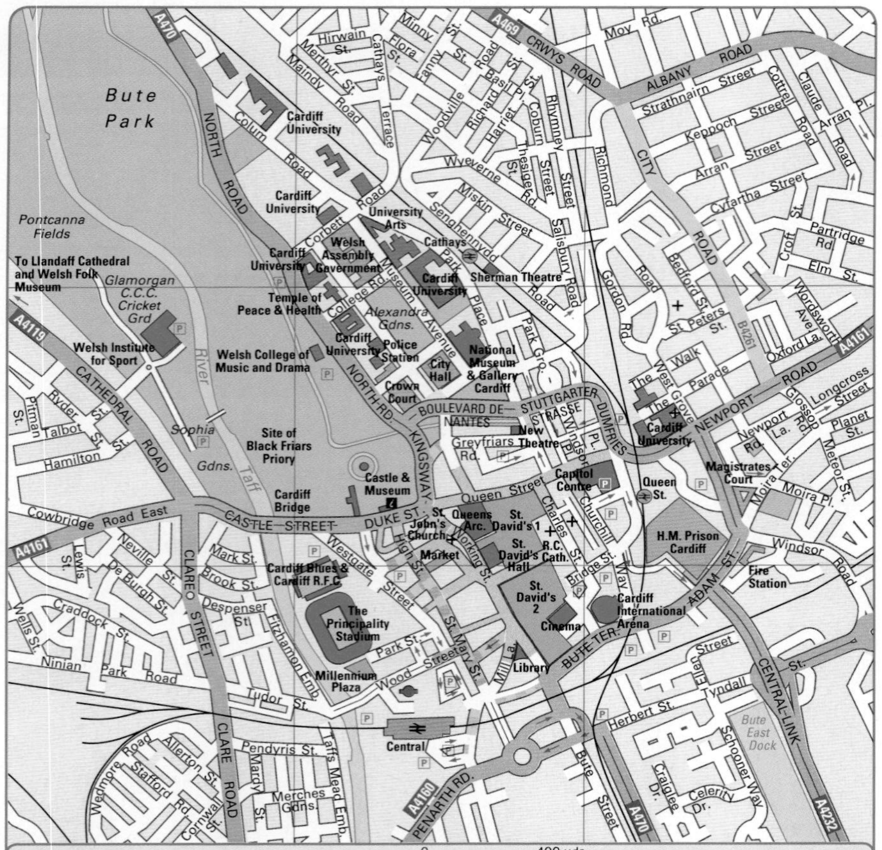

CARDIFF

Appears on main map page 18

400 yds
400m

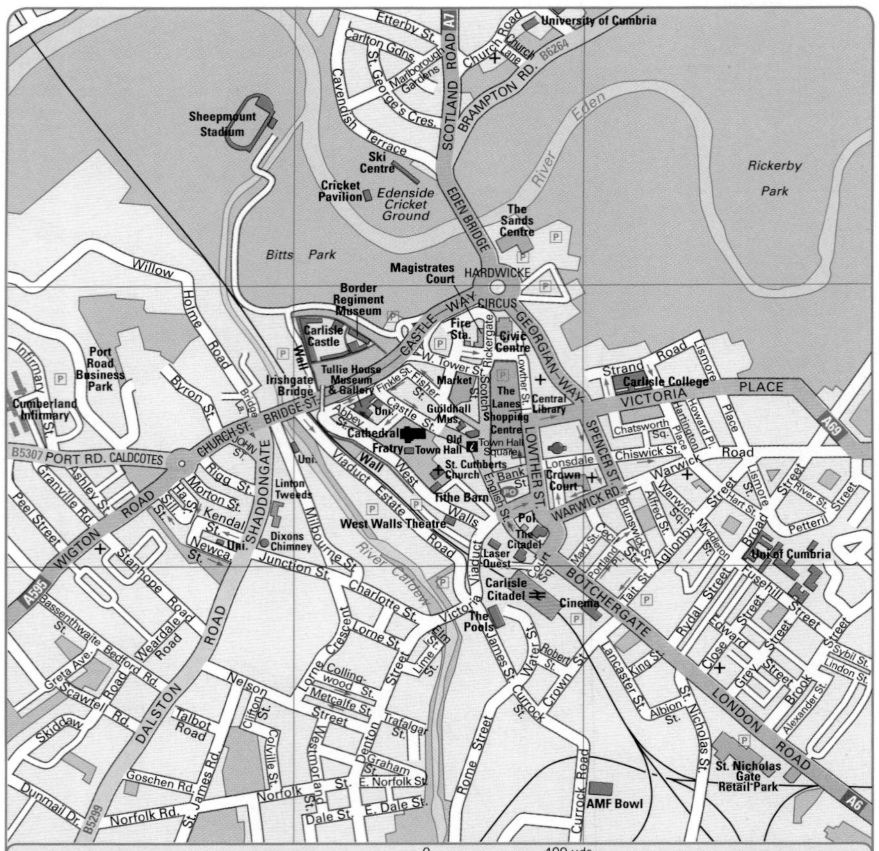

CARLISLE

Appears on main map page 60

400 yds
400m

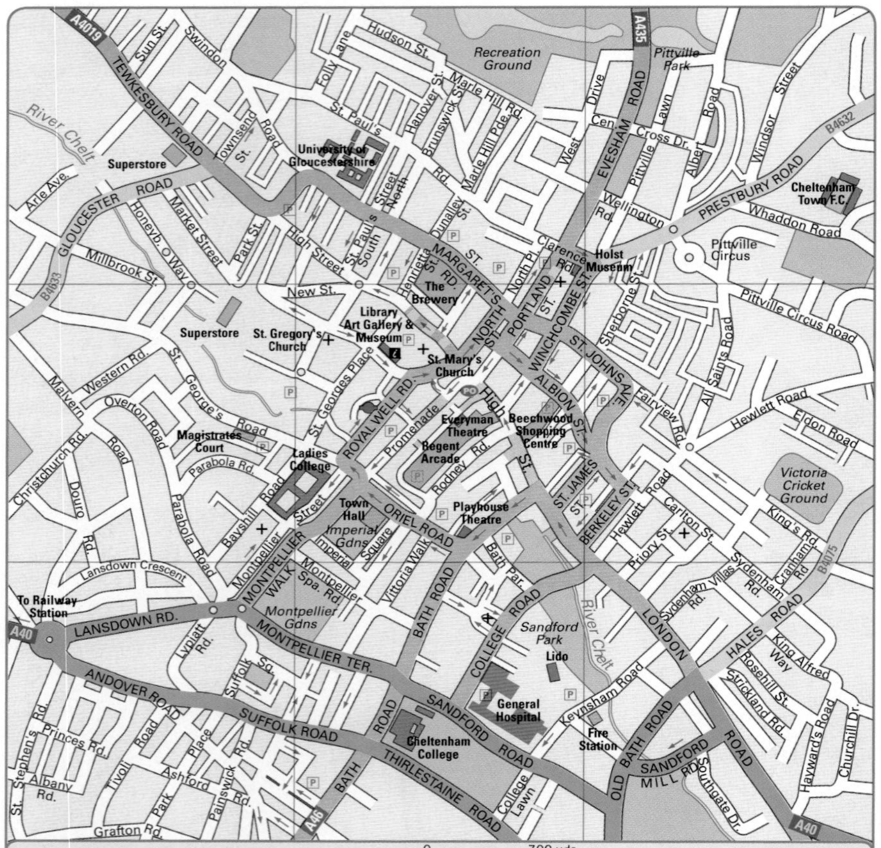

CHELTENHAM

Appears on main map page 29

300 yds
300m

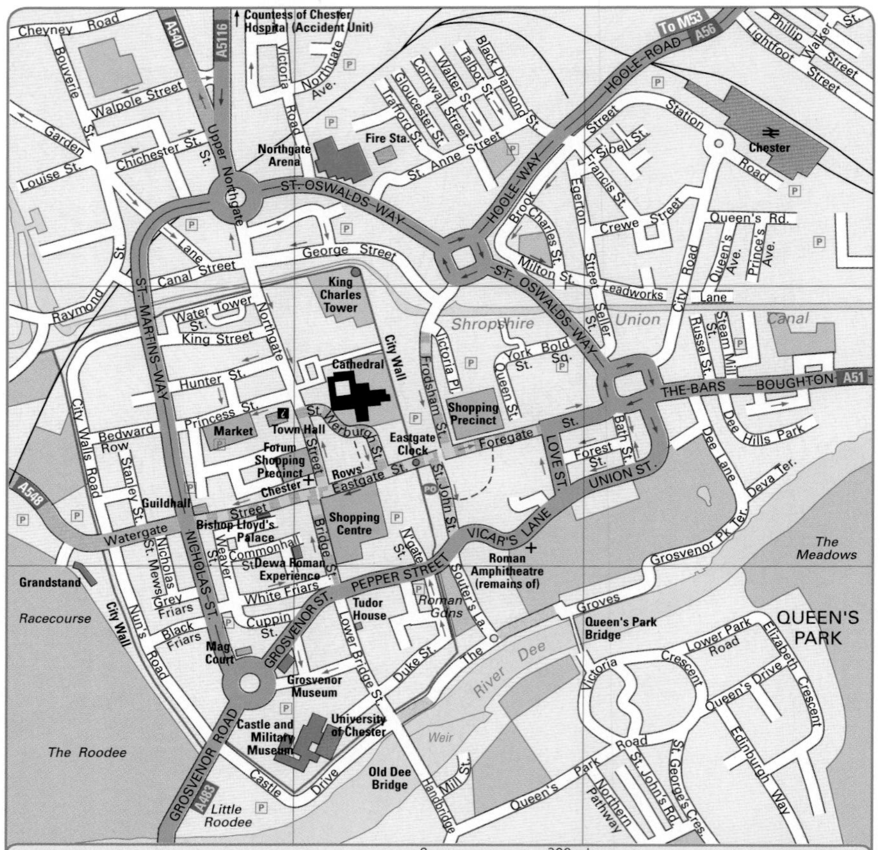

CHESTER

Appears on main map page 48

200 yds
200m

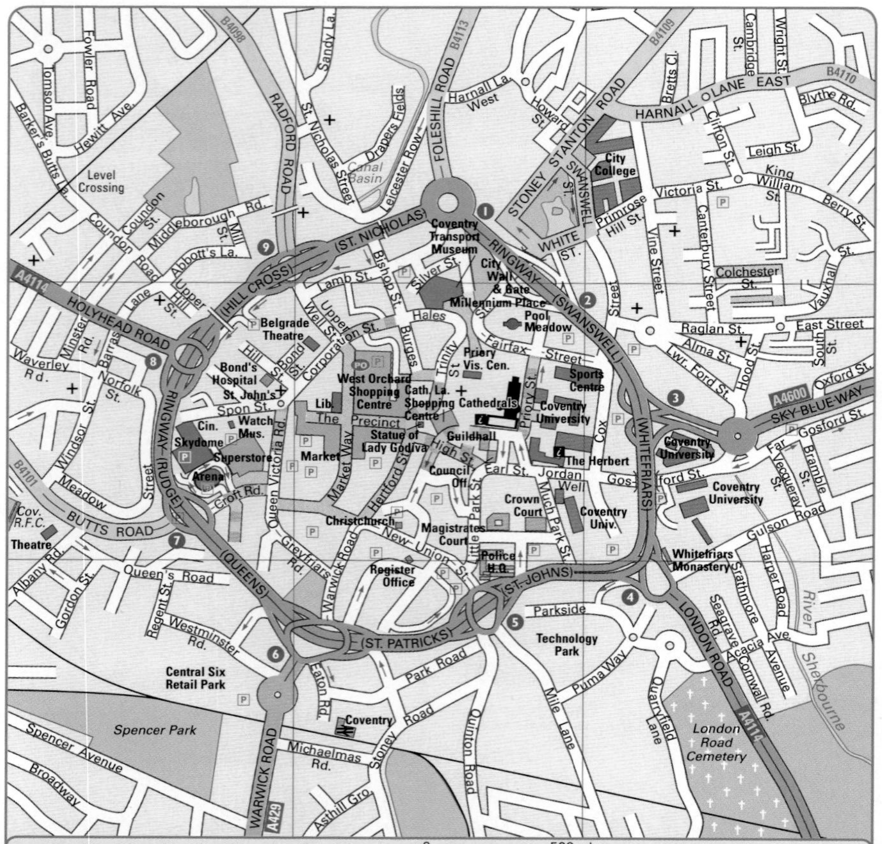

COVENTRY

Appears on main map pages 30/41

500 yds
500m

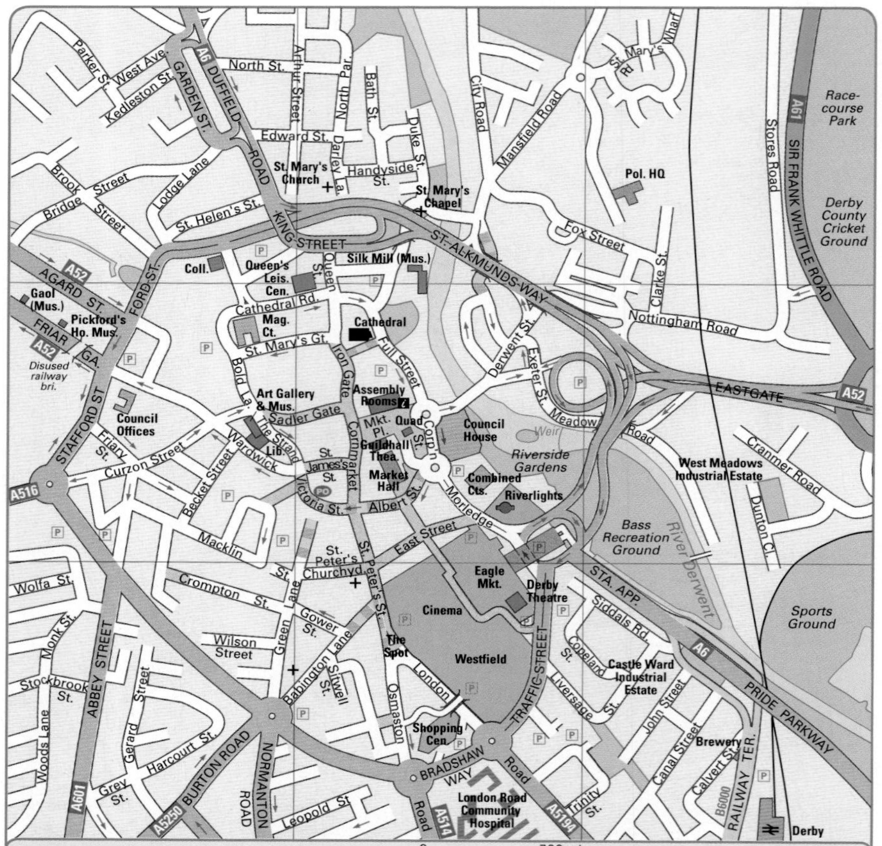

DERBY

Appears on main map page 41

300 yds
300m

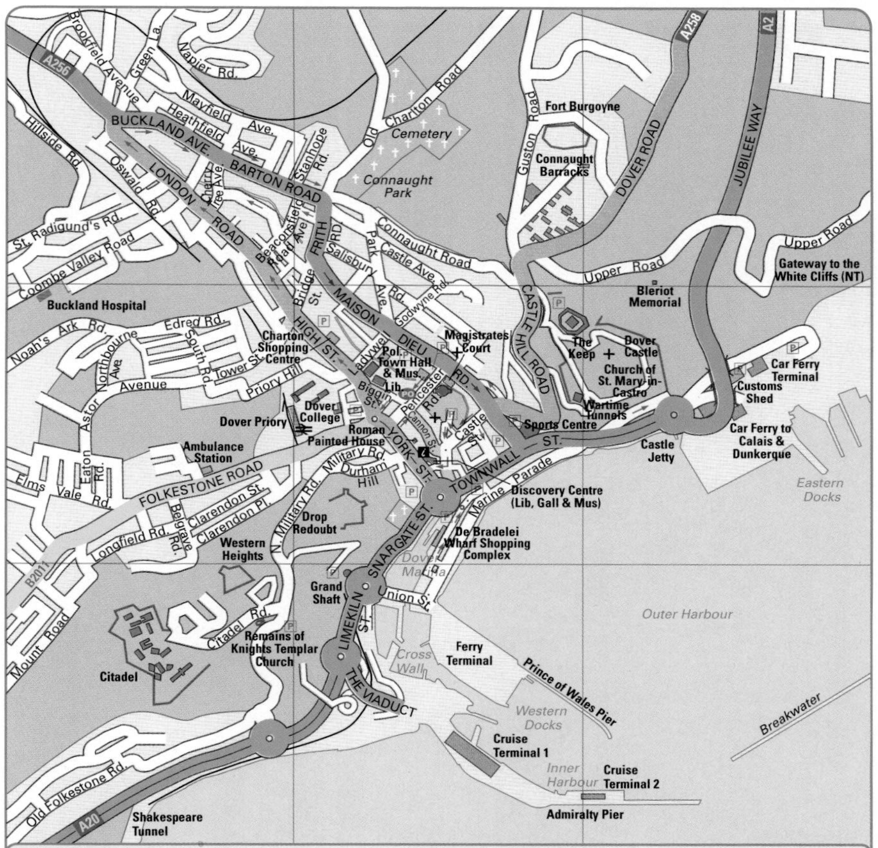

DOVER

0   500 yds
0   500m

Appears on main
map page 15

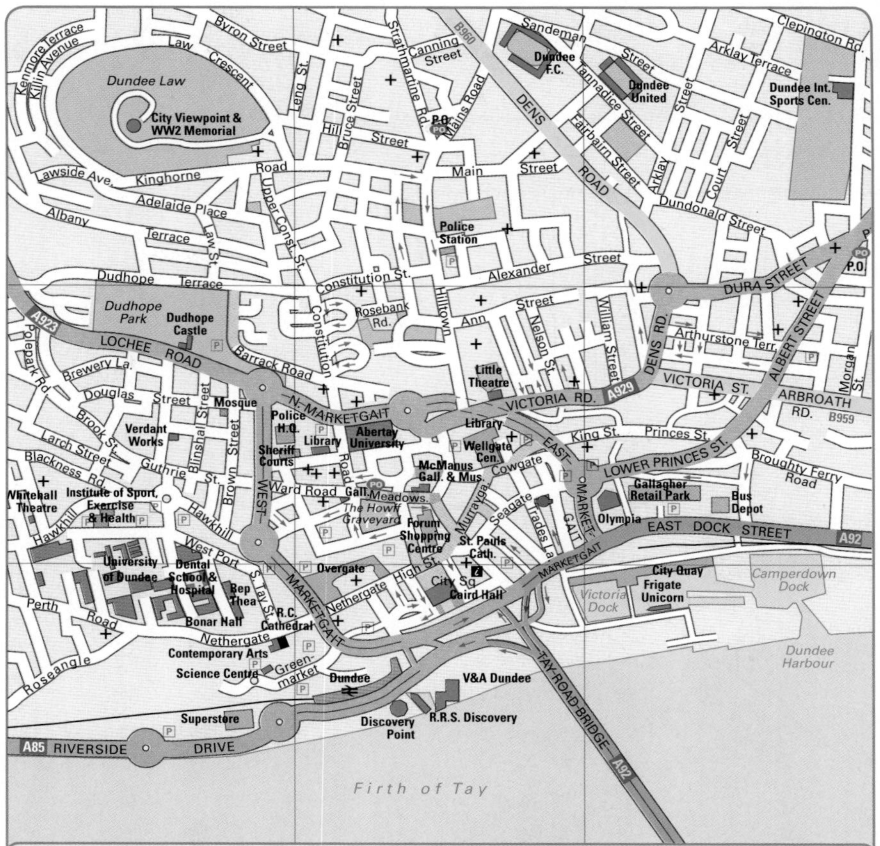

DUNDEE

0   400 yds
0   400m

Appears on main
map page 81

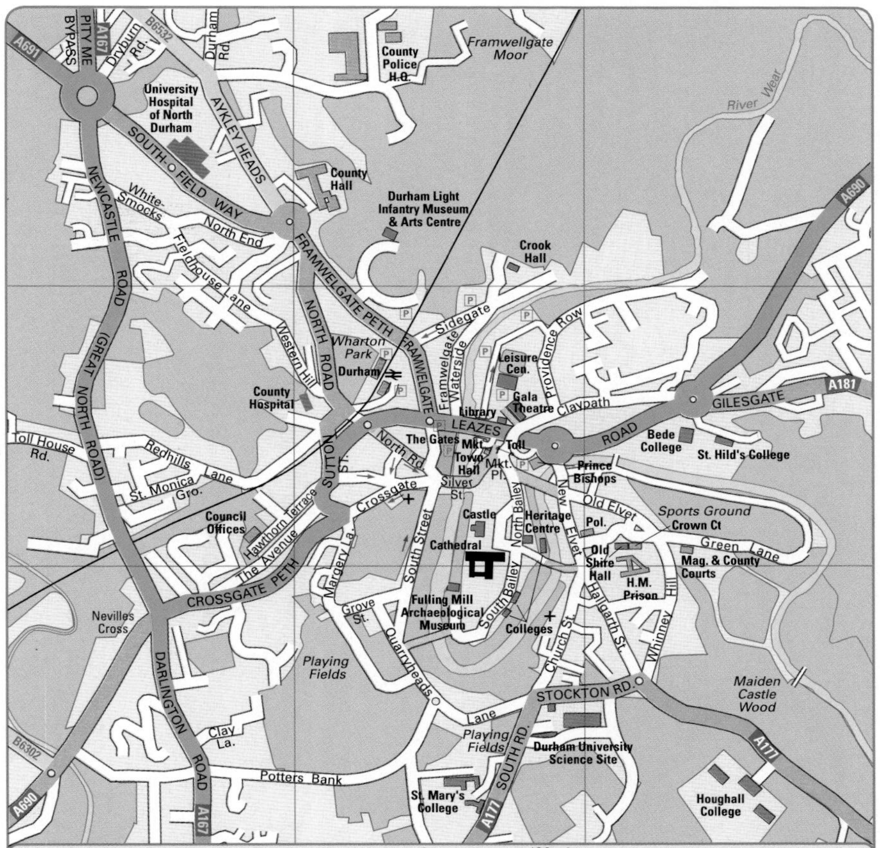

DURHAM

0   400 yds
0   400m

Appears on main
map page 62

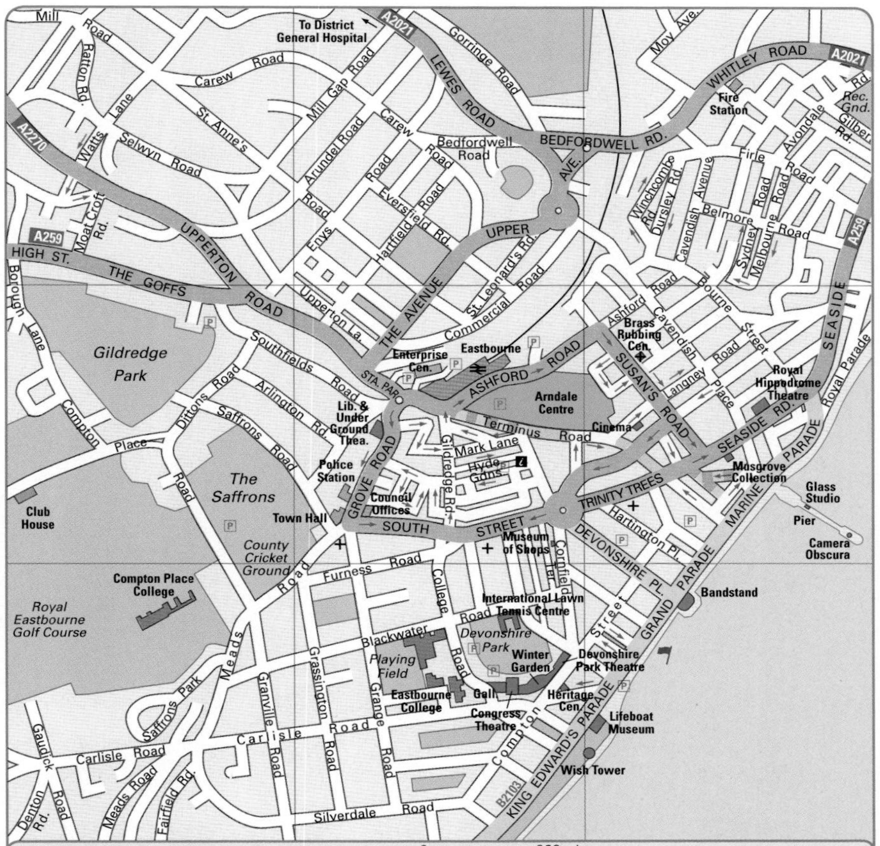

EASTBOURNE

0   200 yds
0   200m

Appears on main
map page 13

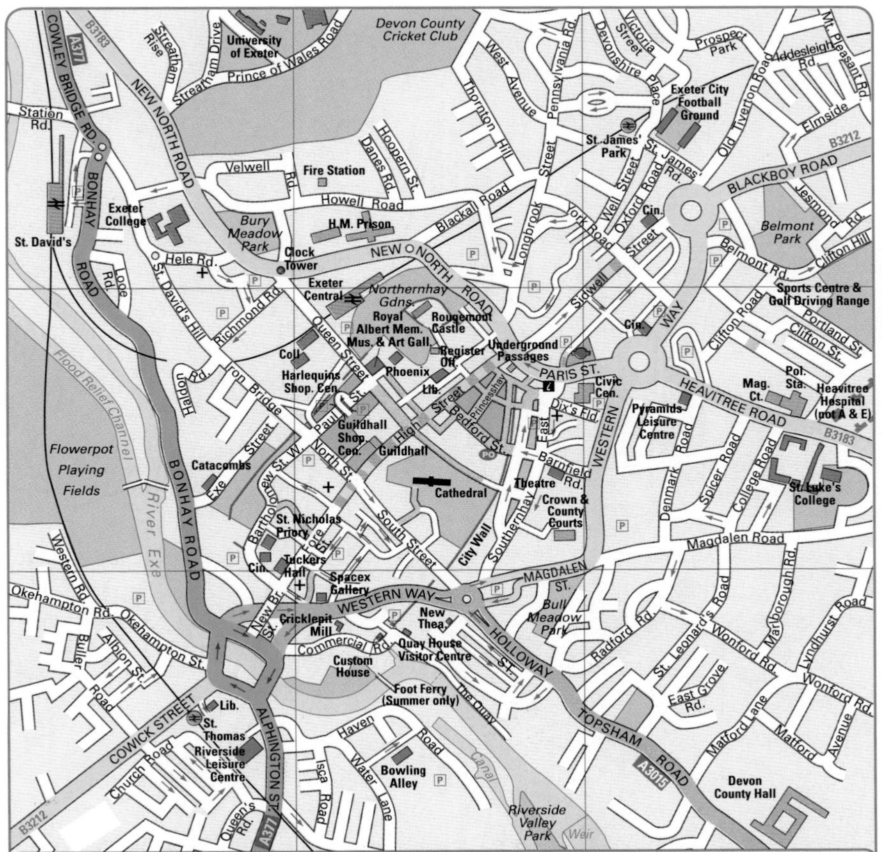

EXETER

0   400 yds
0   400m

Appears on main
map page 7

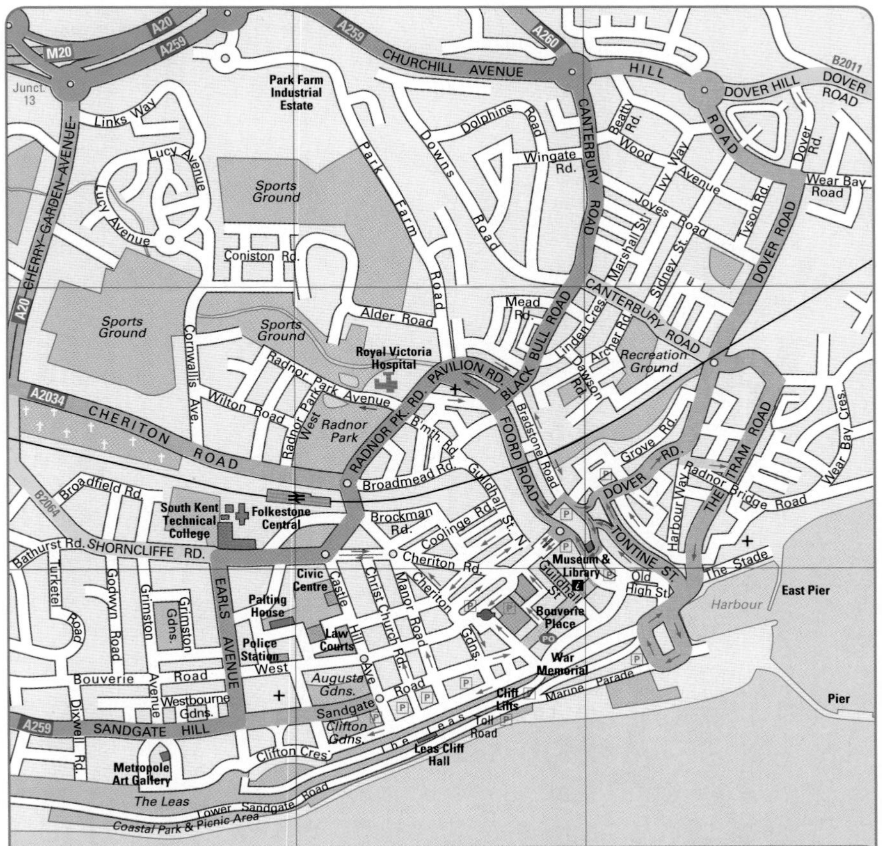

FOLKESTONE

0   200 yds
0   200m

Appears on main
map page 15

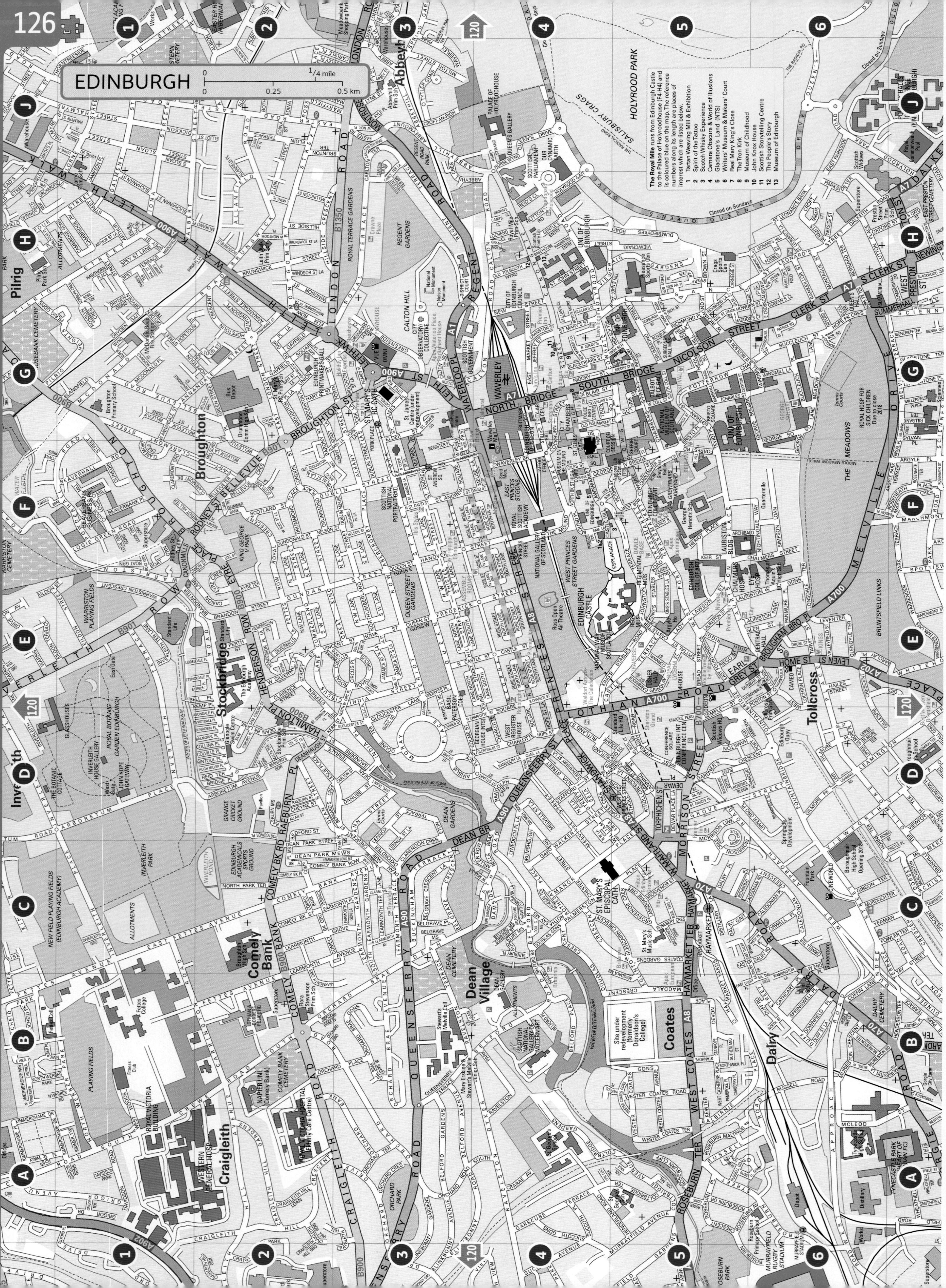
EDINBURGH
0 1/4 mile
0 0.25 0.5 km
The Royal Mile runs from Edinburgh Castle to the Palace of Holyroodhouse (F4-H4) and is coloured blue on the map. The reference numbers along its length are places of interest which are listed below.
1 Tartan Weaving Mill & Exhibition
2 Spirit of the Tattoo
3 Scotch Whisky Experience
4 Camera Obscura & World of Illusions
5 Gladstone's Land (NTS)
6 Writers' Museum & Makars' Court
7 Real Mary King's Close
8 The Tron Kirk
9 Museum of Childhood
10 John Knox House
11 Scottish Storytelling Centre
12 The People's Story
13 Museum of Edinburgh
HOLYROOD PARK
SALISBURY CRAGS
PALACE OF HOLYROODHOUSE
SCOTTISH PARLIAMENT
OUR DYNAMIC EARTH
Closed on Sundays
CALTON HILL
REGENT GARDENS
ROYAL TERRACE GARDENS
WAVERLEY
NORTH BRIDGE
SOUTH BRIDGE
NICOLSON STREET
CLERK ST
UNI OF EDINBURGH
NATIONAL MUSEUM OF SCOTLAND
THE MEADOWS
MELVILLE DRIVE
BRUNTSFIELD LINKS
EDINBURGH CASTLE
WEST PRINCES STREET GARDENS
PRINCES STREET
QUEEN STREET GARDENS
SCOTTISH NATIONAL PORTRAIT GALL
NATIONAL GALLERY OF SCOTLAND
ROYAL SCOTTISH ACADEMY
LOTHIAN ROAD
Tollcross
Broughton
Stockbridge
Pilrig
Inverleith
ROYAL BOTANIC GARDEN EDINBURGH
INVERLEITH PARK
Comely Bank
Craigleith
WESTERN GENERAL HOSP
Dean Village
DEAN CEMETERY
ST. MARY'S EPISCOPAL CATH
HAYMARKET
Coates
Dalry
DALRY CEMETERY
TYNECASTLE PARK (HEART OF MIDLOTHIAN FC)
MURRAYFIELD RUGBY STADIUM
ROSEBURN PARK
LEITH WALK
A1
A7
A70
A90
A700
A702
A900
A902
B900
B901
120

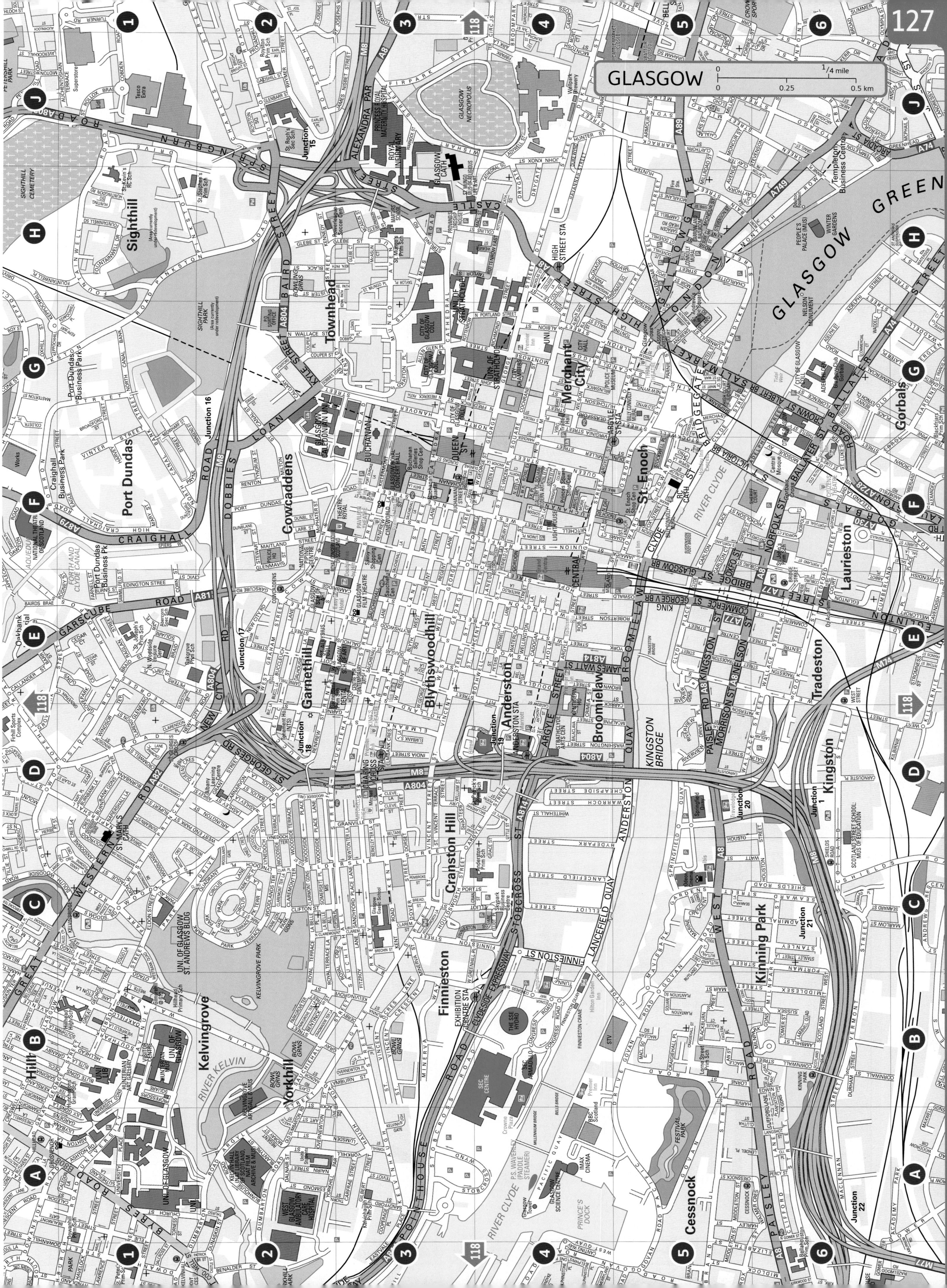
GLASGOW
1/4 mile
0 0.25 0.5 km
Sighthill
Port Dundas
Cowcaddens
Townhead
Merchant City
St. Enoch
Gorbals
Laurieston
Tradeston
Kingston
Kinning Park
Cessnock
Garnethill
Blythswoodhill
Anderston
Bromielaw
Cranston Hill
Finnieston
Yorkhill
Kelvingrove
Hill
GLASGOW GREEN
GLASGOW NECROPOLIS
GLASGOW CATH
ROYAL INFIRMARY
RIVER CLYDE
RIVER KELVIN
KINGSTON BRIDGE
KELVINGROVE PARK
PRINCE'S DOCK
FESTIVAL PARK
THE SSE HYDRO
SEC CENTRE
CENTRAL
HIGH STREET STA
Junction 15
Junction 16
Junction 17
Junction 18
Junction 19
Junction 20
Junction 21
Junction 22
Junction 1
118
A B C D E F G H J
1 2 3 4 5 6

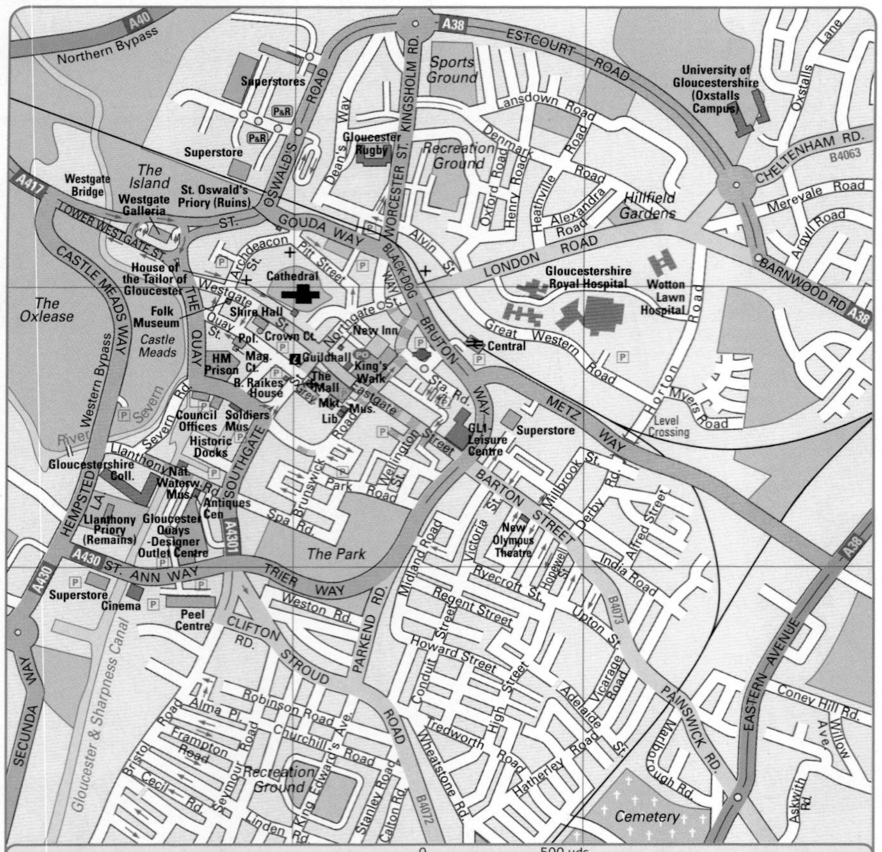

GLOUCESTER

0 ___ 500 yds
0 ___ 500m

Appears on main
map page 29

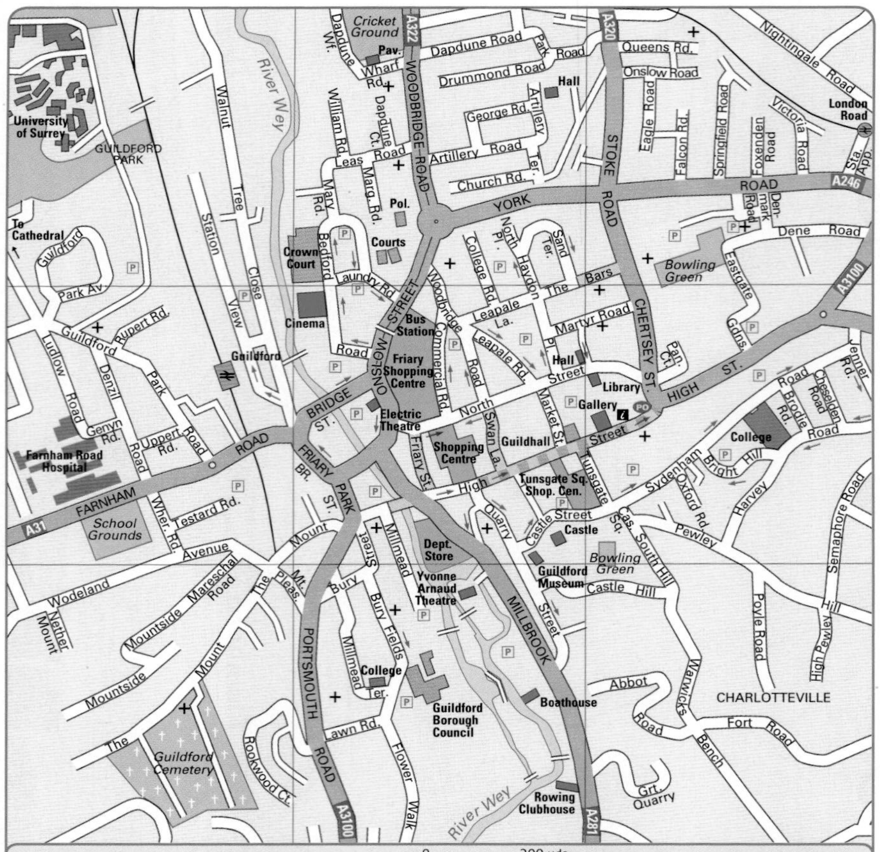

GUILDFORD

0 ___ 200 yds
0 ___ 200m

Appears on main
map page 22

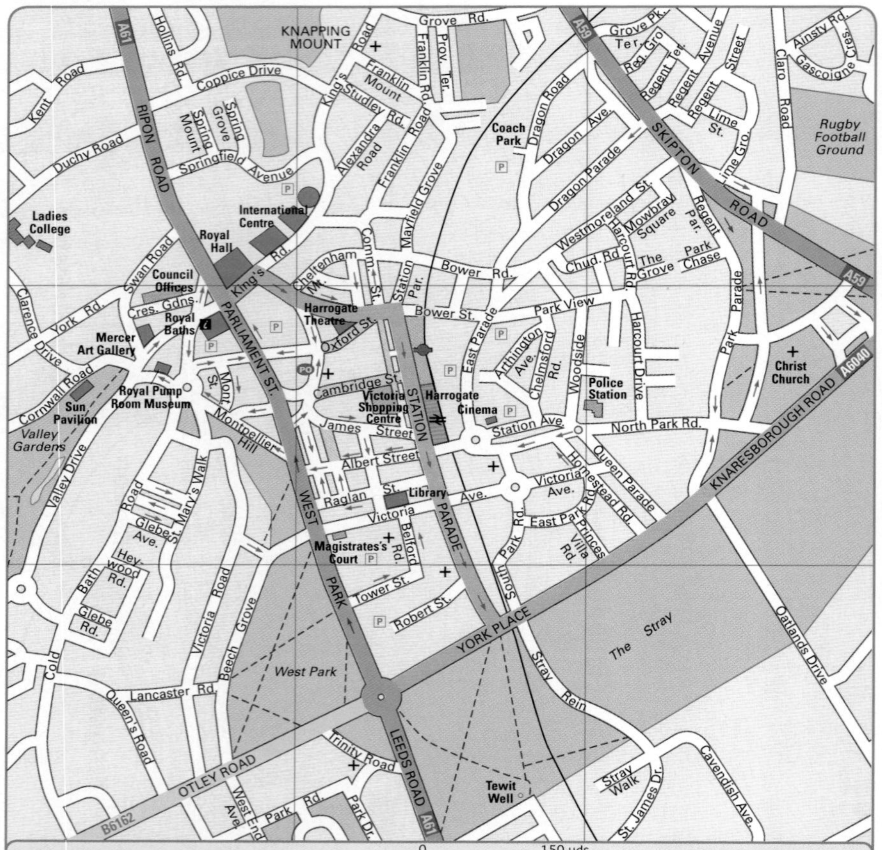

HARROGATE

0 ___ 150 yds
0 ___ 150m

Appears on main
map page 57

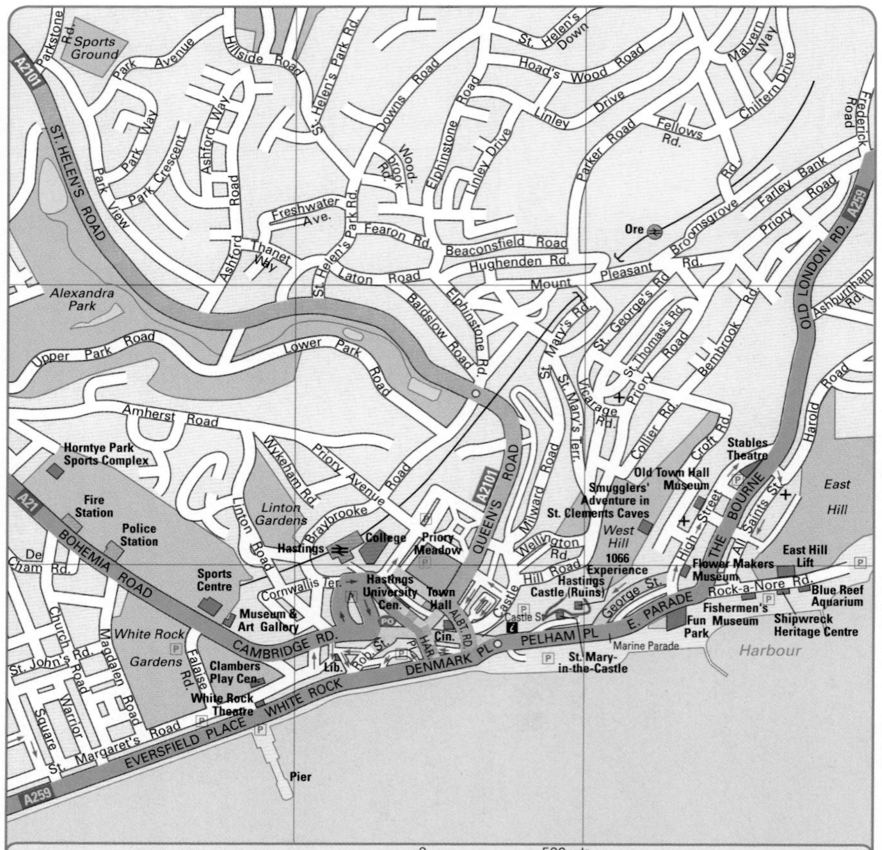

HASTINGS

0 ___ 500 yds
0 ___ 500m

Appears on main
map page 14

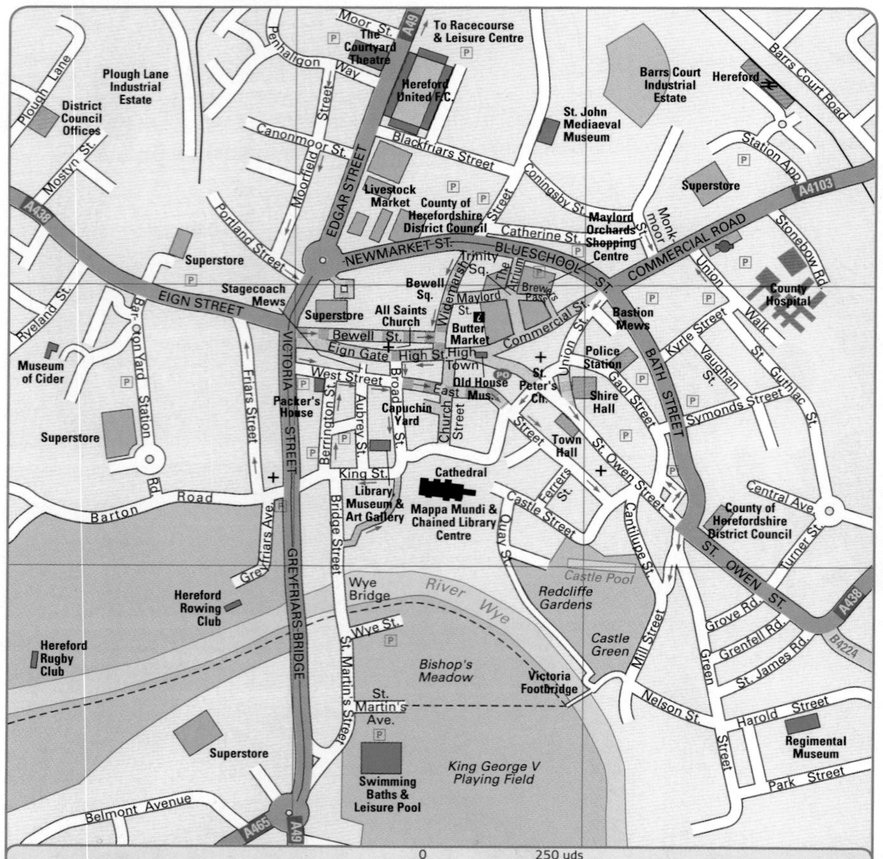

HEREFORD

0 ___ 250 yds
0 ___ 250m

Appears on main
map page 28

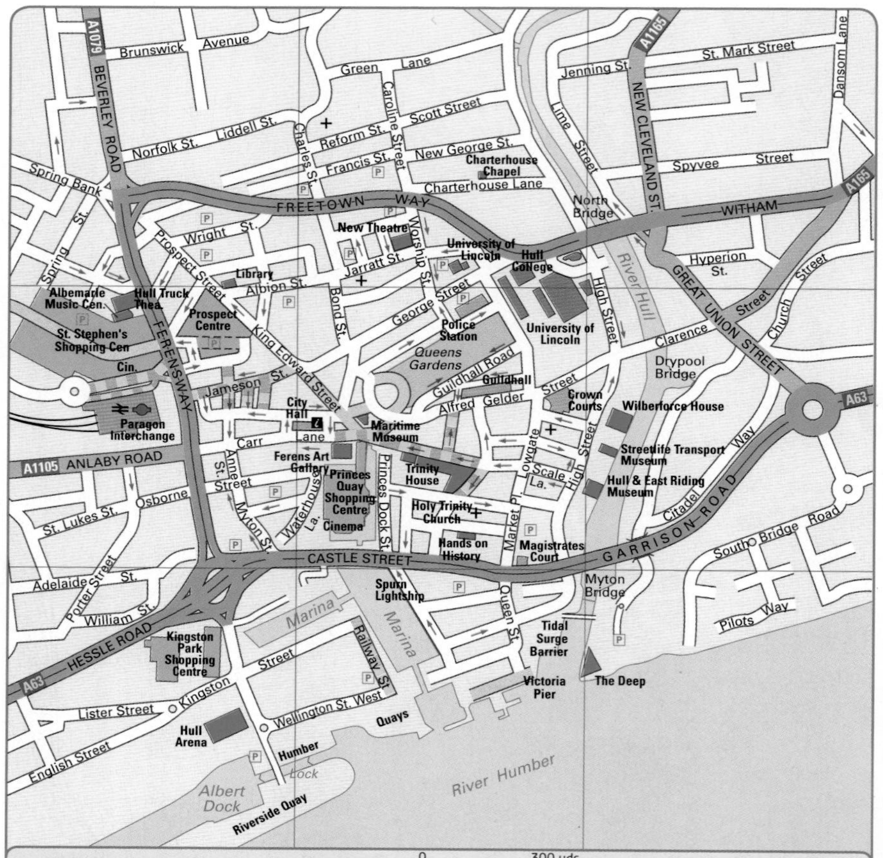

HULL (KINGSTON UPON HULL)

0 ___ 300 yds
0 ___ 300m

Appears on main
map page 59

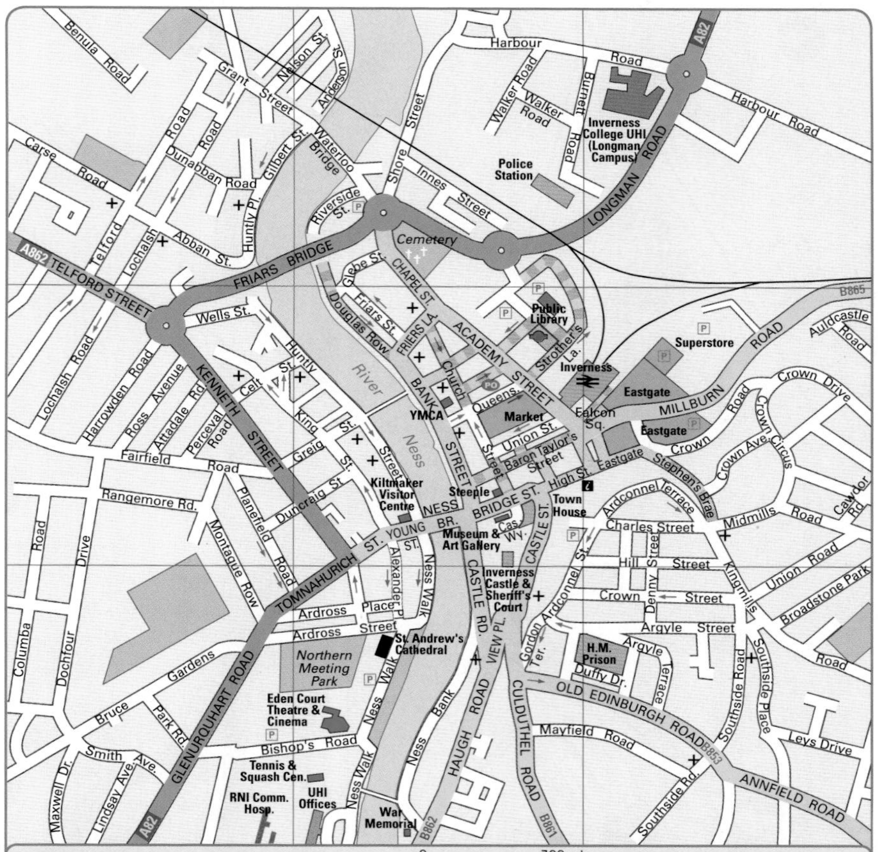

INVERNESS

Appears on main
map page 84

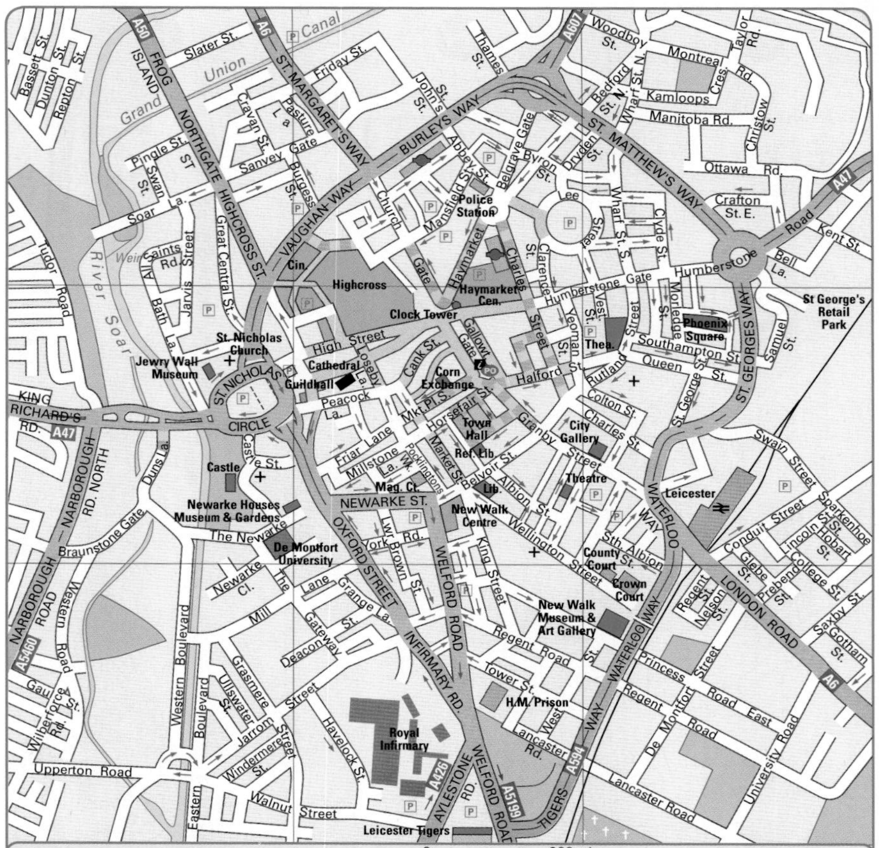

LEICESTER

Appears on main
map page 41

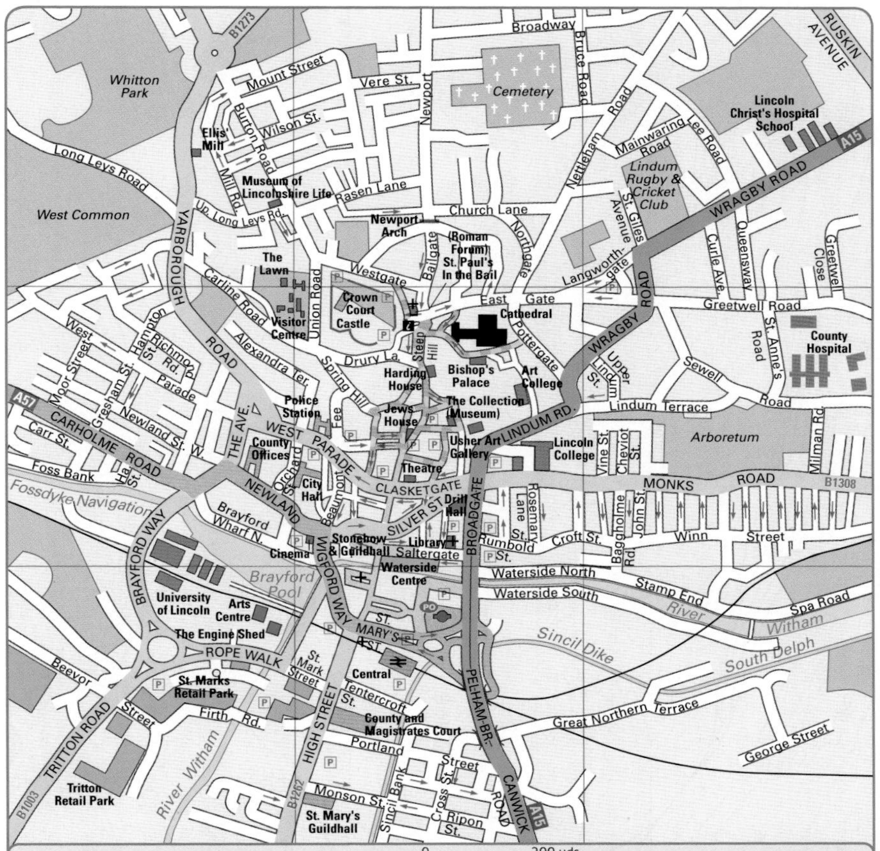

LINCOLN

Appears on main
map page 52

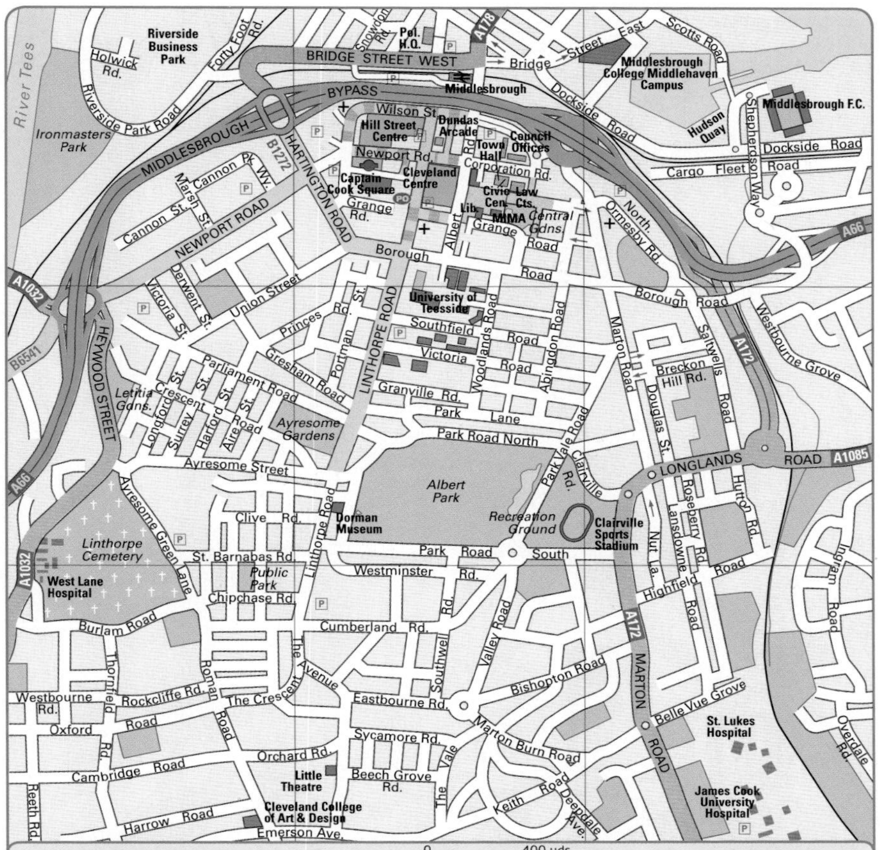

MIDDLESBROUGH

Appears on main
map page 62

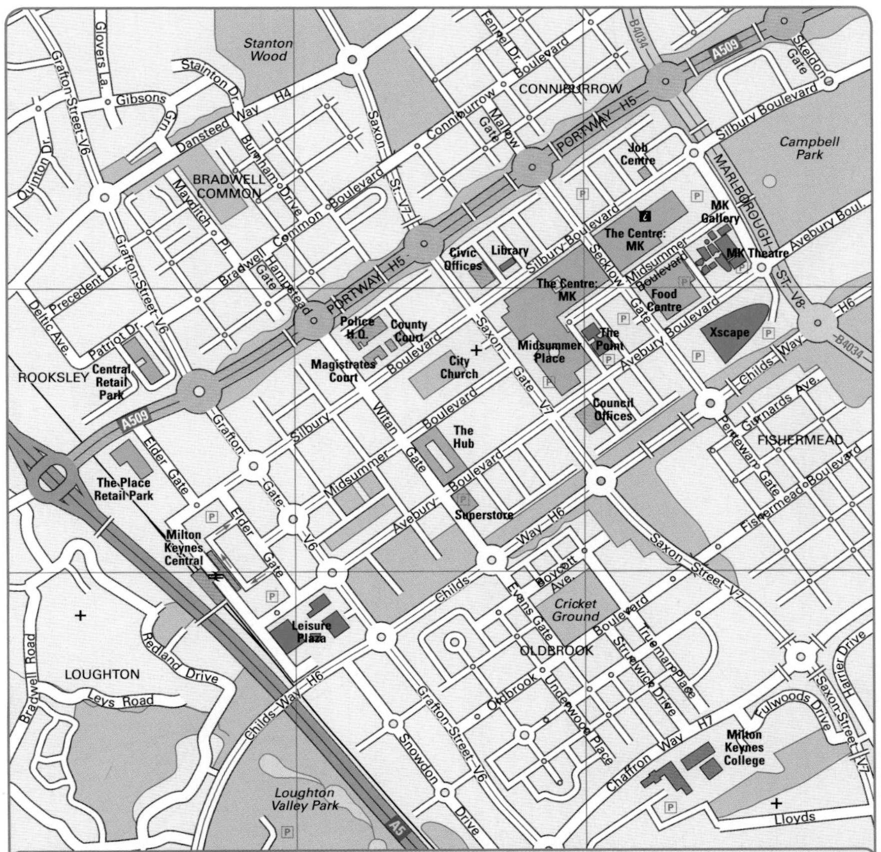

MILTON KEYNES

Appears on main
map page 32

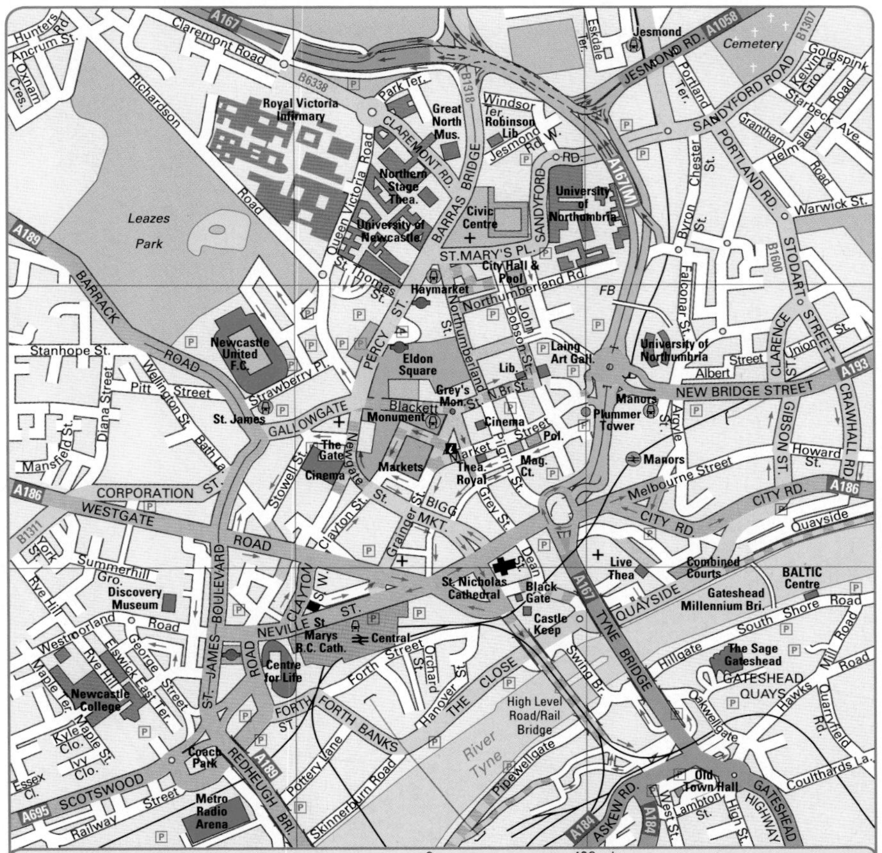

NEWCASTLE UPON TYNE

Appears on main
map page 71

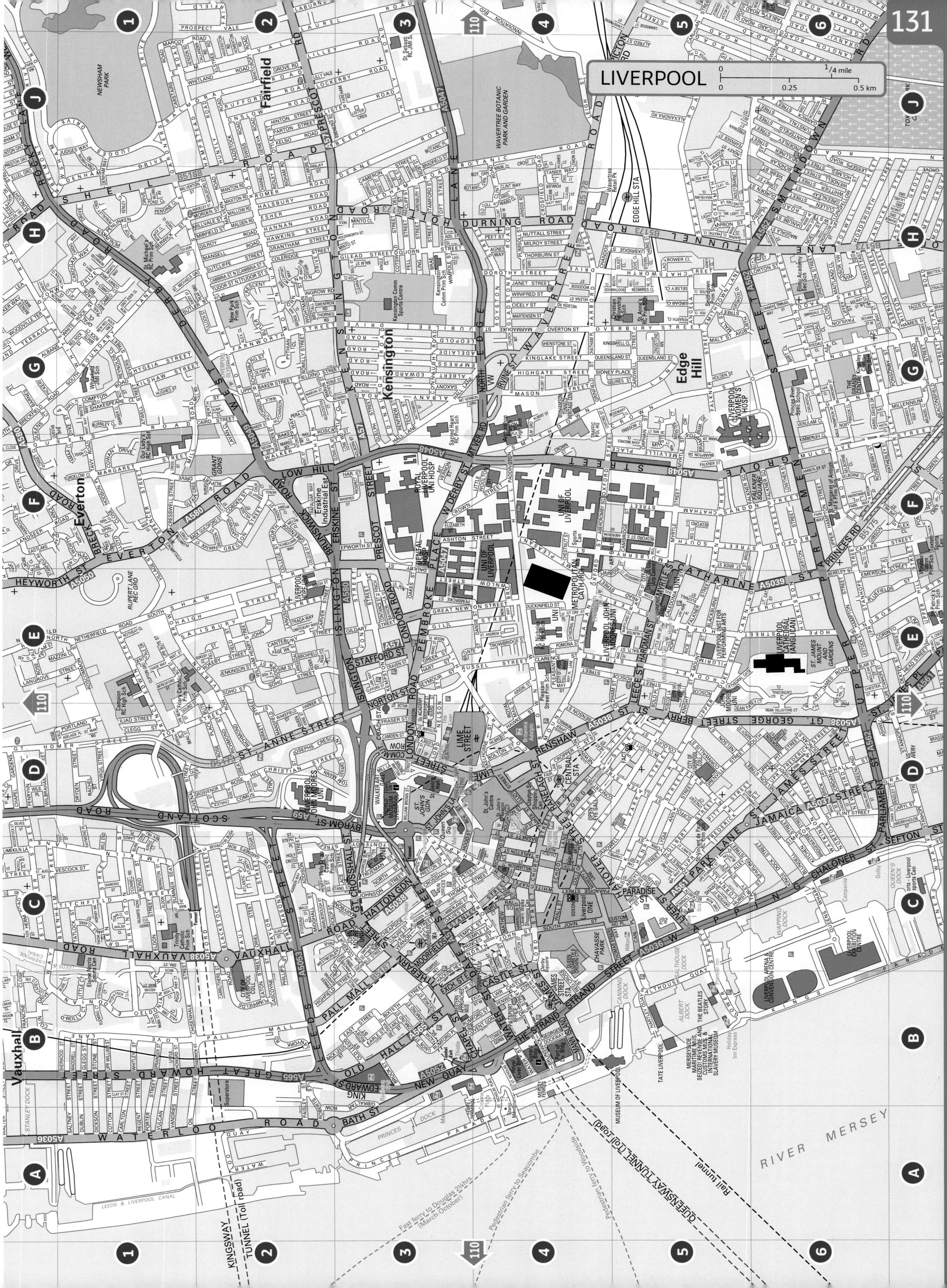
LIVERPOOL
1/4 mile
0 0.25 0.5 km
Fairfield
Kensington
Edge Hill
Everton
Vauxhall
NEWSHAM PARK
WAVERTREE BOTANIC PARK AND GARDEN
EDGE HILL STA
LIME STREET
CENTRAL STA
JAMES STREET STA
MOORFIELDS STA
ALBERT DOCK
CANNING DOCK
SALTHOUSE DOCK
WAPPING DOCK
QUEEN'S DOCK
PRINCES DOCK
STANLEY DOCK
RIVER MERSEY
QUEENSWAY TUNNEL (Toll road)
KINGSWAY TUNNEL (Toll road)
Rail tunnel
LEEDS & LIVERPOOL CANAL
UNI OF LIVERPOOL
ROYAL LIVERPOOL UNI HOSP
METROPOLITAN CATHEDRAL
LIVERPOOL CATHEDRAL (ANGLICAN)
ST. JAMES MOUNT AND GARDENS
LIVERPOOL WOMEN'S HOSP
LIVERPOOL JOHN MOORES UNI
LIVERPOOL INSTITUTE FOR PERFORMING ARTS
Liverpool ONE
CHAVASSE PARK
PARADISE ST
TATE LIVERPOOL
MUSEUM OF LIVERPOOL
THE BEATLES STORY
MERSEYSIDE MARITIME MUS. SEIZED! REVENUE AND CUSTOMS UK & INTERNATIONAL SLAVERY MUSEUM
LIVERPOOL ARENA & CONVENTION CENTRE
LIVERPOOL EXHIBITION CENTRE
RUPERT LANE REC GRD
GRANT GDNS
Erskine Industrial Est
Kensington Comm Sports Centre
Wavertree Retail Pk
Fast ferry to Douglas 2¾hrs (March-October)
Pedestrian ferry to Seacombe
Pedestrian ferry to Woodside
110
SCOTLAND ROAD
GREAT HOWARD STREET
WATERLOO ROAD
VAUXHALL ROAD
ST. ANNE STREET
LONDON ROAD
PEMBROKE PLACE
WEST DERBY ROAD
WEST DERBY STREET
EVERTON ROAD
BRECK ROAD
SHEIL ROAD
KENSINGTON
EDGE LANE
TUNNEL ROAD
SMITHDOWN ROAD
UPPER PARLIAMENT STREET
PRINCES RD
CATHARINE ST
HOPE STREET
RENSHAW ST
BERRY ST
GREAT GEORGE ST
ST. JAMES STREET
PARK LANE
JAMAICA STREET
WAPPING
STRAND STREET
THE STRAND
NEW QUAY
OLD HALL ST
PALL MALL
DALE ST
TITHEBARN ST
HANOVER ST
CHALONER ST
SEFTON ST
DURNING ROAD
MULGRAVE STREET
ISLINGTON
BYROM ST
LOW HILL
A5036 A5038 A5039 A5047 A5048 A5049 A5050 A5052 A5053 A562 A580 A57 A59 A565 A561 A5037 B5173 B5178 B5188 B5175

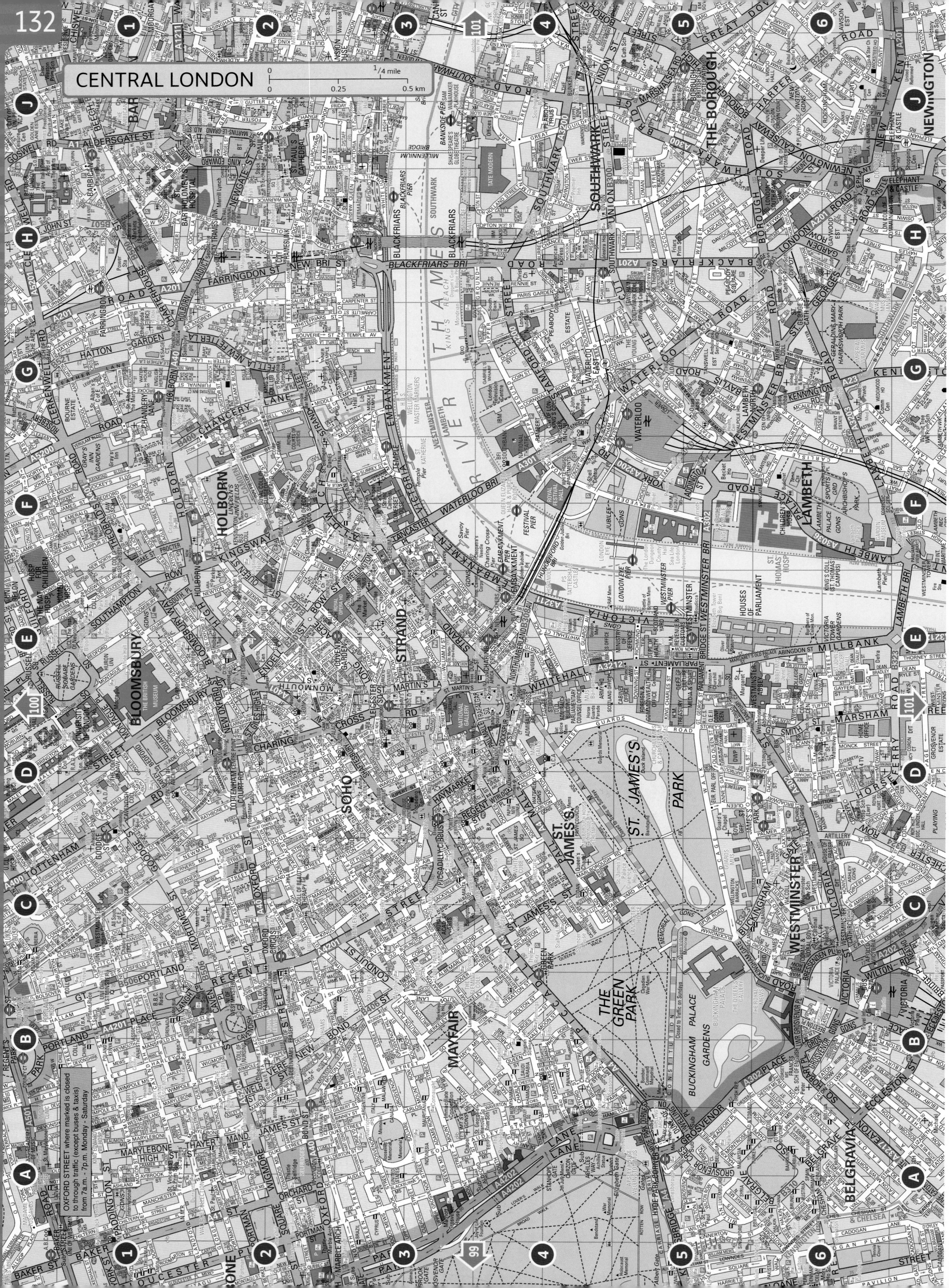
CENTRAL LONDON
1/4 mile
0
0.25
0.5 km
OXFORD STREET where marked is closed to through traffic (except buses & taxis) from 7a.m. - 7p.m. Monday - Saturday
101
100
99
THE BOROUGH
SOUTHWARK
HOLBORN
BLOOMSBURY
SOHO
STRAND
MAYFAIR
ST. JAMES'S
ST. JAMES'S PARK
THE GREEN PARK
BUCKINGHAM PALACE GARDENS
WESTMINSTER
LAMBETH
BELGRAVIA
NEWINGTON
RIVER THAMES
HOUSES OF PARLIAMENT
WATERLOO
TATE MODERN
BLACKFRIARS BRI
WATERLOO BRI
VICTORIA EMBANKMENT
WHITEHALL
MILLBANK
VICTORIA
GREEN PARK
PICCADILLY CIRCUS
OXFORD CIRCUS
TOTTENHAM
KINGSWAY
CHANCERY LANE
FARRINGDON ROAD
HATTON GARDEN
ALDERSGATE ST
BARBICAN
ST. PAUL'S CATHEDRAL
MILLENNIUM BRIDGE
BLACKFRIARS
ELEPHANT & CASTLE
LAMBETH PALACE
ARCHBISHOP'S PARK

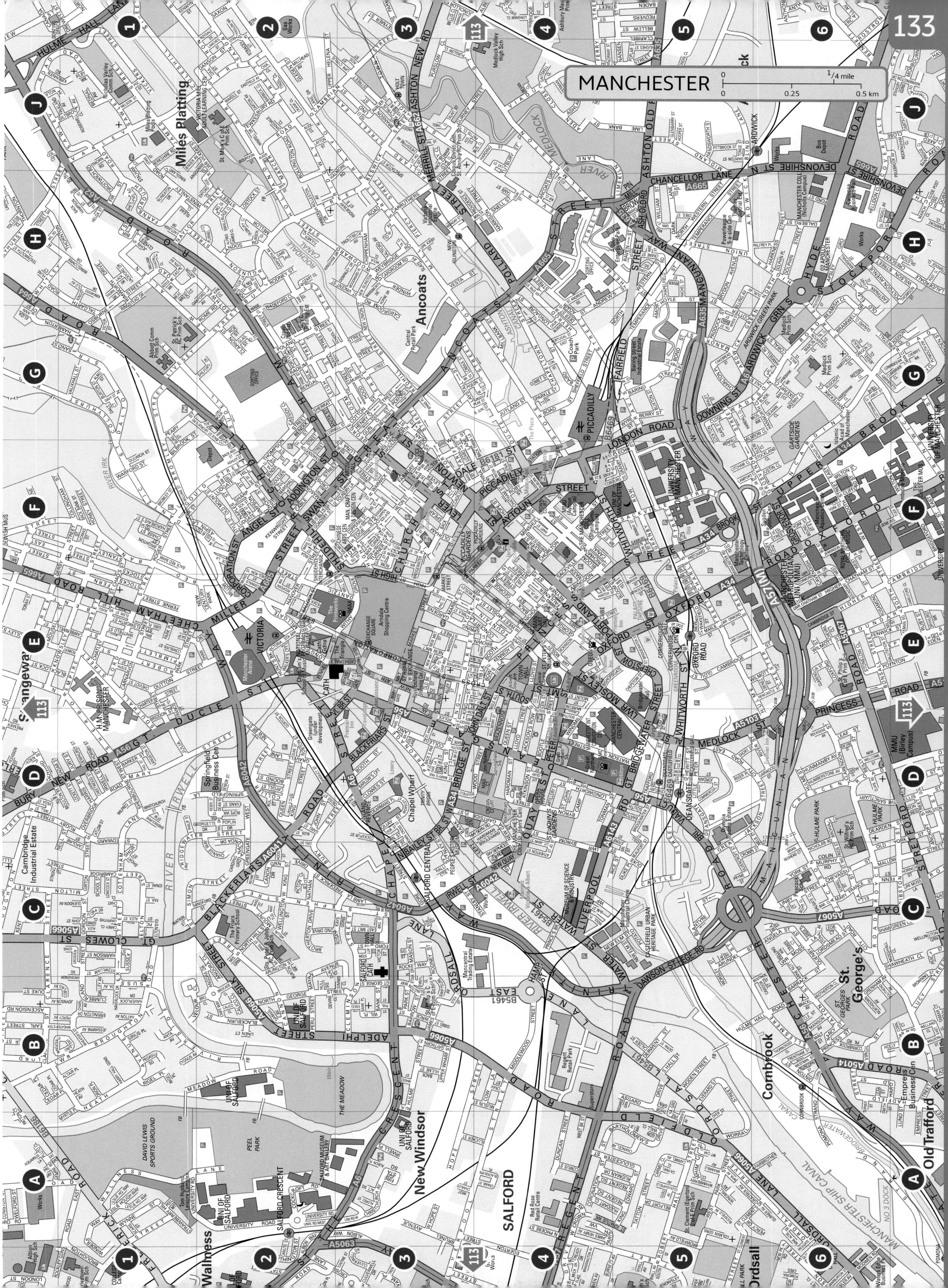
MANCHESTER
0 1/4 mile
0 0.25 0.5 km
Miles Platting
Ancoats
Ardwick
Salford
New Windsor
Cornbrook
Old Trafford
St. George's
Strangeways
Piccadilly
Victoria
Deansgate
Oxford Road
Chapel Wharf
Manchester Arena
Arndale Shopping Centre
Exchange Square
Manchester Metropolitan University
University of Manchester
Museum of Science & Industry
Castlefield Urban Heritage Park
Manchester Central
Piccadilly Gardens
Rochdale Canal
River Irwell
River Medlock
Manchester Ship Canal
Peel Park
David Lewis Sports Ground
The Meadow
Univ. of Salford
H.M. Prison Manchester
Cambridge Industrial Estate
Springfield Business Cen
Hulme Park
Central Retail Park
Empress Business Cen
Regent Retail Park
Red Rose Retail Centre
Mancentral Trading Estate
Gartside Gardens
Cheetham Hill Road
Bury New Road
Great Ancoats Street
Oldham Road
Rochdale Road
Ashton Old Road
Hyde Road
Stockport Road
Upper Brook Street
Oxford Road
Princess Road
Chester Road
Regent Road
Trinity Way
Mancunian Way
Deansgate
Chapel Street
London Road
Whitworth Street
Portland Street
Great Ducie Street
Ordsall Lane
Water Street
Liverpool Road
Bridgewater Street
Medlock Street
Stretford Road
Hulme Hall Road
Chancellor Lane
Devonshire St N
Downing Street
Cambridge Street
Blackfriars Road
Adelphi Street
Great Clowes Street
Salford Crescent
Dawson St
Egerton St
A6 A34 A56 A57(M) A62 A635 A664 A665 A6042 A5063 A5066 A5067 A5103 B6469 B6181 B5461
113

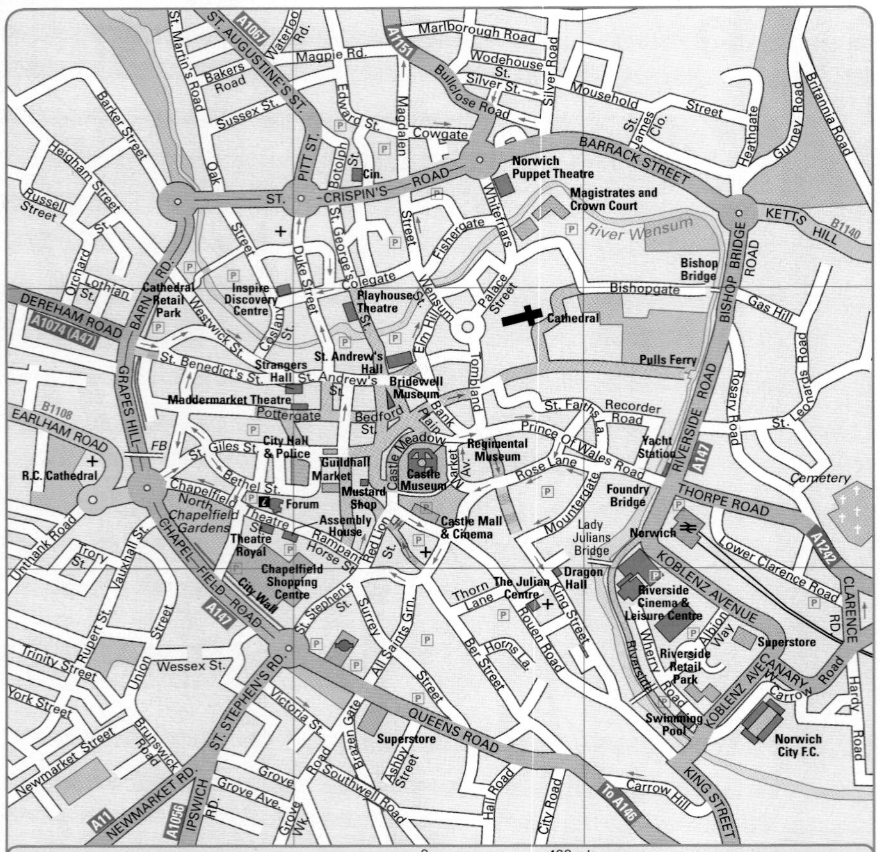

NORWICH

Appears on main map page 45

0 400 yds
0 400m

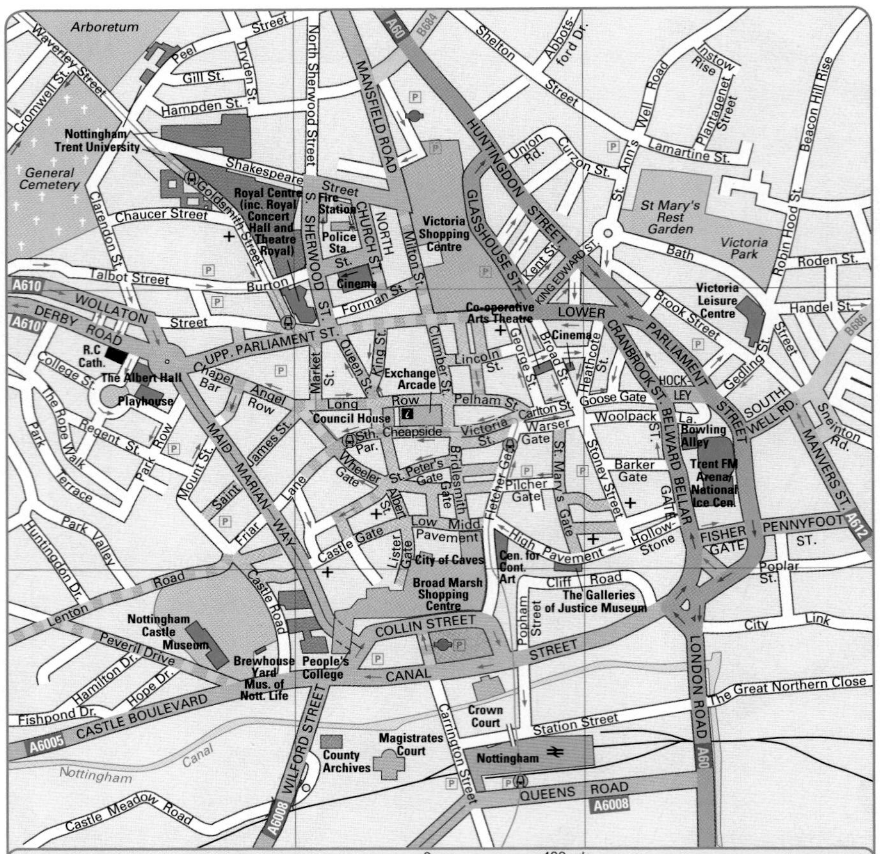

NOTTINGHAM

Appears on main map page 41

0 400 yds
0 400m

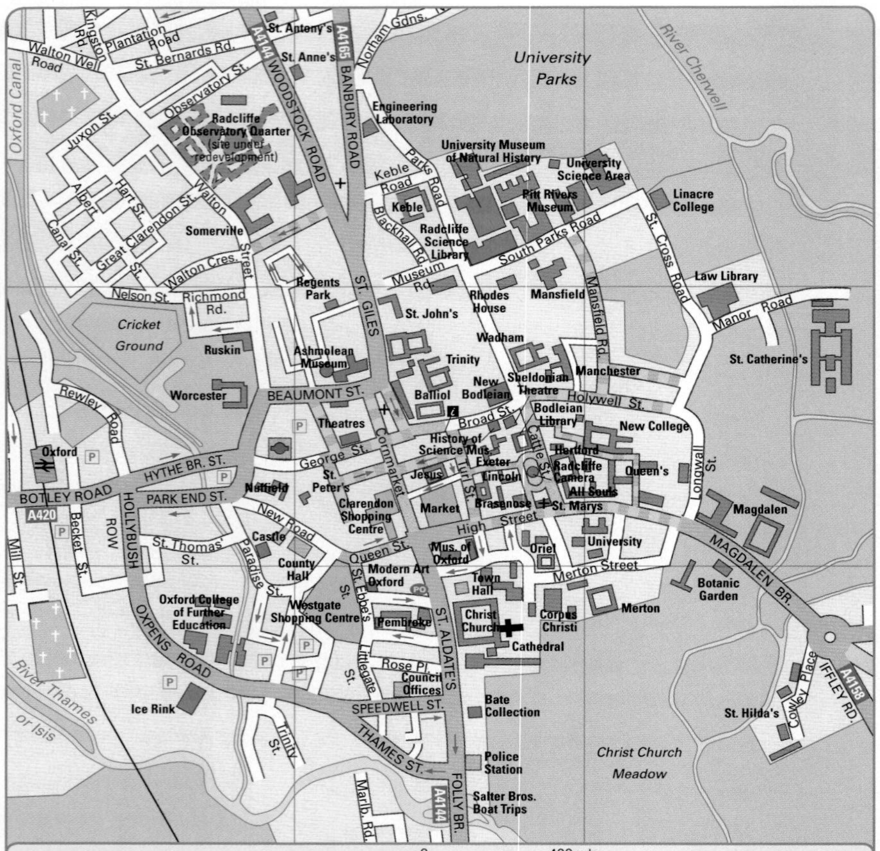

OXFORD

Appears on main map page 21

0 400 yds
0 400m

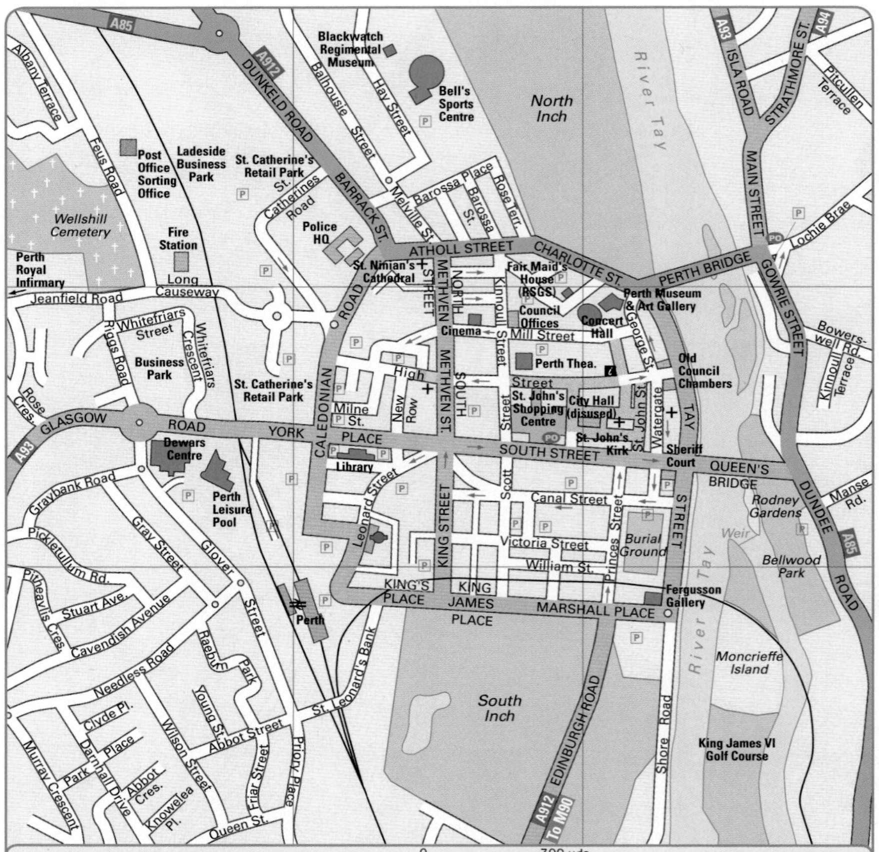

PERTH

Appears on main map page 80

0 300 yds
0 300m

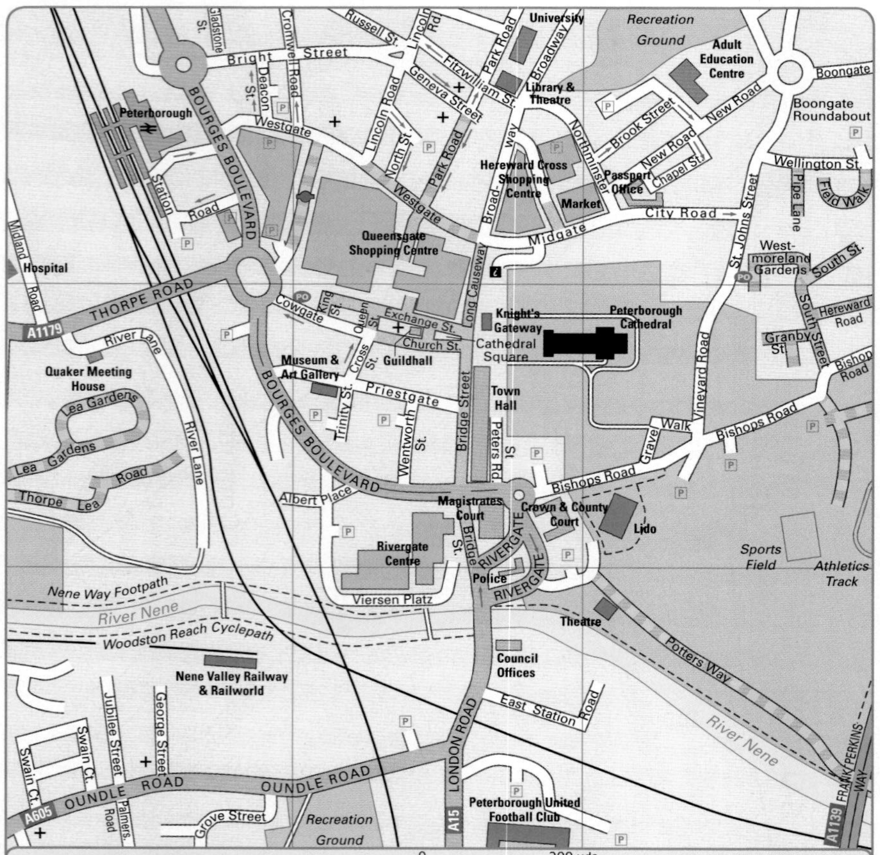

PETERBOROUGH

Appears on main map pages 42/43

0 200 yds
0 200m

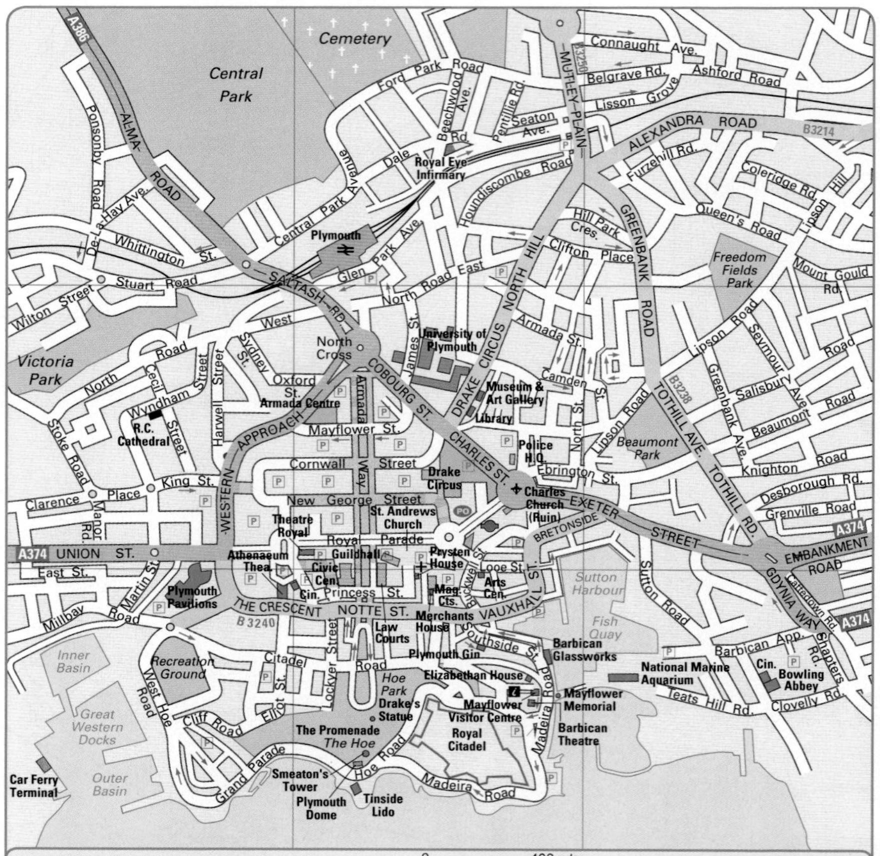

PLYMOUTH

Appears on main map pages 4/5

0 400 yds
0 400m

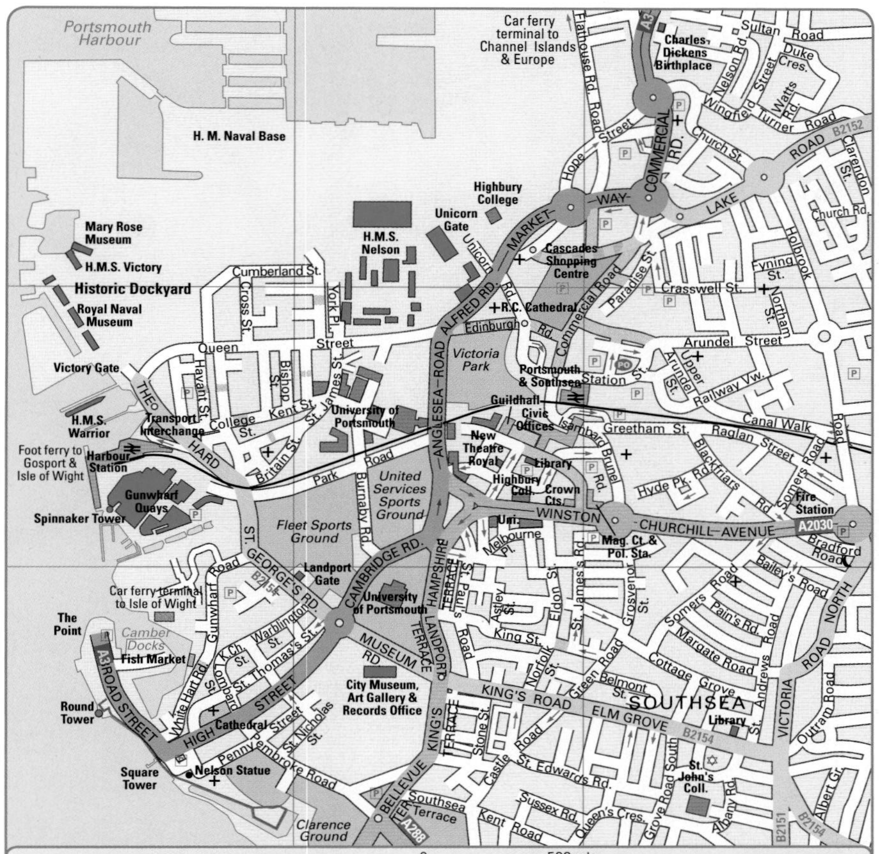

PORTSMOUTH

0 ____ 500 yds
0 ____ 500m

Appears on main map page 11

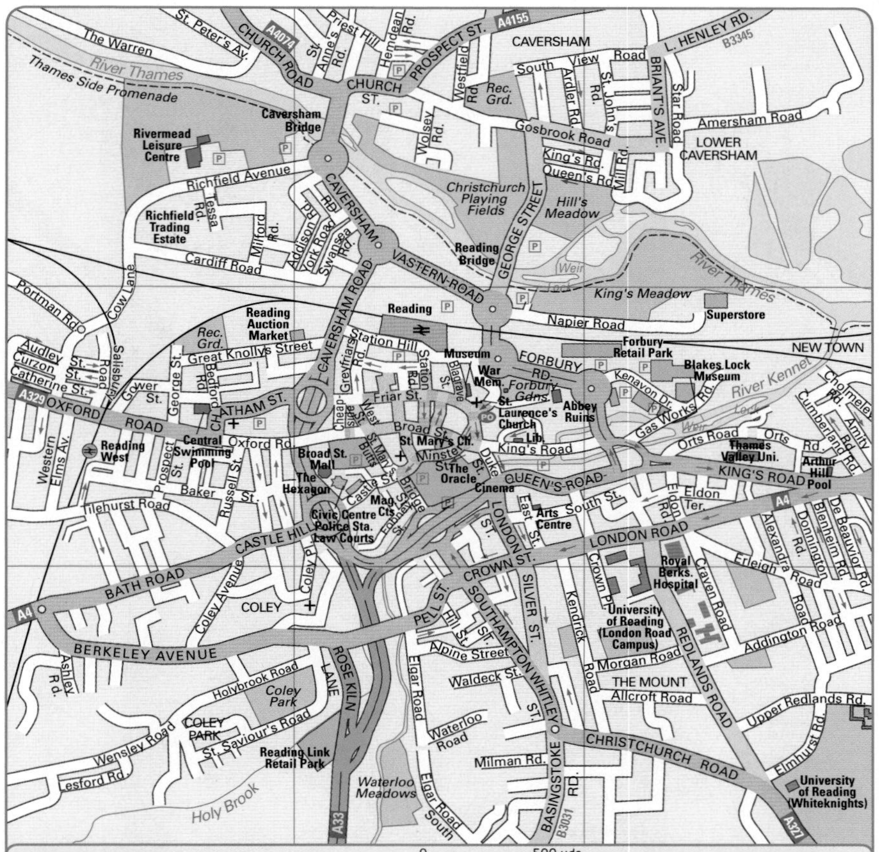

READING

0 ____ 500 yds
0 ____ 500m

Appears on main map page 21

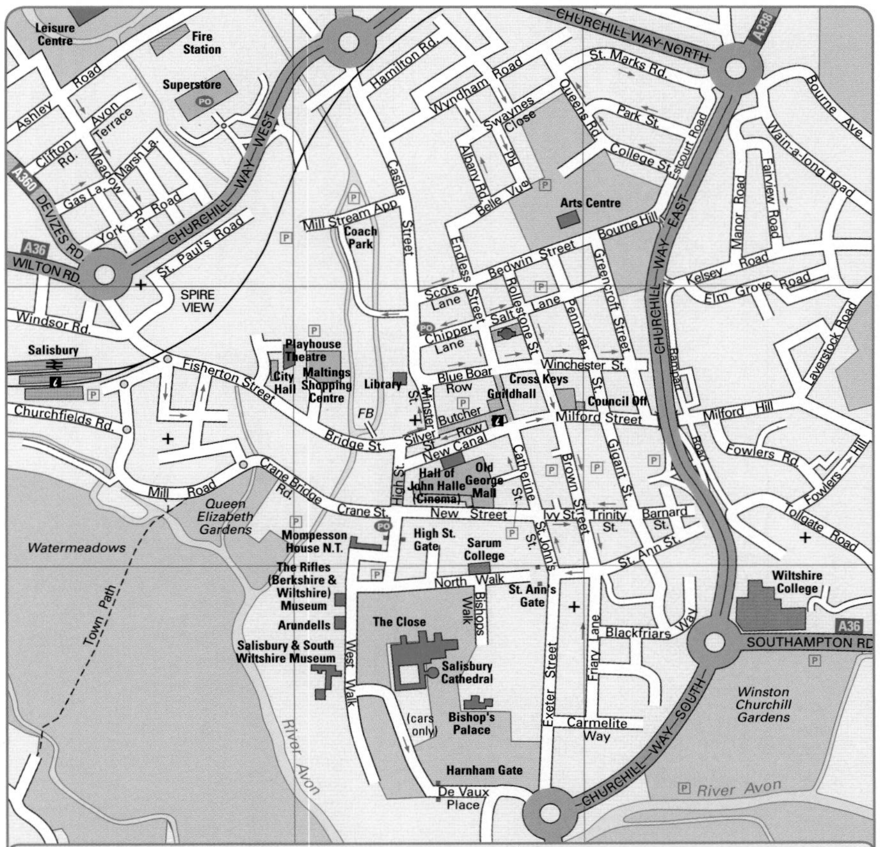

SALISBURY

0 ____ 200 yds
0 ____ 200m

Appears on main map page 10

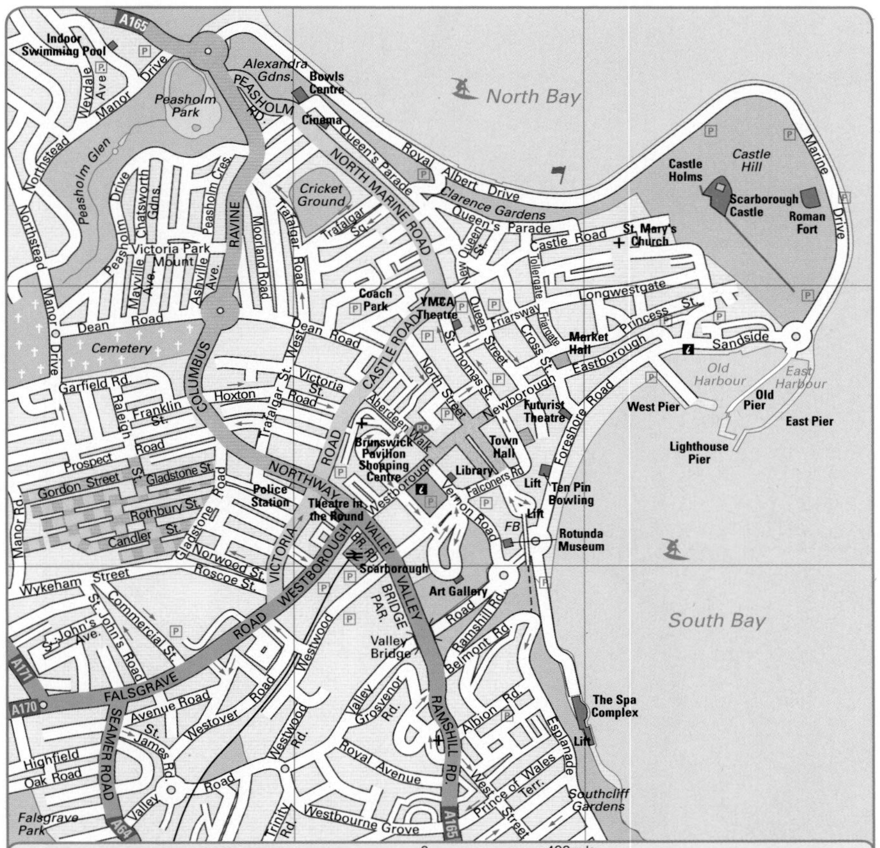

SCARBOROUGH

0 ____ 400 yds
0 ____ 400m

Appears on main map page 59

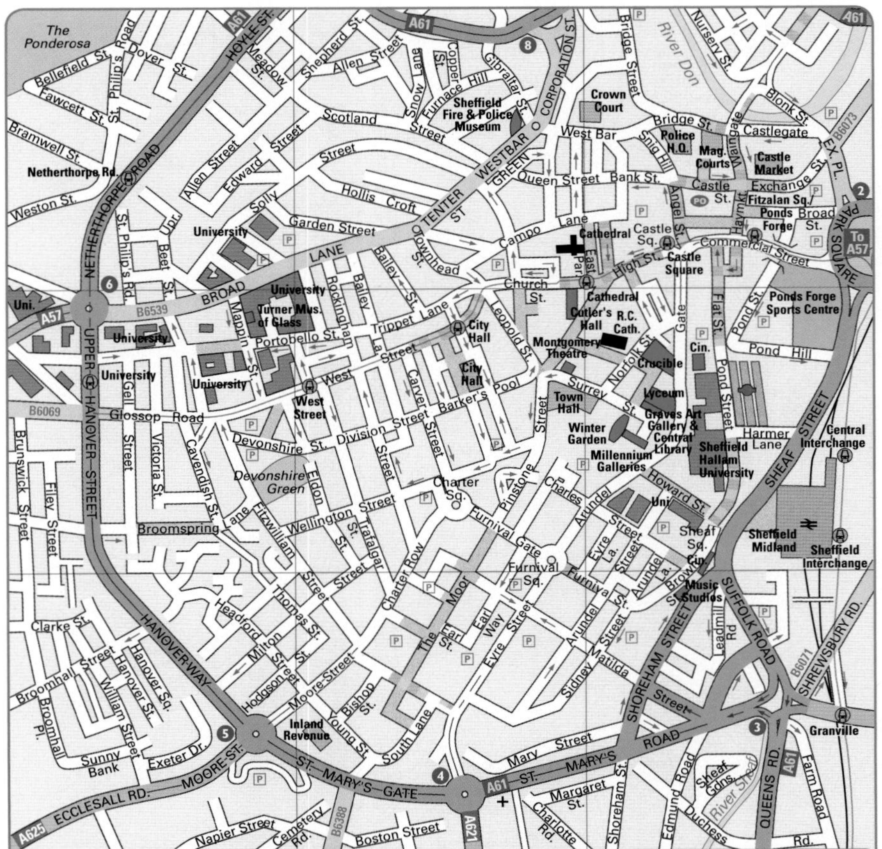

SHEFFIELD

0 ____ 300 yds
0 ____ 300m

Appears on main map page 51

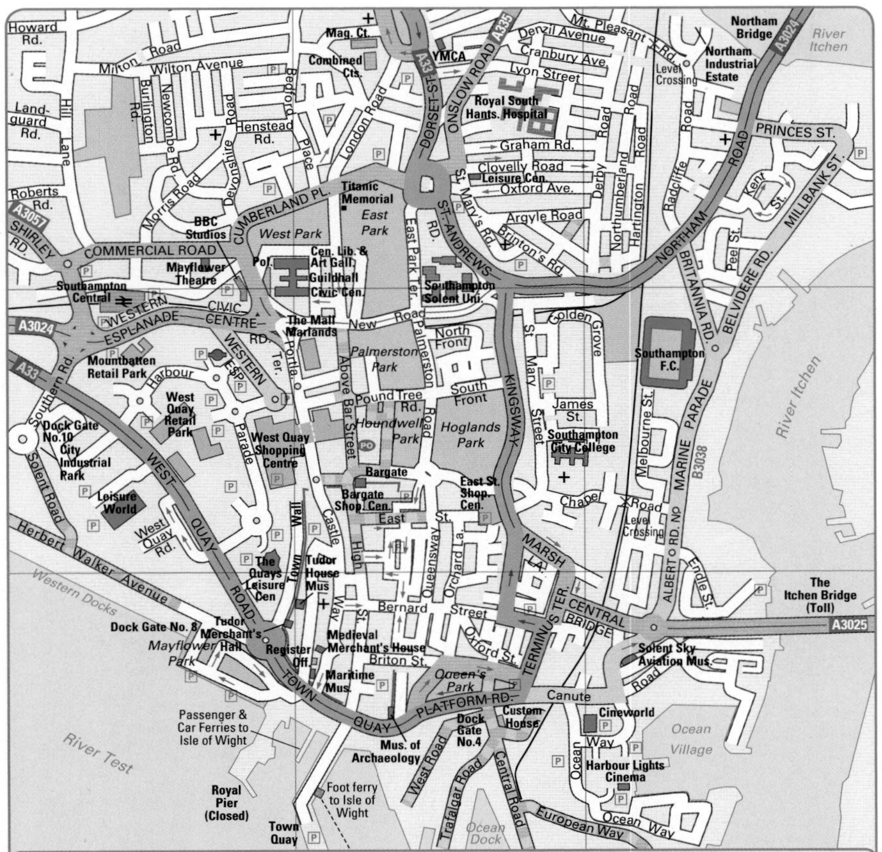

SOUTHAMPTON

0 ____ 400 yds
0 ____ 400m

Appears on main map page 11

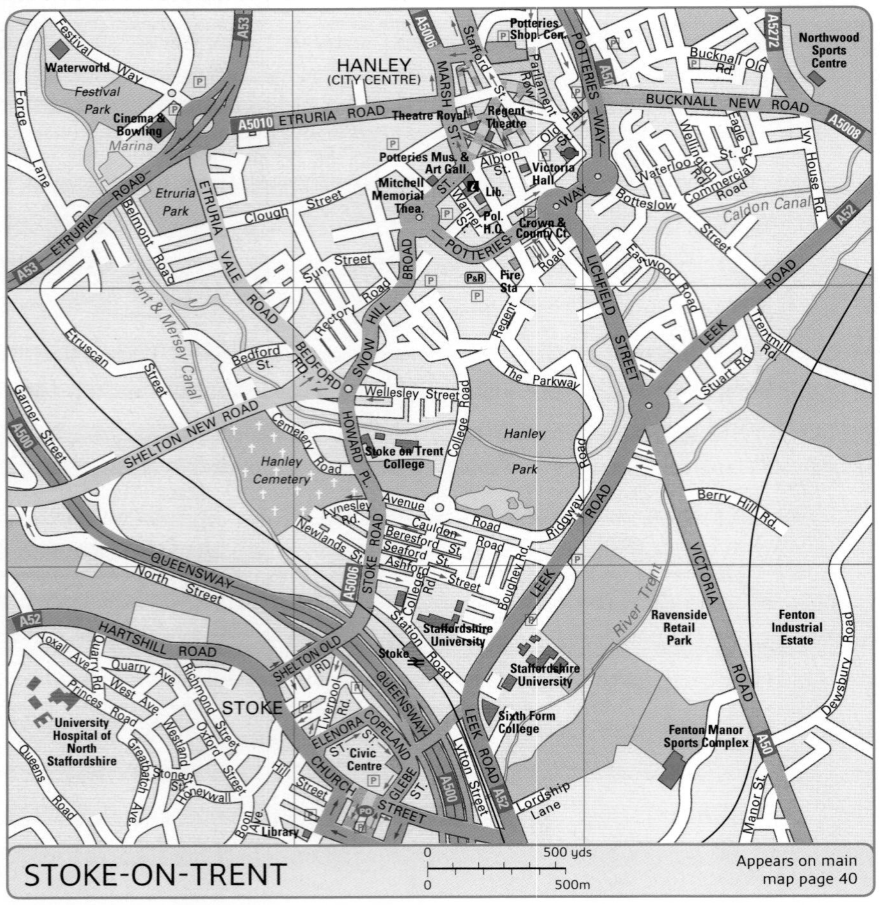

STOKE-ON-TRENT

Appears on main map page 40

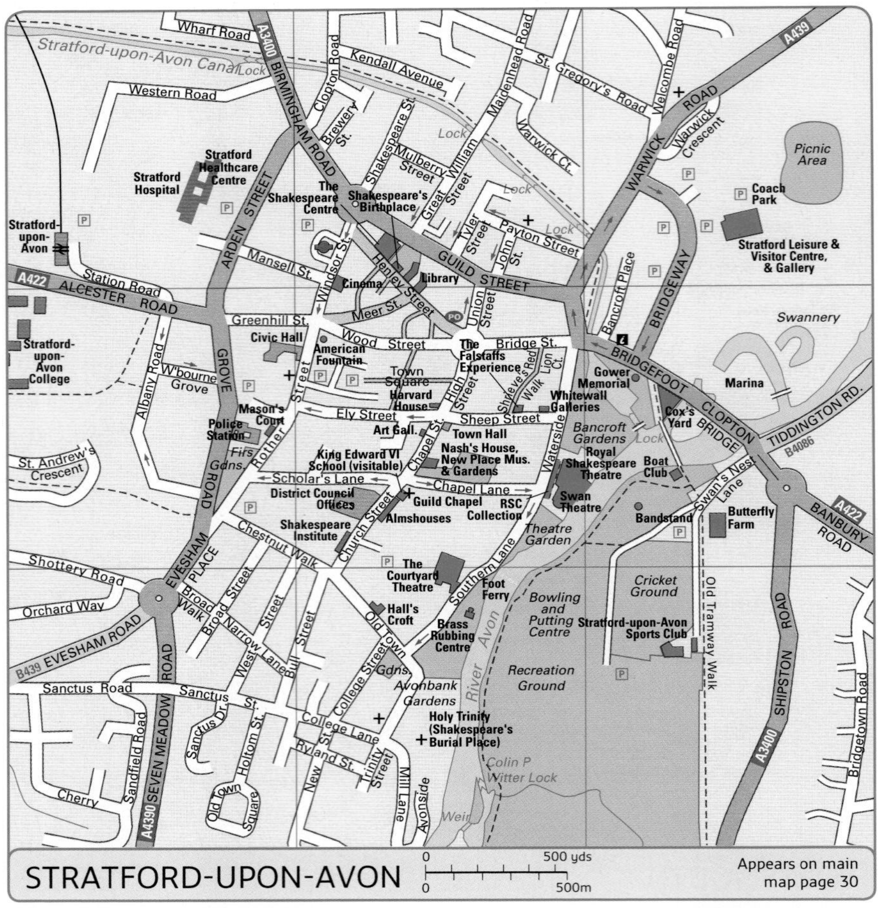

STRATFORD-UPON-AVON

Appears on main map page 30

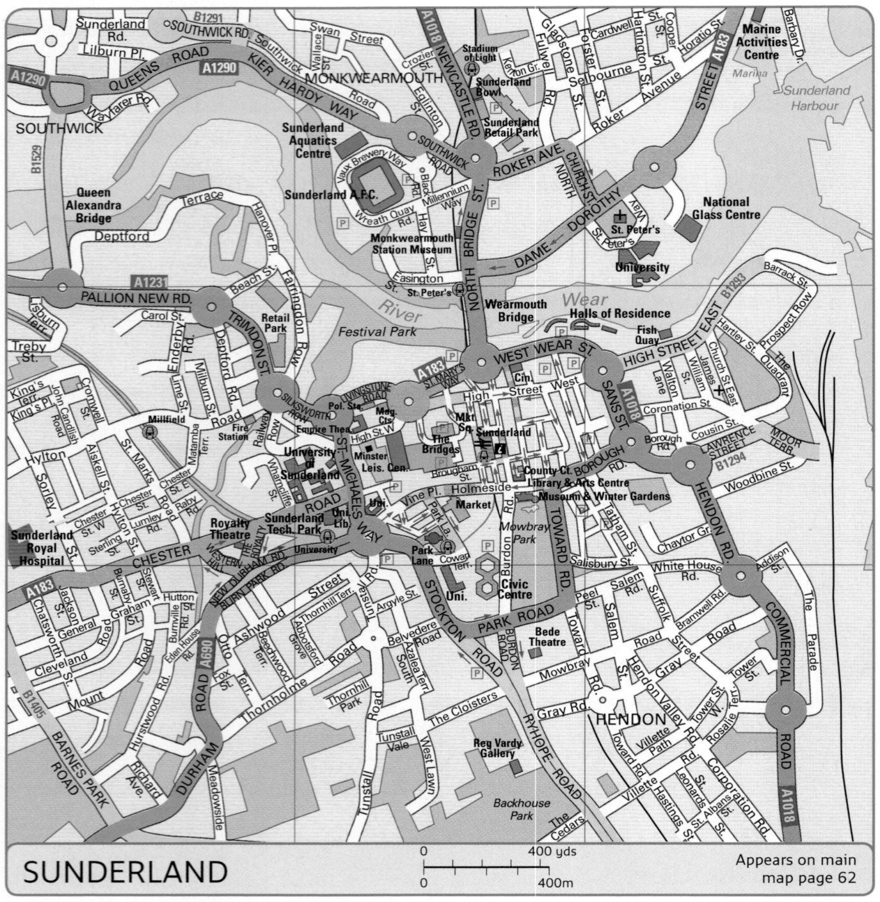

SUNDERLAND

Appears on main map page 62

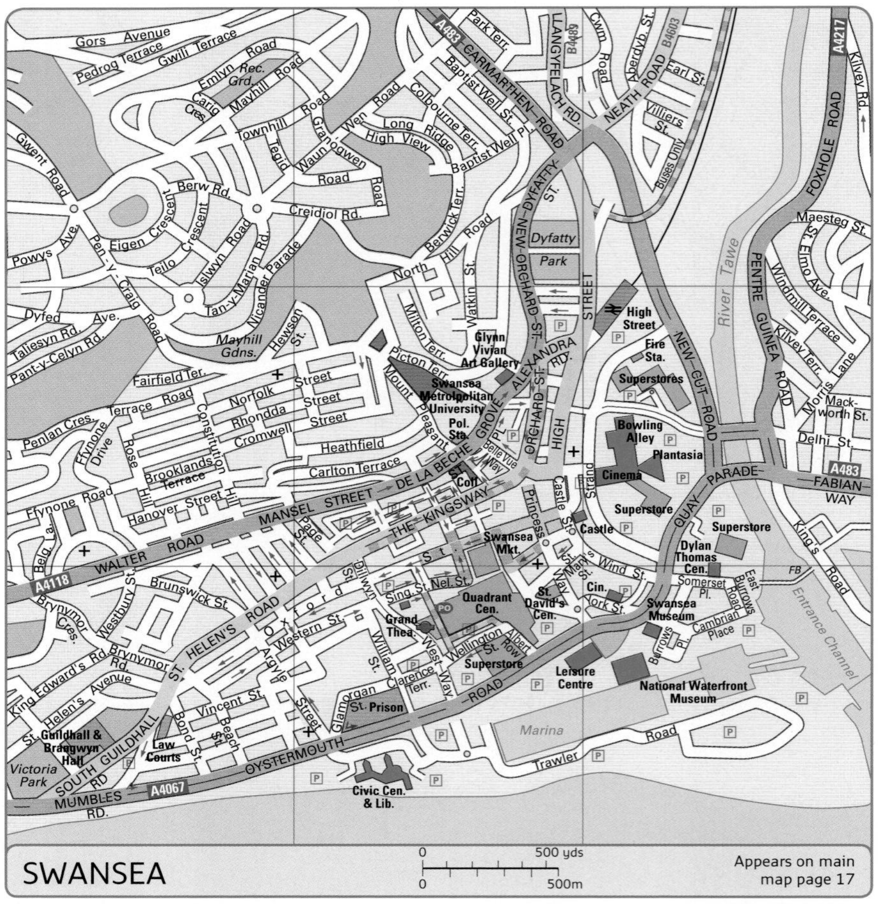

SWANSEA

Appears on main map page 17

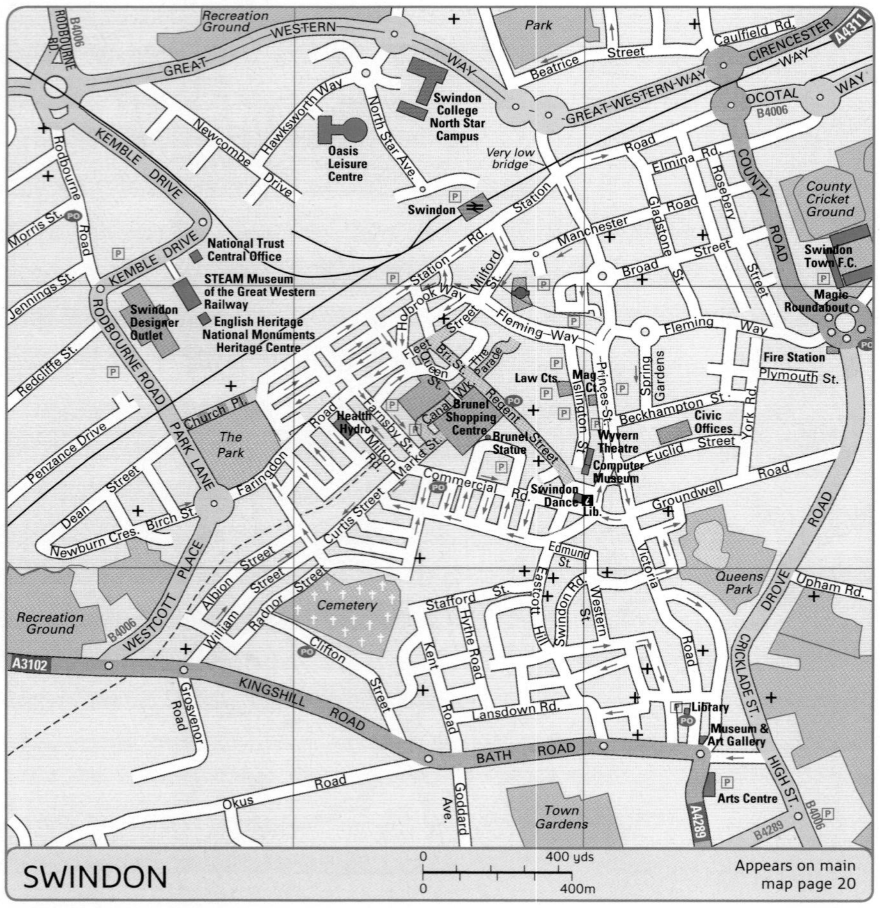

SWINDON

Appears on main map page 20

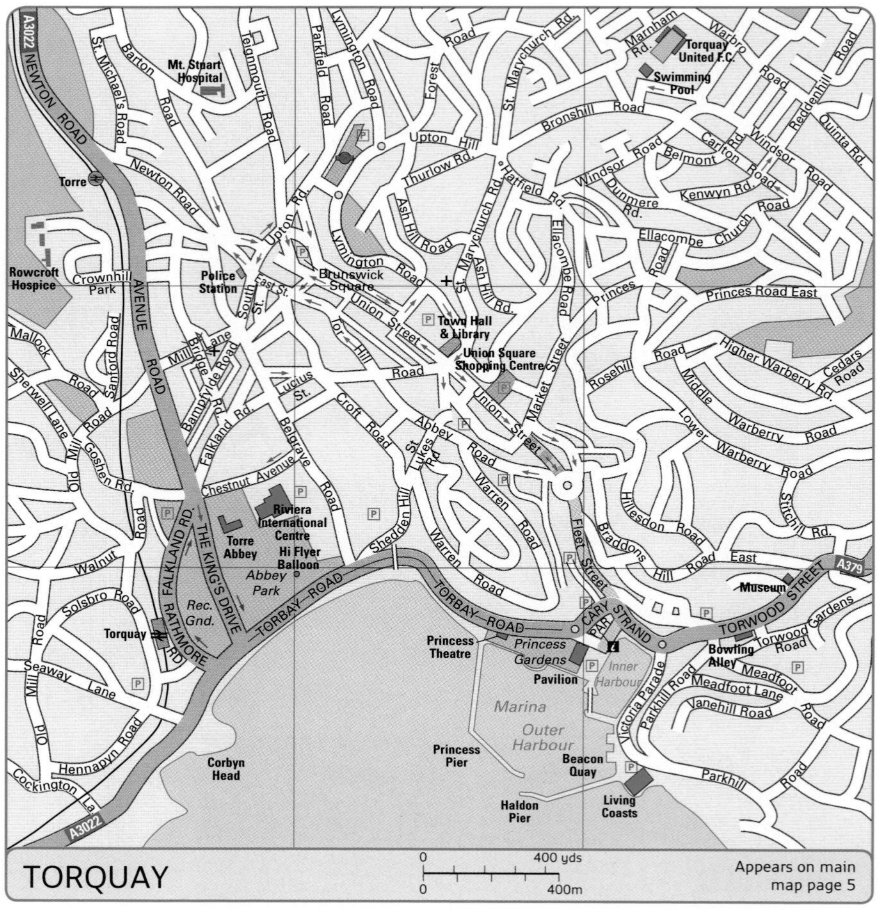

TORQUAY

Appears on main map page 5

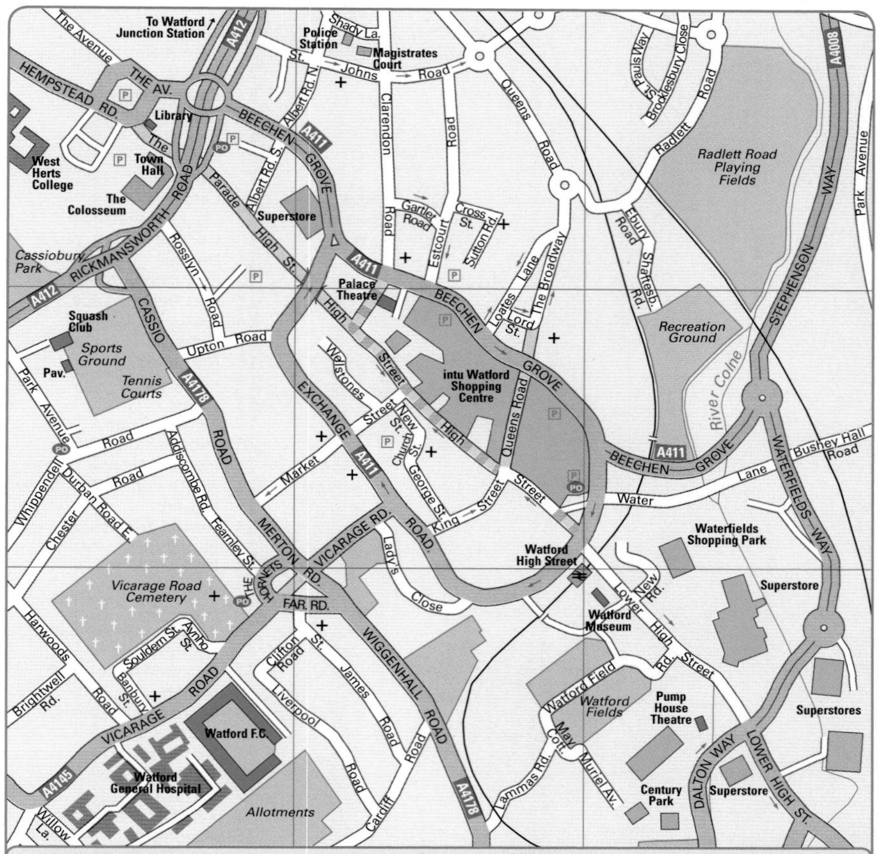

WATFORD

0   200 yds
0   200m

Appears on main map page 22

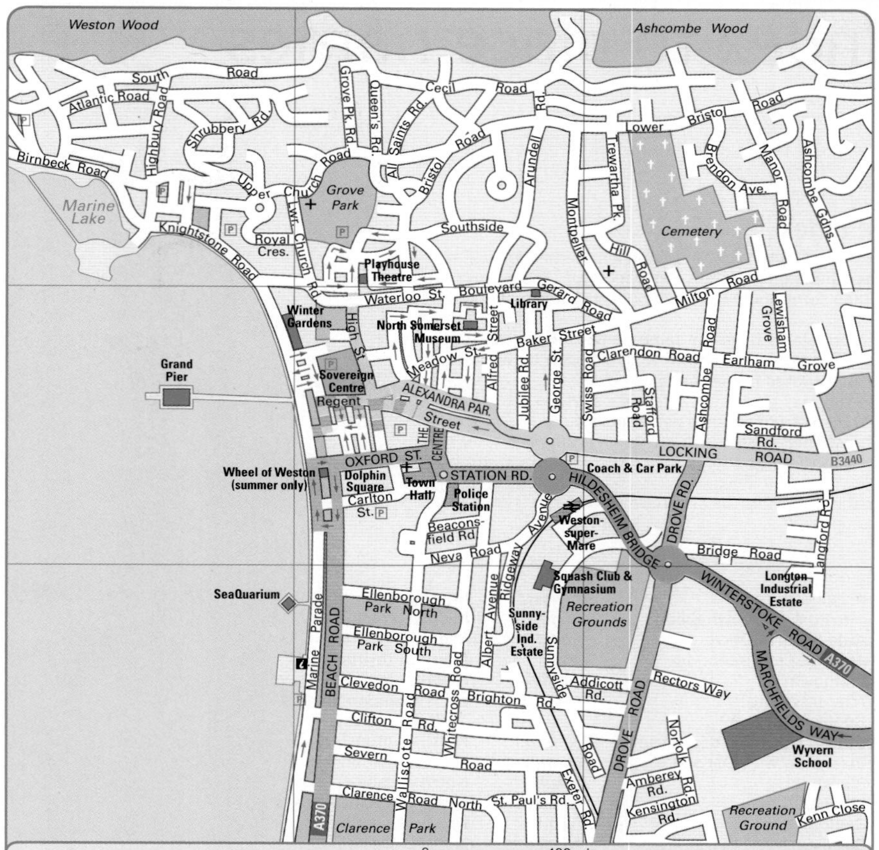

WESTON-SUPER-MARE

0   400 yds
0   400m

Appears on main map page 19

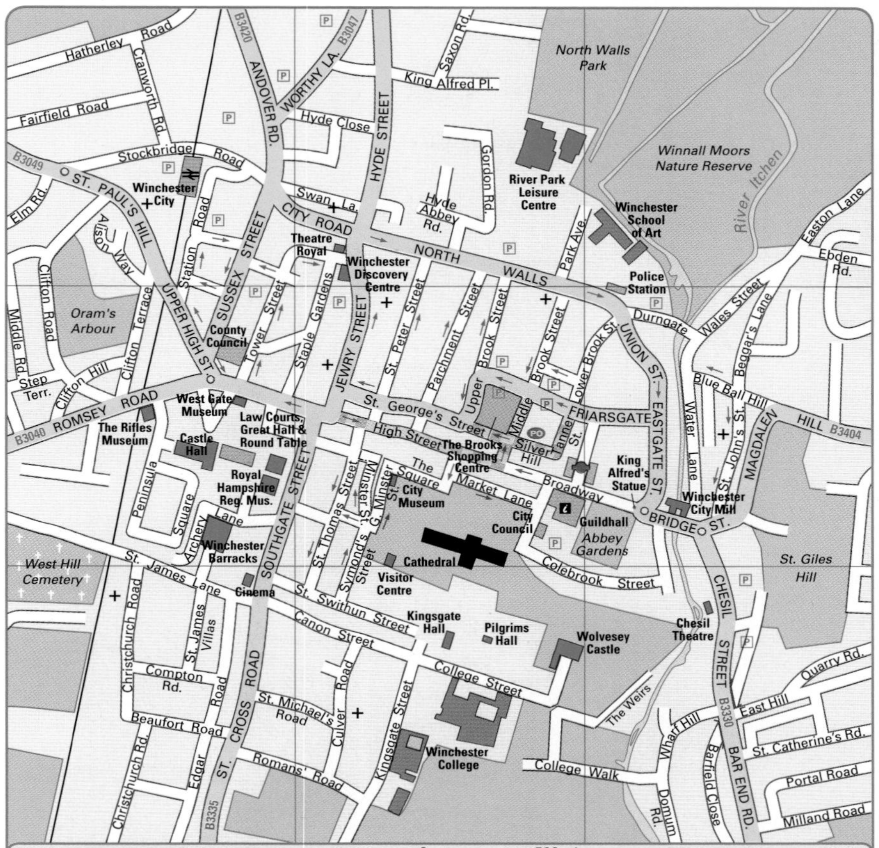

WINCHESTER

0   500 yds
0   500m

Appears on main map page 11

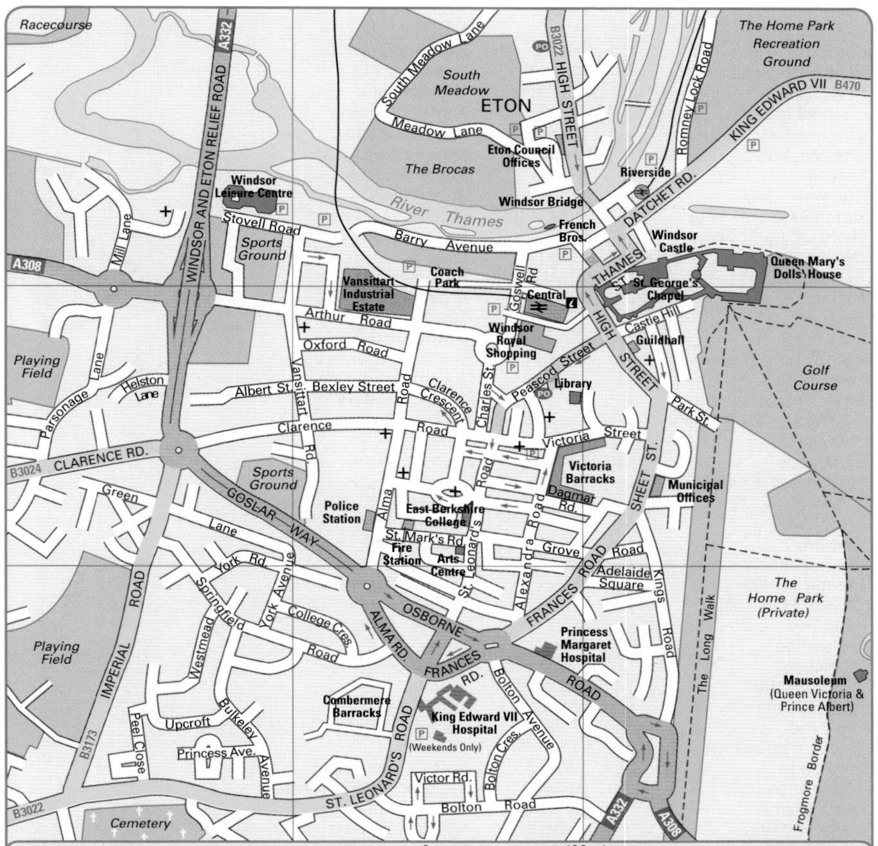

WINDSOR

0   400 yds
0   400m

Appears on main map page 22

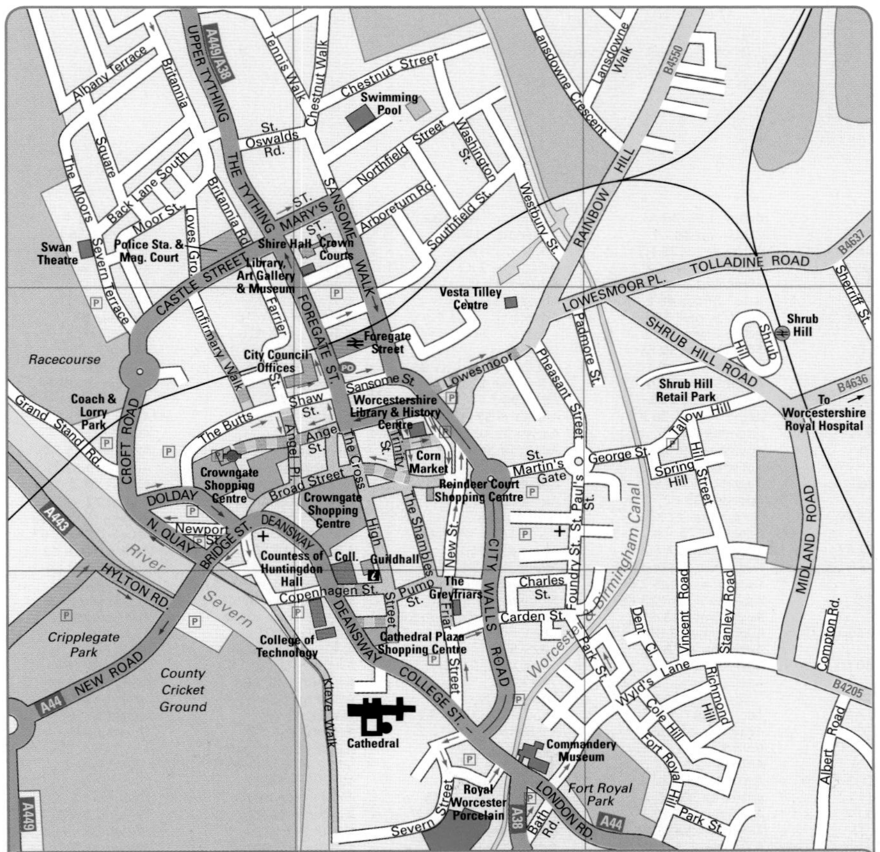

WORCESTER

0   200 yds
0   200m

Appears on main map page 29

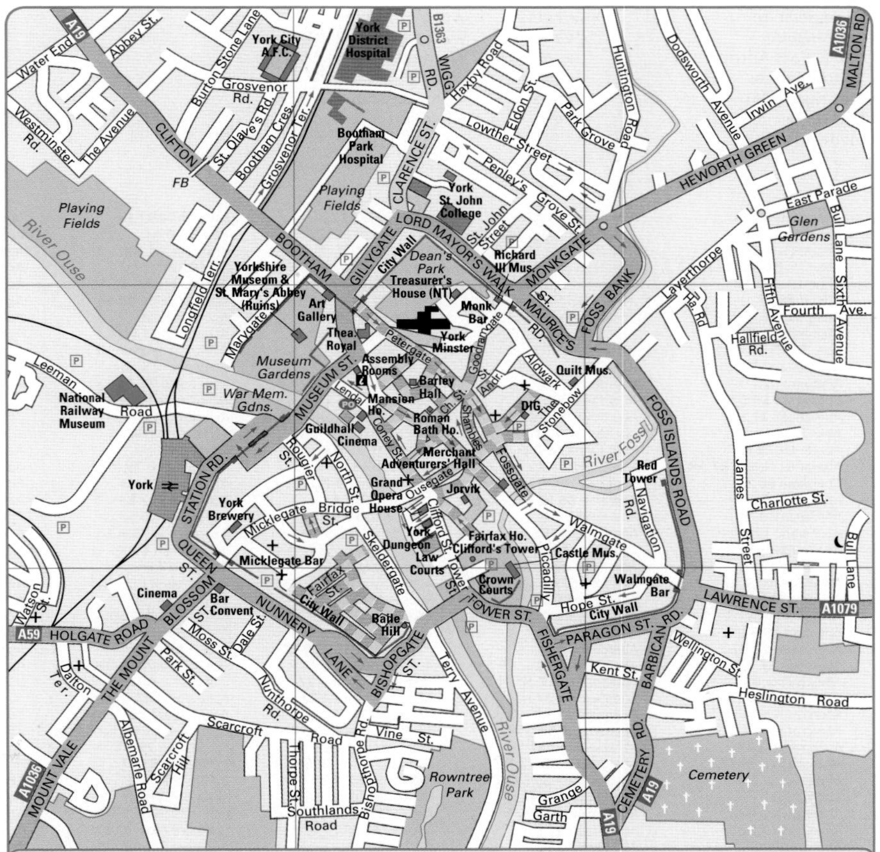

YORK

0   400 yds
0   400m

Appears on main map page 58

Using the index

Place, place of interest and World Heritage Site names are followed by a **page number** and a grid reference in black type. The feature can be found on the map somewhere within the grid square shown.

Where two or more places have the same name the abbreviated *county* or *unitary authority* names are shown to distinguish between them. A list of these abbreviated names appears below.

A selection of the most popular places of interest are shown within the index in blue type. Their postcode information is supplied after the county / unitary authority names to aid integration with satnav systems.

Sites with World Heritage Status are shown within the index in maroon type.

A&B	Argyll & Bute	Mersey	Merseyside
A&N	Antrim & Newtownabbey	Middl	Middlesbrough
A&NDown	Ards & North Down	Midlo	Midlothian
AB&C	Armagh City, Banbridge & Craigavon	Mon	Monmouthshire
		NM&D	Newry, Mourne & Down
Aber	Aberdeenshire	Na H-E. Siar	Na H-Eileanan Siar (Western Isles)
B&H	Brighton & Hove		
B&NESom	Bath & North East Somerset	N'hants	Northamptonshire
B'burn	Blackburn with Darwen	N'umb	Northumberland
B'pool	Blackpool	NAyr	North Ayrshire
BGwent	Blaenau Gwent	NELincs	North East Lincolnshire
Bed	Bedford	NLan	North Lanarkshire
Bourne	Bournemouth	NLincs	North Lincolnshire
BrackF	Bracknell Forest	NPT	Neath Port Talbot
Bucks	Buckinghamshire	NSom	North Somerset
CC&G	Causeway Coast & Glens	NYorks	North Yorkshire
Caerp	Caerphilly	Norf	Norfolk
Cambs	Cambridgeshire	Nott	Nottingham
Carmar	Carmarthenshire	Notts	Nottinghamshire
CenBeds	Central Bedfordshire	Ork	Orkney
Cere	Ceredigion	Oxon	Oxfordshire
Chanl	Channel Islands	P&K	Perth & Kinross
ChesE	Cheshire East	Pembs	Pembrokeshire
ChesW&C	Cheshire West & Chester	Peter	Peterborough
Corn	Cornwall	Plym	Plymouth
Cumb	Cumbria	Ports	Portsmouth
D&G	Dumfries & Galloway	R&C	Redcar & Cleveland
D&S	Derry City & Strabane	RCT	Rhondda Cynon Taff
Darl	Darlington	Read	Reading
Denb	Denbighshire	Renf	Renfrewshire
Derbys	Derbyshire	Rut	Rutland
Dur	Durham	S'end	Southend-on-Sea
EAyr	East Ayrshire	SAyr	South Ayrshire
EDun	East Dunbartonshire	SGlos	South Gloucestershire
ELoth	East Lothian	SLan	South Lanarkshire
ERenf	East Renfrewshire	SYorks	South Yorkshire
ERid	East Riding of Yorkshire	ScBord	Scottish Borders
ESuss	East Sussex	Shet	Shetland
Edin	Edinburgh	Shrop	Shropshire
F&O	Fermanagh & Omagh	Slo	Slough
Falk	Falkirk	Som	Somerset
Flints	Flintshire	Soton	Southampton
Glas	Glasgow	Staffs	Staffordshire
Glos	Gloucestershire	Stir	Stirling
GtLon	Greater London	Stock	Stockton-on-Tees
GtMan	Greater Manchester	Stoke	Stoke-on-Trent
Gwyn	Gwynedd	Suff	Suffolk
Hants	Hampshire	Surr	Surrey
Hart	Hartlepool	Swan	Swansea
Here	Herefordshire	Swin	Swindon
Herts	Hertfordshire	T&W	Tyne & Wear
High	Highland	Tel&W	Telford & Wrekin
Hull	Kingston upon Hull	Thur	Thurrock
Invcly	Inverclyde	VGlam	Vale of Glamorgan
IoA	Isle of Anglesey	W&M	Windsor & Maidenhead
IoM	Isle of Man	W'ham	Wokingham
IoS	Isles of Scilly	WBerks	West Berkshire
IoW	Isle of Wight	WDun	West Dunbartonshire
L&C	Lisburn & Castlereagh	WLoth	West Lothian
Lancs	Lancashire	WMid	West Midlands
Leic	Leicester	WSuss	West Sussex
Leics	Leicestershire	WYorks	West Yorkshire
Lincs	Lincolnshire	Warks	Warwickshire
M&EAnt	Mid & East Antrim	Warr	Warrington
MK	Milton Keynes	Wilts	Wiltshire
MTyd	Merthyr Tydfil	Worcs	Worcestershire
MUlst	Mid Ulster	Wrex	Wrexham
Med	Medway		

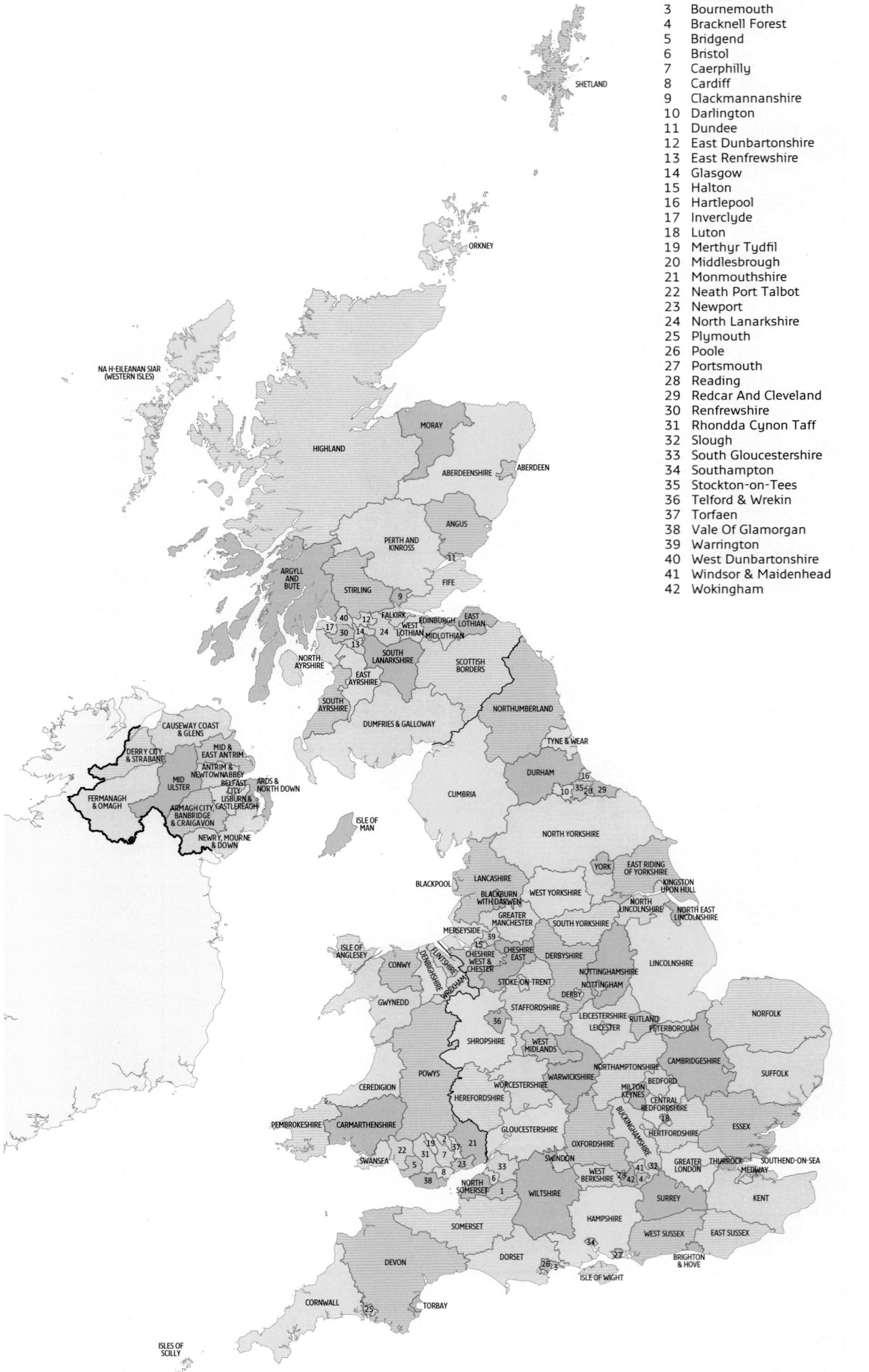

1	Bath & North East Somerset
2	Blaenau Gwent
3	Bournemouth
4	Bracknell Forest
5	Bridgend
6	Bristol
7	Caerphilly
8	Cardiff
9	Clackmannanshire
10	Darlington
11	Dundee
12	East Dunbartonshire
13	East Renfrewshire
14	Glasgow
15	Halton
16	Hartlepool
17	Inverclyde
18	Luton
19	Merthyr Tydfil
20	Middlesbrough
21	Monmouthshire
22	Neath Port Talbot
23	Newport
24	North Lanarkshire
25	Plymouth
26	Poole
27	Portsmouth
28	Reading
29	Redcar And Cleveland
30	Renfrewshire
31	Rhondda Cynon Taff
32	Slough
33	South Gloucestershire
34	Southampton
35	Stockton-on-Tees
36	Telford & Wrekin
37	Torfaen
38	Vale Of Glamorgan
39	Warrington
40	West Dunbartonshire
41	Windsor & Maidenhead
42	Wokingham

Albury Herts 33 H6
Albury Oxon 21 K1
Albury Surr 22 D7
Albury End 33 H6
Albury Heath 22 D7
Albyfield 61 G1
Alcaig 83 R5
Alcaston 38 D7
Alcester 30 B3
Alciston 13 J6
Alcombe 7 H1
Alconbury 32 E1
Alconbury Hill 32 E1
Alconbury Weston 32 E1
Aldborough Norf 45 F2
Aldborough NYorks 57 K3
Aldbourne 21 F4
Aldbrough 59 J6
Aldbrough St. John 62 C5
Aldbury 32 C7
Aldclune 80 E4
Aldeburgh 35 J3
Aldeby 45 J6
Aldenham 22 E2
Aldenham Country Park Herts WD6 3AT 102 D1
Alderbury 10 C2
Alderford 45 F4
Aldergrove 92 G9
Alderholt 10 C3
Alderley 20 A2
Alderley Edge 49 H5
Aldermaston 21 J5
Aldermaston Wharf 21 K5
Alderminster 30 D4
Alderney 3 K4
Alderney Airport 3 J4
Alder's End 29 F5
Aldersey Green 48 D7
Aldershot 22 B6
Alderton Glos 29 J5
Alderton N'hants 31 J4
Alderton Suff 35 H4
Alderton Wilts 20 B3
Alderwasley 51 F7
Aldfield 57 H3
Aldford 48 D7
Aldham Essex 34 D6
Aldham Suff 34 E4
Aldie 85 Q6
Aldingbourne 12 C6
Aldingham 55 F2
Aldington Kent 15 F4
Aldington Worcs 30 B4
Aldochlay 74 B1
Aldons 67 F5
Aldorough 92 F4
Aldous's Corner 45 H7
Aldreth 33 H1
Aldridge 40 C5
Aldringham 35 J2
Aldsworth Glos 20 E1
Aldsworth WSuss 11 J4
Aldunie 84 H8
Aldwark Derbys 50 E7
Aldwark NYorks 57 K3
Aldwick 12 C7
Aldwincle 42 D7
Aldworth 21 J4
Alexandra Palace GtLon N22 7AY 104 A3
Alexandria 74 B3
Aley 7 K2
Aley Green 32 D7
Alfardisworthy 6 A4
Alfington 7 K6
Alfold 12 D3
Alfold Crossways 12 D3
Alford Aber 85 K9
Alford Lincs 53 H5
Alford Som 9 F1
Alfreton 51 G7
Alfrick 29 G3
Alfrick Pound 29 G3
Alfriston 13 J6
Algarkirk 43 F2
Alhampton 9 F1
Alkborough 58 E7
Alkerton 30 E4
Alkham 15 H3
Alkington 38 E2
Alkmonton 40 D2
All Cannings 20 D5
All Saints South Elmham 45 H7
All Stretton 38 D6
Allaleigh 5 J5
Allangillfoot 69 H4
Allanton D&G 68 E5
Allanton EAyr 74 E7
Allanton NLan 75 G5
Allanton ScBord 77 G5
Allanton SLan 75 F5
Allbrook 11 F2
Allendale Town 61 K1
Allenheads 61 K2
Allen's Green 33 H7
Allensford 62 A1
Allensford Country Park Dur DH8 9BA 62 A1
Allensmore 28 D5
Allenton 41 F2
Aller 8 D2
Allerby 60 B3
Allercombe 7 J6
Allerford Devon 6 C7
Allerford Som 7 H1
Allerston 58 E1
Allerthorpe 58 D5
Allerton Mersey 48 D4
Allerton WYorks 57 G6
Allerton Bywater 57 K7
Allerton Mauleverer 57 K4
Allesley 40 E7
Allestree 41 F2
Allet Common 2 E4
Allexton 42 B5
Allgreave 49 J6
Allhallows 24 E4
Allhallows-on-Sea 24 E4
Alligin Shuas 83 J5
Allimore Green 40 A4
Allington Dorset 8 D5
Allington Lincs 42 B1
Allington Wilts 10 D1
Allington Wilts 20 B4
Allington Wilts 20 D5
Allistragh 93 D12
Allithwaite 55 G2
Allnabad 86 G5
Alloa 75 G1
Allonby 60 B2
Allostock 49 G5
Alloway 67 H2
Allowenshay 8 C3
Allscot 39 G6
Allscott 39 F4
Allt na h-Airbhe 83 M1
Alltachonaich 79 J5
Alltforgan 37 J3
Alltmawr 27 K4
Alltnacaillich 86 G5
Alltwalis 17 H2
Alltwen 18 A1
Alltyblaca 17 J1
Allwood Green 34 E1
Almeley 28 C3
Almeley Wooton 28 C3
Almer 9 J5
Almington 39 G2
Almiston Cross 6 B3
Almondbank 80 F8
Almondbury 50 D1
Almondell & Calderwood Country Park WLoth EH52 5PE 75 J4
Almondsbury 19 K3
Alne 57 K3
Alness 84 A4
Alnham 70 E2
Alnmouth 71 H2
Alnwick 71 G2
Alnwick Garden, The N'umb NE66 1YU 71 G2
Alperton 22 E3
Alphamstone 34 C5
Alpheton 34 C3
Alphington 7 H6
Alport 50 E6
Alpraham 48 E7
Alresford 34 E6
Alrewas 40 D4
Alsager 49 G7
Alsagers Bank 40 A1
Alsop en le Dale 50 D7
Alston Cumb 61 J2
Alston Devon 8 C4
Alston Sutton 19 H6
Alstone Glos 29 J5
Alstone Som 19 G7
Alstone Staffs 40 A4
Alstonefield 50 D7
Alswear 7 F3
Alt 49 J2
Altaghoney 90 M6
Altagoaghan 91 L12
Altanduin 87 L7
Altarnun 4 C2
Altass 86 H9
Altens 85 P10
Alterwall 87 Q3
Altham 56 C6
Althorne 25 F2
Althorp House N'hants NN7 4HQ 31 H2
Althorpe 52 B2
Alticry 64 C5
Altishane 90 L7
Altmartin 91 L13
Altnafeadh 79 P5
Altnaharra 86 H6
Altnamackan 93 D14
Altofts 57 J7
Alton Derbys 51 F6
Alton Hants 11 J1
Alton Staffs 40 C1
Alton Barnes 20 E5
Alton Pancras 9 G4
Alton Priors 20 E5
Alton Towers Leisure Park Staffs ST10 4DB 40 C1
Alton Water Reservoir Suff IP9 2RY 35 F5
Altrincham 49 G4
Alva 75 G1
Alvanley 48 D5
Alvaston 41 F2
Alvechurch 30 B1
Alvecote 40 E5
Alvediston 9 J2
Alveley 39 G7
Alverdiscott 6 D3
Alverstoke 11 H5
Alverstone 11 G6
Alverthorpe 57 J7
Alverton 42 A1
Alves 84 F4
Alvescot 21 F1
Alveston SGlos 19 K3
Alveston Warks 30 D3
Alvie 84 C10
Alvingham 53 G3
Alvington 19 K1
Alwalton 42 E6
Alweston 9 F3
Alwington 6 C3
Alwinton 70 E3
Alwoodley 57 J5
Alwoodley Gates 57 J5
Alyth 80 H6
Am Bac (Back) 88 K3
Amalebra 2 B5
Ambaston 41 G2
Amber Hill 43 F1
Ambergate 51 F7
Amberley Glos 20 B1
Amberley WSuss 12 D5
Amble 71 H3
Amblecote 40 A7
Ambleside 60 E6
Ambleston 16 D3
Ambrismore 73 J5
Ambrosden 31 H7
Amcotts 52 B1
Amersham 22 C2
Amerton 40 B3
Amerton Farm Staffs ST18 0LA 40 B3
Amesbury 20 E7
Ameysford 10 B4
Amhuinnsuidhe 88 F7
Amington 40 E5
Amisfield Town 69 F5
Amlwch 46 C3
Amlwch Port 46 C3
Ammanford (Rhydaman) 17 K4
Amotherby 58 D2
Ampfield 10 E2
Ampleforth 58 B2
Ampleforth College 58 B2
Ampney Crucis 20 D1
Ampney St. Mary 20 D1
Ampney St. Peter 20 D1
Amport 21 G7
Ampthill 32 D5
Ampton 34 C1
Amroth 16 E5
Amulree 80 D7
An Cnoc 88 K4
Anaheilt 79 K4
Ancaster 42 C1
Anchor 38 A7
Anchor Corner 44 E6
Ancroft 77 H6
Ancrum 70 B1
Ancton 12 C6
Anderby 53 J5
Anderby Creek 53 J5
Andersea 8 C1
Andersfield 8 B1
Anderson 9 H5
Anderton 49 F5
Anderton Boat Lift ChesW&C CW9 6FW 49 F5
Andover 21 G7
Andover Down 21 G7
Andoversford 30 B7
Andreas 54 D4
Anelog 36 A3
Anfield 48 C3
Angarrack 2 C5
Angarrick 2 E5
Angelbank 28 E1
Angerton 60 D1
Angle 16 B5
Anglers Country Park WYorks WF4 2EB 51 F1
Angler's Retreat 37 G6
Anglesey (Ynys Môn) 46 B4
Anglesey Abbey Cambs CB25 9EJ 33 J2
Anglesey Airport 46 B5
Angmering 12 D6
Angmering-on-Sea 12 D6
Angram NYorks 58 B5
Angram NYorks 61 K7
Anick 70 E7
Anie 80 A9
Animal World & Butterfly House GtMan BL1 5UG 49 F1
Ankerville 84 C3
Anlaby 59 G7
Anmer 44 B3
Anmore 11 H3
Anna Valley 21 G7
Annacloghmullin 93 E14
Annaclone 93 G12
Annacloy 93 K12
Annadorn 93 K12
Annaghbane 93 G13
Annaghmore 93 D10
Annahilt 93 H11
Annalong 93 J15
Annan 69 G7
Annaside 54 D1
Annat A&B 79 M8
Annat High 83 J5
Annbank 67 J1
Anne Hathaway's Cottage Warks CV37 9HH 30 C3
Annesley 51 H7
Annesley Woodhouse 51 G7
Annfield Plain 62 B1
Annisland 74 D4
Annsborough 93 J13
Annscroft 38 D5
Ansdell 55 G7
Ansford 9 F1
Ansley 40 E6
Anslow 40 E3
Anslow Gate 40 D3
Ansteadbrook 12 C3
Anstey Herts 33 H5
Anstey Leics 41 H5
Anstruther 81 L10
Ansty Warks 41 F7
Ansty Wilts 9 J2
Ansty WSuss 13 F4
Ansty Coombe 9 J2
Ansty Cross 9 G4
Anthill Common 11 H3
Anthorn 60 C1
Antingham 45 G2
Anton's Gowt 43 F1
Antonine Wall (Frontiers of the Roman Empire) Central Scotland 118 F2, 75 G3 etc.
Antony 4 D5
Antrim 92 G8
Antrim Castle Gardens BT41 4LH 92 G8
Antrim Round Tower BT41 1BL 92 G8
Antrobus 49 F5
Antynanum 92 H5
Anvil Corner 6 B5
Anvil Green 15 G3
Anwick 52 E7
Anwoth 65 F5
Aonach Mòr Mountain Gondola & Nevis Range Ski Centre High PH33 6SW 79 N3
Aoradh 72 A4
Apethorpe 42 D6
Apeton 40 A4
Apley 52 E5
Apperknowle 51 F5
Apperley 29 H6
Apperley Bridge 57 G6
Appersett 61 K7
Appin (An Apainn) 79 L6
Appleby 52 C1
Appleby Magna 41 F4
Appleby Parva 41 F5
Appleby-in-Westmorland 61 H4
Applecross 82 H6
Appledore Devon 6 C2
Appledore Devon 7 J4
Appledore Kent 14 E5
Appledore Heath 14 E4
Appleford 21 J2
Appleshaw 21 G7
Applethwaite 60 D4
Appleton Halton 48 E4
Appleton Oxon 21 H1
Appleton Roebuck 58 B5
Appleton Thorn 49 F4
Appleton Wiske 62 D6
Appleton-le-Moors 58 D1
Appleton-le-Street 58 D2
Appletreehall 70 A2
Appletreewick 57 F3
Appley 7 J3
Appley Bridge 48 E2
Apse Heath 11 G6
Apsey Green 35 G2
Apsley 22 D1
Apsley End 32 E5
Apuldram 12 B6
Arbeia Roman Fort & Museum (Frontiers of the Roman Empire) T&W NE33 2BB 71 J7
Arbirlot 81 L6
Arborfield 22 A5
Arborfield Cross 22 A5
Arborfield Garrison 22 A5
Arbourthorne 51 F4
Arbroath 81 M6
Arbuthnott 81 N3
Archdeacon Newton 62 C5
Archiestown 84 G6
Arclid 49 G6
Ard a' Chapuill 73 J2
Ardacheranbeg 73 J2
Ardacheranmor 73 J2
Ardachu 87 J9
Ardailly 72 E5
Ardalanish 78 E9
Ardallie 85 Q7
Ardanaiseig 79 M8
Ardaneaskan 83 J7
Ardarroch 83 J7
Ardbeg A&B 72 C6
Ardbeg A&B 73 J4
Ardbeg A&B 73 K2
Ardboe 92 E9
Ardcharnich 83 M2
Ardchiavaig 78 E9
Ardchronie 84 A2
Ardchullarie More 80 A9
Ardchyle 80 A8
Arddlin 38 B4
Ardechvie 83 M11
Ardeley 33 G6
Ardelve 83 J8
Arden 74 B2
Ardens Grafton 30 C3
Ardentinny 73 K2
Ardeonaig 80 B7
Ardersier 84 B5
Ardery 79 J4
Ardessie 83 L2
Ardfern 79 K10
Ardfin 72 C4
Ardgartan 79 P10
Ardgay 84 A1
Ardgenavan 79 N9
Ardglass 93 L13
Ardgour (Corran) 79 M4
Ardgowan 74 A3
Ardhallow 73 K3
Ardindrean 83 M2
Ardingly 13 G4
Ardington 21 H3
Ardington Wick 21 H3
Ardintoul 83 J8
Ardkeen 93 M11
Ardlair 85 K8
Ardlamont 73 H4
Ardleigh 34 E6
Ardleigh Green 23 J3
Ardleigh Heath 34 E5
Ardler 80 H6
Ardley 31 G6
Ardley End 33 J7
Ardlui (Àird Laoigh) 79 Q9
Ardlussa 72 E2
Ardmair 83 M1
Ardmaleish 73 J4
Ardmay 79 P10
Ardmenish 72 D3
Ardmillan 93 L10
Ardminish 72 E6
Ardmolich 79 J3
Ardmore A&B 72 C5
Ardmore A&B 74 B3
Ardmore CC&G 92 C4
Ardnackaig 73 F1
Ardnacross 78 G6
Ardnadam 73 K2
Ardnagoine 86 B9
Ardnahein 73 K1
Ardnahoe 72 C3
Ardnarff 83 J7
Ardnastang 79 K4
Ardnave 72 A3
Ardno 79 N10
Ardoch D&G 68 D3
Ardoch P&K 80 F7
Ardochrig 74 E6
Ardoyne 85 L8
Ardpatrick 73 F4
Ardpeaton 74 A2
Ardquin 93 L11
Ardress 93 E11
Ardrishaig 73 G2
Ardroe 86 C7
Ardross 84 A3
Ardrossan 74 A6
Ardscalpsie 73 J5
Ardsley 51 F2
Ardslignish 78 G4
Ardstraw 90 K8
Ardtalla 72 C5
Ardtalnaig 80 C7
Ardtaraig 73 J2
Ardtoe 78 H3
Ardtole 93 L13
Ardtornish 79 J6
Ardtrostan 80 B8
Arduaine 79 K9
Ardura 78 H7
Ardvasar 82 G10
Ardvorlich 80 B8
Ardwall 65 F5
Ardwell D&G 64 B6
Ardwell SAyr 67 F4
Ardwick 49 H3
Areley Kings 29 H1
Arford 12 B3
Argoed 18 E2
Argoed Mill 27 J2
Argos Hill 13 J4
Argrennan House 65 H5
Argyll & Sutherland Highlanders Museum Stir FK8 1EH 75 F1
Arichonan 73 F1
Arinacrinachd 82 H5
Arinafad Beg 73 F2
Arinagour 78 D5
Arisaig (Àrasaig) 78 H2
Arkendale 57 J3
Arkesden 33 H5
Arkholme 55 J2
Arkle Town 62 A6
Arkleby 60 C3
Arkleside 57 F1
Arkleton 69 J4
Arkley 23 F2
Arksey 51 H2
Arkwright Town 51 G5
Arle 29 J6
Arlecdon 60 B5
Arlesey 32 E5
Arleston 39 F4
Arley 49 F4
Arlingham 29 G7
Arlington Devon 6 E1
Arlington ESuss 13 J6
Arlington Glos 20 E1
Arlington Beccott 6 E1
Armadale High 82 G10
Armadale High 87 K3
Armadale WLoth 75 H4
Armagh 93 D12
Armathwaite 61 G2
Arminghall 45 G5
Armitage 40 C4
Armitage Bridge 50 D1
Armley 57 H6
Armscote 30 D4
Armshead 40 B1
Armston 42 D7
Armthorpe 51 J2
Arnaby 54 E1
Arncliffe 56 E2
Arncliffe Cote 56 E2
Arncroach 81 L10
Arne 9 J6
Arnesby 41 J6
Arney 91 J13
Arngibbon 74 E1
Arngomery 74 E1
Arnicle 73 F7
Arnisdale (Arnasdal) 83 J9
Arnish 82 F6
Arniston Engine 76 B4
Arnol 88 J3
Arnold ERid 59 H5
Arnold Notts 41 H1
Arnolfini Gallery BS1 4QA 123 Bristol
Arnprior 74 E1
Arnside 55 H2
Aros Experience High IV51 9EU 82 E6
Arowry 38 D2
Arrad Foot 55 G1
Arram 59 G5
Arran 73 H7
Arras 59 F5
Arrathorne 62 C7
Arreton 11 G6
Arrington 33 G3
Arrochar 79 Q10
Arrow 30 B3
Arscaig 86 H8
Arscott 38 D5
Arthington 57 H5
Arthingworth 42 A7
Arthog 37 F4
Arthrath 85 P7
Arthurstone 80 H6
Articlave 92 C3
Artigarvan 90 K6
Artikelly 92 B4
Artnagross 92 E5
Aruadh 72 A4
Arundel 12 D6
Arundel Castle WSuss BN18 9AB 12 D6
Arundel Cathedral (R.C.) WSuss BN18 9AY 12 D6
Aryhoulan 79 M4
Asby 60 B4
Ascog 73 K4
Ascot 22 C5
Ascott 30 E5
Ascott d'Oyley 30 E7
Ascott Earl 30 D7
Ascott-under-Wychwood 30 E7
Asenby 57 K2
Asfordby 42 A4
Asfordby Hill 42 A4
Asgarby Lincs 42 E1
Asgarby Lincs 53 G6
Ash Dorset 9 H3
Ash Kent 15 H2
Ash Kent 24 C5
Ash Som 8 D2
Ash Surr 22 B6
Ash Barton 6 D5
Ash Bullayne 7 F5
Ash Green Surr 22 C7
Ash Green Warks 41 F7
Ash Magna 38 E2
Ash Mill 7 F3
Ash Parva 38 E2
Ash Priors 7 K3
Ash Street 34 E4
Ash Thomas 7 J4
Ash Vale 22 B6
Ashampstead 21 J4
Ashbocking 35 F3
Ashbourne 40 D1
Ashbrittle 7 J3
Ashburnham Place 13 K5
Ashburton 5 H4
Ashbury Devon 6 D6
Ashbury Oxon 21 F3
Ashby 52 B2
Ashby by Partney 53 H6
Ashby cum Fenby 53 F2
Ashby de la Launde 52 D7
Ashby de la Zouch 41 F4
Ashby Dell 45 J6
Ashby Folville 42 A4
Ashby Hill 53 F2
Ashby Magna 41 H6
Ashby Parva 41 H7
Ashby Puerorum 53 G5
Ashby St. Ledgers 31 G2
Ashby St. Mary 45 H5
Ashchurch 29 J5
Ashcombe Devon 5 K3
Ashcombe NSom 19 G5
Ashcott 8 D1
Ashdon 33 J4
Ashe 21 J7
Asheldham 25 F1
Ashen 34 B4
Ashenden 14 D4
Ashendon 31 J7
Ashens 73 G3
Ashfield A&B 73 F2
Ashfield Here 28 E6
Ashfield Stir 80 C10
Ashfield Suff 35 G2
Ashfield Green Suff 34 B3
Ashfield Green Suff 35 G1
Ashfold Crossways 13 F4
Ashford Devon 5 G6
Ashford Devon 6 D2
Ashford Hants 10 C3
Ashford Kent 15 F3
Ashford Surr 22 D4
Ashford Bowdler 28 E1
Ashford Carbonel 28 E1
Ashford Hill 21 J5
Ashford in the Water 50 D5
Ashgill 75 F5
Ashiestiel 76 C7
Ashill Devon 7 J4
Ashill Norf 44 C5
Ashill Som 8 C3
Ashingdon 24 E2
Ashington N'umb 71 H5
Ashington Som 8 E2
Ashington WSuss 12 E5
Ashkirk 69 K1
Ashlett 11 F4
Ashleworth 29 H6
Ashleworth Quay 29 H6
Ashley Cambs 33 K2
Ashley ChesE 49 G4
Ashley Devon 6 E4
Ashley Glos 20 C2
Ashley Hants 10 D5
Ashley Hants 10 E1
Ashley Kent 15 J3
Ashley N'hants 42 A6
Ashley Staffs 39 G2
Ashley Wilts 20 B5
Ashley Down 19 J4
Ashley Green 22 C1
Ashley Heath Dorset 10 C4
Ashley Heath Staffs 39 G2
Ashmanhaugh 45 H3
Ashmansworth 21 H6
Ashmansworthy 6 B4
Ashmolean Museum Oxon OX1 2PH 134 Oxford
Ashmore 9 J3
Ashmore Green 21 J5
Ashorne 30 E3
Ashover 51 F6
Ashover Hay 51 F6
Ashow 30 E1
Ashperton 29 F4
Ashprington 5 J5
Ashreigney 6 E4
Ashridge Estate Herts HP4 1LX 32 C7
Ashstead 22 E6
Ashton ChesW&C 48 E6
Ashton Corn 2 D6
Ashton Corn 4 D4
Ashton Hants 11 G3
Ashton Here 28 E2
Ashton Invcly 74 A3
Ashton N'hants 31 J4
Ashton N'hants 42 D7
Ashton Peter 42 E5
Ashton Common 20 B6
Ashton Court Estate NSom BS41 9JN 100 B5
Ashton Keynes 20 D2
Ashton under Hill 29 J5
Ashton upon Mersey 49 G3
Ashton-in-Makerfield 48 E3
Ashton-under-Lyne 49 J3
Ashurst Hants 10 E3
Ashurst Kent 13 J3
Ashurst WSuss 12 E5
Ashurst Bridge 10 E3
Ashurstwood 13 H3
Ashwater 6 B6
Ashwell Herts 33 F5
Ashwell Rut 42 B4
Ashwell End 33 F4
Ashwellthorpe 45 F6
Ashwick 19 K7
Ashwicken 44 B4
Ashybank 70 A2
Askam in Furness 55 F2
Askern 51 H1
Askernish (Aisgernis) 88 B6
Askerswell 8 E5
Askett 22 B1
Askham Cumb 61 G4
Askham Notts 51 K5
Askham Bryan 58 B5
Askham Richard 58 B5
Asknish 73 H1
Askrigg 61 L7
Askwith 57 G5
Aslackby 42 D2
Aslacton 45 F6
Aslockton 42 A1
Aspall 35 F2
Aspatria 60 C2
Aspenden 33 G6
Asperton 43 F2
Aspley Guise 32 C5
Aspley Heath 32 C5
Aspull 49 F2
Asselby 58 D7
Asserby 53 H5
Assington 34 D5
Assington Green 34 B3
Astbury 49 H6
Astcote 31 H3
Asterby 53 F5
Asterley 38 C5
Asterton 38 D6
Asthall 30 D7
Asthall Leigh 30 E7
Astle 49 H5
Astley GtMan 49 G2
Astley Shrop 38 E4
Astley Warks 41 F7
Astley Worcs 29 G2
Astley Abbotts 39 G6
Astley Bridge 49 G1
Astley Cross 29 H2
Astley Green 49 G3
Astley Lodge 38 E4
Aston ChesE 39 F1
Aston ChesW&C 48 E5
Aston Derbys 40 D2
Aston Derbys 50 D4
Aston Flints 48 C6
Aston Here 28 D1
Aston Here 28 D2
Aston Herts 33 F6
Aston Oxon 21 G1
Aston Shrop 38 E3
Aston Shrop 40 A6
Aston Staffs 39 G1
Aston SYorks 51 G4
Aston Tel&W 39 F5
Aston WMid 40 C7
Aston W'ham 22 A3
Aston Abbotts 32 B6
Aston Botterell 39 F7
Aston Cantlow 30 C3
Aston Clinton 32 B7
Aston Crews 29 F6
Aston Cross 29 J5
Aston End 33 F6
Aston Eyre 39 F6
Aston Fields 29 J2
Aston Flamville 41 G6
Aston Heath 48 E5
Aston Ingham 29 F6
Aston juxta Mondrum 49 F7
Aston le Walls 31 F3
Aston Magna 30 C5
Aston Munslow 38 E7
Aston on Carrant 29 J5
Aston on Clun 38 C7
Aston Pigott 38 C5
Aston Rogers 38 C5
Aston Rowant 22 A2
Aston Sandford 22 A1
Aston Somerville 30 B5
Aston Subedge 30 C4
Aston Tirrold 21 J3
Aston Upthorpe 21 J3
Aston-by-Stone 40 B2
Aston-on-Trent 41 G3
Astwick 33 F5
Astwood 32 C4
Astwood Bank 30 B2
Aswarby 42 D1
Aswardby 53 G5
Aswick Grange 43 G4
Atch Lench 30 B3
Atcham 38 E5
Athelhampton 9 G5
Athelington 35 G1
Athelney 8 C2
Athelstaneford 76 D3
Atherington Devon 6 D3
Atherington WSuss 12 D6
Athersley North 51 F2
Atherstone 41 F6
Atherstone on Stour 30 D3
Atherton 49 F2
Atlow 40 E1
Attadale 83 K7
Attahole 90 L8
Attenborough 41 H2
Attenborough Nature Reserve Nott NG9 6DY 109 H6
Atterby 52 C3
Attercliffe 51 F4
Atterley 39 F6
Atterton 41 F6
Attical 93 H15
Attingham Park Shrop SY4 4TP 38 E4
Attleborough Norf 44 E6
Attleborough Warks 41 F6
Attlebridge 45 F4
Attleton Green 34 B3
Atwick 59 H4
Atworth 20 B5
Auberrow 28 D4
Aubourn 52 C6
Auch 79 Q7
Auchairne 67 F5
Auchallater 80 G2
Auchameanach 73 G5
Auchamore 73 G6
Auchattie 85 L11
Auchavan 80 G4
Auchbraad 73 G2
Auchenback 74 D5
Auchenblae 81 N3
Auchenbothie 74 B3
Auchenbrack 68 C4
Auchenbreck 73 J2
Auchencairn 65 H5
Auchencrow 77 G4
Auchendinny 76 A4
Auchendolly 65 H4
Auchenfoyle 74 B3
Auchengillan 74 D2
Auchengray 75 H5
Auchenheath 75 G6
Auchenhessnane 68 D4
Auchenlochan 73 H3
Auchenmalg 64 C5
Auchenrivock 69 J5
Auchentiber 74 B6
Auchenvennel 74 A2
Auchgourish 84 D9
Auchinafaud 73 F5
Auchincruive 67 H1
Auchindarrach 73 G2
Auchindrain 79 M10
Auchindrean 83 M2
Auchinleck 67 K1
Auchinloch 74 E3
Auchinner 80 B9
Auchleven 85 L8
Auchlochan 75 G7
Auchlyne 80 A8
Auchmacoy 85 P7
Auchmantle 64 B4
Auchmithie 81 M6
Auchmull 81 L3
Auchnabony 65 H6
Auchnacree 81 K4
Auchnafree 80 D7
Auchnagallin 84 E7
Auchnagatt 85 P6
Auchnaha 73 H2
Aucholzie 84 H11
Auchrannie 80 H5
Auchraw 80 A8
Auchreoch 79 Q8
Auchronie 81 K2
Auchterarder 80 E9
Auchterderran 76 A1
Auchterless 85 M6
Auchtermuchty 80 H9
Auchterneed 83 Q5
Auchtertool 76 A1
Auchtertyre (Uachdar Thire) High 83 J8
Auchtertyre Stir 79 Q8
Auchtubh 80 A8
Auckengill 87 R3
Auckley 51 J2
Audenshaw 49 J3
Audlem 39 F1
Audley 49 G7
Audley End Essex 33 J5
Audley End Essex 34 C5
Audley End Suff 34 C3
Audmore 40 A3
Auds 85 L4
Aughaboy 92 J6
Aughamullan 93 D10
Aughentaine 91 L11
Augher 91 M11
Aughnacloy 93 B11
Aughnaloopy 93 H15
Aughnaskeagh 93 H12
Aughrim 92 E7
Aughton ERid 58 D6
Aughton Lancs 48 C2
Aughton Lancs 55 J3
Aughton SYorks 51 G4
Aughton Wilts 21 F6
Aughton Park 48 D2
Auldearn 84 D5
Aulden 28 D3
Auldgirth 68 E5
Auldhame 76 D2
Auldhouse 74 E5
Ault a'chruinn 83 K8
Ault Hucknall 51 G6
Aultanrynie 86 F6
Aultbea (An t-Allt Beithe) 83 J2
Aultgrishan 82 H2
Aultguish Inn 83 P3
Aultmore 85 J5
Aultnamain Inn 84 A2
Aultvaich 83 R6
Aunby 42 D4
Aundorach 84 D9
Aunk 7 J5
Aunsby 42 D2
Aust 19 J3
Austerfield 51 J3
Austrey 40 E5
Austwick 56 C3
Authorpe 53 H4
Authorpe Row 53 J5
Avebury 20 E4
Avebury Ring (Stonehenge, Avebury & Associated Sites) Wilts SN8 1RF 20 E5
Avebury Trusloe 20 D5
Aveley 23 J3
Avening 20 B2
Averham 51 K7
Avery Hill 23 H4
Aveton Gifford 5 G6
Aviation Viewing Park GtMan M90 1QX 115 G8
Avielochan 84 D9
Aviemore 84 C9
Avington Hants 11 G1
Avington WBerks 21 G5
Avoch 84 A5
Avon 10 C5
Avon Dassett 31 F3
Avon Heath Country Park Dorset BH24 2DA 95 F2
Avon Valley Railway SGlos BS30 6HD 100 F5
Avonbridge 75 H3
Avoncliff 20 B6
Avonmouth 19 J4
Avonwick 5 H5
Awbridge 10 E2
Awhirk 64 A5
Awkley 19 J3
Awliscombe 7 K5
Awre 20 A1
Awsworth 41 G1
Axbridge 19 H6
Axford Hants 21 K7
Axford Wilts 21 F4
Axminster 8 B5
Axmouth 8 B5
Axton 47 K4
Axtown 5 F4
Aycliffe 62 C4
Aydon 71 F7
Aylburton 19 K1
Ayle 61 J2
Aylesbeare 7 J6
Aylesbury 32 B7
Aylesby 53 F2
Aylesford 14 C2
Aylesham 15 H2
Aylestone 41 H5
Aylmerton 45 F2
Aylsham 45 F3
Aylton 29 F5
Aymestrey 28 D2
Aynho 31 G5
Ayot Green 33 F7
Ayot St. Lawrence 32 E7
Ayot St. Peter 33 F7
Ayr 67 H1
Aysgarth 57 F1
Aysgarth Falls & National Park Centre NYorks DL8 3TH 57 F1
Ayshford 7 J4
Ayside 55 G1
Ayston 42 B5
Aythorpe Roding 33 J7
Ayton 77 H4
Aywick 89 P4
Azerley 57 H2

B

Babbacombe 5 K4
Babbacombe Model Village Torbay TQ1 3LA 5 K4
Babbinswood 38 C2
Babb's Green 33 G7
Babcary 8 E2
Babel 27 H5
Babell 47 K5
Babeny 5 G3
Bablock Hythe 21 H1
Babraham 33 J3
Babworth 51 J4
Bachau 46 C4
Back of Keppoch 78 H2
Back Street 34 B3
Backaland 89 E4
Backbarrow 55 G1
Backe 17 F4
Backfolds 85 Q5
Backford 48 D5
Backies 87 L9
Backwell 19 H5
Backworth 71 H6
Bacon End 33 J7
Baconend Green 33 J7
Baconsthorpe 45 F2
Bacton Here 28 C5
Bacton Norf 45 H2
Bacton Suff 34 E2
Bacton Green 34 E2
Bacup 56 D7
Badachro 82 H3
Badanloch Lodge 87 K6
Badbury 20 E3
Badbury Wick 20 E3
Badby 31 G3
Badcall 86 D5
Badcaul 83 L1
Baddeley Green 49 J7
Badden 73 G2
Baddesley Clinton Warks B93 0DQ 30 C1
Baddesley Clinton 30 C1
Baddesley Ensor 40 E6
Baddidarach 86 C7
Badenscoth 85 M7
Badenyon 84 H9
Badgall 4 C2
Badger 39 G6
Badgerbank 49 H5
Badgers Mount 23 H5
Badgeworth 29 J7
Badgworth 19 G6
Badingham 35 H2
Badintagairt 86 G8
Badlesmere 15 F2
Badley 34 E3
Badlipster 87 Q5
Badluarach 83 K1
Badminton 20 B3
Badnaban 86 C7
Badnabay 86 E5
Badninish 84 B1
Badrallach 83 L1
Badsey 30 B4
Badshot Lea 22 B7
Badsworth 51 G1
Badwell Ash 34 D2
Badworthy 5 G4
Bag Enderby 53 G5
Bagber 9 G3
Bagby 57 K1
Bagendon 20 D1
Baggeridge Country Park Staffs DY3 4HB 106 A3
Bagginswood 39 F7
Baggrave Hall 41 J5
Baggrow 60 C2
Bagillt 48 B5
Baginton 30 E1
Baglan 18 A2
Bagley Shrop 38 D3
Bagley Som 19 H7
Bagmore 21 K7
Bagnall 49 J7
Bagnor 21 H5
Bagpath 20 B2
Bagshot Surr 22 C5
Bagshot Wilts 21 G5
Bagstone 19 K3
Bagthorpe Norf 44 B2
Bagthorpe Notts 51 G7
Baguley 49 H4
Bagworth 41 G5
Bagwyllydiart 28 D6
Baildon 57 G6
Baile Ailein 88 H5
Baile Boidheach 73 F3
Baile Glas 88 C3
Baile Mhàrtainn 88 B1
Baile Mòr 78 D8
Bailiff Bridge 57 G7
Baillieston 74 E4
Bainbridge 61 L7
Bainsford 75 G2
Bainton ERid 59 F4
Bainton Oxon 31 G6
Bainton Peter 42 D5
Bairdstown 93 M9
Bairnkine 70 B2
Baker Street 24 C3
Baker's End 33 G7
Bakewell 50 E6
Bala (Y Bala) 37 J2
Balafark 74 E1
Balavil 84 B10
Balbeg High 83 Q7
Balbeg High 83 Q8
Balblair 84 B4
Balby 51 H2
Balchladich 86 C6
Balchraggan High 83 R6
Balchraggan High 83 R7
Balchrick 86 D4
Balcombe 13 G3
Baldernock 74 D3
Baldersby 57 J2
Baldersby St. James 57 J2
Balderstone GtMan 49 J1
Balderstone Lancs 56 B6
Balderton ChesW&C 48 C6
Balderton Notts 52 B7
Baldhu 2 E4
Baldock 33 F5
Baldon Row 21 J1
Baldovan 81 J7
Baldrine 54 D5
Baldslow 14 C6
Baldwin 54 C5
Baldwinholme 60 E1
Baldwin's Gate 39 G1
Baldwins Hill 13 G3
Bale 44 E2
Balemartine 78 A6
Balephuil 78 A6
Balerno 75 K4
Balernock 74 A2
Baleromindubh 72 B1
Balerominmore 72 B1
Baleshare (Bhaleshear) 88 B2
Balfield 81 L4
Balfour 89 D6
Balfron 74 D2
Balfron Station 74 D2
Balgonar 75 J1
Balgowan D&G 64 B6
Balgowan High 84 A11
Balgown 82 D4
Balgreggan 64 A5
Balgy 83 J5
Balhalgardy 85 M8
Balham 23 F4
Baliasta 89 Q2
Baligill 87 L3
Balintore Angus 80 H5
Balintore High 84 C3
Balivanich (Baile a'Mhanaich) 88 B3
Balix 90 L7
Balkholme 58 D7
Balkissock 67 F5
Ball 38 C3
Ball Haye Green 49 J7
Ball Hill 21 H5
Balla 88 B7
Ballabeg 54 B6
Ballacannell 54 D5
Ballacarnane Beg 54 B5
Ballachulish (Baile a' Chaolais) 79 M5
Balladoole 54 B7
Ballafesson 54 B6
Ballagh 91 L13
Ballagh Bridge 93 J14
Ballagyr 54 B5
Ballajora 54 D4
Ballakilpheric 54 B6
Ballamodha 54 B6
Ballantrae 66 E5
Ballard 93 F14
Ballards Gore 25 F2
Ballasalla IoM 54 B6
Ballasalla IoM 54 C4
Ballater 84 H11
Ballaugh 54 C4
Ballaveare 54 C6
Balleer 93 D13
Ballencrieff 76 C3
Balleny 92 F3
Ballidon 50 E7
Balliekine 73 G6
Balliemore A&B 73 K1
Balliemore A&B 79 K8
Ballig 54 B5
Balliggan 93 M10
Ballimore A&B 73 H2
Ballimore Stir 80 A9
Ballinaby 72 A4
Ballinamallard 91 J11
Ballindarragh 91 K13
Ballinderry 92 E8
Ballingdon 34 C4
Ballinger Common 22 C1
Ballingham 28 E5
Ballingry 75 K1
Ballinlea 92 F3
Ballinluig 80 E5
Ballinran 93 J15
Ballinteer 92 D3
Ballintoy 92 F2
Ballintuim 80 G5
Balloch High 84 B6
Balloch NLan 75 F3
Balloch WDun 74 B2
Ballochan 85 K11
Ballochandrain 73 H2
Ballochgair 66 B1
Ballochmartin 73 K5
Ballochmorrie 67 G5
Ballochmyle 67 K1
Ballochroy 73 F5
Balloo 93 K10
Balloo Lower 92 L8
Balloolymore 93 G12
Balls Cross 12 C4
Balls Green Essex 34 E6
Ball's Green Glos 20 B2
Balls Hill 40 B6
Ballsmill 93 E15
Ballyaghlis 93 J10
Ballyalton 93 L12
Ballyard 91 K11
Ballyardel 93 H15
Ballyaurgan 73 F3
Ballybannan 93 J13
Ballybogy 92 E3
Ballybollen 92 F7
Ballyboyland 92 E4
Ballybrack 90 M9
Ballybriest 92 C8
Ballycarry 92 K7
Ballycassidy 91 J11
Ballycastle 92 G2
Ballyclare 92 H7
Ballycloghan 93 K10
Ballyconnelly 92 F6
Ballycraigy 92 J6
Ballydan 93 K11
Ballydivity 92 E3
Ballydoolagh 91 J12
Ballydrain 93 K10
Ballydugan 93 K12
Ballydullaghan 92 D5
Ballyeaston 92 H7
Ballyesborough A 93 M10
Ballygalley 92 J6
Ballygarvey 92 G6
Ballygawley 93 B11
Ballyginniff 92 G8
Ballygorian 93 G14
Ballygowan A&NDown 93 K10
Ballygowan AB&C 93 G12
Ballygowan NM&D 93 H15
Ballygrant 72 B4
Ballyhalbert 93 M10
Ballyhill 92 H9
Ballyhoe Bridge 92 F4
Ballyholme A&NDown 92 L8
Ballyhome CC&G 92 D3
Ballyhornan 93 L12
Ballyhosset 93 L13
Ballyhushey 91 L10
Ballykeel F&O 90 L8
Ballykeel L&C 93 H11
Ballykeel NM&D 93 J15
Ballykelly 92 B4
Ballykennedy 92 H9
Ballykinler 93 K13
Ballyknock CC&G 92 F4
Ballyknock MUlst 92 D6
Ballyleny 93 E12
Ballylesson 93 J10
Ballylintagh 92 D4
Ballyloughbeg 92 E3
Ballylucas 91 J12
Ballylumford 92 K6
Ballymacashen 93 K10
Ballymackilroy 93 B11
Ballymaconnelly 92 E5
Ballymacormick 93 H11
Ballymacran 92 B4
Ballymagorry 90 K6
Ballymaguigan 92 E8
Ballymartrim AB&C 93 D12
Ballymartin NM&D 93 J15
Ballymeanoch 73 G1
Ballymena 92 G6
Ballymichael 73 H7
Ballymoney 92 E4
Ballymoyer 93 E13
Ballymultimber 92 B3
Ballymultrea 92 E8
Ballymurphy 93 L10
Ballynabragget 93 G11
Ballynagard 90 L4
Ballynagarrick 93 J10
Ballynahatty 91 L10
Ballynahinch 93 J11
Ballynahone Beg 93 D12
Ballynakilly 93 D10
Ballynamallaght 90 L7
Ballynasaggart 91 M11
Ballyneaner 90 M6
Ballynoe A&N 92 G7
Ballynoe NM&D 93 K13
Ballynure 92 J7
Ballyquintin 93 M12
Ballyrashane 92 D3
Ballyreagh F&O 91 K12
Ballyreagh Mid Ulster 93 B11
Ballyrisk 92 C4
Ballyrobert 92 H8
Ballyrogan 92 D5
Ballyronan 92 E8
Ballyroney 93 H13
Ballysallagh 93 H10
Ballyskeagh 93 H10
Ballystrudder 92 K7
Ballytober 92 E3
Ballyvally 93 G14
Ballyveagh 93 J15
Ballyvennox 92 D4
Ballyvoy 92 G2
Ballywalter 93 M10
Ballyward 93 H13
Ballywaternoy 92 F6
Ballywatticock 93 L9
Ballywildrick 92 C3
Balmacara (Baile Mac Ara) 83 J8
Balmaclellan 65 G3
Balmacneil 80 E5
Balmae 65 G6
Balmaha 74 C1
Balmedie 85 P9
Balmedie Country Park Aber AB23 8XG 85 P9
Balmer Heath 38 D2
Balmerino 81 J8
Balmerlawn 10 E4
Balminnoch 64 C4
Balmore EDun 74 E3
Balmore High 83 P7
Balmullo 81 K8
Balnaboth 81 J4
Balnacra 83 K6
Balnafoich 84 A7
Balnaguard 80 E5
Balnahard A&B 72 C1
Balnahard A&B 78 F7
Balnakeil 86 F3
Balnaknock 82 E4
Balnamore 92 E4
Balnapaling 84 B4
Balquhidder 80 A8
Balsall 30 D1
Balsall Common 30 D1
Balsall Heath 40 C7
Balscote 30 E4
Balsham 33 J3
Baltasound 89 Q2
Balterley 49 G7
Balterley Heath 49 G7
Baltersan 64 E4
Baltonsborough 8 E1
Baluachraig 73 G1
Balulive 72 C4
Balvaird 83 R5
Balvicar 79 J9
Bamber Bridge 55 J7
Bamber's Green 33 J6
Bamburgh 77 K7
Bamburgh Castle N'umb NE69 7DF 77 K7
Bamff 80 H5
Bamford Derbys 50 E4
Bamford GtMan 49 H1
Bampton Cumb 61 G5
Bampton Devon 7 H3
Bampton Oxon 21 G1
Bampton Grange 61 G5
Banavie (Banbhaidh) 79 N3
Banbridge 93 G12
Banbury 31 F4
Banbury Museum Oxon OX16 2PQ 31 F5
Bancffosfelen 17 H4
Banchory 85 M11
Banchory Devenick 85 P10
Bancycapel 17 H4
Bancyfelin 17 G4
Bancyffordd 17 H2
Bandrake Head 55 G1
Banff 85 L4
Bangor A&NDown 92 L8
Bangor Gwyn 46 D5
Bangor-on-Dee (Bangor-is-y-coed) 38 C1
Bangor's Green 48 C2
Banham 44 E7
Banham Zoo Norf NR16 2HE 44 E7
Bank 10 D4
Bank End 54 E1
Bank Newton 56 E4
Bank Street 29 F2
Bank Top Lancs 48 E2
Bank Top WYorks 57 G7
Bankend 69 F7
Bankfoot 80 F7
Bankglen 67 K2
Bankhead 65 H6
Bankland 8 C2
Banknock 75 F3
Banks Cumb 70 A7
Banks Lancs 55 G7
Bankshill 69 G5
Bannfoot 93 E10
Banningham 45 G3
Bannister Green 33 K6
Bannockburn 75 G1
Banstead 23 F6
Bantam Grove 57 H7
Bantham 5 G6

Bohemia 10 D3
Bohenie 79 P2
Bohetherick 4 E4
Boho 91 H12
Bohortha 3 F5
Bohuntine 79 P2
Bojewyan 2 A5
Bokiddick 4 A4
Bolam *Dur* 62 B4
Bolam *N'umb* 71 F5
Bolam Lake Country Park *N'umb* NE20 0HE 71 F5
Bolberry 5 G7
Bold Heath 48 E4
Bolderwood 10 D4
Boldon 71 J7
Boldon Colliery 71 J7
Boldre 10 E5
Boldron 62 A5
Bole 51 K4
Bolea 92 C4
Boleigh 2 B6
Bolenowe 2 D5
Boleran 92 D5
Boleside 76 C7
Bolgoed 17 K5
Bolham *Devon* 7 H4
Bolham *Notts* 51 K4
Bolham Water 7 K4
Bolie 90 M5
Bolingey 2 E3
Bollington 49 J5
Bolney 13 F4
Bolnhurst 32 D3
Bolsover 51 G5
Bolsterstone 50 E3
Bolstone 28 E5
Boltby 57 K1
Bolter End 22 A2
Bolton *Cumb* 61 H4
Bolton *ELoth* 76 D3
Bolton *ERid* 58 D4
Bolton *GtMan* 49 G2
Bolton *N'umb* 71 G2
Bolton Abbey 57 F4
Bolton Abbey Estate *NYorks* BD23 6EX 57 F4
Bolton Bridge 57 F4
Bolton by Bowland 56 C5
Bolton Houses 55 H6
Bolton Low Houses 60 D2
Bolton Museum & Art Gallery *GtMan* BL1 1SE 49 G2
Bolton Percy 58 B5
Bolton Priory *NYorks* BD23 6EX 57 F4
Bolton upon Dearne 51 G2
Bolton Wood Lane 60 D2
Boltonfellend 69 K7
Boltongate 60 D2
Bolton-le-Sands 55 H3
Bolton-on-Swale 62 C7
Bolventor 4 B3
Bombie 65 H6
Bomere Heath 38 D4
Bonar Bridge 84 A1
Bonawe (Bun Atha) 79 M7
Bonby 52 D1
Boncath 17 F2
Bonchester Bridge 70 A2
Bonchurch 11 G7
Bondleigh 6 E5
Bonds 55 H5
Bonehill 40 D5
Bo'ness 75 H2
Bonhill 74 B3
Boningale 40 A5
Bonjedward 70 B1
Bonkle 75 G5
Bonning Gate 61 F7
Bonnington *Edin* 75 K4
Bonnington *Kent* 15 F4
Bonnybridge 75 G2
Bonnykelly 85 N5
Bonnyrigg 76 B4
Bonsall 50 E7
Bont 28 C7
Bont Dolgadfan 37 H5
Bont Newydd 37 G3
Bontddu 37 F4
Bont-goch (Elerch) 37 F7
Bonthorpe 53 H5
Bont-newydd *Conwy* 47 J5
Bontnewydd *Gwyn* 46 C6
Bontuchel 47 J7
Bonvilston 18 D4
Bon-y-maen 17 K6
Boode 6 D2
Boohay 5 K5
Booker 22 B2
Booley 38 E3
Boorley Green 11 G3
Boosbeck 63 G5
Boose's Green 34 C5
Boot 60 C6
Boot Street 35 G4
Booth 57 F7
Booth Bank 50 C1
Booth Green 49 J4
Booth Wood 50 C1
Boothby Graffoe 52 C7
Boothby Pagnell 42 C2
Boothstown 49 G2
Boothville 31 J2
Bootle *Cumb* 54 E1
Bootle *Mersey* 48 C3
Booton 45 F3
Boots Green 49 G5
Booze 62 A6
Boquhan 74 D2
Boraston 29 F1
Bordeaux 3 J5
Borden *Kent* 24 E5
Borden *WSuss* 12 B4
Bordley 56 E3
Bordon 11 J1
Boreham *Essex* 24 D1
Boreham *Wilts* 20 B7
Boreham Street 13 K5
Borehamwood 22 E2
Boreland *D&G* 64 D4
Boreland *D&G* 69 G4
Boreley 29 H2
Boreraig 82 B5
Borgh *Na H-E. Siar* 88 A8
Borgh *Na H-E. Siar* 88 E9
Borghastan 88 G3
Borgue *D&G* 65 G6
Borgue *High* 87 P7
Borley 34 C4
Borley Green *Essex* 34 C4
Borley Green *Suff* 34 D2
Borness 65 G6
Borniskeitaig 82 D3
Borough Green 23 K6
Boroughbridge 57 J3
Borras Head 48 C7
Borrowash 41 G2
Borrowby *NYorks* 57 K1
Borrowby *NYorks* 63 H5
Borrowdale 60 D5
Borstal 24 D5
Borth 37 F7
Borthwick 76 B5
Borthwickbrae 69 K2
Borthwickshiels 69 K2
Borth-y-Gest 36 E2
Borve *High* 82 E6
Borve (Borgh) *Na H-E. Siar* 88 K2
Borwick 55 J2
Borwick Rails 54 E2
Bosavern 2 A5
Bosbury 29 F4
Boscarne 4 A4
Boscastle 4 A1
Boscastle Pottery *Corn* PL35 0HE 4 B1
Boscombe *Bourne* 10 C5
Boscombe *Wilts* 10 D1
Bosham 12 B6
Bosham Hoe 12 B6
Bosherston 16 C6
Bosley 49 J6
Bossall 58 D3
Bossiney 4 A2
Bossingham 15 G3
Bossington *Hants* 10 E1
Bossington *Som* 7 G1
Bostock Green 49 F6
Boston 43 G1
Boston Spa 57 K5
Boswarthan 2 B5
Boswinger 3 G4
Bosworth Battlefield Country Park *Leics* CV13 0AD 41 G5
Botallack 2 A5
Botanic Garden *Oxon* OX1 4AZ 134 Oxford
Botany Bay *Lancs* PR6 9AF 48 E1
Botany Bay 23 G2
Botcheston 41 G5
Botesdale 34 E1
Bothal 71 H5
Bothamsall 51 J5
Bothel 60 C3
Bothenhampton 8 D5
Bothwell 75 F5
Botley *Bucks* 22 C1
Botley *Hants* 11 G3
Botley *Oxon* 21 H1
Botloe's Green 29 G6
Botolph Claydon 31 J6
Botolphs 12 E6
Botolph's Bridge 15 G4
Bottesford *Leics* 42 B2
Bottesford *NLincs* 52 B2
Bottisham 33 J2
Bottlesford 20 E6
Bottom Boat 57 J7
Bottom of Hutton 55 H7
Bottom o'th'Moor 49 F1
Bottoms 56 E7
Botton Head 56 B3
Botusfleming 4 E4
Botwnnog 36 B2
Bough Beech 23 H7
Boughrood 28 A5
Boughspring 19 J2
Boughton *Norf* 44 B5
Boughton *Notts* 51 J6
Boughton *N'hants* 31 J2
Boughton Aluph 15 F3
Boughton Lees 15 F3
Boughton Malherbe 14 D3
Boughton Monchelsea 14 C2
Boughton Street 15 F2
Boulby 63 H5
Bouldnor 10 E6
Bouldon 38 E7
Boulge 35 G3
Boulmer 71 H2
Boulston 16 C4
Boultenstone Hotel 85 J9
Boultham 52 C6
Boundary *Derbys* 41 F4
Boundary *Staffs* 40 B1
Bourn 33 G3
Bourne 42 D3
Bourne End *Bucks* 22 B3
Bourne End *CenBeds* 32 C4
Bourne End *Herts* 22 D1
Bournebridge 23 J2
Bournemouth 10 B5
Bournemouth Airport 10 C5
Bournemouth International Centre BH2 5BH 123 Bournemouth
Bournheath 29 J1
Bournmoor 62 D1
Bournville 40 C7
Bourton *Bucks* 31 J5
Bourton *Dorset* 9 G1
Bourton *NSom* 19 G5
Bourton *Oxon* 21 F3
Bourton *Shrop* 38 E6
Bourton *Wilts* 20 D5
Bourton on Dunsmore 31 F1
Bourton-on-the-Hill 30 C5
Bourton-on-the-Water 30 C6
Boustead Hill 60 D1
Bouth 55 G1
Bouthwaite 57 G2
Bovean 93 D10
Bovedy 92 D5
Boveney 22 C4
Boveridge 10 B3
Boverton 18 C5
Bovey Tracey 5 J3
Boviel 92 C6
Bovingdon 22 D1
Bovinger 23 J1
Bovington Camp 9 H6
Bow *Cumb* 60 E1
Bow *Devon* 5 J5
Bow *Devon* 7 F5
Bow *Ork* 89 C8
Bow Brickhill 32 C5
Bow Street *Cere* 37 F7
Bow Street *Norf* 44 E6
Bowbank 61 L4
Bowburn 62 D3
Bowcombe 11 F6
Bowd 7 K6
Bowden *Devon* 5 J6
Bowden *ScBord* 76 D7
Bowden Hill 20 C5
Bowdon 49 G4
Bower 70 C5
Bower Hinton 8 D3
Bower House Tye 34 D4
Bowerchalke 10 B2
Bowerhill 20 C5
Bowermadden 87 Q3
Bowers 40 A2
Bowers Gifford 24 D3
Bowershall 75 J1
Bowertower 87 Q3
Bowes 61 L5
Bowgreave 55 H5
Bowhousebog 75 G5
Bowithick 4 B2
Bowker's Green 48 D2
Bowland Bridge 55 H1
Bowley 28 E3
Bowley Town 28 E3
Bowlhead Green 12 C3
Bowling *WDun* 74 C3
Bowling *WYorks* 57 G6
Bowling Bank 38 C1
Bowlish 19 K7
Bowmanstead 60 E7
Bowmore 72 B4
Bowness-on-Solway 69 H7
Bowness-on-Windermere 60 F7
Bowood House & Gardens *Wilts* SN11 0LZ 20 C5
Bowscale 60 E3
Bowsden 77 H6
Bowside Lodge 87 L3
Bowston 61 F7
Bowthorpe 45 F5
Bowtrees 75 H2
Box *Glos* 20 B1
Box *Wilts* 20 B5
Box End 32 D4
Boxbush *Glos* 29 F6
Boxbush *Glos* 29 G7
Boxford *Suff* 34 D4
Boxford *WBerks* 21 H4
Boxgrove 12 C6
Boxley 14 C2
Boxmoor 22 D1
Box's Shop 6 A5
Boxted *Essex* 34 D5
Boxted *Suff* 34 C3
Boxted Cross 34 D5
Boxwell 20 B2
Boxworth 33 G2
Boxworth End 33 G2
Boyden Gate 25 J5
Boydston 74 C7
Boylestone 40 D2
Boyndie 85 L4
Boynton 59 H3
Boys Hill 9 F4
Boyton *Corn* 6 B6
Boyton *Suff* 35 H4
Boyton *Wilts* 9 J1
Boyton Cross 24 C1
Boyton End 34 B4
Bozeat 32 C3
Braaid 54 C6
Braal Castle 87 P3
Brabling Green 35 G2
Brabourne 15 F3
Brabourne Lees 15 F3
Bracadale 82 D7
Braceborough 42 D4
Bracebridge Heath 52 C6
Braceby 42 D2
Bracewell 56 D5
Brachla 83 R7
Brackenber 61 J5
Brackenbottom 56 D2
Brackenfield 51 F7
Bracklesham 12 B7
Brackley *A&B* 73 G2
Brackley *N'hants* 31 G5
Brackley Gate 41 F1
Brackley Hatch 31 H4
Bracknell 22 B5
Bracky 91 M9
Braco 80 D10
Bracon Ash 45 F6
Bracora 82 H11
Bracorina 82 H11
Bradbourne 50 E7
Bradbury 62 D4
Bradda 54 A6
Bradden 31 H4
Braddock 4 B4
Bradenham *Bucks* 22 B2
Bradenham *Norf* 44 D5
Bradenstoke 20 D4
Bradfield *Devon* 7 J5
Bradfield *Essex* 35 F5
Bradfield *Norf* 45 G2
Bradfield Combust 34 C3
Bradfield Green 49 F7
Bradfield Heath 35 F6
Bradfield Southend (Southend) 21 J4
Bradfield St. Clare 34 D3
Bradfield St. George 34 D2
Bradford *Corn* 4 B3
Bradford *Derbys* 50 E6
Bradford *Devon* 6 C5
Bradford *N'umb* 71 F6
Bradford *N'umb* 77 K7
Bradford *WYorks* 57 G6
Bradford Abbas 8 E3
Bradford Cathedral Church of St. Peter *WYorks* BD1 4EH 123 Bradford
Bradford Leigh 20 B5
Bradford Peverell 9 F5
Bradford-on-Avon 20 B5
Bradford-on-Tone 7 K3
Bradgate Park *Leics* LE6 0HE 41 H4
Bradiford 6 D2
Brading 11 H6
Bradley *ChesW&C* 48 E5
Bradley *Derbys* 40 E1
Bradley *Hants* 21 K7
Bradley *NELincs* 53 F2
Bradley (Low Bradley) *NYorks* 57 F5
Bradley *Staffs* 40 A4
Bradley *WMid* 40 B6
Bradley Fold 49 G2
Bradley Green *Warks* 40 E5
Bradley Green *Worcs* 29 J2
Bradley in the Moors 40 C1
Bradley Mills 50 D1
Bradley Stoke 19 K3
Bradlingill 60 C4
Bradmore *Notts* 41 H2
Bradmore *WMid* 40 A6
Bradney 8 C1
Bradninch 7 J5
Bradnop 50 C7
Bradnor Green 28 B3
Bradpole 8 D5
Bradshaw *GtMan* 49 G1
Bradshaw *WYorks* 57 F6
Bradstone 6 B7
Bradwall Green 49 G6
Bradwell *Derbys* 50 D4
Bradwell *Devon* 6 C1
Bradwell *Essex* 34 C6
Bradwell *MK* 32 B5
Bradwell *Norf* 45 K5
Bradwell Grove 21 F1
Bradwell Waterside 25 F1
Bradwell-on-Sea 25 G1
Bradworthy 6 B4
Brae *D&G* 65 J3
Brae *High* 86 G9
Brae *Shet* 89 M6
Brae of Achnahaird 86 C8
Braeantra 83 R3
Braedownie 80 H3
Braegrum 80 F8
Braehead *D&G* 64 E5
Braehead *Glas* 74 D4
Braehead *SLan* 75 G7
Braehead *SLan* 75 H5
Braehead of Lunan 81 M5
Braeleny 80 B9
Braemar 84 F11
Braemore *High* 83 M3
Braemore *High* 87 N6
Braeswick 89 F4
Brafferton *Darl* 62 C4
Brafferton *NYorks* 57 K2
Brafield-on-the-Green 32 B3
Bragar 88 H3
Bragbury End 33 F6
Bragenham 32 C6
Braichmelyn 46 E6
Braides 55 H4
Braidley 57 F1
Braidwood 75 G6
Braigo 72 A4
Brailsford 40 E1
Brain's Green 19 K1
Braintree 34 B6
Braiseworth 35 F1
Braishfield 10 E2
Braithwaite *Cumb* 60 D4
Braithwaite *SYorks* 51 J1
Braithwaite *WYorks* 57 F5
Braithwell 51 H3
Bramber 12 E5
Bramblety 13 H3
Brambridge 11 F2
Bramcote *Notts* 41 H2
Bramcote *Warks* 41 G7
Bramdean 11 H2
Bramerton 45 G5
Bramfield *Herts* 33 F7
Bramfield *Suff* 35 H1
Bramford 35 F4
Bramhall 49 H4
Bramham 57 K5
Bramhope 57 H5
Bramley *Hants* 21 K6
Bramley *Surr* 22 D7
Bramley *SYorks* 51 G3
Bramley Corner 21 K6
Bramley Head 57 G4
Bramley Vale 51 G6
Bramling 15 H2
Brampford Speke 7 H6
Brampton *Cambs* 33 F1
Brampton *Cumb* 61 H4
Brampton *Cumb* 70 A7
Brampton *Derbys* 51 F5
Brampton *Lincs* 52 B5
Brampton *Norf* 45 G3
Brampton *Suff* 45 J7
Brampton *SYorks* 51 G2
Brampton Abbotts 29 F6
Brampton Ash 42 A7
Brampton Bryan 28 C1
Brampton en le Morthen 51 G4
Brampton Street 45 J7
Brampton Valley Way Country Park *N'hants* NN6 9DG 31 J1
Bramshall 40 C2
Bramshaw 10 D3
Bramshill 22 A5
Bramshott 12 B3
Bramwell 8 D2
Bran End 33 K6
Brancaster 44 B1
Brancaster Staithe 44 B1
Brancepeth 62 C3
Branchill 84 E5
Brand Green 29 G6
Brandelhow 60 D4
Branderburgh 84 G3
Brandesburton 59 H5
Brandeston 35 G2
Brandis Corner 6 C5
Brandiston 45 F3
Brandlingill 60 C4
Brandon *Dur* 62 C3
Brandon *Lincs* 42 C1
Brandon *N'umb* 71 F2
Brandon *Suff* 44 B7
Brandon *Warks* 31 F1
Brandon Bank 44 A7
Brandon Creek 44 A6
Brandon Park *Suff* IP27 0SU 44 B7
Brandon Parva 44 E5
Brandon to Bishop Auckland Walk *Dur* DH7 7RJ 62 C3
Brandsby 58 B2
Brandy Wharf 52 D3
Brane 2 B6
Branksome 10 B5
Branksome Park 10 B5
Bransbury 21 H7
Bransby 52 B5
Branscombe 7 K7
Bransford 29 G3
Bransford Bridge 29 H3
Bransgore 10 C5
Bransholme 59 H6
Branson's Cross 30 B1
Branston *Leics* 42 B3
Branston *Lincs* 52 D6
Branston *Staffs* 40 E3
Branston Booths 52 D6
Branston Water Park *Staffs* DE14 3EZ 40 E3
Brant Broughton 52 C7
Brantham 35 F5
Branthwaite *Cumb* 60 B4
Branthwaite *Cumb* 60 D3
Brantingham 59 F7
Branton *N'umb* 71 F2
Branton *SYorks* 51 J2
Brantwood 60 E7
Branxholm Bridgend 69 K2
Branxholme 69 K2
Branxton 77 G7
Brassey Green 48 E6
Brassington 50 E7
Brasted 23 H6
Brasted Chart 23 H6
Bratoft 53 H6
Brattleby 52 C4
Bratton *Som* 7 H1
Bratton *Tel&W* 39 F4
Bratton *Wilts* 20 C6
Bratton Clovelly 6 C6
Bratton Fleming 6 E2
Bratton Seymour 9 F2
Braughing 33 G6
Brauncewell 52 D7
Braunston *N'hants* 31 G2
Braunston *Rut* 42 B5
Braunstone 41 H5
Braunton 6 C2
Brawby 58 D2
Brawdy 16 B3
Brawith 63 F6
Brawl 87 L3
Brawlbin 87 N4
Bray 22 C4
Bray Shop 4 D3
Bray Wick 22 B4
Braybrooke 42 A7
Braydon Side 20 D3
Brayford 6 E2
Brayshaw 56 C4
Braythorn 57 H5
Brayton 58 C6
Braywoodside 22 B4
Brazacott 4 C1
Brea 2 D4
Breach *Kent* 15 G3
Breach *Kent* 24 E5
Breachwood Green 32 E6
Breaden Heath 38 D2
Breadsall 41 F2
Breadstone 20 A1
Bready 90 K6
Breage 2 D6
Bream 19 K1
Breamore 10 C3
Brean 19 F6
Breanais 88 E5
Brearton 57 J3
Breascleit 88 H4
Breaston 41 G2
Brechfa 17 J2
Brechin 81 M4
Brecklate 66 A2
Breckles 44 D6
Brecon (Aberhonddu) 27 K6
Brecon Beacons Int. Dark Sky Reserve *Carmar/Powys* 27 H7
Brecon Beacons Visitor Centre *Powys* LD3 8ER 27 J6
Breconside 68 D3
Bredbury 49 J3
Brede 14 D6
Bredenbury 29 F3
Bredfield 35 G3
Bredgar 24 E5
Bredhurst 24 D5
Bredon 29 J5
Bredon's Hardwick 29 J5
Bredon's Norton 29 J5
Bredwardine 28 C4
Breedon on the Hill 41 G3
Breibhig 88 K4
Breich 75 H4
Breightmet 49 G2
Breighton 58 D6
Breinton 28 D5
Breinton Common 28 D5
Bremhill 20 C4
Bremhill Wick 20 C4
Brenchley 23 K7
Brendon *Devon* 6 B4
Brendon *Devon* 6 B5
Brendon *Devon* 7 F1
Brenkley 71 H6
Brent Eleigh 34 D4
Brent Knoll 19 G6
Brent Pelham 33 H5
Brentford 22 E4
Brentingby 42 A4
Brentwood 23 J2
Brenzett 15 F5
Brenzett Green 15 F5
Breoch 65 H5
Brereton 40 C4
Brereton Green 49 G6
Brereton Heath 49 H6
Breretonhill 40 C4
Bressay 89 P8
Bressingham 44 E7
Bressingham Common 44 E7
Bressingham Steam Museum & Gardens *Norf* IP22 2AA 44 E7
Bretby 40 E3
Bretford 31 F1
Bretforton 30 B4
Bretherdale Head 61 G6
Bretherton 55 H7
Brettabister 89 N7
Brettenham *Norf* 44 D7
Brettenham *Suff* 34 D3
Bretton *Derbys* 50 D5
Bretton *Flints* 48 C6
Bretton *Peter* 42 E5
Brevig 88 A9
Brewlands Bridge 80 G4
Brewood 40 A5
Briantspuddle 9 H5
Brick End 33 J6
Brickendon 23 G1
Bricket Wood 22 E1
Brickfields Horse Country *IoW* PO33 3TH 11 G5
Brickkiln Green 34 B5
Bricklehampton 29 J4
Bride 54 D3
Bridekirk 60 C3
Bridell 16 E1
Bridestowe 6 D7
Brideswell 85 K7
Bridford 7 G7
Bridge *Corn* 2 D4
Bridge *Kent* 15 G2
Bridge End *Cumb* 55 F1
Bridge End *Devon* 5 G6
Bridge End *Essex* 33 K5
Bridge End *Lincs* 42 E2
Bridge End *Shet* 89 M9
Bridge Hewick 57 J2
Bridge of Alford 85 K9
Bridge of Allan 75 F1
Bridge of Avon 84 F7
Bridge of Awe (Drochaid Abha) 79 M7
Bridge of Balgie 80 A6
Bridge of Brown 84 F8
Bridge of Cally 80 G5
Bridge of Canny 85 L11
Bridge of Craigisla 80 H5
Bridge of Dee 65 H4
Bridge of Don 85 P10
Bridge of Dun 81 M5
Bridge of Dye 81 M2
Bridge of Earn 80 G9
Bridge of Ericht 80 A5
Bridge of Feugh 85 M11
Bridge of Forss 87 N3
Bridge of Gaur 80 A5
Bridge of Orchy (Drochaid Urchaidh) 79 P7
Bridge of Tynet 84 H4
Bridge of Walls 89 L7
Bridge of Weir 74 B4
Bridge Reeve 6 E4
Bridge Sollers 28 D4
Bridge Street 34 C4
Bridge Trafford 48 D5
Bridgefoot *Angus* 81 J7
Bridgefoot *Cambs* 33 H4
Bridgefoot *Cumb* 60 B4
Bridgehampton 8 E2
Bridgehill 62 A1
Bridgemary 11 G4
Bridgemere 39 G1
Bridgend *A&B* 72 B4
Bridgend *A&B* 73 G1
Bridgend *Aber* 85 M6
Bridgend *Angus* 81 L4
Bridgend (Pen-y-bont ar Ogwr) *Bridgend* 18 C4
Bridgend *Corn* 4 B5
Bridgend *Cumb* 60 F5
Bridgend *Moray* 84 H7
Bridgend *WLoth* 75 J3
Bridgend of Lintrathen 80 H5
Bridgerule 6 A5
Bridges 38 C6
Bridgeton 74 E4
Bridgetown *Corn* 6 B7
Bridgetown *Som* 7 H2
Bridgewater Hall, Manchester *GtMan* M2 3WS 133 E5
Bridgeyate 19 K4
Bridgham 44 D7
Bridgnorth 39 G6
Bridgnorth Cliff Railway *Shrop* WV16 4AH 39 G6
Bridgtown 40 B5
Bridgwater 8 B1
Bridlington 59 H3
Bridport 8 D5
Bridstow 28 E6
Brierfield 56 D6
Brierley *Glos* 29 F7
Brierley *Here* 28 D3
Brierley *SYorks* 51 G1
Brierley Hill 40 B7
Brierton 62 E4
Briestfield 50 E1
Brig o'Turk 80 A10
Brigg 52 D2
Briggate 45 H3
Briggswath 63 J6
Brigh 93 D9
Brigham *Cumb* 60 B3
Brigham *ERid* 59 G4
Brighouse 57 G7
Brighstone 11 F6
Brightgate 50 E7
Brighthampton 21 G1
Brightholmlee 50 E3
Brightling 13 K4
Brightlingsea 34 E7
Brighton *B&H* 13 G6
Brighton *Corn* 3 G3
Brighton Centre, The *B&H* BN1 2GR 123 Brighton
Brighton Museum & Art Gallery *B&H* BN1 1EE 123 Brighton
Brighton City (Shoreham) Airport 12 E6
Brighton Pier *B&H* BN2 1TW 123 Brighton
Brightons 75 H3
Brightwalton 21 H4
Brightwalton Green 21 H4
Brightwell 35 G4
Brightwell Baldwin 21 K2
Brightwell Upperton 21 K2
Brightwell-cum-Sotwell 21 J2
Brignall 62 A5
Brigsley 53 F2
Brigsteer 55 H1
Brigstock 42 C7
Brill *Bucks* 31 H7
Brill *Corn* 2 E6
Brilley 28 B4
Brilley Mountain 28 B3
Brimaston 16 C3
Brimfield 28 E2
Brimington 51 G5
Brimington Common 51 G5
Brimley 5 J3
Brimpsfield 29 J7
Brimpton 21 J5
Brimscombe 20 B1
Brimstage 48 C4
Brindham 19 J7
Brindister 89 N9
Brindle 55 J7
Brindley Ford 49 H7
Brineton 40 A4
Bringhurst 42 B6
Brington 32 D1
Brinian 89 D5
Briningham 44 E2
Brinkhill 53 G5
Brinkley *Cambs* 33 K3
Brinkley *Notts* 51 K7
Brinklow 31 F1
Brinkworth 20 D3
Brinscall 56 B7
Brinsea 19 H5
Brinsley 41 G1
Brinsop 28 D4
Brinsworth 51 G3
Brinton 44 E2
Brisco 60 F1
Brisley 44 D3
Brislington 19 K4
Brissenden Green 14 E4
Bristol 19 J4
Bristol Cathedral BS1 5TJ 123 Bristol
Bristol City Museum & Art Gallery *Bristol* BS8 1RL 100 C4
Bristol Filton Airport 19 J3
Bristol International Airport 19 J5
Bristol Zoo *Bristol* BS8 3HA 100 C4
Briston 44 E2
Britannia 56 D7
Britford 10 C2
Brithdir *Caerp* 18 E1
Brithdir *Gwyn* 37 G4
Brithem Bottom 7 J4
British Empire & Commonwealth Museum BS1 6QH 123 Bristol
British Library (St. Pancras) *GtLon* NW1 2DB 104 A6
British Museum *GtLon* WC1B 3DG 132 E1
Briton Ferry (Llansawel) 18 A2
Britwell 22 C3
Britwell Salome 21 K2
Brixham 5 K5
Brixton *Devon* 5 F5
Brixton *GtLon* 23 G4
Brixton Deverill 9 H1
Brixworth 31 J1
Brixworth Country Park *N'hants* NN6 9DG 31 J1
Brize Norton 21 F1
Broad Alley 29 H2
Broad Blunsdon 20 E2
Broad Campden 30 C5
Broad Carr 50 C1
Broad Chalke 10 B2
Broad Ford 14 C4
Broad Green *Cambs* 33 K3
Broad Green *CenBeds* 32 C4
Broad Green *Essex* 33 H5
Broad Green *Essex* 34 C6
Broad Green *Mersey* 48 D3
Broad Green *Suff* 34 E3
Broad Green *Worcs* 29 G3
Broad Haven 16 B4
Broad Hill 33 J1
Broad Hinton 20 E4
Broad Laying 21 H5
Broad Marston 30 C4
Broad Oak *Carmar* 17 J3
Broad Oak *Cumb* 60 C7
Broad Oak *ESuss* 13 K4
Broad Oak *ESuss* 14 D6
Broad Oak *Here* 28 D6
Broad Road 35 G1
Broad Street *ESuss* 14 D6
Broad Street *Kent* 14 D2
Broad Street *Wilts* 20 E6
Broad Street Green 24 E1
Broad Town 20 D4
Broadbottom 49 J3
Broadbridge 12 B6
Broadbridge Heath 12 E3
Broadclyst 7 H6
Broadfield *Lancs* 55 J7
Broadfield *Lancs* 56 C7
Broadford (An t-Ath Leathann) 82 G8
Broadford Airport 82 G8
Broadford Bridge 12 D4
Broadgate 54 E1
Broadhaugh 69 K3
Broadheath *GtMan* 49 G4
Broadheath *Worcs* 29 F2
Broadhembury 7 K5
Broadhempston 5 J4
Broadholme 52 B5
Broadland Row 14 D6
Broadlay 17 G5
Broadley *Lancs* 49 H1
Broadley *Moray* 84 H4
Broadley Common 23 H1
Broadmayne 9 G6
Broadmeadows 76 C7
Broadmere 21 K7
Broadmoor 16 D5
Broadnymett 7 F5
Broadoak *Dorset* 8 D5
Broadoak *Glos* 29 F7
Broadoak *Kent* 25 H5
Broadoak End 33 G7
Broad's Green 33 K7
Broadstairs 25 K5
Broadstone *Poole* 10 B5
Broadstone *Shrop* 38 E7
Broadstreet Common 19 G3
Broadwas 29 G3
Broadwater *Herts* 33 F6
Broadwater *WSuss* 12 E6
Broadwater Down 13 J3
Broadwaters 29 H1
Broadway *Carmar* 17 F4
Broadway *Carmar* 17 G5
Broadway *Pembs* 16 B4
Broadway *Som* 8 C3
Broadway *Suff* 35 H1
Broadway *Worcs* 30 C5
Broadwell *Glos* 30 D6
Broadwell *Oxon* 21 F1
Broadwell *Warks* 31 F2
Broadwell House 61 L1
Broadwey 9 F6
Broadwindsor 8 D4
Broadwood Kelly 6 E5
Broadwoodwidger 6 C7
Brobury 28 C4
Brocastle 18 C4
Brochel 82 F6
Brochloch 67 K4
Brockaghboy 92 D5
Brockamin 29 G3
Brockbridge 11 H3
Brockdish 35 G1
Brockenhurst 10 D4
Brockford Green 35 F2
Brockford Street 35 F2
Brockhall 31 H2
Brockham 22 E7
Brockhampton *Glos* 29 J6
Brockhampton *Glos* 30 B6
Brockhampton *Here* 28 E5
Brockhampton *Here* 29 F3
Brockhampton Green 9 G4
Brockholes *Lancs* PR5 0AG 55 J6
Brockholes 50 D1
Brockhurst *Hants* 11 G4
Brockhurst *WSuss* 13 H3
Brocklebank 60 E2
Brocklesby 52 E1
Brockley *NSom* 19 H5
Brockley *Suff* 34 C3
Brockley Green 34 B4
Brockley Green 34 C3
Brockley's Green 21 H5
Brockton *Shrop* 38 C5
Brockton *Shrop* 38 C7
Brockton *Shrop* 38 E6
Brockton *Shrop* 39 G5
Brockton *Tel&W* 39 G4
Brockweir 19 J1
Brockwood Park 11 H2
Brockworth 29 H7
Brocolitia (Frontiers of the Roman Empire) *N'umb* 70 D6
Brocton 40 B4
Brodick 73 J7
Brodsworth 51 H2
Brogborough 32 C5
Brogden 56 D5
Brogyntyn 38 B2
Broken Cross *ChesE* 49 H5
Broken Cross *ChesW&C* 49 F5
Brokenborough 20 C3
Brokes 62 B7
Bromborough 48 C4
Brome 35 F1
Brome Street 35 F1
Bromeswell 35 H3
Bromfield *Cumb* 60 C2
Bromfield *Shrop* 28 D1
Bromham *Bed* 32 D3
Bromham *Wilts* 20 C5
Bromley *GtLon* 23 H5
Bromley *SYorks* 51 F3
Bromley Cross 49 G1
Bromley Green 14 E4
Brompton *Med* 24 D5
Brompton *NYorks* 59 F1
Brompton *NYorks* 62 D7
Brompton *Shrop* 38 E5
Brompton on Swale 62 C7
Brompton Ralph 7 J2
Brompton Regis 7 H2
Bromsash 29 F6
Bromsberrow 29 G5
Bromsberrow Heath 29 G5
Bromsgrove 29 J1
Bromstead Heath 40 A4
Bromyard 29 F3
Bromyard Downs 29 F3
Bronaber 37 G2
Brondesbury 23 F3
Brongest 17 G1
Bronington 38 D2
Bronllys 28 A5
Bronnant 27 F2
Bronte Weaving Shed *WYorks* BD22 8EP 116 A1
Bronwydd Arms 17 H3
Bronydd 28 B4
Bron-y-gaer 17 G4
Bronygarth 38 B2
Brook *Carmar* 17 F5
Brook *Hants* 10 D3
Brook *Hants* 10 E2
Brook *IoW* 10 E6
Brook *Kent* 15 F3
Brook *Surr* 12 C3
Brook *Surr* 22 D7
Brook Bottom 49 J2
Brook End *Bed* 32 D2
Brook End *Herts* 33 G6
Brook End *MK* 32 C4
Brook End *Worcs* 29 H4
Brook Hill 10 D3
Brook Street *Essex* 23 J2
Brook Street *Kent* 14 E4
Brook Street *Suff* 34 C4
Brook Street *WSuss* 13 G4
Brooke *Norf* 45 G6
Brooke *Rut* 42 B5
Brookeborough 91 K12
Brookend *Glos* 19 J2
Brookend *Glos* 19 K1
Brookfield *Derbys* 50 C3
Brookfield *Mid Ulster* 93 D10
Brookhampton 21 K2
Brookhouse *ChesE* 49 J5
Brookhouse *Denb* 47 J6
Brookhouse *Lancs* 55 J3
Brookhouse *SYorks* 51 H4
Brookhouse Green 49 H6
Brookhouses 40 B1
Brookland 14 E5
Brooklands *D&G* 65 J3
Brooklands *Shrop* 38 E1
Brooklands Museum *Surr* KT13 0QN 22 D5
Brookmans Park 23 F1
Brooks 38 A6
Brooks Green 12 E4
Brooksby 41 J4
Brookside Miniature Railway *ChesE* SK12 1BZ 115 L8
Brookthorpe 29 H7
Brookwood 22 C6
Broom *CenBeds* 32 E4
Broom *Fife* 81 J10
Broom *Warks* 30 B3
Broom Green 44 D3
Broom Hill *Dorset* 10 B4
Broom Hill *Worcs* 29 J1
Broombeg 92 G3
Broomcroft 38 E5
Broome *Norf* 45 H6
Broome *Shrop* 38 D7
Broome *Worcs* 29 J1
Broome Wood 71 G2
Broomedge 49 G4
Broomer's Corner 12 E4
Broomfield *Essex* 34 B7
Broomfield *Kent* 14 D2
Broomfield *Kent* 25 H5
Broomfield *Som* 8 B1
Broomfleet 58 E7
Broomhall Green 39 F1
Broomhaugh 71 F7
Broomhead 85 P4
Broomhill *Bristol* 19 K4
Broomhill *N'umb* 71 H3
Broomielaw 62 A5
Broomley 71 F7
Broompark 62 C2
Broom's Green 29 G5
Brora 87 M9
Broseley 39 F5
Brotherlee 61 L3
Brothertoft 43 F1
Brotherton 57 K7
Brotton 63 G5
Broubster 87 N3
Brough *Cumb* 61 J5
Brough *Derbys* 50 D4
Brough *ERid* 59 F7
Brough *High* 87 Q2
Brough *Notts* 52 B7
Brough *Shet* 89 P6
Brough Lodge 89 P3
Brough Sowerby 61 J5
Broughall 38 E1
Brougham 61 G4
Brougham Hall *Cumb* CA10 2DE 61 G4
Broughderg 92 B8
Broughshane 92 G6
Broughton *Bucks* 32 B7
Broughton *Cambs* 33 F1
Broughton *Flints* 48 C6
Broughton *Hants* 10 E1
Broughton *Lancs* 55 J6
Broughton *MK* 32 B4
Broughton *NLincs* 52 C2
Broughton *NYorks* 56 E4
Broughton *NYorks* 58 D2
Broughton *N'hants* 32 B1
Broughton *Oxon* 31 F5
Broughton *ScBord* 75 K7
Broughton *VGlam* 18 C4
Broughton Astley 41 H6
Broughton Beck 55 F1
Broughton Gifford 20 B5
Broughton Green 29 J2
Broughton Hackett 29 J3
Broughton in Furness 55 F1
Broughton Mills 60 D7
Broughton Moor 60 B3
Broughton Poggs 21 F1
Broughtown 89 F3
Broughty Ferry 81 K7
Brown Candover 11 G1
Brown Edge *Lancs* 48 C1
Brown Edge *Staffs* 49 J7
Brown Heath 48 D6
Brown Lees 49 H7
Brown Street 34 E2
Brownber 61 J6
Browndown 11 G5
Brownheath 38 D3
Brownhills 40 C5
Brownieside 71 G1
Brownlow 49 H6
Brownlow Heath 49 H6
Brown's Bank 39 F1
Brownsea Island *Dorset* BH13 7EE 10 B6
Brownshill 20 B1
Brownshill Green 41 F7
Brownsover 31 G1
Brownston 5 G5
Brownston Green 45 J5
Broxa 63 J3
Broxbourne 23 G1
Broxburn *ELoth* 76 E3
Broxburn *WLoth* 75 J3
Broxholme 52 C5
Broxted 33 J6
Broxton 48 D7
Broxwood 28 C3
Broyle Side 13 H5
Brue (Brù) 88 J3
Bruera 48 D6
Bruern 30 D6
Bruichladdich 72 A4
Bruisyard 35 H2
Bruisyard Street 35 H2
Brumby 52 C1
Brund 50 D6
Brundall 45 H5
Brundish *Norf* 45 H6
Brundish *Suff* 35 G2
Brundish Street 35 G1
Brunstock 60 F1
Brunswick Village 71 H6
Bruntingthorpe 41 J6
Brunton *Fife* 81 J8
Brunton *N'umb* 71 H1
Brunton *Wilts* 21 F6
Brunton Turret (Frontiers of the Roman Empire) *N'umb* NE46 4EJ 70 E7
Bruscarnagh 91 M13
Brushfield 50 D5
Brushford *Devon* 6 E5
Brushford *Som* 7 H3
Bruton 9 F1
Bryansford 93 J13
Bryanston 9 H4
Bryant's Bottom 22 B2
Brydekirk 69 G6
Brymbo 48 B7
Brymor Ice Cream *NYorks* HG4 4PG 57 G1
Brympton 8 E3
Bryn *Caerp* 18 E2
Bryn *Carmar* 17 J5
Bryn *ChesW&C* 49 F5
Bryn *GtMan* 48 E2
Bryn *NPT* 18 B2
Bryn *Shrop* 38 B7
Bryn Bach Country Park *BGwent* NP22 3AY 18 E1
Bryn Bwbach 37 F2
Bryn Gates 48 E2
Bryn Pen-y-lan 38 C1
Brynamman 27 G7
Brynberian 16 E2
Bryncae 18 C3
Bryncethin 18 C3
Bryncir 36 D1
Bryncoch *Bridgend* 18 C3
Bryn-côch *NPT* 18 A2
Bryncroes 36 B2
Bryncrug 37 F5
Bryneglwys 38 A1
Brynford 47 K5
Bryngwran 46 B5
Bryngwyn *Mon* 19 G1
Bryngwyn *Powys* 28 A4
Bryn-henllan 16 D2
Brynhoffnant 26 C3
Bryning 55 H6
Brynithel 19 F1
Brynmawr *BGwent* 28 A7
Bryn-mawr *Gwyn* 36 B2
Brynmelyn 28 A1
Brynmenyn 18 C3
Brynna 18 C3
Brynnau Gwynion 18 C3
Brynog 26 E3
Bryn-penarth 38 A5
Brynrefail *Gwyn* 46 D6
Brynrefail *IoA* 46 C4
Brynsadler 18 D3
Brynsaithmarchog 47 J7
Brynsiencyn 46 C6
Bryn-teg *IoA* 46 C4
Brynteg *Wrex* 48 C7
Bryn-y-cochin 38 C2
Brynygwenin 28 C7
Bryn-y-maen 47 G5
Bubbenhall 30 E1
Bubnell 50 E5
Bubwith 58 D6
Buccleuch 69 J2
Buchan 65 H4
Buchanan Castle 74 C2
Buchanty 80 E8
Buchlyvie 74 D1
Buckabank 60 E2
Buckby Wharf 31 H2
Buckden *Cambs* 32 E2
Buckden *NYorks* 56 E2
Buckenham 45 H5
Buckerell 7 K5
Buckfast 5 H4
Buckfast Abbey *Devon* TQ11 0EE 5 H4
Buckfastleigh 5 H4
Buckhaven 76 B1
Buckholm 76 C7
Buckholt 28 E7
Buckhorn Weston 9 G2
Buckhurst Hill 23 H2
Buckie 85 J4
Buckingham 31 H5
Buckingham Palace *GtLon* SW1A 1AA 132 B5
Buckland *Bucks* 32 B7
Buckland *Devon* 5 G6
Buckland *Glos* 30 B5
Buckland *Hants* 10 E5
Buckland *Here* 28 E3
Buckland *Herts* 33 G5
Buckland *Kent* 15 J3
Buckland *Oxon* 21 G2
Buckland *Surr* 23 F6
Buckland Brewer 6 C3
Buckland Common 22 C1
Buckland Dinham 20 A6
Buckland Filleigh 6 C5
Buckland in the Moor 5 H3
Buckland Monachorum 4 E4
Buckland Newton 9 F4
Buckland Ripers 9 F6
Buckland St. Mary 8 B3
Buckland-tout-Saints 5 H6
Bucklebury 21 J4
Bucklers Hard 11 F5
Bucklesham 35 G4
Buckley (Bwcle) 48 B6
Buckley Green 30 C2
Bucklow Hill 49 G4
Buckman Corner 12 E4
Buckminster 42 B3
Buckna 92 H6
Bucknall 52 E6
Bucknell *Oxon* 31 G6
Bucknell *Shrop* 28 C1
Buckridge 29 G1
Buck's Cross 6 B3
Bucks Green 12 D3
Bucks Hill 22 D1
Bucks Horn Oak 22 B7
Buck's Mills 6 B3
Bucksburn 85 N10
Buckspool 16 C6
Buckton *ERid* 59 H2
Buckton *Here* 28 C1
Buckton *N'umb* 77 J7
Buckton Vale 49 J2
Buckworth 32 E1
Budbrooke 30 D2
Budby 51 J5
Bude 6 A5
Budge's Shop 4 D5
Budlake 7 H5
Budle 77 K7
Budleigh Salterton 7 J7
Budock Water 2 E5
Budore 92 H9
Budworth Heath 49 F5
Buerton 39 F1
Bugbrooke 31 H3
Buggan 91 G11
Bugle 4 A5
Bugthorpe 58 D4
Building End 33 H5
Buildwas 39 F5
Builth Road 27 K3
Builth Wells (Llanfair-ym-Muallt) 27 K3
Bulby 42 D3
Bulcote 41 J1
Buldoo 87 M3
Bulford 20 E7
Bulford Camp 20 E7
Bulkeley 48 E7
Bulkington *Warks* 41 F7
Bulkington *Wilts* 20 C6
Bulkworthy 6 B4
Bull Bay (Porth Llechog) 46 C3
Bull Green 14 E4
Bullbridge 51 F7
Bullbrook 22 B5
Bullen's Green 23 F1
Bulley 29 G7
Bullington 52 D5
Bullpot Farm 56 B1
Bulls Cross 23 G2
Bull's Green *Herts* 33 F7
Bull's Green *Norf* 45 J6
Bullwood 73 K3
Bulmer *Essex* 34 C4
Bulmer *NYorks* 58 C3
Bulmer Tye 34 C5
Bulphan 24 C3
Bulstone 7 K7
Bulverhythe 14 C7
Bulwell 41 H1
Bulwick 42 C6
Bumble's Green 23 H1
Bun 91 K14
Bun Abhainn Eadarra 88 G7
Bunarkaig 79 N2
Bunbury 48 E7
Bunbury Heath 48 E7
Bunchrew 84 A6
Bundalloch 83 J8
Bunessan 78 E8
Bungay 45 H7
Bunker's Hill 53 F7
Bunlarie 73 F7
Bunmhullin 88 B7
Bunnahabhain 72 C3
Bunnell 91 L13
Bunny 41 H3
Buntait 83 P7
Buntingford 33 G6
Bunwell 45 F6
Bunwell Street 45 F6
Burbage *Derbys* 50 C5
Burbage *Leics* 41 G6
Burbage *Wilts* 21 F5
Burbage Common *Leics* LE10 3DD 41 G6
Burchett's Green 22 B3
Burcombe 10 B1
Burcot *Oxon* 21 J2
Burcot *Worcs* 29 J1
Burcott 32 B6
Burdale 58 E3
Burdocks 12 D4
Burdon 62 D1
Burdrop 30 E5
Bure Valley Railway *Norf* NR11 6BW 45 G3
Bures 34 D5
Bures Green 34 D5
Burfa 28 B2
Burford *Oxon* 30 D7
Burford *Shrop* 28 E2
Burg 78 E6
Burgate 34 E1
Burgates 11 J2
Burge End 32 E5
Burgess Hill 13 G5
Burgh 35 G3
Burgh by Sands 60 E1
Burgh Castle 45 J5
Burgh Heath 23 F6
Burgh le Marsh 53 H6
Burgh next Aylsham 45 G3
Burgh on Bain 53 F4
Burgh St. Margaret (Fleggburgh) 45 J4
Burgh St. Peter 45 J6
Burghclere 21 H5
Burghead 84 F4
Burghfield 21 K5
Burghfield Common 21 K5
Burghfield Hill 21 K5
Burghill 28 D4
Burghwallis 51 H1
Burham 24 D5
Buriton 11 J2
Burland 49 F7
Burlawn 3 G2
Burleigh 22 C5
Burlescombe 7 J4
Burleston 9 G5
Burley *Hants* 10 D4
Burley *Rut* 42 B4
Burley *WYorks* 57 H6
Burley Gate 28 E4
Burley in Wharfedale 57 G5
Burley Street 10 D4
Burley Woodhead 57 G5
Burleydam 39 F1
Burlingjobb 28 B3
Burlow 13 J5
Burlton 38 D3
Burmarsh 15 G4
Burmington 30 D5
Burn 58 B7
Burn Naze 55 G5
Burnage 49 H3
Burnaston 40 E2
Burnby 58 E5
Burncross 51 F3
Burndell 12 C6
Burnden 49 G2
Burnedge 49 J1
Burneside 61 G7
Burness 89 F3
Burneston 57 J1
Burnett 19 K5
Burnfoot *CC&G* 92 B5
Burnfoot *ScBord* 69 K2
Burnfoot *ScBord* 70 A2
Burnham *Bucks* 22 C3
Burnham *NLincs* 52 D1
Burnham Deepdale 44 C1
Burnham Green 33 F7
Burnham Market 44 C1
Burnham Norton 44 C1
Burnham Overy Staithe 44 C1
Burnham Overy Town 44 C1
Burnham Thorpe 44 C1
Burnham-on-Crouch 25 F2
Burnham-on-Sea 19 G7
Burnhaven 85 R6
Burnhead *D&G* 67 K5
Burnhead *D&G* 68 D4
Burnhervie 85 M9
Burnhill Green 39 G5
Burnhope 62 B2
Burnhouse 74 B5
Burniston 63 K7
Burnley 56 D6
Burnmouth 77 H4
Burnopfield 62 B1
Burn's Green 33 G6
Burns National Heritage Park *SAyr* KA7 4PQ 67 H2

143

Dufton 61 H4
Duggleby 58 E3
Duiar 84 F7
Duinish 80 B4
Duirinish 82 H7
Duisky 79 M3
Dukestown 28 A7
Dukinfield 49 J3
Dulas 46 C4
Dulcote 19 J7
Dulford 7 J5
Dull 80 D6
Dullaghan 91 K10
Dunaghy 92 E4
Dullatur 75 F3
Dullingham 33 K3
Dullingham Ley 33 K3
Dulnain Bridge 84 D8
Duloe Bed 32 E2
Duloe Corn 4 C5
Dulsie 84 D6
Dulverton 7 H3
Dulwich 23 G4
Dulwich Picture Gallery GtLon SE21 7AD 105 B9
Dumbarton 74 B3
Dumbleton 30 B5
Dumcrieff 69 G3
Dumfin 74 B2
Dumfries 65 K3
Dumgoyne 74 D2
Dummer 21 J7
Dunalastair 80 C5
Dunan A&B 73 K3
Dunan High 82 F8
Dunans 73 J1
Dunball 19 G7
Dunbar 76 E3
Dunbeath 87 P6
Dunblane 80 C10
Dunbog 80 H9
Dunbridge 10 E2
Duncanston Aber 85 K8
Duncanston High 83 R5
Dunchideock 7 G7
Dunchurch 31 F1
Duncote 31 H3
Duncow 68 E5
Duncrun 92 B3
Duncryne 74 C2
Duncton 12 C5
Dundee 81 K7
Dundee Airport 81 J8
Dundee Contemporary Arts DD1 4DY 125 Dundee
Dundon 8 D1
Dundon Hayes 8 D1
Dundonald L&C 93 K9
Dundonald SAyr 74 B7
Dundonnell (Ach-Dà-Dhòmhnaill) 83 L2
Dundraw 60 D2
Dundreggan (Dul Dreagain) 83 P9
Dundrennan 65 H6
Dundridge 11 G3
Dundrod 92 H9
Dundrum AB&C 93 D13
Dundrum NM&D 93 K13
Dundry 19 J5
Duneany 92 F5
Dunearn 76 A2
Dunecht 85 M10
Duneight 93 H10
Dunfermline 75 J2
Dunfield 20 E2
Dunford Bridge 50 D2
Dungannon 93 C10
Dungate 14 E2
Dungavel 74 E7
Dungiven 92 B6
Dungworth 50 E3
Dunham 52 B5
Dunham Massey Hall, Park & Gardens GtMan WA14 4SJ 114 D7
Dunham Town 49 G4
Dunham Woodhouses 49 G4
Dunham-on-the-Hill 48 D5
Dunhampton 29 H2
Dunholme 52 D5
Dunino 81 L9
Dunipace 75 G2
Dunkeld 80 F6
Dunkerton 20 A6
Dunkeswell 7 K5
Dunkeswick 57 J5
Dunkirk ChesW&C 48 C5
Dunkirk Kent 15 F2
Dunk's Green 23 K6
Dunlappie 81 L4
Dunley Hants 21 H6
Dunley Worcs 29 G2
Dunlop 74 C6
Dunloskin 73 K3
Dunloy 92 F5
Dunluce Castle BT57 8UY 92 E2
Dunmere 4 A4
Dunminning 92 F5
Dunmore A&B 73 F4
Dunmore Falk 75 G2
Dunmore Mid Ulster 92 C8
Dunmore NM&D 93 J12
Dunmurry 93 H10
Dunn Street 24 D5
Dunnabie 69 H5
Dunnamore 92 B8
Dunnet 87 Q2
Dunnichen 81 L6
Dunning 80 F9
Dunnington ERid 59 H4
Dunnington Warks 30 B3
Dunnington York 58 C4
Dunnockshaw 56 D7
Dunoon 73 K3
Dunragit 64 B5
Dunrostan 73 F2
Duns 77 F5
Duns Tew 31 F6
Dunsa 50 E5
Dunsby 42 E3
Dunscore 68 D5
Dunscroft 51 J2
Dunsdale 63 G5
Dunsden Green 22 A4
Dunsdeverick 92 E2
Dunsfold 12 D3
Dunsford Devon EX6 7EG 5 J2
Dunsford 7 G7
Dunshalt 80 H9
Dunshill 29 H5
Dunsland Cross 6 C5
Dunsley NYorks 63 K5
Dunsley Staffs 40 A7
Dunsmore 22 B1
Dunsop Bridge 56 B4
Dunstable 32 D6
Dunstable Downs CenBeds LU6 2GY 32 D6
Dunstall 40 D3
Dunstall Green 34 B2
Dunstan 71 H2
Dunstan Steads 71 H1
Dunster 7 H1
Dunster Castle & Gardens Som TA24 6SL 7 H1
Dunston Lincs 52 D6
Dunston Norf 45 G5
Dunston Staffs 40 B4
Dunston Heath 40 B4
Dunston Hill 71 H7
Dunstone Devon 5 F5
Dunstone Devon 5 H3
Dunsville 51 J2
Dunswell 59 G6
Dunsyre 75 J6
Dunterton 4 D3
Duntisbourne Abbots 20 C1
Duntisbourne Leer 20 C1
Duntisbourne Rouse 20 C1
Duntish 9 F4
Duntocher 74 C3
Dunton Bucks 32 B6
Dunton CenBeds 33 F4
Dunton Norf 44 C2
Dunton Bassett 41 H6
Dunton Green 23 J6
Dunton Wayletts 24 C2
Dunure 67 G2
Dunvant 17 J6
Dunvegan 82 C6
Dunvegan Castle High IV55 8WF 82 C6
Dunwich 35 J1
Durdar 60 F1
Durgan 2 E6
Durgates 13 K3
Durham 62 C2
Durham Castle and Cathedral Dur DH1 3RW & DH1 3EH 62 C2
Durham Dales Centre Dur DL13 2FJ 62 A3
Durham Tees Valley Airport 62 D5
Durisdeer 68 D3
Durleigh 8 B1
Durley Hants 11 G3
Durley Wilts 21 F5
Durley Street 11 G3
Durlow Common 29 F5
Durlston Country Park Dorset BH19 2JL 10 B7
Durnamuck 83 L1
Durness 86 G3
Durno 85 M8
Duror 79 L5
Durrants 11 J4
Durrington Wilts 20 E7
Durrington WSuss 12 E6
Dursley 20 A2
Dursley Cross 29 F7
Durston 8 B2
Durweston 9 H4
Duston 31 J2
Duthie Park & David Welch Winter Gardens Aberdeen AB11 7TH 85 P10
Duthil 84 D8
Dutlas 28 B1
Duton Hill 33 K6
Dutson 6 B7
Dutton 48 E5
Duxford 33 H4
Dwygyfylchi 47 F5
Dwyran 46 C6
Dyan 93 C12
Dyce 85 N9
Dyfatty 17 H5
Dyffryn Bridgend 18 B2
Dyffryn Pembs 16 C2
Dyffryn VGlam 18 D4
Dyffryn Ardudwy 36 E3
Dyffryn Castell 37 G7
Dyffryn Ceidrych 27 G6
Dyffryn Cellwen 27 H7
Dyke Devon 6 B3
Dyke Lincs 42 E3
Dyke Moray 84 D5
Dykehead Angus 81 J4
Dykehead NLan 75 G5
Dykehead Stir 74 D1
Dykend 80 H5
Dylan Thomas Centre SA1 1RR 136 Swansea
Dylife 37 H6
Dymchurch 15 G5
Dymock 29 G5
Dyrham 20 A4
Dyrham Park SGlos SN14 8ER 100 H3
Dysart 76 B1
Dyserth 47 J5

E

Eachwick 71 G6
Eadar dha Fhadhail 88 F4
Eagland Hill 55 H5
Eagle 52 B6
Eagle Barnsdale 52 B6
Eagle Moor 52 B6
Eaglescliffe 62 E5
Eaglesfield Cumb 60 B4
Eaglesfield D&G 69 H6
Eaglesham 74 D5
Eaglethorpe 42 D6
Eagley 49 G1
Eairy 54 B6
Eakley 32 B3
Eakring 51 J6
Ealand 51 K1
Ealing 22 E3
Eamont Bridge 61 G4
Earby 56 E5
Earcroft 56 B7
Eardington 39 G6
Eardisland 28 D3
Eardisley 28 C4
Eardiston Shrop 38 C3
Eardiston Worcs 29 F2
Earith 33 G1
Earl Shilton 41 G6
Earl Soham 35 G2
Earl Sterndale 50 C6
Earl Stonham 35 F3
Earle 70 E1
Earlestown 48 E3
Earley 22 A4
Earlham 45 F5
Earlish 82 D4
Earls Barton 32 B2
Earls Colne 34 C6
Earl's Common 29 J3
Earl's Court 23 F4
Earl's Croome 29 H4
Earl's Green 34 E2
Earlsdon 30 E1
Earlsferry 81 K10
Earlsford 85 M7
Earlsheaton 57 H7
Earlston 76 D7
Earlswood Mon 19 H2
Earlswood Surr 23 F7
Earlswood Warks 30 C1
Earnley 12 B7
Earnshaw Bridge 55 J7
Earsairidh 88 B9
Earsdon 71 J6
Earsdon Moor 71 G4
Earsham 45 H7
Earsham Street 35 G1
Earswick 58 C4
Eartham 12 C6
Earthcott Green 19 K3
Easby 63 F6
Easdale 79 J9
Easebourne 12 B4
Easenhall 31 F1
Eashing 22 C7
Easington Bucks 31 H7
Easington Dur 62 E2
Easington ERid 53 G1
Easington N'umb 77 K7
Easington Oxon 21 K2
Easington Oxon 31 F5
Easington R&C 63 H5
Easington Colliery 62 E2
Easington Lane 62 D2
Easingwold 58 B3
Easole Street 15 H2
Eassie 81 J6
East Aberthaw 18 D5
East Acton 23 F3
East Allington 5 H6
East Anstey 7 G3
East Anton 21 G7
East Appleton 62 C7
East Ardsley 57 J7
East Ashey 11 G6
East Ashling 12 B6
East Ayton 59 F1
East Barkwith 52 E4
East Barming 14 C2
East Barnby 63 J5
East Barnet 23 F2
East Barsham 44 D2
East Beckham 45 F2
East Bedfont 22 D4
East Bergholt 34 E5
East Bierley 57 G7
East Bilney 44 D4
East Blatchington 13 H7
East Boldon 71 J7
East Boldre 10 E4
East Bolton 71 G2
East Bower 8 C1
East Brent 19 G6
East Bridge 35 J2
East Bridgford 41 J1
East Buckland 6 E2
East Budleigh 7 J7
East Burnham 22 C3
East Burra 89 M9
East Burrafirth 89 M7
East Burton 9 H6
East Butsfield 62 B2
East Butterleigh 7 H5
East Butterwick 52 B2
East Calder 75 J4
East Carleton 45 F5
East Carlton N'hants 42 B7
East Carlton WYorks 57 H5
East Carlton Countryside Park N'hants LE16 8YF 42 B7
East Chaldon (Chaldon Herring) 9 G6
East Challow 21 G3
East Charleton 5 H6
East Chelborough 8 E4
East Chiltington 13 G5
East Chinnock 8 D3
East Chisenbury 20 E6
East Clandon 22 D6
East Claydon 31 J6
East Coker 8 E3
East Compton Dorset 9 H3
East Compton Som 19 K7
East Coombe 7 G5
East Cornworthy 5 J5
East Cottingwith 58 D5
East Cowes 11 G5
East Cowick 58 C7
East Cowton 62 D6
East Cramlington 71 H6
East Cranmore 19 K7
East Creech 9 J6
East Darlochan 66 A1
East Dean ESuss 13 J7
East Dean Hants 10 D2
East Dean WSuss 12 C5
East Dereham (Dereham) 44 D4
East Down 6 E1
East Drayton 51 K5
East Dundry 19 J5
East Ella 59 G7
East End ERid 59 H6
East End ERid 59 J7
East End Essex 25 G1
East End Hants 10 E5
East End Hants 21 H5
East End Herts 33 H6
East End Kent 14 D4
East End Kent 25 F4
East End MK 32 C4
East End NSom 19 H4
East End Oxon 30 E7
East End Poole 9 J5
East End Som 19 J6
East End Suff 35 F3
East End Suff 35 F5
East Farleigh 14 C2
East Farndon 42 A7
East Ferry 52 B3
East Firsby 52 D4
East Fleetham 71 H1
East Fortune 76 D3
East Garston 21 G4
East Ginge 21 H3
East Goscote 41 J4
East Grafton 21 F5
East Green Suff 33 K3
East Green Suff 35 J2
East Grimstead 10 D2
East Grinstead 13 G3
East Guldeford 14 E5
East Haddon 31 H2
East Hagbourne 21 J3
East Halton 52 E1
East Ham 23 H3
East Hanney 21 H2
East Hanningfield 24 D1
East Hardwick 51 G1
East Harling 44 D7
East Harlsey 62 E7
East Harnham 10 C2
East Harptree 19 J6
East Hartford 71 H6
East Harting 11 J3
East Hatch 9 J2
East Hatley 33 F3
East Hauxwell 62 B7
East Haven 81 L7
East Heckington 42 E1
East Hedleyhope 62 B2
East Hendred 21 H3
East Herrington 62 D1
East Heslerton 59 F2
East Hewish 19 H5
East Hoathly 13 J5
East Holme 9 H6
East Horndon 24 C3
East Horrington 19 J7
East Horsley 22 D6
East Horton 77 J7
East Howe 10 B5
East Huntspill 19 G7
East Hyde 32 E7
East Ilsley 21 H3
East Keal 53 G6
East Kennett 20 E5
East Keswick 57 J5
East Kilbride 74 E5
East Kimber 6 C6
East Kirkby 53 G6
East Knapton 58 E2
East Knighton 9 H6
East Knowstone 7 G3
East Knoyle 9 H1
East Kyloe 77 J7
East Lambrook 8 D3
East Lancashire Railway Lancs BL9 0EY 56 D7
East Langdon 15 J3
East Langton 42 A6
East Langwell 87 K9
East Lavant 12 B6
East Lavington 12 C5
East Layton 62 B5
East Leake 41 H3
East Learmouth 77 G7
East Leigh Devon 5 G5
East Leigh Devon 5 H5
East Leigh Devon 7 F4
East Leigh Devon 7 F5
East Lexham 44 C4
East Lilburn 71 F1
East Linton 76 D3
East Liss 11 J2
East Lockinge 21 H3
East Looe 4 C5
East Lound 51 K2
East Lulworth 9 H6
East Lutton 59 F3
East Lydford 8 E1
East Lyn 7 F1
East Lyng 8 C2
East Malling 14 C2
East Malling Heath 23 K6
East Manley 7 H4
East Marden 12 B5
East Markham 51 K5
East Martin 10 B3
East Marton 56 E4
East Meon 11 H2
East Mere 7 H4
East Mersea 34 E7
East Midlands Airport 41 G3
East Molesey 22 E5
East Moor 57 J7
East Morden 9 J5
East Morriston 76 E6
East Morton 57 G5
East Ness 58 C2
East Newton 59 J6
East Norton 42 A5
East Oakley 21 J6
East Ogwell 5 J3
East Orchard 9 H3
East Ord 77 H5
East Panson 6 B6
East Parley 10 C5
East Peckham 23 K7
East Pennard 8 E1
East Point Pavilion, Lowestoft Suff NR33 0AP 45 K6
East Portlemouth 5 H7
East Prawle 5 H7
East Preston 12 D6
East Pulham 9 G4
East Putford 6 B4
East Quantoxhead 7 K1
East Rainton 62 D2
East Ravendale 53 F3
East Raynham 44 C3
East Retford (Retford) 51 K4
East Rigton 57 J5
East Rolstone 19 G5
East Rounton 62 E6
East Row 63 J5
East Rudham 44 C3
East Runton 45 G1
East Ruston 45 H3
East Saltoun 76 C4
East Shefford 21 G4
East Sleekburn 71 H5
East Somerton 45 J4
East Stockwith 51 K3
East Stoke Dorset 9 H6
East Stoke Notts 42 A1
East Stour 9 H2
East Stourmouth 25 J5
East Stratton 21 J7
East Street 8 E1
East Studdal 15 J3
East Suisnish 82 F7
East Taphouse 4 B4
East Thirston 71 G4
East Tilbury 24 C4
East Tisted 11 J1
East Torrington 52 E4
East Town 19 K7
East Tuddenham 44 E4
East Tytherley 10 D2
East Tytherton 20 C4
East Village 7 G5
East Wall 38 E6
East Walton 44 B4
East Wellow 10 E2
East Wemyss 76 B1
East Whitburn 75 H4
East Wickham 23 H4
East Williamston 16 D5
East Winch 44 A4
East Winterslow 10 D1
East Wittering 11 J5
East Witton 57 G1
East Woodburn 70 E5
East Woodhay 21 H5
East Woodlands 20 A7
East Worldham 11 J1
East Worlington 7 F4
East Youlstone 6 A4
Eastacott 6 E3
Eastbourne 13 K7
Eastbourne Pier ESuss BN21 3EL 125 Eastbourne
Eastbrook 18 E4
Eastburn ERid 59 F4
Eastburn WYorks 57 F5
Eastbury Herts 22 E2
Eastbury WBerks 21 G4
Eastby 57 F4
Eastchurch 25 F4
Eastcombe Glos 20 B1
Eastcombe Som 7 K2
Eastcote GtLon 22 E3
Eastcote N'hants 31 H3
Eastcote WMid 30 C1
Eastcott Corn 6 A4
Eastcott Wilts 20 D6
Eastcourt 20 C2
Eastdown 5 J6
Eastend 30 E6
Easter Ardross 84 A3
Easter Balmoral 84 G11
Easter Buckieburn 75 F2
Easter Compton 19 J3
Easter Drummond 83 Q9
Easter Ellister 72 A5
Easter Fearn 84 A2
Easter Howlaws 77 F6
Easter Kinkell 83 R5
Easter Lednathie 81 J4
Easter Poldar 74 E1
Easter Skeld (Skeld) 89 M8
Easter Suddie 84 A5
Eastergate 12 C6
Easterhouse 74 E4
Easterton 20 D6
Easterton Sands 20 D6
Eastertown 19 G6
Eastfield Bristol 19 J4
Eastfield NLan 75 G4
Eastfield NYorks 59 G1
Eastfield Hall 71 H3
Eastgate Dur 61 L3
Eastgate Lincs 42 E4
Eastgate Norf 45 F3
Easthall 33 F6
Eastham Mersey 48 C4
Eastham Worcs 29 F2
Easthampstead 22 B5
Easthampton 28 D2
Easthaugh 44 E4
Eastheath 22 B5
Easthope 38 E6
Easthorpe Essex 34 D6
Easthorpe Leics 42 B2
Easthorpe Notts 51 K7
Easthouses 76 B4
Eastington Devon 7 F5
Eastington Glos 20 A1
Eastington Glos 30 C7
Eastleach Martin 21 F1
Eastleach Turville 21 F1
Eastleigh Devon 6 C3
Eastleigh Hants 11 F3
Eastling 14 E2
Eastmoor Derbys 51 F5
Eastmoor Norf 44 B5
Eastnor 29 G5
Eastoft 52 B1
Eastoke 11 J5
Easton Cambs 32 E1
Easton Cumb 60 D1
Easton Cumb 69 K6
Easton Devon 7 F7
Easton Dorset 9 F7
Easton Hants 11 G1
Easton IoW 10 E6
Easton Lincs 42 C3
Easton Norf 45 F4
Easton Som 19 J7
Easton Suff 35 G3
Easton Wilts 20 B4
Easton Grey 20 B3
Easton Maudit 32 B3
Easton on the Hill 42 D5
Easton Royal 21 F5
Easton-in-Gordano 19 J4
Eastrea 43 F6
Eastriggs 69 H7
Eastrington 58 D6
Eastry 15 J2
East-the-Water 6 C3
Eastville 19 K4
Eastwell 42 A3
Eastwick 33 H7
Eastwood Notts 41 G1
Eastwood SYorks 51 G3
Eastwood S'end 24 E3
Eastwood WYorks 56 E7
Eastwood End 43 H6
Eathorpe 30 E2
Eaton ChesE 49 H6
Eaton ChesW&C 48 E6
Eaton Leics 42 A3
Eaton Norf 44 A2
Eaton Norf 45 G5
Eaton Notts 51 K5
Eaton Oxon 21 H1
Eaton Shrop 38 C7
Eaton Shrop 38 E6
Eaton Bishop 28 D5
Eaton Bray 32 C6
Eaton Constantine 39 F5
Eaton Ford 32 E3
Eaton Hall 48 D6
Eaton Hastings 21 F2
Eaton Socon 32 E3
Eaton upon Tern 39 F3
Eaves Green 40 E7
Eavestone 57 H3
Ebberston 58 E1
Ebbesborne Wake 9 J2
Ebbw Vale (Glyn Ebwy) 18 E1
Ebchester 62 B1
Ebdon 19 G5
Ebford 7 H7
Ebley 20 B1
Ebnal 38 D1
Ebrington 30 C4
Ebsworthy Town 6 D6
Ecchinswell 21 H6
Ecclaw 77 F4
Ecclefechan 69 G6
Eccles GtMan 49 G3
Eccles Kent 24 D5
Eccles ScBord 77 F6
Eccles Green 28 C4
Eccles Road 44 E6
Ecclesfield 51 F3
Ecclesgreig 81 N4
Eccleshall 40 A3
Eccleshill 57 G6
Ecclesmachan 75 J3
Eccles-on-Sea 45 J3
Eccleston ChesW&C 48 D6
Eccleston Lancs 48 E1
Eccleston Mersey 48 D3
Eccup 57 H5
Echt 85 M10
Eckford 70 C1
Eckington Derbys 51 G5
Eckington Worcs 29 J4
Ecton N'hants 32 B2
Ecton Staffs 50 C7
Edale 50 D4
Eday 89 E4
Eday Airfield 89 E4
Edburton 13 F5
Edderside 60 C2
Edderton 84 B2
Eddington 21 G5
Eddleston 76 A6
Eden D&S 90 M7
Eden M&EAnt 92 K8
Eden Camp NYorks YO17 6RT 58 E2
Eden Park 23 G5
Eden Project Corn PL24 2SG 4 A5
Eden Vale 62 E3
Edenbridge 23 H7
Edendork 93 D10
Edenfield 49 G1
Edenhall 61 G3
Edenham 42 D3
Edensor 50 E5
Edentaggart 74 B1
Edenthorpe 51 J2
Edentrillick 93 H11
Edern 36 B2
Ederny 91 J10
Edgarley 8 E1
Edgbaston 40 C7
Edgcote 31 G4
Edgcott Bucks 31 H6
Edgcott Som 7 G2
Edgcumbe 2 E5
Edge Glos 20 B1
Edge Shrop 38 C5
Edge End 28 E7
Edge Green ChesW&C 48 D7
Edge Green GtMan 48 E3
Edge Green Norf 44 E7
Edgebolton 38 E3
Edgefield 44 E2
Edgehead 76 B4
Edgeley 38 E1
Edgerley 38 C4
Edgerton 50 D1
Edgeworth 20 C1
Edginswell 5 J4
Edgmond 39 G4
Edgmond Marsh 39 G3
Edgton 38 C7
Edgware 23 F2
Edgworth 49 G1
Edinample 80 B8
Edinbane 82 D5
Edinbarnet 74 D3
Edinburgh 76 A3
Edinburgh Airport 75 K3
Edinburgh Castle Edin EH1 2NG 126 E4
Edinburgh Zoo Edin EH12 6TS 120 C2
Edinchip 80 A8
Edingale 40 E4
Edingley 51 J7
Edingthorpe 45 H2
Edingthorpe Green 45 H2
Edington Som 8 C1
Edington Wilts 20 C6
Edistone 6 A3
Edith Weston 42 C5
Edithmead 19 G7
Edlaston 40 D1
Edlesborough 32 C7
Edlingham 71 G3
Edlington 53 F5
Edmondsham 10 B3
Edmondsley 62 C2
Edmondstown 18 D2
Edmondthorpe 42 B4
Edmonstone 89 E5
Edmonton Corn 3 G1
Edmonton GtLon 23 G2
Edmundbyers 62 A1
Ednam 77 F7
Ednaston 40 E1
Edney Common 24 C1
Edrom 77 G5
Edstaston 38 E2
Edstone 30 C2
Edvin Loach 29 F3
Edwalton 41 H2
Edwardstone 34 D4
Edwardsville 18 D2
Edwinsford 17 K2
Edwinstowe 51 J6
Edworth 33 F4
Edwyn Ralph 29 F3
Edzell 81 M4
Efail Isaf 18 D3
Efail-fâch 18 A2
Efailnewydd 36 C2
Efailwen 16 E3
Efenechtyd 47 K7
Effingham 22 E6
Effirth 89 M7
Efflinch 40 D4
Efford 7 G5
Egbury 21 H6
Egdean 12 C4
Egdon 29 J3
Egerton GtMan 49 G1
Egerton Kent 14 E3
Egerton Forstal 14 D3
Egerton Green 48 E7
Egg Buckland 4 E5
Eggborough 58 B7
Eggerness 64 E6
Eggesford Barton 6 E4
Eggington 32 C6
Egginton 40 E3
Egglescliffe 62 E5
Eggleston 61 L4
Egham 22 D4
Egham Wick 22 C4
Egilsay 89 D5
Egleton 42 B5
Eglingham 71 G2
Eglinton D&S 90 M4
Eglinton NAyr 74 B6
Egloshayle 4 A3
Egloskerry 4 C2
Eglwys Cross 38 D1
Eglwys Fach 37 F6
Eglwys Nunydd 18 B3
Eglwysbach 47 G5
Eglwys-Brewis 18 D5
Eglwyswrw 16 E2
Egmanton 51 K6
Egmere 44 D2
Egremont 60 B5
Egton 63 J6
Egton Bridge 63 J6
Egypt 21 H7
Eigg 78 F2
Eight Ash Green 34 D6
Eilanreach 83 J9
Eildon 76 D7
Eilean Donan Castle High IV40 8DX 83 J8
Eilean Shona 78 H3
Einacleit 88 G5
Eisingrug 37 F2
Eisteddfa Gurig 37 G7
Elan Valley Visitor Centre Powys LD6 5HP 27 J2
Elan Village 27 J2
Elberton 19 K3
Elborough 19 G6
Elburton 5 F5
Elcombe 20 E3
Elder Street 33 J5
Eldernell 43 G6
Eldersfield 29 G5
Elderslie 74 C4
Eldon 62 C4
Eldrick 67 G5
Eldroth 56 C3
Eldwick 57 G5
Elemore Vale 62 D2
Eleven Lane Ends 93 F13
Elford N'umb 77 K7
Elford Staffs 40 D4
Elford Closes 33 J1
Elgin 84 G4
Elgol 82 F9
Elham 15 G3
Elie 81 K10
Elilaw 70 E3
Elim 46 B4
Eling Hants 10 E3
Eling WBerks 21 J4
Eling Tide Mill Hants SO40 9HF 96 A3
Eliock 68 D3
Elishaw 70 D4
Elkesley 51 J5
Elkington 31 H1
Elkstone 29 J7
Elland 57 G7
Elland Upper Edge 57 G7
Ellary 73 F3
Ellastone 40 D1
Ellbridge 4 E4
Ellel 55 H4
Ellemford 77 F4
Ellenabeich 79 J9
Ellenborough 60 B3
Ellenhall 40 A3
Ellen's Green 12 D3
Ellerbeck 62 E7
Ellerby 63 H5
Ellerdine 39 F3
Ellerdine Heath 39 F3
Ellerker 59 F7
Ellerton ERid 58 D5
Ellerton NYorks 62 C7
Ellerton Shrop 39 G3
Ellerton Abbey 62 A7
Ellesborough 22 B1
Ellesmere 38 C2
Ellesmere Park 49 G3
Ellesmere Port 48 D5
Ellingham Hants 10 C4
Ellingham Norf 45 H6
Ellingham N'umb 71 G1
Ellingstring 57 G1
Ellington Cambs 32 E1
Ellington N'umb 71 H4
Ellington Thorpe 32 E1
Elliot 81 M7
Elliot's Green 20 A7
Ellisfield 21 K7
Ellishadder 82 E4
Ellistown 41 G4
Ellon 85 P7
Ellonby 60 F3
Ellough 45 J7
Ellough Moor 45 J7
Elloughton 59 F7
Ellwood 19 J1
Elm 43 H5
Elm Park 23 J3
Elmbridge 29 J2
Elmdon Essex 33 H5
Elmdon WMid 40 D7
Elmdon Heath 40 D7
Elmers End 23 G5
Elmer's Green 48 D2
Elmesthorpe 41 G6
Elmhurst 40 D4
Elmley Castle 29 J4
Elmley Lovett 29 H2
Elmore 29 G7
Elmore Back 29 G7
Elmscott 6 A3
Elmsett 34 E4
Elmstead Essex 34 E6
Elmstead GtLon 23 H4
Elmstead Market 34 E6
Elmstone 25 J5
Elmstone Hardwicke 29 J6
Elmswell ERid 59 F4
Elmswell Suff 34 D2
Elmton 51 H5
Elphin 86 E8
Elphinstone 76 B3
Elrick 85 N10
Elrig 64 D6
Elrigbeag 79 N9
Elsdon 70 E4
Elsecar 51 F2
Elsecar Heritage Centre SYorks S74 8HJ 51 F3
Elsenham 33 J6
Elsfield 31 G7
Elsham 52 D1
Elsing 44 E4
Elslack 56 E5
Elson Hants 11 H4
Elson Shrop 38 C2
Elsrickle 75 J6
Elstead 22 C7
Elsted 12 B5
Elsthorpe 42 D3
Elstob 62 D4
Elston Lancs 55 J6
Elston Notts 42 A1
Elstone 6 E4
Elstow 32 D4
Elstree 22 E2
Elstronwick 59 J6
Elswick 55 H6
Elsworth 33 G2
Elterwater 60 E6
Eltham 23 H4
Eltisley 33 F3
Elton Cambs 42 D6
Elton ChesW&C 48 D5
Elton Derbys 50 E6
Elton Glos 29 G7
Elton GtMan 49 G1
Elton Here 28 D1
Elton Notts 42 A2
Elton Stock 62 E5
Elton Green 48 D5
Elvanfoot 68 E2
Elvaston 41 G2
Elvaston Castle Country Park Derbys DE72 3EP 108 D6
Elveden 34 C1
Elvingston 76 C3
Elvington Kent 15 H2
Elvington York 58 D5
Elwick Hart 62 E3
Elwick N'umb 77 K7
Elworth 49 G6
Elworthy 7 J2
Ely Cambs 33 J1
Ely Cardiff 18 E4
Emberton 32 B4
Emberton Country Park MK MK46 5FJ 32 B3
Embleton Cumb 60 C3
Embleton Hart 62 E4
Embleton N'umb 71 H1
Embo 84 C1
Embo Street 84 C1
Emborough 19 K6
Embsay 57 F4
Embsay Steam Railway NYorks BD23 6AF 57 F4
Emerson Park 23 J3
Emery Down 10 D4
Emley 50 E1
Emmington 22 A1
Emneth 43 H5
Emneth Hungate 43 J5
Empingham 42 C5
Empshott 11 J1
Empshott Green 11 J1
Emsworth 11 J4
Enagh 93 F13
Enborne 21 H5
Enborne Row 21 H5
Enchmarsh 38 E6
Enderby 41 H6
Endmoor 55 J1
Endon 49 J7
Endon Bank 49 J7
Enfield 23 G2
Enfield Wash 23 G2
Enford 20 E6
Engine Common 19 K3
Englefield 21 K4
Englefield Green 22 C4
Englesea-brook 49 G7
English Bicknor 28 E7
English Frankton 38 D3
Englishcombe 20 A5
Enham Alamein 21 G7
Enmore 8 B1
Ennerdale Bridge 60 B5
Enniscaven 3 G3
Enniskillen 91 J12
Enniskillen Castle BT74 7ER 91 J12
Ennochdhu 80 F4
Ensdon 38 D4
Ensis 6 D3
Enson 40 B3
Enstone 30 E6
Enterkinfoot 68 D3
Enterpen 62 E6
Enton Green 22 C7
Enville 40 A7
Eòlaigearraidh 88 B8
Eòropaidh 88 L1
Epney 29 G7
Epperstone 41 J1
Epping 23 H1
Epping Green Essex 23 H1
Epping Green Herts 23 F1
Epping Upland 23 H1
Eppleby 62 B5
Eppleworth 59 G6
Epsom 23 F5
Epwell 30 E4
Epworth 51 K2
Epworth Turbary 51 K2
Erbistock 38 C1
Erbusaig 82 H8
Erchless Castle 83 Q6
Erdinagh 91 L12
Erdington 40 D6
Eredine 79 L10
Eriboll 86 G4
Ericstane 69 F2
Eridge Green 13 J3
Eriff 67 K3
Erines 73 G3
Erisey Barton 2 E7
Eriskay (Eiriosgaigh) 88 B7
Eriswell 34 B1
Erith 23 J4
Erlestoke 20 C6
Ermington 5 G5
Ernesettle 4 E4
Erpingham 45 F2
Erringden Grange 56 E7
Errogie (Earagaidh) 83 R8
Errol 80 H8
Erskine 74 C3
Erveny 91 H13
Ervey Cross Roads 90 M5
Ervie 66 D7
Erwarton 35 G5
Erwood 27 K4
Eryholme 62 D6
Eryrys 48 B7
Escart 73 G4
Escart Farm 73 G5
Escomb 62 B4
Escrick 58 C5
Esgair 17 G3
Esgairgeiliog 37 G5
Esgyryn 47 G5
Esh 62 B2
Esh Winning 62 B2
Esher 22 E5
Eshnadarragh 91 M13
Eshnadeelada 91 L13
Eshott 71 H4
Eshton 56 E4
Eskadale 83 Q7
Eskbank 76 B4
Eskdale Green 60 C6
Eskdalemuir 69 H4
Eskham 53 G3
Esknish 72 B4
Eskragh 91 M11
Esperley Lane Ends 62 B4
Espley Hall 71 G4
Esprick 55 H6
Essendine 42 D4
Essendon 23 F1
Essich 84 A7
Essington 40 B5
Eston 63 F5
Etal 77 H7
Etchilhampton 20 D5
Etchingham 14 C5
Etchinghill Kent 15 G4
Etchinghill Staffs 40 C4
Etherdwick Grange 59 J6
Etherley Dene 62 B4
Etherow Country Park GtMan SK6 5JQ 115 M6
Ethie Mains 81 M6
Eton 22 C4
Eton Wick 22 C4
Etteridge 84 A11
Ettiley Heath 49 G6
Ettington 30 D4
Etton ERid 59 F5
Etton Peter 42 E5
Ettrick 69 H2
Ettrickbridge 69 J1
Ettrickhill 69 H2
Etwall 40 E2
Eudon George 39 F7
Eureka! Museum for Children WYorks HX1 2NE 116 C5
Euston 34 C1
Euxton 48 E1
Evanstown 18 C3
Evanton 84 A4
Evedon 42 D1
Evelix 84 B1
Evenjobb 28 B2
Evenley 31 G5
Evenlode 30 D6
Evenwood 62 B4
Evenwood Gate 62 B4
Everbay 89 F5
Evercreech 9 F1
Everdon 31 G3
Everingham 58 E5
Everleigh 21 F6
Everley 59 F1
Eversholt 32 C5
Evershot 8 E4
Eversley 22 A5
Eversley Cross 22 A5
Everthorpe 59 F6
Everton CenBeds 33 F3
Everton Hants 10 D5
Everton Mersey 48 C3
Everton Notts 51 J3
Evertown 69 J6
Eves Corner 25 F2
Evesbatch 29 F4
Evesham 30 B4
Evesham Country Park Shopping & Garden Centre Worcs WR11 4TP 30 B4
Evie 89 C5
Evington 41 J5
Ewart Newtown 77 H7
Ewden Village 50 E3
Ewell 23 F5
Ewell Minnis 15 H3
Ewelme 21 K2
Ewen 20 D2
Ewenny 18 C4
Ewerby 42 E1
Ewerby Thorpe 42 E1
Ewhurst 22 D7
Ewhurst Green ESuss 14 C5
Ewhurst Green Surr 12 D3
Ewloe 48 C6
Ewloe Green 48 B6
Ewood 56 B7
Ewood Bridge 56 C7
Eworthy 6 C6
Ewshot 22 B7
Ewyas Harold 28 C6
Exbourne 6 E5
Exbury 11 F4
Exbury Gardens Hants SO45 1AZ 96 C8
Exceat 13 J7
Exebridge 7 H3
Exelby 57 H1
Exeter 7 H6
Exeter Cathedral Devon EX1 1HS 125 Exeter
Exeter International Airport 7 H6
Exford 7 G2
Exfords Green 38 D5
Exhall Warks 30 C3
Exhall Warks 41 F7
Exlade Street 21 K3
Exminster 7 H7
Exmoor Int. Dark Sky Reserve Devon/Som 7 F1
Exmouth 7 J7
Exnaboe 89 M11
Exning 33 K2
Explore-At-Bristol BS1 5DB 123 Bristol
Exton Devon 7 H7
Exton Hants 11 H2
Exton Rut 42 C4
Exton Som 7 H2
Exwick 7 H6
Eyam 50 E5
Eydon 31 G4
Eye Here 28 D2
Eye Peter 43 F5
Eye Suff 35 F1
Eye Green 43 F5
Eyemouth 77 H4
Eyeworth 33 F4
Eyhorne Street 14 D2
Eyke 35 H3
Eynesbury 32 E3
Eynort 82 D8
Eynsford 23 J5
Eynsham 21 H1
Eype 8 D5
Eyre 82 E5
Eythorne 15 H3
Eyton Here 28 D2
Eyton Shrop 38 C7
Eyton on Severn 38 E5
Eyton upon the Weald Moors 39 F4
Eywood 28 C3

F

Faccombe 21 G6
Faceby 62 E6
Fachwen 46 D6
Facit 49 H1
Faddiley 48 E7
Fadmoor 58 C1
Faebait 83 Q5
Faifley 74 D3
Fail 67 J1
Failand 19 J4
Failford 67 J1
Failsworth 49 H2
Fair Isle 89 K10
Fair Isle Airstrip 89 K10
Fair Oak Devon 7 J4
Fair Oak Hants 11 F3
Fair Oak Hants 21 J5
Fair Oak Green 21 K5
Fairbourne 37 F4
Fairburn 57 K7
Fairfield Derbys 50 C5
Fairfield GtMan 49 J3
Fairfield Kent 14 E5
Fairfield Mersey 48 B4
Fairfield Stock 62 E5
Fairfield Worcs 29 J1
Fairfield Halls, Croydon GtLon CR9 1DG 105 B12
Fairford 20 E1
Fairgirth 65 J5
Fairhaven 55 G7
Fairhill 75 F5
Fairholm 75 F5
Fairlands Valley Park Herts SG2 0BL 33 F6
Fairley 85 N10
Fairlie 74 A5
Fairlight 14 D6
Fairlight Cove 14 D6
Fairmile Devon 7 J6
Fairmile Surr 22 E5
Fairmilehead 76 A4
Fairnington 70 B1
Fairoak 39 G2
Fairseat 24 C5
Fairstead 34 B7
Fairwarp 13 H4
Fairwater 18 E4
Fairy Cross 6 C3
Fairyhill 17 H6
Fakenham 44 D3
Fakenham Magna 34 D1
Fala 76 C4
Fala Dam 76 C4
Falahill 76 B5
Faldingworth 52 D4
Falfield 19 K2
Falin-Wnda 17 G1
Falkenham 35 G5
Falkirk 75 G3
Falkirk Wheel Falk FK1 4RS 75 G2
Falkland 80 H10
Falla 70 C2
Fallgate 51 F6
Fallagloon 92 D6
Fallin 75 G1
Falmer 13 G6
Falmouth 3 F5
Falsgrave 59 G1
Falstone 70 C5
Famous Grouse Experience, Glenturret Distillery P&K PH7 4HA 80 D8
Fanagmore 86 D5
Fancott 32 D6
Fangdale Beck 63 F7
Fangfoss 58 D4
Fankerton 75 F2
Fanmore 78 F6
Fanner's Green 33 K7
Fans 76 E6
Fantasy Island Lincs PE25 1RH 53 J6
Far Cotton 31 J3
Far Forest 29 G1
Far Gearstones 56 C1
Far Green 20 A1
Far Moor 48 E2
Far Oakridge 20 C1
Far Royds 57 H6
Far Sawrey 60 E7
Farcet 43 F6
Farden 28 E1
Fardross 91 M12
Fareham 11 G4
Farewell 40 C4
Farforth 53 G5
Faringdon 21 F2
Farington 55 J7
Farlam 61 G1
Farlary 87 K9
Farleigh NSom 19 J5
Farleigh Surr 23 G5
Farleigh Hungerford 20 B6
Farleigh Wallop 21 K7
Farlesthorpe 53 H5
Farleton Cumb 55 J1
Farleton Lancs 55 J3
Farley Derbys 50 E6
Farley Shrop 38 C5
Farley Staffs 40 C1
Farley Wilts 10 D2
Farley Green Suff 34 B3
Farley Green Surr 22 D7
Farley Hill 22 A5
Farleys End 29 G7
Farlington 58 C3
Farlough 92 F7
Farlow 39 F7
Farm Town 41 F4
Farmborough 19 K5
Farmcote 30 B6
Farmington 30 C7
Farmoor 21 H1
Farmtown 85 K5
Farnborough GtLon 23 H5
Farnborough Hants 22 B6
Farnborough Street 22 B6
Farnborough Warks 31 F4
Farnborough WBerks 21 H3
Farncombe 22 C7
Farndish 32 C2
Farndon ChesW&C 48 D7
Farndon Notts 51 K7
Farne Islands 77 K7
Farnell 81 M5
Farnham Dorset 9 J3
Farnham Essex 33 H6
Farnham NYorks 57 J3
Farnham Suff 35 H2
Farnham Surr 22 B7
Farnham Common 22 C3
Farnham Green 33 H6
Farnham Royal 22 C3
Farningham 23 J5
Farnley NYorks 57 H5
Farnley WYorks 57 H6
Farnley Tyas 50 D1
Farnsfield 51 J7
Farnworth GtMan 49 G2
Farnworth Halton 48 E4
Farr High 84 A7
Farr High 84 C10
Farr High 87 K3
Farraline 83 R8
Farranamucklagh 93 D13
Farrancassidy 91 F11
Farranflugh 92 G7
Farringdon 7 J6
Farrington Gurney 19 K6
Farsley 57 H6
Farthing Corner 24 E5
Farthing Green 14 D3
Farthinghoe 31 G5
Farthingstone 31 H3
Farthorpe 53 F5
Fartown 50 D1
Farway 7 K6
Fascadale 78 G3
Fashion Museum B&NESom BA1 2QH 20 A5
Faslane 74 A2
Fasnakyle 83 P8
Fassfern 79 M3
Fatfield 62 D1
Faugh 61 G1
Fauldhouse 75 H4
Faulkbourne 34 B7
Faulkland 20 A6
Fauls 38 E2
Faulston 10 B2
Faversham 25 G5
Fawdington 57 K2
Fawdon 71 H7
Fawfieldhead 50 C6
Fawkham Green 23 J5
Fawler 30 E7
Fawley Bucks 22 A3
Fawley Hants 11 F4
Fawley WBerks 21 G3
Fawley Chapel 28 E6
Faxfleet 58 E7
Faxton 31 J1
Faygate 13 F3
Fazakerley 48 C3
Fazeley 40 E5
Fearby 57 G1
Fearnan 80 C6
Fearnbeg 82 H5
Fearnhead 49 F3
Fearnmore 82 H4
Fearnoch A&B 73 H2
Fearnoch A&B 73 J3
Featherstone Staffs 40 B5
Featherstone WYorks 57 K7
Featherstone Castle 70 B7
Feckenham 30 B2
Feeny 92 B6
Feering 34 C6
Feetham 61 L7
Feizor 56 C3
Felbridge 13 G3
Felbrigg 45 G2
Felcourt 23 G7
Felden 22 D1
Felhampton 38 D7
Felindre Carmar 17 G2
Felindre Carmar 17 J3
Felindre Carmar 17 K2
Felindre Carmar 27 G6
Felindre Cere 26 E3
Felindre Powys 28 A6
Felindre Powys 38 A7
Felindre Swan 17 K5
Felinfach Cere 26 E3
Felinfach Powys 27 K5
Felinfoel 17 J5
Felingwmisaf 17 J3
Felingwmuchaf 17 J3
Felixkirk 57 K1
Felixstowe 35 H5
Felixstowe Ferry 35 H5
Felkington 77 H6
Felldownhead 6 B7
Felling 71 H7
Felmersham 32 C3
Felmingham 45 G3
Felpham 12 C7
Felsham 34 D3
Felsted 33 K6
Feltham 22 E4
Felthamhill 22 E4

Gors 27 F1
Gorsedd 47 K5
Gorseinon 17 J6
Gorseybank 50 E7
Gorsgoch 26 D3
Gorslas 17 J4
Gorsley 29 F6
Gorsley Common 29 F6
Gorstage 49 F5
Gorstan 83 P4
Gorsty Hill 40 D3
Gortaclare 91 M10
Gortahurk 92 D7
Gortavoy Bridge 93 C10
Gortenorn 78 H4
Gortfin 91 M10
Gortin 90 L8
Gortinreid 90 M5
Gortmullan 91 J14
Gortnacreagh 90 L9
Gortnagallon 92 G9
Gortnahey 92 B5
Gortnalee 91 F11
Gorton 49 H3
Gortreagh 92 C9
Gosbeck 35 F3
Gosberton 43 F2
Gosberton Clough 42 E3
Gosfield 34 B6
Gosford Here 28 E2
Gosford Oxon 31 G7
Gosforth Cumb 60 B6
Gosforth T&W 71 H7
Gosland Green 48 E7
Gosmore 32 E6
Gospel End 40 A6
Gosport 11 H5
Gossabrough 89 P4
Gossington 20 A1
Gossops Green 13 F3
Goswick 77 J6
Gotham 41 H2
Gotherington 29 J6
Gothers 3 G3
Gott 89 N8
Gotton 8 B2
Goudhurst 14 C4
Goulceby 53 F5
Gourdon 81 P3
Gourock 74 A3
Govan 74 D4
Goverton 51 K7
Goveton 5 H6
Govilon 28 B7
Gowdall 58 C7
Gowdystown 93 G11
Gowerton 17 J6
Gowkhall 75 J2
Gowkthrapple 75 F5
Gowthorpe 58 D4
Goxhill ERid 59 H5
Goxhill NLincs 59 H7
Goytre 18 A3
Gozzard's Ford 21 H2
Grabhair 88 J6
Graby 42 D3
Gracefield 92 E8
Gracehill 92 F6
Gradbach 49 J6
Grade 2 E7
Gradeley Green 48 E7
Graffham 12 C5
Grafham Cambs 32 E2
Grafham Surr 22 D7
Grafham Water Cambs PE28 0BH 32 E2
Grafton Here 28 D5
Grafton NYorks 57 K3
Grafton Oxon 21 F1
Grafton Shrop 38 D4
Grafton Worcs 28 E2
Grafton Worcs 29 J5
Grafton Flyford 29 J3
Grafton Regis 31 J4
Grafton Underwood 42 C7
Grafty Green 14 D3
Graianrhyd 48 B7
Graig Carmar 17 H5
Graig Conwy 47 G5
Graig Denb 47 J5
Graig-fechan 47 K7
Grain 24 E4
Grainel 72 A4
Grains Bar 49 J2
Grainsby 53 F3
Grainthorpe 53 G3
Graizelound 51 K3
Grampound 3 G4
Grampound Road 3 G3
Granborough 31 J6
Granby 42 A2
Grand Pier, Teignmouth Devon TQ14 8BB 5 K3
Grandborough 31 F2
Grandes Rocques 3 J5
Grandtully 80 E5
Grange Cumb 60 D5
Grange EAyr 74 C7
Grange High 83 P7
Grange Med 24 D5
Grange Mersey 48 B4
Grange Mid Ulster 93 D9
Grange Blundel 93 D11
Grange Corner 92 F7
Grange de Lings 52 C5
Grange Hill 23 H2
Grange Moor 50 E1
Grange of Lindores 80 H9
Grange Villa 62 C1
Grangee 93 L9
Grangemill 50 E7
Grangemouth 75 H3
Grange-over-Sands 55 H2
Grangeston 67 G4
Grangetown Cardiff 18 E4
Grangetown R&C 63 F4
Gransha AB&C 93 H12
Gransha L&C 93 K10
Gransha M&EAnt 92 K7
Gransmoor 59 H4
Granston 16 B2
Grantchester 33 H3
Grantham 42 C2
Grantley 57 H2
Granton 76 A3
Granton House 69 F3
Grantown-on-Spey 84 E8
Grantsfield 28 E2
Grantshouse 77 G4
Granville 93 C10
Grappenhall 49 F4
Grasby 52 D2
Grasmere 60 E6
Grass Green 34 B5
Grasscroft 49 J2
Grassendale 48 C4
Grassgarth 60 F7
Grassholme 61 L4
Grassington 57 F3
Grassmoor 51 G6
Grassthorpe 51 K6
Grateley 21 F7
Gratwich 40 C2
Gravel Hill 22 D2
Graveley Cambs 33 F2
Graveley Herts 33 F6
Gravelly Hill 40 D6
Gravels 38 C5
Graven 89 N5
Graveney 25 G5
Gravesend 24 C4
Grayingham 52 C3
Grayrigg 61 G7
Grays 24 C4
Grayshott 12 B3
Grayswood 12 C3
Grazeley 21 K5
Greasbrough 51 G3
Greasby 48 B4
Great Aberystwyth Camera Obscura Cere SY23 2DN 36 E7
Great Abington 33 J4
Great Addington 32 C1
Great Alne 30 C3
Great Altcar 48 C2
Great Amwell 33 G7
Great Asby 61 H5
Great Ashfield 34 D2
Great Ayton 63 F5
Great Baddow 24 D1
Great Bardfield 33 K5
Great Barford 32 E3
Great Barr 40 C6
Great Barrington 30 D7
Great Barrow 48 D6
Great Barton 34 C2
Great Barugh 58 D2
Great Bavington 70 E5
Great Bealings 35 G4
Great Bedwyn 21 F5
Great Bentley 35 F6
Great Bernera 88 G4
Great Billing 32 B2
Great Bircham 44 B2
Great Blakenham 35 F3
Great Bolas 39 F3
Great Bookham 22 E6
Great Bourton 31 F4
Great Bowden 42 A7
Great Bradley 33 K3
Great Braxted 34 C7
Great Bricett 34 E3
Great Brickhill 32 C5
Great Bridgeford 40 A3
Great Brington 31 H2
Great Bromley 34 E6
Great Broughton Cumb 60 B3
Great Broughton NYorks 63 F6
Great Buckland 24 C5
Great Budworth 49 F5
Great Burdon 62 D5
Great Burstead 24 C2
Great Busby 63 F6
Great Cambourne 33 G3
Great Canfield 33 J7
Great Canney 24 E1
Great Carlton 53 H4
Great Casterton 42 D5
Great Chalfield 20 B5
Great Chart 14 E3
Great Chatwell 39 G4
Great Chell 49 H7
Great Chesterford 33 J4
Great Cheverell 20 C6
Great Chishill 33 H5
Great Clacton 35 F7
Great Clifton 60 B4
Great Coates 53 F2
Great Comberton 29 J4
Great Corby 61 F1
Great Cornard 34 C4
Great Cowden 59 J5
Great Coxwell 21 F2
Great Crakehall 57 H1
Great Cransley 32 B1
Great Cressingham 44 C5
Great Crosby 48 C2
Great Crosthwaite 60 D4
Great Cubley 40 D2
Great Cumbrae 73 K5
Great Dalby 42 A4
Great Doddington 32 B2
Great Doward 28 E7
Great Dunham 44 C4
Great Dunmow 33 K6
Great Durnford 10 C1
Great Easton Essex 33 K6
Great Easton Leics 42 B6
Great Eccleston 55 H5
Great Edstone 58 D1
Great Ellingham 44 E6
Great Elm 20 A7
Great Eversden 33 G3
Great Fencote 62 C7
Great Finborough 34 E3
Great Fransham 44 C4
Great Gaddesden 32 D7
Great Gidding 42 E7
Great Givendale 58 E4
Great Glemham 35 H2
Great Glen 41 J6
Great Gonerby 42 B2
Great Gransden 33 F3
Great Green Cambs 33 F4
Great Green Norf 45 G7
Great Green Suff 34 D3
Great Green Suff 34 E1
Great Green Suff 35 F1
Great Habton 58 D2
Great Hale 42 E1
Great Hall Hants SO23 8UJ 137 Winchester
Great Hallingbury 33 J7
Great Hampden 22 B1
Great Harrowden 32 B1
Great Harwood 56 C6
Great Haseley 21 K1
Great Hatfield 59 H5
Great Haywood 40 C3
Great Heath 41 F7
Great Heck 58 B7
Great Henny 34 C5
Great Hinton 20 C6
Great Hockham 44 D6
Great Holland 35 G7
Great Horkesley 34 D5
Great Hormead 33 H5
Great Horton 57 G6
Great Horwood 31 J5
Great Houghton N'hants 31 J3
Great Houghton SYorks 51 G2
Great Hucklow 50 D5
Great Kelk 59 H3
Great Kimble 22 B1
Great Kingshill 22 B2
Great Langton 62 C7
Great Leighs 34 B7
Great Limber 52 E2
Great Linford 32 B4
Great Livermere 34 C1
Great Longstone 50 E5
Great Lumley 62 C2
Great Lyth 38 D5
Great Malvern 29 G4
Great Maplestead 34 C5
Great Marton 55 G6
Great Massingham 44 B3
Great Melton 45 F5
Great Milton 21 K1
Great Missenden 22 B1
Great Mongeham 15 J2
Great Moulton 45 F6
Great Munden 33 G6
Great Musgrave 61 J5
Great Ness 38 D4
Great Notley 34 B6
Great Nurcot 7 H2
Great Oak 19 G1
Great Oakley Essex 35 F6
Great Oakley N'hants 42 B7
Great Offley 32 E6
Great Orme Tramway Conwy LL30 2HG 47 F4
Great Ormside 61 J5
Great Orton 60 E1
Great Ouseburn 57 K3
Great Oxendon 42 A7
Great Oxney Green 24 C1
Great Palgrave 44 C4
Great Parndon 23 H1
Great Paxton 33 F2
Great Plumpton 55 G6
Great Plumstead 45 H5
Great Ponton 42 C2
Great Potheridge 6 D4
Great Preston 57 J7
Great Purston 31 G5
Great Raveley 43 F7
Great Rissington 30 C7
Great Rollright 30 E5
Great Ryburgh 44 D3
Great Ryle 71 F2
Great Ryton 38 D5
Great Saling 34 B6
Great Salkeld 61 G3
Great Sampford 33 K5
Great Sankey 48 E4
Great Saredon 40 B5
Great Saxham 34 B2
Great Shefford 21 G4
Great Shelford 33 H3
Great Smeaton 62 D6
Great Snoring 44 D2
Great Somerford 20 C3
Great St. Mary's Church Cambs CB2 3PQ 123 Cambridge
Great Stainton 62 D4
Great Stambridge 25 F2
Great Staughton 32 E2
Great Steeping 53 H6
Great Stonar 15 J2
Great Strickland 61 G4
Great Stukeley 33 F1
Great Sturton 53 F5
Great Sutton ChesW&C 48 C5
Great Sutton Shrop 38 E7
Great Swinburne 70 E6
Great Tew 30 E6
Great Tey 34 C6
Great Thorness 11 F5
Great Thurlow 33 K4
Great Torr 5 G6
Great Torrington 6 C4
Great Tosson 71 F3
Great Totham Essex 34 C7
Great Totham Essex 34 C7
Great Tows 53 F3
Great Urswick 55 F2
Great Wakering 25 F3
Great Waldingfield 34 D4
Great Walsingham 44 D2
Great Waltham 33 K7
Great Warley 23 J2
Great Washbourne 29 J5
Great Weeke 7 F7
Great Welnetham 34 C3
Great Wenham 34 E5
Great Whittington 71 F6
Great Wigborough 34 D7
Great Wigsell 14 C5
Great Wilbraham 33 J3
Great Wilne 41 G2
Great Wishford 10 B1
Great Witcombe 29 J7
Great Witley 29 G2
Great Wolford 30 D5
Great Wratting 33 K4
Great Wymondley 33 F6
Great Wyrley 40 B5
Great Wytheford 38 E4
Great Yarmouth 45 K5
Great Yeldham 34 B5
Greatford 42 D4
Greatgate 40 C1
Greatham Hants 11 J1
Greatham Hart 62 E4
Greatham WSuss 12 D5
Greatness 23 J6
Greatstone-on-Sea 15 F5
Greatworth 31 G4
Green 47 J6
Green Cross 12 B3
Green End Bed 32 E3
Green End Bucks 32 C5
Green End Cambs 33 H1
Green End Cambs 33 G1
Green End Herts 33 G5
Green End Herts 33 G6
Green End Warks 40 E7
Green Hammerton 57 K4
Green Hill 20 D3
Green Lane 30 B2
Green Moor 50 E3
Green Ore 19 J6
Green Quarter 61 F6
Green Street ESuss 14 C6
Green Street Herts 22 E2
Green Street Herts 33 H6
Green Street Worcs 29 H4
Green Street WSuss 12 E4
Green Street Green GtLon 23 H5
Green Street Green Kent 23 J4
Green Tye 33 H7
Greenan 93 G14
Greencastle F&O 90 M8
Greencastle NM&D 93 H15
Greencroft 62 B2
Greendykes 71 F1
Greenend 30 E6
Greenfaulds 75 F3
Greenfield CenBeds 32 D5
Greenfield (Maes-Glas) Flints 47 K5
Greenfield GtMan 50 C2
Greenfield High 83 N10
Greenfield Lincs 53 H5
Greenfield NM&D 93 J15
Greenfield Oxon 22 A2
Greenford 22 E3
Greengairs 75 F3
Greengates 57 G6
Greengill 60 C3
Greenhalgh 55 H6
Greenham 21 H5
Greenhaugh 70 C5
Greenhead 70 B7
Greenheys 49 G2
Greenhill D&G 69 G6
Greenhill GtLon 22 E3
Greenhill SYorks 51 F4
Greenhithe 23 J4
Greenholm 74 D7
Greenholme 61 G6
Greenhow Hill 57 G3
Greenigo 89 D7
Greenisland 92 J8
Greenlands 22 A3
Greenlaw 77 F6
Greenloaning 80 D10
Greenmeadow 19 F2
Greenmoor Hill 21 K3
Greenmount 49 G1
Greenock 74 A3
Greenodd 55 G1
Greens Norton 31 H4
Greenside T&W 71 G7
Greenside WYorks 50 D1
Greenstead 34 E6
Greenstead Green 34 C6
Greensted 23 J1
Greensted Green 23 J1
Greenville 90 K8
Greenway Pembs 16 D2
Greenway Som 8 C2
Greenwell 61 G1
Greenwich 23 G4
Greenwood Forest Park, Y Felinheli Gwyn LL56 4QN 46 D6
Greerstown 93 H10
Greet 30 B5
Greete 28 E1
Greetham Lincs 53 G5
Greetham Rut 42 C4
Greetland 57 F7
Gregson Lane 55 J7
Greinton 8 D1
Grenaby 54 B6
Grendon N'hants 32 B2
Grendon Warks 40 E5
Grendon Common 40 E6
Grendon Green 28 E3
Grendon Underwood 31 H6
Grenitote (Greinetobht) 88 C1
Grenofen 4 E3
Grenoside 51 F3
Greosabhagh 88 G8
Gresford 48 C7
Gresham 45 F2
Greshornish 82 D5
Gress (Griais) 88 K3
Gressenhall 44 D4
Gressingham 55 J3
Greta Bridge 62 A5
Gretna 69 J7
Gretna Green 69 J7
Gretton Glos 30 B5
Gretton N'hants 42 C6
Gretton Shrop 38 E6
Grewelthorpe 57 H2
Greyabbey 93 L10
Greygarth 57 G2
Greylake 8 C1
Greys Green 22 A3
Greysouthen 60 B4
Greystead 70 C5
Greysteel 90 M4
Greystoke 60 F3
Greystone 56 D5
Greystones 51 F4
Greywell 22 A6
Gribthorpe 58 D6
Gribton 68 E5
Griff 41 F7
Griffithstown 19 F2
Grigghall 61 F7
Grimeford Village 49 F1
Grimesthorpe 51 F3
Grimethorpe 51 G2
Griminis (Griminish) 88 B3
Grimister 89 N3
Grimley 29 H2
Grimmet 67 H2
Grimoldby 53 G4
Grimpo 38 C3
Grimsargh 55 J6
Grimsay (Griomsaigh) 88 C3
Grimsbury 31 F4
Grimsby 53 F2
Grimscote 31 H3
Grimscott 6 A5
Grimshader (Griomsiadar) 88 K5
Grimsthorpe 42 D3
Grimston ERid 59 J6
Grimston Leics 41 J3
Grimston Norf 44 B3
Grimstone 9 F5
Grimstone End 34 D2
Grindale 59 H2
Grindiscol 89 N9
Grindle 39 G5
Grindleford 50 E5
Grindleton 56 C5
Grindley 40 C3
Grindley Brook 38 E1
Grindlow 50 D5
Grindon N'umb 77 H6
Grindon Staffs 50 C7
Grindon Stock 62 D4
Grindon T&W 62 D1
Gringley on the Hill 51 K3
Grinsdale 60 E1
Grinshill 38 E3
Grinton 62 A7
Grisdale 61 J7
Gristhorpe 59 G1
Griston 44 D6
Gritley 89 E7
Grittenham 20 D3
Grittleton 20 B4
Grizebeck 55 F1
Grizedale 60 E7
Grizedale Forest Park Cumb LA22 0QJ 60 E7
Grobister 89 F5
Groby 41 H5
Groes 47 J6
Groes-faen 18 D3
Groesffordd 36 B2
Groesffordd Marli 47 J5
Groeslon Gwyn 46 C7
Groeslon Gwyn 46 D6
Groes-lwyd 38 B4
Groes-wen 18 E3
Grogport 73 G6
Groigearraidh 88 B5
Gromford 35 H3
Gronant 47 J4
Groombridge 13 J3
Groombridge Place Gardens Kent TN3 9QG 13 J3
Grosmont Mon 28 D6
Grosmont NYorks 63 J6
Groton 34 D4
Groundistone Heights 69 K2
Grouville 3 K7
Grove Bucks 32 C6
Grove Dorset 9 F7
Grove Kent 25 J5
Grove Notts 51 K5
Grove Oxon 21 H2
Grove End 24 E5
Grove Green 14 C2
Grove Park 23 H4
Grove Town 57 K7
Grovehill 22 D1
Grovesend SGlos 19 K3
Grovesend Swan 17 J5
Gruids 86 H9
Gruline 78 G6
Grumbla 2 B6
Grundisburgh 35 G3
Gruting 89 L8
Grutness 89 N11
Gualachulain 79 N6
Guardbridge 81 K9
Guarlford 29 H4
Gubbergill 60 B7
Gubblecote 32 C7
Guernsey 3 J5
Guernsey Airport 3 H6
Guestling Green 14 D6
Guestling Thorn 14 D6
Guestwick 44 E3
Guestwick Green 44 E3
Guide 56 C7
Guide Post 71 H5
Guilden Down 38 C7
Guilden Morden 33 F4
Guilden Sutton 48 D6
Guildford 22 C7
Guildford House Gallery Surr GU1 3AJ 128 Guildford
Guildtown 80 G7
Guilsborough 31 H1
Guilsfield (Cegidfa) 38 B4
Guilthwaite 51 G4
Guisborough 63 G5
Guiseley 57 G5
Guist 44 E3
Guith 89 E4
Guiting Power 30 B6
Gulberwick 89 N9
Gulladuff 92 D7
Gullane 76 C2
Gullane Bents ELoth EH31 2AZ 76 C2
Gulval 2 B5
Gulworthy 4 E3
Gumfreston 16 E5
Gumley 41 J6
Gunby Lincs 42 C3
Gunby Lincs 53 H6
Gundleton 11 H1
Gunn 6 E2
Gunnersbury 22 E4
Gunnerside 61 L7
Gunnerton 70 E6
Gunness 52 B1
Gunnislake 4 E3
Gunnister 89 M5
Gunstone 40 A5
Gunter's Bridge 12 C4
Gunthorpe Norf 44 E2
Gunthorpe Notts 41 J1
Gunthorpe Rut 42 B5
Gunville 11 F6
Gunwalloe 2 D6
Gupworthy 7 H2
Gurnard 11 F5
Gurnett 49 J5
Gurney Slade 19 K7
Gurnos MTyd 18 D1
Gurnos Powys 18 A1
Gushmere 15 F2
Gussage All Saints 10 B3
Gussage St. Andrew 9 J3
Gussage St. Michael 9 J3
Guston 15 J3
Gutcher 89 P3
Guthram Gowt 42 E3
Guthrie 81 L5
Guyhirn 43 G5
Guy's Head 43 H3
Guy's Marsh 9 H2
Guyzance 71 H3
Gwaelod-y-garth 18 E3
Gwaenysgor 47 J4
Gwaithla 28 B3
Gwalchmai 46 B5
Gwastad 16 D3
Gwastadnant 46 E7
Gwaun-Cae-Gurwen 27 G7
Gwaynynog 47 J6
Gwbert 16 E1
Gweek 2 E6
Gwehelog 19 G1
Gwenddwr 27 K4
Gwendreath 2 E7
Gwennap 2 E4
Gwennap Mining District (Cornwall & West Devon Mining Landscape) Corn 2 E4
Gwenter 2 E7
Gwernaffield 48 B6
Gwernesney 19 H1
Gwernogle 17 J2
Gwernymynydd 48 B6
Gwern-y-Steeple 18 D4
Gwersyllt 48 C7
Gwespyr 47 K4
Gwinear 2 C5
Gwithian 2 C4
Gwredog 46 C4
Gwrhay 18 E2
Gwyddelwern 37 K1
Gwyddgrug 17 H2
Gwynfryn 48 B7
Gwystre 27 K2
Gwytherin 47 G6
Gyfelia 38 C1
Gyre 89 C7
Gyrn Goch 36 D1

H

Habberley 38 C5
Habin 12 B4
Habost (Tabost) 88 L1
Habrough 52 E1
Haccombe 5 J3
Hacconby 42 E3
Haceby 42 D2
Hacheston 35 H3
Hackbridge 23 F5
Hackenthorpe 51 G4
Hackford 44 E5
Hackforth 62 C7
Hackleton 32 B3
Hacklinge 15 J2
Hackness 63 K7
Hackney 23 G3
Hackthorn 52 C4
Hackthorpe 61 G4
Hacton 23 J3
Hadden 77 F7
Haddenham Bucks 22 A1
Haddenham Cambs 33 H1
Haddington ELoth 76 D3
Haddington Lincs 52 C6
Haddiscoe 45 J6
Haddo Country Park Aber AB41 7EQ 85 N7
Haddon 42 E6
Hade Edge 50 D2
Hademore 40 D5
Hadfield 50 C3
Hadham Cross 33 H7
Hadham Ford 33 H6
Hadleigh Essex 24 E3
Hadleigh Suff 34 E4
Hadleigh Castle Country Park Essex SS7 2PP 24 E3
Hadleigh Farm Essex SS7 2AP 24 E3
Hadleigh Heath 34 D4
Hadley Tel&W 39 F4
Hadley Worcs 29 H2
Hadley End 40 D3
Hadley Wood 23 F2
Hadlow 23 K7
Hadlow Down 13 J4
Hadnall 38 E3
Hadrian's Wall (Frontiers of the Roman Empire) Cumb/N'umb 69 K7 & 71 F7
Hadspen 9 F1
Hadstock 33 J4
Hadston 71 H4
Hadzor 29 J2
Haffenden Quarter 14 D3
Hafod Bridge 17 K2
Hafod-Dinbych 47 G7
Hafodunos 47 G6
Hafodyrynys 19 F2
Haggate 56 D6
Haggbeck 69 K6
Haggersta 89 M8
Haggerston GtLon 23 G3
Haggerston N'umb 77 J6
Haggrister 89 M5
Haggs 75 F3
Hagley Here 28 E4
Hagley Worcs 40 B7
Hagnaby Lincs 53 G6
Hagnaby Lincs 53 H5
Hague Bar 49 J4
Hagworthingham 53 G6
Haigh 49 F2
Haigh Hall Country Park GtMan WN2 1PE 48 E2
Haighton Green 55 J6
Hail Weston 32 E2
Haile 60 B6
Hailes 30 B5
Hailey Herts 33 G7
Hailey Oxon 21 K3
Hailey Oxon 30 E7
Hailsham 13 J6
Hainault 23 H2
Hainault Forest Country Park Essex IG7 4QN 104 G2
Haine 25 K5
Hainford 45 G4
Hainton 52 E4
Haisthorpe 59 H3
Hakin 16 B5
Halam 51 J7
Halbeath 75 K2
Halberton 7 J4
Halcro 87 Q3
Hale Cumb 55 J2
Hale GtMan 49 G4
Hale Halton 48 D4
Hale Hants 10 C3
Hale Surr 22 B7
Hale Bank 48 D4
Hale Barns 49 G4
Hale Nook 55 G5
Hale Street 23 K7
Hales Norf 45 H6
Hales Staffs 39 G2
Hales Green 40 D1
Hales Place 15 G2
Halesgate 43 G3
Halesowen 40 B7
Halesworth 35 H1
Halewood 48 D4
Half Way Inn 7 J6
Halford Devon 5 J3
Halford Shrop 38 D7
Halford Warks 30 D4
Halfpenny 55 J1
Halfpenny Green 40 A6
Halfway Carmar 17 J5
Halfway Carmar 17 K2
Halfway Powys 27 H5
Halfway SYorks 51 G4
Halfway WBerks 21 H5
Halfway Bridge 12 C4
Halfway House 38 C4
Halfway Houses Kent 25 F4
Halfway Houses Lincs 52 B6
Halghton Mill 38 D1
Halifax 57 F7
Halistra 82 C5
Halket 74 C5
Halkirk 87 P4
Halkyn 48 B5
Hall 74 C5
Hall Cross 55 H7
Hall Dunnerdale 60 D7
Hall Green ChesE 49 H7
Hall Green Lancs 55 H7
Hall Green WMid 40 D7
Hall Grove 33 F7
Hall of the Forest 38 B7
Halland 13 J5
Hallaton 42 A6
Hallatrow 19 K6
Hallbankgate 61 G1
Hallen 19 J3
Hallfield Gate 51 F7
Hallglen 75 G3
Hallin 82 C5
Halling 24 D5
Hallington Lincs 53 G4
Hallington N'umb 70 E6
Halliwell 49 F1
Halloughton 51 J7
Hallow 29 H3
Hallow Heath 29 H3
Hallrule 70 A2
Halls 76 E3
Halls Green Essex 23 H1
Hall's Green Herts 33 F6
Hallsands 5 J7
Hallthwaites 54 E1
Hallwood Green 29 F5
Hallworthy 4 B2
Hallyne 75 K6
Halmer End 39 G1
Halmond's Frome 29 F4
Halmore 19 K1
Halmyre Mains 75 K6
Halnaker 12 C6
Halsall 48 C1
Halse N'hants 31 G4
Halse Som 7 K3
Halsetown 2 C5
Halsham 59 J7
Halsinger 6 D2
Halstead Essex 34 C5
Halstead Kent 23 H5
Halstead Leics 42 A5
Halstock 8 E4
Halsway 7 K2
Haltemprice Farm 59 G6
Haltham 53 F6
Haltoft End 43 G1
Halton Bucks 32 B7
Halton Halton 48 E4
Halton Lancs 55 J3
Halton N'umb 70 E7
Halton Wrex 38 C2
Halton East 57 F4
Halton Gill 56 D2
Halton Green 55 J3
Halton Holegate 53 H6
Halton Lea Gate 61 H1
Halton Park 55 J3
Halton West 56 D4
Haltwhistle 70 C7
Halvergate 45 J5
Halwell 5 H5
Halwill 6 C6
Halwill Junction 6 C6
Ham Devon 8 B4
Ham Glos 19 K2
Ham Glos 29 J6
Ham GtLon 22 E4
Ham High 87 Q2
Ham Kent 15 J2
Ham Plym 4 E5
Ham Shet 89 H9
Ham Som 8 B2
Ham Som 8 B3
Ham Wilts 21 G5
Ham Common 9 H2
Ham Green Here 29 G4
Ham Green Kent 14 D5
Ham Green Kent 24 E5
Ham Green NSom 19 J4
Ham Green Worcs 30 B2
Ham Hill 24 C5
Ham Hill Country Park Som TA14 6RW 8 D3
Ham Street 8 E1
Hambleden 22 A3
Hambledon Hants 11 H3
Hambledon Surr 12 C3
Hamble-le-Rice 11 F4
Hambleton Lancs 55 G5
Hambleton NYorks 58 B6
Hambridge 8 C2
Hambrook SGlos 19 K4
Hambrook WSuss 11 J4
Hameringham 53 G6
Hamerton 32 E1
Hamilton 75 F5
Hamilton's Bawn 93 E12
Hamlet Devon 7 K6
Hamlet Dorset 8 E4
Hammer 12 B3
Hammerpot 12 D6
Hammersmith 23 F4
Hammersmith Apollo GtLon W6 9QH 103 F8
Hammerwich 40 C5
Hammerwood 13 H3
Hammond Street 23 G1
Hammoon 9 H3
Hamnavoe Shet 89 M9
Hamnavoe Shet 89 N4
Hamnavoe Shet 89 N5
Hamnish Clifford 28 E3
Hamp 8 B1
Hampden Park 13 K6
Hampden Park Stadium Glas G42 9BA 118 E6
Hamperden End 33 J5
Hampnett 30 C7
Hampole 51 H2
Hampreston 10 B5
Hampstead 23 F3
Hampstead Norreys 21 J4
Hampsthwaite 57 H4
Hampton Devon 8 B5
Hampton GtLon 22 E5
Hampton Kent 25 H5
Hampton Peter 42 E6
Hampton Shrop 39 G7
Hampton Swin 20 E2
Hampton Worcs 30 B4
Hampton Bishop 28 E5
Hampton Court Palace & Garden GtLon KT8 9AU 103 D11
Hampton Fields 20 B2
Hampton Heath 38 D1
Hampton in Arden 40 E7
Hampton Loade 39 G7
Hampton Lovett 29 H2
Hampton Lucy 30 D3
Hampton on the Hill 30 D2
Hampton Poyle 31 G7
Hampton Wick 22 E5
Hamptworth 10 D3
Hamsey 13 H5
Hamsey Green 23 G6
Hamstall Ridware 40 D4
Hamstead 10 E5
Hamstead Marshall 21 H5
Hamsteels 62 B2
Hamsterley Dur 62 B1
Hamsterley Dur 62 B3
Hamsterley Forest Dur DL13 3NL 62 A4
Hamstreet 15 F4
Hamworthy 9 J5
Hanbury Staffs 40 D3
Hanbury Worcs 29 J2
Hanbury Woodend 40 D3
Hanby 42 D2
Hanchurch 40 A1
Handa Island 86 D5
Handale 63 H5
Handbridge 48 D6
Handcross 13 F3
Handforth 49 H4
Handley ChesW&C 48 D7
Handley Derbys 51 F6
Handley Green 24 C1
Handsacre 40 C4
Handside 33 F7
Handsworth SYorks 51 G4
Handsworth WMid 40 C6
Handwoodbank 38 D4
Handy Cross 22 B2
Hanford Dorset 9 H3
Hanford Stoke 40 A1
Hanging Bridge 40 D1
Hanging Houghton 31 J1
Hanging Langford 10 B1
Hangingshaw 69 G5
Hanham 19 K4
Hankelow 39 F1
Hankerton 20 C2
Hankham 13 K6
Hanley 40 A1
Hanley Castle 29 H4
Hanley Child 29 F2
Hanley Swan 29 H4
Hanley William 29 F2
Hanlith 56 E3
Hanmer 38 D2
Hannah 53 H5
Hannahstown 93 H9
Hannington Hants 21 J6
Hannington N'hants 32 B1
Hannington Swin 20 E2
Hannington Wick 20 E2
Hanslope 32 B4
Hanthorpe 42 D3
Hanwell GtLon 22 E4
Hanwell Oxon 31 F4
Hanwood 38 D5
Hanworth GtLon 22 E4
Hanworth Norf 45 F2
Happisburgh 45 H2
Happisburgh Common 45 H3
Hapsford 48 D5
Hapton Lancs 56 C6
Hapton Norf 45 F6
Harberton 5 H5
Harbertonford 5 H5
Harbledown 15 G2
Harborne 40 C7
Harborough Magna 31 F1
Harbottle 70 E3
Harbour Park Amusements, Littlehampton WSuss BN17 5LL 12 D6
Harbourneford 5 H4
Harbridge 10 C3
Harbridge Green 10 C3
Harburn 75 J4
Harbury 30 E3
Harby Leics 42 A2
Harby Notts 52 B5
Harcombe 7 K6
Harcombe Bottom 8 C5
Harden WMid 40 C5
Harden WYorks 57 F6
Hardendale 61 G5
Hardenhuish 20 C4
Hardgate Aber 85 M10
Hardgate NYorks 57 H3
Hardham 12 D5
Hardhorn 55 G6
Hardingham 44 E5
Hardingstone 31 J3
Hardington 20 A6
Hardington Mandeville 8 E3
Hardington Marsh 8 E4
Hardington Moor 8 E3
Hardley 11 F4
Hardley Street 45 H5
Hardmead 32 C4
Hardraw 61 K7
Hardstoft 51 G6
Hardway Hants 11 H4
Hardway Som 9 G1
Hardwick Bucks 32 B7
Hardwick Cambs 33 G3
Hardwick Lincs 52 B5
Hardwick Norf 45 G6
Hardwick N'hants 32 B2
Hardwick Oxon 21 G1
Hardwick Oxon 31 G6
Hardwick SYorks 51 G4
Hardwick WMid 40 C6
Hardwick Hall Derbys S44 5QJ 51 G6
Hardwick Hall Country Park, Sedgefield Dur TS21 2EH 62 D4
Hardwick Village 51 J5
Hardwicke Glos 29 G7
Hardwicke Glos 29 J6
Hardwicke Here 28 B4
Hardy's Green 34 D6
Hare Green 34 E6
Hare Hatch 22 B4
Hare Street Herts 33 G6
Hare Street Herts 33 G6
Hareby 53 G6
Harecroft 57 F6
Hareden 56 B4
Harefield 22 D2
Harehill 40 D2
Harehills 57 J6
Harehope 71 F1
Harelaw 75 H6
Hareplain 14 D4
Harescough 61 H2
Harescombe 29 H7
Haresfield 29 H7
Hareshaw NLan 75 G4
Hareshaw SLan 74 E6
Harestock 11 F1
Harewood 57 J5
Harewood End 28 E6
Harewood House WYorks LS17 9LG 57 J5
Harford Devon 5 G5
Harford Devon 7 G6
Hargate 45 F6
Hargatewall 50 D5
Hargrave ChesW&C 48 D6
Hargrave N'hants 32 D1
Hargrave Suff 34 B3
Hargrave Green 34 B3
Harker 69 J7
Harkstead 35 F5
Harlaston 40 E4
Harlaxton 42 B2
Harle Syke 56 D6
Harlech 36 E2
Harlech Castle (Castles & Town Walls of King Edward in Gwynedd) Gwyn LL46 2YH 36 E2
Harlequin 41 J2
Harlescott 38 E4
Harlesden 23 F3
Harleston Devon 5 H6
Harleston Norf 45 G7
Harleston Suff 34 E2
Harlestone 31 J2
Harley Shrop 38 E5
Harley SYorks 51 F3
Harleyholm 75 H7
Harlington CenBeds 32 D5
Harlington GtLon 22 D4
Harlington SYorks 51 G2
Harlosh 82 C6
Harlow 23 H1
Harlow Hill 71 F7
Harlthorpe 58 D6
Harlton 33 G3
Harlyn 3 F1
Harman's Cross 9 J6
Harmby 57 G1
Harmer Green 33 F7
Harmer Hill 38 D3
Harmondsworth 22 D4
Harmston 52 C6
Harnage 38 E5
Harnham 10 C2
Harnhill 20 D1
Harold Hill 23 J2
Harold Park 23 J2
Harold Wood 23 J2
Haroldston West 16 B4
Haroldswick 89 Q1
Harome 58 C1
Harpenden 32 E7
Harpford 7 J6
Harpham 59 G3
Harpley Norf 44 B3
Harpley Worcs 29 F2
Harpole 31 H2
Harprigg 56 B1
Harpsden 22 A3
Harpswell 52 C4
Harpur Hill 50 C5
Harpurhey 49 H2
Harracott 6 D3
Harrietfield 80 E8
Harrietsham 14 D2
Harringay 23 G3
Harrington Cumb 60 A4
Harrington Lincs 53 G5
Harrington N'hants 31 J1
Harringworth 42 C6
Harris 82 D11
Harris Green 45 G6
Harris Museum & Art Gallery, Preston Lancs PR1 2PP 55 J7
Harriseahead 49 H7
Harriston 60 C2
Harrogate 57 J4
Harrogate International Centre NYorks HG1 5LA 128 Harrogate
Harrold 32 C3
Harrold-Odell Country Park Bed MK43 7DS 32 C3
Harrop Fold 56 C5
Harrow 22 E3
Harrow Green 34 C3
Harrow Museum GtLon HA2 6PX 102 C4
Harrow on the Hill 22 E3
Harrow Weald 22 E2
Harrowbarrow 4 E3
Harrowden 32 D4
Harrowgate Hill 62 C5
Harry Stoke 19 K4
Harston Cambs 33 H3
Harston Leics 42 B2
Harswell 58 E5
Hart 62 E3
Hartburn 71 F5
Hartest 34 C3
Hartfield 13 H3
Hartford Cambs 33 F1
Hartford ChesW&C 49 F5
Hartford Som 7 H3
Hartford End 33 K7
Hartfordbridge 22 A6
Hartforth 62 B6
Hartgrove 9 H3
Harthill ChesW&C 48 E7
Harthill NLan 75 H4
Harthill SYorks 51 G4
Hartington 50 D6
Hartington Hall 71 F5
Hartland 6 A3
Hartland Quay 6 A3
Hartlebury 29 H1
Hartlepool 63 F3
Hartlepool's Maritime Experience Hart TS24 0XZ 63 F3
Hartley Cumb 61 J6
Hartley Kent 14 C4
Hartley Kent 24 C5
Hartley N'umb 71 J6
Hartley Green 40 B3
Hartley Mauditt 11 J1
Hartley Wespall 21 K6
Hartley Wintney 22 A6
Hartlington 57 F3
Hartlip 24 E5
Hartoft End 63 H7
Harton NYorks 58 D3
Harton Shrop 38 D7
Harton T&W 71 J7
Hartpury 29 H6
Hartrigge 70 B1
Hartshead 57 G7
Hartshill 41 F6
Hartsholme Country Park Lincs LN6 0EY 52 C6
Hartshorne 41 F3
Hartsop 60 F5
Hartwell Bucks 31 J7
Hartwell ESuss 13 H3
Hartwell N'hants 31 J3
Hartwith 57 H3
Hartwood 75 G5
Harvel 24 C5
Harvington Worcs 29 H1
Harvington Worcs 30 B4
Harwell Notts 51 J3
Harwell Oxon 21 H3
Harwich 35 G5
Harwood Dur 61 K3
Harwood GtMan 49 G1
Harwood Dale 63 K7
Harwood on Teviot 69 K3
Harworth 51 J3
Hasbury 40 B7
Hascombe 22 D7
Haselbech 31 J1
Haselbury Plucknett 8 D3
Haseley 30 D2
Haseley Knob 30 D1
Haselor 30 C3
Hasfield 29 H6
Hasguard 16 B5
Haskayne 48 C2
Hasketon 35 G3
Hasland 51 F6
Hasland Green 51 F6
Haslemere 12 C3
Haslingden 56 C7
Haslingden Grane 56 C7
Haslingfield 33 H3
Haslington 49 G7
Hassall 49 G7
Hassall Green 49 G7
Hassell Street 15 F3
Hassendean 70 A1
Hassingham 45 H5
Hassocks 13 G5
Hassop 50 E5
Hasthorpe 53 H6
Hastigrow 87 Q3
Hastingleigh 15 F3
Hastings ESuss 14 D7
Hastings Som 8 C3
Hastings Fishermen's Museum ESuss TN34 3DW 128 Hastings
Hastingwood 23 H1
Hastoe 22 C1
Haswell 62 D2
Haswell Plough 62 D2
Hatch CenBeds 32 E4
Hatch Hants 21 K6
Hatch Beauchamp 8 C2
Hatch End 22 E2
Hatch Green 8 C3
Hatching Green 32 E7
Hatchmere 48 E5
Hatcliffe 53 F2
Hatfield Here 28 E3
Hatfield Herts 23 F1
Hatfield SYorks 51 J2
Hatfield Broad Oak 33 J7
Hatfield Heath 33 J7
Hatfield House Herts AL9 5NF 23 F1
Hatfield Peverel 34 B7
Hatfield Woodhouse 51 J2
Hatford 21 G2
Hatherden 21 G6
Hatherleigh 6 D5
Hathern 41 G3
Hatherop 20 E1
Hathersage 50 E4
Hathersage Booths 50 E4
Hathershaw 49 J2
Hatherton ChesE 39 F1
Hatherton Staffs 40 B4
Hatley St. George 33 F3
Hatt 4 D4
Hattingley 11 H1
Hatton Aber 85 Q7
Hatton Derbys 40 E2
Hatton GtLon 22 E4
Hatton Lincs 52 E5
Hatton Shrop 38 D6
Hatton Warks 30 D2
Hatton Warr 48 E4
Hatton Country World Warks CV35 8XA 30 D2
Hatton Heath 48 D6
Hatton of Fintray 85 N9
Haugh 53 H5
Haugh Head 71 F1
Haugh of Glass 85 J7
Haugh of Urr 65 J4
Haugham 53 G4
Haughhead 74 E3
Haughley 34 E2
Haughley Green 34 E2
Haughley New Street 34 E2
Haughton ChesE 48 E7
Haughton Notts 51 J5
Haughton Powys 38 C4
Haughton Shrop 38 C3
Haughton Shrop 38 E4
Haughton Shrop 39 F6
Haughton Staffs 40 A3
Haughton Green 49 J3
Haughton Le Skerne 62 D5
Haultwick 33 G6
Haunton 40 E4
Hauxton 33 H3
Havannah 49 H6
Havant 11 J4
Haven 28 D3
Havenstreet 11 G5
Havercroft 51 F1
Haverfordwest (Hwlffordd) 16 C4
Haverhill 33 K4
Haverigg 54 E2
Havering Park 23 H2
Havering-atte-Bower 23 J2
Haversham 32 B4
Haverthwaite 55 G1
Haverton Hill 62 E4
Haviker Street 14 C3
Havyat 8 E1
Hawarden (Penarlâg) 48 C6
Hawbridge 29 J4
Hawbush Green 34 B6
Hawcoat 55 F2
Hawes 56 D1
Hawe's Green 45 G6
Hawick 70 A2
Hawkchurch 8 C4
Hawkedon 34 B3
Hawkenbury Kent 13 J3
Hawkenbury Kent 14 D3
Hawkeridge 20 B6
Hawkerland 7 J7
Hawkes End 40 E7
Hawkesbury 20 A3
Hawkesbury Upton 20 A3
Hawkhill 71 H2
Hawkhurst 14 C4
Hawkinge 15 H3
Hawkley 11 J2
Hawkridge 7 G2
Hawkshead 60 E7
Hawkshead Hill 60 E7
Hawksheads 55 H3
Hawksland 75 G6
Hawkswick 56 E2
Hawksworth Notts 42 A1
Hawksworth WYorks 57 G5
Hawksworth WYorks 57 H6
Hawkwell Essex 24 E2
Hawkwell N'umb 71 F6
Hawley Hants 22 B6
Hawley Kent 23 J4
Hawley's Corner 23 H6
Hawling 30 B6
Hawnby 58 B1
Haworth 57 F6
Hawstead 34 C3
Hawstead Green 34 C3
Hawthorn Dur 62 E2
Hawthorn Hants 11 H1
Hawthorn RCT 18 D3
Hawthorn Wilts 20 B5
Hawthorn Hill BrackF 22 B4
Hawthorn Hill Lincs 53 F7
Hawthorpe 42 D3
Hawton 51 K7
Haxby 58 C4
Haxey 51 K2
Haxted 23 H7
Haxton 20 E7
Hay Green 43 J4
Hay Mills 40 D7
Hay Street 33 G6
Haydock 48 E3
Haydon Dorset 9 F3
Haydon Swin 20 E3
Haydon Bridge 70 D7
Haydon Wick 20 E3
Hayes GtLon 22 D3
Hayes GtLon 23 H5
Hayes End 22 D3
Hayfield Derbys 50 C4
Hayfield Fife 76 A1
Haygrove 8 B1
Hayhillock 81 L6
Hayle 2 C5
Hayling Island 11 J4
Haymoor Green 49 F7
Hayne 7 H4
Haynes 32 E4
Haynes Church End 32 D4
Haynes West End 32 D4
Hay-on-Wye (Y Gelli Gandryll) 28 B4
Hayscastle 16 B3
Hayscastle Cross 16 C3
Hayton Cumb 60 C2
Hayton Cumb 61 G1
Hayton ERid 58 E5
Hayton Notts 51 K4
Hayton's Bent 38 E7
Haytor Vale 5 H3
Hayward Gallery GtLon SE1 8XZ 132 F4
Haywards Heath 13 G4
Haywood Oaks 51 J7
Hazel End 33 H6
Hazel Grove 49 J4
Hazel Street 13 K3
Hazelbank 75 G6
Hazelbury Bryan 9 G4
Hazeleigh 24 E1
Hazeley 22 A6
Hazelhurst 49 G1
Hazelside 68 D1
Hazelslack 55 H2
Hazelslade 40 C4
Hazelwood Derbys 41 F1
Hazelwood GtLon 23 H5
Hazlefield 65 H6
Hazlehead Aberdeen 85 N10
Hazlehead SYorks 50 D2
Hazlemere 22 B2
Hazlerigg 71 H6
Hazleton 30 B7
Hazon 71 G3
Heacham 44 A2
Head Bridge 6 E4
Headbourne Worthy 11 F1
Headcorn 14 D3

Impington **33** H2
Ince **48** D5
Ince Blundell **48** C2
Ince-in-Makerfield **48** E2
Inch Kenneth **78** F7
Inchbare **81** M4
Inchberry **84** H5
Inchbraoch **81** N5
Inchgrundle **81** K3
Inchinagh **92** B6
Inchinnan **74** C4
Inchlaggan **83** M10
Inchmarnock **73** J5
Inchnacardoch Hotel **83** P9
Inchnadamph **86** E7
Inchree **79** M4
Inchrory **84** F10
Inchture **80** H8
Indian Queens **3** G3
Inerval **72** B6
Ingatestone **24** C2
Ingbirchworth **50** E2
Ingerthorpe **57** H3
Ingestre **40** B3
Ingham *Lincs* **52** C4
Ingham *Norf* **45** H3
Ingham *Suff* **34** C1
Ingham Corner **45** H3
Ingleborough **43** H4
Ingleby *Derbys* **41** F3
Ingleby *Lincs* **52** B5
Ingleby Arncliffe **62** E6
Ingleby Barwick **62** E5
Ingleby Cross **62** E6
Ingleby Greenhow **63** F6
Ingleigh Green **6** E5
Inglesbatch **20** A5
Inglesham **21** F2
Ingleton *Dur* **62** B4
Ingleton *NYorks* **56** B2
Inglewhite **55** J5
Ingliston **75** K3
Ingmire Hall **61** H7
Ingoe **71** F6
Ingoldisthorpe **44** A2
Ingoldmells **53** J6
Ingoldsby **42** D2
Ingon **30** D3
Ingram **71** F2
Ingrave **24** C2
Ingrow **57** F6
Ings **60** F7
Ingst **19** J3
Ingworth **45** F3
Inhurst **21** J5
Inisclan **90** J8
Inishrush **92** E6
Injebreck **54** C5
Inkberrow **30** B3
Inkersall **51** G5
Inkersall Green **51** G5
Inkpen **21** G5
Inkstack **87** Q2
Inmarsh **20** C5
Innellan **73** K4
Innerhadden **80** B5
Innerleithen **76** B7
Innerleven **81** J10
Innermessan **64** A4
Innerwick *ELoth* **77** F3
Innerwick *P&K* **80** A6
Innsworth **29** H6
Insch **85** L8
Insh **84** C10
Inskip **55** H6
Instow **6** C2
Intake **51** H2
Intech, Winchester *Hants* SO21 1HX **11** G2
International Centre, The, Telford *Tel&W* TF3 4JH **39** G5
Intwood **45** F5
Inver *Aber* **84** G11
Inver *High* **84** C2
Inver Mallie **79** N2
Inverailort **79** J2
Inverallign **83** J5
Inverallochy **85** Q4
Inveraray (Inbhir Aora) **79** M10
Inverarish **82** F7
Inverarity **81** K6
Inverarnan (Inbhir Àirnein) **79** Q9
Inverasdale **83** J2
Inverbeg **74** B1
Inverbervie **81** P3
Inverbroom **83** M2
Invercassley **86** G9
Inverchaolain **73** J3
Invercharnan **79** N6
Inverchoran **83** N5
Invercreran **79** M6
Inverdruie **84** D9
Inveresk **76** B3
Inverey **80** F2
Inverfarigaig **83** R8
Invergarry (Inbhir Garadh) **83** P10
Invergeldie **80** C8
Invergloy **79** P2
Invergordon **84** B4
Invergowrie **81** J7
Inverharroch Farm **84** H7
Inverie **82** H10
Inverinan **79** L9
Inverinate **83** K8
Inverkeilor **81** M6
Inverkeithing **75** K2
Inverkeithny **85** L6
Inverkip **74** A3
Inverkirkaig **86** C8
Inverlael **83** M2
Inverlauren **74** B2
Inverlochlarig **79** R9
Inverlussa **72** E2
Invermore **92** J6
Invermoriston (Inbhir Moireasdan) **83** Q9
Invernaver **87** K3
Inverneil **73** G2
Inverness (Inbhir Nis) **84** A6
Inverness Airport **84** B5
Invernoaden **73** K1
Inveroran Hotel (Inbhir Orain) **79** P6
Inverquharity **81** K5
Inverquhomery **85** Q6
Inverroy **79** P2
Inversnaid Hotel **79** Q10
Inverugie **85** R6
Inveruglas (Inbhir Dhubhghlais) **79** Q10
Inverurie **85** M8
Invervar **80** B6
Invervegain **73** J3
Invwardleigh **6** D6
Inworth **34** C7
Iochdar (Eochar) **88** B4
Iona **78** D8
Iping **12** B4
Ipplepen **5** J4
Ipsden **21** K3
Ipstones **40** C1
Ipswich **35** F4
Irby **48** B4
Irby Hill **48** B4
Irby in the Marsh **53** H6
Irby upon Humber **52** E2
Irchester **32** C2
Irchester Country Park *N'hants* NN29 7DL **32** C2
Ireby *Cumb* **60** D3
Ireby *Lancs* **56** B2
Ireland **89** M10
Ireland's Cross **39** G1
Ireleth **55** F2
Ireshopeburn **61** K3
Irish Hill **92** J8
Irlam **49** G3
Irnham **42** D3
Iron Acton **19** K3
Iron Cross **30** B3
Ironbridge **39** F5
Ironbridge Gorge *Tel&W* TF8 7DQ **39** F5
Irons Bottom **23** F7
Ironville **51** G7
Irstead **45** H3
Irthington **69** K7
Irthlingborough **32** C1
Irton **59** G1
Irvine **74** B7
Irvinestown **91** J11
Isauld **87** M3
Isbister *Ork* **89** B5
Isbister *Shet* **89** M3
Isbister *Shet* **89** P6
Isfield **13** H5
Isham **32** B1
Isington **22** A7
Island of Stroma **87** R2
Islawr-dref **37** F4
Islay **72** A4
Islay Airport **72** B5
Islay House **72** B4
Isle Abbotts **8** C2
Isle Brewers **8** C2
Isle of Bute Discovery Centre *A&B* PA20 0AH **73** J4
Isle of Lewis (Eilean Leodhais) **88** J3
Isle of Man **54** C5
Isle of Man Airport **54** B7
Isle of May **76** E1
Isle of Noss **89** P8
Isle of Sheppey **25** F4
Isle of Walney **54** E3
Isle of Whithorn **64** E7
Isle of Wight **11** F6
Isle of Wight (Sandown Airport) **11** G6
Isle of Wight Pearl *IoW* PO30 4DD **11** F6
Isle of Wight Zoo *IoW* PO36 8QB **11** H6
Isleham **33** K1
Isleornsay (Eilean Iarmain) **82** G9
Isles of Scilly (Scilly Isles) **2** C1
Isleworth **22** E4
Isley Walton **41** G3
Islibhig **88** E5
Islip *N'hants* **32** C1
Islip *Oxon* **31** G7
Isombridge **39** F4
Istead Rise **24** C5
Itchen **11** F3
Itchen Abbas **11** G1
Itchen Stoke **11** G1
Itchen Valley Country Park *Hants* SO30 3HQ **96** D2
Itchingfield **12** E4
Itchington **19** K3
Itteringham **45** F2
Itton *Devon* **6** E6
Itton *Mon* **19** H2
Itton Common **19** H2
Ivegill **60** F2
Ivelet **61** L7
Iver **22** D3
Iver Heath **22** D3
Iveston **62** B1
Ivetsey Bank **40** A4
Ivinghoe **32** C7
Ivinghoe Aston **32** C7
Ivington **28** D3
Ivington Green **28** D3
Ivy Hatch **23** J6
Ivy Todd **44** C5
Ivybridge **5** G5
Ivychurch **15** F5
Iwade **25** F5
Iwerne Courtney (Shroton) **9** H3
Iwerne Minster **9** H3
Ixworth **34** D1
Ixworth Thorpe **34** D1

J

Jack Hill **57** G4
Jackfield **39** F5
Jacksdale **51** G7
Jackton **74** D5
Jacobstow **4** B1
Jacobstowe **6** D5
Jacobswell **22** C6
James Hamilton Heritage Park *SLan* G74 5LB **119** G7
James Pringle Weavers of Inverness *High* IV2 4RB **84** A6
Jameston **16** D6
Jamestown *D&G* **69** J4
Jamestown *WDun* **74** B2
Janefield **84** B5
Janetstown **87** R4
Janus Stones BT93 8AA **91** G10
Jarrow **71** J7
Jarvis Brook **13** J3
Jasper's Green **34** B6
Jawcraig **75** G3
Jayes Park **22** E7
Jaywick **35** F7
Jealott's Hill **22** B4
Jeater Houses **62** E7
Jedburgh **70** B1
Jeffreyston **16** D5
Jemimaville **84** B4
Jephson Gardens *Warks* CV32 4ER **30** E2
Jericho **49** H1
Jerrettspass **93** F13
Jersay **75** G4
Jersey **3** J7
Jersey Airport **3** J7
Jersey Marine **18** A2
Jerviswood **75** G6
Jesmond **71** H7
Jevington **13** J6
Jinney Ring Craft Centre, The *Worcs* B60 4BU **29** J2
Jockey End **32** D7
Jodrell Bank **49** G5
Jodrell Bank Observatory & Arboretum *ChesE* SK11 9DL **49** G5
John Muir Country Park *ELoth* EH42 1UW **76** E3
John o' Groats **87** R2
Johnby **60** F3
John's Cross **14** C5
Johnshaven **81** N4
Johnson Street **45** H4
Johnston **16** C4
Johnstone **74** C4
Johnstone Castle **74** C4
Johnstonebridge **69** F4
Johnstons Cashmere Visitor Centre *Moray* IV30 4AF **84** G4
Johnstown *Carmar* **17** G4
Johnstown *Wrex* **38** C1
Jonesborough **93** F15
Joppa **67** J2
Jordans **22** C2
Jordanston **16** C2
Jorvik YO1 9WT **137** York
Jorvik Glass *NYorks* YO60 7DA **58** D3
Joy's Green **29** F7
Jumpers Common **10** C5
Juniper Green **75** K4
Juniper Hill **31** G5
Jura **72** D2
Jura House **72** C4
Jurby East **54** C4
Jurby West **54** C4

K

Kaber **61** J5
Kaimes **76** A4
Kames *A&B* **73** H3
Kames *EAyr* **68** B1
Katesbridge **93** H12
Kea **3** F4
Keadby **52** B1
Keady **93** D13
Keal Cotes **53** G6
Kearney **93** M11
Kearsley **49** G2
Kearstwick **56** B2
Kearton **62** A7
Keasden **56** C3
Keckwick **48** E4
Keddington **53** G4
Keddington Corner **53** G4
Kedington **34** B4
Kedleston **41** F1
Keelby **52** E1
Keele **40** A1
Keeley Green **32** D4
Keelham **57** F6
Keenaghan **91** F11
Keenans Bridge **92** E6
Keenthorne **8** B1
Keeran **91** J10
Keeres Green **33** J7
Keeston **16** B4
Keevil **20** C6
Kegworth **41** G3
Kehelland **2** D4
Keighley **57** F5
Keighley & Worth Valley Railway *WYorks* BD22 8NJ **57** F5
Keil **66** A3
Keilhill **85** M5
Keillmore **72** E2
Keills **72** C4
Keils **72** D4
Keinton Mandeville **8** E1
Keir House **75** F1
Keir Mill **68** D4
Keisby **42** D3
Keisley **61** J4
Keiss **87** R3
Keith **85** J5
Kelbrook **56** E5
Kelby **42** D1
Keld *Cumb* **61** G5
Keld *NYorks* **61** K6
Keldholme **58** D1
Keldy Castle **63** H7
Kelfield *NLincs* **52** B2
Kelfield *NYorks* **58** B6
Kelham **51** K7
Kella **54** C4
Kellacott **6** C7
Kellan **78** G6
Kellas *Angus* **81** K7
Kellas *Moray* **84** F5
Kellaton **5** H7
Kellaways **20** C4
Kelleth **61** H6
Kelleythorpe **59** G4
Kelling **44** E1
Kellington **58** B7
Kelloe **62** D3
Kelloholm **68** C2
Kelly *Corn* **4** A3
Kelly *Devon* **6** B7
Kelly Bray **4** D3
Kelmarsh **31** J1
Kelmscott **21** F2
Kelsale **35** H2
Kelsall **48** E6
Kelsay **72** A5
Kelshall **33** G5
Kelsick **60** D1
Kelso **77** F7
Kelstedge **51** F6
Kelstern **53** F3
Kelston **20** A5
Kelton **65** K3
Kelton Hill (Rhonehouse) **65** H5
Kelty **75** K1
Kelvedon **34** C7
Kelvedon Hatch **23** J2
Kelvin Hall *Glas* G3 8AW **127** A2
Kelvingrove Art Gallery & Museum *Glas* G3 8AG **127** B2
Kelvinside **74** D4
Kelynack **2** A6
Kemacott **6** E1
Kemback **81** K9
Kemberton **39** G5
Kemble **20** C2
Kemerton **29** J5
Kemeys Commander **19** G1
Kemeys Inferior **19** G2
Kemnay **85** M9
Kemp Town **13** G6
Kempe's Corner **15** F3
Kempley **29** F6
Kempley Green **29** F6
Kemps Green **30** C1
Kempsey **29** H4
Kempsford **20** E2
Kempshott **21** J7
Kempston **32** D4
Kempston Hardwick **32** D4
Kempston West End **32** C4
Kempton **38** C7
Kemsing **23** J6
Kemsley **25** F5
Kenardington **14** E4
Kenchester **28** D4
Kencot **21** F1
Kendal **61** G7
Kenderchurch **28** D6
Kendleshire **19** K4
Kenfig **18** A3
Kenfig Hill **18** B3
Kenidjack **2** A5
Kenilworth **30** D1
Kenilworth Castle *Warks* CV8 1NE **30** D1
Kenknock **79** R7
Kenley *GtLon* **23** G5
Kenley *Shrop* **38** E5
Kenmore *High* **82** H5
Kenmore *P&K* **80** C6
Kenn *Devon* **7** H7
Kenn *NSom* **19** H5
Kennacraig **73** G4
Kennall Vale (Cornwall & West Devon Mining Landscape) *Corn* **2** E5
Kennavay **88** H8
Kenneggy Downs **2** C6
Kennerleigh **7** G5
Kennet **75** H1
Kennethmont **85** K8
Kennett **33** K2
Kennford **7** H7
Kenninghall **44** E7
Kennington *Kent* **15** F3
Kennington *Oxon* **21** J1
Kennoway **81** J10
Kenny **8** C3
Kennyhill **33** K1
Kennythorpe **58** D3
Kenovay **78** A6
Kensaleyre **82** E5
Kensington **23** F4
Kensington Palace *GtLon* W8 4PX **103** G7
Kenstone **38** E3
Kensworth **32** D7
Kent & East Sussex Railway *Kent* TN30 6HE **14** D5
Kent Street *ESuss* **14** C6
Kent Street *Kent* **23** K6
Kentallen (Ceann an t-Sàilein) **79** M5
Kentchurch **28** D6
Kentford **34** B2
Kentisbeare **7** J5
Kentisbury **6** E1
Kentisbury Ford **6** E1
Kentish Town **23** F3
Kentmere **61** F6
Kenton *Devon* **7** H7
Kenton *Suff* **35** F2
Kenton *T&W* **71** H7
Kenton Corner **35** G2
Kentra **78** H4
Kents Bank **55** G2
Kent's Green **29** G6
Kent's Oak **10** E2
Kenwick **38** D2
Kenwood House *GtLon* NW3 7JR **102** H4
Kenwyn **3** F4
Kenyon **49** F3
Keoldale **86** F3
Keose (Ceòs) **88** J5
Keppoch *A&B* **74** B3
Keppoch *High* **83** J8
Keprigan **66** A2
Kepwick **62** E7
Keresley **41** F7
Keresley Newlands **41** F7
Kernborough **5** H6
Kerrera **79** K8
Kerridge **49** J5
Kerris **2** B6
Kerry (Ceri) **38** A6
Kerrycroy **73** K4
Kerry's Gate **28** C5
Kersall **51** K6
Kersey **34** E4
Kersey Vale **34** E4
Kershopefoot **69** K5
Kersoe **29** J4
Kerswell **7** J5
Kerswell Green **29** H4
Kerthen Wood **2** C5
Kesgrave **35** G4
Kesh **91** H10
Kessingland **45** K7
Kessingland Beach **45** K7
Kestle **3** G4
Kestle Mill **3** F3
Keston **23** H5
Keswick *Cumb* **60** D4
Keswick *Norf* **45** G5
Keswick *Norf* **45** H2
Ketley Bank **39** F4
Ketsby **53** G5
Kettering **32** B1
Ketteringham **45** F5
Kettins **80** H7
Kettle Corner **14** C2
Kettlebaston **34** D3
Kettlebrook **40** E5
Kettleburgh **35** G2
Kettlehill **81** J10
Kettleholm **69** G6
Kettleness **63** J5
Kettleshulme **49** J5
Kettlesing **57** H4
Kettlesing Bottom **57** H4
Kettlesing Head **57** H4
Kettlestone **44** D2
Kettlethorpe **52** B5
Kettletoft **89** F4
Kettlewell **56** E2
Ketton **42** C5
Kevingtown **23** H5
Kew **22** E4
Kewstoke **19** G5
Kexbrough **51** F2
Kexby *Lincs* **52** B4
Kexby *York* **58** D4
Key Green **49** H6
Keyham **41** J5
Keyhaven **10** E5
Keyingham **59** J7
Keymer **13** G5
Keynsham **19** K5
Key's Toft **53** H7
Keysoe **32** D2
Keysoe Row **32** D2
Keyston **32** D1
Keyworth **41** J2
Kibblesworth **62** C1
Kibworth Beauchamp **41** J6
Kibworth Harcourt **41** J6
Kidbrooke **23** H4
Kidderminster Green **40** A5
Kidderminster **29** H1
Kiddington **31** F6
Kidlington **31** F7
Kidmore End **21** K4
Kidnal **38** D1
Kidsdale **64** E7
Kidsgrove **49** H7
Kidstones **56** E1
Kidwelly (Cydweli) **17** H5
Kielder **70** B4
Kielder Forest *N'umb* NE48 1ER **70** B4
Kielder Water *N'umb* NE48 1BX **70** C5
Kilbarchan **74** C4
Kilberry **73** F4
Kilbirnie **74** B5
Kilbride *A&B* **73** J4
Kilbride *A&B* **79** K8
Kilbride *A&N* **92** H7
Kilbride Farm **73** H4
Kilbridemore **73** J1
Kilburn *Derbys* **41** F1
Kilburn *GtLon* **23** F3
Kilburn *NYorks* **58** B2
Kilby **41** J6
Kilchattan Bay **73** K5
Kilchenzie **66** A1
Kilcheran **79** K7
Kilchiaran **72** A4
Kilchoan *A&B* **79** J9
Kilchoan *High* **78** F4
Kilchoman **72** A4
Kilchrenan (Cill Chrèanain) **79** M8
Kilchrist **66** A2
Kilclief **93** L12
Kilconquhar **81** K10
Kilcoo **93** H13
Kilcorig **93** H10
Kilcot **29** F6
Kilcoy **83** R5
Kilcreggan **74** A2
Kilcross **92** H9
Kildale **63** G6
Kildary **84** B3
Kildavie **66** B2
Kildonan **66** E1
Kildonan Lodge **87** M7
Kildonnan **78** F2
Kildrochet House **64** A5
Kildress **92** C9
Kildrum **92** G7
Kildrummy **85** J9
Kildwick **57** F5
Kilfinan **73** H3
Kilfinnan **83** N11
Kilgetty **16** E5
Kilgwrrwg Common **19** H2
Kilham *ERid* **59** G3
Kilham *N'umb* **77** G7
Kilkeel **93** J15
Kilkenneth **78** A6
Kilkenny **30** B7
Kilkerran *A&B* **66** B2
Kilkerran *SAyr* **67** H3
Kilkhampton **6** A4
Kilkinamurry **93** H12
Killadeas **91** J11
Killagan Bridge **92** F4
Killaloo **90** M6
Killamarsh **51** G4
Killarbran **91** L12
Killard **92** E7
Killay **17** K6
Killead **92** G8
Killeague **92** D4
Killean **72** E6
Killearn **74** D2
Killeen *AB&C* **93** E12
Killeen *Mid Ulster* **93** D10
Killeen *NM&D* **93** F14
Killeeshil **93** B11
Killellan **66** A2
Killen *D&S* **90** J8
Killen *High* **84** A5
Killerby **62** B4
Killerton *Devon* EX5 3LE **7** H5
Killerton **7** H5
Killeter **90** J8
Killichonan **80** A5
Killiechonate **79** P2
Killiechronan **78** G6
Killiecrankie **80** E4
Killilan **83** K7
Killimster **87** R4
Killin **80** A7
Killinallan **72** B3
Killinchy **93** L10
Killinghall **57** H4
Killington *Cumb* **56** B1
Killington *Devon* **6** E1
Killingworth **71** H6
Killochyett **76** C6
Killocraw **72** E7
Killough **93** L13
Killowen **93** G15
Killucan **92** B9
Killundine **78** G6
Killure **92** D4
Killyclogher **91** L9
Killycolp **93** D9
Killycolpy **93** E9
Killycor **90** M6
Killycurragh **92** C8
Killyharry **93** C10
Killykergan **92** D5
Killylane **90** M4
Killylea **93** C12
Killyleagh **93** L11
Killymallaght **90** L6
Killynether **93** K9
Killyrammer **92** E4
Kilmacolm **74** B4
Kilmahamogue **92** F3
Kilmahog **80** B10
Kilmalieu **79** K5
Kilmaluag **82** E3
Kilmany **81** J8
Kilmarie **82** F9
Kilmarnock **74** C7
Kilmartin **73** G1
Kilmaurs **74** C6
Kilmelford **79** K9
Kilmeny **72** B4
Kilmersdon **19** K6
Kilmeston **11** G2
Kilmichael **66** A1
Kilmichael Glassary **73** G1
Kilmichael of Inverlussa **73** F2
Kilmington *Devon* **8** B5
Kilmington *Wilts* **9** G1
Kilmington Common **9** G1
Kilmood **93** K10
Kilmorack **83** Q6
Kilmore (A' Chille Mhòr) *A&B* **79** K8
Kilmore *AB&C* **93** E11
Kilmore *High* **82** G10
Kilmore *NM&D* **93** K11
Kilmory *A&B* **73** F3
Kilmory *High* **78** G3
Kilmory *High* **82** D10
Kilmory *NAyr* **66** D1
Kilmuir *High* **84** A6
Kilmuir *High* **84** B3
Kilmun **73** K2
Kiln Green *Here* **29** F7
Kiln Green *W'ham* **22** B4
Kiln Pit Hill **62** A1
Kilnave **72** A3
Kilncadzow **75** G6
Kilndown **14** C4
Kilnhurst **51** G3
Kilninian **78** F6
Kilninver **79** K8
Kilnsea **53** H1
Kilnsey **56** E3
Kilnwick **59** F5
Kilnwick Percy **58** E4
Kiloran **72** B1
Kilpatrick **66** D1
Kilpeck **28** D5
Kilphedir **87** M8
Kilpin **58** D7
Kilpin Pike **58** D7
Kilraghts **92** F4
Kilrea **92** E5
Kilrenny **81** L10
Kilroot **92** K8
Kilsally **93** D9
Kilsby **31** G1
Kilskeery **91** J11
Kilspindie **80** H8
Kilstay **64** B7
Kilsyth **75** F3
Kiltarlity **83** R6
Kilton *Notts* **51** H5
Kilton *R&C* **63** G5
Kilton *Som* **7** K1
Kilton Thorpe **63** G5
Kiltyrie **80** B7
Kilvaxter **82** D4
Kilve **7** K1
Kilverstone **44** C7
Kilvington **42** B1
Kilwaughter **92** J6
Kilwinning **74** B6
Kimberley *Norf* **44** E5
Kimberley *Notts* **41** H1
Kimberworth **51** G3
Kimble Wick **22** B1
Kimblesworth **62** C2
Kimbolton *Cambs* **32** D2
Kimbolton *Here* **28** E2
Kimbridge **10** E2
Kimcote **41** H7
Kimmeridge **9** J7
Kimmerston **77** H7
Kimpton *Hants* **21** F7
Kimpton *Herts* **32** E7
Kinakelly **91** K14
Kinallen **93** H12
Kinawley **91** J13
Kinbrace **87** L6
Kinbuck **80** C10
Kincaple **81** K9
Kincardine *Fife* **75** H2
Kincardine *High* **84** A2
Kincardine O'Neil **85** K11
Kinclaven **80** G7
Kincorth **85** P10
Kincraig **84** C10
Kindallachan **80** E5
Kineton *Glos* **30** B6
Kineton *Warks* **30** E3
Kineton Green **40** D7
Kinfauns **80** G8
King Sterndale **50** C5
Kingarth **73** J5
Kingcoed **19** H1
Kingerby **52** D3
Kingham **30** D6
Kingholm Quay **65** K3
Kinghorn **76** A2
Kinglassie **76** A1
Kingoodie **81** J8
King's Acre **28** D4
King's Bank **14** D5
King's Bromley **40** D4
Kings Caple **28** E6
King's Cliffe **42** D6
King's College Chapel, Cambridge *Cambs* CB2 1ST **33** H3
King's Coughton **30** B3
King's Green **29** G5
King's Heath **40** C7
King's Hill *Kent* **23** K6
King's Hill *Warks* **30** E1
King's Hill *WMid* **40** B6
Kings Langley **22** D1
King's Lynn **44** A3
King's Meaburn **61** H4
Kings Mills **3** H5
King's Moss **48** E2
Kings Muir **76** A7
King's Newnham **31** F1
King's Newton **41** F3
King's Norton *Leics* **41** J5
King's Norton *WMid* **30** B1
King's Nympton **6** E4
King's Pyon **28** D3
Kings Ripton **33** F1
King's Somborne **10** E1
King's Stag **9** G3
King's Stanley **20** B1
King's Sutton **31** F5
King's Tamerton **4** E5
Kings Walden **32** E6
Kings Worthy **11** F1
Kingsand **4** E5
Kingsbarns **81** L9
Kingsbridge *Devon* **5** H6
Kingsbridge *Som* **7** H2
Kingsburgh **82** D5
Kingsbury *GtLon* **22** E3
Kingsbury *Warks* **40** E6
Kingsbury Episcopi **8** D2
Kingsbury Water Park *Warks* B76 0DY **40** E6
Kingscavil **75** J3
Kingsclere **21** J6
Kingscote **20** B2
Kingscott **6** D4
Kingscross **66** E1
Kingsdon **8** E2
Kingsdown *Kent* **15** J3
Kingsdown *Swin* **20** E3
Kingsdown *Wilts* **20** B5
Kingseat **75** K1
Kingsey **22** A1
Kingsfold *Pembs* **16** C6
Kingsfold *WSuss* **12** E3
Kingsford *Aberdeen* **85** N10
Kingsford *EAyr* **74** C6
Kingsford *Worcs* **40** A7
Kingsgate **25** K4
Kingshall Street **34** D2
Kingsheanton **6** D2
Kingshouse **80** A8
Kingshouse Hotel **79** P5
Kingshurst **40** D7
Kingskerswell **5** J4
Kingskettle **81** J10
Kingsland *Here* **28** D2
Kingsland *IoA* **46** A4
Kingsley *ChesW&C* **48** E5
Kingsley *Hants* **11** J1
Kingsley *Staffs* **40** C1
Kingsley Green **12** B3
Kingsley Holt **40** C1
Kingslow **39** G6
Kingsmill **92** D9
Kingsmuir *Angus* **81** K6
Kingsmuir *Fife* **81** L10
Kingsnorth **15** F4
Kingsnorth Power Station **24** E4
Kingstanding **40** C6
Kingsteignton **5** J3
Kingsthorne **28** D5
Kingsthorpe **31** J2
Kingston *Cambs* **33** G3
Kingston *Corn* **4** D3
Kingston *Devon* **5** G6
Kingston *Devon* **7** J7
Kingston *Dorset* **9** G4
Kingston *Dorset* **9** J7
Kingston *ELoth* **76** D2
Kingston *GtMan* **49** J3
Kingston *Hants* **10** C4
Kingston *IoW* **11** F6
Kingston *Kent* **15** G2
Kingston *MK* **32** C5
Kingston *Moray* **84** H4
Kingston *WSuss* **12** D6
Kingston Bagpuize **21** H2
Kingston Blount **22** A2
Kingston by Sea **13** F6
Kingston Deverill **9** H1
Kingston Gorse **12** D6
Kingston Lacy *Dorset* BH21 4EA **95** A2
Kingston Lisle **21** G3
Kingston Maurward **9** G5
Kingston near Lewes **13** G6
Kingston on Soar **41** H3
Kingston Russell **8** E5
Kingston Seymour **19** H5
Kingston St. Mary **8** B2
Kingston Stert **22** A1
Kingston upon Hull **59** H7
Kingston upon Thames **22** E5
Kingston Warren **21** G3
Kingstone *Here* **28** D5
Kingstone *Here* **29** F6
Kingstone *Som* **8** C3
Kingstone *Staffs* **40** C3
Kingstone Winslow **21** F3
Kingstown **60** E1
Kingswear **5** J5
Kingswell **74** D6
Kingswinford **40** A7
Kingswood *Bucks* **31** H7
Kingswood *Glos* **20** A2
Kingswood *Here* **28** B3
Kingswood *Kent* **14** D2
Kingswood *Powys* **38** B5
Kingswood *SGlos* **19** K4
Kingswood *Som* **7** K2
Kingswood *Surr* **23** F6
Kingswood *Warks* **30** C1
Kingthorpe **52** E5
Kington *Here* **28** B3
Kington *Worcs* **29** J3
Kington Langley **20** C4
Kington Magna **9** G2
Kington St. Michael **20** C4
Kingussie **84** B10
Kingweston **8** E1
Kinharvie **65** K4
Kinkell **74** E3
Kinlet **39** G7
Kinloch *High* **82** E11
Kinloch *High* **86** F6
Kinloch *P&K* **80** G6
Kinloch Hourn (Ceann Loch Shubhairne) **83** K10
Kinloch Laggan **80** A3
Kinloch Rannoch **80** B5
Kinlochard **79** R10
Kinlochbervie **86** E4
Kinlocheil **79** L3
Kinlochewe **83** L4
Kinlochleven (Ceann Loch Liobhann) **79** N4
Kinlochmoidart **79** J3
Kinlochmorar **83** J11
Kinloss **84** E4
Kinmel Bay (Bae Cinmel) **47** H4
Kinmuck **85** N9
Kinnaber **81** N4
Kinnadie **85** P6
Kinnaird **80** H8
Kinneff **81** P3
Kinnelhead **69** F3
Kinnersley **38** C3
Kinnersley *Here* **28** C4
Kinnersley *Worcs* **29** H4
Kinnerton **28** B2
Kinnerton Green **48** C6
Kinnesswood **80** G10
Kinninvie **62** A4
Kinnoulton **41** J2
Kinross **80** G10
Kinrossie **80** G7
Kinsbourne Green **32** E7
Kinsham *Here* **28** C2
Kinsham *Worcs* **29** J5
Kinsley **51** G1
Kinson **10** B5
Kintbury **21** G5
Kintessack **84** D4
Kintillo **80** G9
Kintocher **85** K10
Kinton *Here* **28** D1
Kinton *Shrop* **38** C4
Kintore **85** M9
Kintour **72** C5
Kintra *A&B* **72** B6
Kintra *A&B* **78** E8
Kinuachdrachd **73** F1
Kinveachy **84** D9
Kinver **40** A7
Kinwarton **30** C3
Kiplaw Croft **85** Q7
Kippax **57** K6
Kippen **74** E1
Kippford (Scaur) **65** J5
Kipping's Cross **23** K7
Kippington **23** J6
Kirbister **89** C7
Kirbuster **89** B5
Kirby Bedon **45** G5
Kirby Bellars **42** A4
Kirby Cane **45** H6
Kirby Corner **30** D1
Kirby Cross **35** G6
Kirby Fields **41** H5
Kirby Green **45** H6
Kirby Grindalythe **59** F3
Kirby Hill *NYorks* **57** J3
Kirby Hill *NYorks* **62** B6
Kirby Knowle **57** K1
Kirby le Soken **35** G6
Kirby Misperton **58** D2
Kirby Muxloe **41** H5
Kirby Row **45** H6
Kirby Sigston **62** E7
Kirby Underdale **58** E4
Kirby Wiske **57** J1
Kircubbin **93** L10
Kirdford **12** D4
Kirk **87** Q4
Kirk Bramwith **51** J1
Kirk Deighton **57** J4
Kirk Ella **59** G7
Kirk Hallam **41** G1
Kirk Hammerton **57** K4
Kirk Ireton **50** E7
Kirk Langley **40** E2
Kirk Merrington **62** C3
Kirk Michael **54** C4
Kirk of Shotts **75** G4
Kirk Sandall **51** J2
Kirk Smeaton **51** H1
Kirk Yetholm **70** D1
Kirkabister **89** N9
Kirkandrews **65** G6
Kirkandrews-upon-Eden **60** E1
Kirkbampton **60** E1
Kirkbean **65** K5
Kirkbride **60** D1
Kirkbuddo **81** L6
Kirkburn *ERid* **59** F4
Kirkburn *ScBord* **76** A7
Kirkburton **50** D1
Kirkby *Lincs* **52** D3
Kirkby *Mersey* **48** D3
Kirkby *NYorks* **63** F6
Kirkby Fleetham **62** C7
Kirkby Green **52** D7
Kirkby in Ashfield **51** G7
Kirkby la Thorpe **42** D1
Kirkby Lonsdale **56** B2
Kirkby Malham **56** D3
Kirkby Mallory **41** G5
Kirkby Malzeard **57** H2
Kirkby on Bain **53** F6
Kirkby Overblow **57** J5
Kirkby Stephen **61** J6
Kirkby Thore **61** H4
Kirkby Underwood **42** D3
Kirkby Wharfe **58** B5
Kirkby Woodhouse **51** G7
Kirkby-in-Furness **55** F1
Kirkbymoorside **58** C1
Kirkcaldy **76** A1
Kirkcambeck **70** A7
Kirkcolm **64** A4
Kirkconnel **68** C2
Kirkconnell **65** K4
Kirkcowan **64** D4
Kirkcudbright **65** G5
Kirkdale House **65** F5
Kirkdean **75** K6
Kirkfieldbank **75** G6
Kirkgunzeon **65** J4
Kirkham *Lancs* **55** H6
Kirkham *NYorks* **58** D3
Kirkhamgate **57** J7
Kirkharle **71** F5
Kirkhaugh **61** H2
Kirkheaton *N'umb* **71** F6
Kirkheaton *WYorks* **50** D1
Kirkhill **83** R6
Kirkhope **69** J1
Kirkibost (Circebost) **88** G4
Kirkinner **64** E5
Kirkinriola **92** G6
Kirkintilloch **74** E3
Kirkistown **93** M11
Kirkland *Cumb* **60** B5
Kirkland *Cumb* **61** H3
Kirkland *D&G* **68** C2
Kirkland *D&G* **68** D4
Kirkland *D&G* **69** F5
Kirkland of Longcastle **64** D6
Kirkleatham **63** F4
Kirklevington **62** E5
Kirkley **45** K6
Kirklington *Notts* **51** J7
Kirklington *NYorks* **57** J1
Kirklinton **69** K7
Kirkliston **75** K3
Kirkmaiden **64** B7
Kirkmichael *P&K* **80** F4
Kirkmichael *SAyr* **67** H3
Kirkmuirhill **75** F6
Kirknewton *N'umb* **77** H7
Kirknewton *WLoth* **75** K4
Kirkney **85** K7
Kirkoswald *Cumb* **61** G2
Kirkoswald *SAyr* **67** G3
Kirkpatrick Durham **65** H3
Kirkpatrick-Fleming **69** H6
Kirksanton **54** E1
Kirkstall **57** H6
Kirkstead **52** E6
Kirkstile **69** J4
Kirkstyle **87** R2
Kirkthorpe **57** J7
Kirkton *Aber* **85** L5
Kirkton *Aber* **85** L8
Kirkton *Angus* **81** K6
Kirkton *D&G* **68** E5
Kirkton *High* **83** J8
Kirkton *High* **84** B1
Kirkton *ScBord* **70** A2
Kirkton Manor **76** A7
Kirkton of Auchterhouse **81** J7
Kirkton of Bourtie **85** N8
Kirkton of Craig **81** N5
Kirkton of Culsalmond **85** L7
Kirkton of Durris **85** M11
Kirkton of Glenbuchat **84** H9
Kirkton of Glenisla **80** H4
Kirkton of Kingoldrum **81** J5
Kirkton of Kinnettles **81** K6
Kirkton of Lethendy **80** G6
Kirkton of Logie Buchan **85** P8
Kirkton of Maryculter **85** N11
Kirkton of Menmuir **81** L4
Kirkton of Rayne **85** L7
Kirkton of Skene **85** N10
Kirkton of Tealing **81** K7
Kirktonhill **74** B3
Kirktown **85** Q5
Kirktown of Alvah **85** L4
Kirktown of Deskford **85** K4
Kirktown of Fetteresso **81** P2
Kirktown of Slains **85** Q8
Kirkwall **89** D6
Kirkwall Airport **89** D7
Kirkwhelpington **70** E5
Kirmington **52** E1
Kirmond le Mire **52** E3
Kirn **73** K3
Kirriemuir **81** J5
Kirstead Green **45** G6
Kirtlebridge **69** H6
Kirtleton **69** H5
Kirtling **33** K3
Kirtling Green **33** K3
Kirtlington **31** G7
Kirtomy **87** K3
Kirton *Lincs* **43** G2
Kirton *Notts* **51** J6
Kirton *Suff* **35** G5
Kirton End **43** F1
Kirton Holme **43** F1
Kirton in Lindsey **52** C3
Kiscadale **66** E1
Kislingbury **31** H3
Kismeldon Bridge **6** B4
Kit Hill Country Park *Corn* PL17 8AX **4** D3
Kites Hardwick **31** F2
Kitley **5** F5
Kittisford **7** J3
Kittisford Barton **7** J3
Kittle **17** J7
Kitt's End **23** F2
Kitt's Green **40** D7
Kitwood **11** H1
Kivernoll **28** D5
Kiveton Park **51** G4
Klibreck **86** H6
Knabbygates **85** K5
Knaith **52** B4
Knaith Park **52** B4
Knap Corner **9** H2
Knaphill **22** C6
Knaplock **7** G2
Knapp *P&K* **80** H7
Knapp *Som* **8** C2
Knapthorpe **51** K7
Knaptoft **41** J7
Knapton *Norf* **45** H2
Knapton *York* **58** B4
Knapton Green **28** D3
Knapwell **33** G2
Knaresborough **57** J4
Knarsdale **61** H1
Knayton **57** K1
Knebworth **33** F6
Knebworth House *Herts* SG3 6PY **33** F6
Knedlington **58** D7
Kneesall **51** K6
Kneesworth **33** G4
Kneeton **42** A1
Knelston **17** H7
Knenhall **40** B2
Knettishall **44** D7
Knettishall Heath Country Park *Suff* IP22 2TQ **44** D7
Knightacott **6** E2
Knightcote **31** F3
Knightley **40** A3
Knightley Dale **40** A3
Knighton *Devon* **5** F6
Knighton *Dorset* **9** F3
Knighton *Leic* **41** H5
Knighton *Poole* **10** B5
Knighton (Tref-y-clawdd) *Powys* **28** B1
Knighton *Som* **7** K1
Knighton *Staffs* **39** G1
Knighton *Staffs* **39** G3
Knighton *Wilts* **21** F4
Knighton on Teme **29** F1
Knightswood **74** D4
Knightwick **29** G3
Knill **28** B2
Knipton **42** B2
Knitsley **62** B2
Kniveton **50** E7
Knock *A&B* **78** G7
Knock *Cumb* **61** H4
Knock *Moray* **85** K5
Knockalava **73** H1
Knockally **87** P7
Knockaloe Moar **54** B5
Knockan *CC&G* **92** B6
Knockan *High* **86** E8
Knockandhu **84** G8
Knockanorane **91** L13
Knockanully **92** G5
Knockarevan **91** K14
Knockarthur **87** K9
Knockavannon **93** E14
Knockbain **84** A5
Knockban **83** N4
Knockbrack **90** L5
Knockbrex **65** F6
Knockcloghrim **92** D7
Knockdee **87** P3
Knockdow **73** K3
Knockdown **20** B3
Knockenkelly **66** E1
Knockentiber **74** B7
Knockgray **67** K4
Knockholt **23** H6
Knockholt Pound **23** H6
Knockin **38** C3
Knockinelder **93** M11
Knockinlaw **74** C7
Knockintorran (Cnoc an Torrain) **88** B2
Knocklearn **65** H3
Knockmany Passage Grave BT76 0XJ **91** M11
Knockmill **23** J5
Knockmoyle **90** L9
Knocknacarry **92** H3
Knocknaha **66** A2
Knocknain **66** D7
Knocknalling **67** K5
Knocknashangan **91** F12
Knockrome **72** D3
Knocks **91** K13
Knocksharry **54** B5
Knockville **64** D3
Knodishall **35** J2
Knodishall Common **35** J2
Knodishall Green **35** J2
Knole **8** D2
Knolls Green **49** H5
Knolton **38** C2
Knook **20** C7
Knossington **42** B5
Knott End-on-Sea **55** G5
Knotting **32** D2
Knotting Green **32** D2
Knottingley **58** B7
Knotts **56** C4
Knotty Green **22** C2
Knowbury **28** E1
Knowe **64** D3
Knowehead **92** L9
Knowesgate **70** E5
Knoweside **67** G2
Knowetownhead **70** A2
Knowl Green **34** B4
Knowl Hill **22** B4
Knowl Wall **40** A2
Knowle *Bristol* **19** K4
Knowle *Devon* **6** C2
Knowle *Devon* **7** F5
Knowle *Devon* **7** J7
Knowle *Shrop* **28** E1
Knowle *Som* **7** H1
Knowle *WMid* **30** C1
Knowle Cross **7** J6
Knowle Green **56** B6
Knowle Hall **19** G7
Knowle St. Giles **8** C3
Knowlton *Dorset* **10** B3
Knowlton *Kent* **15** H2
Knowsley **48** D3
Knowsley Safari Park *Mersey* L34 4AN **113** G3
Knowstone **7** G3
Knox Bridge **14** C3
Knucklas (Cnwclas) **28** B1
Knutsford **49** G5
Knypersley **49** H7
Krumlin **50** C1
Kuggar **2** E7
Kyle of Lochalsh (Caol Loch Aillse) **82** H8
Kyleakin (Caol Acain) **82** H8
Kylerhea (Ceol Reatha) **82** H8
Kyles Scalpay (Caolas Scalpaigh) **88** H8
Kylesku **86** E6
Kylesmorar **83** J11
Kylestrome **86** E6
Kynaston **38** C3
Kynnersley **39** F4
Kyre Park **29** F2

L

Labost **88** H3
Lacasaigh **88** J5
Lace Market Centre NG1 1HF **134** Nottingham
Laceby **53** F2
Lacey Green **22** B1
Lach Dennis **49** G5
Lack **91** J10
Lackagh **92** B5
Lackalee (Leac a' Li) **88** G8
Lackford **34** B1
Lacock **20** C5
Ladbroke **31** F3
Laddingford **23** K7
Lade Bank **53** G7
Ladies Hill **55** H5
Ladock **3** F3
Lady Hall **54** E1
Lady Lever Art Gallery *Mersey* CH62 5EQ **112** B6
Ladybank **81** J9
Ladycross **6** B7
Ladykirk **77** G6
Ladysford **85** P4
Ladywood **29** H2
Lagavara **92** F2
Lagavulin **72** C6
Lagg *A&B* **72** D3
Lagg *NAyr* **66** D1
Lagg *SAyr* **67** G2
Laggan *A&B* **72** A5
Laggan (An Lagan) *High* **83** N11
Laggan *High* **84** A11
Laggan *Moray* **84** H7
Lagganulva **78** F6
Laghy Corner **93** D10
Lagrae **68** C2
Laide **83** K1
Laig **78** F2
Laight **68** B2
Laindon **24** C3
Laing Art Gallery *T&W* NE1 8AG **129** Newcastle upon Tyne
Lairg **86** H9
Lairigmor **79** N4
Laisterdyke **57** G6
Laithes **61** F3
Lake *Devon* **5** F4
Lake *Devon* **6** D2
Lake *IoW* **11** G6
Lake *Wilts* **10** C1
Lake District Visitor Centre at Brockhole *Cumb* LA23 1LJ **60** F6
Lakenham **45** G5
Lakenheath **44** B7
Lakes Aquarium *Cumb* LA12 8AS **55** G1
Lakes End **43** J6
Lakes Glass Centre, Ulverston *Cumb* LA12 7LY **55** F2
Lakeside *Cumb* **55** G1
Lakeside *Thur* **23** J4
Lakeside & Haverthwaite Railway *Cumb* LA12 8AL **55** G1
Laleham **22** D5
Laleston **18** B4
Lamancha **76** A5
Lamarsh **34** C5
Lamas **45** G3
Lamb Corner **34** E5
Lamb Roe **56** C6
Lambden **77** F6
Lambeg **93** H10
Lamberhurst **13** K3
Lamberhurst Quarter **13** K3
Lamberton **77** H5
Lambfell Moar **54** B5
Lambley *Notts* **41** J1
Lambley *N'umb* **61** H1
Lambourn **21** G4
Lambourn Woodlands **21** G4
Lambourne End **23** H2
Lambs Green **13** F3
Lambston **16** C4
Lambtón **62** C1
Lamellion **4** C4
Lamerton **4** E3
Lamesley **62** C1
Lamington **75** H7
Lamlash **73** J7
Lamloch **67** K4
Lamonby **60** F3
Lamorna **2** B6
Lamorran **3** F4
Lampert **70** B6
Lampeter (Llanbedr Pont Steffan) **17** J1
Lampeter Velfrey **16** E4
Lamphey **16** D5
Lamplugh **60** B4
Lamport **31** J1
Lamyatt **9** F1
Lana *Devon* **6** B5
Lana *Devon* **6** B6
Lanark **75** G6
Lanarth **2** E6
Lancaster **55** H3
Lancaster Leisure Park *Lancs* LA1 3LA **55** H3
Lancaster Priory *Lancs* LA1 1YZ **55** H3
Lanchester **62** B2
Lancing **12** E6
Landbeach **33** H2
Landcross **6** C3
Landerberry **85** M10
Landewednack **2** E7
Landford **10** D3
Landican **48** B4
Landimore **17** H6
Landkey **6** D2
Landmoth **62** E7
Landore **17** K6
Landrake **4** D4
Land's End *Corn* TR19 7AA **2** A6
Land's End Airport **2** A6
Landscove **5** H4
Landshipping **16** D4
Landulph **4** E4
Landwade **33** K2
Landywood **40** B5
Lane Bottom **56** D6
Lane End *Bucks* **22** B2
Lane End *Cumb* **60** C7
Lane End *Derbys* **51** G6
Lane End *Dorset* **9** H5
Lane End *Hants* **11** G2
Lane End *Here* **29** F7
Lane End *Kent* **23** J4
Lane End *Wilts* **20** B7
Lane Ends *Derbys* **40** E2
Lane Ends *GtMan* **49** J3
Lane Ends *Lancs* **56** C6
Lane Ends *NYorks* **56** E5
Lane Green **40** A5
Lane Head *Dur* **62** A4
Lane Head *Dur* **62** B5
Lane Head *GtMan* **49** F3
Lane Head *WYorks* **50** D2
Lane Heads **55** H6
Lane Side **56** C7
Laneast **4** C2
Lane-end **4** A4
Laneham **52** B5
Lanehead *Dur* **61** K2

Lanehead N'umb 70 C5
Lanesend 16 D5
Lanesfield 40 B6
Laneshawbridge 56 E5
Langar 42 A2
Langbank 74 B3
Langbar 57 F4
Langbaurgh 63 F5
Langcliffe 56 D3
Langdale End 63 K7
Langdon Corn 4 C1
Langdon Corn 6 B7
Langdon Beck 61 K3
Langdon Hills 24 C3
Langdon Hills Country Park Essex SS17 9NH 24 C3
Langdon House 5 K3
Langford CenBeds 32 E4
Langford Essex 24 E1
Langford Notts 52 B7
Langford Oxon 21 F1
Langford Budville 7 K3
Langham Essex 34 E5
Langham Norf 44 E1
Langham Rut 42 B4
Langham Suff 34 D2
Langham Moor 34 E5
Langho 56 B6
Langholm 69 J5
Langland 17 K7
Langlands 65 G5
Langlee 70 B2
Langleeford 70 E1
Langley ChesE 49 J5
Langley Derbys 41 G1
Langley Essex 33 H5
Langley Glos 30 B6
Langley GtMan 49 H2
Langley Hants 11 F4
Langley Herts 33 F6
Langley Kent 14 C2
Langley N'umb 70 D7
Langley Oxon 30 E7
Langley Slo 22 D4
Langley Som 7 J3
Langley Warks 30 C2
Langley WSuss 12 B4
Langley Burrell 20 C4
Langley Corner 22 D3
Langley Green Derbys 40 E2
Langley Green Warks 30 D2
Langley Green WSuss 13 F3
Langley Heath 14 D2
Langley Marsh 7 J3
Langley Mill 41 G1
Langley Moor 62 C2
Langley Park Bucks SL3 6DW 22 D3
Langley Park 62 C2
Langley Street 45 H5
Langney 13 K6
Langold 51 H4
Langore 4 C2
Langport 8 D2
Langrick 43 F1
Langrick Bridge 43 F1
Langridge B&NESom 20 A5
Langridge Devon 6 D3
Langridgeford 6 D3
Langrigg 60 C2
Langrish 11 J2
Langsett 50 E2
Langshaw 76 D7
Langshawburn 69 H3
Langside 74 D4
Langstone Hants 11 J4
Langstone Newport 19 G2
Langthorne 62 C7
Langthorpe 57 J3
Langthwaite 62 A6
Langtoft ERid 59 G3
Langtoft Lincs 42 E4
Langton Dur 62 B5
Langton Lincs 53 F6
Langton Lincs 53 G5
Langton NYorks 58 D3
Langton by Wragby 52 E5
Langton Green Kent 13 J3
Langton Green Suff 35 F1
Langton Herring 9 F6
Langton Long Blandford 9 H4
Langton Matravers 9 J7
Langtree 6 C4
Langtree Week 6 C4
Langwathby 61 G3
Langwell House 87 P7
Langwith 51 H5
Langworth 52 D5
Lanhydrock Corn PL30 5AD 4 A4
Lanivet 4 A4
Lank 4 A3
Lanlivery 4 A5
Lanner 2 E4
Lanoy 4 C3
Lanreath 4 B5
Lansallos 4 B5
Lansdown 20 A5
Lanteglos 4 A2
Lanteglos Highway 4 B5
Lanton N'umb 77 H7
Lanton ScBord 70 B1
Lanvean 3 F2
Lapford 7 F5
Laphroaig 72 B6
Lapley 40 A4
Lapworth 30 C1
Larach na Gaibhre 73 F3
Larachbeg 78 H6
Larchmount 93 D11
Laragh 92 D6
Larbert 75 G2
Larbreck 55 H5
Larden Green 48 E7
Larg 64 D3
Largie 85 L7
Largiemore 73 H2
Largoward 81 K10
Largs 74 A5
Largybaan 66 A2
Largybeg 66 E1
Largymore 66 E1
Lark Hall 33 J3
Larkfield 74 A3
Larkhall 75 F5
Larkhill F&O 91 G10
Larkhill Wilts 20 E7
Larklands 41 G1
Larling 44 D7
Larne 92 J6
Larriston 70 A4
Lartington 62 A5
Lasborough 20 B2
Lasham 21 K7
Lashbrook 6 C5
Lashenden 14 D3
Lassington 29 G6
Lassintullich 80 C5
Lassodie 75 K1
Laswade 76 B4
Lastingham 63 H7
Latchford 49 F4
Latchingdon 24 E1
Latchley 4 E3
Lately Common 49 F3
Lathbury 32 B4
Latheron 87 P6
Latheronwheel 87 P6
Latimer 22 D2
Latteridge 19 K3
Lattiford 9 F2
Latton 20 D2
Lauchentyre 65 F5
Lauder 76 D6
Laugharne (Lacharn) 17 G4
Laughterton 52 B5
Laughton ESuss 13 J5
Laughton Leics 41 J7
Laughton Lincs 42 D2
Laughton Lincs 52 B3
Laughton en le Morthen 51 H4
Launcells 6 A5
Launcells Cross 6 A5
Launceston 6 B7
Launde Abbey 42 A5
Launton 31 H6
Laurelvale 93 F12
Laurencekirk 81 N3
Laurieston D&G 65 G4
Laurieston Falk 75 H3
Lavendon 32 C3
Lavenham 34 D4
Laverhay 69 G4
Lavernock 18 E5
Laversdale 69 K7
Laverstock 10 C1
Laverstoke 21 H7
Laverton Glos 30 B5
Laverton NYorks 57 H2
Laverton Som 20 A6
Lavister 48 C7
Law 75 G5
Lawers 80 B7
Lawford Essex 34 E5
Lawford Som 7 K2
Lawhitton 6 B7
Lawkland 56 C3
Lawkland Green 56 C3
Lawley 39 F5
Lawnhead 40 A3
Lawrence Weston 19 J4
Lawrencetown 93 F12
Lawrenny 16 D5
Lawshall 34 C3
Lawshall Green 34 C3
Lawton 28 D3
Laxdale (Lacasdal) 88 K4
Laxey 54 D5
Laxfield 35 G1
Laxford Bridge 86 E5
Laxo 89 N6
Laxton ERid 58 D7
Laxton Notts 51 K6
Laxton N'hants 42 C6
Laycock 57 F5
Layde 92 H4
Layer Breton 34 D7
Layer de la Haye 34 D7
Layer Marney 34 D7
Layham 34 E4
Laymore 8 C4
Layter's Green 22 C2
Layton 55 G6
Lazenby 63 F4
Lazonby 61 G3
Lea Derbys 51 F7
Lea Here 29 F6
Lea Lincs 52 B4
Lea Shrop 38 C7
Lea Shrop 38 D5
Lea Wilts 20 C3
Lea Bridge 51 F7
Lea Green 29 F2
Lea Marston 40 E6
Lea Town 55 H6
Lea Yeat 56 C1
Leachd 73 J1
Leachkin (An Leacainn) 84 A6
Leadburn 76 A5
Leaden Roding 33 J7
Leadenham 52 C7
Leaderfoot 76 D7
Leadgate Cumb 61 J2
Leadgate Dur 62 B1
Leadgate N'umb 62 B1
Leadhills 68 D2
Leadingcross Green 14 D2
Leafield 30 E7
Leagrave 32 D6
Leake Commonside 53 G7
Leake Hurn's End 43 H1
Lealands 13 J5
Lealholm 63 H6
Lealt A&B 72 E1
Lealt High 82 F4
Leam 50 E5
Leamington Hastings 31 F2
Leamington Spa 30 E2
Leamington Spa Art Gallery & Museum Warks CV32 4AA 30 E2
Leamoor Common 38 D7
Leanach 73 J1
Leargybreck 72 D3
Leasgill 55 H1
Leasingham 42 D1
Leason 17 H6
Leasowe 48 B3
Leat 6 B7
Leatherhead 22 E6
Leathley 57 H5
Leaton Shrop 38 D4
Leaton Tel&W 39 F4
Leaveland 15 F2
Leavenheath 34 D5
Leavening 58 D3
Leaves Green 23 H5
Leavesden Green 22 E1
Lebberston 59 G1
Lechlade-on-Thames 21 F2
Leck CC&G 92 D4
Leck Lancs 56 B2
Leckford 10 E1
Leckfurin 87 K4
Leckgruinart 72 A4
Leckhampstead Bucks 31 J5
Leckhampstead Thicket 21 H4
Leckhampstead WBerks 21 H4
Leckhampton 29 J7
Leckie 74 E1
Leckmelm (Leac Mailm) 83 M2
Leckuary 73 G1
Leckwith 18 E4
Leconfield 59 G5
Ledaig (Leideag) 79 L7
Ledburn 32 B6
Ledbury 29 G5
Ledgemoor 28 D3
Ledicot 28 D2
Ledmore 86 E8
Ledsham ChesW&C 48 C5
Ledsham WYorks 57 K7
Ledston 57 K7
Ledstone 5 H6
Ledwell 31 F6
Lee A&B 78 F8
Lee Devon 6 C1
Lee Hants 10 E3
Lee Lancs 55 J4
Lee Shrop 38 D2
Lee Brockhurst 38 E3
Lee Chapel 24 C3
Lee Clump 22 C1
Lee Mill Bridge 5 F5
Lee Moor 5 F4
Lee Valley Park Essex EN9 1XQ 23 G1
Leebotten 89 N10
Leebotwood 38 D6
Leece 55 F3
Leeds Kent 14 D2
Leeds WYorks 57 H6
Leeds Art Gallery WYorks LS1 3AA 130 E3
Leeds Bradford International Airport 57 H5
Leeds Castle & Gardens Kent ME17 1PL 14 D2
Leedstown 2 D5
Leegomery 39 F4
Leek 49 J7
Leek Wootton 30 D2
Leekbrook 49 J7
Leeke 92 B5
Leeming NYorks 57 H1
Leeming WYorks 57 F6
Leeming Bar 57 H1
Lee-on-the-Solent 11 G4
Lees Derbys 40 E2
Lees GtMan 49 J2
Leeswood 48 B7
Leftwich 49 F5
Legacurry 93 H11
Legamaddy 93 K13
Legamaghery 91 L11
Leganany 93 H12
Legars 77 F6
Legbourne 53 G4
Legerwood 76 D6
Leggs 91 G10
Legoland Windsor W&M SL4 4AY 22 C4
Legsby 52 E4
Leicester 41 H5
Leicester Forest East 41 H5
Leigh Dorset 9 F4
Leigh Dorset 10 B5
Leigh GtMan 49 F2
Leigh Kent 23 J7
Leigh Shrop 38 C5
Leigh Surr 23 F7
Leigh Wilts 20 D2
Leigh Worcs 29 G3
Leigh Beck 24 E3
Leigh Common 9 G2
Leigh Delamere 20 B4
Leigh Green 14 E4
Leigh Park 11 J4
Leigh Sinton 29 G3
Leigh upon Mendip 19 K7
Leigh Woods 19 J4
Leigham 5 F5
Leighland Chapel 7 J2
Leigh-on-Sea 24 E3
Leighterton 20 B2
Leighton NYorks 57 G2
Leighton (Tre'r Llai) Powys 38 B5
Leighton Shrop 39 F5
Leighton Som 20 A7
Leighton Bromswold 32 E1
Leighton Buzzard 32 C6
Leinthall Earls 28 D2
Leinthall Starkes 28 D2
Leintwardine 28 D1
Leire 41 H7
Leirinmore 86 G3
Leiston 35 J2
Leith 76 A3
Leitholm 77 F6
Leitrim F&O 91 L14
Leitrim NM&D 93 J12
Leitrim NM&D 93 J13
Lelant 2 C5
Lelley 59 J6
Lemington 71 G7
Lempitlaw 77 F7
Lemsford 33 F7
Lenaderg 93 G12
Lenagh 90 M8
Lenchwick 30 B4
Lendalfoot 67 F4
Lenham 14 D2
Lenham Heath 14 E3
Lenie 83 R8
Lenimore 73 G6
Lennel 77 G6
Lennox Plunton 65 G5
Lennoxtown 74 E3
Lent Rise 22 C3
Lenton Lincs 42 D2
Lenton Nott 41 H2
Lenton Abbey 41 H2
Lenwade 44 E4
Lenzie 74 E3
Leochel-Cushnie 85 K9
Leominster 28 D3
Leonard Stanley 20 B1
Leorin 72 B6
Lepe 11 F5
Lephinchapel 73 H1
Lephinmore 73 H1
Leppington 58 D3
Lepton 50 E1
Lerryn 4 B5
Lerwick 89 N8
Lesbury 71 H2
Leslie Aber 85 K8
Leslie Fife 80 H10
Lesmahagow 75 G7
Lesnewth 4 B1
Lessingham 45 H3
Lessness Heath 23 H4
Lessonhall 60 D1
Leswalt 64 A4
Letchmore Heath 22 E2
Letchworth Garden City 33 F5
Letcombe Bassett 21 G3
Letcombe Regis 21 G3
Letham Angus 81 L6
Letham Falk 75 G2
Letham Fife 81 J9
Lethanhill 67 J2
Letheringham 35 G3
Letheringsett 44 E2
Lettaford 7 F7
Letter 91 G10
Letter Finlay 83 N11
Letterbreen 91 H12
Letterfearn (Leitir Fheàrna) 83 J8
Letterkeen 91 H10
Letterloan 92 D4
Lettermore 87 J5
Lettershaws 68 D1
Lettershendony 90 M5
Letterston 16 C3
Lettoch 84 F8
Letton Here 28 C1
Letton Here 28 C4
Letty Green 33 F7
Letwell 51 H4
Leuchars 81 K8
Leumrabhagh 88 J6
Leurbost (Liurbost) 88 J5
Leusdon 5 H3
Levedale 40 A4
Level's Green 33 H6
Leven ERid 59 H5
Leven Fife 81 J10
Levencorroch 66 E1
Levenhall 76 B3
Levens 55 H1
Levens Green 33 G6
Levenshulme 49 H3
Levenwick 89 N10
Leverburgh (An t-Ób) 88 F9
Leverington 43 H4
Leverstock Green 22 D1
Leverton 43 G1
Leverton Lucasgate 43 H1
Leverton Outgate 43 H1
Levington 35 G5
Levisham 63 J7
Levishie 83 Q9
Lew 21 G1
Lewannick 4 C2
Lewcombe 8 E4
Lewdown 6 C7
Lewes 13 H5
Leweston 16 C3
Lewisham 23 G4
Lewiston (Blàr na Maigh) 83 R8
Lewistown 18 C3
Lewknor 22 A2
Leworthy 6 F2
Lewson Street 25 F5
Lewth 55 H6
Lewtrenchard 6 C7
Ley 4 B4
Ley Green 32 E6
Leybourne 23 K6
Leyburn 62 B7
Leyland 55 J7
Leylodge 85 M9
Leymoor 50 D1
Leysdown-on-Sea 25 G4
Leysmill 81 M6
Leysters 28 E2
Leyton 23 G3
Leytonstone 23 G3
Lezant 4 D3
Lezerea 2 D5
Lhanbryde 84 G4
Libanus 27 J6
Libberton 75 H6
Libbery 29 J3
Liberton 76 A4
Lichfield 40 D5
Lichfield Cathedral Staffs WS13 7LD 40 D5
Lickey 29 J1
Lickey End 29 J1
Lickey Hills Country Park Worcs B45 8ER 106 E8
Lickfold 12 C4
Liddaton Green 6 C7
Liddesdale 79 J5
Liddington 21 F3
Lidgate Derbys 51 F5
Lidgate Suff 34 B3
Lidgett 51 J6
Lidlington 32 C5
Lidsey 12 C6
Lidsing 24 D5
Lidstone 30 E6
Lieurary 87 N3
Liff 81 J7
Liffock 92 C3
Lifton 6 B7
Liftondown 6 B7
Ligfordrum 90 L7
Ligg 90 L5
Lightcliffe 57 G7
Lighthorne 30 E3
Lighthorne Heath 30 E3
Lighthouse, The - Poole's Centre for the Arts Poole BH15 1UG 95 B6
Lighthouse, The, Glasgow Glas G1 3NU 127 F4
Lightwater 22 C5
Lightwater Valley Park NYorks HG4 3HT 57 H2
Lightwood 40 B1
Lightwood Green ChesE 39 F1
Lightwood Green Wrex 38 C1
Ligoniel 92 J9
Lilbourne 31 G1
Lilburn Tower 71 F1
Lillesdon 8 C2
Lilleshall 39 G4
Lilley Herts 32 E6
Lilley WBerks 21 H4
Lilliesleaf 70 A1
Lilling Green 58 C3
Lillingstone Dayrell 31 J5
Lillingstone Lovell 31 J4
Lillington Dorset 9 F3
Lillington Warks 30 E2
Lilliput 10 B6
Lilly 6 D2
Lilstock 7 K1
Lilyhurst 39 G4
Limavady 92 B4
Limbury 32 D6
Lime Hill 93 B9
Lime Side 49 J2
Limefield 49 H1
Limehurst 49 J2
Limekilnburn 75 F5
Limekilns 75 J2
Limerigg 75 G3
Limerstone 11 F6
Liminary 92 G7
Limington 8 E2
Limpenhoe 45 H5
Limpley Stoke 20 A5
Limpsfield 23 H6
Limpsfield Chart 23 H6
Linacre Reservoirs Derbys S42 7JW 51 F5
Linbriggs 70 D3
Linby 51 H7
Linchmere 12 B3
Lincluden 65 K3
Lincoln 52 C5
Lincoln Castle Lincs LN1 3AA 129 Lincoln
Lincoln Cathedral Lincs LN2 1PL 129 Lincoln
Lincomb 29 H2
Lincombe Devon 5 H5
Lincombe Devon 5 H6
Lindal in Furness 55 F2
Lindale 55 H1
Lindean 76 C7
Lindfield 13 G4
Lindford 12 B3
Lindisfarne (Holy Island) 77 K6
Lindley 57 H5
Lindow End 49 H5
Lindridge 29 F2
Lindsaig 73 H3
Lindsell 33 K6
Lindsey 34 D4
Lindsey Tye 34 D4
Linfitts 49 J2
Linford Hants 10 C4
Linford Thur 24 C4
Linford Wood 32 B4
Lingague 54 B6
Lingards Wood 50 C1
Lingdale 63 G5
Lingen 28 C2
Lingfield 23 G7
Lingley Green 48 E4
Lingwood 45 H5
Linhope 69 K3
Liniclate (Lionacleit) 88 B4
Linicro 82 D4
Linkend 29 H5
Linkenholt 21 G6
Linkhill 14 D5
Linkinhorne 4 D3
Linksness 89 B7
Linktown 76 A1
Linley Shrop 38 C6
Linley Shrop 39 F6
Linley Green 29 F3
Linlithgow 75 J3
Linlithgow Bridge 75 H3
Linn of Muick Cottage 81 J2
Linnels 70 E7
Linney 16 B6
Linshiels 70 D3
Linsiadar 88 H4
Linsidemore 83 R1
Linslade 32 C6
Linstead Parva 35 H1
Linstock 60 F1
Linthwaite 50 D1
Lintlaw 77 G5
Lintmill 85 K4
Linton Cambs 33 J4
Linton Derbys 40 E4
Linton Here 29 F6
Linton Kent 14 C3
Linton NYorks 56 E3
Linton ScBord 70 C1
Linton WYorks 57 J5
Linton-on-Ouse 57 K3
Lintzford 62 B1
Linwood Hants 10 C4
Linwood Lincs 52 E4
Linwood Renf 74 C4
Lionel (Lional) 88 L1
Liphook 12 B3
Lipley 39 G2
Lisadian AB&C 93 D12
Lisadian L&C 93 H11
Lisbane 93 K10
Lisbarnet 93 K10
Lisbellaw 91 K12
Lisburn 93 H10
Liscall 92 D5
Liscard 48 C3
Liscloon 90 L6
Liscombe 7 G2
Liscolman 92 E3
Lisconrea 91 K11
Lisdoart 93 B11
Lisk 90 K7
Liskeard 4 C4
Lislane 92 C5
Lislea Mid Ulster 92 E6
Lislea NM&D 93 F14
Lisleen 93 K10
L'Islet 3 J5
Lismore 79 K7
Lisnadill 93 D13
Lisnafin 90 L8
Lisnagat 93 E13
Lisnagunogue 92 E2
Lisnamuck 92 D7
Lisnarrick 91 H11
Lisnaskea 91 K13
Lisnatunny 90 K8
Lisrodden 92 E6
Liss 11 J2
Liss Forest 11 J2
Lissan 92 C8
Lissett 59 H4
Lissington 52 E4
Liston 34 C4
Listooder 93 K11
Lisvane 18 E3
Liswerry 19 G3
Litcham 44 C4
Litchborough 31 H3
Litchfield 21 H6
Litherland 48 C3
Litlington Cambs 33 G4
Litlington ESuss 13 J6
Little Abington 33 J4
Little Addington 32 C1
Little Alne 30 C2
Little Altcar 48 C2
Little Amwell 33 G7
Little Ann 21 G7
Little Ashy 61 H6
Little Aston 40 C6
Little Atherfield 11 F7
Little Ayton 63 F5
Little Baddow 24 D1
Little Badminton 20 B3
Little Ballinluig 80 E5
Little Bampton 60 D1
Little Bardfield 33 K5
Little Barford 32 E3
Little Barningham 45 F2
Little Barrington 30 D7
Little Barrow 48 D6
Little Barugh 58 D2
Little Bavington 70 E6
Little Bealings 35 G4
Little Bedwyn 21 F5
Little Beeby 41 J5
Little Bentley 35 F6
Little Berkhamsted 23 F1
Little Billing 32 B2
Little Birch 28 E5
Little Bispham 55 G5
Little Blakenham 35 F4
Little Bloxwich 40 C5
Little Bollington 49 G4
Little Bookham 22 E6
Little Bourton 31 F4
Little Bowden 42 A7
Little Bradley 33 K3
Little Brampton 38 C7
Little Braxted 34 C7
Little Brechin 81 L4
Little Brickhill 32 C5
Little Bridge 92 D9
Little Bridgeford 40 A3
Little Brington 31 H2
Little Bromley 34 E6
Little Broughton 60 B3
Little Budworth 48 E6
Little Burdon 62 D5
Little Burstead 24 C2
Little Burton 59 H5
Little Bytham 42 D4
Little Canford 10 B5
Little Carlton Lincs 53 G4
Little Carlton Notts 51 K7
Little Casterton 42 D4
Little Catwick 59 H5
Little Catworth 32 D1
Little Cawthorpe 53 G4
Little Chalfield 20 B5
Little Chalfont 22 C2
Little Chart 14 E3
Little Chesterford 33 J4
Little Chesterton 31 G6
Little Cheverell 20 C6
Little Clacton 35 F7
Little Clanfield 21 F1
Little Clifton 60 B4
Little Coates 53 F2
Little Comberton 29 J4
Little Common 14 C7
Little Compton 30 D5
Little Corby 61 F1
Little Cornard 34 C5
Little Cowarne 29 F3
Little Coxwell 21 F2
Little Crakehall 62 C7
Little Cransley 32 B1
Little Crawley 32 C4
Little Creaton 31 J1
Little Cressingham 44 C6
Little Crosby 48 C2
Little Crosthwaite 60 D4
Little Cubley 40 D2
Little Dalby 42 A4
Little Dewchurch 28 E5
Little Ditton 33 K3
Little Doward 28 E7
Little Down 21 G6
Little Downham 43 J7
Little Drayton 39 F2
Little Driffield 59 G4
Little Dunham 44 C4
Little Dunkeld 80 F6
Little Dunmow 33 K6
Little Easton 33 K6
Little Eaton 41 F1
Little Eccleston 55 H6
Little Ellingham 44 E6
Little End 23 J1
Little Everdon 31 G3
Little Eversden 33 G3
Little Faringdon 21 F1
Little Fencote 62 C7
Little Fenton 58 B6
Little Finborough 34 E3
Little Fransham 44 D4
Little Gaddesden 32 C7
Little Garway 28 D6
Little Gidding 42 E7
Little Glemham 35 H3
Little Glenshee 80 E7
Little Gorsley 29 F6
Little Gransden 33 F3
Little Green Cambs 33 F4
Little Green Notts 42 A1
Little Green Suff 34 E1
Little Green Suff 35 F1
Little Green Wrex 38 D1
Little Grimsby 53 G3
Little Gringley 51 K4
Little Gruinard 83 K2
Little Habton 58 D2
Little Hadham 33 H6
Little Hale 42 E1
Little Hallingbury 33 H7
Little Hampden 22 B1
Little Haresfield 20 B1
Little Harrowden 32 B1
Little Haseley 21 K1
Little Hatfield 59 H5
Little Hautbois 45 G3
Little Haven Pembs 16 B4
Little Haven WSuss 12 E3
Little Hay 40 D5
Little Hayfield 50 C4
Little Haywood 40 C3
Little Heath 41 F7
Little Hereford 28 E2
Little Hockham 44 D6
Little Horkesley 34 D5
Little Hormead 33 H6
Little Horsted 13 H5
Little Horton 20 D5
Little Horwood 31 J5
Little Houghton 32 B3
Little Hucklow 50 D5
Little Hulton 49 G2
Little Hungerford 21 J4
Little Hutton 57 K2
Little Irchester 32 C2
Little Keyford 20 A7
Little Kimble 22 B1
Little Kineton 30 E3
Little Kingshill 22 B2
Little Langdale 60 E6
Little Langford 10 B1
Little Laver 23 J1
Little Lawford 31 F1
Little Leigh 49 F5
Little Leighs 34 B7
Little Lever 49 G2
Little Ley 85 L9
Little Linford 32 B4
Little Linton 33 J4
Little London Bucks 31 H7
Little London Essex 33 H6
Little London ESuss 13 J5
Little London Hants 21 G7
Little London IoM 54 C5
Little London Lincs 43 F3
Little London Lincs 43 H3
Little London Lincs 52 E4
Little London Lincs 53 G5
Little London Norf 43 J3
Little London Norf 44 B6
Little London Oxon 21 J1
Little London Powys 37 K7
Little London Suff 34 E3
Little London WYorks 57 H6
Little Longstone 50 D5
Little Lyth 38 D5
Little Malvern 29 G4
Little Maplestead 34 C5
Little Marcle 29 F5
Little Marland 6 D4
Little Marlow 22 B3
Little Marsden 56 D6
Little Massingham 44 B3
Little Melton 45 F5
Little Milford 16 C4
Little Mill 19 G1
Little Milton 21 K1
Little Missenden 22 C2
Little Musgrave 61 J5
Little Ness 38 D4
Little Neston 48 B5
Little Newcastle 16 C3
Little Newsham 62 B5
Little Oakley Essex 35 G6
Little Oakley N'hants 42 B7
Little Odell 32 C3
Little Offley 32 E6
Little Onn 40 A4
Little Orton Cumb 60 E1
Little Orton Leics 41 F5
Little Ouse 44 A7
Little Ouseburn 57 K3
Little Overton 38 C1
Little Packington 40 E7
Little Parndon 33 H7
Little Paxton 32 E2
Little Petherick 3 G1
Little Plumpton 55 G6
Little Plumstead 45 H4
Little Ponton 42 C2
Little Posbrook 11 G4
Little Potheridge 6 D4
Little Preston 31 G3
Little Raveley 43 F7
Little Ribston 57 J4
Little Rissington 30 C7
Little Rollright 30 D5
Little Ryburgh 44 D3
Little Ryle 71 F2
Little Ryton 38 D5
Little Salkeld 61 G3
Little Sampford 33 K5
Little Saxham 34 C2
Little Scatwell 83 P5
Little Shelford 33 H3
Little Shrawardine 38 C4
Little Silver 7 H5
Little Singleton 55 G6
Little Smeaton NYorks 51 H1
Little Smeaton NYorks 62 D6
Little Snoring 44 D2
Little Sodbury 20 A3
Little Sodbury End 20 A3
Little Somborne 10 E1
Little Somerford 20 C3
Little Soudley 39 G3
Little Stainforth 56 D3
Little Stainton 62 D5
Little Stanney 48 D5
Little Staughton 32 E2
Little Steeping 53 H6
Little Stoke 40 B2
Little Stonham 35 F3
Little Street 43 J7
Little Stretton Leics 41 J5
Little Stretton Shrop 38 D6
Little Strickland 61 G5
Little Stukeley 33 F1
Little Sugnall 40 A2
Little Sutton 48 C5
Little Swinburne 70 E6
Little Tarrington 29 F4
Little Tew 30 E6
Little Tey 34 C6
Little Thetford 33 J1
Little Thornage 44 E2
Little Thornton 55 G5
Little Thorpe 62 E2
Little Thurlow 33 K3
Little Thurlow Green 33 K3
Little Thurrock 24 C4
Little Torboll 84 B1
Little Torrington 6 C4
Little Tosson 71 F3
Little Totham 34 C7
Little Town Cumb 60 D5
Little Town Lancs 56 B6
Little Town Warr 49 F3
Little Twycross 41 F5
Little Urswick 55 F2
Little Wakering 25 F3
Little Walden 33 J4
Little Waldingfield 34 D4
Little Walsingham 44 D2
Little Waltham 34 B7
Little Warley 24 C2
Little Washbourne 29 J5
Little Weighton 59 F6
Little Welland 29 H5
Little Welnetham 34 C2
Little Wenham 34 E5
Little Wenlock 39 F5
Little Whittington 70 E7
Little Wilbraham 33 J3
Little Wishford 10 B1
Little Witcombe 29 J7
Little Witley 29 G2
Little Wittenham 21 J2
Little Wittingham Green 35 G1
Little Wolford 30 D5
Little Woodcote 23 F5
Little Wratting 33 K4
Little Wymington 32 C2
Little Wymondley 33 F6
Little Wyrley 40 C5
Little Wytheford 38 E4
Little Yeldham 34 B5
Littlebeck 63 J6
Littleborough Devon 7 G4
Littleborough GtMan 49 J1
Littleborough Notts 52 B4
Littlebourne 15 H2
Littlebredy 8 E6
Littlebury 33 J5
Littlebury Green 33 H5
Littledean 29 F7
Littleferry 84 C1
Littleham Devon 6 C3
Littleham Devon 7 J7
Littlehampton 12 D6
Littlehempston 5 J4
Littlehoughton 71 H2
Littlemill EAyr 67 J2
Littlemill High 84 D5
Littlemoor Derbys 51 F6
Littlemoor Dorset 9 F6
Littlemore 21 J1
Littlemoss 49 J3
Littleover 41 F2
Littleport 43 J7
Littlestead Green 22 A4
Littlestone-on-Sea 15 F5
Littlethorpe 57 J3
Littleton ChesW&C 48 D6
Littleton Hants 11 F1
Littleton Som 8 D1
Littleton Surr 22 D5
Littleton Drew 20 B3
Littleton Panell 20 D6
Littleton-on-Severn 19 J2
Littletown Dur 62 D2
Littletown IoW 11 G5
Littlewick Green 22 B4
Littlewindsor 8 D4
Littleworth Glos 30 C5
Littleworth Oxon 21 G2
Littleworth Staffs 40 C4
Littleworth SYorks 51 J3
Littleworth Worcs 29 H4
Littley Green 33 K7
Litton Derbys 50 D5
Litton NYorks 56 E2
Litton Som 19 J6
Litton Cheney 8 E5
Liverpool 48 C3
Liverpool Cathedral Mersey L1 7AZ 131 E6
Liverpool John Lennon Airport 48 D4
Liverpool - Maritime Mercantile City Mersey L3 4AF 112 C4
Liverpool Metropolitan Cathedral (RC) Mersey L3 5TQ 131 E4
Liversedge 57 H7
Liverton Devon 5 J3
Liverton R&C 63 H5
Liverton Street 14 D3
Living Coasts, Torquay Torbay TQ1 2BG 5 K4
Livingston 75 J4
Livingston Village 75 J4
Lixwm 47 K5
Lizard 2 E7
Llaingarreglwyd 26 D3
Llaingoch 46 A4
Llaithddu 37 K7
Llampha 18 C4
Llan 37 H5
Llanaber 37 F4
Llanaelhaearn 36 C1
Llanaeron 26 D2
Llanafan 27 F1
Llanafan-fawr 27 J3
Llanafan-fechan 27 J3
Llanallgo 46 C4
Llanarmon 36 D2
Llanarmon Dyffryn Ceiriog 38 A2
Llanarmon-yn-Ial 47 K7
Llanarth Cere 26 D3
Llanarth Mon 28 C7
Llanarthney 17 J3
Llanasa 47 K4
Llanbabo 46 B4
Llanbadarn Fawr 36 E7
Llanbadarn Fynydd 27 K1
Llanbadarn-y-garreg 28 A4
Llanbadoc 19 G1
Llanbadrig 46 B3
Llanbeder 19 G2
Llanbedr Gwyn 36 E3
Llanbedr Powys 28 A4
Llanbedr Powys 28 B6
Llanbedr-Dyffryn-Clwyd 47 K7
Llanbedrgoch 46 D4
Llanbedrog 36 C2
Llanbedr-y-cennin 47 F6
Llanberis 46 D7
Llanbethery 18 D5
Llanbister 28 A1
Llanblethian 18 C4
Llanboidy 17 F3
Llanbradach 18 E2
Llanbryn-mair 37 H5
Llancadle 18 D5
Llancarfan 18 D4
Llancayo 19 G1
Llancynfelyn 37 F6
Llandafal 18 E1
Llandaff 18 E4
Llandaff North 18 E4
Llandanwg 36 E3
Llandawke 17 F4
Llanddaniel Fab 46 C5
Llanddarog 17 H4
Llanddeiniol 26 E1
Llanddeiniolen 46 D6
Llandderfel 37 J2
Llanddeusant Carmar 27 G6
Llanddeusant IoA 46 B4
Llanddew 27 K5
Llanddewi 17 H7
Llanddewi Rhydderch 28 C7
Llanddewi Skirrid 28 C7
Llanddewi Velfrey 16 E4
Llanddewi Ystradenni 28 A2
Llanddewi-Brefi 27 F3
Llanddewi'r Cwm 27 K4
Llanddoged 47 G6
Llanddona 46 D5
Llanddowror 17 F4
Llanddulas 47 H5
Llanddwywe 36 E3
Llanddyfnan 46 D5
Llandefaelog Fach 27 K5
Llandefaelog-tre'r-graig 28 A6
Llandefalle 28 A5
Llandegfan 46 D5
Llandegfedd Reservoir Mon NP4 0TA 19 G2
Llandegla 47 K7
Llandegley 28 A2
Llandegveth 19 G2
Llandegwning 36 B2
Llandeilo 17 K3
Llandeilo Abercywyn 17 G4
Llandeilo Graban 27 K4
Llandeilo'r-Fan 27 H5
Llandeloy 16 B3
Llandenny 19 H1
Llandevaud 19 H2
Llandevenny 19 H3
Llandinabo 28 E6
Llandinam 37 K7
Llandissilio 16 E3
Llandogo 19 J1
Llandough VGlam 18 C4
Llandough VGlam 18 E4
Llandovery (Llanymddyfri) 27 G5
Llandow 18 C4
Llandre Carmar 16 E3
Llandre Carmar 17 K1
Llandre Cere 37 F7
Llandrillo 37 K2
Llandrindod Wells 27 K2
Llandrinio 38 B4
Llandudno 47 F4
Llandudno Junction 47 F5
Llandwrog 46 C7
Llandybie 17 K4
Llandyfaelog 17 H4
Llandyfan 17 K4
Llandyfriog 17 G1
Llandyfrydog 46 C4
Llandygai 46 D5
Llandygwydd 17 F1
Llandyrnog 47 K6
Llandyry 17 H5
Llandysilio 38 B4
Llandyssil 38 A6
Llandysul 17 H1
Llanedeyrn 19 F3
Llanedy 17 J5
Llaneglwys 27 K5
Llanegryn 37 F5
Llanegwad 17 J3
Llaneilian 46 C3
Llanelian-yn-Rhos 47 G5
Llanelidan 47 K7
Llanelieu 28 A5
Llanellen 28 C7
Llanelli 17 J5
Llanelli Millennium Coastal Park Carmar SA15 2LF 17 H6
Llanelltyd 37 G4
Llanelly 28 B7
Llanelly Hill 28 B7
Llanelwedd 27 K3
Llanenddwyn 36 E3
Llanengan 36 B3
Llanerfyl 37 K5
Llaneuddog 46 C4
Llanfachraeth 46 B4
Llanfachreth 37 G3
Llanfaelog 46 B5
Llanfaelrhys 36 B3
Llanfaenor 28 D7
Llanfaes IoA 46 E5
Llanfaes Powys 27 K6
Llanfaethlu 46 B4
Llanfaglan 46 C6
Llanfair 36 E3
Llanfair Caereinion 38 A5
Llanfair Clydogau 27 F3
Llanfair Dyffryn Clwyd 47 K7
Llanfair Talhaiarn 47 H5
Llanfair Waterdine 28 B1
Llanfairfechan 46 E5
Llanfair-Nant-Gwyn 16 E2
Llanfair-Orllwyn 17 G1
Llanfairpwllgwyngyll 46 D5
Llanfairynghornwy 46 B3
Llanfair-yn-neubwll 46 B5
Llanfallteg 16 E4
Llanfaredd 27 K3
Llanfarian 26 E1
Llanfechain 38 A3
Llanfechell 46 B3
Llanfendigaid 36 E5
Llanferres 47 K6
Llanfflewyn 46 B4
Llanfigael 46 B4
Llanfihangel Glyn Myfyr 37 J1
Llanfihangel Nant Bran 27 J5
Llanfihangel Rhydithon 28 A2
Llanfihangel Rogiet 19 H3
Llanfihangel Tal-y-llyn 28 A6
Llanfihangel-ar-arth 17 H1
Llanfihangel-nant-Melan 28 A3
Llanfihangel-uwch-Gwili 17 H3
Llanfihangel-y-Creuddyn 27 F1
Llanfihangel-yng-Ngwynfa 37 K4
Llanfihangel-yn-Nhywyn 46 B5
Llanfihangel-y-pennant Gwyn 36 E1
Llanfihangel-y-pennant Gwyn 37 F5
Llanfilo 28 A5
Llanfoist 28 B7
Llanfor 37 J2
Llanfrechfa 19 G2
Llanfrothen 37 F1
Llanfrynach 27 K6
Llanfwrog Denb 47 K7
Llanfwrog IoA 46 B4
Llanfyllin 38 A4
Llanfynydd Carmar 17 J3
Llanfynydd Flints 48 B7
Llanfyrnach 17 F2
Llangadfan 37 K4
Llangadog 27 G6
Llangadwaladr IoA 46 B6
Llangadwaladr Powys 38 A2
Llangaffo 46 C6
Llangain 17 G4
Llangammarch Wells 27 J4
Llangan 18 C4
Llangarron 28 E6
Llangasty-Talyllyn 28 A6
Llangathen 17 J3
Llangattock 28 B7
Llangattock Lingoed 28 C7
Llangattock-Vibon-Avel 28 D7
Llangedwyn 38 A3
Llangefni 46 C5
Llangeinor 18 C3
Llangeitho 27 F3
Llangeler 17 G2
Llangelynin 36 E5
Llangendeirne 17 H4
Llangennech 17 J5
Llangennith 17 H6
Llangenny 28 B7
Llangernyw 47 G6
Llangian 36 B3
Llangiwg 18 A1
Llangloffan 16 C2
Llanglydwen 16 E3
Llangoed 46 E5
Llangoedmor 16 E1
Llangollen 38 B1
Llangollen Railway Denb LL20 8SN 38 B1
Llangolman 16 E3
Llangorse 28 A6
Llangorwen 37 F7
Llangovan 19 H1
Llangower 37 J2
Llangrannog 26 C3
Llangristiolus 46 C5
Llangrove 28 E7
Llangua 28 C6
Llangunllo 28 B1
Llangunnor 17 H3
Llangurig 27 J1
Llangwm Conwy 37 J1
Llangwm Mon 19 H1
Llangwm Pembs 16 C5
Llangwnnadl 36 B2
Llangwyfan 47 K6
Llangwyllog 46 C5
Llangwyryfon 27 F1
Llangybi Cere 27 F3
Llangybi Gwyn 36 D1
Llangybi Mon 19 G2
Llangyfelach 17 K6
Llangynhafal 47 K6
Llangynidr 28 A7
Llangyniew 38 A5
Llangynin 17 F4
Llangynllo 17 G1
Llangynog Carmar 17 G4
Llangynog Powys 37 K3
Llangynwyd 18 B3
Llanhamlach 27 K6
Llanharan 18 D3
Llanharry 18 D3
Llanhennock 19 G2
Llanhilleth 19 F1
Llanidloes 37 J7
Llaniestyn 36 B2
Llanigon 28 B5
Llanilar 27 F1
Llanilid 18 C3
Llanishen Cardiff 18 E3
Llanishen Mon 19 H1
Llanllawddog 17 H3
Llanllechid 46 E6
Llanlleonfel 27 J3
Llanllugan 37 K5
Llanllwch 17 G4
Llanllwchaiarn 38 A6
Llanllwni 17 H1
Llanllyfni 46 C7
Llanllywel 19 G2
Llanmadoc 17 H6
Llanmaes 18 C5
Llanmartin 19 G3
Llanmerewig 38 A6
Llanmihangel 18 C4
Llan-mill 16 E4
Llanmiloe 17 F5
Llanmorlais 17 J6
Llannefydd 47 H5
Llannerch Hall 47 J5
Llannerch-y-medd 46 C4
Llannerch-y-Môr 47 K5
Llannon Carmar 17 J5
Llan-non Cere 26 E2
Llannor 36 C2
Llanover 19 G1
Llanpumsaint 17 H3
Llanreithan 16 B3
Llanrhaeadr 47 J6
Llanrhaeadr-ym-Mochnant 38 A3
Llanrhian 16 B2
Llanrhidian 17 H6
Llanrhyddlad 46 B4
Llanrhystud 26 E2
Llanrothal 28 D7
Llanrug 46 D6
Llanrumney 19 F3
Llanrwst 47 F6
Llansadurnen 17 F4
Llansadwrn Carmar 17 K2
Llansadwrn IoA 46 D5
Llansaint 17 G5
Llansamlet 17 K6
Llansanffraid 26 E2
Llansanffraid Glan Conwy 47 G5
Llansannan 47 H6
Llansannor 18 C4
Llansantffraed 28 A6
Llansantffraed-Cwmdeuddwr 27 J2
Llansantffraed-in-Elwel 27 K3
Llansantffraid-ym-Mechain 38 B3
Llansawel 17 K2
Llansilin 38 B3
Llansoy 19 H1
Llanspyddid 27 K6
Llanstadwell 16 C5
Llansteffan 17 G4
Llanstephan 28 A4
Llantarnam 19 G2
Llanteg 16 E4
Llanthony 28 B6
Llantilio Crossenny 28 C7
Llantilio Pertholey 28 C7
Llantood 16 E1
Llantrisant IoA 46 B4
Llantrisant Mon 19 G2
Llantrisant RCT 18 D3
Llantrithyd 18 D4
Llantwit Fardre 18 D3
Llantwit Major 18 C5
Llantysilio 38 A1
Llanuwchllyn 37 H3
Llanvaches 19 H2
Llanvair-Discoed 19 H2
Llanvapley 28 C7
Llanvetherine 28 C7
Llanveynoe 28 C5
Llanvihangel Crucorney (Llanfihangel Crucornau) 28 C6
Llanvihangel Gobion 19 G1
Llanvihangel-Ystern-Llewern 28 D7
Llanvithyn 18 D4
Llanwarne 28 E6
Llanwddyn 37 K4
Llanwenog 17 H1
Llanwern 19 G3
Llanwinio 17 F3
Llanwnda Gwyn 46 C7
Llanwnda Pembs 16 C2
Llanwnnen 17 J1
Llanwnog 37 K6
Llanwonno 18 D2
Llanwrda 27 G5
Llanwrin 37 G5
Llanwrthwl 27 J2
Llanwrtyd 27 H4
Llanwrtyd Wells 27 H4
Llanwyddelan 37 K5
Llanyblodwel 38 B3
Llanybri 17 G4
Llanybydder 17 J1
Llanycefn 16 E3
Llanychaer Bridge 16 C2
Llanycil 37 J2
Llanycrwys 17 K1
Llanymawddwy 37 H4
Llanymynech 38 B3
Llanynghenedl 46 B4
Llanynys 47 K6
Llan-y-pwll 48 C7
Llanyre 27 K2
Llanystumdwy 36 D2
Llanywern 28 A6
Llawhaden 16 D4
Llawndy 47 K4
Llawnt 38 B2
Llawr-y-dref 36 B3
Llawryglyn 37 J6
Llay 48 C7
Llechcynfarwy 46 B4
Llecheiddior 36 D1
Llechfaen 27 K6
Llechryd Caerp 18 E1
Llechryd Cere 17 F1
Llechrydau 38 B2
Llechwedd Slate Caverns Gwyn LL41 3NB 37 G1
Lledrod Cere 27 F1
Lledrod Powys 38 B3
Llethryd 17 J6
Llidiad-Nenog 17 J2
Llidiardau 37 H2
Llithfaen 36 C1
Lloc 47 K5
Llong 48 B6
Llowes 28 A4
Lloyney 28 B1
Llundain-fach 26 E3
Llwydcoed 18 C1
Llwydiarth 37 K4
Llwyn 38 B7
Llwyncelyn 26 D3
Llwyn-croes 17 H3
Llwyndafydd 26 C3
Llwynderw 38 B5
Llwyndyrys 36 C1
Llwyneinion 38 B1
Llwyngwril 36 E5
Llwynhendy 17 J6
Llwyn-Madoc 27 J3
Llwynmawr 38 B2
Llwyn-onn Cere 26 D3
Llwyn-onn MTyd 27 K7
Llwyn-y-brain Carmar 16 E4
Llwyn-y-brain Carmar 27 G5
Llwyn-y-groes 26 E3
Llwynypia 18 C2
Llyn Brenig Conwy LL21 9TT 47 H7
Llyn Llech Owain Country Park Carmar SA14 7NF 17 J4
Llynclys 38 B3
Llynfaes 46 C5
Llysfaen 47 G5
Llyswen 28 A5
Llysworney 18 C4
Llys-y-frân 16 D3
Llywel 27 H5
Load Brook 50 E4
Loanend 77 H5
Loanhead 76 A4
Loans 74 B7
Lobb 6 C2
Lobhillcross 6 C7
Loch a' Charnain 88 C4
Loch an Eilein Visitor Centre & Forest Trail High PH22 1QT 84 C10
Loch Choire Lodge 87 J6
Loch Eil Outward Bound 79 M3
Loch Head D&G 64 D6
Loch Head D&G 67 J4
Loch Lomond Shores & Gateway Centre WDun G83 8QL 74 B2

Loch Ness Centre and Exhibition *High* IV63 6TU **83** R8
Loch of the Lowes *P&K* PH8 0HH **80** F6
Loch Sgioport **88** C5
Lochailort (Ceann Loch Ailleart) **79** J2
Lochaline (Loch Àlainn) **78** H6
Lochans **64** A5
Locharbriggs **68** E5
Lochawe (Loch Obha) **79** N8
Lochboisdale (Loch Baghasdail) **88** B7
Lochbuie **78** H8
Lochcarron (Loch Carrann) **83** J6
Lochdhu Hotel **87** N5
Lochdon **79** J7
Lochearnhead (Ceann Loch Èireann) **80** A8
Lochee **81** J7
Lochend (Ceann Loch) *High* **83** R7
Lochfoot **68** C2
Lochfoot **65** K3
Lochgair **73** H1
Lochgarthside **83** R9
Lochgelly **75** K1
Lochgilphead (Ceann Loch Gilb) **73** G2
Lochgoilhead **79** P10
Lochgoyn **74** D7
Lochhill *EAyr* **67** K2
Lochhill *Moray* **84** G4
Lochinch Castle **64** B4
Lochinver (Loch an Inbhir) **86** C7
Lochlea **74** C7
Lochmaben **69** F5
Lochmaddy **88** D2
Lochore **75** K1
Lochore Meadows Country Park *Fife* KY5 8BA **75** K1
Lochportain **88** D1
Lochranza **73** H5
Lochside *Aber* **81** N4
Lochside *High* **86** G4
Lochside *High* **87** L6
Lochton **67** G5
Lochuisge **79** J5
Lochurr **68** C5
Lochussie **83** Q5
Lochwinnoch **74** B5
Lockengate **4** A4
Lockerbie **69** G5
Lockeridge **20** E5
Lockerley **10** D2
Lockhills **61** G2
Locking **19** G6
Lockington *ERid* **59** F5
Lockington *Leics* **41** G3
Locks Heath **11** G4
Locksbottom **23** H5
Locksgreen **11** F5
Lockton **58** E1
Locomotive: The National Railway Museum at Shildon *Dur* DL4 1PQ **62** D4
Loddington *Leics* **42** A5
Loddington *N'hants* **32** B1
Loddiswell **5** H6
Loddon **45** H6
Lode **33** J2
Loders **8** E5
Lodsworth **12** C4
Loftus House *NYorks* **57** G2
Loftus House *WYorks* **57** J7
Loftus **63** H5
Logan *D&G* **64** A6
Logan *EAyr* **67** K1
Loganlea **75** H4
Loggerheads **39** G2
Loggerheads Country Park *Denb* CH7 5LH **47** K6
Logie Coldstone **85** J10
Logierait **80** E5
Login **16** E3
Lolworth **33** G2
Lonbain **82** G5
Londesborough **58** E5
London **23** G3
London Apprentice **4** A6
London Ashford Airport **15** F5
London Beach **14** D4
London Biggin Hill Airport **23** H5
London City Airport **23** H3
London Colney **22** E1
London Eye *GtLon* SE1 7PB **132** E5
London Gatwick Airport **23** F7
London Heathrow Airport **22** D4
London Luton Airport **32** E6
London Minstead **10** D3
London Motor Museum *GtLon* UB3 4SB **103** B7
London Oxford Airport **31** F7
London Southend Airport **24** E3
London Stansted Airport **33** J6
London Transport Museum *GtLon* WC2E 7BB **132** E3
Londonderry (Derry) *D&S* **90** L5
Londonderry *NYorks* **57** H1
Londonthorpe **42** C2
Londubh **83** J2
Long Ashton **19** J4
Long Bank **29** G1
Long Bennington **42** B1
Long Bredy **8** E5
Long Buckby **31** H2
Long Clawson **42** A3
Long Compton *Staffs* **40** A2
Long Compton *Warks* **30** D5
Long Crendon **21** K1
Long Crichel **9** J3
Long Dean **20** B4
Long Downs **2** E5
Long Drax **58** C7
Long Duckmanton **51** G5
Long Gill **56** D4
Long Green *ChesW&C* **48** D5
Long Green *Essex* **34** D6
Long Green *Worcs* **29** H5
Long Hanborough **31** F7
Long Itchington **31** F2
Long Lane **39** F4
Long Lawford **31** F1
Long Load **8** D2
Long Marston *Herts* **32** B7

Long Marston *NYorks* **58** B4
Loughton *Warks* **30** C4
Long Marston **61** H4
Long Meadowend **38** D7
Long Melford **34** C4
Long Newton **20** C2
Long Preston **56** D4
Long Riston **59** H5
Long Stratton **45** F6
Long Street **31** J4
Long Sutton *Hants* **22** A7
Long Sutton *Lincs* **43** H3
Long Sutton *Som* **8** D2
Long Thurlow **34** E2
Long Whatton **41** G3
Long Wittenham **21** J2
Longbenton **71** H7
Longborough **30** C6
Longbridge *Plym* **5** F5
Longbridge *Warks* **30** B2
Longbridge *WMid* **30** B1
Longbridge Deverill **20** B7
Longburgh **60** E1
Longburton **9** F3
Longcliffe **50** E7
Longcombe **5** J5
Longcot **21** F2
Longcroft **75** F3
Longcross *Devon* **4** E3
Longcross *Surr* **22** C5
Longden **38** D5
Longden *Staffs* **40** C4
Longden upon Tern **39** F4
Longdown **7** G7
Longdowns *Ork* **89** C8
Longdon on Tern **39** F4
Longdon **7** G6
Longdon *Staffs* **40** C4
Longdon Green **40** C4
Longdon upon Tern **39** F4
Longdown **7** G7
Longdowns **2** E5
Longfield *Kent* **24** C5
Longfield *NM&D* **93** F15
Longfield Hill **24** C5
Longfleet **10** B5
Longford *Derbys* **40** E2
Longford *Glos* **29** H6
Longford *GtLon* **22** D4
Longford *Shrop* **39** F2
Longford *Tel&W* **39** G4
Longforgan **81** J8
Longformacus **76** E5
Longframlington **71** G3
Longham *Dorset* **10** B5
Longham *Norf* **44** D4
Longhirst **71** H5
Longhope *Glos* **29** F7
Longhope *Ork* **89** C8
Longhorsley **71** G4
Longhoughton **71** H2
Longlands *Cumb* **60** D3
Longlands *GtLon* **23** H4
Longlane *Derbys* **40** E2
Longlane *WBerks* **21** H4
Longleat House *Wilts* BA12 7NW **20** B7
Longleat Safari Park *Wilts* BA12 7NW **20** B7
Longlevens **29** H7
Longley **50** D2
Longley Green **29** G3
Longmanhill **85** M4
Longmoor Camp **11** J1
Longmorn **84** G5
Longnewton *ScBord* **70** A1
Longnewton *Stock* **62** D5
Longney **29** G7
Longniddry **76** C3
Longnor *Shrop* **38** D5
Longnor *Staffs* **50** C6
Longparish **21** H7
Longridge *Lancs* **56** B6
Longridge *Staffs* **40** B4
Longridge *WLoth* **75** H4
Longridge End **29** H6
Longridge Towers **77** H5
Longriggend **75** G3
Longrock **2** C5
Longsdon **49** J7
Longshaw **48** E2
Longside **85** Q6
Longslow **39** F2
Longstanton **33** H2
Longstock **10** E1
Longstone **2** C5
Longstowe **33** G3
Longstreet **20** E6
Longthorpe **42** E6
Longton *Lancs* **55** H7
Longton *Stoke* **40** B1
Longtown *Cumb* **69** J7
Longtown *Here* **28** C6
Longville in the Dale **38** E6
Longwell Green **19** K4
Longwick **22** A1
Longwitton **71** F5
Longworth **21** G2
Longyester **76** D4
Lonmay **85** Q5
Looe **4** C5
Look Out Discovery Park, Bracknell *BrackF* RG12 7QW **22** B5
Loose **14** C2
Loosebeare **7** F5
Loosegate **43** G3
Loosley Row **22** B1
Lopcombe Corner **10** D1
Lopen **8** D3
Loppington **38** D3
Lorbottle **71** F3
Lorbottle Hall **71** F3
Lordington **11** J4
Lord's Cricket Ground & Museum *GtLon* NW8 8QN **102** G6
Lord's Hill **10** E3
Lorn **74** B2
Loscoe **41** G1
Loscombe **8** D5
Losgaintir (Luskentyre) **88** F8
Lossiemouth **84** G3
Lossit **72** A1
Lostock Gralam **49** F5
Lostock Green **49** F5
Lostock Junction **49** F2
Lostwithiel **4** B5
Loth **89** F4
Lothbeg **87** M8
Lothersdale **56** E5
Lothmore **87** M8
Loudwater **22** C2
Lough Gilly **93** F13
Loughan **92** D4
Loughans **93** B11
Loughash **90** H6
Loughborough **41** H4
Loughbrickland **93** G12
Loughgall **93** E11
Loughguile **92** F2
Loughinisland **93** K12
Loughmacrory **90** M9
Loughor **17** J6

Loughton *Essex* **23** H2
Loughton *MK* **32** B5
Loughton *Shrop* **39** F7
Louis Tussaud's Waxworks FY1 5AA **121** Blackpool
Lound *Lincs* **42** D4
Lound *Notts* **51** J4
Lound *Suff* **45** K6
Lount **41** F4
Louth **53** G4
Love Clough **56** D7
Lovedean **11** H3
Lover **10** D3
Loversall **51** H3
Loves Green **24** C1
Lovesome Hill **62** D7
Loveston **16** D5
Lovington **8** E1
Low Ackworth **51** G1
Low Angerton **71** F5
Low Ballevain **66** A1
Low Barlay **65** F5
Low Barlings **52** D5
Low Bentham (Lower Bentham) **56** B3
Low Bolton **62** A7
Low Bradfield **50** E3
Low Bradley (Bradley) **57** F5
Low Braithwaite **60** F2
Low Brunton **70** E6
Low Burnham **51** K2
Low Burton **57** H1
Low Buston **71** H3
Low Catton **58** D4
Low Coniscliffe **62** D5
Low Craighead **67** G3
Low Dinsdale **62** D5
Low Ellington **57** H1
Low Entercommon **62** D6
Low Etherley **62** C4
Low Fell **62** C1
Low Gate **70** E7
Low Grantley **57** H2
Low Green **34** C2
Low Habberley **29** H1
Low Ham **8** D2
Low Hawsker **63** K6
Low Haygarth **61** H7
Low Hesket **61** G2
Low Hutton **58** D3
Low Kingthorpe **58** E1
Low Laithe **57** G3
Low Langton **52** E5
Low Leighton **50** C4
Low Lorton **60** C4
Low Marishes **58** E2
Low Marnham **52** B6
Low Middleton **77** K7
Low Mill **63** G7
Low Moor *Lancs* **56** C5
Low Moor *WYorks* **57** G7
Low Moorsley **62** D2
Low Moresby **60** A4
Low Newton-by-the-Sea **71** H1
Low Row *Cumb* **70** A7
Low Row *NYorks* **61** L7
Low Stillaig **73** H4
Low Street **44** E5
Low Tharston **45** F6
Low Torry **75** J2
Low Town **71** G3
Low Toynton **53** F5
Low Wood **55** G1
Low Worsall **62** D6
Lowbands **29** G5
Lowbridge **4** C3
Lowdham **41** J1
Lowe **38** E2
Lowe Hill **49** J7
Lower Aisholt **8** B1
Lower Apperley **29** H6
Lower Arncott **31** H7
Lower Ashtead **22** E6
Lower Ashton **7** G7
Lower Assendon **22** A3
Lower Auchalick **73** H3
Lower Ballam **55** G6
Lower Ballinderry **93** G10
Lower Barewood **28** C3
Lower Bartle **55** H6
Lower Bayble (Pabail Iarach) **88** L4
Lower Beeding **13** F4
Lower Benefield **42** C7
Lower Bentham (Low Bentham) **56** B3
Lower Bentley **29** J2
Lower Berry Hill **28** E7
Lower Birchwood **51** G7
Lower Boddington **31** F3
Lower Boscaswell **2** A5
Lower Bourne **22** B7
Lower Brailes **30** E5
Lower Breakish **82** G8
Lower Bredbury **49** J3
Lower Broadheath **29** H3
Lower Brynamman **27** G7
Lower Bullingham **28** E5
Lower Bullington **21** H7
Lower Burgate **10** C3
Lower Burrow **8** D2
Lower Burton **28** D3
Lower Caldecote **32** E4
Lower Cam **20** A1
Lower Cambourne **33** G3
Lower Chapel **27** K5
Lower Cheriton **7** K5
Lower Chicksgrove **9** J1
Lower Chute **21** G6
Lower Clent **40** B1
Lower Creedy **7** G5
Lower Cumberworth **50** E2
Lower Darkley **93** D13
Lower Darwen **56** B7
Lower Dean **32** D2
Lower Diabaig **82** H4
Lower Dicker **13** J5
Lower Dinchope **38** D7
Lower Down **38** C7
Lower Drift **2** B6
Lower Dunsforth **57** K3
Lower Earley **22** A4
Lower Edmonton **23** G2
Lower Elkstone **50** C7
Lower End *Bucks* **31** K1
Lower End *MK* **32** C5
Lower End *N'hants* **32** B3
Lower Everleigh **20** E6
Lower Eythorne **15** H2
Lower Failand **19** J4
Lower Farringdon **11** J1
Lower Fittleworth **12** C5
Lower Foxdale **54** B6
Lower Freystrop **16** C4
Lower Froyle **22** A7
Lower Gabwell **5** K4
Lower Gledfield **83** R1
Lower Godney **19** H7
Lower Gravenhurst **32** E5
Lower Green *Essex* **33** H5
Lower Green *Kent* **23** K7
Lower Green *Kent* **23** J7
Lower Green *Norf* **44** D2
Lower Green *Staffs* **40** B5
Lower Green Bank **55** J4
Lower Hacheston **35** H3
Lower Halstock Leigh **8** E4
Lower Halstow **24** E5
Lower Hardres **15** G2

Luddington *NLincs* **52** B1
Lyonshall **28** C3
Lydtham St. Anne's **55** G7
Ludford *Lincs* **52** E4
Ludford *Shrop* **28** E1
Ludgershall *Bucks* **31** H7
Ludgershall *Wilts* **21** F6
Ludgvan **2** C5
Ludham **45** H4
Ludlow **28** D1
Ludney **53** G3
Ludstock **29** F5
Ludwell **9** J2
Ludworth **62** D2
Luffincott **6** B6
Luffness **76** C3
Lufton **8** E3
Lugar **67** K1
Lugate **76** D3
Luggate Burn **76** E3
Luggiebank **75** F3
Lugton **74** C5
Lugwardine **28** E4
Luib **82** F8
Luing **79** J9
Lulham **28** D5
Lullington *Derbys* **40** E4
Lullington *Som* **20** A6
Lulsgate Bottom **19** J5
Lulsley **29** G3
Lulworth Camp **9** H6
Lulworth Cove & Heritage Centre *Dorset* BH20 5RQ **9** H7
Lumb *Lancs* **56** D7
Lumb *WYorks* **57** F7
Lumbutts **56** E7
Lumby **57** K6
Lumphanan **85** K10
Lumphinnans **75** K1
Lumsdaine **77** G4
Lumsden **85** J9
Lunan **81** M5
Lunanhead **81** K5
Luncarty **80** F8
Lund *ERid* **59** F5
Lund *NYorks* **58** C6
Lundavra **79** M4
Lundie **81** J7
Lundin Links **81** K10
Lundwood **51** F2
Lundy **6** A1
Lunga *P&K* **80** A8
Lunga *ScBord* **73** G10
Lunga **89** N6
Lunna **89** P6
Lunning **89** P6
Lunnon **17** J7
Lunsford **14** C6
Lunsford's Cross **14** C6
Lunt **48** C2
Luntley **28** C3
Luppitt **7** K5
Lupset **51** F1
Lupton **55** J1
Lurgan **93** F11
Lurgashall **12** C4
Lurignich **79** K4
Lurley **7** H4
Lusby **53** G6
Luss **74** B1
Lussagiven **72** E2
Lusta **82** C5
Lustleigh **7** F7
Luston **28** D2
Luthermuir **81** M4
Luthrie **81** J9
Luton *Devon* **5** K4
Luton *Devon* **7** J5
Luton *Luton* **32** E6
Luton *Med* **24** D5
Luton Airport **32** E6
Lutterworth **41** H7
Lutton *Devon* **5** F4
Lutton *Lincs* **43** H3
Lutton *N'hants* **42** E7
Luxborough **7** H2
Luxulyan **4** A5
Lybster **87** Q6
Lydacott **6** C5
Lydbury North **38** C7
Lydcott **6** E2
Lydd **15** F5
Lydden **15** H3
Lyddington **42** B6
Lydd-on-Sea **15** F5
Lydeard St. Lawrence **7** K2
Lydford **6** D7
Lydford-on-Fosse **8** E1
Lydgate *GtMan* **49** J2
Lydgate *WYorks* **56** E7
Lydham **38** C6
Lydiard Millicent **20** D3
Lydiard Tregoze **20** E3
Lydiate **48** C2
Lydlinch **9** G3
Lydney **19** K1
Lydstep **16** D6
Lye **40** B1
Lye Cross **19** H5
Lye Green *Bucks* **22** C1
Lye Green *ESuss* **13** J3
Lye Green *Warks* **30** C2
Lye's Green **20** B7
Lyford **21** G2
Lymbridge Green **15** G3
Lyme Regis **8** C5
Lymekilns **74** E5
Lyminge **15** G3
Lymington **10** E5
Lyminster **12** C6
Lymm **49** F4
Lymore **10** D5
Lympne **15** G4
Lympsham **19** G6
Lympstone **7** H7
Lynaberack **84** B11
Lynch **7** H1
Lynch Green **45** F5
Lynchat **84** B10
Lyndhurst **10** E4
Lyndon **42** C5
Lyne *ScBord* **76** A6
Lyne *Surr* **22** D5
Lyne Down **29** F5
Lyne of Gorthleck **83** R8
Lyne of Skene **85** M9
Lyneal **38** D2
Lyneham *Oxon* **30** D6
Lyneham *Wilts* **20** D4
Lyneholmeford **70** A6
Lynemore **84** F8
Lynemouth **71** H4
Lyness **89** C8
Lynford **44** C6
Lyng *Norf* **44** E4
Lyng *Som* **8** C2
Lyngate **45** H3
Lynmouth **7** F1
Lynn **39** G4
Lynsted **25** F5
Lynstone **6** A4
Lynton **7** F1
Lynton & Lynmouth Cliff Railway *Devon* EX35 6EP **7** F1
Lyon's Gate **9** F4

M

Mabe Burnthouse **2** E5
Mabie **65** K3
Mablethorpe **53** J4
Macclesfield **49** J5
Macclesfield Forest **49** J5
Macduff **85** M4
Macfin **92** D4
Machan **75** F5
Macharioch **66** B3
Machen **18** E3
Machie *A&B* **72** A4
Machie *A&B* **72** B6
Machrihanish **66** A1
Machrins **72** B1
Machynlleth **37** G5
Mackan **91** J7
Mackerye End **32** E7
Mackworth **41** F2
Macmerry **76** C3
Macosquin **92** D4
Madame Tussauds *GtLon* NW1 5LR **102** H6
Maddan **93** D13
Madderty **80** E8
Maddiston **75** H3
Madehurst **12** C5
Madeley *Staffs* **39** G1
Madeley *Tel&W* **39** G5
Madeley Heath **39** G1
Madford **7** K4
Madingley **33** G2
Madjeston **9** H2
Madley **28** D5
Madresfield **29** H4
Madron **2** B5
Maenaddwyn **46** C4
Maenclochog **16** D3
Maendy **18** D4
Maenporth **2** E6
Maentwrog **37** F1
Maen-y-groes **26** C3
Maer *Corn* **6** A5
Maer *Staffs* **39** G2
Maerdy *Carmar* **17** K3
Maerdy *Carmar* **17** K3
Maerdy *Conwy* **37** K1
Maerdy *RCT* **18** C2
Maes-glas **19** F3
Maesgwynne **17** F3
Maeshafn **48** B6
Maesllyn **17** G1
Maesmynis **27** K4
Maesteg **18** B2
Maes-Treylow **28** B2
Maesybont **17** J4
Maesycrugiau **17** H1
Maesycwmmer **18** E2
Magdalen Laver **23** J1
Maggieknockater **84** H6
Maggots End **33** H6
Magham Down **13** K5
Maghaberry **93** G10
Magham Down **13** K5
Maghera *Mid Ulster* **92** D7
Maghera *NM&D* **93** J13
Magherabane **92** D7
Magherabeg **93** G11
Magherafelt **92** D7
Magheragall **93** G10
Magheralin **93** G11
Magheralough *D&S* **90** K8
Magheralough *F&O* **91** K11
Magheramason **90** K6
Magheramayo **93** H13
Magheramorne **92** D5
Magherasaul **93** J13
Magheraveely **91** L14
Maghery *AB&C* **93** E10
Maghery *AB&C* **93** E10
Maghery *NM&D* **93** H15
Maghull **48** C2
Magilligan **92** B3
Maghull **48** C2
Magna Park **41** H7
Magor **19** H3
Magpie Green **34** E1
Maguiresbridge **91** K13
Maiden Bradley **9** H1
Maiden Head **19** J5
Maiden Law **62** B2
Maiden Newton **8** E5
Maiden Wells **16** C6
Maidencombe **5** K4
Maidenhayne **8** B5
Maidenhead **22** B3
Maidens **67** G3
Maiden's Green **22** B4
Maidensgrove **22** A3
Maidenwell *Corn* **4** B4
Maidenwell *Lincs* **53** G5
Maidford **31** H3
Maids' Moreton **31** J5
Maidstone **14** C2
Maidwell **31** J1
Mail **89** N10
Maindee **19** G3
Maine **90** M9
Mainland *Ork* **89** C7
Mainland *Shet* **89** M7
Mains of Watten **87** Q4
Mainsforth **62** D3
Mainsriddle **65** K5
Mainstone **38** B7
Maisemore **29** H6
Maizetown **92** E6
Major's Green **30** C1
Makendon **70** D3
Makeney **41** F1
Makerstoun **76** E7
Malborough **5** H7
Malcoff **50** C4
Malden Rushett **22** E5
Maldon **24** E1
Malham **56** E3
Mallaig (Malaig) **82** G11
Malleny Mills **75** K4
Mallaigvaig **82** G11
Mallow **91** G11
Mallusk **92** H6
Mallwyd **37** H4

Meeson **39** F3
Meeth **6** D5
Meeting House Hill **45** H3
Megarrystown **93** G11
Meggethead **69** G1
Meidrim **17** F3
Meifod *Denb* **47** J7
Meifod *Powys* **38** A4
Meigh **93** F14
Meigle **80** H6
Meikle Earnock **75** F5
Meikle Grenach **73** J4
Meikle Kilmany **73** J4
Meikle Rahane **74** A2
Meikle Wartle **85** M7
Meikleour **80** G7
Meikleyard **74** D2
Meinciau **17** H4
Meir **40** B1
Meir Heath **40** B1
Meirheath **40** B1
Melbost **88** K4
Melbost Borve (Mealabost) **88** K2
Melbourn **33** G4
Melbourne *Derbys* **41** F3
Melbourne *ERid* **58** D5
Melbury *Devon* **6** C4
Melbury Abbas **9** H3
Melbury Bubb **8** E4
Melbury Osmond **8** E4
Melbury Sampford **8** E4
Melby **89** K7
Melchbourne **32** D2
Melcombe Bingham **9** G4
Melcombe Regis **9** F6
Meldon *Devon* **6** D6
Meldon *N'umb* **71** G5
Meldreth **33** G4
Meledor **3** G3
Melfort **79** K9
Melgarve **83** Q11
Meliden (Gallt Melyd) **47** J4
Melincourt **18** B1
Melin-y-coed **47** G6
Melin-y-ddol **37** K5
Melin-y-grug **37** K5
Melin-y-Wig **37** K1
Melkinthorpe **61** G4
Melkridge **70** C7
Melksham **20** C5
Melksham Forest **20** C5
Melldalloch **73** H3
Melling *Lancs* **55** H2
Melling *Mersey* **48** C2
Melling Mount **48** D2
Mellis **34** E1
Mellon Charles **83** J1
Mellon Udrigle **83** J1
Mellor *Gtman* **49** J4
Mellor *Lancs* **56** B6
Mellor Brook **56** B6
Mells **20** A7
Melmerby *Cumb* **61** H3
Melmerby *NYorks* **57** F1
Melmerby *NYorks* **57** J2
Melplash **8** D5
Melrose *Aber* **85** M4
Melrose *ScBord* **76** D7
Melsetter **89** B9
Melsonby **62** B6
Meltham **50** C1
Melton *ERid* **59** F7
Melton *Suff* **35** G3
Melton Constable **44** E2
Melton Mowbray **42** A4
Melton Ross **52** D1
Meltonby **58** D4
Melvaig **82** H2
Melverley **38** C4
Melverley Green **38** C4
Melvich **87** L3
Membury **8** B4
Memsie **85** P4
Memus **81** K5
Menabilly **4** A5
Menai Bridge (Porthaethwy) **46** D5
Mendham **45** G7
Mendlesham **35** F2
Mendlesham Green **34** E2
Menethorpe **58** D3
Menheniot **4** C4
Menithwood **29** G2
Mennock **68** D3
Menston **57** G5
Menstrie **75** G1
Menthorpe **58** C6
Meoble **79** J2
Meole Brace **38** D4
Meon **11** G4
Meonstoke **11** H3
Meopham **24** C5
Meopham Green **24** C5
Mepal **43** H7
Meppershall **32** E5
Merbach **28** C4
Mercaston **40** E1
Mere *ChesE&* **49** G4
Mere *Wilts* **9** H1
Mere Brow **48** D1
Mere Green **40** D6
Mere Heath **49** F5
Mereclough **56** D6
Mereside **55** G6
Meretown **39** G3
Mereworth **23** K6
Mergie **81** N2
Meriden **40** E7
Merkadale **82** D7
Merkland **65** H3
Merley **10** B5
Merlin's Bridge **16** C4
Merridge **8** B1
Merrifield **5** J6
Merrington **38** D3
Merrion **16** C6
Merriott **8** D3
Merrivale **5** F3
Merry Hill *Herts* **22** E2
Merry Hill *WMid* **40** A7
Merry Hill *WMid* **40** B7
Merrymeet **4** C4
Mersea Island **34** E7
Mersey Ferries *Mersey* CH44 6QY **131** A4
Mersham **15** F4
Merstham **23** F6
Merston **12** B6
Merstone **11** G6
Merther **3** G4
Merthyr **17** G3
Merthyr Cynog **27** J5
Merthyr Dyfan **18** E5
Merthyr Mawr **18** B4
Merthyr Tydfil **18** D1
Merthyr Vale **18** D2
Merton *Devon* **6** D4
Merton *Norf* **44** D5
Merton *Oxon* **31** G7
Mervinslaw **70** B2
Meshaw **7** F4
Messing **34** D7
Messingham **52** B2
Metcombe **7** J6
Metfield **45** G7
Metherell **4** E4

Metheringham 52 D6
Methil 76 B1
Methlem 36 A2
Methley 57 J7
Methley Junction 57 J7
Methlick 85 N7
Methven 80 F8
Methwold 44 B6
Methwold Hythe 44 B6
MetroCentre 71 H7
Mettingham 45 H7
Metton 45 F2
Mevagissey 4 A6
Mewith Head 56 C3
Mexborough 51 G3
Mey 87 Q2
Meysey Hampton 20 E1
Miavaig (Miabhaig) 88 F4
Michaelchurch 28 E6
Michaelchurch Escley 28 C5
Michaelchurch-on-Arrow 28 B3
Michaelston-le-Pit 18 E4
Michaelston-super-Ely 18 E4
Michaelston-y-Fedw 19 F3
Michaelstow 4 A3
Michelcombe 5 G4
Micheldever 11 G1
Michelmersh 10 E2
Mickfield 35 F2
Mickle Trafford 48 D6
Micklebring 51 H3
Mickleby 63 J5
Micklefield 57 K6
Micklefield Green 22 D2
Mickleham 22 E6
Micklehurst 49 J2
Mickleover 41 F2
Micklethwaite Cumb 60 D1
Micklethwaite WYorks 57 F5
Mickleton Dur 61 L4
Mickleton Glos 30 C4
Mickletown 57 J7
Mickley Derbys 51 F5
Mickley NYorks 57 H2
Mickley Green 34 C3
Mickley Square 71 F7
Mid Ardlaw 85 P4
Mid Beltie 85 L10
Mid Calder 75 J4
Mid Hants Railway Hants SO24 9JG 11 H1
Mid Lambrook 8 D3
Mid Lavant 12 B6
Mid Letter 79 M10
Mid Mossdale 61 K7
Mid Yell 89 P3
Midbea 89 D3
Middle Assendon 22 A3
Middle Aston 31 F6
Middle Barton 31 F6
Middle Bickenhill 40 E7
Middle Bockhampton 10 C5
Middle Claydon 31 J6
Middle Drift 4 B4
Middle Duntisbourne 20 C1
Middle Handley 51 G5
Middle Harling 44 D7
Middle Kames 73 H2
Middle Littleton 30 B4
Middle Maes-coed 28 C5
Middle Marwood 6 D2
Middle Mill 16 B3
Middle Quarter 14 D4
Middle Rasen 52 D4
Middle Salter 56 B3
Middle Sontley 38 C1
Middle Stoford 7 K3
Middle Taphouse 4 B4
Middle Town 2 C1
Middle Tysoe 30 E4
Middle Wallop 10 D1
Middle Winterslow 10 D1
Middle Woodford 10 C1
Middlebie 69 H6
Middlecliff 51 G2
Middlecott 6 C5
Middleham 57 G1
Middlehill 4 C4
Middlehope 38 E7
Middlemarsh 9 F4
Middlemoor 4 E3
Middlesbrough 62 E4
Middlesceugh 60 F2
Middleshaw 55 J1
Middlesmoor 57 F2
Middlestone 62 C3
Middlestone Moor 62 C3
Middlestown 50 E1
Middleton Angus 81 L6
Middleton Cumb 56 B1
Middleton Derbys 50 D6
Middleton Derbys 50 E7
Middleton Essex 34 C4
Middleton GtMan 49 H2
Middleton Hants 21 H7
Middleton Here 28 E2
Middleton Lancs 55 H4
Middleton Midlo 76 B5
Middleton Norf 44 A4
Middleton NYorks 58 D1
Middleton N'hants 42 B7
Middleton N'umb 71 F5
Middleton N'umb 77 J7
Middleton P&K 80 G6
Middleton Shrop 28 E1
Middleton Shrop 38 B6
Middleton Shrop 38 C3
Middleton Suff 35 J2
Middleton Swan 17 H7
Middleton Warks 40 D6
Middleton WYorks 57 G5
Middleton WYorks 57 J7
Middleton Baggot 39 F6
Middleton Bank Top 71 F5
Middleton Cheney 31 F4
Middleton Green 40 B2
Middleton Hall 70 E1
Middleton Moor 35 J2
Middleton on the Hill 28 E2
Middleton One Row 62 D5
Middleton Priors 39 F7
Middleton Quernhow 57 J2
Middleton Scriven 39 F7
Middleton St. George 62 D5
Middleton Stoney 31 G6
Middleton Tyas 62 C6
Middleton-in-Teesdale 61 L4
Middleton-on-Leven 62 E5
Middleton-on-Sea 12 C6
Middleton-on-the-Wolds 59 F5
Middletown AB&C 93 C13
Middletown Cumb 60 A6
Middletown Powys 38 C4
Middlewich 49 G6
Middlewood ChesE 49 J4
Middlewood SYorks 51 F3
Middlewood Green 34 E2
Middlezoy 8 C1
Midfield 86 H3
Midford 20 A5
Midge Hall 55 J7
Midgeholme 61 H1
Midgham 21 J5
Midgley WYorks 50 E1
Midgley WYorks 57 F7
Midhopestones 50 E3
Midhurst 12 B4
Midland Railway Centre Derbys DE5 3QZ 51 G7
Midlem 70 A1
Midloe Grange 32 E2
Midpark 73 J5
Midsomer Norton 19 K6
Midthorpe 53 F5
Midtown High 83 J2
Midtown High 86 H3
Midville 53 G7
Midway 41 F3
Migvie 85 J10
Milarrochy 74 C1
Milber 5 J3
Milborne Port 9 F3
Milborne St. Andrew 9 G5
Milborne Wick 9 F2
Milbourne N'umb 71 G6
Milbourne Wilts 20 C3
Milburn 61 H4
Milbury Heath 19 K2
Milcombe 31 F5
Milden 34 D4
Mildenhall Suff 34 B1
Mildenhall Wilts 21 F5
Mile Elm 20 C5
Mile End Essex 34 D6
Mile End Glos 28 E7
Mile End Park GtLon E3 4HL 104 C6
Mile Oak 23 K7
Mile Town 25 F4
Milebrook 28 C1
Milebush Kent 14 C3
Milebush M&EAnt 92 K8
Mileham 44 D4
Miles Green 40 A1
Miles Hope 28 E2
Milesmark 75 J2
Miles's Green 21 J5
Milfield 77 H7
Milford Derbys 41 F1
Milford Devon 6 A3
Milford Shrop 38 D3
Milford Staffs 40 B3
Milford Surr 22 C7
Milford Haven (Aberdaugleddau) 16 B5
Milford on Sea 10 D5
Milkwall 19 J1
Milky Way Adventure Park Devon EX39 5RY 6 B3
Mill Bank 57 F7
Mill Brow 49 J4
Mill End Bucks 22 A3
Mill End Cambs 33 K3
Mill End Herts 33 G5
Mill End Green 33 K6
Mill Green Cambs 33 K4
Mill Green Essex 24 C1
Mill Green Herts 23 F1
Mill Green Norf 45 F7
Mill Green Shrop 39 F3
Mill Green Staffs 40 C3
Mill Green Suff 34 D3
Mill Green Suff 35 F3
Mill Green Suff 35 H2
Mill Green WMid 40 C5
Mill Hill B'burn 56 B7
Mill Hill Cambs 33 F3
Mill Hill GtLon 23 F2
Mill Houses 56 B3
Mill Lane 22 A6
Mill of Camsail 74 A2
Mill of Colp 85 M6
Mill of Uras 81 P2
Mill Side 55 H1
Mill Street Kent 23 K6
Mill Street Norf 44 E4
Mill Town 92 G8
Milland 12 B4
Millbay 92 K7
Millbeck 60 D4
Millbounds 89 E4
Millbreck 85 Q6
Millbridge 22 B7
Millbrook CenBeds 32 D5
Millbrook Corn 4 E5
Millbrook Devon 8 C4
Millbrook M&EAnt 92 J6
Millbrook Soton 10 E3
Millcombe 5 J6
Millcorner 14 D5
Milldale 50 D7
Millden 81 L5
Millearne 80 E9
Millend 30 E6
Millenheath 38 E2
Millennium Seed Bank, Wakehurst Place WSuss RH17 6TN 13 G3
Millerhill 76 B4
Miller's Dale 50 D5
Millers Green Derbys 50 E7
Miller's Green Essex 23 J1
Millford 93 D12
Millgate 56 D7
Millhalf 28 B4
Millhayes Devon 7 K4
Millhayes Devon 8 B4
Millholme 61 G7
Millhouse A&B 73 H3
Millhouse Cumb 60 E3
Millhouse Green 50 E2
Millhousebridge 69 G5
Millikenpark 74 C4
Millin Cross 16 C4
Millington 58 E4
Millington Green 40 E1
Millisle 92 L9
Millmeece 40 A2
Millom 54 E1
Millow 33 F4
Millpool 4 B3
Millport 73 K5
Millthorpe 51 F5
Millthrop 61 H7
Milltown A&N 92 F7
Milltown AB&C 93 E10
Milltown AB&C 93 D11
Milltown AB&C 93 E12
Milltown AB&C 93 G13
Milltown CC&G 92 C3
Milltown CC&G 92 E4
Milltown Corn 4 B5
Milltown Derbys 51 F6
Milltown D&S 90 K6
Milltown Devon 6 D2
Milltown D&G 69 J6
Milltown F&O 91 E10
Milltown F&O 91 H11
Milltown L&C 93 H11
Milltown M&EAnt 92 E6
Milltown M&EAnt 92 F7
Milltown NM&D 93 F14
Milltown NM&D 93 G14
Milltown of Aberdalgie 80 F8
Milltown of Auchindoun 84 H7
Milltown of Edinvillie 84 G6
Milltown of Kildrummy 85 J9
Milltown of Rothiemay 85 K6
Milnathort 80 G10
Milners Heath 48 D6
Milngavie 74 D3
Milnrow 49 J1
Milnsbridge 50 D1
Milnthorpe 55 H1
Milovaig 82 B5
Milrig 74 D7
Milson 29 F1
Milstead 14 E2
Milston 20 E7
Milton Angus 81 J6
Milton Cambs 33 H2
Milton Cumb 70 A7
Milton Derbys 41 F3
Milton D&G 64 C5
Milton D&G 65 J3
Milton D&G 68 D5
Milton High 82 H6
Milton High 83 P5
Milton (Baile a' Mhuilinn) High 83 Q7
Milton High 83 R6
Milton High 84 B3
Milton Mid Ulster 93 C9
Milton Moray 85 K4
Milton Newport 19 G3
Milton Notts 51 K5
Milton NSom 19 G5
Milton Oxon 21 H2
Milton Oxon 31 F5
Milton Pembs 16 D5
Milton P&K 80 F7
Milton Ports 11 H5
Milton Som 8 D2
Milton Stir 80 A10
Milton Stoke 49 J7
Milton WDun 74 C3
Milton Abbas 9 H4
Milton Abbot 4 E3
Milton Bridge 76 A4
Milton Bryan 32 C5
Milton Clevedon 9 F1
Milton Combe 4 E4
Milton Country Park Cambs CB24 6AZ 33 H2
Milton Damerel 6 B4
Milton End 29 G7
Milton Ernest 32 D3
Milton Green 48 D7
Milton Hill 21 H2
Milton Keynes 32 B5
Milton Keynes Village 32 B5
Milton Lilbourne 20 E5
Milton Malsor 31 J3
Milton of Auchinhove 85 K10
Milton of Balgonie 81 J10
Milton of Buchanan 74 C1
Milton of Cairnborrow 85 J6
Milton of Campfield 85 L10
Milton of Campsie 74 E3
Milton of Cullerlie 85 M10
Milton of Cushnie 85 K9
Milton of Tullich 84 H11
Milton on Stour 9 G2
Milton Regis 24 E5
Milton Street 13 J6
Miltonduff 84 F4
Miltonise 64 B3
Milton-Lockhart 75 G6
Milton-under-Wychwood 30 D7
Milverton Som 7 K3
Milverton Warks 30 E2
Milwich 40 B2
Mimbridge 22 C5
Minack Theatre Corn TR19 6JU 2 A6
Minard 73 H1
Minard Castle 73 H1
Minchington 9 J3
Minchinhampton 20 B1
Mindrum 77 G7
Mindrummill 77 G7
Minehead 7 H1
Minera 48 B7
Minerstown 93 K13
Minety 20 D2
Minety Lower Moor 20 D2
Minffordd Gwyn 36 E2
Minffordd Gwyn 37 G4
Minffordd Gwyn 46 D5
Mingearraidh 88 B6
Miningsby 53 G6
Minions 4 C3
Minishant 67 H2
Minley Manor 22 B6
Minllyn 37 H4
Minnigaff 64 E4
Minskip 57 J3
Minstead 10 D3
Minsted 12 B4
Minster Kent 25 F4
Minster Kent 25 K5
Minster Lovell 30 E7
Minsteracres 62 A1
Minsterley 38 C5
Minsterworth 29 G7
Minterburn 93 C11
Minterne Magna 9 F4
Minterne Parva 9 F4
Minting 52 E5
Mintlaw 85 Q6
Minto 70 A1
Minton 38 D6
Minwear 16 D4
Minworth 40 D6
Mirehouse 60 A5
Mireland 87 R3
Mirfield 57 H7
Miserden 20 C1
Miskin RCT 18 D2
Miskin RCT 18 D3
Misselfore 10 B2
Misson 51 J3
Misterton Leics 41 H7
Misterton Notts 51 K3
Misterton Som 8 D4
Mistley 35 F5
Mitcham 23 F5
Mitchel Troy 28 D7
Mitcheldean 29 F7
Mitchell 3 F3
Mitchelland 60 F7
Mitcheltroy Common 19 H1
Mitford 71 G5
Mithian 2 E3
Mitton 40 A4
Mixbury 31 H5
Mixenden 57 F7
Moat 69 K6
Moats Tye 34 E3
Mobberley ChesE 49 G5
Mobberley Staffs 40 C1
Moccas 28 C4
Mochdre Conwy 47 G5
Mochdre Powys 37 K7
Mochrum 64 D6
Mockbeggar Hants 10 C4
Mockbeggar Kent 14 C3
Mockerkin 60 B4
Modbury 5 G5
Moddershall 40 B2
Modern Art Oxford Oxon OX1 1BP 134 Oxford
Moel Famau Country Park Denb LL15 1US 47 K6
Moelfre IoA 46 D4
Moelfre Powys 38 A3
Moffat 69 F3
Mogerhanger 32 E4
Moin'a'choire 72 B4
Moine House 86 H4
Moira L&C 93 G10
Moira Leic 41 F4
Molash 15 F2
Mol-chlach 82 E9
Mold (Yr Wyddgrug) 48 B6
Molehill Green Essex 33 J6
Molehill Green Essex 34 B6
Molescroft 59 G5
Molesden 71 G5
Molesworth 32 D1
Mollance 65 H4
Molland 7 G3
Mollington ChesW&C 48 C5
Mollington Oxon 31 F4
Mollinsburn 75 F3
Monach Islands (Heisker Islands) 88 A2
Monachty 26 E2
Monanclogh 92 F3
Monea 91 H12
Monehanegan 90 M5
Monewden 35 G3
Moneycanon 90 L6
Moneycarragh 93 J13
Moneydig 92 D5
Moneyglass 92 F7
Moneymore 92 D8
Moneyneany 92 C7
Moneynick 92 F8
Moneyreagh 93 K10
Moneyrod 92 F7
Moneyrow Green 22 B4
Moneysharvan 92 D6
Moneyslane 93 H13
Moniaive 68 C4
Monifieth 81 L7
Monikie 81 L7
Monikie Country Park Angus DD5 3QN 81 K7
Monimail 80 H9
Monington 16 E1
Monk Bretton 51 F2
Monk Fryston 58 B7
Monk Hesleden 62 E3
Monk Sherborne 21 K6
Monk Soham 35 G2
Monk Soham Green 35 G2
Monk Street 33 K6
Monken Hadley 23 F2
Monkerton 7 H6
Monkey Mates W'ham RG41 1JA 22 A4
Monkey World, Wareham Dorset BH20 6HH 9 H6
Monkhide 29 F4
Monkhill 60 E1
Monkhopton 39 F6
Monkland 28 D3
Monkleigh 6 C3
Monknash 18 C4
Monkokehampton 6 D5
Monks Eleigh 34 D4
Monks Eleigh Tye 34 D4
Monk's Gate 13 F4
Monks' Heath 49 H5
Monk's Hill 14 D3
Monks Horton 15 G4
Monks Kirby 41 G7
Monks Risborough 22 B1
Monkscross 4 D3
Monkseaton 71 J6
Monksilver 7 J2
Monkstadt 82 D4
Monkstown 92 J8
Monkswood 19 G1
Monkton Devon 7 K5
Monkton Kent 25 J5
Monkton Pembs 16 C5
Monkton SAyr 67 H1
Monkton T&W 71 J7
Monkton VGlam 18 C4
Monkton Combe 20 A5
Monkton Deverill 9 H1
Monkton Farleigh 20 B5
Monkton Heathfield 8 B2
Monkton Up Wimborne 10 B3
Monkton Wyld 8 C5
Monkwearmouth 62 D1
Monkwood 11 H1
Monlough 93 J10
Monmouth (Trefynwy) 28 E7
Monnington Court 28 C5
Monnington on Wye 28 C4
Monreith 64 D6
Montacute 8 E3
Montacute House Som TA15 6XP 8 E3
Monteith 93 G12
Montford 38 D4
Montford Bridge 38 D4
Montgarrie 85 K9
Montgomery (Trefaldwyn) 38 B6
Montgreenan 74 B6
Montpellier Gallery Warks CV37 6EP 136 Stratford-upon-Avon
Montrave 81 J10
Montrose 81 N5
Monxton 21 G7
Monyash 50 D6
Monymusk 85 L9
Monzie 80 D8
Moodiesburn 74 E3
Moons Moat North 30 B2
Moor Allerton 57 J6
Moor Cock 56 B3
Moor Crichel 9 J4
Moor End Bed 32 D3
Moor End CenBeds 32 C6
Moor End Cumb 55 J2
Moor End ERid 58 E6
Moor End Lancs 55 G5
Moor End NYorks 58 B6
Moor End WYorks 57 F7
Moor Green Wilts 20 B5
Moor Green WMid 40 C7
Moor Head 57 G6
Moor Monkton 58 B4
Moor Row 60 B5
Moor Side Cumb 55 F2
Moor Side Lancs 55 H6
Moor Side Lancs 55 J6
Moor Side Lincs 53 F7
Moor Street 24 E5
Moorby 53 F6
Moorcot 28 C3
Moordown 10 B5
Moore 48 E4
Moorend 93 G11
Moorends 51 J1
Moorfield 50 C3
Moorfields 92 G7
Moorgreen 41 G1
Moorhall 51 F5
Moorhampton 28 C4
Moorhouse Cumb 60 E1
Moorhouse Notts 51 K6
Moorland (Northmoor Green) 8 C1
Moorlinch 8 C1
Moors Centre, Danby NYorks YO21 2NB 63 H6
Moors Valley Country Park Dorset BH24 2ET 95 E1
Moors Valley Railway Dorset BH24 2ET 95 E1
Moorsholm 63 G5
Moorside Dorset 9 G3
Moorside GtMan 49 J2
Moorside WYorks 57 H6
Moorthorpe 51 G1
Moortown IoW 11 F6
Moortown Lincs 52 D3
Moortown Mid Ulster 92 E9
Moortown Tel&W 39 F4
Morar 82 G11
Morborne 42 E6
Morchard Bishop 7 F5
Morcombelake 8 D5
Morcott 42 C5
Morda 38 B3
Morden Dorset 9 J5
Morden GtLon 23 F5
Morden Hall Park GtLon SM4 5JD 103 G11
Morden Park 23 F5
Mordiford 28 E5
Mordington Holdings 77 H5
Mordon 62 D4
More 38 C6
Morebath 7 H3
Morebattle 70 C1
Morecambe 55 H3
Morefield 83 M1
Moreleigh 5 H5
Morenish 80 B7
Moresby Parks 60 A5
Morestead 11 G2
Moreton Dorset 9 H6
Moreton Essex 23 J1
Moreton Here 28 E2
Moreton Mersey 48 B4
Moreton Oxon 21 K1
Moreton Staffs 39 G4
Moreton Staffs 40 D2
Moreton Corbet 38 E3
Moreton Jeffries 29 F4
Moreton Mill 38 E3
Moreton Morrell 30 E3
Moreton on Lugg 28 E4
Moreton Paddox 30 E3
Moreton Pinkney 31 G4
Moreton Say 39 F2
Moreton Valence 20 A1
Moretonhampstead 7 F7
Moreton-in-Marsh 30 D5
Morfa Carmar 17 J4
Morfa Cere 26 C3
Morfa Bychan 36 E2
Morfa Glas 18 B1
Morfa Nefyn 36 B1
Morgan's Vale 10 C2
Morganstown 18 E3
Mork 19 J1
Morland 61 G4
Morley Derbys 41 F1
Morley Dur 62 B4
Morley WYorks 57 H7
Morley Green 49 H4
Morley St. Botolph 44 E6
Mornick 4 D3
Morningside Edin 76 A3
Morningside NLan 75 G5
Morningthorpe 45 G6
Morpeth 71 H5
Morrey 40 D4
Morridge Side 50 C7
Morrilow Heath 40 B2
Morriston SAyr 67 G3
Morriston Swan 17 K6
Morristown 18 E4
Morston 44 E1
Mortehoe 6 C1
Morthen 51 G4
Mortimer 21 K5
Mortimer West End 21 K5
Mortimer's Cross 28 D2
Mortlake 23 F4
Morton Derbys 51 G6
Morton Lincs 42 D3
Morton Lincs 52 B3
Morton Lincs 52 B6
Morton Notts 51 K7
Morton SGlos 19 K2
Morton Shrop 38 B3
Morton Bagot 30 C2
Morton on the Hill 45 F4
Morton Tinmouth 62 B4
Morton-on-Swale 62 D7
Morvah 2 B5
Morval 4 C5
Morvich (A'Mhormhaich) High 83 K8
Morvich High 87 K9
Morvil 16 D2
Morville 39 F6
Morwellham 4 E4
Morwellham Quay Museum Devon PL19 8JL 4 E3
Morwenstow 6 A4
Morwick Hall 71 H3
Mosborough 51 G4
Moscow 74 C6
Mosedale 60 E3
Moselden Height 50 C1
Moseley WMid 40 B6
Moseley Worcs 29 H3
Moses Gate 49 G2
Moss A&B 78 A6
Moss SYorks 51 H1
Moss Wrex 48 C7
Moss Bank 48 E3
Moss Houses 49 H5
Moss Nook 49 H4
Moss Side GtMan 49 H3
Moss Side Lancs 55 G6
Moss Side Mersey 48 C2
Mossat 85 J9
Mossbank 89 N5
Mossblown 67 J1
Mossburnford 70 B2
Mossdale 65 G3
Mossend 75 F4
Mosser 60 C4
Mossgiel 67 J1
Mossley A&N 92 J8
Mossley ChesE 49 H6
Mossley GtMan 49 J2
Mossley Hill 48 C4
Mosspaul Hotel 69 J4
Moss-side CC&G 92 F3
Moss-side High 84 C5
Mosstodloch 84 H4
Mossy Lea 48 E1
Mosterton 8 D4
Moston GtMan 49 H3
Moston Shrop 38 E3
Moston Green 49 G6
Mostyn 47 K4
Motcombe 9 H2
Mothecombe 5 G6
Mother Shipton's Cave NYorks HG5 8DD 57 J4
Motherby 60 F4
Motherwell 75 F5
Mottingham 23 H4
Mottisfont 10 E2
Mottisfont Abbey Hants SO51 0LP 10 E2
Mottistone 11 F6
Mottram in Longdendale 49 J3
Mottram St. Andrew 49 H5
Mouldsworth 48 E5
Moulin 80 E5
Moulsecoomb 13 G6
Moulsford 21 J3
Moulsham 24 D1
Moulsoe 32 C4
Moulton ChesW&C 49 F6
Moulton Lincs 43 G3
Moulton NYorks 62 C6
Moulton N'hants 31 J2
Moulton Suff 33 K2
Moulton VGlam 18 D4
Moulton Chapel 43 F4
Moulton Seas End 43 G3
Moulton St. Mary 45 J5
Mount Corn 2 E3
Mount Corn 4 B4
Mount Kent 15 G3
Mount WYorks 50 D1
Mount Ambrose 2 E4
Mount Bures 34 D5
Mount Charles 4 A5
Mount Edgcumbe Country Park Corn PL10 1HZ 94 B4
Mount Hamilton CC&G 92 F5
Mount Hamilton D&S 92 B7
Mount Hawke 2 E4
Mount Manisty 48 C5
Mount Norris 93 E13
Mount Oliphant 67 H2
Mount Pleasant AB&C 93 E12
Mount Pleasant ChesE 49 H7
Mount Pleasant Derbys 40 E4
Mount Pleasant Derbys 41 F1
Mount Pleasant ESuss 13 H5
Mount Pleasant Flints 48 B5
Mount Pleasant GtLon 22 D2
Mount Pleasant Hants 10 E5
Mount Pleasant Norf 44 D6
Mount Pleasant Suff 34 B4
Mount Ross 93 M11
Mount Sorrel 10 B2
Mount Stewart (NT) BT22 2AN 93 L10
Mount Tabor 57 F7
Mountain 57 F6
Mountain Ash (Aberpennar) 18 D2
Mountain Cross 75 K6
Mountain Water 16 C3
Mountbenger 69 J1
Mountblow 74 C3
Mountcastle 90 L6
Mountfield ESuss 14 C5
Mountfield F&O 90 M9
Mountgerald 83 R4
Mountjoy Corn 3 F2
Mountjoy F&O 90 L9
Mountjoy Mid Ulster 93 E10
Mountnessing 24 C2
Mounton 19 J2
Mountsandel Fort BT52 1TW 92 D3
Mountsorrel 41 H4
Mousa 89 N10
Mousehole 2 B6
Mouswald 69 F6
Mow Cop 49 H7
Mowden 62 C5
Mowhan 93 E13
Mowhaugh 70 D1
Mowsley 41 J7
Mowtie 81 P2
Moxley 40 B6
Moy High 79 R2
Moy High 84 B7
Moy Mid Ulster 93 D11
Moyad 93 H15
Moyagoney 92 E6
Moyallon 93 F11
Moyarget 92 F3
Moybane F&O 91 H12
Moybane NM&D 93 E15
Moygashel 93 D10
Moylagh 91 M10
Moylgrove 16 E1
Moys 92 B5
Muasdale 72 E6
Much Birch 28 E5
Much Cowarne 29 F4
Much Dewchurch 28 D5
Much Hadham 33 H7
Much Hoole 55 H7
Much Hoole Town 55 H7
Much Marcle 29 F5
Much Wenlock 39 F5
Muchalls 85 P11
Muchelney 8 D2
Muchelney Ham 8 D2
Muchlarnick 4 C5
Muchra 69 H2
Muchrachd 83 N7
Muck 78 F3
Mucking 24 C3
Muckle Roe 89 M6
Muckleford 9 F5
Mucklestone 39 G2
Muckleton 38 E3
Muckletown 85 K8
Muckley 39 F6
Muckley Corner 40 C5
Muckton 53 G4
Mudale 86 H6
Muddiford 6 D2
Muddles Green 13 J5
Muddleswood 13 F5
Mudeford 10 C5
Mudford 8 E3
Mudgley 19 H7
Mugdock 74 D3
Mugdock Country Park Stir G62 8EL 118 D1
Mugeary 82 E7
Muggington 40 E1
Muggintonlane End 40 E1
Muggleswick 62 A2
Mugswell 23 F6
Muie 87 J9
Muir of Fowlis 85 K9
Muir of Ord (Am Blàr Dubh) 83 R5
Muiravonside Country Park Falk EH49 6LW 75 H3
Muirdrum 81 L7
Muiredge 76 B1
Muirhead 74 E4
Muirhouses 75 J2
Muirkirk 68 B1
Muirmill 75 F2
Muirton 80 G8
Muirton of Ardblair 80 G6
Muker 61 L7
Mulbarton 45 F5
Mulben 84 H5
Mull 78 G7
Mullabrack 93 F12
Mullacott Cross 6 D1
Mullaghbane 93 E15
Mullaghboy Mid Ulster 92 E7
Mullaghboy M&EAnt 92 K6
Mullaghduff 93 D14
Mullaghglass 93 F14
Mullaghmassa 91 M10
Mullaghmore 93 G14
Mullan 91 H14
Mullanmore 93 B9
Mullans Town 93 B10
Mullartown 93 J14
Mullion 2 D7
Mullion Cove 2 D7
Mullnagore 93 C10
Mumby 53 J5
Munderfield Row 29 F3
Munderfield Stocks 29 F3
Mundesley 45 H2
Mundford 44 C6
Mundham 45 H6
Mundon 24 E1
Munerigie 83 N10
Mungasdale 83 K1
Mungoswells 76 C3
Mungrisdale 60 E3
Munlochy 84 A5
Munnoch 74 A6
Munsley 29 F4
Munslow 38 E7
Murchington 6 E7
Murcott Oxon 31 G7
Murcott Wilts 20 C2
Murdostoun 75 G5
Murieston 75 J4
Murkle 87 P3
Murlaggan 83 L11
Murley 91 L11
Murrell Green 22 A6
Murrow 43 G5
Mursley 32 B6
Murston 25 F5
Murthly 80 F7
Murton Cumb 61 J4
Murton Dur 62 D2
Murton N'umb 77 H6
Murton Swan 17 J7
Murton York 58 C4
Musbury 8 B5
Muscliff 10 B5
Museum in Docklands GtLon E14 4AL 105 C7
Museum of Childhood Edin EH1 1TG 126 G4
Museum of Childhood GtLon E2 9PA 104 C6
Museum of Flight ELoth EH39 5LF 76 D3
Museum of Garden History, London GtLon SE1 7LB 132 F6
Museum of London GtLon EC2Y 5HN 132 J1
Museum of Science & Industry, Manchester GtMan M3 4FP 133 C4
Museum of Transport Glas G3 8DP 127 A2
Musselburgh 76 B3
Mustard Hyrn 45 J4
Mustard Shop Norf NR2 1NQ 134 Norwich
Muston Leics 42 B2
Muston NYorks 59 G2
Mustow Green 29 H1
Mutford 45 J7
Muthill 80 D9
Mutley 4 E5
Mutterton 7 J5
Muxton 39 G4
M.V. Princess Pocahontas Kent DA11 0BS 24 C4
Mybster 87 P4
Myddfai 27 G5
Myddle 38 D3
Myddlewood 38 D3
Mydroilyn 26 D3
Myerscough College 55 H6
Myerscough Smithy 56 B6
Mylor 3 F5
Mylor Bridge 3 F5
Mynachdy 18 E4
Mynachlog-ddu 16 E2
Myndtown 38 C7
Mynydd Llandygai 46 E6
Mynydd Mechell 46 B4
Mynydd-bach Mon 19 H2
Mynydd-bach Swan 17 K6
Mynyddygarreg 17 H5
Mynytho 36 C2
Mytchett 22 B6
Mytholm 56 E7
Mytholmroyd 57 F7
Mythop 55 G6
Myton-on-Swale 57 K3
Mytton 38 D4

N

Na Gearrannan (Garenin) 88 G3
Naast 83 J2
Nab's Head 56 B7
Na Buirgh 88 F8
Naburn 58 B5
Nackington 15 G2
Nacton 35 G4
Nadderwater 7 G6
Nafferton 59 G4
Nailbridge 29 F7
Nailsbourne 8 B2
Nailsea 19 H4
Nailstone 41 G5
Nailsworth 20 B2
Nairn 84 C5
Nancegollan 2 D5
Nancekuke 2 D4
Nancledra 2 B5
Nanhoron 36 B2
Nannau 37 G3
Nannerch 47 K6
Nanpantan 41 H4
Nanpean 3 G3
Nanstallon 4 A4
Nant Peris 46 E7
Nant-ddu 27 K7
Nanternis 26 C3
Nantgaredig 17 H3
Nantgarw 18 E3
Nant-glas 27 J2
Nantglyn 47 J6
Nantgwyn 27 J1
Nantlle 46 D7
Nantmawr 38 B3
Nantmel 27 K2
Nantmor 37 F1
Nantwich 49 F7
Nantycaws 17 H4
Nant-y-derry 19 G1
Nant-y-dugoed 37 J4
Nantyffyllon 18 B2
Nantyglo 28 A7
Nant-y-Gollen 38 B3
Nant-y-groes 27 K2
Nant-y-moel 18 C2
Nant-y-Pandy 46 E5
Naphill 22 B2
Napley Heath 39 G2
Nappa 56 D4
Napton on the Hill 31 F2
Narberth (Arberth) 16 E4
Narborough Leics 41 H6
Narborough Norf 44 B4
Narkurs 4 D5
Nasareth 36 D1
Naseby 31 H1
Nash Bucks 31 J5
Nash Here 28 C2
Nash Newport 19 G3
Nash Shrop 29 F1
Nash VGlam 18 C4
Nash Street 24 C5
Nassington 42 D6
Nasty 33 G6
Nateby Cumb 61 J6
Nateby Lancs 55 H5
Nately Scures 22 A6
National Agricultural Centre, Stoneleigh Warks CV8 2LZ 30 E1
National Army Museum GtLon SW3 4HT 103 H8
National Botanic Garden of Wales Carmar SA32 8HG 17 J4
National Botanic Gardens BT7 1LP 93 J9
National Coal Mining Museum for England WYorks WF4 4RH 117 H8
National Exhibition Centre WMid B40 1NT 107 M6
National Fishing Heritage Centre, Grimsby NELincs DN31 1UZ 53 F2
National Gallery GtLon WC2N 5DN 132 D3
National Gallery of Scotland Edin EH2 2EL 126 F4
National Indoor Arena, Birmingham WMid B1 2AA 122 D3
National Marine Aquarium PL4 0LF 134 Plymouth
National Maritime Museum Cornwall Corn TR11 3QY 3 F5
National Maritime Museum, Greenwich GtLon SE10 9NF 105 D8
National Media Museum WYorks BD1 1NQ 123 Bradford
National Memorial Arboretum, Alrewas Staffs DE13 7AR 40 D4
National Motorcycle Museum, Solihull WMid B92 0EJ 107 M6
National Museum Cardiff CF10 3NP 124 Cardiff
National Museum of Scotland Edin EH1 1JF 126 G5
National Portrait Gallery GtLon WC2H 0HE 132 D3
National Railway Museum YO26 4XJ 137 York
National Sea Life Centre, Birmingham WMid B1 2JB 122 D3
National Seal Sanctuary Corn TR12 6UG 2 E6
National Slate Museum, Llanberis Gwyn LL55 4TY 46 D7
National Space Centre Leic LE4 5NS 41 H5
National Wallace Monument Stir FK9 5LF 75 G1
National War Museum Edin EH1 2NG 126 E4
National Waterfront Museum SA1 3RD 136 Swansea
National Wildflower Centre, Liverpool Mersey L16 3NA 112 E4
Natland 55 J1
Natural History Museum at Tring Herts HP23 6AP 32 C7
Natural History Museum, London GtLon SW7 5BD 103 G7
Natureland Seal Sanctuary Lincs PE25 1DB 53 J6
Naughton 34 E4
Naunton Glos 30 C6
Naunton Worcs 29 H5
Naunton Beauchamp 29 J3
Navan 93 D12
Navan Fort Armagh City BT60 4LD 93 D12
Navenby 52 C7
Navestock 23 J2
Navestock Side 23 J2
Navidale 87 N8
Nawton 58 C1
Nayland 34 D5
Nazeing 23 H1
Neacroft 10 C5
Neal's Green 41 F7
Neap House 52 B1
Near Sawrey 60 E7
Nearton End 32 B6
Neasden 23 F3
Neasham 62 D5
Neat Enstone 30 E6
Neath (Castell-nedd) 18 A2
Neatham 22 A7
Neatishead 45 H3
Nebo Cere 26 E2
Nebo Conwy 47 G7
Nebo Gwyn 46 C7
Nebo IoA 46 C3
Necton 44 C5
Ned 92 B4
Nedd 86 D6
Nedderton 71 H5
Nedging 34 D4
Nedging Tye 34 E4
Needham 45 G7
Needham Lake Suff IP6 8NU 34 E3
Needham Market 34 E3
Needham Street 34 B2
Needingworth 33 G1
Needles Pleasure Park IoW PO39 0JD 10 E6
Needwood 40 D3
Neen Savage 29 F1
Neen Sollars 29 F1
Neenton 39 F7
Nefyn 36 C1
Neighbourne 19 K7
Neilston 74 C5
Neithrop 31 F4
Nelsherry 91 J10
Nelson Caerp 18 E2
Nelson Lancs 56 D6
Nelson Village 71 H6
Nemphlar 75 G6
Nempnett Thrubwell 19 J5
Nenthall 61 J2
Nenthead 61 J2
Nenthorn 76 E7
Neopardy 7 F6
Nerabus 72 A5
Nercwys 48 B6
Neriby 72 B4
Nerston 74 E5
Nesbit 77 H7
Nesfield 57 F5
Ness 48 C5
Ness Botanic Gardens ChesW&C CH64 4AY 112 A8
Nesscliffe 38 C4
Neston ChesW&C 48 B5
Neston Wilts 20 B5
Nether Alderley 49 H5
Nether Auchendrane 67 H2
Nether Barr 64 E4
Nether Blainslie 76 D6
Nether Broughton 41 J3
Nether Burrow 56 B2
Nether Cerne 9 F5
Nether Compton 8 E3
Nether Dalgliesh 69 H3
Nether Dallachy 84 H4
Nether Edge 51 F4
Nether End 50 E5
Nether Exe 7 H6
Nether Glasslaw 85 N5
Nether Haugh 51 G3
Nether Heage 51 F7
Nether Heselden 56 D2
Nether Heyford 31 H3
Nether Kellet 55 J3
Nether Kinmundy 85 Q6
Nether Langwith 51 H5
Nether Loads 51 F6
Nether Moor 51 F6
Nether Padley 50 E5
Nether Poppleton 58 B4
Nether Silton 62 E7
Nether Skyborry 28 B1
Nether Stowey 7 K2
Nether Wallop 10 E1
Nether Wasdale 60 C6
Nether Wellwood 68 B1
Nether Welton 60 E2
Nether Westcote 30 D6
Nether Whitacre 40 E6
Nether Winchendon (Lower Winchendon) 31 J7
Nether Worton 31 F6
Netheravon 20 E7
Netherburn 75 G6
Netherbury 8 D5
Netherby Cumb 69 J6
Netherby NYorks 57 J5
Nethercott 31 F6
Netherfield ESuss 14 C6
Netherfield Notts 41 J1
Netherfield SLan 75 F6
Netherhall 74 A4
Netherhampton 10 C2
Netherhay 8 D4
Netherland Green 40 D2
Netherley 85 N11
Nethermill 69 F5
Netherseal 40 E4
Nethershield 67 K1
Netherstreet 20 C5
Netherthird D&G 65 H5
Netherthird EAyr 67 K2
Netherthong 50 D2
Netherthorpe 51 H4
Netherton Angus 81 L5
Netherton ChesW&C 48 E5
Netherton Devon 5 J3
Netherton Hants 21 G6
Netherton Mersey 48 C2
Netherton NLan 75 F5
Netherton N'umb 70 E3
Netherton Oxon 21 H1
Netherton P&K 80 G5
Netherton SLan 75 H5
Netherton WMid 40 B7
Netherton Worcs 29 J4
Netherton WYorks 50 E1
Netherton WYorks 50 D1
Netherton Burnfoot 70 E3
Netherton Northside 70 E3
Nethertown Cumb 60 A6
Nethertown Staffs 40 D4
Netherwitton 71 G4
Netherwood D&G 65 K3
Netherwood EAyr 68 B1
Nethy Bridge 84 E8
Netley Abbey 11 F4
Netley Marsh 10 E3
Nettlebed 21 K3
Nettlebridge 19 K7
Nettlecombe Dorset 8 E5
Nettlecombe IoW 11 G7
Nettlecombe Som 7 J2
Nettleden 32 D7
Nettleham 52 D5
Nettlestead Kent 23 K6
Nettlestead Suff 34 E4
Nettlestead Green 23 K6
Nettlestone 11 H5
Nettlesworth 62 C2
Nettleton Lincs 52 E2
Nettleton Wilts 20 B4
Nettleton Hill 50 C1
Netton Devon 5 F6
Netton Wilts 10 C1
Neuadd Cere 26 D3
Neuadd IoA 46 B3
Neuadd Powys 27 J4
Nevendon 24 D2
Nevern 16 D2
Nevill Holt 42 B6
New Abbey 65 K4
New Aberdour 85 N4
New Addington 23 G5
New Alresford 11 G1
New Alyth 80 H6
New Arley 40 E6
New Arram 59 G5
New Ash Green 24 C5
New Balderton 52 B7
New Barn 24 C5
New Belses 70 A1
New Bewick 71 F1
New Bolingbroke 53 G7
New Boultham 52 C5
New Bradwell 32 B4
New Brancepeth 62 C2
New Bridge Devon 5 H3
New Bridge D&G 65 K3
New Brighton Flints 48 B6
New Brighton Hants 11 J4
New Brighton Mersey 48 C3
New Brighton Wrex 48 B7
New Brighton WYorks 57 H7
New Brinsley 51 G7
New Broughton 48 C7
New Buckenham 44 E6
New Buildings 90 L5
New Byth 85 N5
New Cheriton 11 G2
New Cross Cere 27 F1
New Cross GtLon 23 G4
New Cumnock 68 B2
New Deer 85 N6
New Duston 31 J2
New Earswick 58 C4
New Edlington 51 H3
New Elgin 84 G4
New Ellerby 59 H6
New Eltham 23 H4
New End 30 B2
New Farnley 57 H6
New Ferry Mersey 48 C4
New Ferry M&EAnt 92 E7
New Galloway 65 G3
New Gilston 81 K10
New Greens 22 E1
New Grimsby 2 B1
New Hartley 71 J6
New Haw 22 D5
New Heaton 77 G7
New Hedges 16 E5
New Herrington 62 D1
New Hinksey 21 J1
New Holland 59 G7
New Houghton Derbys 51 H6
New Houghton Norf 44 B3
New Houses 56 D2
New Hunwick 62 B3
New Hutton 61 G7
New Hythe 14 C2
New Inn Carmar 17 H2
New Inn Mon 19 H1
New Inn Torfaen 19 F2
New Invention Shrop 28 B1
New Invention WMid 40 B5
New Lanark 75 G6
New Lanark SLan ML11 9DB 75 G6
New Lane 48 D1
New Lane End 49 F3
New Leake 53 H7
New Leeds 85 P5
New Lodge 51 F2
New Longton 55 J7
New Luce 64 B4
New Mains 75 G7
New Malden 23 F5
New Marske 63 G4
New Marton 38 C2
New Mill Corn 2 B5
New Mill Herts 32 C7
New Mill WYorks 50 D2
New Mill End 32 E7
New Mills Corn 3 F3
New Mills Derbys 50 C4
New Mills Glos 19 K1
New Mills Mon 19 J1
New Mills (Y Felin Newydd) Powys 37 K5
New Milton 10 D5
New Mistley 35 F5
New Moat 16 D3
New Ollerton 51 J6
New Orleans 66 B2
New Oscott 40 C6
New Palace & Adventureland, New Brighton Mersey CH45 2JX 112 A2
New Park Corn 4 B2
New Park NYorks 57 H4
New Pitsligo 85 N5
New Polzeath 3 G1
New Quay (Ceinewydd) 26 C2
New Rackheath 45 G4
New Radnor (Maesyfed) 28 B2
New Rent 61 F3
New Ridley 71 F7
New Road Side 56 E5
New Romney 15 F5
New Rossington 51 J3
New Row Cere 27 G1
New Row Lancs 56 B6
New Sawley 41 G2
New Shoreston 77 K7
New Silksworth 62 D1
New Stevenston 75 F5
New Swanington 41 G4
New Totley 51 F5
New Town CenBeds 32 E4
New Town Cere 16 E1
New Town Dorset 9 J3
New Town Dorset 9 J4
New Town ELoth 76 C3
New Town ESuss 13 H4
New Town Glos 30 B5
New Town Mid Ulster 92 E6
New Tredegar 18 E1
New Tupton 51 F6
New Ulva 73 F2
New Valley 88 K4
New Village 51 H2
New Walk Museum & Art Gallery LE1 7EA 129 Leicester
New Walsoken 43 H5
New Waltham 53 F2
New Walton Pier Essex CO14 8ES 35 G6
New Winton 76 C3
New World 43 G6
New Yatt 30 E7
New York Lincs 53 F7
New York T&W 71 J6
Newall 57 H5
Newark Ork 89 G3
Newark Peter 43 F5
Newark Castle, Newark-on-Trent Notts NG24 1BG 51 K7
Newark-on-Trent 52 B7
Newarthill 75 F5
Newball 52 D5
Newbarn 15 G4
Newbarns 55 F2
Newbattle 76 B4
Newbiggin Cumb 55 F3
Newbiggin Cumb 60 B7
Newbiggin Cumb 61 F4
Newbiggin Cumb 61 G2
Newbiggin Cumb 61 H4
Newbiggin Dur 61 L4
Newbiggin NYorks 57 F1
Newbiggin NYorks 61 L7
Newbiggin N'umb 70 E7
Newbiggin-by-the-Sea 71 J5
Newbigging Angus 81 K7
Newbigging SLan 75 J6
Newbiggin-on-Lune 61 J6
Newbold Derbys 51 F5
Newbold Leics 41 G4
Newbold on Avon 31 F1
Newbold on Stour 30 D4
Newbold Pacey 30 D3
Newbold Verdon 41 G5
Newborough (Niwbwrch) IoA 46 C6
Newborough Peter 43 F5
Newborough Staffs 40 D3
Newbottle N'hants 31 G5
Newbottle T&W 62 D1
Newbourne 35 G4
Newbridge (Cefn Bychan) Caerp 19 F2
Newbridge Corn 2 B5
Newbridge Corn 4 D4
Newbridge Edin 75 K3

Newbridge ESuss 13 H3
Newbridge Hants 10 D3
Newbridge IoW 11 F6
Newbridge NYorks 58 E1
Newbridge Oxon 21 H1
Newbridge Pembs 16 C2
Newbridge Wrex 38 B1
Newbridge Green 29 H5
Newbridge on Wye 27 K3
Newbridge-on-Usk 19 G2
Newbrough 70 D7
Newbuildings 7 F5
Newburgh Aber 85 P8
Newburgh Fife 80 H9
Newburgh Lancs 48 D1
Newburgh ScBord 69 J1
Newburn 71 G7
Newbury Som 19 K6
Newbury WBerks 21 H5
Newbury Wilts 20 B7
Newbury Park 23 H3
Newby Cumb 61 G4
Newby Lancs 56 D5
Newby NYorks 56 C3
Newby NYorks 59 G1
Newby NYorks 63 F5
Newby Bridge 55 G1
Newby Cote 56 C2
Newby Cross 60 E1
Newby East 61 F1
Newby Hall NYorks HG4 5AE 57 J3
Newby West 60 E1
Newby Wiske 57 J1
Newcastle A&NDown 93 M11
Newcastle Mon 28 D7
Newcastle NM&D 93 J13
Newcastle Shrop 38 B7
Newcastle Bridgend 18 B4
Newcastle Emlyn (Castell Newydd Emlyn) 17 G1
Newcastle International Airport 71 G6
Newcastle upon Tyne 71 H7
Newcastleton 69 K5
Newcastle-under-Lyme 40 A1
Newchapel Pembs 17 F2
Newchapel Staffs 49 H7
Newchapel Surr 23 G7
Newchurch Carmar 17 G3
Newchurch IoW 11 G6
Newchurch Kent 15 F4
Newchurch Lancs 56 D6
Newchurch Lancs 56 D7
Newchurch Mon 19 H2
Newchurch Powys 28 B3
Newchurch Staffs 40 D3
Newcott 8 B4
Newcraighall 76 B3
Newdigate 22 E7
Newell Green 22 B4
Newenden 14 D5
Newent 29 G6
Newerne 19 K1
Newfield Dur 62 C1
Newfield Dur 62 C3
Newfound 21 J6
Newgale 16 B3
Newgate 44 E1
Newgate Street 23 G1
Newhall ChesE 39 F1
Newhall Derbys 40 E3
Newham 71 G1
Newham Hall 71 G1
Newhaven 13 H6
Newhey 49 J1
Newholm 63 J5
Newhouse 75 F4
Newick 13 H4
Newingreen 15 G4
Newington Edin 76 A3
Newington Kent 15 G4
Newington Kent 24 E5
Newington Notts 51 J3
Newington Oxon 21 K2
Newington Bagpath 20 B2
Newland Cumb 55 G2
Newland Glos 19 J1
Newland Hull 59 G6
Newland NYorks 58 C7
Newland Oxon 30 E7
Newland Worcs 29 G4
Newlandrig 76 B4
Newlands Cumb 60 E3
Newlands Essex 24 E3
Newlands N'umb 62 A1
Newlands ScBord 70 A4
Newland's Corner 22 D7
Newlands of Geise 87 N3
Newlyn 2 B6
Newmachar 85 N9
Newmains 75 G5
Newman's End 33 J7
Newman's Green 34 C4
Newmarket Na H-E. Siar 88 K4
Newmarket Suff 33 K2
Newmill Aber 81 N2
Newmill A&N 92 H8
Newmill Moray 85 J5
Newmill ScBord 69 K2
Newmillerdam 51 F1
Newmillerdam Country Park WYorks WF2 6QP 117 L8
Newmills 93 D10
Newmills 80 G7
Newmilns 74 D7
Newney Green 24 C1
Newnham Glos 29 F7
Newnham Hants 22 A6
Newnham Herts 33 F5
Newnham Kent 14 E2
Newnham N'hants 31 G3
Newnham Bridge 29 F2
Newnham Paddox 41 G7
Newport Corn 6 B7
Newport Devon 6 D2
Newport ERid 58 E6
Newport Essex 33 J5
Newport Glos 19 K2
Newport High 87 P7
Newport IoW 11 G6
Newport (Casnewydd) Newport 19 G3
Newport Norf 45 K4
Newport (Trefdraeth) Pembs 16 D2
Newport Som 8 C2
Newport Tel&W 39 G4
Newport Pagnell 32 B4
Newport-on-Tay 81 K8
Newpound Common 12 D4
Newquay 3 F2
Newquay Zoo Corn TR7 2LZ 3 F2
Newry 93 F14
Newsbank 49 H6
Newseat 85 M7
Newsells 33 G5
Newsham Lancs 55 J6
Newsham NYorks 57 J1
Newsham NYorks 62 B5
Newsham N'umb 71 H6
Newsholme ERid 58 D7
Newsholme Lancs 56 D4
Newsome 50 D1
Newstead Notts 51 H7
Newstead N'umb 71 G1
Newstead ScBord 76 D7
Newstead Abbey Notts NG15 8NA 51 H7
Newthorpe Notts 41 G1
Newthorpe NYorks 57 K6
Newtoft 52 D4
Newton A&B 73 J1
Newton Bridgend 18 B4
Newton Cambs 33 H4
Newton Cambs 43 H4
Newton Cardiff 19 F4
Newton ChesW&C 48 E5
Newton ChesW&C 48 E7
Newton ChesW&C 48 D6
Newton Cumb 55 F2
Newton Derbys 51 G7
Newton D&G 69 G4
Newton GtMan 49 J3
Newton Here 28 C2
Newton Here 28 C5
Newton Here 28 E3
Newton High 83 R5
Newton High 84 B4
Newton High 84 B6
Newton High 87 R5
Newton Lancs 55 G6
Newton Lancs 55 J2
Newton Lancs 56 B4
Newton Lincs 42 D2
Newton NAyr 73 H5
Newton Norf 44 C4
Newton Notts 41 J1
Newton N'hants 42 B7
Newton N'umb 70 E3
Newton N'umb 71 F7
Newton Pembs 16 B3
Newton Pembs 16 C5
Newton ScBord 70 B1
Newton SGlos 19 K2
Newton Shrop 38 D2
Newton SLan 75 H7
Newton Som 7 K2
Newton Staffs 40 C3
Newton Suff 34 D4
Newton Swan 17 K7
Newton Warks 31 G1
Newton Wilts 10 D2
Newton WLoth 75 J3
Newton WYorks 57 K7
Newton Abbot 5 J3
Newton Arlosh 60 D1
Newton Aycliffe 62 C4
Newton Bewley 62 E4
Newton Blossomville 32 C3
Newton Bromswold 32 C2
Newton Burgoland 41 F5
Newton by Toft 52 D4
Newton Ferrers 5 F6
Newton Flotman 45 G6
Newton Green 19 J2
Newton Harcourt 41 J6
Newton Kyme 57 K5
Newton Longville 32 B5
Newton Mearns 74 D5
Newton Morrell NYorks 62 C6
Newton Morrell Oxon 31 H6
Newton Mountain 16 C5
Newton Mulgrave 63 H5
Newton of Leys 84 B7
Newton on the Hill 38 D3
Newton on Trent 52 B5
Newton Poppleford 7 J7
Newton Purcell 31 H5
Newton Regis 40 E5
Newton Reigny 61 F3
Newton Solney 40 E3
Newton St. Cyres 7 G6
Newton St. Faith 45 G4
Newton St. Loe 20 A5
Newton St. Petrock 6 C4
Newton Stacey 21 H7
Newton Stewart 64 E4
Newton Tony 21 F7
Newton Tracey 6 D3
Newton under Roseberry 63 F5
Newton Underwood 71 G5
Newton upon Derwent 58 D5
Newton Valence 11 J1
Newton with Scales 55 H6
Newtonairds 68 D5
Newtongrange 76 B4
Newtonhill 85 P11
Newton-in-the-Isle 43 H4
Newton-le-Willows Mersey 48 E3
Newton-le-Willows NYorks 57 H1
Newtonmore (Baile Ùr an t-Slèibh) 84 B11
Newton-on-Ouse 58 B4
Newton-on-Rawcliffe 63 J7
Newton-on-the-Moor 71 G3
Newtown Bucks 22 C1
Newtown ChesW&C 48 E7
Newtown Corn 2 C6
Newtown Corn 4 C3
Newtown Cumb 70 A7
Newtown Derbys 49 J4
Newtown Devon 7 J6
Newtown Devon 7 J6
Newtown Dorset 8 D4
Newtown Glos 19 K1
Newtown GtMan 48 E2
Newtown GtMan 49 G2
Newtown Hants 10 D3
Newtown Hants 10 E2
Newtown Hants 11 G3
Newtown Hants 11 H3
Newtown Hants 21 H5
Newtown Here 28 D4
Newtown Here 29 F4
Newtown High 83 P10
Newtown IoM 54 C6
Newtown IoW 11 F5
Newtown NM&D 93 F14
Newtown N'umb 71 F1
Newtown N'umb 71 F3
Newtown Oxon 22 A3
Newtown (Y Drenewydd) Powys 38 A6
Newtown RCT 18 D2
Newtown Shrop 38 D2
Newtown Som 8 B1
Newtown Som 8 B3
Newtown Staffs 40 B5
Newtown Staffs 49 J6
Newtown Staffs 50 C6
Newtown Wilts 9 J2
Newtown Wilts 21 G5
Newtown Crommelin 92 G5
Newtown Linford 41 H5
Newtown St. Boswells 76 D7
Newtown Saville 91 M11
Newtown Unthank 41 G5
Newtownabbey 92 J8
Newtownards 93 K9
Newtownbreda 93 J9
Newtownbutler 91 L14
Newtownhamilton 93 E14
Newtown-in-St-Martin 2 E6
Newtownstewart 90 L8
Newtyle 80 H6
Newyears Green 22 D3
Neyland 16 C5
Nibley Glos 19 K1
Nibley SGlos 19 K3
Nibley Green 20 A2
Nicholashayne 7 K4
Nicholaston 17 J7
Nidd 57 J3
Nigg Aberdeen 85 P10
Nigg High 84 C3
Nightcott 7 G3
Nilig 47 J7
Nilston Rigg 70 D7
Nimlet 20 A4
Nine Ashes 23 J1
Nine Elms 20 E3
Nine Mile Burn 75 K5
Ninebanks 61 J1
Ninemile Bar (Crocketford) 65 J3
Nineveh 29 F2
Ninfield 14 C6
Ningwood 11 F6
Nisbet 70 B1
Niton 11 G7
Nitshill 74 D4
Nizels 23 J6
No Man's Heath ChesW&C 38 E1
No Man's Heath Warks 40 E5
No Man's Land 4 C5
Noah's Ark 23 J6
Noak Hill 23 J2
Noblehill 65 K3
Noblethorpe 50 E2
Nobottle 31 H2
Nocton 52 D6
Noddsdale 74 A4
Nogdam End 45 H5
Noke 31 G7
Nolton 16 B4
Nolton Haven 16 B4
Nomansland Devon 7 G4
Nomansland Wilts 10 D3
Noneley 38 D3
Nonington 15 H2
Nook Cumb 55 J1
Nook Cumb 69 K6
Norbreck 55 G5
Norbury ChesE 38 E1
Norbury Derbys 40 D1
Norbury GtLon 23 G4
Norbury Shrop 38 C6
Norbury Staffs 39 G3
Norbury Common 38 E1
Norbury Junction 39 G3
Norchard 16 D6
Norcott Brook 49 F4
Nordelph 43 J5
Norden Dorset 9 J6
Norden GtMan 49 H1
Nordley 39 F6
Norfolk Lavender, Heacham Norf PE31 7JE 44 A2
Norham 77 H6
Norland Town 57 F7
Norley 48 E5
Norleywood 10 E5
Norlington 13 H5
Norman Cross 42 E6
Normanby NLincs 52 B1
Normanby NYorks 58 D1
Normanby R&C 63 F5
Normanby by Stow 52 B4
Normanby Hall Country Park NLincs DN15 9HU 52 B1
Normanby le Wold 52 E3
Normanby-by-Spital 52 D4
Normandy 22 C6
Norman's Bay 13 K6
Norman's Green 7 J5
Normanston 45 K6
Normanton Derby 41 F2
Normanton Leics 42 B1
Normanton Lincs 42 C1
Normanton Notts 51 K7
Normanton WYorks 57 J7
Normanton le Heath 41 F4
Normanton on Soar 41 H3
Normanton on Trent 51 K6
Normanton-on-the-Wolds 41 J2
Normoss 55 G6
Norrington Common 20 B5
Norris Green 4 E4
Norris Hill 41 F4
Norristhorpe 57 H7
North Acton 23 F3
North Anston 51 H4
North Ascot 22 C5
North Aston 31 F6
North Baddesley 10 E3
North Ballachulish (Baile a' Chaolais a Tuath) 79 M4
North Balloch 67 H4
North Barrow 9 F2
North Barsham 44 D2
North Bay Miniature Railway NYorks YO12 6PF 59 G1
North Benfleet 24 D3
North Bersted 12 C6
North Berwick 76 D2
North Boarhunt 11 H3
North Boisdale 88 B7
North Bovey 7 F7
North Bradley 20 B6
North Brentor 6 C7
North Brewham 9 G1
North Bridge 12 C3
North Buckland 6 C1
North Burlingham 45 H4
North Cadbury 9 F2
North Cairn 66 D6
North Camp 22 B6
North Carlton Lincs 52 C5
North Carlton Notts 51 H4
North Cave 58 E6
North Cerney 20 D1
North Chailey 13 G4
North Charford 10 C3
North Charlton 71 G1
North Cheriton 9 F2
North Chideock 8 D5
North Cliffe 58 E6
North Clifton 52 B5
North Cockerington 53 G3
North Coker 8 E3
North Collafirth 89 M4
North Common SGlos 19 K4
North Common Suff 34 D1
North Connel 79 L7
North Coombe 7 G5
North Cornelly 18 B3
North Corner 19 K3
North Cotes 53 G2
North Cove 45 J7
North Cowton 62 C6
North Crawley 32 C4
North Cray 23 H4
North Creake 44 C2
North Curry 8 C2
North Dalton 59 F4
North Deighton 57 J4
North Dell (Dail Bho Thuath) 88 K1
North Duffield 58 C6
North Elkington 53 F3
North Elmham 44 D3
North Elmsall 51 G1
North End Bucks 32 B6
North End Dorset 9 H2
North End ERid 59 H4
North End ERid 59 H5
North End ERid 59 J6
North End Essex 33 K7
North End Hants 10 C3
North End Hants 11 G2
North End Leics 41 H4
North End Norf 44 E6
North End NSom 19 H5
North End N'umb 71 G3
North End Ports 11 H4
North End WSuss 12 C6
North End WSuss 12 E5
North Erradale 82 H2
North Fambridge 24 E2
North Ferriby 59 F7
North Frodingham 59 H4
North Gorley 10 C3
North Green Norf 45 G7
North Green Suff 35 H1
North Green Suff 35 H2
North Green Suff 35 H2
North Grimston 58 E3
North Halling 24 D5
North Harby 52 B5
North Hayling 11 J4
North Hazelrigg 77 J7
North Heasley 7 F2
North Heath WBerks 21 H4
North Heath WSuss 12 D4
North Hill 4 C3
North Hillingdon 22 D3
North Hinksey 21 H1
North Holmwood 22 E7
North Houghton 10 E1
North Huish 5 H5
North Hykeham 52 C6
North Johnston 16 C4
North Kelsey 52 D2
North Kessock 84 A6
North Killingholme 52 E1
North Kilvington 57 K1
North Kilworth 41 J7
North Kingston 10 C4
North Kyme 52 E7
North Lancing 12 E6
North Lee 22 B1
North Lees 57 J2
North Leigh 30 E7
North Leverton with Habblesthorpe 51 K4
North Littleton 30 B4
North Lopham 44 E7
North Luffenham 42 C5
North Marden 12 B5
North Marston 31 J6
North Middleton Midlo 76 B5
North Middleton N'umb 71 F1
North Molton 7 F3
North Moreton 21 J3
North Mundham 12 B6
North Muskham 51 K7
North Newbald 59 F6
North Newington 31 F5
North Newnton 20 E6
North Newton 8 B1
North Nibley 20 A2
North Norfolk Railway Norf NR26 8RA 45 F1
North Oakley 21 J6
North Ockendon 23 J3
North Ormesby 63 F5
North Ormsby 53 F3
North Otterington 57 J1
North Owersby 52 D3
North Perrott 8 D4
North Petherton 8 B1
North Petherwin 4 C2
North Pickenham 44 C5
North Piddle 29 J3
North Plain 69 G7
North Pool 5 H6
North Poorton 8 E5
North Quarme 7 H2
North Queensferry 75 K2
North Radworthy 7 F2
North Rauceby 42 D1
North Reston 53 G4
North Riding Forest Park NYorks YO18 7LT 63 J7
North Rigton 57 H5
North Rode 49 H6
North Roe 89 M4
North Ronaldsay 89 G2
North Ronaldsay Airfield 89 G2
North Runcton 44 A4
North Sandwick 89 P3
North Scale 54 E3
North Scarle 52 B6
North Seaton 71 H5
North Shields 71 J7
North Shoebury 25 F3
North Side 43 F6
North Skelton 63 G5
North Somercotes 53 H3
North Stainley 57 H2
North Stainmore 61 K5
North Stifford 24 C3
North Stoke B&NESom 20 A5
North Stoke Oxon 21 K3
North Stoke WSuss 12 D5
North Stoneham 11 F3
North Street Hants 11 H1
North Street Kent 15 F2
North Street Med 24 E4
North Street WBerks 21 K4
North Sunderland 77 K7
North Tamerton 6 B6
North Tawton 6 E5
North Third 75 F2
North Thoresby 53 F3
North Tidworth 21 F7
North Togston 71 H3
North Town Devon 6 D5
North Town Hants 22 B6
North Town W&M 22 B3
North Tuddenham 44 E4
North Uist (Uibhist a Tuath) 88 C1
North Walsham 45 G2
North Waltham 21 J7
North Warnborough 22 A6
North Watten 87 Q4
North Weald Bassett 23 H1
North Wembley 22 E3
North Wheatley 51 K4
North Whilborough 5 J4
North Wick 19 J5
North Widcombe 19 J6
North Willingham 52 E4
North Wingfield 51 G6
North Witham 42 C3
North Wootton Dorset 9 F3
North Wootton Norf 44 A3
North Wootton Som 19 J7
North Wraxall 20 B4
North Wroughton 20 E3
North Yardhope 70 E3
North Yorkshire Moors Railway NYorks YO18 7AJ 58 E1
Northacre 44 D6
Northall 32 C6
Northall Green 44 D4
Northallerton 62 D7
Northam Devon 6 C3
Northam Soton 11 F3
Northam Burrows Country Park Devon EX39 1XR 6 C2
Northampton 31 J2
Northaw 23 F1
Northay Devon 8 C4
Northay Som 8 B3
Northbay 88 B8
Northbeck 42 D1
Northborough 42 E5
Northbourne Kent 15 J2
Northbourne Oxon 21 J3
Northbridge Street 14 C5
Northbrook Hants 11 G1
Northbrook Oxon 31 F6
Northchapel 12 C4
Northchurch 22 C1
Northcote Manor 6 E4
Northcott 6 B6
Northcourt 21 J2
Northedge 51 F6
Northend B&NESom 20 A5
Northend Bucks 22 A2
Northend Warks 30 E3
Northfield Hull 59 G7
Northfield ScBord 77 H4
Northfield Som 8 B1
Northfield WMid 30 B1
Northfields 42 D5
Northfleet 24 C4
Northhouse 69 K3
Northiam 14 D5
Northill 32 E4
Northington Glos 20 A1
Northington Hants 11 G1
Northlands 53 G7
Northleach 30 C7
Northleigh Devon 6 E2
Northleigh Devon 7 K6
Northlew 6 D6
Northmoor 21 H1
Northmoor Green (Moorland) 8 C1
Northmuir 81 J5
Northney 11 J4
Northolt 22 E3
Northop (Llaneurgain) 48 B6
Northop Hall 48 B6
Northorpe Lincs 42 D4
Northorpe Lincs 43 F2
Northorpe Lincs 52 B3
Northover Som 8 D1
Northover Som 8 E2
Northowram 57 G7
Northport 9 J6
Northrepps 45 G2
Northton (Taobh Tuath) 88 E9
Northumberland Dark Sky Park N'umb 70 B4
Northumbria Craft Centre, Morpeth N'umb NE61 1PD 71 H5
Northway Glos 29 J5
Northway Som 7 K3
Northwich 49 F5
Northwick SGlos 19 J3
Northwick Som 19 G7
Northwick Worcs 29 H3
Northwold 44 B6
Northwood GtLon 22 D2
Northwood IoW 11 F5
Northwood Kent 25 K5
Northwood Mersey 48 D3
Northwood Shrop 38 D2
Northwood Green 29 G7
Northwood Hills 22 E2
Norton Glos 29 H6
Norton Halton 48 E4
Norton Herts 33 F5
Norton IoW 10 E6
Norton Mon 28 D6
Norton Notts 51 H5
Norton NSom 19 G5
Norton N'hants 31 H2
Norton NYorks 58 D2
Norton Powys 28 C2
Norton Shrop 38 D7
Norton Shrop 38 E5
Norton Shrop 39 G5
Norton Stock 62 E4
Norton Suff 34 D2
Norton Swan 17 K7
Norton SYorks 51 F4
Norton SYorks 51 H1
Norton VGlam 18 B4
Norton Wilts 20 B3
Norton WMid 40 A7
Norton Worcs 29 H3
Norton Worcs 30 B4
Norton WSuss 12 B7
Norton WSuss 12 C6
Norton Bavant 20 C7
Norton Bridge 40 A2
Norton Canes 40 C5
Norton Canon 28 C4
Norton Disney 52 B7
Norton Ferris 9 G1
Norton Fitzwarren 7 K3
Norton Green Herts 33 F6
Norton Green IoW 10 E6
Norton Green Stoke 49 J7
Norton Hawkfield 19 J5
Norton Heath 24 C1
Norton in Hales 39 G2
Norton in the Moors 49 H7
Norton Lindsey 30 D2
Norton Little Green 34 D2
Norton Malreward 19 K5
Norton Mandeville 23 J1
Norton St. Philip 20 A6
Norton Subcourse 45 J6
Norton Wood 28 C4
Norton Woodseats 51 F4
Norton-Juxta-Twycross 41 F5
Norton-le-Clay 57 K2
Norton's Cross Roads 93 D13
Norton-sub-Hamdon 8 D3
Norwell 51 K6
Norwell Woodhouse 51 K6
Norwich 45 G5
Norwich Castle Museum & Art Gallery Norf NR1 3JU 134 Norwich
Norwich Cathedral Norf NR1 4DH 134 Norwich
Norwich International Airport 45 G4
Norwick 89 Q1
Norwood End 23 J1
Norwood Green GtLon 22 E4
Norwood Green WYorks 57 G7
Norwood Hill 23 F7
Norwood Park 8 E1
Noseley 42 A6
Noss Mayo 5 F6
Nosterfield 57 H1
Nosterfield End 33 K4
Nostie 83 J8
Notgrove 30 C6
Nottage 18 B4
Notting Hill 23 F3
Nottingham 41 H1
Nottingham Castle Museum & Art Gallery NG1 6EL 134 Nottingham
Nottington 9 F6
Notton Wilts 20 C5
Notton WYorks 51 F1
Nottswood Hill 29 G7
Nounsley 34 B7
Noutard's Green 29 G2
Nowton 34 C2
Nowton Park Suff IP29 5LU 34 C2
Nox 38 D4
Noyadd Trefawr 17 F1
Nuffield 21 K3
Nun Monkton 58 B4
Nunburnholme 58 E5
Nuneaton 41 F6
Nuneham Courtenay 21 J2
Nunney 20 A7
Nunnington Here 28 E4
Nunnington NYorks 58 C2
Nunnington Park 7 J3
Nunnykirk 71 F4
Nuns Quarter 93 L10
Nunsthorpe 53 F2
Nunthorpe Middl 63 F5
Nunthorpe York 58 B4
Nunton 10 C2
Nunwick NYorks 57 J2
Nunwick N'umb 70 D6
Nup End 33 F7
Nupend 20 A1
Nursling 10 E3
Nursted 11 J2
Nurton 40 A6
Nutbourne WSuss 11 J4
Nutbourne WSuss 12 D5
Nutfield 23 G6
Nuthall 41 H1
Nuthampstead 33 H5
Nuthurst Warks 30 C1
Nuthurst WSuss 12 E4
Nutley ESuss 13 H4
Nutley Hants 21 K7
Nutwell 51 J2
Nyadd 75 F1
Nyetimber 12 B7
Nyewood 11 J2
Nymans WSuss RH17 6EB 13 F4
Nymet Rowland 7 F5
Nymet Tracey 7 F5
Nympsfield 20 B1
Nynehead 7 K3
Nythe 8 D1
Nyton 12 C6

O
O2, The GtLon SE10 0BB 105 D7
Oad Street 24 E5
Oadby 41 J5
Oak Cross 6 D6
Oak Tree 62 D5
Oakamoor 40 C1
Oakbank 75 J4
Oakdale Caerp 18 E2
Oakdale Poole 10 B5
Oake 7 K3
Oaken 40 A5
Oakenclough 55 J5
Oakengates 39 G4
Oakenholt 48 B5
Oakenshaw Dur 62 C3
Oakenshaw WYorks 57 G7
Oakerthorpe 51 F7
Oakes 50 D1
Oakfield IoW 11 G5
Oakfield Torfaen 19 F2
Oakford Cere 26 D3
Oakford Devon 7 H3
Oakfordbridge 7 H3
Oakgrove 49 J6
Oakham 42 B5
Oakhanger 11 J1
Oakhill 19 K7
Oakington 33 H2
Oaklands Conwy 47 G7
Oaklands Herts 33 F7
Oakle Street 29 G7
Oakley Bed 32 D3
Oakley Bucks 31 H7
Oakley Fife 75 J2
Oakley Hants 21 J6
Oakley Oxon 22 A1
Oakley Poole 10 B5
Oakley Suff 35 F1
Oakley Green 22 C4
Oakley Park 37 J7
Oakridge Lynch 20 C1
Oaks 38 D5
Oaks Green 40 D2
Oaksey 20 C2
Oakshaw Ford 70 A6
Oakshott 11 J2
Oakthorpe 41 F4
Oaktree Hill 62 D7
Oakwell Hall & Country Park WYorks WF17 9LG 117 G5
Oakwood Leisure Park Pembs SA67 8DE 16 D4
Oakwoodhill 12 E3
Oakworth 57 F6
Oare Kent 25 G5
Oare Som 7 G1
Oare Wilts 20 E5
Oasby 42 D2
Oatfield 66 A2
Oath 8 C2
Oathlaw 81 K5
Oatlands 57 J4
Oban (An t-Òban) 79 K8
Obley 28 C1
Oborne 9 F3
Obthorpe 42 D4
Occlestone Green 49 F6
Occold 35 F1
Occumster 87 Q6
Oceanarium BH2 5AA 123 Bournemouth
Ochiltree 67 K1
Ochr-y-foel 47 J5
Ochtertyre P&K 80 D8
Ochtertyre Stir 75 F1
Ockbrook 41 G2
Ockeridge 29 G2
Ockham 22 D6
Ockle 78 G3
Ockley 12 E3
Ocle Pychard 28 E4
Octon 59 G2
Odcombe 8 E3
Odd Down 20 A5
Oddendale 61 H5
Oddingley 29 J3
Oddington 31 G7
Oddsta 89 P3
Odell 32 C3
Odham 6 C5
Odiham 22 A6
Odsey 33 F5
Odstock 10 C2
Odstone 41 F5
Offchurch 30 E2
Offenham 30 B4
Offerton 49 J4
Offham ESuss 13 G5
Offham Kent 23 K6
Offham WSuss 12 D6
Offley Hoo 32 E6
Offleymarsh 39 G3
Offord Cluny 33 F2
Offord D'Arcy 33 F2
Offton 34 E4
Offwell 7 K6
Ogbourne Maizey 20 E4
Ogbourne St. Andrew 20 E4
Ogbourne St. George 20 E4
Ogden Water WYorks HX2 8YA 116 B3
Oghill 90 M5
Ogil 71 G6
Oglet 48 D4
Ogmore 18 B4
Ogmore Vale 18 C2
Ogmore-by-Sea 18 B4
Ogston Reservoir Derbys DE55 6EL 51 F6
Oil Terminal 89 C8
Okeford Fitzpaine 9 H3
Okehampton 6 D6
Okehampton Camp 6 D6
Olchard 5 J3
Olchfa 17 K6
Old 31 J1
Old Aberdeen 85 P10
Old Alresford 11 G1
Old & New Towns of Edinburgh Edin 120 D2
Old Arley 40 E6
Old Basford 41 H1
Old Basing 21 K6
Old Belses 70 A1
Old Bewick 71 F1
Old Blacksmith's Shop, Gretna Green D&G DG16 5DY 69 J7
Old Blair 80 D4
Old Bolingbroke 53 G6
Old Bramhope 57 H5
Old Brampton 51 F5
Old Bridge of Urr 65 H4
Old Buckenham 44 E6
Old Burdon 62 D1
Old Burghclere 21 H6
Old Bushmills Distillery BT1 2LB 92 E2
Old Byland 58 B1
Old Cassop 62 D3
Old Church Stoke 38 B6
Old Cleeve 7 J1
Old Clipstone 51 J6
Old Colwyn 47 G5
Old Craighall 76 B3
Old Dailly 67 G4
Old Dalby 41 J3
Old Dam 50 D5
Old Deer 85 P6
Old Dilton 20 B7
Old Down SGlos 19 K3
Old Down Som 19 K6
Old Edlington 51 H3
Old Eldon 62 C4
Old Ellerby 59 H6
Old Felixstowe 35 H5
Old Fletton 42 E6
Old Ford 23 G3
Old Glossop 50 C3
Old Goginan 37 F7
Old Goole 58 D7
Old Gore 29 F6
Old Grimsby 2 B1
Old Hall 53 F1
Old Hall Green 33 G6
Old Hall Street 45 H2
Old Harlow 33 H7
Old Heath 34 E6
Old Heathfield 13 J4
Old Hill Mid Ulster 92 C8
Old Hill WMid 40 B7
Old Hurst 33 G1
Old Hutton 55 J1
Old Kea 3 F4
Old Kilpatrick 74 C3
Old Knebworth 33 F6
Old Leake 53 H7
Old Malton 58 E2
Old Mill 92 J6
Old Milton 10 D5
Old Milverton 30 D2
Old Montsale 25 G2
Old Netley 11 F3
Old Newton 34 E2
Old Philpstoun 75 J3
Old Radnor (Pencraig) 28 B3
Old Rayne 85 L8
Old Romney 15 F5
Old Royal Naval College, Greenwich GtLon SE10 9LW 105 D8
Old Scone 80 G8
Old Shields 75 G3
Old Sodbury 20 A3
Old Somerby 42 C2
Old Station, The, Tintern Parva Mon NP16 7NX 19 J1
Old Stratford 31 J4
Old Sunderlandwick 59 G4
Old Swarland 71 G3
Old Swinford 40 B7
Old Thirsk 57 K1
Old Town Cumb 55 J1
Old Town IoS 2 C1
Old Town Farm 70 D4
Old Tupton 51 F6
Old Warden 32 E4
Old Weston 32 D1
Old Windsor 22 C4
Old Wives Lees 15 F2
Old Woking 22 D6
Old Woodhall 53 F6
Old Woods 38 D3
Oldberrow 30 C2
Oldborough 7 F5
Oldbury Kent 23 J6
Oldbury Shrop 39 G6
Oldbury Warks 41 F6
Oldbury WMid 40 B7
Oldbury Court Estate Bristol BS16 2JH 100 E3
Oldbury Naite 19 K2
Oldbury on the Hill 20 B3
Oldbury-on-Severn 19 K2
Oldcastle Bridgend 18 C4
Oldcastle Mon 28 C6
Oldcastle Heath 38 D1
Oldcotes 51 H4
Oldcroft 19 K1
Oldeamere 43 G6
Oldfield 29 H2
Oldford 20 A6
Oldhall 85 J11
Oldham 49 J2
Oldham Edge 49 J2
Oldhamstocks 77 F3
Oldland 19 K4
Oldmeldrum 85 N8
Oldpark 39 F5
Oldridge 7 G6
Oldshore Beg 86 D4
Oldstead 58 B2
Oldstone 92 G8
Oldtown of Ord 85 L5
Oldwalls 17 H6
Oldways End 7 G3
Oldwhat 85 N5
Oldwich Lane 30 D1
Olgrinmore 87 P4
Oliver 69 G1
Oliver's Battery 11 F2
Ollaberry 89 M4
Ollerton ChesE 49 G5
Ollerton Notts 51 J6
Ollerton Shrop 39 F3
Olmstead Green 33 K4
Olney 32 B3
Olrig House 87 P3
Olton 40 D7
Olveston 19 K3
Olympia GtLon W14 8UX 103 G7
Omagh 91 L9
Ombersley 29 H2
Ompton 51 J6
Onchan 54 C6
Onecote 50 C7
Onehouse 34 E3
Ongar Hill 43 J3
Ongar Street 28 C2
Onibury 28 D1
Onich (Omhanaich) 79 M4
Onllwyn 27 H7
Onneley 39 G1
Onslow Green 33 K7
Onslow Village 22 C7
Oona Bridge 93 C12
Opinan High 82 H3
Opinan High 83 J1
Orange Lane 77 F6
Orbliston 84 H5
Orbost 82 C6
Orby 53 H6
Orcadia 73 K4
Orchard 73 K2
Orchard Portman 8 B2
Orchardtown 90 M4
Orcheston 20 D7
Orcop 28 D6
Orcop Hill 28 D6
Ord 82 G9
Ordhead 85 L9
Ordie 85 J10
Ordiequish 84 H5
Ordsall 51 J5
Ore 14 D6
Oreham Common 13 F5
Oreston 5 F5
Oreton 29 F1
Orford Suff 35 J4
Orford Warr 49 F3
Organford 9 J5
Orgreave 40 D4
Oritor 92 C9
Orkney Islands 89 C5
Orlestone 14 E4
Orleton Here 28 D2
Orleton Worcs 29 F2
Orleton Common 28 D2
Orlingbury 32 B1
Ormesby 63 F5
Ormesby St. Margaret 45 J4
Ormesby St. Michael 45 J4
Ormidale 73 J2
Ormiston 76 C4
Ormsaigmore 78 F4
Ormsary 73 F3
Ormskirk 48 D2
Oronsay 72 B2
Orpington 23 H5
Orrell GtMan 48 E2
Orrell Mersey 48 C3
Orrisdale 54 C4
Orroland 65 H6
Orsett 24 C3
Orsett Heath 24 C4
Orslow 40 A4
Orston 42 A1
Orton Cumb 61 H6
Orton N'hants 32 B1
Orton Longueville 42 E6
Orton Rigg 60 E1
Orton Waterville 42 E6
Orton-on-the-Hill 41 F5
Orwell 33 G3
Osbaldeston 56 B6
Osbaldwick 58 C4
Osbaston Leics 41 G5
Osbaston Shrop 38 C3
Osbaston Tel&W 38 E4
Osbaston Hollow 41 G5
Osborne 11 G5
Osborne House IoW PO32 6JX 11 G5
Osbournby 42 D2
Oscroft 48 E6
Ose 82 D6
Osgathorpe 41 G4
Osgodby Lincs 52 D3
Osgodby NYorks 58 C6
Osgodby NYorks 59 G1
Oskaig 82 F7
Osleston 40 E2
Osmaston Derby 41 F2
Osmaston Derbys 40 D1
Osmington 9 G6
Osmington Mills 9 G6
Osmondthorpe 57 J6
Osmotherley 62 E7
Osnaburgh (Dairsie) 81 K9
Osprings 25 G5
Ossett 57 H7
Ossett Street Side 57 H7
Ossian's Grave BT44 0TG 92 H4
Ossington 51 K6
Ostend 25 F2
Osterley 22 E4
Osterley Park & House GtLon TW7 4RB 103 C8
Oswaldkirk 58 C2
Oswaldtwistle 56 C7
Oswestry 38 B3
Oteley 38 D2
Otford 23 J6
Otham 14 C2
Othery 8 C1
Otley Suff 35 G3
Otley WYorks 57 H5
Otter 73 H3
Otter Ferry 73 H2
Otterbourne 11 F2
Otterburn NYorks 56 D4
Otterburn N'umb 70 D4
Otterburn Camp 70 D4
Otterden Place 14 E2
Otterham 4 B1
Otterham Quay 24 E5
Otterhampton 19 F7
Ottershaw 22 D5
Otterswick 89 P4
Otterton 7 J7
Otterton Mill Devon EX9 7HG 7 J7
Otterwood 11 F4
Ottery St. Mary 7 J6
Ottinge 15 G3
Ottringham 59 J7
Oughterby 60 D1
Oughtershaw 56 D1
Oughterside 60 C2
Oughtibridge 51 F3
Oulston 58 B2
Oulton Cumb 60 D1
Oulton Norf 45 F3
Oulton Staffs 39 G3
Oulton Staffs 40 B2
Oulton Suff 45 K6
Oulton WYorks 57 J7
Oulton Broad 45 K6
Oulton Grange 40 B2
Oulton Park 48 E6
Oultoncross 40 B2
Oundle 42 D7
Our Dynamic Earth Edin EH8 8AS 126 J4
Ousby 61 H3
Ousdale 87 N7
Ousden 34 B3
Ousefleet 58 E7
Ouston Dur 62 C1
Ouston N'umb 71 F6
Out Newton 59 K7
Out Rawcliffe 55 H5
Out Skerries Airstrip 89 Q5
Outcast 55 G2
Outchester 77 K7
Outgate 60 E7
Outhgill 61 J6
Outlands 39 G3
Outlane 50 C1
Outwell 43 J5
Outwood Surr 23 G7
Outwood WYorks 57 J7
Outwoods 39 G4
Ouzlewell Green 57 J7
Ovenden 57 F7
Over Cambs 33 G1
Over ChesW&C 49 F6
Over Glos 29 H7
Over SGlos 19 J3
Over Burrows 40 E2
Over Compton 8 E3
Over Dinsdale 62 D5
Over End 50 E5
Over Green 40 D6
Over Haddon 50 E6
Over Hulton 49 F2
Over Kellet 55 J3
Over Kiddington 31 F6
Over Monnow 28 D7
Over Norton 30 E6
Over Peover 49 G5
Over Silton 62 E7
Over Stowey 7 K2
Over Stratton 8 D3
Over Tabley 49 G4
Over Wallop 10 D1
Over Whitacre 40 E6
Over Winchendon (Upper Winchendon) 31 J7
Over Worton 31 F6
Overbury 29 J5
Overcombe 9 F6
Overgreen 51 F5
Overleigh 8 D1
Overpool 48 C5
Overseal 40 E4
Overslade 31 F1
Oversland 15 F2
Overslev Green 30 B3
Overstone 32 B2
Overstrand 45 G1
Overthorpe 31 F4
Overton ChesW&C 48 E5
Overton Hants 21 J7
Overton Lancs 55 H4
Overton NYorks 58 B4
Overton Shrop 28 E1
Overton Swan 17 H7
Overton (Owrtyn) Wrex 38 C1
Overton WYorks 50 E1
Overton Bridge 38 C1
Overtown Lancs 56 B2
Overtown NLan 75 G5
Overtown Swin 20 E4
Overy 21 J2
Oving Bucks 31 J6
Oving WSuss 12 C6
Ovingdean 13 G6
Ovingham 71 F7
Ovington Dur 62 B5
Ovington Essex 34 B4
Ovington Hants 11 G1
Ovington Norf 44 D5
Ovington N'umb 71 F7
Ower Hants 10 E3
Ower Hants 11 F4
Owermoigne 9 G6
Owler Bar 50 E5
Owlpen 20 A2
Owl's Green 35 G2
Owlswick 22 A1
Owmby 52 D4
Owmby-by-Spital 52 D4
Owslebury 11 G2
Owston 42 A5
Owston Ferry 52 B2
Owstwick 59 J6
Owthorpe 41 J2
Oxborough 44 B5
Oxcliffe Hill 55 H3
Oxcombe 53 G5
Oxen End 33 K6
Oxen Park 55 G1
Oxenhope 57 G7
Oxenhall 29 G6
Oxenholme 61 G7
Oxenhope 57 F6
Oxenpill 19 H7
Oxenton 29 J5
Oxenwood 21 G6
Oxford 21 J1
Oxford Cathedral Oxon OX1 1AB 134 Oxford
Oxford Story Oxon OX1 3AJ 134 Oxford
Oxford University Museum of Natural History Oxon OX1 3PW 134 Oxford
Oxhey 22 E2
Oxhill 30 E4
Oxley 40 B5
Oxley Green 34 D7
Oxley's Green 13 K4
Oxnam 70 C2
Oxnead 45 G3
Oxnop Ghyll 61 L7
Oxshott 22 E5
Oxspring 50 E2
Oxted 23 G6
Oxton Mersey 48 C4
Oxton Notts 51 J7
Oxton ScBord 76 C5
Oxwich 17 H7
Oxwich Green 17 H7
Oxwick 44 D3
Oykel Bridge 86 F9
Oyne 85 L8
Ozleworth 20 A2

P
Pabbay 88 E9
Packington 41 F4
Packwood 30 C1
Padanaram 81 K5
Padarn Country Park Gwyn LL55 4TY 46 D6
Padbury 31 J5
Paddington 23 F3
Paddlesworth 15 G3
Paddock 14 E2
Paddock Wood 23 K7
Paddockhole 69 H5
Paddolgreen 38 E2
Padeswood 48 B6
Padfield 50 C3
Padiham 56 C6
Padside 57 G4
Padstow 3 G1
Padworth 21 K5
Paganhill 20 B1
Pagham 12 B7
Paglesham Churchend 25 F2
Paglesham Eastend 25 F2
Paignton 5 J4
Paignton & Dartmouth Steam Railway Torbay TQ4 6AF 5 J5
Paignton Pier Torbay TQ4 6BW 5 J4
Paignton Zoo Torbay TQ4 7EU 5 J5
Pailton 41 G7
Paine's Corner 13 K4
Painscastle 28 A4
Painshawfield 71 F7
Painswick 20 B1
Pairc Shiaboist 88 H3
Paisley 74 C4
Pakefield 45 K6
Pakenham 34 D2
Palace of Holyroodhouse Edin EH8 8DX 126 J4
Palace of Westminster (Palace of Westminster Abbey inc. St Margaret's Church) GtLon SW1A 0AA 105 A7
Palacerigg Country Park NLan G67 3HU 119 M1
Pale 37 J2
Palehouse Common 13 H5
Palestine 21 F7
Paley Street 22 B4
Palgowan 67 H5
Palgrave 35 F1
Pallinsburn House 77 G7
Palmarsh 15 G4
Palmers Cross 22 D7
Palmers Green 23 G2
Palmerstown 18 E4
Palnackie 65 J5
Palnure 64 E4
Palterton 51 G6
Pamber End 21 K6
Pamber Green 21 K6
Pamber Heath 21 K5
Pamington 29 J5
Pamphill 9 J4
Pampisford 33 H4
Panborough 19 H7
Panbride 81 L7
Pancrasweek 6 A5
Pancross 18 D5
Pandy Gwyn 37 F5
Pandy Mon 28 C6
Pandy Powys 37 J5
Pandy Wrex 38 A2
Pandy Tudur 47 G6
Pandy'r Capel 47 J7
Panfield 34 B6
Pangbourne 21 K4
Pannal 57 J4
Pannal Ash 57 H4
Panshanger 33 F7
Pant 38 B3
Pant Glas 36 D1
Pant Gwyn 37 H3
Pant Mawr 37 H7
Pantasaph 47 K5
Panteg 19 G2
Pantglas 37 G6
Pantgwyn Carmar 17 J3
Pantgwyn Cere 17 F1
Pant-lasau 17 K5
Panton 52 E5
Pant-pastynog 47 J6
Pantperthog 37 G5
Pant-y-dwr 27 J1
Pantyffordd 48 B7
Pant-y-ffridd 38 A5
Pantyffynnon 17 K4
Pantygasseg 19 F2
Pantygelli 28 C7
Pantymwyn 47 K6
Panxworth 45 H4
Papa Stour 89 K6
Papa Stour Airstrip 89 K6
Papa Westray 89 D2
Papa Westray Airfield 89 D2
Papcastle 60 C3
Papple 76 D3
Papplewick 51 H7
Papworth Everard 33 F2
Papworth St. Agnes 33 F2
Par 4 A5
Paradise Park, Newhaven ESuss BN9 0DH 13 H6
Paradise Wildlife Park, Broxbourne Herts EN10 7QA 23 G1
Parbold 48 D1
Parbrook Som 8 E1
Parbrook WSuss 12 D4
Parc 37 H2
Parcllyn 26 B3
Parc-rhydderch 27 F3
Parc-Seymour 19 H2
Parc-y-rhôs 17 J1
Pardshaw 60 B4
Parham 35 H2
Parish Holm 68 C1
Park Aber 85 N10
Park D&S 90 M6

Ramsey Island Essex 25 F1
Ramsey Island Pembs 16 A3
Ramsey Mereside 43 F7
Ramsey St. Mary's 43 F7
Ramsgate 25 K5
Ramsgate Street 44 E2
Ramsgill 57 G2
Ramsholt 35 H4
Ramshorn 40 C1
Ramsnest Common 12 C3
Ranaghan 92 C7
Ranby Lincs 53 F5
Ranby Notts 51 J4
Rand 52 E5
Rand Farm Park Lincs LN8 5NJ 52 E5
Randalstown 92 F7
Randwick 20 B1
Ranelly 91 L10
Rangemore 40 D3
Rangeworthy 19 K3
Ranish (Ranais) 88 K5
Rankinston 67 J2
Rank's Green 34 B7
Ranmoor 51 F4
Rannoch School 80 A5
Ranscombe 7 H1
Ranskill 51 J4
Ranton 40 A3
Ranton Green 40 A3
Ranworth 45 H4
Rapness 89 E3
Rapps 8 C3
Rascarrel 65 H6
Rash 56 B1
Rasharkin 92 E5
Rashee 92 H7
Rashwood 29 J2
Raskelf 57 K2
Rassau 28 A7
Rastrick 57 G7
Ratagan 83 K9
Ratby 41 H5
Ratcliffe Culey 41 F6
Ratcliffe on Soar 41 G3
Ratcliffe on the Wreake 41 J4
Ratford Bridge 16 B4
Ratfyn 20 E7
Rathen 85 P4
Rathfriland 93 G13
Rathillet 81 J8
Rathkeel 92 G6
Rathmell 56 D3
Ratho 75 K3
Ratho Station 75 K3
Rathven 85 J4
Ratley 30 E4
Ratling 15 H2
Ratlinghope 38 D6
Ratsloe 7 H6
Rattar 87 Q2
Ratten Row Cumb 60 E2
Ratten Row Lancs 55 H5
Rattery 5 H4
Rattlesden 34 D3
Rattray 80 G6
Raughton Head 60 E2
Raunds 32 C1
Ravenfield 51 G3
Ravenglass 60 B7
Ravenglass & Eskdale Railway Cumb CA18 1SW 60 B7
Raveningham 45 H6
Raven's Green 35 F6
Ravenscar 63 K6
Ravensdale 54 C4
Ravensden 32 D3
Ravenshaw 56 E5
Ravenshayes 7 H5
Ravenshead 51 H7
Ravensmoor 49 F7
Ravensthorpe N'hants 31 H1
Ravensthorpe WYorks 57 H7
Ravenstone Leics 41 G4
Ravenstone MK 32 B3
Ravenstonedale 61 J6
Ravenstruther 75 H6
Ravensworth 62 B6
Ravernet 93 H10
Raw F&O 91 L12
Raw NYorks 63 K6
Rawcliffe ERid 58 C7
Rawcliffe York 58 B4
Rawcliffe Bridge 58 C7
Rawdon 57 H6
Rawmarsh 51 G3
Rawnsley 40 C4
Rawreth 24 D2
Rawridge 8 B4
Rawson Green 41 F1
Rawtenstall 56 D7
Rawyards 75 F4
Raydon 34 E5
Raylees 70 E4
Rayleigh 24 E2
Raymond's Hill 8 C5
Rayne 34 B6
Rayners Lane 22 E3
Raynes Park 23 F5
Reach 33 J2
Read 56 C6
Reading 22 A4
Reading Green 35 F1
Reading Street 14 E4
Reagill 61 H5
Real Mary King's Close, The Edin EH1 1PG 126 F4
Rearquhar 84 B1
Rearsby 41 J4
Rease Heath 49 F7
Reaveley 71 F2
Reawick 89 M8
Reay 87 M3
Reculver 25 J5
Red Ball 7 J4
Red Bull 49 H7
Red Dial 60 D2
Red Hill Hants 11 J3
Red Hill Warks 30 C3
Red Lodge 33 K1
Red Lumb 49 H1
Red Oaks Hill 33 J5
Red Point 82 H4
Red Post Corn 6 A5
Red Post Devon 5 J4
Red Rail 28 E6
Red Rock 48 E2
Red Roses 17 F4
Red Row 71 H4
Red Street 49 H7
Red Wharf Bay (Traeth Coch) 46 D4
Redberth 16 D5
Redbourn 32 E7
Redbourne 52 C3
Redbrook Glos 28 E7
Redbrook Wrex 38 E1
Redbrook Street 14 E4
Redburn High 83 R4
Redburn High 84 D6
Redburn N'umb 70 C7
Redcar 63 G4
Redcastle Angus 81 M5
Redcastle High 83 R6
Redcliff Bay 19 H4
Reddingmuirhead 75 H3
Reddish 49 H3
Redditch 30 B2
Rede 34 C3
Redenhall 45 G7
Redesmouth 70 D5
Redford Angus 81 L6
Redford Dur 62 A3
Redford WSuss 12 B4
Redgrave 34 E1
Redhill L&C 93 G11
Redhill Notts 41 H1
Redhill NSom 19 H5
Redhill Surr 23 F6
Redhill Aerodrome & Heliport 23 F7
Redhouse 73 G4
Redhouses 72 B4
Redisham 45 J7
Redland Bristol 19 J4
Redland Ork 89 C5
Redlingfield 35 F1
Redlynch Som 9 G1
Redlynch Wilts 10 D2
Redmarley D'Abitot 29 G5
Redmarshall 62 D4
Redmile 42 A2
Redmire 62 A7
Redmoor 4 A4
Rednal 38 C3
Redpath 76 D7
Redruth 2 D4
Redscarhead 76 A6
Redshaw 68 D1
Redstone Bank 16 E4
Redwick Newport 19 H3
Redwick SGlos 19 J3
Redworth 62 C4
Reed 33 G5
Reed End 33 G5
Reedham 45 J5
Reedley 56 D6
Reedness 58 D7
Reepham Lincs 52 D5
Reepham Norf 44 E3
Reeth 62 A7
Regaby 54 D4
Regil 19 J5
Regoul 84 C5
Reiff 86 B8
Reigate 23 F6
Reighton 59 H2
Reiss 87 R4
Rejerrah 3 F3
Relan 91 M13
Releath 2 D5
Relubbus 2 C5
Relugas 84 D6
Remenham 22 A3
Remenham Hill 22 A3
Rempstone 41 H3
Rendcomb 30 B7
Rendham 35 H2
Rendlesham 35 H3
Renfrew 74 D4
Renhold 32 D3
Renishaw 51 G5
Rennington 71 H2
Renton 74 B3
Renwick 61 G2
Repps 45 J4
Repton 41 F3
Rescobie 81 L5
Rescorla 4 A5
Resipole 79 J4
Resolis 84 A4
Resolven 18 B1
Resourie 79 K2
Respryn 4 B4
Reston 77 G4
Restormel 4 B4
Reswallie 81 L5
Reterth 3 G2
Retew 3 G3
Retford (East Retford) 51 K4
Rettendon 24 D2
Rettendon Place 24 D2
Retyn 3 F3
Revesby 53 F6
Revesby Bridge 53 G6
Rew 5 H3
Rew Street 11 F5
Rewe Devon 7 G6
Rewe Devon 7 H6
Reybridge 20 C5
Reydon 35 J1
Reydon Smear 35 K1
Reymerston 44 E5
Reynalton 16 D5
Reynoldston 17 H7
Rezare 4 D3
Rhadyr 19 G1
Rhandirmwyn 27 G4
Rhayader (Rhaeadr Gwy) 27 J2
Rhedyn 36 B2
Rheged - the Village in the Hill Cumb CA11 0DQ 61 F4
Rhemore 78 G5
Rhenigidale (Reinigeadal) 88 H7
Rheola 18 B1
Rhes-y-cae 47 K6
Rhewl Denb 38 A1
Rhewl Denb 47 K6
Rhewl Shrop 38 C2
Rhian 86 H8
Rhiconich 86 E4
Rhicullen 84 A4
Rhidorroch 83 M1
Rhifail 87 K5
Rhigos 18 C1
Rhiston 38 B6
Rhiw 36 B3
Rhiwargor 37 J3
Rhiwbina 18 E3
Rhiwbryfdir 37 F1
Rhiwderin 19 F3
Rhiwinder 18 D3
Rhiwlas Gwyn 37 J2
Rhiwlas Gwyn 46 D6
Rhiwlas Powys 38 B2
Rhode 8 B1
Rhodes Minnis 15 G3
Rhodesia 51 H5
Rhodiad-y-brenin 16 A3
Rhodmad 26 E1
Rhonadale 73 F7
Rhonehouse (Kelton Hill) 65 H5
Rhoose 18 D5
Rhos Carmar 17 G2
Rhos NPT 18 A1
Rhos Common 38 B4
Rhosaman 27 G7
Rhoscolyn 46 A5
Rhoscrowther 16 C5
Rhosesmor 48 B6
Rhos-fawr 36 C2
Rhosgadfan 46 D7
Rhos-goch IoA 46 C4
Rhosgoch Powys 28 A4
Rhos-hill 16 E1
Rhoshirwaun 36 A3
Rhoslan 36 D1
Rhoslefain 36 E5
Rhosllanerchrugog 38 B1
Rhoslligwy 46 C4
Rhosmaen 17 K3
Rhosmeirch 46 C5
Rhosneigr 46 B5
Rhosnesni 48 C7
Rhôs-on-Sea 47 G4
Rhossili 17 H7
Rhosson 16 A3
Rhostrehwfa 46 C5
Rhostryfan 46 C7
Rhostyllen 38 C1
Rhos-y-bol 46 C4
Rhos-y-brithdir 38 A3
Rhosycaerau 16 C2
Rhos-y-garth 27 F1
Rhos-y-gwaliau 37 J2
Rhos-y-llan 36 B2
Rhos-y-mawn 47 G6
Rhos-y-Meirch 28 B2
R.H.S. Garden Harlow Carr NYorks HG3 1QB 57 H4
R.H.S. Garden Hyde Hall Essex CM3 8ET 24 D2
R.H.S. Garden Rosemoor Devon EX38 8PH 6 D4
R.H.S. Garden Wisley Surr GU23 6QB 22 D6
Rhu 74 A2
Rhuallt 47 J5
Rhubodach 73 J3
Rhuddall Heath 48 E6
Rhuddlan 47 J5
Rhue 83 M1
Rhulen 28 A4
Rhunahaorine 73 F6
Rhyd Gwyn 37 F1
Rhyd Powys 37 J5
Rhydargaeau 17 H3
Rhydcymerau 17 J2
Rhyd-Ddu 46 D7
Rhydding 18 A2
Rhydgaled 47 H6
Rhydlanfair 47 G7
Rhydlewis 17 G1
Rhydlios 36 A2
Rhydlydan Conwy 47 G7
Rhydlydan Powys 37 K6
Rhydolion 36 B3
Rhydowen 17 H1
Rhyd-Rosser 26 E2
Rhydspence 28 B4
Rhydtalog 48 B7
Rhyd-uchaf 37 H2
Rhyd-wen 37 J3
Rhyd-wyn 46 B4
Rhyd-y-ceirw 48 B7
Rhyd-y-clafdy 36 C2
Rhydycroesau 38 B2
Rhydyfelin Cere 26 E1
Rhydyfelin RCT 18 D3
Rhyd-y-foel 47 H5
Rhyd-y-fro 18 A1
Rhyd-y-groes 46 D6
Rhydymain 37 H3
Rhydymwyn 48 B6
Rhyd-yr-onnen 37 F5
Rhyd-y-sarn 37 F1
Rhydywrach 16 E4
Rhyl 47 J4
Rhyl Sun Centre Denb LL18 3AQ 47 J4
Rhymney 18 E1
Rhyn 38 C2
Rhynd 80 G8
Rhynie Aber 85 J8
Rhynie High 84 C3
Ribbesford 29 G1
Ribchester 56 B6
Ribigill 86 H4
Riby 52 E2
Riccall 58 C6
Riccarton 74 C7
Richards Castle 28 D2
Robin Hill Countryside Adventure Park IoW PO30 2NU 11 G6
Richings Park 22 D4
Richmond GtLon 22 E4
Richmond NYorks 62 B6
Richmond SYorks 51 G4
Rich's Holford 7 K2
Rickarton 81 P2
Rickerscote 40 B3
Rickford 19 H6
Rickinghall 34 E1
Rickleton 62 C1
Rickling 33 H5
Rickling Green 33 J6
Rickmansworth 22 D2
Riddell 70 A1
Riddings 51 G7
Riddlecombe 6 E4
Riddlesden 57 F5
Ridge Dorset 9 J6
Ridge Herts 23 F1
Ridge Wilts 9 J1
Ridge Green 23 G7
Ridge Lane 40 E6
Ridgebourne 27 K2
Ridgeway 51 G4
Ridgeway Cross 29 G4
Ridgeway Moor 51 G4
Ridgewell 34 B4
Ridgewood 13 H4
Ridgmont 32 C5
Ridham Dock 25 F5
Riding Gate 9 G2
Riding Mill 71 F7
Ridley 24 C5
Ridleywood 48 C7
Ridlington Norf 45 H2
Ridlington Rut 42 B5
Ridsdale 70 E5
Riechip 80 F6
Rievaulx 58 B1
Rift House 62 E3
Rigg 69 H7
Riggend 75 F4
Rigmaden Park 56 B1
Rigsby 53 H5
Rigside 75 G7
Riley Green 56 B7
Rileyhill 40 D4
Rilla Mill 4 C3
Rillaton 4 C3
Rillington 58 E2
Rimington 56 D5
Rimpton 9 F2
Rimswell 59 K7
Rinaston 16 C3
Ring o' Bells 48 D1
Ring of Brodgar (Heart of Neolithic Orkney) Ork KW16 3JZ 89 B6
Ringboy 93 M11
Ringford 65 G5
Ringinglow 50 E4
Ringland 45 F4
Ringles Cross 13 H4
Ringmer 13 H5
Ringmore Devon 5 G6
Ringmore Devon 5 K3
Ring's End 43 G5
Ringsend 92 D4
Ringsfield 45 J7
Ringsfield Corner 45 J7
Ringshall Herts 32 C7
Ringshall Suff 34 E3
Ringshall Stocks 34 E3
Ringstead Norf 44 B1
Ringstead N'hants 32 C1
Ringwood 10 C4
Ringwould 15 J3
Rinloan 84 G10
Rinsey 2 C6
Ripe 13 J6
Ripley Derbys 51 F7
Ripley Hants 10 C5
Ripley NYorks 57 H3
Ripley Surr 22 D6
Riplingham 59 F6
Ripon 57 J2
Rippingale 42 E3
Ripple Kent 15 J3
Ripple Worcs 29 H5
Ripponden 50 C1
Risabus 72 B6
Risbury 28 E3
Risby ERid 59 G6
Risby Suff 34 B2
Risca 19 F2
Rise 59 H5
Riseden 14 C4
Risegate 43 F3
Riseholme 52 C5
Riseley Bed 32 D2
Riseley W'ham 22 A5
Rishangles 35 F2
Rishton 56 C6
Rishworth 50 C1
Risinghurst 21 J1
Risley Derbys 41 G2
Risley Warr 49 F3
Risplith 57 H3
Rispond 86 G3
Rivar 21 G5
Rivenhall 34 C7
Rivenhall End 34 C7
River Kent 15 H3
River WSuss 12 C4
River Bank 33 J2
River Bridge 19 G7
River Link Boat Cruises Devon TQ6 9AJ 5 J6
Riverford Bridge 5 H4
Riverhead 23 J6
Riverside Cardiff 18 E4
Riverside NM&D 93 J15
Riverside Country Park Med ME7 2XH 24 E5
Riverside Museum & Tall Ship Glenlee Glas G3 8RS 118 D4
Riverton 6 E2
Riverview Park 24 C4
Riviera International Centre Torbay TQ2 5LZ 136 Torquay
Rivington 49 F1
Roa Island 55 F3
Roach Bridge 55 J7
Road Green 45 G6
Road Weedon 31 H3
Roade 31 J3
Roadhead 70 A6
Roadside High 87 P3
Roadside Ork 89 F3
Roadside of Kinneff 81 P3
Roadwater 7 J2
Roag 82 C6
Roast Green 33 H5
Roath 18 E4
Robert Burns Birthplace Museum SAyr KA7 4PQ 67 H2
Roberton ScBord 69 K2
Roberton SLan 68 E1
Robertsbridge 14 C5
Robertstown 18 D1
Roberttown 57 G7
Robeston Cross 16 B5
Robeston Wathen 16 D4
Robeston West 16 B5
Robin Hill Countryside Adventure Park IoW PO30 2NU 11 G6
Robin Hood Derbys 50 E5
Robin Hood Lancs 48 E1
Robin Hood WYorks 57 J7
Robin Hood's Bay 63 K6
Robinhood End 34 B5
Robins 12 B4
Robinsons Town 93 E10
Robinswood Hill Country Park Glos GL4 6SX 29 H7
Roborough Devon 6 D4
Roborough Plym 5 F4
Roby 48 D3
Roby Mill 48 E2
Rocester 40 D2
Roch 16 B3
Roch Bridge 16 B3
Roch Gate 16 B3
Rochdale 49 H1
Roche 3 G2
Rochester Med 24 D5
Rochester N'umb 70 D4
Rochester Cathedral Med ME1 1SX 24 D5
Rochford Essex 24 E2
Rochford Worcs 29 F2
Rock Corn 3 G1
Rock N'umb 71 H2
Rock Worcs 29 G1
Rock Ferry 48 C4
Rockbeare 7 J6
Rockbourne 10 C3
Rockcliffe Cumb 69 J7
Rockcliffe D&G 65 J5
Rockcliffe Cross 69 J7
Rockfield A&B 73 G5
Rockfield High 84 D2
Rockfield Mon 28 D7
Rockford 10 C4
Rockhampton 19 K2
Rockhead 4 A2
Rockingham 42 B6
Rockland All Saints 44 D6
Rockland St. Mary 45 H5
Rockland St. Peter 44 D6
Rockley 20 E4
Rockside 72 A4
Rockspring 92 D8
Rockstown 93 B9
Rockwell End 22 A3
Rockwell Green 7 K4
Rodborough 20 B1
Rodbourne 20 C3
Rodbridge Corner 34 C4
Rodd 28 C2
Roddam 71 F1
Rodden 9 F6
Rode 20 B6
Rode Heath 49 H7
Rodeheath 49 H6
Rodel (Roghadal) 88 F9
Roden 38 E4
Rodhuish 7 J2
Rodington 38 E4
Rodington Heath 38 E4
Rodley 29 G7
Rodmarton 20 C2
Rodmell 13 H6
Rodmersham 25 F5
Rodmersham Green 25 F5
Rodney Stoke 19 H6
Rodsley 40 E1
Rodway 19 F7
Roe Cross 49 J3
Roe Green 33 G5
Roecliffe 57 J3
Roehampton 23 F4
Roesound 89 M6
Roffey 12 E3
Rogart 87 K9
Rogate 12 B4
Rogerstone 19 F3
Rogiet 19 H3
Rokemarsh 21 K2
Roker 62 E1
Rollesby 45 J4
Rolleston Leics 42 A5
Rolleston Notts 51 K7
Rollestone 20 D7
Rolleston-on-Dove 40 E3
Rolston 59 J5
Rolstone 19 G5
Rolvenden 14 D4
Rolvenden Layne 14 D4
Romaldkirk 61 L4
Roman Bath House (Frontiers of the Roman Empire) EDun 119 D2
Roman Baths & Pump Room B&NESom BA1 1LZ 20 A5
Roman Fort (Frontiers of the Roman Empire) Falk 75 F3
Romanby 62 D7
Romanno Bridge 75 K6
Romansleigh 7 F3
Romesdal 82 E5
Romford Dorset 10 B4
Romford GtLon 23 J3
Romiley 49 J3
Romney Street 23 J5
Romney, Hythe & Dymchurch Railway Kent TN28 8PL 15 G4
Romsey 10 E2
Romsley Shrop 39 G7
Romsley Worcs 29 J1
Rona 82 G5
Ronachan 73 F5
Ronague 54 B6
Ronnachmore 72 B5
Rood End 40 C7
Rookhope 61 L2
Rookley 11 G6
Rookley Green 11 G6
Rooks Bridge 19 G6
Rook's Nest 7 J2
Rookwith 57 H1
Roos 59 J6
Roose 55 F3
Roosebeck 55 F3
Roosecote 55 F3
Rootham's Green 32 D3
Rootpark 75 H5
Ropley 11 H1
Ropley Dean 11 H1
Ropley Soke 11 H1
Ropsley 42 C2
Rora 85 Q5
Rorrington 38 C5
Roscavey 91 M10
Rose 2 E3
Rose Ash 7 F3
Rose Green Essex 34 D6
Rose Green WSuss 12 C7
Rose Hill 13 H5
Roseacre Kent 14 C2
Roseacre Lancs 55 H6
Rosebank 75 G6
Rosebrough 71 G1
Rosebush 16 D3
Rosecare 4 B1
Rosecliston 3 F3
Rosedale Abbey 63 H7
Roseden 71 F1
Rosehearty 85 P4
Rosehill 38 D4
Roselands 13 K6
Rosemarket 16 C5
Rosemarkie 84 B5
Rosemary Lane 7 K4
Rosemeilan 91 L12
Rosemount P&K 80 G6
Rosemount SAyr 67 H1
Rosenannon 3 G2
Rosenithon 3 F6
Rosevean 4 A5
Roseville 40 B6
Rosewell 76 A4
Roseworth 62 E4
Rosgill 61 G5
Roshven 79 J3
Roskhill 82 C6
Roskorwell 2 E6
Rosley 60 E2
Roslin 76 A4
Rosliston 40 E4
Rosliston Forestry Centre Derbys DE12 8JX 40 E4
Rosneath 74 A2
Ross D&G 65 G6
Ross N'umb 77 K7
Ross P&K 80 C8
Ross Priory 74 C2
Rosscor 91 F11
Rossdhu House 74 B2
Rossett 48 C7
Rossett Green 57 J4
Rosside 55 F2
Rossington 51 J3
Rosslea 91 M13
Rosslyn Chapel Midlo EH25 9PU 120 E6
Rossmore 10 B5
Ross-on-Wye 29 F6
Roster 87 Q6
Rostherne 49 G4
Rosthwaite Cumb 60 D5
Roston 40 D1
Rostrevor 93 G15
Rosudgeon 2 C6
Rosyth 75 K2
Rothbury 71 F3
Rother Valley Country Park SYorks S26 5PQ 51 F5
Rotherby 41 J4
Rotherfield 13 J3
Rotherfield Greys 22 A3
Rotherfield Peppard 22 A3
Rotherham 51 G3
Rothersthorpe 31 J3
Rotherwick 22 A6
Rothes 84 G6
Rothesay 73 J4
Rothiemurchus High PH22 1QH 84 D10
Rothienorman 85 M7
Rothiesholm 89 F5
Rothley Leics 41 H4
Rothley N'umb 71 F5
Rothney 85 L8
Rothwell Lincs 52 E3
Rothwell N'hants 42 B7
Rothwell WYorks 57 J7
Rotsea 59 G4
Rottal 81 J4
Rotten Row Bucks 22 A3
Rotten Row WMid 30 C1
Rottingdean 13 G6
Rottington 60 A5
Roud 11 G6
Roudham 44 D7
Rough Castle (Frontiers of the Roman Empire) Falk 75 G3
Rough Close 40 B2
Rough Common 15 G2
Rougham Norf 44 C3
Rougham Suff 34 D2
Rougham Green 34 D2
Roughburn 79 Q2
Roughhoft 92 H8
Roughlee 56 D5
Roughley 40 D6
Roughton Lincs 53 F6
Roughton Norf 45 G2
Roughton Shrop 39 G6
Round Bush 22 E2
Roundbush Green 33 J7
Roundham 8 D4
Roundhay 57 J6
Roundstreet Common 12 D4
Roundway 20 D5
Rous Lench 30 B3
Rousay 89 D4
Rousdon 8 B5
Rousham 31 F6
Rousham Gap 31 F6
Rousky 90 M8
Routenburn 73 K4
Routh 59 G5
Rout's Green 22 A2
Row Corn 4 A3
Row Cumb 55 H1
Row Cumb 61 H3
Row Heath 35 F7
Row Town 22 D5
Rowanburn 69 K6
Rowardennan Lodge 74 B1
Rowarth 50 C4
Rowbarton 8 B2
Rowberrow 19 H6
Rowde 20 C5
Rowden 6 E6
Rowen 47 F5
Rowfields 40 D1
Rowfoot 70 B7
Rowhedge 34 E6
Rowhook 12 E3
Rowington 30 D2
Rowland 50 E5
Rowland's Castle 11 J3
Rowlands Gill 62 B1
Rowledge 22 B7
Rowlestone 28 C6
Rowley Devon 7 F4
Rowley Dur 62 A2
Rowley Shrop 38 C5
Rowley Park 40 B3
Rowley Regis 40 B7
Rowly 22 D7
Rowner 11 G4
Rowney Green 30 B1
Rownhams 10 E3
Rowrah 60 B5
Rowsham 32 B7
Rowsley 50 E6
Rowstock 21 H3
Rowston 52 D7
Rowthorne 51 G6
Rowton ChesW&C 48 D6
Rowton Shrop 38 C4
Rowton Tel&W 39 F4
Roxburgh 77 F7
Roxby NLincs 52 C1
Roxby NYorks 63 H5
Roxhill 92 F7
Roxton 32 E3
Roxwell 24 C1
Royal Academy of Arts GtLon W1J 0BD 132 C3
Royal Albert Hall GtLon SW7 2AP 103 G7
Royal Albert Memorial Museum & Art Gallery Devon EX4 3RX 125 Exeter
Royal Armouries Museum, Leeds WYorks LS10 1LT 130 G5
Royal Artillery Barracks GtLon SE18 5DP 105 E8
Royal Bath & West Showground Som BA4 6QN 9 F1
Royal Botanic Garden Edin EH3 5LR 126 D1
Royal Botanic Gardens, Kew GtLon TW9 3AB 103 E8
Royal British Legion Village 14 C2
Royal Centre NG1 5ND 134 Nottingham
Royal Cornwall Museum Corn TR1 2SJ 3 F4
Royal Festival Hall GtLon SE1 8XX 132 F4
Royal Highland Showground Edin EH28 8NB 120 A2
Royal Horticultural Halls GtLon SW1P 2PB 132 D6
Royal Hospital Chelsea GtLon SW3 4SR 103 H8
Royal Leamington Spa 30 E2
Royal Mews, Buckingham Palace GtLon SW1W 0QH 132 B6
Royal Naval Museum PO1 3NH 135 Portsmouth
Royal Oak 48 D2
Royal Observatory Greenwich GtLon SE10 8XJ 105 D8
Royal Opera House GtLon WC2E 9DD 132 E3
Royal Pavilion B&H BN1 1EE 123 Brighton
Royal Scots Regimental Museum, The Edin EH1 2YT 126 E5
Royal Scottish Academy Edin EH2 2EL 126 F4
Royal Tunbridge Wells 13 J3
Royal Victoria Country Park Hants SO31 5GA 11 F4
Royal Welch Fusiliers Regimental Museum Gwyn LL55 2AY 46 C6
Royal Wootton Bassett 20 D3
Royal Yacht Britannia Edin EH6 6JJ 120 D1
Roybridge (Drochaid Ruaidh) 79 P2
Roydon Essex 33 H7
Roydon Norf 44 B3
Roydon Norf 44 E7
Roydon Hamlet 23 H1
Royston Herts 33 G4
Royston SYorks 51 F1
Royton 49 J2
Rozel 3 K6
Ruabon (Rhiwabon) 38 C1
Ruaig 78 B6
Ruan Lanihorne 3 F4
Ruan Major 2 D7
Ruan Minor 2 E7
Ruanaich 78 D8
Ruardean 29 F7
Ruardean Hill 29 F7
Ruardean Woodside 29 F7
Rubery 29 J1
Rubha Ban 79 M10
Ruckcroft 61 G2
Ruckinge 15 F4
Ruckland 53 G5
Rucklers Lane 22 D1
Ruckley 38 E5
Rudbaxton 16 C3
Rudby 62 E6
Rudchester 71 G7
Ruddington 41 H2
Ruddlemoor 4 A5
Rudford 29 G6
Rudge 20 B6
Rudgeway 19 K3
Rudgwick 12 D3
Rudhall 29 F6
Rudheath 49 F5
Rudley Green 24 E1
Rudloe 20 B4
Rudry 18 E3
Rudston 59 G3
Rudyard 49 J7
Rudyard Lake Staffs ST13 8RT 49 J7
Rufford 48 D1
Rufford Country Park Notts NG22 9DF 51 J6
Rufforth 58 B4
Ruffside 61 L1
Rugby 31 G1
Rugby Football Union, Twickenham GtLon TW1 1DZ 103 D9
Rugeley 40 C4
Ruishton 8 B2
Ruislip 23 D3
Ruislip Gardens 22 D3
Ruislip Manor 22 E3
Rum 82 D11
Rumbling Bridge 75 J1
Rumburgh 45 H7
Rumford 3 F1
Rumleigh 4 E4
Rumney 19 F4
Rumwell 7 K3
Runacraig 80 A9
Runcorn 48 E4
Runcton 12 B6
Runcton Holme 44 A5
Rundlestone 5 F3
Runfold 22 B7
Runhall 44 E5
Runham Norf 45 J4
Runham Norf 45 K5
Runnington 7 K3
Runsell Green 24 D1
Runshaw Moor 48 E1
Runswick Bay 63 J5
Runtaleave 80 H4
Runwell 24 D2
Ruscombe Glos 20 B1
Ruscombe W'ham 22 A4
Rush Green GtLon 23 J3
Rush Green Herts 33 F6
Rushall Here 29 F5
Rushall Norf 45 F7
Rushall Wilts 20 E6
Rushall WMid 40 C5
Rushbrooke 34 C2
Rushbury 38 E6
Rushden Herts 33 G5
Rushden N'hants 32 C2
Rushford Devon 4 E3
Rushford Norf 44 D7
Rushgreen 49 F4
Rushlake Green 13 K5
Rushmere 45 J7
Rushmere St. Andrew 35 G4
Rushmoor 22 B7
Rushock 29 H1
Rusholme 49 H3
Rushton ChesW&C 48 E6
Rushton N'hants 42 B7
Rushton Shrop 39 F5
Rushton Spencer 49 J6
Rushwick 29 H3
Rushy Green 13 H5
Rushyford 62 C4
Ruskie 80 B10
Ruskington 52 D7
Rusko 65 F5
Rusland 55 G1
Rusper 13 F3
Ruspidge 29 F7
Russ Hill 23 F7
Russell Green 34 B7
Russell's Green 14 C6
Russell's Water 22 A2
Russel's Green 35 G1
Rusthall 13 J3
Rustington 12 D6
Ruston 59 F1
Ruston Parva 59 G3
Ruswarp 63 J6
Rutherend 74 E5
Rutherford 76 E7
Rutherglen 74 E4
Ruthernbridge 4 A4
Ruthin (Rhuthun) Denb 47 K7
Ruthin VGlam 18 C4
Ruthrieston 85 P10
Ruthven Aber 85 K6
Ruthven Angus 80 H6
Ruthven High 84 B11
Ruthvoes 3 G2
Ruthwaite 60 D3
Ruthwell 69 F7
Rutland Water Rut LE15 8QL 42 B5
Ruyton-XI-Towns 38 C3
Ryal 71 F6
Ryal Fold 56 B7
Ryall Dorset 8 D5
Ryall Worcs 29 H4
Ryarsh 23 K6
Rydal 60 E6
Ryde 11 G5
Rydon 6 B5
Rye 14 E5
Rye Foreign 14 D5
Rye Harbour ESuss TN31 7TX 14 E6
Rye Harbour 14 E6
Rye Park 23 G1
Rye Street 29 G5
Ryebank 38 E2
Ryeford 29 F6
Ryehill 59 J7
Ryhall 42 D4
Ryhill 51 F1
Ryhope 62 E1
Rylands 41 H2
Rylstone 56 E4
Ryme Intrinseca 8 E3
Ryther 58 B6
Ryton Glos 29 G5
Ryton NYorks 58 D2
Ryton Shrop 39 G5
Ryton T&W 71 G7
Ryton-on-Dunsmore 30 E1

S

Sabden 56 C6
Sabden Fold 56 D6
Sackers Green 34 D5
Sacombe 33 G7
Sacombe Green 33 G7
Sacriston 62 C2
Sadberge 62 D5
Saddell 73 F7
Saddington 41 J6
Saddle Bow 44 A4
Sadgill 61 F6
Saffron Walden 33 J5
Sageston 16 D5
Saham Hills 44 D5
Saham Toney 44 C5
Saighdinis 88 C2
Saighton 48 D6
St. Abbs 77 H4
St. Agnes 2 E3
St Agnes Mining District (Cornwall & West Devon Mining Landscape) Corn 2 E3
St. Aidan's Winery N'umb TD15 2RX 77 K6
St. Albans 22 E1
St. Albans Cathedral Herts AL1 1BY 22 E1
St. Allen 3 F3
St. Andrews 81 L9
St. Andrew's & Blackfriars Halls Norf NR3 1AU 134 Norwich
St. Andrews Major 18 E4
St. Anne 3 J4
St. Anne's 55 G7
St. Ann's 69 F4
St. Ann's Chapel Corn 4 E3
St. Ann's Chapel Devon 5 G6
St. Anthony 3 F5
St. Anthony-in-Meneage 2 E6
St. Anthony's Hill 13 K6
St. Arvans 19 J2
St. Asaph (Llanelwy) 47 J5
St. Athan 18 D5
St. Aubin 3 J7
St. Audries 7 K1
St Augustine's Abbey (Canterbury Cathedral, St Augustine's Abbey, & St Martin's Church) Kent CT1 1PF 15 G2
St. Austell 4 A5
St. Bees 60 A5
St. Blazey 4 A5
St. Blazey Gate 4 A5
St. Boswells 76 D7
St. Botolph's Church, Boston Lincs PE21 6NP 43 G1
St. Brelade 3 J7
St. Breock 3 G1
St. Breward 4 A3
St. Briavels 19 J1
St. Brides 16 B4
St. Brides Major 18 B4
St. Bride's Netherwent 19 H3
St. Brides Wentlooge 19 F3
St. Bride's-super-Ely 18 D4
St. Budeaux 4 E5
St. Buryan 2 B6
St. Catherine 20 A5
St. Catherines 79 N10
St. Clears (Sanclêr) 17 F4
St. Cleer 4 C4
St. Clement Corn 3 F4
St. Clement Chanl 3 K7
St. Clether 4 C2
St. Colmac 73 J4
St. Columb Major 3 G2
St. Columb Minor 3 F2
St. Columb Road 3 G3
St. Combs 85 Q4
St. Cross South Elmham 45 G7
St. Cyrus 81 N4
St. Davids Fife 75 K2
St. David's (Tyddewi) Pembs 16 A3
St. David's P&K 80 E8
St. David's Hall CF10 1AH 124 Cardiff
St. Day 2 E4
St. Decumans 7 J1
St. Dennis 3 G3
St. Denys 11 F3
St. Dogmaels (Llandudoch) 16 E1
St. Dogwells 16 C3
St. Dominick 4 E4
St. Donats 18 C5
St. Edith's Marsh 20 C5
St. Endellion 3 G1
St. Enoder 3 F3
St. Erme 3 F4
St. Erney 4 D5
St. Erth 2 C5
St. Erth Praze 2 C5
St. Ervan 3 F1
St. Eval 3 F2
St. Ewe 3 G4
St. Fagans 18 E4
St. Fagans National History Museum Cardiff CF5 6XB 99 A5
St. Fergus 85 Q5
St. Fillans 80 B8
St. Florence 16 D5
St. Gennys 4 B1
St. George Bristol 19 K4
St. George Conwy 47 H5
St. Georges NSom 19 G5
St. George's Tel&W 39 G4
St. George's VGlam 18 D4
St. George's Hall, Liverpool Mersey L1 1JJ 131 D3
St. Germans 4 D5
St. Giles' Cathedral Edin EH1 1RE 126 F4
St. Giles in the Wood 6 D4
St. Giles on the Heath 6 B6
St. Harmon 27 J1
St. Helen Auckland 62 B4
St. Helena 45 F4
St. Helen's ESuss 14 D6
St. Helens IoW 11 H6
St. Helens Mersey 48 E3
St. Helier Chanl 3 J7
St. Helier GtLon 23 F5
St. Hilary Corn 2 C5
St. Hilary VGlam 18 D4
St. Hill 13 G3
St. Ibbs 32 E6
St. Illtyd 19 F1
St. Ippollitts 32 E6
St. Ishmael 17 G5
St. Ishmael's 16 B5
St. Issey 3 G1
St. Ive 4 D4
St. Ives Cambs 33 G1
St. Ives Corn 2 C4
St. Ives Dorset 10 C4
St. James South Elmham 45 H7
St. John Chanl 3 J6
St. John Corn 4 E5
St. John the Baptist Church, Cirencester Glos GL7 2NX 20 D1
St. John's GtLon 23 G4
St. John's IoM 54 B5
St. John's Surr 22 C6
St. John's Worcs 29 H3
St. John's Chapel Devon 6 D3
St. John's Chapel Dur 61 K3
St. John's Fen End 43 J4
St. John's Hall 62 A3
St. John's Highway 43 J4
St. John's Kirk 75 H7
St. John's Town of Dalry 68 B5
St. Judes 54 C4
St. Just 2 A5
St. Just in Roseland 3 F5
St Just Mining District (Cornwall & West Devon Mining Landscape) Corn 2 A5
St. Katherines 85 M7
St. Keverne 2 E6
St. Kew 4 A3
St. Kew Highway 4 A3
St. Keyne 4 C4
St. Lawrence Corn 4 A4
St. Lawrence Essex 25 F1
St. Lawrence IoW 11 G7
St. Lawrence's Church, Eyam Derbys S32 5QH 50 E5
St. Leonards Bucks 22 C1
St. Leonards Dorset 10 C4
St. Leonards ESuss 14 D7
St. Leonards Grange 11 F5
St. Leonard's Street 23 K6
St. Levan 2 A6
St. Lythans 18 E4
St. Mabyn 4 A3
St. Madoes 80 G8
St. Margaret South Elmham 45 H7
St. Margarets Here 28 C5
St. Margarets Herts 33 G7
St. Margarets Wilts 21 F5
St. Margaret's at Cliffe 15 J3
St Margaret's Church (Palace of Westminster & Westminster Abbey inc. St Margaret's Church) GtLon SW1P 3JX 105 A7
St. Margaret's Hope 89 D8
St. Mark's 54 B6
St. Martin Chanl 3 J5
St. Martin Chanl 3 K7
St. Martin Corn 2 E6
St. Martin Corn 4 C5
St. Martin-in-the-Fields Church GtLon WC2N 4JH 132 E3
St. Martin's IoS 2 C1
St. Martins P&K 80 G7
St. Martin's Shrop 38 C2
St Martin's Church (Canterbury Cathedral, St Augustine's Abbey, & St Martin's Church) Kent CT1 1PW 15 G2
St. Mary 3 J6
St. Mary Bourne 21 H6
St. Mary Church 18 D4
St. Mary Cray 23 H5
St. Mary Hill 18 C4
St. Mary Hoo 24 D4
St. Mary in the Marsh 15 F5
St. Mary Magdalene Chapel, Sandringham Norf PE35 6EH 44 A3
St. Mary the Virgin Church, Holy Island N'umb TD15 2RX 77 K6
St. Mary the Virgin Church, Oxford Oxon OX1 4AH 21 J1
St. Mary the Virgin Church, Rye ESuss TN31 7HE 14 E6
St. Marychurch 5 K4
St. Mary's IoS 2 C1
St. Mary's Ork 89 D7
St. Mary's Airport 2 C1
St. Mary's Bay 15 F5
St. Mary's Church, Whitby NYorks YO22 4JT 63 K5
St. Mary's Grove 19 H5
St. Maughans Green 28 D7
St. Mawes 3 F5
St. Mawgan 3 F2
St. Mellion 4 D4
St. Mellons 19 F3
St. Merryn 3 F1
St. Mewan 3 G3
St. Michael Church 8 C1
St. Michael Penkevil 3 F4
St. Michael South Elmham 45 H7
St. Michaels Fife 81 K8
St. Michaels Kent 14 D4
St. Michaels Worcs 28 E2
St. Michael's Church, Hathersage Derbys S32 1AJ 50 E4
St. Michael's Mount Corn TR17 0HT 2 C5
St. Michael's on Wyre 55 H5
St. Mildred's Church, Whippingham IoW PO32 6LP 11 G5
St. Minver 3 G1
St. Monans 81 L10
St. Mungo Museum of Religious Life & Art Glas G4 0RH 127 H3
St. Mungo's Cathedral Glas G4 0QZ 127 J3
St. Neot 4 B4
St. Neots 32 E2
St. Newlyn East 3 F3
St. Nicholas Pembs 16 C2
St. Nicholas VGlam 18 D4
St. Nicholas at Wade 25 J5
St. Ninians 75 F1
St. Osyth 35 F7
St. Ouen 3 J7
St. Owen's Cross 28 E6
St. Paul's Cathedral, London GtLon EC4M 8AD 132 J2
St. Paul's Cray 23 H5
St. Paul's Walden 32 E6
St. Peter 3 J7
St. Peter Port 3 J5
St. Peter's 25 K5
St. Petrox 16 C6
St. Pinnock 4 C4
St. Quivox 67 H1
St. Ruan 2 E7
St. Sampson 3 J5
St. Saviour Chanl 3 H5
St. Saviour Chanl 3 K7
St. Stephen 3 G3
St. Stephens Corn 4 E5
St. Stephens Corn 6 B7
St. Stephens Herts 22 E1
St. Teath 4 A2
St. Thomas 7 H6
St. Tudy 4 A3
St. Twynnells 16 C6
St. Veep 4 B5
St. Vigeans 81 M6
St. Wenn 3 G2
St. Weonards 28 D6
St. Winnow 4 B5
St. Winwaloe's Church, Gunwalloe Corn TR12 7QE 2 D6
Saintbury 30 C5
Saintfield 93 K11
Salachail 79 M5
Salcombe 5 H7
Salcombe Regis 7 K7
Salcott 34 D7
Sale 49 G3
Sale Green 29 J3
Saleby 53 H5
Salehurst 14 C5
Salem Carmar 17 K3
Salem Cere 37 F7
Salem Gwyn 46 D7
Salen A&B 78 G6
Salen High 78 H4
Salendine Nook 50 D1
Salesbury 56 B6
Saleway 29 J3
Salford CenBeds 32 C5
Salford GtMan 49 H3
Salford Oxon 30 D6
Salford Priors 30 B3
Salfords 23 F7
Salhouse 45 H4
Saline 75 J1
Salisbury 10 C2
Salisbury Cathedral Wilts SP1 2EF 135 Salisbury
Salkeld Dykes 61 G3
Sallachy High 83 K7
Sallachy High 86 H9
Salle 45 F3
Salmonby 53 G5
Salperton 30 B6
Salph End 32 D3
Salsburgh 75 G4
Salt 40 B3
Salt Hill 22 C3
Salt Holme 62 E4
Saltaire WYorks BD17 7EF 57 G6
Saltaire 57 G6
Saltash 4 E5
Saltburn 84 B3
Saltburn-by-the-Sea 63 G4
Saltburn Cliff Lift R&C TS12 1DP 63 G4
Saltby 42 B3
Saltcoats Cumb 60 B7
Saltcoats NAyr 74 A6
Saltcotes 55 G7
Saltdean 13 G6
Salterbeck 60 A4
Salterforth 56 D5
Saltergate 63 J7
Salterswall 49 F6
Saltfleet 53 H3
Saltfleetby All Saints 53 H3
Saltfleetby St. Clements 53 H3
Saltfleetby St. Peter 53 H4
Saltford 19 K5
Salthaugh Grange 59 J7
Salthouse 44 E1
Saltley 40 C7
Saltmarshe 58 D7
Saltney 48 C6
Salton 58 D1
Saltrens 6 C3
Saltwick 71 G6
Saltwood 15 G4
Salvington 12 E6
Salwarpe 29 H2
Salwayash 8 D5
Sambourne 30 B2
Sambrook 39 G3
Samlesbury 56 B6
Sampford Arundel 7 K4
Sampford Brett 7 J1
Sampford Courtenay 6 E5
Sampford Moor 7 K4
Sampford Peverell 7 J4
Sampford Spiney 5 F3
Samsonagh 91 H12
Samuelston 76 C3
Sanaigmore 72 A3
Sancreed 2 B6
Sancton 59 F6
Sand 19 H7
Sand Hutton 58 C4
Sandaig A&B 78 A6
Sandaig High 82 H10
Sandal Magna 51 F1
Sanday 89 F3
Sanday Airfield 89 F3
Sandbach 49 G6
Sandbank 73 K2
Sandbanks 10 B6
Sandend 85 K4
Sanderstead 23 G5
Sandford Cumb 61 J5
Sandford Devon 7 G5
Sandford Dorset 9 J6
Sandford IoW 11 G6
Sandford NSom 19 H6
Sandford Shrop 38 C3
Sandford Shrop 38 E2
Sandford SLan 75 F6
Sandford Orcas 9 F2
Sandford St. Martin 31 F6
Sandford-on-Thames 21 J1
Sandgarth 89 E6
Sandgate 15 H4
Sandgreen 65 F5
Sandhaven 85 P4
Sandhead 64 A5
Sandhills Dorset 8 E4
Sandhills Dorset 9 F3
Sandhills Surr 12 C3
Sandhills WYorks 57 J6
Sandhoe 70 E7
Sandholme ERid 58 E6
Sandholme Lincs 43 G2
Sandhurst BrackF 22 B5
Sandhurst Glos 29 H6
Sandhurst Kent 14 C5

Sandhurst Cross 14 C5
Sandhutton 57 J1
Sandiacre 41 G2
Sandilands 53 J4
Sandiway 49 F5
Sandleheath 10 C3
Sandleigh 21 H1
Sandling 14 C2
Sandlow Green 49 G6
Sandness 89 K7
Sandon Essex 24 D1
Sandon Herts 33 G5
Sandon Staffs 40 B3
Sandown 11 H6
Sandplace 4 C5
Sandquoy 89 G3
Sandridge Devon 5 J5
Sandridge Herts 32 E7
Sandridge Wilts 20 C5
Sandringham 44 A3
Sandrocks 13 G4
Sandsend 63 J5
Sandside 55 H1
Sandsound 89 M8
Sandtoft 51 K2
Sanduck 7 F7
Sandway 14 D2
Sandwell 40 C7
Sandwell Park Farm WMid B71 4BG 106 F3
Sandwell Valley Country Park WMid B71 4BG 106 F3
Sandwich 15 J2
Sandwick Cumb 60 F5
Sandwick Shet 89 N10
Sandwick (Sanndabhaig) Na H-E. Siar 88 K4
Sandwith 60 A5
Sandy Carmar 17 H5
Sandy CenBeds 32 E4
Sandy Bank 53 F7
Sandy Haven 16 B5
Sandy Lane Wilts 20 C5
Sandy Lane Wrex 38 D1
Sandy Lane WYorks 57 G6
Sandy Way 11 F6
Sandycroft 48 C6
Sandygate Devon 5 J3
Sandygate IoM 54 C4
Sandyhills 65 J5
Sandylands 55 H3
Sandypark 7 F7
Sandyway 28 D6
Sangobeg 86 G3
Sankyn's Green 29 G2
Sanna 72 D4
Sannox 73 J6
Sanquhar 68 C3
Santon Bridge 60 C6
Santon Downham 44 C7
Sant-y-Nyll 18 D4
Sapcote 41 G6
Sapey Common 29 G2
Sapiston 34 D1
Sapperton Derbys 40 D2
Sapperton Glos 20 C1
Sapperton Lincs 42 D2
Saracen's Head 43 G3
Sarclet 87 R5
Sardis 16 C5
Sarisbury 11 G4
Sark 3 K6
Sark Dark Sky Island Channel Islands 3 K6
Sarn Bridgend 18 C3
Sarn Powys 38 B6
Sarn Bach 36 C3
Sarn Meyllteyrn 36 B2
Sarnau Carmar 17 G4
Sarnau Cere 26 C3
Sarnau Gwyn 37 J2
Sarnau Powys 27 K5
Sarnau Powys 38 B4
Sarnesfield 28 C3
Saron Carmar 17 G2
Saron Carmar 17 K4
Saron Gwyn 46 C7
Saron Gwyn 46 D6
Sarratt 22 D2
Sarre 25 J5
Sarsden 30 D6
Sartfield 54 C4
Satley 62 B2
Satron 61 L7
Satterleigh 6 E3
Satterthwaite 60 E7
Sauchen 85 L9
Sauchie 75 G1
Sauchrie 67 H2
Saughall 48 C5
Saughall Massie 48 B4
Saughtree 70 A4
Saul Glos 20 A1
Saul NM&D 93 L12
Saundby 51 K4
Saundersfoot 16 E5
Saunderton 22 A1
Saunton 6 C2
Sausthorpe 53 G6
Saval 86 H9
Savalbeg 86 H9
Saverley Green 40 B2
Savile Town 57 H7
Sawbridge 31 G2
Sawbridgeworth 33 H7
Sawdon 59 F1
Sawley Derbys 41 G2
Sawley Lancs 56 C5
Sawley NYorks 57 H3
Sawston 33 H4
Sawtry 42 E7
Saxby Leics 42 B4
Saxby Lincs 52 D4
Saxby All Saints 52 C1
Saxelbye 41 J3
Saxham Street 34 E2
Saxilby 52 B5
Saxlingham 44 E2
Saxlingham Green 45 G6
Saxlingham Nethergate 45 G6
Saxlingham Thorpe 45 G6
Saxmundham 35 H2
Saxon Street 33 K3
Saxondale 41 J2
Saxtead 35 G2
Saxtead Green 35 G2
Saxtead Little Green 35 G2
Saxthorpe 45 F2
Saxton 57 K6
Sayers Common 13 F5
Scackleton 58 C2
Scadabhagh 88 G8
Scaddy 93 K11
Scaftworth 51 J3
Scagglethorpe 58 E2
Scaitcliffe 56 C7
Scalasaig 72 B1
Scalby ERid 58 E7
Scalby NYorks 59 G1
Scaldwell 31 J1
Scale Houses 61 G2
Scaleby 69 K7
Scalebyhill 69 K7
Scales Cumb 55 F2
Scales Cumb 60 E4
Scalford 42 A3
Scaling 63 H5
Scaliscro 88 G5
Scalloway 89 M9
Scalpay (Eilean Scalpaigh) 88 H8
Scamblesby 53 F5
Scampston 58 E2
Scampton 52 C5
Scaniport 84 A7
Scapa 89 D7
Scapegoat Hill 50 C1
Scarborough 59 G1
Scarborough Sea Life & Marine Sanctuary NYorks YO12 6RP 59 G1
Scarcewater 3 G3
Scarcliffe 51 G6
Scarcroft 57 J5
Scardroy 83 N5
Scarfskerry 87 Q2
Scargill 62 A5
Scarinish 78 B6
Scarisbrick 48 C1
Scarning 44 D4
Scarrington 42 A1
Scarrowhill 61 G1
Scarth Hill 48 D2
Scarthingwell 57 K6
Scartho 53 F2
Scaur D&G 65 J3
Scaur (Kippford) D&G 65 J5
Scarva 93 F12
Scawby 52 C2
Scawby Brook 52 C2
Scawton 58 B1
Scayne's Hill 13 G4
Scethrog 28 A6
Schaw 67 J1
Scholar Green 49 H7
Scholes SYorks 51 F3
Scholes WYorks 50 D2
Scholes WYorks 57 G7
Scholes WYorks 57 J6
School Green 49 F6
School House 8 C4
Schoose 60 B4
Sciberscross 87 K9
Science Museum GtLon SW7 2DD 103 G7
Scilly Isles (Isles of Scilly) 2 C1
Scissett 50 E1
Scleddau 16 C2
Sco Ruston 45 G3
Scofton 51 J4
Scolboa 92 G7
Scole 35 F1
Scollogstown 93 K13
Scone 80 G8
Sconser 82 F7
Scopwick 52 D7
Scoraig 83 L1
Scorborough 59 G5
Scorrier 2 E4
Scorriton 5 H4
Scorton Lancs 55 J5
Scorton NYorks 62 C6
Scot Hay 39 G1
Scotby 60 F1
Scotch Corner 62 C6
Scotch Street 93 E11
Scotch Town 90 M8
Scotch Whisky Heritage Centre Edin EH1 2NE 126 F4
Scotforth 55 H4
Scothern 52 D5
Scotland 42 D2
Scotland End 30 E5
Scotland Street 34 D5
Scotland Street School Museum of Education Glas G5 8QB 127 C6
Scotlandwell 80 G10
Scotnish 73 F2
Scots' Gap 71 F5
Scotston 80 E6
Scotstoun 74 D4
Scotstown 79 K4
Scott Willoughby 42 D2
Scotter 52 B2
Scotterthorpe 52 B2
Scottish Exhibition & Conference Centre (S.E.C.C.) Glas G3 8YW 127 B4
Scottish National Gallery of Modern Art Edin EH4 3DR 126 B4
Scottish National Portrait Gallery Edin EH2 1JD 126 F3
Scottish Parliament Edin EH99 1SP 126 H4
Scottish Seabird Centre, North Berwick ELoth EH39 4SS 76 D2
Scottish Wool Centre, Aberfoyle Stir FK8 3UQ 80 A10
Scottlethorpe 42 D3
Scotton Lincs 52 B3
Scotton NYorks 57 J4
Scotton NYorks 62 B7
Scottow 45 G3
Scoughall 76 E2
Scoulton 44 D5
Scounslow Green 40 C3
Scourie 86 D5
Scousburgh 89 M11
Scouthead 49 J2
Scrabster 87 P2
Scrafield 53 G6
Scraghy 91 J9
Scrainwood 70 E3
Scralea 90 J9
Scrane End 43 G1
Scraptoft 41 J5
Scratby 45 K4
Scrayingham 58 D4
Scredington 42 D1
Scremby 53 H6
Scremerston 77 J6
Screveton 42 A1
Scribbagh 91 F12
Scriven 57 J4
Scronkey 55 H5
Scrooby 51 J3
Scropton 40 D2
Scrub Hill 53 F7
Scruton 62 D7
Sculthorpe 44 C2
Scunthorpe 52 B1
Scurlage 17 H7
Sea 8 C3
Sea Life Centre, Blackpool FY1 5AA 121 Blackpool
Sea Life Centre, Brighton B&H BN2 1TB 123 Brighton
Sea Life Centre, Great Yarmouth Norf NR30 3AH 45 K5
Sea Life London Aquarium GtLon SE1 7PD 132 F5
Sea Life Sanctuary, Hunstanton Norf PE36 5BH 44 A1
Sea Mills 19 J4
Sea Palling 45 J3
Seaborough 8 D4
Seaburn 71 K7
Seacombe 48 C3
Seacroft Lincs 53 J6
Seacroft WYorks 57 J6
Seadyke 43 G2
Seafield A&B 73 F2
Seafield NM&D 93 H15
Seafield SAyr 67 H1
Seafield WLoth 75 J4
Seaford 13 H7
Seaforde 93 K12
Seaforth 48 C3
Seagrave 41 J4
Seagry Heath 20 C3
Seaham 62 E2
Seaham Grange 62 E1
Seahouses 77 K7
Seal 23 J6
Sealand 48 C6
Seale 22 B7
Sea-Life Adventure S'end SS1 2ER 24 E3
Sealyham 16 C3
Seamer NYorks 59 G1
Seamer NYorks 62 E5
Seamill 73 K6
Seapatrick 93 G12
SeaQuarium, Rhyl Denb LL18 3AF 47 J4
Searby 52 D2
Seasalter 25 G5
Seascale 60 B6
Seathorne 53 J6
Seathwaite Cumb 60 D5
Seathwaite Cumb 60 D7
Seatle 55 G1
Seatoller 60 D5
Seaton Corn 4 D5
Seaton Cumb 60 B3
Seaton Devon 8 B5
Seaton Dur 62 D1
Seaton ERid 59 H5
Seaton N'umb 71 J6
Seaton Rut 42 C6
Seaton Burn 71 H6
Seaton Carew 63 F4
Seaton Delaval 71 J6
Seaton Junction 8 B5
Seaton Ross 58 D5
Seaton Sluice 71 J6
Seaton Tramway Devon EX12 2NQ 8 B5
Seatown 8 D5
Seave Green 63 F6
Seaview 11 H5
Seaville 60 C1
Seavington St. Mary 8 D3
Seavington St. Michael 8 D3
Seawick 35 F7
Sebastopol 19 F2
Sebergham 60 E2
Seckington 40 E5
Second Coast 83 K1
Sedbergh 61 H7
Sedbury 19 J2
Sedbusk 61 K7
Seddington 32 E4
Sedgeberrow 30 B5
Sedgebrook 42 B2
Sedgefield 62 D4
Sedgeford 44 B2
Sedgehill 9 H2
Sedgemere 30 D1
Sedgley 40 B6
Sedgwick 55 J1
Sedlescombe 14 C6
Sedlescombe Street 14 C6
Seend 20 C5
Seend Cleeve 20 C5
Seer Green 22 C2
Seething 45 H6
Sefton 48 C2
Seghill 71 H6
Seifton 38 D7
Seighford 40 A3
Seil 79 J9
Seilebost 88 F8
Seion 46 D6
Seisdon 40 A6
Seisiadar 88 L4
Seized! Revenue & Customs Uncovered Mersey L3 4AQ 131 B5
Selattyn 38 B2
Selborne 11 J1
Selby 58 C6
Selham 12 C4
Selhurst 23 G5
Selkirk 69 K1
Sellack 28 E6
Sellafield 60 B6
Sellafield Visitors Centre Cumb CA20 1PG 60 B6
Sellafirth 89 P3
Sellindge 15 G4
Selling 15 F2
Sells Green 20 C5
Selly Oak 40 C7
Selmeston 13 J6
Selsdon 23 G5
Selsey 12 B7
Selsfield Common 13 G3
Selside Cumb 61 G7
Selside NYorks 56 C2
Selsley 20 B1
Selstead 15 H3
Selston 51 G7
Selworthy 7 H1
Semblister 89 M7
Semer 34 D4
Semington 20 B5
Semley 9 H2
Send 22 D6
Send Marsh 22 D6
Senghenydd 18 E2
Sennen 2 A6
Sennen Cove 2 A6
Sennybridge 27 J6
Senwick 65 G6
Sequer's Bridge 5 G5
Serlby 51 J4
Serpentine Gallery GtLon W2 3XA 103 G7
Serrington 10 B1
Seskinore 91 L10
Sessay 57 K2
Setchey 44 A4
Setley 10 E4
Settiscarth 89 C6
Settle 56 D3
Settrington 58 E2
Seven Ash 7 K2
Seven Bridges 20 E2
Seven Kings 23 H3
Seven Sisters 18 B1
Seven Springs 29 J7
Sevenhampton Glos 30 B6
Sevenhampton Swin 21 F2
Sevenoaks 23 J6
Sevenoaks Weald 23 J6
Severn Beach 19 J3
Severn Stoke 29 H4
Severn Valley Railway Shrop DY12 1BG 29 H1
Sevick End 32 D3
Sevington 15 F3
Sewards End 33 J5
Sewardstone 23 G2
Sewerby 59 H3
Sewerby Hall & Gardens ERid YO15 1EA 59 J3
Seworgan 2 E5
Sewstern 42 B3
Seymour Villas 6 C1
Sezincote 30 C5
Sgarasta Mhòr 88 F8
Sgiogarstaigh (Skigersta) 88 L1
Shabbington 21 K1
Shackerley 40 A5
Shackerstone 41 F5
Shackleford 22 C7
Shadfen 71 H5
Shadforth 62 D2
Shadingfield 45 J7
Shadoxhurst 14 E4
Shadsworth 56 C7
Shadwell Norf 44 D7
Shadwell WYorks 57 J5
Shaftenhoe End 33 H5
Shaftesbury 9 H2
Shafton 51 F1
Shakespeare's Birthplace Warks CV37 6QW 136 Stratford-upon-Avon
Shakespeare's Globe Theatre GtLon SE1 9DT 132 J3
Shalbourne 21 G5
Shalcombe 10 E6
Shalden 21 K7
Shalden Green 22 A7
Shaldon 5 K3
Shalfleet 11 F6
Shalford Essex 34 B6
Shalford Surr 22 D7
Shalford Green 34 B6
Shallowford Devon 7 F1
Shallowford Staffs 40 A3
Shalmsford Street 15 F2
Shalstone 31 H5
Shalunt 73 J3
Shambellie 65 K4
Shamley Green 22 D7
Shanaghy 91 K14
Shandon 74 A2
Shandwick 84 C3
Shangton 42 A6
Shankend 70 A3
Shankhouse 71 H6
Shankill 93 G13
Shanklin 11 G6
Shanklin Chine IoW PO37 6BW 11 G6
Shannochie 66 D1
Shantron 74 B2
Shap 61 G5
Shapinsay 89 E6
Shapwick Dorset 9 J4
Shapwick Som 8 D1
Sharcott 20 E6
Shard End 40 D7
Shardlow 41 G2
Shareshill 40 B5
Sharlston 51 F1
Sharlston Common 51 F1
Sharnal Street 24 D4
Sharnbrook 32 C3
Sharneyford 56 D7
Sharnford 41 G6
Sharnhill Green 9 G4
Sharow 57 J2
Sharp Street 45 H3
Sharpenhoe 32 D5
Sharperton 70 E3
Sharpham House 5 J5
Sharpness 19 K1
Sharpthorne 13 G3
Sharrington 44 E2
Shatterford 39 G7
Shatterling 15 H2
Shaugh Prior 5 F4
Shave Cross 8 D5
Shavington 49 G7
Shaw GtMan 49 J2
Shaw Swin 20 E3
Shaw WBerks 21 H5
Shaw Wilts 20 B5
Shaw Green Herts 33 F5
Shaw Green NYorks 57 H4
Shaw Mills 57 H3
Shaw Side 49 J2
Shawbost (Siabost) 88 H3
Shawbury 38 E3
Shawell 41 H7
Shawfield GtMan 49 H1
Shawfield Staffs 50 C6
Shawford 11 F2
Shawforth 56 D7
Shawhead 65 J3
Shawtonhill 74 E6
Shean 93 F15
Sheanachie 66 B2
Shearington 69 F7
Shearsby 41 J6
Shebbear 6 C5
Shebdon 39 G3
Shebster 87 N3
Shedfield 11 G3
Sheen 50 D6
Sheepridge 50 D1
Sheepscombe 29 H7
Sheepstor 5 F4
Sheepwash Devon 6 C5
Sheepwash N'umb 71 H5
Sheepway 19 H4
Sheepy Magna 41 F5
Sheepy Parva 41 F5
Sheering 33 J7
Sheerness 25 F4
Sheet 11 J2
Sheetrim AB&C 93 C13
Sheetrim F&O 91 J14
Sheffield 51 F4
Sheffield Botanic Gardens SYorks S10 2LN 111 B4
Sheffield Bottom 21 K5
Sheffield Green 13 H4
Sheffield Park Garden ESuss TN22 3QX 13 H4
Shefford 32 E5
Shefford Woodlands 21 G4
Sheigra 86 D3
Sheinton 39 F5
Shelderton 28 D1
Sheldon Derbys 50 D6
Sheldon Devon 7 K5
Sheldon WMid 40 D7
Sheldwich 15 F2
Sheldwich Lees 15 F2
Shelf Bridgend 18 C3
Shelf WYorks 57 G7
Shelfanger 45 F7
Shelfield Warks 30 C2
Shelfield WMid 40 C5
Shelfield Green 30 C2
Shelford 41 J1
Shellbrook 41 F4
Shellbrook Hill 38 C1
Shelley Essex 23 J1
Shelley Suff 34 E5
Shelley WYorks 50 E1
Shellingford 21 G2
Shellow Bowells 24 C1
Shelsley Beauchamp 29 G2
Shelsley Walsh 29 G2
Shelswell 31 H5
Shelthorpe 41 H4
Shelton Bed 32 D2
Shelton Norf 45 G6
Shelton Notts 42 A1
Shelton Shrop 38 D4
Shelve 38 C6
Shelwick 28 E4
Shelwick Green 28 E4
Shenfield 24 C2
Shenington 30 E4
Shenley 22 E1
Shenley Brook End 32 B5
Shenley Church End 32 B5
Shenleybury 22 E1
Shenmore 28 C5
Shennanton 64 D4
Shenstone Staffs 40 D5
Shenstone Worcs 29 H1
Shenstone Woodend 40 D5
Shenton 41 F5
Shenval 84 G8
Shepeau Stow 43 G4
Shephall 33 F6
Shepherd's Bush 23 F4
Shepherd's Green 22 A3
Shepherd's Patch 20 A1
Shepherdswell (Sibertswold) 15 H3
Shepley 50 D2
Shepperdine 19 K2
Shepperton 22 D5
Shepreth 33 G4
Shepreth Wildlife Park Cambs SG8 6PZ 33 G4
Shepshed 41 G4
Shepton Beauchamp 8 D3
Shepton Mallet 19 K7
Shepton Montague 9 F1
Shepway 14 C2
Sheraton 62 E3
Sherborne Dorset 9 F3
Sherborne Glos 30 C7
Sherborne St. John 21 K6
Sherbourne 30 D2
Sherbourne Street 34 D4
Sherburn Dur 62 D2
Sherburn NYorks 59 F2
Sherburn Hill 62 D2
Sherburn in Elmet 57 K6
Shere 22 D7
Shereford 44 C3
Sherfield English 10 D2
Sherfield on Loddon 21 K6
Sherford Devon 5 H6
Sherford Som 8 B2
Sheriff Hutton 58 C3
Sheriffhales 39 G4
Sheringham 45 F1
Sheringham Park Norf NR26 8TL 45 F1
Sherington 32 B4
Shernal Green 29 J2
Shernborne 44 B2
Sherramore 83 R11
Sherrington 9 J1
Sherston 20 B3
Sherwood 41 H1
Sherwood Forest Country Park Notts NG21 9HN 51 J6
Sherwood Forest Fun Park Notts NG21 9QA 51 J6
Sherwood Green 6 D3
Sherwood Pines Forest Park Notts NG21 9JL 51 J6
Shetland Islands 89 L7
Shevington 48 E2
Shevington Moor 48 E1
Sheviock 4 D5
Shide 11 G6
Shiel Bridge (Drochaid Sheile) 83 K9
Shieldaig High 83 J3
Shieldaig High 83 J5
Shieldhill 75 G3
Shielfoot 78 H3
Shifford 21 G1
Shifnal 39 G5
Shilbottle 71 G3
Shildon 62 C4
Shillanavogy 92 H6
Shillingford Devon 7 H3
Shillingford Oxon 21 J2
Shillingford Abbot 7 H7
Shillingford St. George 7 H7
Shillingstone 9 H3
Shillington 32 E5
Shillmoor 70 D3
Shilstone 6 D5
Shilton Oxon 21 F1
Shilton Warks 41 G7
Shimpling Norf 45 F7
Shimpling Suff 34 C3
Shimpling Street 34 C3
Shincliffe 62 D2
Shiney Row 62 D1
Shinfield 22 A5
Shingay 33 G4
Shingham 44 B5
Shingle Street 35 H4
Shinn 93 G13
Shinness Lodge 86 H8
Shipbourne 23 J6
Shipbrookhill 49 F5
Shipdham 44 D5
Shipham 19 H6
Shiphay 5 J4
Shiplake 22 A4
Shiplake Row 22 A4
Shiplate 19 G6
Shipley N'umb 71 G2
Shipley Shrop 40 A6
Shipley WSuss 12 E4
Shipley WYorks 57 G6
Shipley Bridge Devon 5 G4
Shipley Bridge Surr 23 G7
Shipley Common 41 G1
Shipley Country Park Derbys DE75 7GX 108 E2
Shipmeadow 45 H6
Shippea Hill 44 A7
Shippon 21 H2
Shipston on Stour 30 D4
Shipton Glos 30 B7
Shipton NYorks 58 B4
Shipton Shrop 38 E6
Shipton Bellinger 21 F7
Shipton Gorge 8 D5
Shipton Green 12 B6
Shipton Moyne 20 B3
Shipton Oliffe 30 B7
Shipton Solers 30 B7
Shipton-on-Cherwell 31 F7
Shiptonthorpe 58 E5
Shipton-under-Wychwood 30 D7
Shirburn 21 K2
Shirdley Hill 48 C1
Shire Hall Gallery, Stafford Staffs ST16 2LD 40 B3
Shire Oak 40 C5
Shirebrook 51 H6
Shirecliffe 51 F3
Shiregreen 51 F3
Shirehampton 19 J4
Shiremoor 71 J6
Shirenewton 19 H2
Shireoaks 51 H4
Shirl Heath 28 D3
Shirland 51 F7
Shirley Derbys 40 E1
Shirley GtLon 23 G5
Shirley Hants 10 C5
Shirley Soton 11 F3
Shirley WMid 30 C1
Shirley Heath 30 C1
Shirley Warren 10 E3
Shirleywich 40 B3
Shirrell Heath 11 G3
Shirwell 6 D2
Shirwell Cross 6 D2
Shiskine 66 D1
Shittlehope 62 A3
Shobdon 28 C2
Shobley 10 C4
Shobrooke 7 G5
Shocklach 38 D1
Shocklach Green 38 D1
Shoeburyness 25 F3
Sholden 15 J2
Sholing 11 F3
Shoot Hill 38 D4
Shooter's Hill 23 H4
Shop Corn 3 F1
Shop Corn 6 A4
Shop Corner 35 G5
Shopnoller 7 K2
Shoptown 92 H7
Shore 49 J1
Shoreditch 23 G3
Shoreham 23 J5
Shoreham-by-Sea 13 F6
Shoresdean 77 H6
Shoreswood 77 H6
Shorley 11 G2
Shorncote 20 D2
Shorne 24 C4
Shorne Ridgeway 24 C4
Short Cross 38 B5
Short Green 44 E7
Short Heath Derbys 41 F4
Short Heath WMid 40 C6
Shortacombe 6 D7
Shortbridge 13 H4
Shortfield Common 22 B7
Shortgate 13 H5
Shortgrove 33 J5
Shorthampton 30 E6
Shortlands 23 G5
Shortlanesend 3 F4
Shorton 5 J4
Shorwell 11 F6
Shoscombe 20 A6
Shotatton 38 C3
Shotesham 45 G6
Shotgate 24 D2
Shotley N'hants 42 C6
Shotley Suff 35 G5
Shotley Bridge 62 A1
Shotley Gate 35 G5
Shotleyfield 62 A1
Shottenden 15 F2
Shottermill 12 B3
Shottery 30 C3
Shotteswell 31 F4
Shottisham 35 H4
Shottle 51 F7
Shottlegate 41 F1
Shotton Dur 62 D4
Shotton Dur 62 E3
Shotton Flints 48 C6
Shotton N'umb 71 H6
Shotton N'umb 77 G7
Shotton Colliery 62 D2
Shotts 75 G4
Shotwick 48 C5
Shouldham 44 A5
Shouldham Thorpe 44 A5
Shoulton 29 H3
Shover's Green 13 K3
Shrawardine 38 C4
Shrawley 29 H2
Shreding Green 22 D3
Shrewley 30 D2
Shrewsbury 38 D4
Shrewton 20 D7
Shri Venkateswara (Balaji Temple of the United Kingdom) WMid B69 3DU 106 E3
Shrigley 93 L11
Shrine of Our Lady of Walsingham (Anglican) Norf NR22 6EF 44 D2
Shripney 12 C6
Shrivenham 21 F3
Shropham 44 D6
Shroton (Iwerne Courtney) 9 H3
Shrub End 34 D6
Shucknall 28 E4
Shudy Camps 33 K4
Shugborough Estate Staffs ST17 0XB 40 B3
Shurdington 29 J7
Shurlock Row 22 B4
Shurnock 30 B2
Shurrery 87 N3
Shurrery Lodge 87 N4
Shurton 19 F7
Shustoke 40 E6
Shut Heath 40 A3
Shute Devon 7 G5
Shute Devon 8 B5
Shutford 30 E4
Shuthonger 29 H5
Shutlanger 31 J4
Shutt Green 40 A5
Shuttington 40 E5
Shuttlewood 51 G5
Shuttleworth 49 G1
Siadar Iarach 88 J2
Sibbaldbie 69 G5
Sibbertoft 41 J7
Sibdon Carwood 38 D7
Sibertswold (Shepherdswell) 15 H3
Sibford Ferris 30 E5
Sibford Gower 30 E5
Sible Hedingham 34 B5
Sibley's Green 33 K6
Sibsey 53 G7
Sibson Cambs 42 D6
Sibson Leics 41 F5
Sibster 87 R4
Sibthorpe 42 A1
Sibton 35 H2
Sibton Green 35 H1
Sicklesmere 34 C2
Sicklinghall 57 J5
Sidbury Devon 7 K6
Sidbury Shrop 39 F7
Sidcot 19 H6
Sidcup 23 H4
Siddal 57 G7
Siddington ChesE 49 H5
Siddington Glos 20 D2
Sidemoor 29 J1
Sidestrand 45 G2
Sidford 7 K6
Sidlesham 12 B7
Sidley 14 C7
Sidlow 23 F7
Sidmouth 7 K7
Sigford 5 H3
Sigglesthorne 59 H5
Sigingstone 18 C4
Signet 30 D7
Silbury Hill (Stonehenge, Avebury & Associated Sites) Wilts SN8 1QH 20 E5
Silchester 21 K5
Sileby 41 J4
Silecroft 54 E1
Silent Valley BT33 0HU 93 J14
Silfield 45 F6
Silian 26 E3
Silk Willoughby 42 D1
Silkstead 11 F2
Silkstone 50 E2
Silkstone Common 50 E2
Sill Field 55 J1
Silloth 60 C1
Sills 70 D3
Silpho 63 K7
Silsden 57 F5
Silsoe 32 D5
Silver End CenBeds 32 E4
Silver End Essex 34 C6
Silver Green 45 G6
Silver Hill 91 J12
Silver Street Kent 24 E5
Silver Street Som 8 E1
Silverbridge 93 E15
Silverbrook 90 L6
Silverburn 76 A4
Silvercraigs 73 G2
Silverdale Lancs 55 H2
Silverdale Staffs 40 A1
Silvergate 45 F3
Silverhill 14 C6
Silverlace Green 35 H3
Silverley's Green 35 G1
Silverstone 31 H4
Silverton 7 H5
Silvington 29 F1
Simister 49 H2
Simmondley 50 C3
Simonburn 70 D6
Simonsbath 7 F2
Simonside 71 J7
Simonstone Bridgend 18 C3
Simonstone Lancs 56 C6
Simprim 77 G6
Simpson 32 B5
Sinclair's Hill 77 G5
Sinclairston 67 J2
Sinderby 57 J1
Sinderhope 61 K1
Sindlesham 22 A5
Sinfin 41 F2
Singdean 70 A3
Singleton Lancs 55 G6
Singleton WSuss 12 B5
Singlewell 24 C4
Singret 48 C7
Sinkhurst Green 14 D3
Sinnahard 85 J9
Sinnington 58 D1
Sinton Green 29 H2
Sion Mills 90 K7
Sipson 22 D4
Sirhowy 28 A7
Sirhowy Valley Country Park Caerp NP11 7BD 99 C1
Sisland 45 H6
Sissinghurst 14 C4
Sissinghurst Castle Garden Kent TN17 2AB 14 D4
Siston 19 K4
Sithney 2 D6
Sittingbourne 25 F5
Siulaisiadar 88 L4
Six Ashes 39 G7
Six Hills 41 J3
Six Mile Bottom 33 J3
Six Road Ends 92 L9
Six Roads End 40 D3
Sixhills 52 E4
Sixmile 15 G3
Sixmilecross 91 M10
Sixpenny Handley 10 B3
Sizewell 35 J2
Skail 87 K5
Skaill Ork 89 B6
Skaill Ork 89 E7
Skara Brae (Heart of Neolithic Orkney) Ork KW16 3LR 89 B6
Skares Aber 85 L7
Skares EAyr 67 K2
Skateraw 77 F3
Skeabost 82 E6
Skeeby 62 C6
Skeffington 42 A5
Skeffling 53 G1
Skegby 51 H6
Skegness 53 J6
Skelberry 89 N6
Skelbo 84 B1
Skelbo Street 84 B1
Skelbrooke 51 H1
Skeld (Easter Skeld) 89 M8
Skeldon 67 H2
Skeldyke 43 G2
Skellingthorpe 52 C5
Skellister 89 N7
Skellow 51 H1
Skelmanthorpe 50 E1
Skelmersdale 48 D2
Skelmorlie 73 K4
Skelpick 87 K4
Skelton Cumb 60 F3
Skelton ERid 58 D7
Skelton NYorks 62 B6
Skelton (Skelton-in-Cleveland) R&C 63 G5
Skelton York 58 B4
Skelton-in-Cleveland (Skelton) R&C 63 G5
Skelton-on-Ure 57 J3
Skelwick 89 D3
Skelwith Bridge 60 E6
Skendleby 53 H6
Skendleby Psalter 53 H5
Skenfrith 28 D6
Skerne 59 G4
Skeroblingarry 66 B1
Skerray 87 J3
Skerries 93 C13
Skerton 55 H3
Sketchley 41 G6
Sketty 17 K6
Skewen 18 A2
Skewsby 58 C2
Skeyton 45 G3
Skeyton Corner 45 G3
Skidbrooke 53 H3
Skidbrooke North End 53 H3
Skidby 59 G6
Skilgate 7 H3
Skillington 42 B3
Skinburness 60 C1
Skinflats 75 H2
Skinningrove 63 H5
Skipness 73 G5
Skippool 55 G5
Skipsea 59 H4
Skipsea Brough 59 H4
Skipton 56 E4
Skipton Castle NYorks BD23 1AW 56 E4
Skipton-on-Swale 57 J2
Skipwith 58 C6
Skirbeck 43 G1
Skirbeck Quarter 43 G1
Skirethorns 56 E3
Skirlaugh 59 H6
Skirling 75 J7
Skirmett 22 A3
Skirpenbeck 58 D4
Skirwith Cumb 61 H3
Skirwith NYorks 56 C2
Skirza 87 R3
Skittle Green 22 A1
Skomer Island 16 A5
Skullomie 87 J3
Skyborry Green 28 B1
Skye 82 E7
Skye Green 34 C6
Skyreholme 57 F3
Slack Derbys 51 F6
Slack WYorks 56 E7
Slackhall 50 C4
Slackhead 85 J4
Slad 20 B1
Slade Devon 6 D1
Slade Devon 7 K5
Slade Pembs 16 C4
Slade Swan 17 H7
Slade Green 23 J4
Slade Hooton 51 H4
Sladesbridge 4 A3
Slaggyford 61 H1
Slaidburn 56 C4
Slaithwaite 50 C1
Slaley 61 L1
Slamannan 75 G3
Slane 92 H5
Slapton Bucks 32 C6
Slapton Devon 5 J6
Slapton N'hants 31 H4
Slatepit Dale 51 F6
Slatmore 91 M12
Slattadale 83 J3
Slaugham 13 F4
Slaughden 35 J3
Slaughterford 20 B4
Slawston 42 A6
Sleaford Hants 12 B3
Sleaford Lincs 42 D1
Sleagill 61 G5
Sleap 38 D3
Sledge Green 29 H5
Sledmere 59 F3
Sleights 63 J6
Slepe 9 J5
Slerra 6 B3
Slickly 87 Q3
Sliddery 66 D1
Slievenisky 93 J12
Sligachan 82 E8
Slimbridge 20 A1
Slimbridge Wildfowl & Wetlands Trust Glos GL2 7BT 20 A1
Slindon Staffs 40 A2
Slindon WSuss 12 C6
Slinfold 12 E3
Sling 19 J1
Slingsby 58 C2
Slip End CenBeds 32 D7
Slip End Herts 33 F5
Slipper Chapel, Houghton St. Giles Norf NR22 6AL 44 D2
Slipton 32 C1
Slitting Mill 40 C4
Slochd 84 B8
Slockavullin 73 G1
Slogarie 65 G4
Sloley 45 G3
Slongaber 65 J3
Sloothby 53 H5
Slough 22 C3
Slough Green Som 8 B2
Slough Green WSuss 13 F4
Sluggan 84 C8
Slyne 55 H3
Smailholm 76 E7
Small Dole 13 F5
Small Hythe 14 D4
Smallbridge 49 J1
Smallbrook 7 G6
Smallburgh 45 H3
Smallburn 68 B1
Smalldale 50 C5
Smalley 41 G1
Smallfield 23 G7
Smallford 22 E1
Smallridge 8 B4
Smallthorne 49 H7
Smallworth 44 E7
Smannell 21 G7
Smardale 61 J6
Smarden 14 D3
Smaull 72 A4
Smeatharpe 7 K4
Smeeth 15 F4
Smeeton Westerby 41 J6
Smestow 40 A6
Smethwick 40 C7
Smethwick Green 49 H6
Smirisary 78 H3
Smisby 41 F4
Smith End Green 29 G3
Smithfield 69 K7
Smithies 51 F2
Smithincott 7 J4
Smith's End 33 G5
Smith's Green Essex 33 J6
Smith's Green Essex 33 K4
Smithton 84 B6
Smithy Green 49 G5
Smockington 41 G7
Smugglers Adventure ESuss TN34 3HY 128 Hastings
Smyrton 67 F5
Smythe's Green 34 D7
Snailbeach 38 C5
Snailwell 33 K2
Snainton 59 F1
Snaith 58 C7
Snape NYorks 57 H1
Snape Suff 35 H3
Snape Green 48 C1
Snape Watering 35 H3
Snarestone 41 F5
Snarford 52 D4
Snargate 14 E5
Snave 15 F5
Sneachill 29 J3
Snead 38 C6
Snead's Green 29 H2
Sneath Common 45 F7
Sneaton 63 J6
Sneatonthorpe 63 K6
Snelland 52 D4
Snellings 60 A6
Snelston 40 D1
Snetterton 44 D6
Snettisham 44 A2
Snipeshill 25 F5
Snitter 71 F3
Snitterby 52 C3
Snitterfield 30 D3
Snitterton 50 E6
Snittlegarth 60 D3
Snitton 28 E1
Snodhill 28 C4
Snodland 24 D5
Snow End 33 H5
Snow Street 44 E7
Snowden Hill 50 E2
Snowdon Mountain Railway Gwyn LL55 4TY 46 D7
Snowshill 30 B5
Snowshill Manor Glos WR12 7JU 30 B5
Soar Cardiff 18 D3
Soar Carmar 17 K3
Soar Devon 5 H7
Soay 82 E9
Soberton 11 H3
Soberton Heath 11 H3
Sockbridge 61 G4
Sockburn 62 D6
Sodom 47 J5
Sodylt Bank 38 C2
Softley 62 A4
Soham 33 J1
Soham Cotes 33 J1
Soldierstown 93 G10
Soldon 6 B4
Soldon Cross 6 B4
Soldridge 11 H1
Sole Street Kent 15 F3
Sole Street Kent 24 C5
Soleburn 64 A4
Solihull 30 C1
Solihull Lodge 30 B1
Sollas (Solas) 88 C1
Sollers Dilwyn 28 D3
Sollers Hope 29 F5
Sollom 48 D1
Solomon's Tump 29 G7
Solsgirth 75 H1
Solva 16 A3
Solwaybank 69 J6
Somerby Leics 42 A4
Somerby Lincs 52 D2
Somercotes 51 G7
Somerford 10 C5
Somerford Keynes 20 D2
Somerley 12 B7
Somerleyton 45 J6
Somersal Herbert 40 D2
Somersby 53 G5
Somerset House GtLon WC2R 1LA 132 F3
Somersham Cambs 33 G1
Somersham Suff 34 E4
Somerton Newport 19 G3
Somerton Oxon 31 F6
Somerton Som 8 D2
Somerton Suff 34 C3
Sompting 12 E6
Sompting Abbotts 12 E6
Sonning 22 A4
Sonning Common 22 A3
Sonning Eye 22 A4
Sontley 38 C1
Sookholme 51 H6
Sopley 10 C5
Sopworth 20 B3
Sorbie 64 E6
Sordale 87 P3
Sorisdale 78 D4
Sorn 67 K1
Sornhill 74 D7
Sortat 87 Q3
Sotby 53 F5
Sots Hole 52 E6
Sotterley 45 J7
Soudley 39 G3
Soughton 48 B6
Soulbury 32 B6
Soulby 61 J5
Souldern 31 G5
Souldrop 32 C2
Sound ChesE 39 F1
Sound Shet 89 N8
Sourhope 70 D1
Sourin 89 D4
Sourton 6 D6
Soutergate 55 F1
South Acre 44 C4
South Acton 22 E4
South Alkham 15 H3
South Allington 5 H7
South Alloa 75 G1
South Ambersham 12 C4
South Anston 51 H4
South Ascot 22 C5
South Baddesley 10 E5
South Balloch 67 H4
South Bank 63 F4
South Barrow 9 F2
South Bellsdyke 75 H2
South Benfleet 24 D3
South Bersted 12 C6
South Bockhampton 10 C5
South Boisdale 88 B7
South Bowood 8 D5
South Brent 5 G4
South Brentor 6 C7
South Brewham 9 G1
South Broomhill 71 H4
South Burlingham 45 H5
South Cadbury 9 F2
South Cairn 66 D7
South Carlton 52 C5
South Cave 59 F6
South Cerney 20 D2
South Chard 8 C4
South Charlton 71 G1
South Cheriton 9 F2
South Church 62 C4
South Cliffe 58 E6
South Clifton 52 B5
South Cockerington 53 G4
South Common 13 G5
South Cornelly 18 B3
South Corriegills 73 J7
South Cove 45 J7
South Creake 44 C2
South Crosland 50 D1
South Croxton 41 J4
South Croydon 23 G5
South Dalton 59 F5
South Darenth 23 J4
South Dell (Dail Bho Dheas) 88 K1
South Duffield 58 C6
South Elkington 53 F4
South Elmsall 51 G1
South End Bucks 32 B6
South End Cumb 55 F3
South End Hants 10 C3
South End NLincs 59 H7
South Erradale 82 H3
South Fambridge 24 E2
South Fawley 21 G3
South Ferriby 59 F7
South Field 59 G7
South Godstone 23 G7
South Gorley 10 C3
South Green Essex 24 C2
South Green Essex 34 E7
South Green Norf 44 E4
South Green Suff 35 F1
South Gyle 75 K3
South Hall 73 J3
South Hanningfield 24 D2
South Harefield 22 D3
South Harting 11 J3
South Hayling 11 J5
South Hazelrigg 77 J7
South Heath 22 C1
South Heighton 13 H6
South Hetton 62 D2
South Hiendley 51 F1
South Hill 4 D3
South Hinksey 21 J1
South Hole 6 A4
South Holme 58 C2
South Holmwood 22 E7
South Hornchurch 23 J3
South Hourat 74 A5
South Huish 5 G6
South Hykeham 52 C6
South Hylton 62 D1
South Kelsey 52 D3
South Killingholme 52 E1
South Kilvington 57 K1
South Kilworth 41 J7
South Kirkby 51 G1
South Kirkton 85 M10
South Knighton 5 J3
South Kyme 42 E1
South Lakes Wild Animal Park Cumb LA15 8JR 55 F2
South Lancing 12 E6
South Leigh 21 G1
South Leverton 51 K4
South Littleton 30 B4
South Lopham 44 E7
South Luffenham 42 C5
South Malling 13 H5
South Marston 20 E3
South Middleton 70 E1
South Milford 57 K6
South Milton 5 G6
South Mimms 23 F1
South Molton 7 F3
South Moor 62 B1
South Moreton 21 J3
South Mundham 12 B6
South Muskham 51 K7
South Newbald 59 F6
South Newington 31 F5
South Newton 10 B1
South Normanton 51 G7
South Norwood 23 G5
South Nutfield 23 G7
South Ockendon 23 J3
South Ormsby 53 G5
South Ossett 50 E1
South Otterington 57 J1
South Owersby 52 D3
South Oxhey 22 E2
South Park 23 F7
South Perrott 8 D4
South Petherton 8 D3
South Petherwin 6 B7
South Pickenham 44 C5
South Pool 5 H6
South Queensferry (Queensferry) 75 K3
South Radworthy 7 F2
South Rauceby 42 D1
South Raynham 44 C3
South Reston 53 H4
South Ronaldsay 89 D9
South Ruislip 22 E3
South Runcton 44 A5
South Scarle 52 B6
South Shields 71 J7
South Shields Museum & Art Gallery T&W NE33 2JA 71 J7
South Somercotes 53 H3
South Somercotes Fen Houses 53 H3
South Stainley 57 J3
South Stoke B&NESom 20 A5
South Stoke Oxon 21 K3
South Stoke WSuss 12 D6
South Street ESuss 13 G5
South Street GtLon 23 H6
South Street Kent 24 C5
South Street Kent 24 E5
South Street Kent 25 H5
South Tawton 6 E6
South Thoresby 53 H5
South Tidworth 21 F7
South Tottenham 23 G3
South Town Devon 7 H7
South Town Hants 11 H1
South Uist (Uibhist a Deas) 88 B5
South View 21 K6
South Walsham 45 H4
South Warnborough 22 A7
South Weald 23 J2
South Weston 22 A2
South Wheatley Corn 4 C1
South Wheatley Notts 51 K4
South Wigston 41 H6
South Willingham 52 E4
South Wingfield 51 F7
South Witham 42 C4
South Wonston 11 F1
South Woodham Ferrers 24 E2
South Wootton 44 A3
South Wraxall 20 B5
South Yardle 40 D7
South Zeal 6 E6
Southall 22 E3
Southam Glos 29 J6
Southam Warks 31 F2
Southampton 11 F3
Southampton Airport 11 F3
Southbar 74 C4
Southborough GtLon 23 H5
Southborough Kent 23 J7
Southbourne Bourne 10 C5
Southbourne WSuss 11 J4
Southbrook 7 J6
Southburgh 44 E5
Southburn 59 F4
Southchurch 25 F3
Southcott Devon 6 D6
Southcott Wilts 20 E6
Southcourt 32 B7
Southdean 70 B3
Southdene 48 D3
Southease 13 H6
Southend A&B 66 A3
Southend Bucks 22 A3
Southend (Bradfield Southend) WBerks 21 J4
Southend Wilts 20 E4
Southend Airport 24 E3
Southend Pier S'end SS1 1EE 24 E3
Southend-on-Sea 24 E3
Southerfield 60 C2
Southerly 6 D7
Southern Green 33 G5
Southerndown 18 B4
Southerness 65 K5
Southery 44 A6
Southfield 76 A1
Southfields 23 F4
Southfleet 24 C4
Southgate Cere 36 E7
Southgate GtLon 23 G2
Southgate Norf 44 A2
Southgate Norf 45 F3
Southgate Swan 17 J7
Southill 32 E4
Southington 21 J7
Southleigh 8 B5
Southmarsh 9 G1
Southminster 25 F2
Southmoor 21 G2
Southoe 32 E2
Southolt 35 F2
Southorpe 42 D5
Southowram 57 G7
Southport 48 C1

Southport Pier Mersey PR8 1QX 48 C1
Southrepps 45 G2
Southrey 52 E6
Southrop 20 E1
Southrope 21 K7
Southsea Ports 11 H5
Southsea Wrex 48 B7
Southtown Norf 45 K5
Southtown Ork 89 D8
Southwaite Cumb 61 F2
Southwaite Cumb 61 J6
Southwark Cathedral GtLon SE1 9DA 105 B7
Southwater 12 E4
Southwater Street 12 E4
Southway 19 J7
Southwell Dorset 9 F7
Southwell Notts 51 J7
Southwell Minster Notts NG25 0HD 51 K7
Southwick D&G 65 K5
Southwick Hants 11 H4
Southwick N'hants 42 D6
Southwick Som 19 G7
Southwick T&W 62 D1
Southwick Wilts 20 B6
Southwick WSuss 13 F6
Southwold 35 K1
Southwood 8 E1
Sowden 7 H7
Sower Carr 55 G5
Sowerby NYorks 57 K1
Sowerby WYorks 57 F7
Sowerby Bridge 57 F7
Sowerby Row 60 E2
Sowerhill 7 G3
Sowley Green 34 B3
Sowood 50 C1
Sowton 7 H6
Spa Common 45 G2
Spa Complex NYorks YO11 2HD 135 Scarborough
Spadeadam 70 A6
Spalding 43 F3
Spaldington 58 D6
Spaldwick 32 E1
Spalford 52 B6
Spamount 90 J8
Spanby 42 D2
Sparham 44 E4
Spark Bridge 55 G1
Sparkford 9 F2
Sparkhill 40 C7
Sparkwell 5 F5
Sparrow Green 44 D4
Sparrowpit 50 C4
Sparrow's Green 13 K3
Sparsholt Hants 11 F1
Sparsholt Oxon 21 G3
Spartylea 61 K2
Spath 40 C2
Spaunton 58 D1
Spaxton 8 B1
Spean Bridge (Drochaid an Aonachain) 79 P2
Spean Bridge Woollen Mill High PH34 4EP 79 P2
Spear Hill 12 E5
Speddoch 68 D5
Speedwell 19 K4
Speen Bucks 22 B1
Speen WBerks 21 H5
Speeton 59 H2
Speke 48 D4
Speldhurst 23 J7
Spellbrook 33 H7
Spelsbury 30 E6
Spen Green 49 H6
Spencers Wood 22 A5
Spennithorne 57 G1
Spennymoor 62 C3
Spernall 30 B2
Spetchley 29 H3
Spetisbury 9 J4
Spexhall 45 H7
Spey Bay 84 H4
Spilsby 53 G6
Spindlestone 77 K7
Spinkhill 51 G5
Spinnaker Tower PO1 3TN 135 Portsmouth
Spinningdale 84 A2
Spirthill 20 C4
Spital High 87 P4
Spital W&M 22 C4
Spital in the Street 52 C3
Spitalbrook 23 G1
Spitfire & Hurricane Memorial, R.A.F. Manston Kent CT12 5DF 25 K5
Spithurst 13 H5
Spittal D&G 64 D5
Spittal D&G 64 E4
Spittal ELoth 76 C3
Spittal N'umb 77 J5
Spittal Pembs 16 C3
Spittal of Glenmuick 81 J2
Spittal of Glenshee 80 G4
Spittalfield 80 G6
Spixworth 45 G4
Splayne's Green 13 H4
Splott 19 F4
Spofforth 57 J4
Spondon 41 G2
Spooner Row 44 E6
Spoonley 39 F2
Sporle 44 C4
Sportsman's Arms 47 H7
Spott 76 E3
Spratton 31 J1
Spreakley 22 B7
Spreyton 6 E6
Spriddlestone 5 F5
Spridlington 52 D4
Spring Grove 22 E4
Spring Vale 11 H5
Springburn 74 E4
Springfield A&B 73 J3
Springfield D&G 69 J7
Springfield F&O 91 H12
Springfield Fife 81 J9
Springfield Moray 84 E5
Springfield WMid 40 C7
Springhill Staffs 40 B5
Springhill Staffs 40 C5
Springholm 65 J4
Springkell 69 H6
Springside 74 B7
Springthorpe 52 B4
Springwell 62 C1
Sproatley 59 H6
Sproston Green 49 G6
Sprotbrough 51 H2
Sproughton 35 F4
Sprouston 77 F7
Sprowston 45 G4
Sproxton Leics 42 B3
Sproxton NYorks 58 C1
Sprytown 6 C7
Spurlands End 22 B2
Spurstow 48 E7
Spyway 8 E5
Square Point 65 H3
Squires Gate 55 G6
Srannda 88 F9
Sròndoire 73 G3
Sronphadruig Lodge 80 C3
S.S. Great Britain Bristol BS1 6TY 100 C5
Stableford Shrop 39 G6
Stableford Staffs 40 A2
Stacey Bank 50 E3
Stackhouse 56 D3
Stackpole 16 C6
Stacksteads 56 D7
Staddiscombe 5 F5
Staddlethorpe 58 E7
Staden 50 C5
Stadhampton 21 K2
Staffield 61 G2
Staffin 82 E4
Stafford 40 B3
Staffordstown 92 F8
Stagden Cross 33 K7
Stagsden 32 C4
Stagshaw Bank 70 E7
Stainburn Cumb 60 B4
Stainburn NYorks 57 H5
Stainby 42 C3
Staincross 51 F1
Staindrop 62 B4
Staines-upon-Thames 22 D4
Stainfield Lincs 42 D3
Stainfield Lincs 52 E5
Stainforth NYorks 56 D3
Stainforth SYorks 51 J1
Staining 55 G6
Stainland 50 C1
Stainsacre 63 K6
Stainsby Derbys 51 G6
Stainsby Lincs 53 G5
Stainton Cumb 55 J1
Stainton Cumb 61 F4
Stainton Dur 62 A5
Stainton Middl 62 E5
Stainton NYorks 62 B7
Stainton SYorks 51 H3
Stainton by Langworth 52 D5
Stainton le Vale 52 E3
Stainton with Adgarley 55 F2
Staintondale 63 K7
Stair Cumb 60 D4
Stair EAyr 67 J1
Stairfoot 51 F2
Staithes 63 H5
Stake Pool 55 H5
Stakeford 71 H5
Stakes 11 H4
Stalbridge 9 G3
Stalbridge Weston 9 G3
Stalham 45 H3
Stalham Green 45 H3
Stalisfield Green 14 E2
Stalling Busk 56 E1
Stallingborough 52 E1
Stallington 40 B2
Stalmine 55 G5
Stalybridge 49 J3
Stambourne 34 B5
Stamford Lincs 42 D5
Stamford N'umb 71 H2
Stamford Bridge ChesW&C 48 D6
Stamford Bridge ERid 58 D4
Stamfordham 71 F6
Stanah 55 G5
Stanborough 33 F7
Stanborough Park Herts AL8 6XF 33 F7
Stanbridge Dorset 10 B4
Stanbridge Earls 10 E2
Stanbridge CenBeds 32 C6
Stanbury 57 F6
Stand 75 F4
Standalone Farm, Letchworth Garden City Herts SG6 4JN 33 F5
Standburn 75 H3
Standedge Tunnel & Visitor Centre WYorks HD7 6NQ 50 C1
Standeford 40 B5
Standen 14 D4
Standen Street 14 D4
Standerwick 20 B6
Standford 12 B3
Standford Bridge 39 G3
Standish Glos 20 B1
Standish GtMan 48 E1
Standlake 21 G1
Standon Hants 11 F2
Standon Herts 33 G6
Standon Staffs 40 A2
Standon Green End 33 G7
Stane 75 G5
Stanecastle 74 B7
Stanfield 44 D3
Stanford CenBeds 32 E4
Stanford Kent 15 G4
Stanford Shrop 38 C4
Stanford Bishop 29 F3
Stanford Bridge 29 G2
Stanford Dingley 21 J4
Stanford End 22 A5
Stanford in the Vale 21 G2
Stanford on Avon 31 G1
Stanford on Soar 41 H3
Stanford on Teme 29 G2
Stanford Rivers 23 J1
Stanford-le-Hope 24 C3
Stanfree 51 G5
Stanghow 63 G5
Stanground 43 F6
Stanhoe 44 C2
Stanhope Dur 61 L3
Stanhope ScBord 69 G1
Stanion 42 C7
Stanklyn 29 H1
Stanley Derbys 41 G1
Stanley Dur 62 B1
Stanley Notts 51 G6
Stanley P&K 80 G7
Stanley Staffs 49 J7
Stanley Wilts 20 C4
Stanley WYorks 57 J7
Stanley Common 41 G1
Stanley Crook 62 B3
Stanley Gate 48 D2
Stanley Hill 29 F4
Stanleygreen 38 E2
Stanlow ChesW&C 48 D5
Stanlow Shrop 39 G6
Stanmer 13 G5
Stanmore GtLon 22 E2
Stanmore WBerks 21 H4
Stannersburn 70 C5
Stanningfield 34 C3
Stannington N'umb 71 H6
Stannington SYorks 51 F4
Stansbatch 28 C2
Stansfield 34 B3
Stanshope 50 D7
Stanstead 34 C4
Stanstead Abbotts 33 G7
Stansted 24 C5
Stansted Mountfitchet 33 J6
Stanton Derbys 40 E4
Stanton Glos 30 B5
Stanton N'umb 71 G4
Stanton Staffs 40 D1
Stanton Suff 34 D1
Stanton by Bridge 41 F3
Stanton by Dale 41 G2
Stanton Drew 19 J5
Stanton Fitzwarren 20 E2
Stanton Harcourt 21 H1
Stanton Hill 51 G6
Stanton in Peak 50 E6
Stanton Lacy 28 D1
Stanton Lees 50 E6
Stanton Long 38 E6
Stanton Prior 19 K5
Stanton St. Bernard 20 D5
Stanton St. John 21 J1
Stanton St. Quintin 20 C4
Stanton Street 34 D2
Stanton under Bardon 41 G4
Stanton upon Hine Heath 38 E3
Stanton Wick 19 K5
Stanton-on-the-Wolds 41 J2
Stanwardine in the Fields 38 D3
Stanwardine in the Wood 38 D3
Stanway Essex 34 D6
Stanway Glos 30 B5
Stanway Green Essex 34 D6
Stanway Green Suff 35 G1
Stanwell 22 D4
Stanwell Moor 22 D4
Stanwick 32 C1
Stanwix 60 F1
Staoinebrig 88 B5
Stapeley 39 F1
Stapenhill 40 E3
Staple Kent 15 H2
Staple Som 7 K1
Staple Cross 7 J3
Staple Fitzpaine 8 B3
Staplecross 14 C5
Staplefield 13 F4
Stapleford Cambs 33 H3
Stapleford Herts 33 G7
Stapleford Leics 42 B4
Stapleford Lincs 52 B7
Stapleford Notts 41 G2
Stapleford Wilts 10 B1
Stapleford Abbotts 23 H2
Stapleford Tawney 23 J2
Staplegrove 8 B2
Staplehay 8 B2
Staplehurst 14 C3
Staplers 11 G6
Staplestreet 25 G5
Stapleton Cumb 70 A6
Stapleton Here 28 C2
Stapleton Leics 41 G6
Stapleton NYorks 62 C5
Stapleton Shrop 38 D5
Stapleton Som 8 D2
Stapley 7 K4
Staploe 32 E2
Staplow 29 F4
Star Pembs 17 F2
Star Som 19 H6
Starbotton 56 E2
Starcross 7 H7
Stareton 30 E1
Starkholmes 51 F7
Starling 49 G1
Starling's Green 33 H5
Starr 67 J4
Starston 45 G7
Startforth 62 A5
Startley 20 C3
Statham 49 F4
Stathe 8 C2
Stathern 42 A2
Station Town 62 E3
Staughton Green 32 E2
Staughton Highway 32 E2
Staunton Glos 28 E7
Staunton Glos 29 G6
Staunton Harold Hall 41 F3
Staunton Harold Reservoir Derbys DE73 8DN 41 F3
Staunton in the Vale 42 B1
Staunton on Arrow 28 C2
Staunton on Wye 28 C4
Staveley Cumb 61 F7
Staveley Derbys 51 G5
Staveley NYorks 57 J3
Staveley-in-Cartmel 55 G1
Staverton Devon 5 H4
Staverton Glos 29 H6
Staverton N'hants 31 G2
Staverton Wilts 20 B5
Staverton Bridge 29 H6
Stawell 8 C1
Stawley 7 J3
Staxigoe 87 R4
Staxton 59 G2
Staylittle (Penffordd-las) 37 H6
Staynall 55 G5
Staythorpe 51 K7
Stean 57 F2
Steane 31 G5
Stearsby 58 C2
Steart 19 F7
Stebbing 33 K6
Stebbing Green 33 K6
Stechford 40 D7
Stedham 12 B4
Steel Cross 13 J3
Steel Green 54 E2
Steele Road 70 A4
Steen's Bridge 28 E3
Steep 11 J2
Steep Marsh 11 J2
Steeple Dorset 9 J6
Steeple Essex 25 F1
Steeple Ashton 20 C6
Steeple Aston 31 F6
Steeple Barton 31 F6
Steeple Bumpstead 33 K4
Steeple Claydon 31 H6
Steeple Gidding 42 E7
Steeple Langford 10 B1
Steeple Morden 33 F4
Steeraway 39 F5
Steeton 57 F5
Stella 71 G7
Stelling Minnis 15 G3
Stembridge 8 D2
Stenalees 4 A5
Stenhill 7 J4
Stenhousemuir 75 G2
Stenigot 53 F4
Stenness 89 L5
Stenscholl 82 E4
Stenson 41 F3
Stenton 76 E3
Stepaside Pembs 16 E5
Stepaside Powys 37 K7
Stepney 23 G3
Steppingley 32 D5
Stepps 74 E4
Sternfield 35 H2
Sterridge 6 D1
Stert 20 D6
Stetchworth 33 K3
Stevenage 33 F6
Stevenston 74 A6
Steventon Hants 21 J7
Steventon Oxon 21 H2
Steventon End 33 K4
Stevington 32 C3
Stewart Park Middl TS7 8AR 63 F5
Stewartby 32 D4
Stewarton D&G 64 E6
Stewarton EAyr 74 C6
Stewartstown 93 D9
Stewkley 32 B6
Stewley 8 C3
Stewton 53 G4
Steyning 12 E5
Steynton 16 C5
Stibb 6 A4
Stibb Cross 6 C4
Stibb Green 21 F5
Stibbard 44 D3
Stibbington 42 D6
Stichill 77 F7
Sticker 3 G3
Stickford 53 G6
Sticklepath Devon 6 E6
Sticklepath Som 8 C3
Stickling Green 33 H5
Stickney 53 G7
Stiff Street 24 E5
Stiffkey 44 D1
Stifford's Bridge 29 G4
Stileway 19 H7
Stillingarry (Stadhlaigearraidh) 88 B5
Stillingfleet 58 B5
Stillington NYorks 58 B3
Stillington Stock 62 D4
Stilton 42 E7
Stinchcombe 20 A2
Stinsford 9 G5
Stirchley Tel&W 39 G5
Stirchley WMid 40 C7
Stirling (Sruighlea) 75 F1
Stirling Castle Stir FK8 1EJ 75 F1
Stirling Visitor Centre Stir FK8 1EH 75 F1
Stirton 56 E4
Stisted 34 C6
Stitchcombe 21 F5
Stithians 2 E5
Stivichall 30 E1
Stixwould 52 E6
Stobo 75 K7
Stoborough 9 J6
Stoborough Green 9 J6
Stobwood 75 H5
Stock 24 C2
Stock Green 29 J3
Stock Lane 21 F4
Stock Wood 30 B3
Stockbridge Hants 10 E1
Stockbridge WSuss 12 B6
Stockbury 24 E5
Stockcross 21 H5
Stockdale 2 E5
Stockdalewath 60 E2
Stockerston 42 B6
Stockgrove Country Park CenBeds LU7 0BA 32 C6
Stocking Green Essex 33 J5
Stocking Green MK 32 B4
Stocking Pelham 33 H6
Stockingford 41 F6
Stockland Cardiff 18 E4
Stockland Devon 8 B4
Stockland Bristol 19 F7
Stockleigh English 7 G5
Stockleigh Pomeroy 7 G5
Stockley 20 D5
Stocklinch 8 C3
Stockport 49 H3
Stocksbridge 50 E3
Stocksfield 71 F7
Stockton Here 28 E2
Stockton Norf 45 H6
Stockton Shrop 38 B5
Stockton Shrop 39 G6
Stockton Tel&W 39 G4
Stockton Warks 31 F2
Stockton Wilts 9 J1
Stockton Heath 49 F4
Stockton on Teme 29 G2
Stockton on the Forest 58 C4
Stockton-on-Tees 62 E5
Stockwell 29 J7
Stockwell Heath 40 C3
Stockwood Bristol 19 K5
Stockwood Dorset 8 E4
Stodday 55 H4
Stodmarsh 25 J5
Stody 44 E2
Stoer 86 C7
Stoford Som 8 E3
Stoford Wilts 10 B1
Stogumber 7 J2
Stogursey 19 F7
Stoke Devon 6 A3
Stoke Hants 11 J4
Stoke Hants 21 H6
Stoke Med 24 E4
Stoke Plym 4 E5
Stoke WMid 30 E1
Stoke Abbott 8 D4
Stoke Albany 42 B7
Stoke Ash 35 F1
Stoke Bardolph 41 J1
Stoke Bishop 19 J4
Stoke Bliss 29 F2
Stoke Bruerne 31 J3
Stoke by Clare 34 B4
Stoke Canon 7 H6
Stoke Charity 11 F1
Stoke Climsland 4 D3
Stoke D'Abernon 22 E6
Stoke Doyle 42 D7
Stoke Dry 42 B6
Stoke Edith 29 F4
Stoke Farthing 10 B2
Stoke Ferry 44 B6
Stoke Fleming 5 J6
Stoke Gabriel 5 J5
Stoke Gifford 19 K4
Stoke Golding 41 F6
Stoke Goldington 32 B4
Stoke Green 22 C3
Stoke Hammond 32 B6
Stoke Heath Shrop 39 F3
Stoke Heath Worcs 29 J2
Stoke Holy Cross 45 G5
Stoke Lacy 29 F4
Stoke Lyne 31 G6
Stoke Mandeville 32 B7
Stoke Newington 23 G3
Stoke on Tern 39 F3
Stoke Orchard 29 J6
Stoke Pero 7 G1
Stoke Poges 22 C3
Stoke Pound 29 J2
Stoke Prior Here 28 E3
Stoke Prior Worcs 29 J2
Stoke Rivers 6 E2
Stoke Rochford 42 C3
Stoke Row 21 K3
Stoke St. Gregory 8 C2
Stoke St. Mary 8 B2
Stoke St. Michael 19 K7
Stoke St. Milborough 38 E7
Stoke sub Hamdon 8 D3
Stoke Talmage 21 K2
Stoke Trister 9 G2
Stoke Villice 19 J5
Stoke Wake 9 G4
Stoke-by-Nayland 34 D5
Stokeford 9 H6
Stokeham 51 K5
Stokeinteignhead 5 K3
Stokenchurch 22 A2
Stokenham 5 J6
Stoke-on-Trent 40 A1
Stokesay 38 D7
Stokesby 45 J4
Stokesley 63 F6
Stolford 19 F7
Ston Easton 19 K6
Stonar Cut 25 K5
Stondon Massey 23 J1
Stone Bucks 31 J7
Stone Glos 19 K2
Stone Kent 14 E5
Stone Kent 23 J4
Stone Som 8 E1
Stone Staffs 40 B2
Stone SYorks 51 H4
Stone Worcs 29 H1
Stone Allerton 19 H6
Stone Cross Dur 62 A5
Stone Cross ESuss 13 J4
Stone Cross ESuss 13 K6
Stone Cross Kent 13 J3
Stone Cross Kent 15 F4
Stone House 56 C1
Stone Street Kent 23 J6
Stone Street Suff 34 D5
Stone Street Suff 45 H7
Stonea 43 H6
Stonebridge ESuss 13 J4
Stonebridge NSom 19 G6
Stonebridge Warks 40 E7
Stonebroom 51 G7
Stonecross Green 34 C3
Stonefield A&B 73 G3
Stonefield Staffs 40 B2
Stonegate ESuss 13 K4
Stonegate NYorks 63 H6
Stonegrave 58 C2
Stonehaugh 70 C6
Stonehaven 81 P2
Stonehenge (Stonehenge, Avebury & Associated Sites) Wilts SP4 7DE 20 E7
Stonehill 22 C5
Stonehouse ChesW&C 48 E5
Stonehouse D&G 65 J4
Stonehouse Glos 20 B1
Stonehouse N'umb 61 H1
Stonehouse Plym 4 E5
Stonehouse SLan 75 F6
Stoneleigh Surr 23 F5
Stoneleigh Warks 30 E1
Stoneley Green 49 F7
Stonely 32 E2
Stoner Hill 11 J2
Stones 56 E7
Stones Green 35 F6
Stones of Stenness (Heart of Neolithic Orkney) Ork KW16 3JZ 89 C6
Stonesby 42 B3
Stonesfield 30 E7
Stonestreet Green 15 F4
Stonethwaite 60 D5
Stoney Cross 10 D3
Stoney Middleton 50 E5
Stoney Stanton 41 G6
Stoney Stoke 9 G1
Stoney Stratton 9 F1
Stoney Stretton 38 C5
Stoneyburn 75 H4
Stoneyford 7 J7
Stoneygate 41 J5
Stoneyhills 25 F2
Stoneykirk 64 A5
Stoneywood 85 N9
Stonham Aspal 35 F3
Stonham Barns Suff IP14 6AT 35 F3
Stonnall 40 C5
Stonor 22 A3
Stonton Wyville 42 A6
Stony Houghton 51 G6
Stony Stratford 31 J4
Stonybreck 89 K10
Stonyford 93 H9
Stoodleigh Devon 6 E2
Stoodleigh Devon 7 H4
Stopham 12 D5
Stopsley 32 E6
Stoptide 3 G1
Storeton 48 C4
Stormontfield 80 G8
Stornoway (Steòrnabhagh) 88 K4
Stornoway Airport 88 K4
Storridge 29 G4
Storrington 12 D5
Storrs 50 E4
Storth 55 H1
Storwood 58 D5
Stotfield 84 G3
Stotfold 33 F5
Stottesdon 39 F7
Stoughton Leics 41 J5
Stoughton Surr 22 C6
Stoughton WSuss 11 J3
Stoughton Cross 19 H7
Stoul 82 H11
Stoulton 29 J4
Stour Provost 9 G2
Stour Row 9 H2
Stourbridge 40 A7
Stourhead Wilts BA12 6QD 9 G1
Stourpaine 9 H4
Stourport-on-Severn 29 H1
Stourton Staffs 40 A7
Stourton Warks 30 D5
Stourton Wilts 9 G1
Stourton Caundle 9 G3
Stoven 45 J7
Stow Lincs 52 B4
Stow ScBord 76 C6
Stow Bardolph 44 A5
Stow Bedon 44 D6
Stow cum Quy 33 J2
Stow Longa 32 E1
Stow Maries 24 E2
Stow Pasture 52 B4
Stowbridge 43 J5
Stowe Glos 19 J1
Stowe Shrop 28 C1
Stowe Staffs 40 D4
Stowe Landscape Gardens Bucks MK18 5DQ 31 H5
Stowe-by-Chartley 40 C3
Stowehill 31 H3
Stowell Glos 30 B7
Stowell Som 9 F2
Stowey 19 J6
Stowford Devon 6 C7
Stowford Devon 6 E3
Stowford Devon 7 K7
Stowlangtoft 34 D2
Stowmarket 34 E3
Stow-on-the-Wold 30 C6
Stowting 15 G3
Stowupland 34 E3
Straad 73 J4
Strabane 90 K7
Stracathro 81 M4
Strachan 85 L11
Strachur (Clachan Strachur) 79 M10
Stradbroke 35 G1
Stradhavern 92 G9
Stradishall 34 B3
Stradsett 44 A5
Stragglethorpe 52 C7
Straid A&N 92 J7
Straid CC&G 92 F2
Straid M&EAnt 92 F7
Straidbilly 92 E3
Straidkilly 92 H5
Straight Soley 21 G4
Straiton Edin 76 A4
Straiton SAyr 67 H3
Straloch 80 F4
Stramshall 40 C2
Stranagalwilly 90 M6
Strands 54 E1
Strang 54 C6
Strangford Here 28 E6
Strangford NM&D 93 L12
Stranocum 92 F3
Stranraer 64 A4
Strata Florida 27 G2
Stratfield Mortimer 21 K5
Stratfield Saye 21 K5
Stratfield Turgis 21 K6
Stratford CenBeds 32 E4
Stratford Glos 29 H5
Stratford GtLon 23 G3
Stratford St. Andrew 35 H3
Stratford St. Mary 34 E5
Stratford sub Castle 10 C1
Stratford Tony 10 B2
Stratford-upon-Avon 30 D3
Stratford-upon-Avon Butterfly Farm Warks CV37 7LS 136 Stratford-upon-Avon
Strath 87 Q4
Strathan High 83 K11
Strathan High 86 C7
Strathaven 75 F6
Strathblane 74 D3
Strathcanaird 86 D9
Strathcarron 83 K6
Strathclyde Country Park NLan ML1 3ED 119 K6
Strathdon 84 H9
Strathkinness 81 K9
Strathmiglo 80 H9
Strathpeffer (Strath Pheofhair) 83 Q5
Strathtay 80 E5
Strathwhillan 73 J7
Strathy 87 L3
Strathyre 80 A9
Stratton Corn 6 A5
Stratton Dorset 9 F5
Stratton Glos 20 D1
Stratton Audley 31 H6
Stratton Hall 35 G5
Stratton St. Margaret 20 E3
Stratton St. Michael 45 G6
Stratton Strawless 45 G3
Stratton-on-the-Fosse 19 K6
Stravanan 73 J5
Straw 92 C7
Strawberry Hill 22 E4
Stream 7 J2
Streat 13 G5
Streatham 23 F4
Streatham Ice and Leisure Centre GtLon SW16 6HX 105 A10
Streatham Vale 23 F4
Streatley CenBeds 32 D6
Streatley WBerks 21 J3
Street Devon 7 K7
Street Lancs 55 J4
Street NYorks 63 H6
Street Som 8 C4
Street Som 8 D1
Street Ashton 41 G7
Street Dinas 38 C2
Street End 12 B7
Street Gate 62 C1
Street Houses 58 B5
Street Lane 41 F1
Street on the Fosse 9 F1
Streethay 40 D4
Streethouse 57 J7
Streetlam 62 D7
Streetly 40 C6
Streetly End 33 K4
Strefford 38 D7
Strelley 41 H1
Strensall 58 C3
Strensham 29 J4
Stretcholt 19 F7
Strete 5 J6
Stretford GtMan 49 G3
Stretford Here 28 D3
Stretford Here 28 E3
Strethall 33 H5
Stretham 33 J1
Strettington 12 B6
Stretton ChesW&C 48 D7
Stretton Derbys 51 F6
Stretton Rut 42 C4
Stretton Staffs 40 A4
Stretton Staffs 40 E3
Stretton Warr 49 F4
Stretton en le Field 41 F4
Stretton Grandison 29 F4
Stretton Heath 38 C4
Stretton Sugwas 28 D4
Stretton under Fosse 41 G7
Stretton Westwood 38 E6
Stretton-on-Dunsmore 31 F1
Stretton-on-Fosse 30 D5
Stribers 55 G1
Strichen 85 P5
Strines 49 J4
Strinesdale Countryside Area GtMan OL4 2JJ 115 L1
Stringston 7 K1
Strixton 32 C2
Stroanbrack 90 M7
Stroat 19 J2
Stromeferry 83 J7
Stromemore 83 J7
Stromness 89 B7
Stronaba 79 P2
Stronachlachar 79 R9
Strone A&B 73 K2
Strone High 83 R8
Stronlonag 73 K2
Stronmilchan (Sròn nam Mialchon) 79 N8
Stronsay 89 F5
Stronsay Airfield 89 F5
Strontian (Sròn an t-Sìthein) 79 K4
Strood 24 D5
Strood Green Surr 23 F7
Strood Green WSuss 12 D4
Strood Green WSuss 12 E3
Stroquhan 68 D5
Stroud Glos 20 B1
Stroud Hants 11 J2
Stroud Common 22 D7
Stroud Green Essex 24 E2
Stroud Green Glos 20 B1
Stroude 22 D5
Stroul 74 A2
Stroxton 42 C2
Struan 80 C4
Strubby Lincs 52 E5
Strubby Lincs 53 H4
Strumpshaw 45 H5
Struy 83 Q7
Stryd y Facsen 46 B4
Stryt-cae-rhedyn 48 B6
Stryt-issa 38 B1
Stuart & Waterford Crystal Factory Shop, Crieff P&K PH7 4HQ 80 D8
Stuart Line Cruises, Exmouth Devon EX8 1EJ 7 J7
Stuartfield 85 P6
Stub Place 60 B7
Stubber's Green 40 C5
Stubbington 11 G4
Stubbins 49 G1
Stubbs Green 45 H6
Stubhampton 9 J3
Stubley 51 F5
Stubshaw Cross 48 E2
Stubton 42 B1
Stuck A&B 73 J4
Stuck A&B 73 K1
Stuckbeg 74 A1
Stuckreoch 73 J1
Stuckton 10 C3
Stud Green 22 B4
Studdon 61 K1
Studfold 56 D2
Studham 32 D7
Studholme 60 D1
Studland 10 B6
Studland & Godlingston Heath NNR Dorset BH19 3AX 10 B6
Studley Warks 30 B2
Studley Wilts 20 C4
Studley Common 30 B2
Studley Green 22 A2
Studley Roger 57 H2
Studley Royal Park & Ruins of Fountains Abbey NYorks HG4 3DY 57 H3
Stuggadhoo 54 C6
Stughan 93 D10
Stump Cross Essex 33 J4
Stump Cross Lancs 55 J6
Stuntney 33 J1
Stunts Green 13 K5
Sturbridge 40 A2
Sturgate 52 B4
Sturmer 33 K4
Sturminster Common 9 G3
Sturminster Marshall 9 J4
Sturminster Newton 9 G3
Sturry 25 H5
Sturton by Stow 52 B4
Sturton le Steeple 51 K4
Stuston 35 F1
Stutton NYorks 57 K5
Stutton Suff 35 F5
Styal 49 H4
Styrrup 51 J3
Suardail 88 K4
Succoth 79 P10
Succothmore 79 N10
Suckley 29 G3
Suckley Green 29 G3
Suckley Knowl 29 G3
Sudborough 42 C7
Sudbourne 35 J3
Sudbrook Lincs 42 C1
Sudbrook Mon 19 J3
Sudbrooke 52 D5
Sudbury Derbys 40 D2
Sudbury GtLon 22 E3
Sudbury Suff 34 C4
Sudbury Hall Derbys DE6 5HT 40 D2
Sudden 49 H1
Sudgrove 20 C1
Suffield Norf 45 G2
Suffield NYorks 63 K7
Sugarloaf 14 E4
Sugnall 39 G2
Sugwas Pool 28 D4
Suie Lodge Hotel 79 R8
Sulby IoM 54 C4
Sulby IoM 54 C6
Sulgrave 31 G4
Sulham 21 K4
Sulhamstead 21 K5
Sullington 12 D5
Sullom 89 M5
Sullom Voe Oil Terminal 89 M5
Sully 18 E5
Sumburgh 89 M11
Sumburgh Airport 89 M11
Summer Bridge 57 H3
Summer Isles 86 B9
Summer Lodge 61 L7
Summercourt 3 F3
Summerfield Norf 44 B2
Summerfield Worcs 29 H1
Summerhill 48 C7
Summerhouse 62 C5
Summerlands 55 J1
Summerleaze 19 H3
Summertown 21 J1
Summit 49 J1
Sun Green 49 J3
Sunadale 73 G6
Sunbiggin 61 H6
Sunbury-on-Thames 22 E5
Sundaywell 68 D5
Sunderland Cumb 60 C3
Sunderland Lancs 55 H4
Sunderland T&W 62 D1
Sunderland Bridge 62 C3
Sunderland Museum & Winter Gardens T&W SR1 1PP 136 Sunderland
Sundhope 69 J1
Sundon Park 32 D6
Sundown Adventure Land Notts DN22 0HX 51 K5
Sundridge 23 H6
Sundrum Mains 67 J1
Sunhill 20 E1
Sunk Island 53 F1
Sunningdale 22 C5
Sunninghill 22 C5
Sunningwell 21 H1
Sunniside Dur 62 B3
Sunniside T&W 62 C1
Sunny Bank 60 D7
Sunny Brow 62 B3
Sunnylaw 75 F1
Sunnyside N'umb 70 E7
Sunnyside SYorks 51 G3
Sunnyside WSuss 13 G3
Sunton 21 F6
Sunwick 77 G5
Surbiton 22 E5
Surfleet 43 F3
Surfleet Seas End 43 F3
Surlingham 45 H5
Sustead 45 F2
Susworth 52 B2
Sutcombe 6 B4
Sutcombemill 6 B4
Suton 44 E6
Sutors of Cromarty 84 C4
Sutterby 53 G5
Sutterton 43 F2
Sutton Cambs 33 H1
Sutton CenBeds 33 F4
Sutton Devon 5 H6
Sutton Devon 7 F5
Sutton GtLon 23 F5
Sutton Kent 15 J3
Sutton Lincs 52 B7
Sutton Norf 45 H3
Sutton Notts 42 A2
Sutton Notts 51 J4
Sutton Oxon 21 H1
Sutton Pembs 16 C4
Sutton Peter 42 D6
Sutton Shrop 38 C3
Sutton Shrop 38 E4
Sutton Shrop 39 F2
Sutton Shrop 39 G7
Sutton Staffs 39 G3
Sutton Suff 35 H4
Sutton SYorks 51 H1
Sutton WSuss 12 C5
Sutton Abinger 22 E7
Sutton at Hone 23 J4
Sutton Bank National Park Centre NYorks YO7 2EH 58 B1
Sutton Bassett 42 A7
Sutton Benger 20 C4
Sutton Bingham 8 E3
Sutton Bonington 41 H3
Sutton Bridge 43 H3
Sutton Cheney 41 G5
Sutton Coldfield 40 D6
Sutton Courtenay 21 J2
Sutton Crosses 43 H3
Sutton Grange 57 H2
Sutton Green Oxon 21 H1
Sutton Green Surr 22 D6
Sutton Green Wrex 38 D1
Sutton Holms 10 B4
Sutton Howgrave 57 J2
Sutton in Ashfield 51 G7
Sutton in the Elms 41 H6
Sutton Ings 59 H6
Sutton Lane Ends 49 J5
Sutton le Marsh 53 J4
Sutton Leach 48 E3
Sutton Maddock 39 G5
Sutton Mallet 8 C1
Sutton Mandeville 9 J2
Sutton Montis 9 F2
Sutton on Sea 53 J4
Sutton on the Hill 40 E2
Sutton on Trent 51 K6
Sutton Poyntz 9 G6
Sutton Scarsdale 51 G6
Sutton Scotney 11 F1
Sutton St. Edmund 43 G4
Sutton St. James 43 H4
Sutton St. Nicholas 28 E4
Sutton upon Derwent 58 D5
Sutton Valence 14 D3
Sutton Veny 20 B7
Sutton Waldron 9 H3
Sutton Weaver 48 E5
Sutton Wick B&NESom 19 J6
Sutton Wick Oxon 21 H2
Sutton-in-Craven 57 F5
Sutton-on-Hull 59 H6
Sutton-on-the-Forest 58 B3
Sutton-under-Brailes 30 E5
Sutton-under-Whitestonecliffe 57 K1
Swaby 53 G5
Swadlincote 41 F4
Swaffham 44 C5
Swaffham Bulbeck 33 J2
Swaffham Prior 33 J2
Swafield 45 G2
Swainbost (Suainebost) 88 L1
Swainby 62 E6
Swainshill 28 D4
Swainsthorpe 45 G5
Swainswick 20 A5
Swalcliffe 30 E5
Swalecliffe 25 H5
Swallow 52 E2
Swallow Beck 52 C6
Swallow Falls Conwy LL24 0DW 47 F7
Swallowcliffe 9 J2
Swallowfield 22 A5
Swallows Cross 24 C2
Swampton 21 H6
Swan Green ChesW&C 49 G5
Swan Green Suff 35 G1
Swan Street 34 C6
Swanage 10 B7
Swanage Railway Dorset BH19 1HB 10 B7
Swanbach 39 F1
Swanbourne 32 B6
Swanbridge 18 E5
Swancote 39 G6
Swanland 59 F7
Swanlaws 70 C2
Swanley 23 J5
Swanley Village 23 J5
Swanmore Hants 11 G3
Swanmore IoW 11 G5
Swannington Leics 41 G4
Swannington Norf 45 F4
Swanscombe 24 C4
Swansea (Abertawe) 17 K6
Swansea Museum SA1 1SN 136 Swansea
Swanston 76 A4
Swanton Abbot 45 G3
Swanton Morley 44 E4
Swanton Novers 44 E2
Swanton Street 14 D2
Swanwick Derbys 51 G7
Swanwick Hants 11 G4
Swanwick Green 38 E1
Swarby 42 D1
Swardeston 45 G5
Swarkestone 41 F3
Swarland 71 G3
Swarraton 11 G1
Swarthmoor 55 F2
Swaton 42 E2
Swatragh 92 D6
Swavesey 33 G2
Sway 10 D5
Swayfield 42 C3
Swaythling 11 F3
Swaythorpe 59 G3
Sweetham 7 G6
Sweethay 8 B2
Sweetshouse 4 A4
Sweffling 35 H2
Swell 8 C2
Swepstone 41 F4
Swerford 30 E5
Swettenham 49 H6
Swffryd 19 F2
Swift's Green 14 D3
Swiftsden 14 C5
Swilland 35 F3
Swillington 57 J6
Swimbridge 6 E3
Swimbridge Newland 6 D2
Swinbrook 30 D7
Swincliffe 57 H4
Swincombe 6 E1
Swinden 56 D4
Swinderby 52 B6
Swindon Staffs 40 A6
Swindon Swin 20 E3
Swindon Village 29 J6
Swine 59 H6
Swinefleet 58 D7
Swineford 19 K5
Swineshead Bed 32 D2
Swineshead Lincs 43 F1
Swineshead Bridge 43 F1
Swineside 57 F1
Swiney 87 Q6
Swinford Leics 31 G1
Swinford Oxon 21 H1
Swingate 41 H1
Swingfield Minnis 15 H3
Swingleton Green 34 D4
Swinhoe 71 H1
Swinhope 53 F3
Swinithwaite 57 F1
Swinscoe 40 D1
Swinside Hall 70 C2
Swinstead 42 D3
Swinton GtMan 49 G2
Swinton NYorks 57 H2
Swinton NYorks 58 D2
Swinton ScBord 77 G6
Swinton SYorks 51 G3
Swinton Quarter 77 G6
Swintonmill 77 G6
Swithland 41 H4
Swordale 83 R4
Swordland 82 H11
Swordly 87 K3
Sworton Heath 49 F4
Swyddffynnon 27 F2
Swyncombe 21 K2
Swynnerton 40 A2
Swyre 8 E6
Sychnant 27 J1
Syde 29 J7
Sydenham Belfast City 92 J9
Sydenham GtLon 23 G4
Sydenham Oxon 22 A1
Sydenham Damerel 4 E3
Syderstone 44 C2
Sydling St. Nicholas 9 F5
Sydmonton 21 H6
Sydney 49 G7
Syerston 42 A1
Sykehouse 51 J1
Sykes 56 B4
Sylen 17 J5
Symbister 89 P6
Symington SAyr 74 B7
Symington SLan 75 H7
Symonds Yat 28 E7
Symondsbury 8 D5
Synod Inn (Post-mawr) 26 D3
Syre 87 J5
Syreford 30 B6
Syresham 31 H4
Syston Leics 41 J4
Syston Lincs 42 C1
Sytchampton 29 H2
Sywell 32 B2
Sywell Country Park N'hants NN6 0QX 32 B2

T

Tableyhill 49 G5
Tachbrook Mallory 30 E2
Tackley 31 F6
Tacolneston 45 F6
Tadcaster 57 K5
Tadden 9 J4
Taddington Derbys 50 D5
Taddington Glos 30 B5
Taddiport 6 C4
Tadley 21 K5
Tadlow 33 F4
Tadmarton 30 E5
Tadpole Bridge 21 G1
Tadworth 23 F6
Tafarnaubach 28 A7
Tafarn-y-bwlch 16 D2
Tafarn-y-Gelyn 47 K6
Taff Merthyr Garden Village 18 E2
Taff's Well (Ffynnon Taf) 18 E3
Tafolwern 37 H5
Taibach NPT 18 A3
Tai-bach Powys 38 A3
Taicynhaeaf 37 F4
Tain 84 B2
Tai'n Lôn 36 D1
Tai'r Bull 27 J6
Tairgwaith 27 G7
Tai'r-heol 18 E2
Tairlaw 67 J3
Tai'r-ysgol 17 K6
Takeley 33 J6
Takeley Street 33 J6
Talachddu 27 K5
Talacre 47 K4
Talardd 37 H3
Talaton 7 J6
Talbenny 16 B4
Talbot Green 18 D3
Talbot Village 10 B5
Talerddig 37 J5
Talgarreg 26 D3
Talgarth 28 A5
Taliesin 37 F6
Talisker 82 D7
Talke Pits 49 H7
Talkin 61 G1
Talkin Tarn Country Park Cumb CA8 1HN 61 G1
Talla Linnfoots 69 G1
Talladale 83 K3
Talland 4 C5
Tallarn Green 38 D1
Tallentire 60 C3
Talley (Talyllychau) 17 K2
Tallington 42 D5
Talmine 86 H3
Talog 17 G3
Tal-sarn 26 E3
Talsarnau 37 F2
Talskiddy 3 G2
Talwrn IoA 46 C5
Talwrn Wrex 38 B1
Talwrn Wrex 38 C1
Talybont Cere 37 F7
Tal-y-bont Conwy 47 F6
Tal-y-bont Gwyn 36 E3
Tal-y-bont Gwyn 46 E5
Talybont-on-Usk 28 A6
Tal-y-Cae 46 E6
Tal-y-cafn 47 F5
Tal-y-coed 28 D7
Talygarn 18 D3
Tal-y-llyn Gwyn 37 G5
Talyllyn Powys 28 A6
Talysarn 46 C7
Tal-y-wern 37 H5
Tamar Valley Mining District (Cornwall & West Devon Mining Landscape) Corn/Devon 4 E3
Tamavoid 74 D1
Tamerton Foliot 4 E4
Tamlaght CC&G 92 E6
Tamlaght F&O 91 J12
Tamlaght O'Crilly 92 E6
Tamnamore 93 D10
Tamnavally 93 E9
Tamniarn 92 C6
Tamnyrankin 92 D6
Tamworth 40 E5
Tamworth Green 43 G1
Tan Office Green 34 B3
Tandem 50 D1
Tandragee 93 F12
Tandridge 23 G6
Tanerdy 17 H3
Tanfield 62 B1
Tanfield Lea 62 B1
Tang 57 H4
Tang Hall 58 C4
Tangiers 16 C4
Tangley 21 G6
Tangmere 12 C6
Tangy 66 A1
Tank Museum, Bovington Dorset BH20 6JG 9 H6
Tankersley 51 F2
Tankerton 25 H5
Tan-lan 37 F1
Tannach 87 R5
Tannadice 81 K5
Tannington 35 G2
Tannochside 74 E4
Tansley 51 F7
Tansley Knoll 51 F7
Tansor 42 D6
Tantobie 62 B1
Tanton 63 F5
Tanworth in Arden 30 C1
Tan-y-fron 47 H6
Tan-y-graig 36 C2
Tanygrisiau 37 F1
Tan-y-groes 17 F1
Tan-y-pistyll 37 K3
Tan-yr-allt 47 J4
Taobh Siar 88 G7
Tapeley 6 C3
Taplow 22 C3
Tapton Grove 51 G5
Taransay (Tarasaigh) 88 F7
Tarbert A&B 72 E2
Tarbert A&B 72 E5
Tarbert A&B 73 G4
Tarbert Na H-E. Siar 88 G7
Tarbet (An Tairbeart) A&B 79 Q10
Tarbet High 82 H11
Tarbet High 86 D5
Tarbock Green 48 D4
Tarbolton 67 J1
Tarbrax 75 J5
Tardebigge 29 J2
Tardy Gate 55 J7
Tarfside 81 K3
Tarland 85 J10
Tarleton 55 H7
Tarlscough 48 D1
Tarlton 20 C2
Tarnbrook 55 J4
Tarnock 19 G6
Tarporley 48 E6
Tarr 7 K2
Tarrant Crawford 9 J4
Tarrant Gunville 9 J3
Tarrant Hinton 9 J3
Tarrant Keyneston 9 J4
Tarrant Launceston 9 J4
Tarrant Monkton 9 J4
Tarrant Rawston 9 J4
Tarrant Rushton 9 J4
Tarrel 84 C2
Tarring Neville 13 H6
Tarrington 29 F4
Tarrnacraig 73 H7
Tarskavaig 82 F10
Tarves 85 N7
Tarvie (Tairbhidh) High 83 Q5
Tarvie P&K 80 F4
Tarvin 48 D6
Tarvin Sands 48 D6
Tasburgh 45 G6
Tasley 39 F6
Tassagh 93 D13
Taston 30 E6
Tate Britain GtLon SW1P 4RG 105 A7
Tate Liverpool Mersey L3 4BB 131 B5
Tate Modern GtLon SE1 9TG 132 H4
Tate St. Ives Corn TR26 1TG 2 C4
Tatenhill 40 E3
Tathall End 32 B4
Tatham 56 B3
Tathwell 53 G4
Tatsfield 23 H6
Tattenhall 48 D7
Tattenhoe 32 B5
Tatterford 44 C3
Tattersett 44 C2
Tattershall 53 F7
Tattershall Bridge 52 E7
Tattershall Thorpe 53 F7
Tattingstone 35 F5
Tattinweer 91 K12
Tatton Park ChesE WA16 6QN 49 G4
Tatworth 8 C4
Tauchers 84 H6
Taughblane 93 H11
Taunton 8 B2
Tavelty 85 M9
Taverham 45 F4
Tavernspite 16 E4
Tavistock 4 E3
Tavistock (Cornwall & West Devon Mining Landscape) Devon 4 E3
Taw Bridge 6 E5
Taw Green 6 E6
Tawstock 6 D3
Taxal 50 C5
Tayburn 74 D6
Tayinloan 72 E6
Taylors Cross 6 A4
Taynish 73 F2
Taynton Glos 29 G6
Taynton Oxon 30 D7
Taynuilt (Taigh an Uillt) 79 M7
Tayock 81 M5

Union Mills 54 C6
Union Street 14 C4
University of Glasgow Visitor Centre Glas G12 8QQ 127 B1
Unst 89 Q1
Unst Airport 89 Q2
Unstone 51 F5
Unstone Green 51 F5
Unsworth 49 H2
Unthank Cumb 61 F3
Unthank Derbys 51 F5
Up Cerne 9 F4
Up Exe 7 H5
Up Hatherley 29 J6
Up Holland 48 E2
Up Marden 11 J3
Up Mudford 8 E3
Up Nately 21 K6
Up Somborne 10 E1
Up Sydling 9 F4
Upavon 20 E6
Upchurch 24 E5
Upcott Devon 6 C6
Upcott Devon 6 D2
Upcott Here 28 C3
Upcott Som 7 H3
Upend 33 K3
Upgate 45 F4
Upgate Street Norf 44 E6
Upgate Street Norf 45 G6
Uphall Dorset 8 E4
Uphall WLoth 75 J3
Uphall Station 75 J4
Upham Devon 7 G5
Upham Hants 11 G2
Uphampton Here 28 C2
Uphampton Worcs 29 H2
Uphempston 5 J4
Uphill 19 G6
Uplands Glos 20 B1
Uplands Swan 17 K6
Uplawmoor 74 C5
Upleadon 29 G6
Upleatham 63 G5
Uplees 25 G5
Uploders 8 E5
Uplowman 7 J4
Uplyme 8 C5
Upminster 23 J3
Upottery 8 B4
Upper Affcot 38 D7
Upper Ardroscadale 73 J4
Upper Arley 39 G7
Upper Arncott 31 H7
Upper Astley 38 E4
Upper Aston 40 A6
Upper Astrop 31 G5
Upper Ballinderry 93 G10
Upper Basildon 21 K4
Upper Bayble (Pabail Uarach) 88 L4
Upper Beeding 12 E5
Upper Benefield 42 C7
Upper Bentley 29 J2
Upper Berwick 38 D4
Upper Boat 18 E3
Upper Boddam 85 L7
Upper Boddington 31 F3
Upper Borth 37 F7
Upper Boyndlie 85 P4
Upper Brailes 30 E5
Upper Breakish 82 G8
Upper Breinton 28 D4
Upper Broadheath 29 H3
Upper Broughton 41 J3
Upper Brynamman 27 G7
Upper Bucklebury 21 J5
Upper Burgate 10 C3
Upper Caldecote 32 E4
Upper Canada 19 G6
Upper Catesby 31 G3
Upper Catshill 29 J1
Upper Chapel 27 K4
Upper Cheddon 8 B2
Upper Chicksgrove 9 J1
Upper Chute 21 F6
Upper Clatford 21 G7
Upper Coberley 29 J7
Upper Colwall 29 G4
Upper Cotton 40 C1
Upper Cound 38 E5
Upper Cumberworth 50 E2
Upper Cwmbran 19 F2
Upper Dean 32 D2
Upper Denby 50 E2
Upper Denton 70 B7
Upper Derwent Reservoirs Derbys S33 0AQ 50 D4
Upper Diabaig 83 J4
Upper Dicker 13 J5
Upper Dovercourt 35 G5
Upper Dunsforth 57 K3
Upper Dunsley 32 C7
Upper Eastern Green 40 E7
Upper Egleton 29 F4
Upper Elkstone 50 C7
Upper End 50 C5
Upper Enham 21 G7
Upper Farringdon 11 J1
Upper Framilode 29 G7
Upper Froyle 22 A7
Upper Godney 19 H7
Upper Gornal 40 B6
Upper Gravenhurst 32 E5
Upper Green Essex 33 H5
Upper Green Essex 33 J5
Upper Green Mon 28 C7
Upper Green WBerks 21 G5
Upper Grove Common 28 E6
Upper Hackney 50 E6
Upper Halliford 22 D5
Upper Halling 24 C5
Upper Hambleton 42 C5
Upper Harbledown 15 G2
Upper Hardres Court 15 G2
Upper Hartfield 13 H3
Upper Hatton 40 A2
Upper Hayesden 23 J7
Upper Hayton 38 E7
Upper Heath 38 E7
Upper Heaton 50 D1
Upper Hellesdon 45 G4
Upper Helmsley 58 C4
Upper Hengoed 38 B2
Upper Hergest 28 B3
Upper Heyford N'hants 31 H3
Upper Heyford Oxon 31 F6
Upper Hill Here 28 D3
Upper Hill SGlos 19 K2
Upper Horsebridge 13 J5
Upper Howsell 29 G4
Upper Hulme 50 C6
Upper Inglesham 21 F2
Upper Kilchattan 72 B1
Upper Killay 17 J6
Upper Knockando 84 F6
Upper Lambourn 21 G3
Upper Langford 19 H6
Upper Langwith 51 H6
Upper Leigh 40 C2
Upper Ley 29 G7
Upper Loads 51 F6
Upper Longdon 40 C4
Upper Longwood 39 F5
Upper Ludstone 40 A6
Upper Lybster 87 Q6
Upper Lydbrook 29 F7
Upper Lyde 28 D4
Upper Lye 28 C2
Upper Maes-coed 28 C5
Upper Midhope 50 E3
Upper Milton 30 D7
Upper Minety 20 D2
Upper Moor 29 J4
Upper Morton 19 K2
Upper Nash 16 D5
Upper Newbold 51 F5
Upper North Dean 22 B2
Upper Norwood 23 G4
Upper Oddington 30 D6
Upper Padley 50 E5
Upper Pennington 10 D5
Upper Pollicott 31 J7
Upper Poppleton 58 B4
Upper Quinton 30 C4
Upper Ratley 10 E2
Upper Rissington 30 D6
Upper Rochford 29 F2
Upper Sanday 89 E7
Upper Sapey 29 F2
Upper Scolton 16 C3
Upper Seagry 20 C3
Upper Shelton 32 C4
Upper Sheringham 45 F1
Upper Shuckburgh 31 F2
Upper Siddington 20 D2
Upper Skelmorlie 74 A4
Upper Slaughter 30 C6
Upper Soudley 29 F7
Upper Staploe 32 E3
Upper Stoke 45 G5
Upper Stondon 32 E5
Upper Stowe 31 H3
Upper Street Hants 10 C3
Upper Street Norf 35 F1
Upper Street Norf 45 H4
Upper Street Suff 35 F5
Upper Strensham 29 J5
Upper Sundon 32 D6
Upper Swanmore 11 G3
Upper Swell 30 C6
Upper Tean 40 C2
Upper Tirkane 92 D6
Upper Thurnham 55 H4
Upper Tooting 23 F4
Upper Town Derbys 50 E6
Upper Town Derbys 50 E7
Upper Town Here 28 E4
Upper Town NSom 19 J5
Upper Tysoe 30 E4
Upper Upham 21 F4
Upper Upnor 24 D4
Upper Vobster 20 A7
Upper Wardington 31 F4
Upper Waterhay 20 D2
Upper Weald 32 B5
Upper Weedon 31 H3
Upper Welson 28 B3
Upper Weston 20 A5
Upper Whiston 51 G4
Upper Wick 29 H3
Upper Wield 11 H1
Upper Winchendon (Over Winchendon) 31 J7
Upper Witton 40 C6
Upper Woodford 10 C1
Upper Woolhampton 21 J5
Upper Wootton 21 J6
Upper Wraxall 20 B4
Upper Wyche 29 G4
Upperby 60 F1
Upperlands 92 D6
Uppermill 49 J2
Upperthong 50 D2
Upperton 12 C4
Uppertown CC&G 92 F5
Uppertown Derbys 51 F6
Uppingham 42 B5
Uppington 38 E5
Upsall 57 K1
Upsettlington 77 G6
Upshire 23 H1
Upstreet 25 J5
Upthorpe 34 D1
Upton Bucks 31 J7
Upton Cambs 32 E1
Upton ChesW&C 48 D6
Upton Corn 4 C3
Upton Corn 6 A5
Upton Devon 5 H6
Upton Devon 7 J5
Upton Dorset 9 G6
Upton Dorset 9 J5
Upton ERid 59 H4
Upton Hants 10 E3
Upton Hants 21 G6
Upton Leics 41 F6
Upton Lincs 52 B4
Upton Mersey 48 B4
Upton Norf 45 H4
Upton Notts 51 K5
Upton Notts 51 K7
Upton N'hants 31 J2
Upton Oxon 21 J3
Upton Oxon 30 D7
Upton Pembs 16 D5
Upton Peter 42 E5
Upton Slo 22 C4
Upton Som 7 H3
Upton Som 8 D2
Upton Wilts 9 H1
Upton WYorks 51 G1
Upton Bishop 29 F6
Upton Cheyney 19 K5
Upton Country Park Poole BH17 7BJ 95 B5
Upton Cressett 39 F6
Upton Crews 29 F6
Upton Cross 4 C3
Upton End 32 E5
Upton Grey 21 K7
Upton Hellions 7 G5
Upton Lovell 20 C7
Upton Magna 38 E4
Upton Noble 9 G1
Upton Park 23 H3
Upton Pyne 7 H6
Upton Scudamore 20 B7
Upton Snodsbury 29 J3
Upton St. Leonards 29 H7
Upton upon Severn 29 H4
Upton Warren 29 J2
Upwaltham 12 C5
Upware 33 J1
Upwell 43 J5
Upwey 9 F6
Upwick Green 33 H6
Upwood 43 F7
Urafirth 89 M5
Urbis, Manchester GtMan M4 3BG 133 E2
Urchfont 20 D6
Urdimarsh 28 E4
Urgha 88 G8
Urlay Nook 62 E5
Urmston 49 G3
Urpeth 62 C1
Urquhart 84 G4
Urquhart Castle High IV63 6XJ 83 R8
Urra 63 F6
Ushaw Moor 62 C2
Usher Hall Edin EH1 2EA 126 E5
Usk (Brynbuga) 19 G1
Usselby 52 D3
Usworth 62 D1
Utley 57 F5
Uton 7 G6
Utterby 53 G3
Uttoxeter 40 C2
Uwchmynydd 36 A3
Uxbridge 22 D3
Uyeasound 89 P2
Uzmaston 16 C4

V
Valley (Y Fali) 46 A5
Valley Truckle 4 B2
Valleyfield D&G 65 G5
Valleyfield Fife 75 J2
Valsgarth 89 Q1
Vange 24 D3
Vardre 17 K5
Varteg (Y Farteg) 19 F1
Vatersay (Bhatarsaigh) 88 A9
Vatten 82 C6
Vaul 78 B6
Vaynor 27 K7
Vaynor Park 38 A5
Veaullt 28 A3
Veensgarth 89 N8
Velindre Pembs 16 D2
Velindre Powys 28 A5
Vellow 7 J2
Venn 5 H6
Venn Ottery 7 J6
Venngreen 6 B4
Vennington 38 C5
Venny Tedburn 7 G6
Venterdon 4 D3
Ventnor 11 G7
Ventnor Botanic Gardens IoW PO38 1UL 11 G7
Venton 5 F5
Venton 5 F5
Venue Cymru, Llandudno Conwy LL30 1BB 47 F4
Vernham Dean 21 G6
Vernham Street 21 G6
Vernolds Common 38 D7
Verwood 10 B4
Veryan 3 G5
Veryan Green 3 G4
Vickerstown 54 E3
Victoria 3 G2
Victoria & Albert Dundee 125 Dundee
Victoria & Albert Museum GtLon SW7 2RL 103 G7
Victoria Bridge 90 K7
Vidlin 89 N6
Viewpark 75 F4
Vigo 40 C5
Vigo Village 24 C5
Villavin 6 D4
Vindobala (Frontiers of the Roman Empire) N'umb 71 G7
Vindolandia (Chesterholm) (Frontiers of the Roman Empire) N'umb NE47 7JN 70 C7
Vinehall Street 14 C5
Vine's Cross 13 J5
Viney Hill 19 K1
Virginia Water 22 C5
Virginstow 6 B6
Virley 34 D7
Vobster 20 A7
Voe 89 N6
Vogrie Country Park Midlo EH23 4NU 120 H5
Voirrey Embroidery Mersey CH63 6JA 112 A6
Volks Electric Railway B&H BN2 1EN 13 G6
Vow 92 E5
Vowchurch 28 C5
Voy 89 B6
Vron Gate 38 C5

W
Waberthwaite 60 C7
Wackerfield 62 B4
Wacton 45 F6
Wadbister 89 N8
Wadborough 29 J4
Waddesdon 31 J7
Waddesdon Manor Bucks HP18 0JH 31 J7
Waddeton 5 J5
Waddicar 48 C3
Waddingham 52 C3
Waddington Lancs 56 C5
Waddington Lincs 52 C6
Waddingworth 52 E5
Waddon Devon 5 J3
Waddon GtLon 23 G5
Wadebridge 3 G1
Wadeford 8 C3
Wadenhoe 42 D7
Wadesmill 33 G7
Wadhurst 13 K3
Wadshelf 51 F5
Wadworth 51 H3
Wadworth Hill 59 J7
Waen Denb 47 H6
Waen Denb 47 K6
Waen Aberwheeler 47 J6
Waen-fâch 38 B4
Waen-wen 46 D6
Wainfleet All Saints 53 H7
Wainfleet Bank 53 H7
Wainfleet St. Mary 53 H7
Wainford 45 H6
Waingroves 41 G1
Wainhouse Corner 4 B1
Wainscott 24 D4
Wainstalls 57 F7
Waitby 61 J6
Wakefield 57 J7
Wakehurst Place WSuss RH17 6TN 13 G3
Wakerley 42 C6
Wakes Colne 34 C6
Walberswick 35 J1
Walberton 12 C6
Walbottle 71 G7
Walcot Lincs 42 D2
Walcot Lincs 52 E7
Walcot NLincs 58 E7
Walcot Shrop 38 C7
Walcot Tel&W 38 E4
Walcot Green 45 F7
Walcote Leics 41 H7
Walcote Warks 30 C3
Walcott 45 H2
Walcott Dales 52 E7
Walden 57 F1
Walden Head 56 E1
Walden Stubbs 51 H1
Walderslade 24 D5
Walderton 11 J3
Walditch 8 D5
Waldley 40 D2
Waldridge 62 C2
Waldringfield 35 G4
Waldron 13 J5
Wales 51 G4
Wales Millennium Centre Cardiff CF10 5AL 99 C6
Walesby Lincs 52 E3
Walesby Notts 51 J5
Waleswood 51 G4
Walford Here 28 C1
Walford Here 28 E6
Walford Shrop 38 D3
Walford Staffs 40 A2
Walford Heath 38 D4
Walgherton 39 F1
Walgrave 32 B1
Walhampton 10 E5
Walk Mill 56 D6
Walkden 49 G2
Walker 71 H7
Walker Art Gallery, Liverpool Mersey L3 8EL 131 D3
Walker Fold 56 B5
Walkerburn 76 B7
Walkeringham 51 K3
Walkerith 51 K3
Walkern 33 F6
Walker's Green 28 E4
Walkford 10 D5
Walkhampton 5 F4
Walkingham Hill 57 J3
Walkington 59 F6
Walkwood 30 B2
Wall Corn 2 D5
Wall N'umb 70 E7
Wall Staffs 40 D5
Wall End 55 F1
Wall Heath 40 A7
Wall Houses 71 F7
Wall under Heywood 38 E6
Wallace Collection, London GtLon W1U 3BN 132 A2
Wallacehall 69 H6
Wallacetown 67 G3
Wallasey 48 B3
Wallaston Green 16 C5
Wallend 24 E4
Waller's Green 29 F5
Wallingford 21 K3
Wallington GtLon 23 F5
Wallington Hants 11 G4
Wallington Herts 33 F5
Wallington Wrex 38 D1
Wallingwells 51 H4
Wallis 16 D3
Wallisdown 10 B5
Walliswood 12 E3
Walls 89 L8
Walls of Derry BT48 6PR 90 L5
Wallsend 71 J7
Wallyford 76 B3
Walmer 15 J2
Walmer Bridge 55 H7
Walmersley 49 H1
Walmley 40 D6
Walmsgate 53 G5
Walpole 35 H1
Walpole Cross Keys 43 J4
Walpole Highway 43 J4
Walpole Marsh 43 H4
Walpole St. Andrew 43 J4
Walpole St. Peter 43 J4
Walrond's Park 8 C2
Walrow 19 G7
Walsall 40 C6
Walsall Wood 40 C5
Walsden 56 E7
Walsgrave on Sowe 41 F7
Walsham le Willows 34 E1
Walshaw 49 G1
Walshford 57 K4
Walsoken 43 H4
Walston 75 J6
Walsworth 32 E5
Walter's Ash 22 B2
Walterston 18 D4
Walterstone 28 C6
Waltham Kent 15 G3
Waltham NELincs 53 F2
Waltham Abbey 23 G1
Waltham Chase 11 G3
Waltham Cross 23 G1
Waltham on the Wolds 42 A3
Waltham St. Lawrence 22 B4
Walthamstow 23 G3
Walton Bucks 32 B7
Walton Cumb 70 A7
Walton Derbys 51 F6
Walton Leics 41 H7
Walton Mersey 48 C3
Walton MK 32 B5
Walton Peter 42 E5
Walton Powys 28 B3
Walton Shrop 28 D1
Walton Som 8 D1
Walton Staffs 40 A2
Walton Suff 35 H5
Walton Tel&W 38 E4
Walton Warks 30 D3
Walton WYorks 51 F1
Walton WYorks 57 K5
Walton Cardiff 29 J5
Walton East 16 D3
Walton Elm 9 G3
Walton Hall Gardens Warr WA4 6SN 113 M5
Walton Highway 43 H4
Walton Lower Street 35 G5
Walton on the Hill 23 F6
Walton on the Naze 35 G6
Walton on the Wolds 41 H4
Walton Park D&G 65 H3
Walton Park NSom 19 H4
Walton West 16 B4
Walton-in-Gordano 19 H4
Walton-le-Dale 55 J7
Walton-on-Thames 22 E5
Walton-on-the-Hill 40 B3
Walton-on-Trent 40 E4
Walwen Flints 47 K5
Walwen Flints 48 B5
Walwick 70 E6
Walworth CC&G 92 B4
Walworth Darl 62 C5
Walworth Gate 62 C4
Walwyn's Castle 16 B4
Wambrook 8 B4
Wanborough Surr 22 C7
Wanborough Swin 21 F3
Wandel 68 E1
Wandon 71 F1
Wandon End 32 E6
Wandsworth 23 F4
Wandylaw 71 G1
Wangford Suff 35 J1
Wangford Suff 44 B7
Wanlip 41 H4
Wanlockhead 68 D2
Wannock 13 J6
Wansbeck Riverside Park N'umb NE63 8TX 71 H5
Wansford ERid 59 G4
Wansford Peter 42 D6
Wanshurst Green 14 C3
Wanstrow 20 A7
Wanswell 19 K1
Wantage 21 G3
Wapley 20 A4
Wappenbury 30 E2
Wappenham 31 H4
Warblebank 60 D2
Warbleton 13 K5
Warblington 11 J4
Warborough 21 J2
Warboys 43 G7
Warbreck 55 G6
Warbstow 4 C1
Warburton 49 F4
Warcop 61 J5
Ward End 40 D7
Ward Green 34 E2
Warden Kent 25 G4
Warden N'umb 70 E7
Warden Hill 29 J6
Warden Street 32 E4
Wardington 31 F4
Wardle ChesE 49 F7
Wardle GtMan 49 J1
Wardley GtMan 49 G2
Wardley Rut 42 B5
Wardley T&W 71 J7
Wardlow 50 D5
Wardsend 49 J4
Wardy Hill 43 H7
Ware Herts 33 G7
Ware Kent 25 J5
Wareham 9 J6
Warehorne 14 E4
Waren Mill 77 K7
Warenford 71 G1
Warenton 77 K7
Wareside 33 G7
Waresley Cambs 33 F3
Waresley Worcs 29 H1
Warfield 22 B4
Wargrave Mersey 48 E3
Wargrave W'ham 22 A4
Warham Here 28 D5
Warham Norf 44 D1
Waringsford 93 H12
Waringstown 93 G11
Wark N'umb 70 D6
Wark N'umb 77 G7
Warkleigh 6 E3
Warkton 32 B1
Warkworth N'hants 31 F4
Warkworth N'umb 71 H3
Warland 56 E7
Warleggan 4 B4
Warley Essex 23 J2
Warley WMid 40 C7
Warley Town 57 F7
Warlingham 23 G6
Warmfield 57 J7
Warmingham 49 G6
Warminghurst 12 E5
Warmington N'hants 42 D6
Warmington Warks 31 F4
Warminster 20 B7
Warmlake 14 D3
Warmley 19 K4
Warmley Hill 19 K4
Warmsworth 51 H2
Warmwell 9 G6
Warndon 29 H3
Warners End 22 D1
Warnford 11 H2
Warnham 12 E3
Warningcamp 12 D6
Warninglid 13 F4
Warren ChesE 49 H5
Warren Pembs 16 C6
Warren House 6 E7
Warren Row 22 B3
Warren Street 14 E2
Warrenby 63 F4
Warrenpoint 93 G15
Warren's Green 33 F6
Warrington MK 32 B3
Warrington Warr 49 F4
Warsash 11 F4
Warslow 50 C7
Warsop Vale 51 H6
Warter 58 E4
Warthill 58 C4
Wartling 13 K6
Wartnaby 42 A3
Warton Lancs 55 H7
Warton Lancs 55 J2
Warton N'umb 71 F3
Warton Warks 40 E5
Warton Bank 55 H7
Warwick 30 D2
Warwick Bridge 61 F1
Warwick Castle Warks CV34 4QU 30 D2
Warwick Wold 23 G6
Warwick-on-Eden 61 F1
Wasbister 89 C4
Wasdale Head 60 C6
Waseley Hills Country Park Worcs B45 9AT 106 D8
Wash 50 C4
Wash Common 21 H5
Washall Green 33 H5
Washaway 4 A4
Washbourne 5 H5
Washbrook 19 H7
Washfield 7 H4
Washfold 62 A6
Washford Som 7 J1
Washford Warks 30 B2
Washford Pyne 7 G4
Washingborough 52 D5
Washington T&W 62 D1
Washington WSuss 12 E5
Washmere Green 34 D4
Wasing 21 J5
Waskerley 62 A2
Wasperton 30 D3
Wasps Nest 52 D6
Wass 58 B2
Wat Tyler Country Park Essex SS16 4UH 24 D3
Watchet 7 J1
Watchfield Oxon 21 F2
Watchfield Som 19 G7
Watchgate 61 G7
Watcombe 5 K4
Watendlath 60 D5
Water 56 D7
Water Eaton MK 32 B5
Water Eaton Oxon 31 G7
Water End Bed 32 E4
Water End CenBeds 32 D5
Water End ERid 58 D6
Water End Essex 33 J4
Water End Herts 23 F1
Water End Herts 32 D7
Water Newton 42 E6
Water Orton 40 D6
Water Stratford 31 H5
Water Yeat 55 F1
Waterbeach 33 H2
Waterbeck 69 H6
Watercombe 9 G6
Waterend 22 A2
Waterfall 50 C7
Waterfoot ERenf 74 D5
Waterfoot Lancs 56 D7
Waterford 33 G7
Watergate 4 B2
Waterhead Cumb 60 E6
Waterhead D&G 68 C5
Waterheath 45 J6
Waterhouses Dur 62 B2
Waterhouses Staffs 50 C7
Wateringbury 23 K6
Waterlane 20 C1
Waterloo Derbys 51 G6
Waterloo GtMan 49 J2
Waterloo High 82 G8
Waterloo Mersey 48 C3
Waterloo N.Lan 75 G5
Waterloo Norf 45 G4
Waterloo Pembs 16 C5
Waterloo P&K 80 F7
Waterloo Poole 10 B5
Waterloo Cross 7 J4
Waterloo Port 46 C6
Waterlooville 11 H3
Watermead Country Park Leics LE7 4PF 41 J4
Watermeetings 68 E2
Watermillock 60 F4
Watermouth Castle Devon EX34 9SL 6 D1
Waterperry Oxon OX33 1JZ 21 K1
Waterperry 21 K1
Waterrow 7 J3
Waters Upton 39 F4
Watersfield 12 D5
Watershed Mill Visitor Centre, Settle NYorks BD24 9LR 56 D3
Watersheddings 49 J2
Waterside Aber 85 Q8
Waterside Bucks 22 C1
Waterside B'burn 56 C7
Waterside D&S 90 L5
Waterside EAyr 67 J3
Waterside EAyr 74 C6
Waterside EDun 74 E3
Watersmeet House Devon EX35 6NT 7 F1
Waterstock 21 K1
Waterston 16 C5
Waterthorpe 51 G4
Waterworld, Hanley ST1 5PU 136 Stoke-on-Trent
Watford Herts 22 E2
Watford N'hants 31 H2
Watford Park 18 E3
Wath NYorks 57 G3
Wath NYorks 57 J2
Wath Brow 60 B5
Wath upon Dearne 51 G2
Watley's End 19 K3
Watlington Norf 44 A4
Watlington Oxon 21 K2
Watnall 41 H1
Watten 87 Q4
Wattisfield 34 E1
Wattisham 34 E3
Wattlebridge 91 L14
Watton Dorset 8 D5
Watton ERid 59 G5
Watton Norf 44 D5
Watton at Stone 33 G7
Watton Green 44 D5
Watton's Green 23 J2
Wattston 75 F4
Wattstown 18 D2
Wattsville 19 F2
Waun Fawr 37 F7
Waun y Clyn 17 H5
Waunarlwydd 17 K6
Waunclunda 17 K2
Waunfawr 46 D7
Waun-Lwyd 18 E1
Wavendon 32 C5
Waverbridge 60 D2
Waverton ChesW&C 48 D6
Waverton Cumb 60 D2
Wavertree 48 C4
Wawne 59 G6
Waxham 45 J3
Waxholme 59 K7
Way Gill 56 E3
Way Village 7 G4
Way Wick 19 G5
Wayford 8 D4
Waytown 8 D5
Weacombe 7 K1
Weald 21 G1
Weald & Downland Open Air Museum WSuss PO18 0EU 12 B5
Weald Country Park Essex CM14 5QS 23 J2
Wealdstone 22 E2
Weardley 57 H5
Weare 19 H6
Weare Giffard 6 C3
Wearhead 61 K3
Wearne 8 D2
Weasenham All Saints 44 C3
Weasenham St. Peter 44 C3
Weathercote 56 C2
Weatheroak Hill 30 B1
Weaverham 49 F5
Weaverthorpe 59 F2
Webheath 30 B2
Webton 28 D5
Weddington 41 F6
Wedhampton 20 D6
Wedmore 19 H7
Wednesbury 40 B6
Wednesfield 40 B6
Weedon 32 B7
Weedon Bec 31 H3
Weedon Lois 31 H4
Weeford 40 D5
Week Devon 5 H4
Week Devon 7 F4
Week Som 7 H2
Week Orchard 6 A5
Week St. Mary 4 C1
Weeke 11 F1
Weekley 42 B7
Weel 59 G6
Weeley 35 F6
Weeley Heath 35 F6
Weem 80 D5
Weeping Cross 40 B3
Weethley 30 B3
Weeting 44 B7
Weeton ERid 59 K7
Weeton Lancs 55 G6
Weeton NYorks 57 H5
Weetwood 57 H6
Weir Essex 24 E3
Weir Lancs 56 D7
Weir Quay 4 E4
Weirbrook 38 C3
Weisdale 89 M7
Welbeck Abbey 51 H5
Welborne 44 E5
Welbourn 52 C7
Welburn NYorks 58 C1
Welburn NYorks 58 D3
Welbury 62 D6
Welby 42 C2
Welches Dam 43 H7
Welcombe 6 A4
Weldon 42 C7
Welford N'hants 41 J7
Welford WBerks 21 H4
Welford-on-Avon 30 C3
Welham Leics 42 A6
Welham Notts 51 K4
Welham Green 23 F1
Well Hants 22 A7
Well Lincs 53 H5
Well NYorks 57 H1
Well End Bucks 22 B3
Well End Herts 23 F2
Well Hill 23 H5
Well Street 23 K6
Well Town 7 H5
Welland 29 G4
Wellesbourne 30 D3
Wellhill 84 D4
Wellhouse WBerks 21 J4
Wellhouse WYorks 50 C1
Welling 23 H4
Wellingborough 32 B2
Wellingham 44 C3
Wellingore 52 C7
Wellington Cumb 60 B6
Wellington Here 28 D4
Wellington Som 7 K3
Wellington Tel&W 39 F4
Wellington Heath 29 G4
Wellington Marsh 28 D4
Wellow B&NESom 20 A6
Wellow IoW 10 E6
Wellow Notts 51 J6
Wells 19 J7
Wells Cathedral Som BA5 2UE 19 J7
Wells Green 40 D7
Wellsborough 41 F5
Wells-next-the-Sea 44 D1
Wellstyle Green 33 K7
Wellwood 75 J2
Welney 43 J6
Welsh Bicknor 28 E7
Welsh End 38 E2
Welsh Frankton 38 C2
Welsh Hook 16 C3
Welsh Mountain Zoo Conwy LL28 5UY 47 G5
Welsh Newton 28 D7
Welsh St. Donats 18 D4
Welshampton 38 D2
Welshpool (Y Trallwng) 38 B5
Welton B&NESom 19 K6
Welton Cumb 60 E2
Welton ERid 59 F7
Welton Lincs 52 D4
Welton N'hants 31 G2
Welton le Marsh 53 H6
Welton le Wold 53 F4
Welwick 59 K7
Welwyn 33 F7
Welwyn Garden City 33 F7
Wem 38 E3
Wembdon 8 B1
Wembley GtLon HA9 0WS 102 E5
Wembley 22 E3
Wembley Park 22 E3
Wembury 5 F6
Wembworthy 6 E4
Wemyss Bay 73 K4
Wenallt Cere 27 F1
Wenallt Gwyn 37 J1
Wendens Ambo 33 J5
Wendlebury 31 G7
Wendling 44 D4
Wendover 22 B1
Wendover Dean 22 B1
Wendron 2 D5
Wendron Mining District (Cornwall & West Devon Mining Landscape) Corn 2 D5
Wendy 33 G4
Wenfordbridge 4 A3
Wenhaston 35 J1
Wenlli 47 G6
Wennington Cambs 33 F1
Wennington GtLon 23 J3
Wennington Lancs 56 B2
Wensley Derbys 50 E6
Wensley NYorks 57 F1
Wensleydale Cheese Visitor Centre, Hawes NYorks DL8 3RN 56 D1
Wentbridge 51 G1
Wentnor 38 C6
Wentworth Cambs 33 H1
Wentworth SYorks 51 F3
Wenvoe 18 E4
Weobley 28 C3
Weobley Marsh 28 D3
Weoley Castle 40 C7
Wepham 12 D6
Wepre 48 B6
Wepre Country Park Flints CH5 4HL 48 B6
Wereham 44 A5
Wergs 40 A5
Wern Gwyn 36 E2
Wern Powys 28 A7
Wern Powys 38 B4
Wern Shrop 38 B2
Wernffrwd 17 J6
Wern-olau 17 J6
Wernrheolydd 28 C7
Wern-y-cwrt 19 G1
Werrington Corn 6 B7
Werrington Peter 42 E5
Werrington Staffs 40 B1
Wervil Grange 26 C3
Wervin 48 D5
Wesham 55 H6
Wessington 51 F7
West Aberthaw 18 D5
West Acre 44 B4
West Acton 22 E3
West Allerdean 77 H6
West Alvington 5 H6
West Amesbury 20 E7
West Anstey 7 G3
West Ashby 53 F5
West Ashford 6 D2
West Ashling 12 B6
West Ashton 20 B6
West Auckland 62 B4
West Ayton 59 F1
West Bagborough 7 K2
West Barkwith 52 E4
West Barnby 63 J5
West Barns 76 E3
West Barsham 44 D2
West Bay 8 D5
West Beckham 45 F2
West Benhar 75 G4
West Bergholt 34 D6
West Bexington 8 E6
West Bilney 44 B4
West Blatchington 13 F6
West Boldon 71 J7
West Bourton 9 G2
West Bowling 57 G6
West Brabourne 15 F3
West Bradford 56 C5
West Bradley 8 E1
West Bretton 50 E1
West Bridgford 41 H2
West Bromwich 40 C6
West Buckland Devon 6 E2
West Buckland Som 7 K3
West Burrafirth 89 L7
West Burton NYorks 57 F1
West Burton WSuss 12 C5
West Butsfield 62 A2
West Butterwick 52 B2
West Byfleet 22 D5
West Caister 45 K4
West Calder 75 J4
West Camel 8 E2
West Carbeth 74 D3
West Carr Houses 51 K2
West Cauldcoats 74 E6
West Chaldon 9 G6
West Challow 21 G3
West Charleton 5 H6
West Chevington 71 H4
West Chiltington 12 D5
West Chiltington Common 12 D5
West Chinnock 8 D3
West Chisenbury 20 E6
West Clandon 22 D6
West Cliffe 15 J3
West Clyne 87 L9
West Coker 8 E3
West Compton Dorset 8 E5
West Compton Som 19 J7
West Cowick 58 C7
West Cross 17 K7
West Crudwell 20 C2
West Curry 4 C1
West Curthwaite 60 E2
West Dean Wilts 10 D2
West Dean WSuss 12 B5
West Deeping 42 E5
West Derby 48 C3
West Dereham 44 A5
West Ditchburn 71 G1
West Down 6 D1
West Drayton GtLon 22 D4
West Drayton Notts 51 K5
West Edington 71 G5
West Ella 59 G7
West End Bed 32 C3
West End BrackF 22 B4
West End Caerp 19 F2
West End Cambs 43 H6
West End ERid 59 G3
West End Hants 11 F3
West End Herts 23 F1
West End Lancs 55 H3
West End Lincs 53 G3
West End Norf 44 D5
West End Norf 45 J4
West End NSom 19 H5
West End NYorks 57 G4
West End Oxon 21 H1
West End Oxon 21 J3
West End SLan 75 H6
West End Suff 45 J7
West End Surr 22 C5
West End Surr 22 E5
West End Wilts 9 J2
West End Wilts 9 J2
West End Wilts 20 C4
West End Green 21 K5
West Farleigh 14 C2
West Farndon 31 G3
West Felton 38 C3
West Firle 13 H6
West Fleetham 71 G1
West Flotmanby 59 G2
West Garforth 57 J6
West Ginge 21 H3
West Glen 73 H3
West Grafton 21 F5
West Green GtLon 23 G3
West Green Hants 22 A6
West Grimstead 10 D2
West Grinstead 12 E4
West Haddlesey 58 B7
West Haddon 31 H1
West Hagbourne 21 J3
West Hagley 40 B7
West Hall 70 A7
West Hallam 41 G1
West Halton 59 F7
West Ham 23 G3
West Handley 51 F5
West Hanney 21 H2
West Hanningfield 24 D2
West Hardwick 51 G1
West Harnham 10 C2
West Harptree 19 J6
West Harrow 22 E3
West Harting 11 J2
West Hatch Som 8 B2
West Hatch Wilts 9 J2
West Head 43 J5
West Heath ChesE 49 H6
West Heath GtLon 23 H4
West Heath Hants 21 J6
West Heath Hants 22 B6
West Heath WMid 30 B1
West Helmsdale 87 N8
West Hendon 23 F3
West Hendred 21 H3
West Heslerton 59 F2
West Hewish 19 G5
West Hill Devon 7 J6
West Hill ERid 59 H3
West Hill NSom 19 H4
West Hoathly 13 G3
West Holme 9 H6
West Horndon 24 C3
West Horrington 19 J7
West Horsley 22 D6
West Horton 77 J7
West Hougham 15 H4
West Howe 10 B5
West Howetown 7 H2
West Huntspill 19 G7
West Hyde 22 D2
West Hythe 15 G4
West Ilsley 21 H3
West Itchenor 11 J4
West Keal 53 G6
West Kennet Long Barrow (Stonehenge, Avebury & Associated Sites) Wilts SN8 1QH 20 E5
West Kennett 20 E5
West Kilbride 74 A6
West Kingsdown 23 J5
West Kington 20 B4
West Kingston Wick 20 B4
West Kirby 48 B4
West Knapton 58 E2
West Knighton 9 G6
West Knoyle 9 H1
West Kyloe 77 J6
West Lambrook 8 D3
West Langdon 15 J3
West Langwell 87 J9
West Lavington Wilts 20 D6
West Lavington WSuss 12 B4
West Layton 62 B6
West Leake 41 H3
West Learmouth 77 G7
West Lees 62 E6
West Leigh Devon 5 H5
West Leigh Devon 6 E5
West Leigh Som 7 K2
West Leith 32 C7
West Lexham 44 C4
West Lilling 58 C3
West Linton 75 K5
West Liss 11 J2
West Littleton 20 A4
West Lockinge 21 H3
West Looe 4 C5
West Lulworth 9 H6
West Lutton 59 F3
West Lydford 8 E1
West Lyn 7 F1
West Lyng 8 C2
West Lynn 44 A4
West Mains 77 J6
West Malling 23 K6
West Malvern 29 G4
West Marden 11 J3
West Markham 51 K5
West Marsh 53 F2
West Marton 56 D4
West Melbury 9 H2
West Melton 51 G2
West Meon 11 H2
West Meon Hut 11 H2
West Mersea 34 E7
West Midland Safari Park & Leisure Park Worcs DY12 1LF 29 H1
West Milton 8 D5
West Minster 25 F4
West Molesey 22 E5
West Monkton 8 B2
West Moors 10 B4
West Morden 9 J5
West Morriston 76 E6
West Morton 57 F5
West Mostard 61 J7
West Mudford 8 E2
West Ness 58 C2
West Newbiggin 62 D5
West Newton ERid 59 H6
West Newton Norf 44 A3
West Norwood 23 G4
West Ogwell 5 J4
West Orchard 9 H3
West Overton 20 E5
West Panson 6 B6
West Park 48 E3
West Parley 10 B5
West Peckham 23 K6
West Pelton 62 C1
West Pennard 8 E1
West Pentire 2 E2
West Perry 32 E2
West Porlock 7 G1
West Prawle 5 H7
West Preston 12 D6
West Pulham 9 G4
West Putford 6 B4
West Quantoxhead 7 K1
West Raddon 7 G5
West Rainton 62 D2
West Rasen 52 D4
West Raynham 44 C3
West Retford 51 J4
West Rounton 62 E6
West Row 33 K1
West Rudham 44 C3
West Runton 45 F1
West Saltoun 76 C4
West Sandford 7 G5
West Sandwick 89 N4
West Scrafton 57 F1
West Shepton 19 K7
West Somerset Railway Som TA24 5BG 7 K2
West Somerton 45 J4
West Stafford 9 G6
West Stockwith 51 K3
West Stoke 12 B6
West Stonesdale 61 K6
West Stoughton 19 H7
West Stour 9 G2
West Stourmouth 25 J5
West Stow 34 C1
West Stow Country Park Suff IP28 6HG 34 B1
West Stowell 20 E5
West Stratton 21 J7
West Street Kent 14 E2
West Street Med 24 D4
West Street Suff 34 D1
West Tanfield 57 H2
West Taphouse 4 B4
West Tarbert 73 G4
West Tarring 12 E6
West Thirston 71 G3
West Thorney 11 J4
West Thurrock 23 J4
West Tilbury 24 C4
West Tisted 11 H2
West Tofts Norf 44 C6
West Tofts P&K 80 G7
West Torrington 52 E4
West Town B&NESom 19 J5
West Town Hants 11 J5
West Town NSom 19 H5
West Town Som 8 E1
West Tytherley 10 D2
West Walton 43 H4
West Wellow 10 D3
West Wembury 5 F6
West Wemyss 76 B1
West Wick 19 G5
West Wickham Cambs 33 K4
West Wickham GtLon 23 G5
West Williamston 16 D5
West Winch 44 A4
West Winterslow 10 D1
West Wittering 11 J5
West Witton 57 F1
West Woodburn 70 D5
West Woodhay 21 G5
West Woodlands 20 A7
West Worldham 11 J1
West Worlington 7 F4
West Worthing 12 E6
West Wratting 33 K3
West Wycombe 22 B2
West Yatton 20 B4
West Yell 89 N4
Westbere 25 H5
Westborough 42 B1
Westbourne Bourne 10 B5
Westbourne WSuss 11 J4
Westbourne Green 23 F3
Westbrook Kent 25 K4
Westbrook WBerks 21 H4
Westbrook Wilts 20 C5
Westbury Bucks 31 H5
Westbury Shrop 38 C5
Westbury Wilts 20 B6
Westbury Leigh 20 B6
Westbury on Trym 19 J4
Westbury-on-Severn 29 G7
Westbury-sub-Mendip 19 J7
Westby Lancs 55 G6
Westby Lincs 42 C3
Westcliff-on-Sea 24 E3
Westcombe 9 F1
Westcot 21 G3
Westcott Bucks 31 J7
Westcott Devon 7 J5
Westcott Surr 22 E7
Westcott Barton 31 F6
Westcourt 21 F5
Westcroft 32 B5
Westdean 13 J7
Westdowns 4 A2
Westend Town 20 A4
Wester Balgedie 80 G10
Wester Dechmont 75 J3
Wester Gruinards 83 R1
Wester Hailes 76 A4
Wester Skeld 89 L8
Westerdale High 87 P4
Westerdale NYorks 63 G6
Westerfield 35 F4
Westergate 12 C6
Westerham 23 H6
Westerhope 71 G7
Westerleigh 19 K4
Westerloch 87 R4
Westerton Aber 85 M11
Westerton Dur 62 C3
Westerton P&K 80 D9
Westerwick 89 L8
Westfield Cumb 60 A4
Westfield ESuss 14 D6
Westfield High 87 N3
Westfield NLan 75 F3
Westfield Norf 44 D5
Westfield WLoth 75 H3
Westfield WYorks 57 H7
Westfield Sole 24 D5
Westgate Dur 61 L3
Westgate NLincs 51 K2
Westgate Norf 44 D1
Westgate N'umb 71 G6
Westgate Hill 57 H7
Westgate on Sea 25 K4
Westhall Aber 85 L8
Westhall Suff 45 J7
Westham Dorset 9 F7
Westham ESuss 13 K6
Westham Som 19 H7
Westhampnett 12 B6
Westhay Devon 8 C4
Westhay Som 19 H7
Westhead 48 D2
Westhide 28 E4
Westhill 85 N10
Westhope Here 28 D3
Westhope Shrop 38 D7
Westhorp 31 G3
Westhorpe Lincs 43 F2
Westhorpe Notts 51 J7
Westhorpe Suff 34 E2
Westhoughton 49 F2
Westhouse 56 B2
Westhouses 51 G7
Westhumble 22 E6
Westing 89 P2
Westlake 5 G5
Westlands 40 A1
Westlea 20 E3
Westleigh Devon 6 C3
Westleigh Devon 7 J4
Westleigh GtMan 49 F2
Westleton 35 J2
Westley Shrop 38 C5
Westley Suff 34 C2
Westley Heights 24 C3
Westley Waterless 33 K3
Westlington 31 J7
Westlinton 69 J7
Westloch 76 A5
Westmancote 29 J5
Westmarsh 25 J5
Westmeston 13 G5
Westmill 33 G6
Westminster 23 F4
Westminster Abbey (Palace of Westminster & Westminster Abbey inc. St Margaret's Church) GtLon SW1P 3PA 105 A7
Westminster Cathedral GtLon SW1P 2QW 132 C6
Westmuir 81 J5
Westness 89 C5
Westnewton Cumb 60 C2
Westnewton N'umb 77 H7
Westoe 71 J7
Weston B&NESom 20 A5
Weston ChesE 49 G7
Weston Devon 7 K5
Weston Devon 7 K7
Weston Dorset 9 F7
Weston Halton 48 E4
Weston Hants 11 J2
Weston Here 28 C3
Weston Herts 33 F5
Weston Lincs 43 F3
Weston Notts 51 K6
Weston NYorks 57 G5
Weston N'hants 31 G4
Weston Shrop 28 C1
Weston Shrop 38 E3
Weston Shrop 38 E6
Weston Soton 11 F3
Weston Staffs 40 B3
Weston WBerks 21 H4
Weston Bampfylde 9 F2
Weston Beggard 28 E4
Weston by Welland 42 A6
Weston Colville 33 K3
Weston Corbett 21 K7
Weston Coyney 40 B1
Weston Favell 31 J2
Weston Green Cambs 33 K3
Weston Green Norf 45 F4
Weston Heath 39 G4
Weston Hills 43 F3
Weston in Arden 41 F7
Weston Jones 39 G3
Weston Longville 45 F4
Weston Lullingfields 38 D3
Weston Park Staffs TF11 8LE 40 A4
Weston Patrick 21 K7
Weston Point 48 D4
Weston Rhyn 38 B2
Weston Subedge 30 C4
Weston Town 20 A7
Weston Turville 32 B7
Weston under Penyard 29 F6
Weston under Wetherley 30 E2
Weston Underwood Derbys 40 E1
Weston Underwood MK 32 B3
Westonbirt - The National Arboretum Glos GL8 8QS 20 B3
Westoning 32 D5
Weston-in-Gordano 19 H4
Weston-on-Avon 30 C3
Weston-on-the-Green 31 G7
Weston-on-Trent 41 G3
Weston-super-Mare 19 G5
Weston-under-Lizard 40 A4

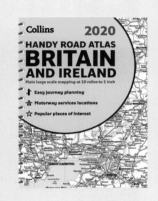
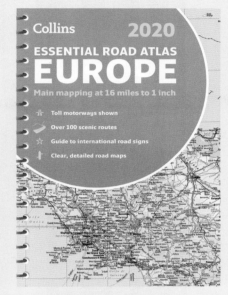
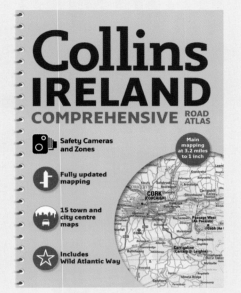

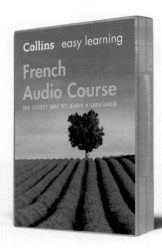 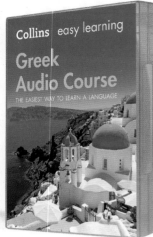  
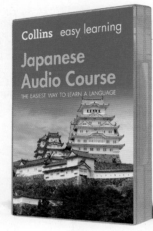   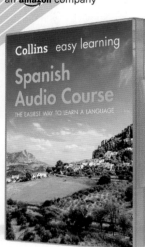